Insurance and Employee Benefits

Second Edition

by Mandell S. Winter, Jr. & Jeffrey B. Mershon

ISBN: 978-0-9726772-5-7

TABLE OF CONTENTS

Preface vii

Acknowledgments ix

About the Authors x

Chapter 1: Risk and Insurance

Risk 2

Insurance 11

Legal Aspects of Insurance 16

Chapter 2: Introduction to Life Insurance

Managing Personal Risks 30

General Types of Life Insurance 31

Life Insurance Contracts 45

Income and Estate Tax Implications of Life Insurance 57

Chapter 3: Life Insurance Needs Analysis

Determining the Need: General Methods 66

Life Insurance Needs Analysis 69

Chapter 4: Life Insurance Policy Selection and Annuities

Selecting the Right Policy 88

Analyzing Insurance Policies 91

Life Insurance Policy Replacement 101

Accelerated Death Benefits and Viatical Settlements 103

Annuities 106

Chapter 5: Life Insurance Company Selection

Choosing in a Competitive Market 117

When There Is No Choice 129

Chapter 6: Individual Health Care Plans: Medical Expense Coverage

Basic Health Insurance Terms 134

Group and Individual Plans 141

Health Care Plans for Individuals 142

Which Plan? 158

Taxation of Health Plans 161

Caveat 163

Chapter 7: Individual Health Care Plans: Disability Income Insurance

Disability Income Insurance: The Basics 168

Chapter 8: Individual Health Care Plans: Long-Term Care

What Is Long-Term Care? 192

Levels and Locations of Care 197

Buying Long-Term Care Policies 200

The Faces of Long-Term Care 206

Chapter 9: Homeowners Insurance

The Field of Property and Liability Insurance 212

Property and Liability Basics 212

Homeowners Coverage by Section 214

Homeowners Forms 222

Endorsements 228

Exclusions 230

Homeowners Insurance Needs Analysis 237

Chapter 10: Automobile Insurance: The Personal Auto Policy

The Personal Auto Policy 242

Buying Auto Insurance 254

Making Claims 259

Chapter 11: Personal and Professional Liability Insurance

Legal Liability 264

Comprehensive Personal Liability Insurance 271

Professional Liability Insurance 280

Umbrella Liability Insurance 282

Why Liability? 283

Liability Insurance: Needs Analysis 284

Chapter 12: Commercial Insurance Lines

General Introduction to Commercial Lines 290

Chapter 13: Introduction to Employee Benefits and Group Insurance

The Basics of Employee Benefits 312

Group Insurance 319

Chapter 14: Group Life, Medical, and Disability

Group Life Insurance 328

Group Health Care 336

Group Disability Income Insurance 350

Chapter 15: Other Insurance Benefits: Cafeteria Plans, FSAs, and Group Dental

Cafeteria Plans 358

Flexible Spending Accounts (FSA) 361

General Notes 365

Group Dental Coverage 367

Chapter 16: Non-Insurance Benefits and Benefits Taxation

Pay for Time Not Worked 374

Family and Medical Leave Act: FMLA 381

Statutory Fringe Benefits 383

Other Fringe Benefits 393

Income Tax Ramifications of Employee Benefits 401

Non-Insurance Benefits and Financial Planning 402

Chapter 17: Nonqualified Deferred Compensation

Executive Benefit Alternatives 406

Nonqualified Deferred Compensation 407

Chapter 18: Equity-Based Compensation: Stock Options and Stock Purchase Plans

Equity-Based Compensation 422

Employee Stock Purchase Plan 428

Chapter 19: Equity-Based Compensation: Restricted Stock, Shadow Stock Arrangements, and Performance Unit or Share Plans

Restricted Stock Plans 436

Shadow Stock Arrangements 439

Performance Units and Performance Shares 443

Chapter 20: Business Applications of Insurance

Key Person Life Insurance 448

Transfer for Value 450

Business Ownership Transfer Issues 453

Split Dollar Life Insurance 468

IRC § 162 Plans 474

Death Benefit Only Plans 475

Overhead Expense Insurance 476

Index

Index 481

PREFACE

Personal financial planning is a process. Financial planners work with individuals for the purpose of providing them with a plan for financial stability and independence. While the exciting parts of financial planning are often in the realm of investment planning, the more mundane aspects of a financial plan are no less important. Insurance and employee benefits are critical parts of every financial plan. Even if a client is financially successful, insurance is necessary to protect his or her assets. Death, disability, liability, property loss, or health problems can create a substantial financial void in the absence of adequate protection— especially when that client must provide for a family.

Financial planners who purport to provide comprehensive financial planning must assist clients in developing an adequate insurance plan as part of the foundation of their overall financial plan. Any planner who ignores these issues or gives them inadequate attention runs the risk of leaving his or her clients with substantial financial exposures. If a client suffers financial reversals because of inadequate insurance, the planner is likely to be held responsible if he or she does not recommend adequate protection or refer the client to competent insurance professionals.

Employee benefits, beyond salary or wages, generally increase total compensation by 30-40 percent, and failure to understand and take advantage of these valuable benefits is a costly mistake. This text is written in an effort to help aspiring financial planners understand employee benefits well enough to encourage their clients to recognize their value and take advantage of those offered.

Insurance is not the sum total of a financial plan, but there is no other financial product or combination of products that can provide the security insurance provides. Many individuals have learned negative attitudes about insurance, and it is the job of the broad-based financial planner to show them the flexibility and freedom insurance provides. Without an adequate insurance program, decades of successful planning and investing can be wiped out by a single accident or error.

This book is designed to serve primarily as the textbook for the second course of a personal financial planning education program registered with Certified Financial Planner Board of Standards Inc. (CFP Board) and satisfying the education component of CFP Board's requirements for earning the CERTIFIED FINANCIAL PLANNER™ certification*. Specifically, it covers topic numbers 21 through 39 of the 101 topics appearing in the CFP Board's 1999 Job Study Analysis.

This book has been written at the upper undergraduate level (junior and senior) and may be used in introductory courses in risk management, insurance, and employee benefits offered at colleges and universities. Also, it may be used by individuals interested simply in enhancing their knowledge of individual risk management, insurance, and employee benefits. Each of the 20 chapters opens with an introduction of the chapter subject and a list of learning objectives. At the end of each chapter, there is a list of important concepts, questions and problems for review, and suggested additional readings.

This book is used as the textbook for Insurance and Employee Benefits, the second course in Kaplan University's Online Certificate in Financial Planning program. In that course, it is supplemented by brief online readings, exercises, quizzes at the end of each of 10 lessons, and a Final Exam containing 60 multiple-choice questions (some of which are related to a case situation) similar to those appearing on CFP Board's Certification Examination. Students in Kaplan's financial planning education program also have the use of a message board where they can pose questions online to qualified instructors.

ACKNOWLEDGMENTS

Anyone who writes a book will realize early on that it is not a one-person project. To reach a point in one's career where writing a book is possible requires years of support from all of those teachers of the past. Some were teachers in classrooms; others were teachers in everyday life. Every day, each person can learn something from someone else. I have been blessed with many great teachers.

A book such as this does not start on its own. I am very grateful to Keith Fevurly and Jeff Mershon for giving me the opportunity to be the instructor of the course for which this text was initially written and for the opportunity to write the text. Jeff Mershon, my co-author and technical reviewer, provided invaluable assistance in making this text a sound educational tool, ensuring accuracy and currency of the material.

My editors, Dana and Daniel, helped in many ways. Without them, this text would not flow as well as it does and a number of sections would be much less clear. Their patience and suggestions were greatly appreciated.

The Internet is an exceptional resource when writing in this field. Many unnamed authors provided explanations and information that made it possible for me to better describe products, regulations, terminology, and processes.

Finally, I must thank Pat and Ben for their unfailing encouragement and willingness to put up with some of the late hours that went into writing this text. And I must tip my hat to Dell for showing me the power of focus and clarity.

Mandell S. Winter, Jr.
MBA, CLU, ChFC, RFC

ABOUT THE AUTHORS

Mandell S. Winter, Jr. is an instructor in the Online Certificate in Financial Planning program at Kaplan University, where he teaches Insurance and Employee Benefits. He received his bachelor of science in business at the University of Colorado, Boulder, and earned his M.B.A. at Golden Gate University while serving as an officer in the U.S. Air Force. He has published numerous articles in nationally distributed financial services periodicals as well as periodicals focused on the construction industry. He also wrote "Ownership and Beneficiary Designations for Life Insurance", part of the Harcourt Brace Professional Publishing's Personal Financial Planning Portfolio.

Prior to joining the faculty at Kaplan University, he spent 17 years working full time in the insurance/financial-planning arena. While continuing to serve his clients, he worked on the faculty of the College for Financial Planning for over six years, where he taught financial planning and insurance as well as estate and insurance planning for business owners. He also redeveloped the financial planning process and insurance courses into a single course. Mandell taught at Metropolitan State College of Denver and Westwood College of Technology. He has earned his Chartered Life Underwriter and Chartered Financial Consultant designations as well as being a Registered Financial Consultant. He is also a member of the national and local associations of Insurance and Financial Advisors and The Society of Financial Service Professionals.

Jeffrey B. Mershon is Associate Executive Director of the Certificate in Financial Planning Online Education Program at Kaplan University, a subsidiary of Kaplan Higher Education Corporation, which in turn is wholly-owned by Kaplan, Inc. Kaplan, Inc. is wholly-owned by The Washington Post Company. Mr. Mershon received his Bachelor of Arts degree in English Literature from Cornell University's College of Arts and Sciences and his Master of Business Administration degree in Accounting and Finance from Cornell University's Johnson Graduate School of Management. He developed Kaplan University's Insurance and Employee Benefits course, Income Tax Planning course, and a substantial portion of the Online Review course and Live Review materials.

Prior to joining Kaplan University, Mr. Mershon was Director of Curriculum Development at the College for Financial Planning, supervising the development and maintenance of the College's Certified Financial Planner™ and Master of Science in Financial Planning education courses and other education offerings. He served for five years as Assistant Executive Director and Director of Post-Certification at Certified Financial Planner Board of Standards in Denver, where he was instrumental in the development of CFP Board's *Code of Ethics* and *Professional Responsibility and Financial Planning Practice Standards*. He has practiced as a financial planner, consultant to various financial planning organizations, and as a partner in a local CPA firm, as well as in senior financial management in private industry. In addition to being a CPA, he has earned both the Certified Financial Planner™ certification and the Personal Financial Specialist designation. He is a member of the Financial Planning Association and the American Institute of CPAs.

Mr. Mershon is the author of *Fundamentals of Personal Financial Planning* (2nd edition) used in the introductory course of Kaplan University's Certificate in Financial Planning Online Education Program and by other educational institutions. He is co-author of *Individual Income Tax Planning* used in the Income Tax Planning course of Kaplan's Certificate in Financial Planning Online Education Program and is currently writing a textbook for Kaplan's Planning for Retirement course.

CHAPTER ONE

Risk and Insurance

• • •

When building a home or an office building, the stability of the structure is only as good as its base. Before the plans are drawn, engineers carefully determine what problems the foundation might face. All potential perils are researched to ensure that the foundation is up to the task.

Recognizing and analyzing personal risks are the engineering of a financial plan's foundation. A financial planner must work with each client to identify his or her personal risks and come up with a plan to manage them before moving on to building and retaining wealth. If it is not done, the foundation may crack and all of the work above it will have been for naught.

Upon completing this chapter, you should be able to:

- Define risk, distinguishing it from peril and hazard, and identify the principal classifications

- Explain the types of risk to which an individual may be exposed

- Identify and describe the rules of risk management, including their applications, as well as the general methods of handling risk

- Define insurance, from both an individual and a societal perspective, explaining its nature and identifying its functions

- Explain what constitutes an insurable risk

- Describe the law of large numbers

- Identify and explain the legal aspects of insurance, including the characteristics of an insurance contract

RISK

If there were no risks, there would be no need for insurance.

Pick up the newspaper any day in any location and you might find stories about natural disasters, homes burning, auto wrecks, or burglaries. You might also see an obituary alerting you that someone famous has succumbed to cancer or heart disease. While driving, you might hear emergency vehicles as they head to an unknown location, maybe to assist with something relatively minor or maybe to find disaster. In any of these situations, someone likely suffered a loss. It may be as minor as time away from work and the cost of a doctor's visit or as major as the destruction of a home or the ending of a life.

Everyone faces various risks every day-some are serious, some are not. Dealing with risk can be done consciously or unconsciously. The important thing to remember as a financial planner is that risks exist, and the planner's job is to make sure clients are aware of financial risks they might face so that they can manage those risks effectively.

What Is Risk?

The word *risk*, as both a noun and a verb, has many different definitions. For a lender, risk might represent the chance that a given debt will not be repaid. An investor might consider his or her risk to be the potential loss on an investment. An insurance company might say that risk is the chance that its actuarial calculations are inaccurate or might even refer to a particular policyholder as a risk. A property holder might define risk as the probability or danger that a loss might occur. One might simply define risk as uncertainty: the possibility that an outcome might be different than what is expected.

For our purposes, we will borrow a definition of risk from Emmett and Therese Vaughan:

Risk *is a condition in which there is a possibility of an adverse deviation from a desired outcome that is expected or hoped for.*[1] This definition takes the position that risk exists whether or not anyone is aware of it. Additionally, it includes the requirement that there is a result that individuals either expect or hope for and that the desired result might not occur. An **adverse deviation** is a deviation that is contrary to the desired outcome. The deviation may result in a minor variance or a completely different result.

For example, in a windstorm, a homeowner hopes for no damage to occur to his or her home. If a tree branch breaks off and cracks a window, that would be a minor deviation. A complete deviation would occur if a tree fell across power lines, snapping them, and then caused a break in a natural gas line, the sparking wire igniting the gas and burning the house to the ground. **Uncertainty** as to whether a loss will occur creates risk: When one expects things to continue as they are, but there is a chance of loss, risk exists. If the loss is certain, there is no risk, only the assurance that the loss will occur.

---

[1]Vaughan and Vaughan, *Fundamentals of Risk and Insurance*, Wiley, 9th ed., 2003

Perils and Hazards

Sometimes individuals incorrectly use the words "peril" and "hazard" as synonyms for risk. These two words are related but are important terms in their own right.

A **peril** is the specific cause of a loss. Fires, tornados, floods, hail, thefts, and heart attacks are all perils.

Hazard is a bit more complex because there are different types of hazards. In general, a hazard is something that increases the chance that a peril will cause a loss. There are three generally recognized categories of hazards.

Physical hazards are self explanatory: They are physical in nature. Oily rags kept in an open container in a garage, log construction of a building, high blood pressure, and tightrope walking without a net are all physical hazards. They all increase the likelihood that a peril will result in a serious loss.

Moral hazard is the hazard of intentional dishonesty. Individuals who make claims for losses that they intentionally caused, such as burning down their own houses or destroying jewelry they no longer want. Individuals have even been caught boarding buses after an accident and claiming they were injured.

Similar to the moral hazard is the **morale hazard**. This is a hazard of attitude. People expend less effort to prevent losses when those losses are insured and often select more expensive procedures than they otherwise might use to correct those losses. An estimator might use more expensive methods for a repair estimate since insurance will cover it. A physician might prescribe a relatively expensive treatment rather than an equally effective treatment that costs much less because insurance will cover the cost. A car owner might leave his car unprotected when hail is expected, knowing the insurance company will cover it. The attitude is often "The insurance company can afford it better than I can" or "Don't worry about it, it's insured."

Can something be a hazard and a peril? Yes. Consider a serious illness such as cancer. It is a peril in that it causes the loss of income or the loss of accumulated sick leave in order to obtain treatment. It is a hazard in that it increases the chance that the individual will die.

Classifications of Risk

There are many ways to classify risks, and a particular risk can be defined by a combination of these classifications:

Financial and Nonfinancial Risks

Some risks have the potential of causing a financial loss. Others involve losses that are not financial. In the study of financial planning, the primary concern is with financial risks.

In-Depth: Categories of Personal Peril

Premature Death: While this obviously does not create a financial problem for the decedent, it may create severe financial problems for his or her survivors. Many households depend on the income or services of an individual; when that person dies, his or her contributions cease. If adequate financial reserves or insurance have not been put in place to cover the lost income or services, the survivors will suffer more than emotional loss. Losses may also occur in a business where he or she was an owner or a key person to the business.

Illness/Disability: Some would separate these two, but one may well lead to the other. When someone is ill or disabled, his or her earning capacity is compromised, and his or her ability to provide services to the household is likewise compromised. The seriousness of the condition will dictate the extent to which the contributions are reduced. It may be that the reduction is minor. It may be that the reduction is complete. Combined with the added expenses of treating the condition and the need for others to provide for the ill or disabled person, the financial impact of an illness or disability can be severe.

Unemployment: The effect of unemployment can be widely varied. Is the unemployed individual the sole source of income for the household? Is the unemployment short term or protracted? Is the household able to cut back on expenses, or has every paycheck been spent on fixed bills before it was earned? All of these factors will affect the impact of unemployment.

Dependent Old Age: One of the greatest fears of senior citizens is running out of money. Many seniors care much less about how much money they have month to month than whether their pension and savings will be used up while they are still alive. It is a frightening proposition to think that you might be a burden to your children or be forced into selling assets to survive and end up being supported by the state.

Dynamic and Static Risks

Dynamic risks are those that arise from societal changes, such as shifts in taxation policy, the economy, or regulation. These changes could be in the form of style changes, inflation, and national priorities. These changes affect many people and are not particularly predictable.

An example of a dynamic risk was a change in tax laws in the 1980s. Laws that radically changed the way investment real estate was taxed caused a substantial drop in the price of investment real estate properties. Because many limited partnerships had been created to take advantage of the generous taxation rules, many of the limited partnerships became worthless when the tax rules changed.

Static risks are typically losses to individuals or small groups caused by fires, natural disasters, crimes such as theft or murder, and other incidents of limited scope. It is possible to find some predictability in the overall impact of these losses to a large number of individuals but not for a specific individual. In general, financial planners should consider insurance for many static risks, but dynamic risks are often uninsurable.

A simple example of a static risk is an earthquake , which generally affects a certain number of people in its geographic location. While an earthquake may affect hundreds or thousands of people, it generally will not affect an entire nation or even everyone within 50 miles of the epicenter.

Fundamental and Particular Risks

A risk of loss that would be suffered by the community as a whole, such as economic or political loss, is a **fundamental risk**. These risks are essentially impersonal, not affecting one person without affecting his or her neighbor. Citywide floods or tornados that destroy large areas are fundamental risks. A **particular risk** is one that affects an individual or a business in a community. The loss is personal. The potential of a home being burglarized or an individual being hurt in an auto accident is an example of a particular risk.

Speculative and Pure Risks

This is where insurance and gambling part ways. Gambling is a **speculative risk**. There is clearly a possibility of loss, but there is also a possibility of gain. Investing most often also involves speculative risk. With **pure risk**, there are only two options: loss or no loss. Under most circumstances, only pure risks are insurable, but not even all pure risks are insurable. There are four types of pure risks that are considered insurable **risk exposures**.

First, **personal risks** are typically related to the loss of the ability to earn an income. Earning power may be curtailed because of four perils: premature death, illness/disability, unemployment, and dependent old age (see "In Depth: Categories of Personal Peril").

Property risk, whether for real property or personal property, is the second classification of risk exposures. **Real property** is land and buildings. Cars, clothes, furniture, tools, jewelry, a boat, computers, etc. are **personal property**. The most obvious loss occurs if the property is damaged, stolen, or destroyed. These losses would be **direct losses**. However, there may also be **indirect losses** from a loss of use of the property. If you have a computer stolen or destroyed, not only do you have to replace the computer as a result of the direct loss, but you may suffer indirect loss from important documentation stored on the computer that is difficult or impossible to replace. If you use your computer for business, you may be unable to work effectively until the computer is replaced, suffering further indirect losses. Likewise, if your car is stolen, damaged, or destroyed, you will have additional transportation expenses until the car is found, repaired, or replaced.

We are all exposed to potential **liability risks**, the third type, because the laws in the United States generally make individuals responsible for any losses they cause to others by injuring them or damaging their property. While few people intentionally injure others or damage the property of others, accidents do happen. The liability, or responsibility, exists regardless of the intent of the person causing the damage. Generally, it is only unintentional liability losses that are insurable. Damages for which a person may be held responsible include the costs of medical care, lost income, or the cost of repairing or replacing damaged or destroyed property.

On the other side of the liability risk coin are risks individuals face because others do not fulfill their responsibilities. This fourth area encompasses the **risks associated with the failure of others**. If a homeowner hires a company to replace the roof on the house, there is a chance the roofer will not finish the job. While the company is liable for completing the work, if the contractor cannot be found or if there is no possibility of getting repaid or getting the work finished, it is the homeowner who suffers the loss and may have to pay twice for work that needs to be done. If a person is in an accident caused by an uninsured driver with few assets, there is little chance of receiving compensation for damage or medical expenses from that driver even if it can be proven that he or she was at fault in the accident.

Managing Risks

As stated above, the risks of loss exist even if we choose to ignore them or are unaware of them. It is better to identify those risks and make a conscious choice regarding how to deal with them rather than to wait until a loss occurs before realizing that such a loss was possible. There are five methods of handling risk:

- Risk Avoidance
- Risk Retention
- Risk Transfer
- Risk Sharing
- Risk Reduction

Risk Avoidance

If you want to avoid the risks associated with owning a recreational vehicle, do not buy one. If you own one now, you could get rid of it. A manufacturer of swing sets can avoid product liability risk for swing sets by not manufacturing them. Obviously, you cannot avoid all risks because, carried to an extreme, nothing would be produced, and no one would go anywhere or do anything to expose themselves to the possibility of getting hurt or causing a loss to someone else.

Risk Retention

If an individual does not take action to avoid, reduce, share, or transfer a risk, any loss associated with that risk is retained and will be paid out of pocket. Risk retention may be voluntary or involuntary. Insurance policy deductibles are a form of risk retention that may be partially voluntary and partially involuntary. An auto insurance company may have a minimum $250 deductible on each auto policy. That part is involuntary: You must retain that part of the risk. To lower the premium, you may choose to have a $500 deductible-the extra $250 is voluntary risk retention. When you face a risk that you choose to ignore or not manage in another way, you voluntarily retain the risk. If there is no other way to manage a risk or if you are unaware of a risk, you involuntarily retain it.

Risk Transfer

This is what insurance accomplishes. The risk of financial loss is transferred from a person or business to another—the insurance company—which is more willing, or able, to bear that risk. Insurance is the primary method of shifting or transferring risk. In return for a specified payment (the premium) by the insured, the insurance company agrees to indemnify (cover the losses of) the insured for losses that may occur (up to a specified limit). Hedging and hold-harmless agreements also involve transfer of risk. Hedging is when a seller of a commodity wants to be assured of a certain price for his or her goods. A hedging contract is sold to an investor. The investor pays the seller a fee for the right to purchase the commodity at a certain price. If the price of the commodity goes up, the seller gets that price and the investor gets the difference. If the price goes down, the investor will not buy the commodity, but the seller gets to keep the fee paid plus whatever the commodity brings. A hold-harmless agreement is one where one party agrees to accept the responsibility that otherwise would belong to another party.

Risk Sharing

The most common example of risk sharing is the corporation. The investments of many people are pooled; each individual's risk is limited to his or her investment. Insurance is another device designed to deal with risk through sharing losses. Some small private insurance plans consist of a group of similar businesses that agree to cover any specified losses incurred by a member of the group. Each member is assessed a "fair share" of the loss when one member suffers a loss. A "fair share" will generally be defined in the agreement. It may be based on (1) an equal amount from each participating individual or (2) the relative potential loss of each individual. If all of the businesses are the same size and about the same value, their fair share of a loss may be the same for all. If Company B is three times as large as Company A, and Company C is twice as large as Company A, Company B's fair share would be three times as much as Company A's and Company C's share would be twice as much as Company A's. Any definition will work if all members agree to it.

Risk Reduction

There are two general approaches to risk reduction:

(i) **Loss prevention**: This is an attempt to reduce the risk by preventing losses or reducing the chance that losses will occur. Examples might include safety programs, night security guards, less fragile materials, higher quality control, more obvious and extensive warnings, and/or burglar alarms.

(ii) **Severity reduction**, a.k.a. **loss control**: This involves reducing the severity of a loss once it has occurred. A sprinkler system does not stop fires from starting, but it can reduce the amount of damage caused by a fire. Automobiles are now built to reduce the injuries of passengers if the car is involved in a collision.

Rules of Risk Management

We all practice risk management every day. For example, let us assume that in a plastic container, deep in your refrigerator, is some leftover chicken Dijon. You are ready to warm it in the microwave when you stop to think. When did I have this? How long has it been in there? It smells okay, but it may have been hiding in there for as long as two weeks.

You could retain the risk, heat it up, and enjoy it. This will have one of two results. You will enjoy your meal or snack, as the case may be, and be fine. Or, you may enjoy your meal and end up with food poisoning and spend a few hours in the bathroom or even the emergency room, being very unhappy with your choice.

You could also avoid the risk by following the age-old axiom: "When in doubt, throw it out." You might resolve that next time you will write the date on the container when you put your favorite food back in the refrigerator.

The potential loss if you choose choice one is being very ill. The potential loss with choice two is that you have to find something else to eat, and you are out the cost of a piece of chicken and some sauce.

Those are the alternatives. Most of us would probably decide that the economic and personal costs of eating "bad" food far outweigh the economic cost of avoiding the risk. This is risk management at its simplest.

Most experts agree that there are three basic rules of risk management:
- Do not risk more than you can afford to lose
- Consider the odds
- Do not risk a lot for a little

Do Not Risk More Than You Can Afford to Lose

Many people rationalize that the "safe" way to visit Las Vegas, Atlantic City, or any of the other gambling towns is to decide in advance how much you are willing to lose. That amount is the cost of the entertainment of gambling. When investing, most advisers would suggest that you should not put so much into high-risk investments that if you lose it, you will face severe financial difficulty. If you own a home and cannot afford to replace it if it is destroyed, insure it. Put simply: If you can afford to manage the loss from current income or other assets, then you can afford to retain the risk. If you cannot afford the loss, then retention of the risk is not advisable.

What happens if you can afford some risk but not all of the potential loss? If you enter the casino with $500 in your pocket and lose it at the roulette wheel, you have limited your losses to $500. As long as you knew going in that you could afford to lose it, you have not risked more than you could afford to lose. However, if you also took your credit cards into the casino, there is the risk that you will be caught up in the excitement and walk out with thousands of dollars of credit card debt. You reduce the risk by leaving the credit cards at home. In simple, insurance-related terms, if you cannot afford to rebuild your home if it is destroyed, then you should buy insurance: The potential loss could be two to three hundred times the premium.

Consider the Odds

Think about how likely it is that a specific loss may occur. If the chances of loss are virtually nonexistent, it is not worth thinking about. If a loss is certain to occur, it is not insurable and you need to think of other ways to deal with it. Some people get upset when they cannot insure against something they know will happen. If a loss is certain to occur, the cost of insuring it will have to be 100 percent of the loss plus the cost of administration. If you build a building in a flood plain that floods every year, you will not be able to buy insurance for that building because it is virtually certain that it will be destroyed within a year. Individual health insurance policies that have maternity coverage are quite expensive, since only those who expect to use it want it included in their policies.

Most potential losses fall between nonexistent and certain. The more likely the loss, the greater the cost to insure it. By knowing the probability that a loss will occur, the individual has a better appreciation of whether insurance or some other form of risk management is best. In the aftermath of the terrorist attacks on the World Trade Center, we all learned that certain "nonexistent risks" actually existed. Among the numerous unforeseeable events that were caused by the attacks, safe deposit boxes at the bottom of the World Trade Center were destroyed. We have always been taught that a safe deposit box is where we keep irreplaceable documents and heirlooms. Many people who own valuable jewelry keep those items in safe deposit boxes and have them insured only when they are out of the box. Any items so insured were, for the most part, lost in the collapse of the towers, without compensation to the owners. Now may be the time to rethink the meaning of safety. Maybe using a safe deposit box in a small bank building makes more sense than one in a high-rise building. Maybe a safe in the basement of your home is safer. This was likely the first time in history that safe deposit boxes, built of steel, in a steel reinforced concrete safe have been destroyed. The odds are still against it happening: One vault, in one building, out of thousands of vaults throughout the country. A safe deposit box is likely still the safest place for irreplaceable items, but now some people will insure these items when they are locked up as well. Considering the odds, the cost will probably be relatively small.

Do Not Risk a Lot for a Little

This refers to the relationship of the cost of managing the risk to the potential loss. If you own a home that would cost $250,000 to rebuild, the insurance might be $1,500 per year to protect the building and its contents and provide liability insurance. If you have no claims, you have spent $1,500 for peace of mind. If you do not have the insurance and the house is destroyed, you have lost $250,000. Even if you have severe weather that damages your roof, that could easily cost $4,000 to $10,000 to repair if you did not pay your $1,500 premium.

The opposite could also be true: A 12-year-old car may run well and look great. While your specific vehicle may be running perfectly, have no rust spots, great paint, new upholstery, new battery, and even a recently rebuilt transmission, the cost to buy another car of the same model that runs, may be $1,500. Insuring the car against damage will be $700 per year. If you plan to keep the car until it dies, it is not likely that spending $700 a year for a $1,500 payment makes any sense. If you keep it for three more years, you will have spent $2,100 for the possibility of receiving $1,500 or less if the car is damaged or destroyed. If the car is in an accident and would cost $1,600 to repair, the insurance company will consider it a total loss.

That means you would give up the car for a check in the amount of $1,500 (minus the deductible). If you want to keep the car and get it repaired anyway, the insurance company will likely give you less than the $1,500 because they will not receive the salvage value. All in all, you would be risking a lot on an insurance premium payment for the possibility of very little money in the event of an accident.

Choosing the Tools of Risk Management

When dealing with risk, placing a specific risk in the following matrix helps determine what the options are.

Table 1.1: Risk Management Matrix

	High Frequency	Low Frequency
High Severity	1	2
Low Severity	3	4

The following guidelines may help in determining which method of risk management to use.

Scenario 1: High Severity and High Frequency
A risk of loss that is severe and likely to happen needs to be dealt with. However, acquiring insurance will not be possible or will be very expensive. These risks must be retained, reduced, or avoided. Insurance against catastrophically high losses with a large retention may be appropriate: In hail- or earthquake-prone areas, insurance companies have relatively high deductibles, some being a percentage of the loss rather than a fixed dollar amount. This is because from the insurance company's point of view, the losses will occur, and they will be expensive to fix.

Scenario 2: High Severity and Low Frequency
These are the ideal circumstances for insurance. The likelihood of a home being totally destroyed is low, however the loss when it does happen is substantial.

Scenario 3: Low Severity and High Frequency
This costs very little but happens all the time. Hotels having towels stolen might be an example. Insurance will not be the best solution for this type of situation. Much of the risk will probably be retained, but risk reduction or risk avoidance could reduce some of the cost.

Scenario 4: Low Severity and Low Frequency
This type of situation happens quite seldom, costs little to fix, and is the perfect application of risk retention. These are all the little annoying things that happen every so often, such as when a light switch stops working; when someone stubs a toe, causing him or her to drop and break a plate; or when a broken tree limb is too high to retrieve without hiring someone.

INSURANCE

What is insurance? One individual might see it as peace of mind or a source of security. Another might see it as various contract forms that are intended to indemnify for specific losses. As a financial planner, you should see it as a critical part of the foundation of any financial plan. As a whole, insurance is a toolbox full of specialized tools, with each form of insurance as a tool that is used to deal with certain insurable risks when called for.

Insurance is a financial arrangement with two fundamental characteristics:
  • Risk of substantial financial loss is transferred from the individual to a group.
  • Losses are equitably shared by all members of the group.

Look at Sametown: There are 1,000 homes in Sametown, each with the same square footage and made out of the same materials. Though purchase costs ranged from $180,000 to $275,000 because of location, location, location: each house would cost $150,000 to rebuild.

All of the homeowners in Sametown signed an agreement when they bought their homes that if any of their neighbors suffered the loss of their home to a fire, windstorm, or flood, each of the homeowners would ante up $150 to defray the cost of rebuilding the lost home. Everyone in Sametown shares the risk that everyone else faces. When house #437 burned to the ground, everyone paid his or her $150. The losses were borne equitably. Everyone had the same potential risk—the loss of a house that would cost $150,000 to replace. If the houses were different sizes and the risks were different for the 1,000 residents, the contribution from each would have to be adjusted to be equitable.

This obviously simplified illustration assumes that everyone will pay his or her share when called upon to do so. In reality, someone would have to take the time to verify that the loss took place, was due to one of the listed perils, and then would have to collect everyone's share. With 999 households to contact, this could take a while. In addition, if a major disaster struck, the cost of paying for the replacement of only 150 of the homes (15 percent) would be $22,500 (150 homes times $150) for each homeowner. While this example illustrates the benefits of shared loss and transfer of the risk, it leaves many questions unanswered. Are there any natural hazards that exist that might increase the chances of disaster? Faults in the area that may lead to earthquakes? A history of high winds or tornados? Is the town on a flood plain? What will happen if all or almost all of the homes are lost at one time? Who will pay the cost then?

Insurance attempts to deal with these questions. Individuals purchase insurance to obtain security, and security has a price-the premium. Individuals trade dollars to the insurance company to ensure that if they are hit with a disaster, the money will be there to recover. Each insured individual pays the premium regardless of whether or not he or she submits a claim. This ensures that, when someone does file a claim, the claim will be paid and that individual will not be wiped out financially, even if multiple claims are made at once.

While the premiums are paid whether or not the policyholder makes a claim, how many people would consider the unused policy a waste? People may pay their homeowners insurance premium for years with no claims. However, one hailstorm that results in a $10,000 re-roofing job is a great reminder of the value of that insurance. Not many people consider health insurance premiums wasted, even if all they have paid for were a few blood tests to find out they were in perfect health. Would they really want to trade places with someone who had a blood test that led to more tests and eventually surgery with total costs of $30,000 or more? Most people understand that they are insuring against the possibility that something might happen whether they end up making a claim or not. Those who are insured who have no claims, as well as those who need to make claims, are the winners.

How Insurance Works

Probability theory is the foundation on which the insurance industry determines the likelihood of losses occurring. This permits actuaries to calculate appropriate premiums. Sometimes it is relatively easy; other times it is quite difficult.

One approach is called the **relative frequency interpretation**. This determines how often a certain type of loss occurs by analyzing how often something is likely to happen, given enough separate, independent trials. This can be done in two ways. The first way is based on the nature of the event under consideration. The second is based on a look at history to observe the outcomes of the actual events.

The easiest example of analyzing the nature of the event is to consider the flip of a coin. Assuming it will not land on its edge, it will be heads or tails. If the coin is balanced, we know intuitively that it will land on one side half of the time and on the other side the other half of the time. On any given flip, it could come up heads or tails. In 10 flips it might come up five and five, eight and two, or any other combination. However, we can surmise that the more times we flip it, the more likely it will be that the number of heads and tails will be the same or at least more evenly split. This is called the **Law of Large Numbers**. Clearly stated: As the number of events approaches infinity, the more accurate is the resulting prediction.

With insurance risks, the nature of the occurrences is such that history is a much better predictor of the frequency of various losses. By looking at many years' worth of outcomes (losses), insurance company actuaries can develop a **probability distribution**. Just as with the first method, this historical approach is able to provide more accurate information the more occurrences and exposures used. A company will have a much better idea of expected losses to homes if it insures 50,000 homes than if it insures 10,000 homes. If the statistics are gathered over 10 years, they will be more accurate than if they are gathered over only three years.

Once the probability distribution has been developed, expected claims can be determined. When these are added to the administrative costs of providing the insurance, and an allowance is made for variations in the year-to-year claims, the premiums are developed. Adjustments are made based on various risk factors. With automobiles, the age of the driver, the location of the vehicle, the vehicle's use, annual mileage, type of vehicle, etc. are used to determine the premium for each specific driver. For homeowners insurance, the square footage of the home, method of construction, distance to fire hydrant, security systems, age of structure, construction costs in the area, geographic differences in claims, use of smoke alarms, etc. are used to determine the premium for each home to be insured.

Each insured pays his or her premium. The insurance company puts the insurance concept into practice: It collects the premiums, invests the money, and waits for the claims. While most policyholders hope to never have to submit a claim, the insurance company knows to expect claims and hopes projected claims closely match actual claims. Individuals hope they suffer no losses. Insurance companies hope they do not suffer more losses than expected even though no company expects the actual claims to be exactly equal to the projected claims: Claims will be higher than expected in some years and lower than expected in others.

Adverse Selection

If you were the sole income earner for your family, and your job put you in life and death situations on a regular basis, you would probably be more likely to purchase life insurance than someone who lives and works in such a manner that the likelihood of his or her death by other than natural causes is minimal. However, for an insurance company to accept you as a standard risk would be financial suicide: You would ultimately not be contributing a fair share to the pool of funds. An insurance company that does not carefully screen applicants to ensure that they are of average risk will almost certainly be a victim of adverse selection, harming both the insurance company and its policyholders. Some people think this might apply to firefighters and members of a police force. Typical members of these groups are well trained to protect themselves and are usually not considered higher than average risks. A test pilot or members of a bomb squad may well be considered higher than average risks.

Adverse selection happens when an individual who is suffering a loss or who knows a loss is likely to occur is permitted to buy insurance at the same price as those who are not likely to suffer a similar loss. Poor risk individuals usually want insurance more than individuals with average or better-than-average risks. But if too many poor-risk policies are sold, claims are relatively high, making premiums high. People in this group are either denied insurance or charged a higher premium. They are said to be "rated" when this happens.

Knowing premiums are calculated on claims expenses, would you want your agent selling a homeowners policy to someone whose neighborhood was already on fire? Would you want your insurer to allow someone to buy coverage a week before a scheduled surgery and then drop it after the operation? Most likely, you would not: The actions of these individuals would be at odds with the concept of insurance. They would be taking the benefit of insurance but not sharing the costs. Insurance only works when all policyholders share in the losses of the few, so that if they suffer a loss, their out-of-pocket costs will be manageable. Avoiding adverse selection benefits policyholders.

If one person slips through now and then, with thousands of individuals being insured, the insurance company may not suffer too much. If too many below-average or poor risks are accepted, it will adversely affect the company and its insureds. The company will have to raise the premiums for the rest of the insurance buyers to make up for the lax controls of the insurer and/or the dishonesty of those who unfairly benefited. It is the failure to understand this that leads to the moral and morale risks facing insurers and insureds.

The Function of Insurance

What is the function of insurance? Without insurance, every business and family would have to maintain a very large cash reserve in case they suffered a loss. Without that reserve, a company might be put out of business if one truckload of product were destroyed, a product injured a customer, or a fire destroyed company equipment. A family could face financial ruin if the key breadwinner died or became unable to work because of illness or injury.

While losses for a group, or even all homeowners in a city, are relatively predictable, those for individuals are not. Insurance reduces the individual risks faced by everyone by trading small payments—the premiums—for the assurance that financial disaster will not strike when a loss occurs: Everyone accepts a small loss so that if they are hit with a large loss, the financial impact will be limited.

Losses will still occur, but the existence of insurance will likely increase the number and amount of losses due to moral and morale hazards. Insurance companies also make efforts to encourage loss prevention and severity reduction among their insureds. For example, discounts are given to owners of cars with anti-lock brakes, airbags, anti-theft devices, and for those who have taken driver's safety courses. So, while the effect of insurance on aggregate losses is not certain, it is predictable that some claims will be filed because of the moral and morale hazards that exist when insurance is in place. However, insurance's function is not to eliminate losses, but to permit individuals and businesses to free up reserves they would otherwise have to maintain for spending and investing. In that regard, insurance can be said to keep the economy moving.

Identifying an Insurable Risk

As we discussed in the section on risk, many losses are not insurable. In order for a loss to be insurable, an insurer must be willing to offer the coverage and an insured must be willing to pay an appropriate premium to obtain the coverage. There are four key factors in determining whether a risk is insurable from the standpoint of the insurance company. These four factors help minimize the potential for adverse selection, moral and morale hazards, and financially devastating risks. In other words, they help maintain a high proportion of good risks relative to bad risks in an insurable group.

The Risk of Loss Must Be Definable and Measurable

In most cases, potential losses are easily measurable. If a car is damaged, the direct loss is the cost to repair or replace it—add to that the cost of the indirect loss of alternate transportation until the car is repaired or replaced. If hail destroys a roof, the loss is the cost to repair it. The cost of medical care and long-term disability are all relatively easy to measure. Even the financial impact of the premature death of a family breadwinner can be estimated. However, it will be difficult to find an insurer willing to write a $1,000,000 life insurance policy on a family pet: The moral hazards involved are not difficult to imagine.

There Must Be a Large Number of Similar (Homogeneous) Exposure Units to Make Potential Losses Somewhat Predictable

Not only does the company need to have a large enough pool to make the losses predictable, the insurance company needs to have enough insured risks to spread the risk among an adequate number of insurable risks for the concept of insurance to work.

The Potential Loss Must Be Fortuitous or Accidental

If something is certain to happen, it will not be insurable. Even if it is just expected to happen, it is not insurable. Remember the definition of risk: *the possibility that something might happen that is not expected or wanted.* An individual is generally not permitted to insure against his or her own intentional acts. For example, liability insurance will generally not pay damages incurred when an insured punches someone.

The Loss Must Not Be Catastrophic

Remember, the determination of an insurable risk is from the point of view of the company, not the individual. If the insurance company has catastrophic losses, the policyholders will lose their insurance and some may not receive benefits in a timely manner because it will not be able to pay them. In other words, while a loss may be catastrophic to an individual, that same loss cannot be catastrophic to an insurance company and still be an insurable risk. For example, in 1992, Hurricane Andrew hit Southern Florida. And again in 2004, Florida experienced the effects of four hurricanes. Thousands of homes were damaged or destroyed. A number of insurance companies had sold homeowners policies in the area but not enough in other areas to keep them from becoming insolvent because too many of their insured risks filed major claims.

LEGAL ASPECTS OF INSURANCE

This section deals with a number of topics. First are a number of legal terms that often relate to insurance; second is a discussion of what constitutes a contract; and finally, are listed terms that directly describe contracts of insurance.

Terminology

Understanding the following legal terms is helpful in understanding the practical application of insurance.

An **intentional tort** is a purposeful infringement on the rights of others, such as assault, battery, libel, slander, false arrest or imprisonment, trespass, or invasion of privacy. Some of these are criminal offenses punishable by fine or imprisonment, and anyone who suffers damages as a result of an intentional tort has the right to sue for compensation.

A **trespasser** is one who is on someone's property without the owner's permission. An owner owes a minimal duty to a trespasser. The owner is not allowed to intentionally cause harm to a trespasser, such as setting a booby trap, and must warn the trespasser if he or she sees a trespasser walking toward a known hazard. Otherwise, a trespasser must accept the conditions of the property as they are. An owner can use reasonable force to expel a trespasser.

A **licensee** is a person who comes onto a property with the presumed approval or permission of the owner but not for the benefit of the owner. A door-to-door salesperson is a licensee. The property owner is generally under no duty to go out of his or her way to make the property safe for a licensee but must give the licensee reasonable warning of known unsafe conditions, such as posting a "Beware of Dog" sign.

An **invitee** is a person who has been "invited" to come onto the land or premises for the purpose or benefit of the owner. Store customers are invitees. The duty owed to an invitee is to keep the premises in a safe condition and to warn the invitee of any dangerous conditions. The property owner owes a greater duty or responsibility to an invitee than to a licensee. The owner must warn a licensee of any unsafe condition of which the owner has knowledge. But an invitee must be warned of any unsafe condition. This means that the owner must make an effort to find and identify any and all unsafe conditions. Failure to discover an existing unsafe condition does not excuse the owner from this responsibility.

An **attractive nuisance** is any dangerous place, condition, or object that is likely to entice or allure children (for example, earth-moving equipment, a swimming pool, or a great climbing tree). Property owners are expected to recognize the hazardous nature of such attractions and exposures and take special precautions to prevent children from gaining entrance to the property where they might be injured. The property owner may be held liable for failure to take adequate steps to prevent children from having access to the attractive nuisance.

Survival of tort actions means that the right to initiate legal action for damages continues after the death of the plaintiff, the defendant, or both. If Bob and Jack are walking around Jack's property, and dynamite stored in a shed explodes and kills them, Bob's estate and/or heirs have a right to sue Jack's estate for the loss.

Negligence (unintentional tort) is behavior or conduct that does not meet the standard expected from a reasonable and prudent person. If someone is injured by the negligence of another or suffers damage to his or her property, the negligent party may be held legally liable for the damage. For example, a reasonable person would not burn leaves on a windy day because he or she would understand the possibility that the wind might carry the fire to the property of others.

Negligence as a matter of law generally exists when a person violates a statute. **Negligence per se** exists when the injured party is one of a class of persons whom the law was intended to protect and if the resulting harm is one of the types that the law was intended to prevent. An example is the speed limits established by law around schools, put in place to protect children. If someone is speeding through a school zone and injures a child (not an adult), there is a presumption that the injury was caused by the speeder. What the child may have done is generally held to be irrelevant. Another example occurs when state law presumes that if while driving, your car hits another car from the rear, you are at fault. The presumption is that you were following too closely. If the rules are violated, the violation is referred to as negligence per se, and the injured party is relieved of the obligation of proving that the action was unreasonable. In this case, the presumption of innocence is modified.

Absolute liability (strict liability) is sometimes referred to as "liability without fault." A person who participates in certain types of activities will be liable for any injury inflicted on another by those activities, regardless of whether that person was negligent. Absolute liability applies to certain hazardous activities such as the keeping of wild animals, explosives manufacturing, oil well drilling, and aerial crop spraying.

Vicarious liability involves ascribing the acts of one person or entity to another. It is well known that a corporation is generally responsible for the negligent acts of its employees. A principal may be held vicariously liable for the tortious conduct or negligence of his or her agent. Parents are not generally liable for the acts of their children. However, they may be liable for failing to supervise their children.

Under *res ipsa loquitur* (translated "the thing speaks for itself"), a person can be found to be negligent because an accident would not normally have happened without negligence on the part of the person accused of negligence. In the eyes of the law, the fact that the accident happened is prima facie evidence that the individual was negligent. This principle applies only in the rare circumstance in which the injured party was not in a position to witness the negligent act, the accused person was in exclusive control of the instrumentality that caused the harm, and the harm would not normally have occurred without negligence. For example, suppose that an x-ray showed that a scalpel was in a person's chest cavity a week after surgery. No additional proof of wrongdoing is needed.

Defenses Against Claims of Liability

The great American lottery has become finding someone else to pay for one's misfortunes. Someone sues a car manufacturer when injured in a car accident instead of suing the person who caused the accident because the automaker has deeper pockets (more money). A skier who crosses a fence that is well marked with warnings sues the ski area after getting injured because the ski area did not prevent him from skiing out of bounds. What defense is there when someone is accused of negligence?

If it can be shown that an injured party reasonably should have recognized and understood the danger involved in an activity and voluntarily chose to pursue the activity anyway, this is called an **assumption of the risk**, and the defendant escapes liability. For example, if a bungee jumper sues the manufacturer of the bungee cord, the manufacturer could raise this defense. Some (but not all) jurisdictions permit the following two defenses based on negligence on the part of the injured party. If there is *any* negligence on the part of the injured party, called **contributory negligence**, it may bar a recovery by that injured party. If negligence on the part of the injured party is such that it should justify reducing any amount of damages payable by the defendant, it is referred to as **comparative negligence**. There are three common variations of the comparative negligence rule, depending on the jurisdiction:

Pure comparative negligence reduces a claimant's recovery by his or her proportion of total negligence. If the claimant is found to be 35 percent negligent, then the defendant has to pay only 65 percent of the claimant's loss.

The **50 percent rule** allows a claimant to recover damages from a defendant as long as the claimant's negligence is not greater than that of the defendant. The plaintiff does not recover anything if he or she is found to be 51 percent responsible.

The **49 percent rule** allows the plaintiff to recover reduced damages as long as his or her negligence is *less than* (or *not as great as*-depending on the statute language) that of the defendant. There is no recovery for the plaintiff if his or her negligence is found to be 50 percent. The contributory negligence of an injured party will not keep him or her from recovery of damages if the defendant, immediately prior to the accident, had a **last clear chance** to prevent the accident but did nothing to prevent it. If a defendant owns a small dock on a river and sees a stranger in a swim suit walk out on the dock (despite the "No Diving-Submerged Hazard" signs), the defendant is negligent if he or she does not take the last clear chance to tell the stranger of the hazard. Let us say you are driving down the street and see your neighbor backing out of the driveway rather quickly and you continue to drive on anyway. If this action results in the two of you having an accident, you might be found liable even though the other driver was driving carelessly and you had the right of way, because you did not take the last clear chance to avoid the collision.

Contracts

Many agreements made in the course of a day are contracts. Some are formal, some informal. Some are enforceable in a court of law, others are not. Insurance policies are contracts. They have all of the necessary components for enforceable contracts and also have certain contractual provisions and legal concepts that particularly apply to them. For any agreement to be enforceable, these five components must exist:

- Offer and Acceptance
- Consideration
- A Legal Purpose
- Competent Parties
- Legal Form

Offer and Acceptance

One entity (individual/business/trust/etc.) must make a definite offer, and the other party must accept this offer without changing any of its terms. If the second party wants to make a change to the offer, it becomes a new offer or a counteroffer.

With property and liability insurance, the offer is made by the prospect by making application for coverage. The offer is accepted when the agent binds coverage or when the policy is issued. The property-liability insurance binder can be written or oral (by telephone, for example). Thus, a property-liability insurance contract does not necessarily have to be in writing when the oral binder is used. However, if later the insurance company sends a written policy and bills a different premium, it is in effect making a counteroffer. Payment of the premium by the insured is an indication of acceptance of the counteroffer made by the insurer.

With life insurance, either the insured or the company may make the initial offer. When an application for life insurance is completed and the initial premium is paid, the applicant is making the offer. Issuance of the policy as applied for is an acceptance by the insurance company. If the company offers a policy that is different from the one originally applied for, the company is making a counteroffer. Subsequent payment of the premium then becomes acceptance by the policy owner. If the applicant submits the application without an initial premium, he or she is effectively asking the insurance company to make an offer. When the policy comes back, that is the offer, and payment of the premium shows acceptance.

Consideration

The consideration for a legal contract is whatever is given to one party as an inducement for him or her to complete the contract. It is some form of payment or obligation. The payment may be in money, services, goods, or a promise. For insurance contracts, the consideration provided by the applicant is the premium plus the statements in the application. The insurance company's consideration is the promise to pay valid claims.

A Legal Purpose

A contract to deliver illegal drugs or take the life of a person is not for a legal purpose and would therefore not be enforceable in the courts.

Competent Parties

For a contract to be enforceable, the parties must be capable of entering into the contract in the eyes of the law. Basically, the rules of competency deal with minors and the mentally incompetent. The reasoning is that some parties are not capable of understanding the contracts into which they enter. Therefore, the courts have ruled that incompetent parties are not bound by such agreements. A minor's contracts are generally voidable at his or her option at any time while still a minor and for "a reasonable period of time" after reaching the age of majority. Many states have reduced the legal age for purposes of negotiating a contract for life and health insurance, among others. Therefore, if the applicant resides in one of the states permitting a reduced legal age for life insurance, the minor applicant who meets the minimum requirement can negotiate a binding contract.

Legal Form

In general, contracts can run the gamut from oral to formal, written documents. If an agreement made over a handshake or written on a dirty bar napkin has all the required parts to be a valid contract, and the terms can be proven, it is enforceable. However, insurance contracts must use language that approximates that prescribed by state law if state law addresses that type of contract. An insurer must also follow the proper procedure for filing and gaining state approval of its contracts.

Void and Voidable Contracts

When a scam artist starts waving a contract in someone's face, threatening to sue, it is good to know what makes a contract void or, at least, voidable.

A **void** contract has no legal standing because it lacks one or more of the requirements specified by law for a valid contract. It cannot be enforced by either party. For example, a contract to have one person steal another's property is void and neither party can enforce it because any contract contrary to law is void and unenforceable.

A **voidable** contract is binding on one party but the other party may elect out of the contract. For example, a contract an adult makes with a minor child is generally voidable by the child but not voidable by the adult. Many states have specific statutes that bind minors to their contracts for life and health insurance but not for property-liability insurance. For this reason, most contracts with minors must be co-signed by an adult. Otherwise, a 17-year-old could borrow $5,000 to buy a car, wreck it, and then decide not to pay. Although the lender might try to collect, the courts may choose to not enforce the contract.

Insurance Contract Terms

Insurance contracts are described or affected by a number of legal and technical terms that specifically apply to them. The terms and concepts shown below are important in understanding how insurance policies operate.

Insurance contracts are **contracts of indemnity**. The concept of indemnity is to make someone whole: to put him or her back in the place he or she occupied before a loss occurred. This means the insurer promises to reimburse the insured up to the amount of the insured's covered financial loss or the amount of coverage, whichever is less. Life insurance policies are sometimes referred to as **valued policies** since they pay the face amount. However, the underwriting process, to some extent, determines the "value" of the insured by limiting the amount of insurance it will issue on his or her life. Some property insurance policies are also valued policies. Such property insurance policies may not be helpful in preserving the principle of indemnity because they pay the policy owner the face amount, regardless of the policy owner's actual financial loss. However, these policies are normally based on the appraised value of the insured items. These are generally issued on expensive jewelry, classic automobiles, art, and the like.

An insurance contract is a **personal contract**. This means that the policy is personally issued to the insured and is between the insured and the insurance company. With the exception of life insurance, these contracts may not be assigned to anyone else without the approval of the insurer. It can be as important for the insurer to underwrite for a new insured as it is for the insurer to initially pass judgment on the condition of the property insured. The life insurance policy is personal in a different sense. The contract will insure the same person unless the insurance company approves a change of insureds. Unlike other forms of insurance, life insurance may be assigned to anyone the policy owner chooses. For example, a life insurance policy may be assigned to a creditor as security for a debt.

A life insurance contract can be assigned in two ways. An **absolute assignment** is a complete transfer of ownership. It is the same as signing over the title of a car to someone else. The original owner no longer owns the contract. The alternative is a **collateral assignment**. When a car is purchased with a loan, the car is collaterally assigned to the lender. If the borrower defaults on the loan, the lender gets the car, sells it, pays off the debt, and gives the borrower anything that is left. When a policy owner borrows against a life insurance policy, the policy is collaterally assigned to the insurance company. Many small business loans require the

> **NEED TO KNOW: WHAT IS PERSONAL PROPERTY WORTH?**
>
> When a client wants to know what an item of personal property is worth, he or she generally seeks an appraisal. For insurance purposes, the appraised value is the cost of replacing the item with one of like kind and condition. The appraiser will usually ask the purpose of the appraisal. If the client seeks the appraisal for an estate value, then he or she would want a low value appraised for the item so that the value of the item in the estate would be reduced. The appraised value is also the price the appraiser believes can be realized if the item were to be sold. Even this value may vary among appraisers. If the estate needed to sell assets quickly for liquidity, then the price realized might be less than if the estate can take its time selling the assets. In that situation, the estate value might be half or less of replacement value.

business owner to assign life insurance to the lender. In this case, if the borrower were to die, the lender would get paid back first with the named beneficiary getting any money that is left.

Contracts may be **unilateral** or **bilateral**. Under the definition of a unilateral contract, only one party can be forced to comply with the contract. Under the terms of a bilateral contract, both parties make promises that are legally enforceable. Insurance contracts are unilateral. Only the insurer is legally bound to do something. The insured makes no enforceable promise to do anything. Of course, if the insured does not pay the renewal premium, the policy is cancelled. There are also policy conditions that must be met by the policy owner to obtain the policy benefits promised in the contract.

An insurance contract is a **contract of adhesion**. If one party (the insurer) writes a contract and the second party (the insured) has only an option to accept or reject the contract as written, the contract is not considered to have been drawn up through negotiation. Because the drafter of the contract decides on the policy language, the courts, under the doctrine of adhesion, interpret all ambiguous language as favorably as possible for the other party. In other words, if the words of the contract are your words, you are stuck with them—they adhere to you.

Insurance contracts are **aleatory contracts**. An aleatory contract provides one party with potential benefits greatly in excess of the benefits to be received by the other party. Gambling contracts are aleatory contracts: A winner may receive benefits far in excess of the money paid and the outcome is affected by chance. Likewise, because of chance, an insured may receive more benefits than he or she paid in premiums. A **commutative contract** is the opposite. A typical sales contract is commutative: Both parties receive essentially equivalent benefits. It is important to recognize that while it is by chance that a particular insured may receive far more in benefits than the amount paid in premiums, insurance contracts are not gambling contracts. From the insurer's point of view, premiums paid by all insureds are expected to be adequate to pay expected claims and all the administrative and sales costs, while still leaving a profit. There is no gamble on the part of the insurer.

Insurance contracts are also contracts of **utmost good faith**: Both parties expect the other to behave honestly. However, the concept of utmost good faith probably applies more to the honesty of the insured. In making an underwriting decision whether to insure and how to rate an applicant, the insurer relies on the complete truthfulness of the applicant in providing information concerning the proposed loss exposure. If the information provided by the applicant is false or incomplete, the underwriter will not be able to properly assess the risk. If this happens, the insurer may be able to void the contract on grounds of breach of warranty, misrepresentation, or concealment.

A **misrepresentation** is a false statement. If a misrepresentation is material, it may be a basis for voiding the contract. For example, when a property loss occurs, a property insurance policy insurer may refuse to pay a claim on the grounds of misrepresentation made by the insured at the time of application. An example might be a homeowner who tells the company he used fire retardant roofing materials when he did not, resulting in his house burning to the ground because a cinder landed on his roof. Another example might be that the insured tells the insurance company that a specific car is for casual use only, when in fact it is driven 45 miles a day in a heavy traffic commute.

However, with life insurance policies, any misrepresentation must be discovered within the one- or two-year contestable period. Otherwise, the life insurance policy is valid despite a misrepresentation of the applicant-policy owner. As a result of at least one court case, an insurance company was required to pay a death claim on a policy that was more than two years old, even though the insured sent someone else for the physical exam, committing intentional fraud.

A **warranty** is a promise that a fact or condition exists exactly as stated in the contract, or implied by the nature of the contract. If any statement that is subject to the warranty is determined to be untrue, it renders the policy voidable by the other party. For most insurance policies, the remedy of voiding a contract for any fact that is not absolutely correct is too severe in the eyes of most courts. This harsh interpretation is most commonly seen in ocean marine policies (discussed later in the text). A warranty must generally be in writing and be a part of the written contract to be enforceable. State laws generally specify that an insurance policy must include language that all statements by the applicant will be construed to be representations and not warranties. Courts today generally hold that insurance contracts may not be voided because of a breach of warranty or misrepresentation unless the violation was material, caused the loss, and/or increased the risk that contributed to the loss. This position is obviously more favorable for the insured. Otherwise, if a life insurance application included a notation that the applicant saw a physician for a sprained ankle in June of 1998, but the appointment was actually in May of 1998, the company could void the contract.

Concealment is the failure to disclose known material information. If the withheld information, had it been known, would have led the insurer to make a different underwriting decision, it is material. If an applicant for insurance fails to disclose known material facts, this constitutes concealment. Intentional concealment is grounds for voiding the contract. It is difficult for an insurance company to void an insurance contract on the grounds of concealment because the insurer would have to prove that the insured knew a particular fact, that it was material, and that the insured intentionally failed to inform the insurer. For instance, an insured runs a business involving wood finishing in his basement. The storage of combustible materials and the creation of sawdust is material in determining the risk of insuring the structure. Failing to inform the insurer of this business would be concealment.

Assurance of Indemnity

The concept of **indemnity** centers on the idea that individuals are to be made whole—and no more than whole—when they suffer a loss, to be put in no better than the financial position they would have been in had a loss not occurred. As stated above, insurance contracts are contracts of indemnity. Insurance policies use four concepts, listed below, or policy provisions, to help ensure that the principle of indemnity will be maintained. It would lead to adverse selection and an increased number of fraudulent claims if insureds were able to make a profit when a loss occurred. Property insurance policies are strictly contracts of indemnity. The insurer is willing to reimburse the insured for the amount of his or her financial loss but no more. It can be argued that settling a property insurance claim on the basis of the replacement cost of a destroyed building is not indemnity. Replacing an old building with a new building may put the insured in a better financial position than before the loss. However, it is virtually impossible to replace the workmanship and materials used 50 or 100 years ago when replacing a home with current materials and building methods. While a replaced home may be new, it may not have the quality of construction or touches of craftsmanship of the one that was destroyed. Therefore, companies underwrite the policies carefully, investigate claims closely and, in some cases, pay only if the building is actually repaired or replaced.

Doctrine of Insurable Interest

Insurance is issued only when an applicant has an insurable interest in the subject being insured. An insurable interest exists between a policy owner and the subject matter of the insurance if the policy owner will suffer a financial loss if the subject matter is damaged or destroyed. For example, a homeowner has an insurable interest in his or her home because he or she would suffer a financial loss if the home were damaged or destroyed. A creditor also has an insurable interest in the life of a debtor because the creditor might not collect the amount of the loan if the debtor dies before repaying the debt. Everyone is presumed to have an insurable interest in his or her own life, health, and property.

In property insurance, the insurable interest in the property insured must exist at the time of the loss. Assume a person owned a car that was insured and then sold the car. If the new owner destroyed the car 20 minutes after the purchase, the original owner would suffer no loss. Since he or she had no insurable interest in the car at the time of its destruction, he or she would collect nothing from the insurer, even if the policy had not been cancelled.

For life insurance, an insurable interest in the insured life must exist at the time the policy is issued. Thus, a woman will have an insurable interest in the life of her husband at the time the policy is issued. However, if the couple were to divorce later, she could keep the policy and collect at his death, even though she might suffer no financial loss at his death.

In property insurance, the insurable interest must be based on a financial interest in the property. In life insurance, however, an insurable interest may be based on certain family relationships even though the policy owner may derive no financial benefit from the continued life of the insured. An insurable interest is generally assumed to exist between an applicant for insurance and his or her spouse, children, and parents. In general, an insurable interest in other relatives is not assumed and, therefore, a potential financial loss would need to exist. However, even family members are not generally able to purchase insurance on someone without their knowledge. Applications for individual life insurance generally must be signed by the proposed insured.

Actual Cash Value

The actual cash value (ACV) of a loss is the maximum reimbursement that will be paid to a claimant under most property insurance contracts. ACV is the property's replacement cost minus physical depreciation (not the same as depreciation the accountant shows in financial statements). This arrangement ensures enforcement of the principle of indemnity because the insured is not reimbursed by providing him or her with a new asset as a replacement for an old asset. Depreciation of old property is recognized and the insured is reimbursed accordingly. However, this could result in a very low value being placed upon old furniture that is still functional and which the insured will need to replace. For this reason, many homeowners policies are written with replacement cost coverage.

Other Insurance Provisions

This provision is often found in property insurance policies and health care plans. It provides that the insurer will pay a proportion of any loss that the amount of the policy's coverage applicable to the loss bears to the total amount of coverage for the loss provided by all insurers, whether the other insurance is collectible or not. This means that if someone has three policies that could equally cover the same loss, each insurance company will pay, at most, a third of the loss. So, the insured cannot purchase multiple policies and hope to profit if he or she suffers damage to insured property or has substantial medical claims. Health care plans operate a bit differently and will be discussed later in the text.

Subrogation

The final provision used to enforce the concept of indemnity is **subrogation**. This common law doctrine gives an insurer the rights of the insured against anyone who caused a loss for the insured that was covered by the insurer. This means if someone else injures you and if your health insurance pays the bills, your health care plan has the right to sue the person who injured you to get paid back before you can collect anything from that person. This often happens following auto accidents. For example, an insured is in an accident and his insurer pays to repair his or her car and pays for medical expenses. If the other party was at fault, the injured person's auto insurer is first in line to collect from the at-cause driver's insurance

Other Legal and Contract Provisions

There are other legal and contract provisions and concepts that can be applied directly to insurance but generally are not specified in any policy.

The **parol evidence rule** is sometimes used to put an end to disputes involving contracts. The rule states that the written contract is the final word in an agreement between two parties. It is presumed that each party had an equal opportunity to include whatever he or she wanted in the contract before it was signed. Therefore the contract, as written, is binding on both parties. Any prior oral agreements, notes on napkins, emails, faxes or the like, between the parties are assumed to have been considered when creating the final version. Neither party is permitted to bring in evidence subsequent to the contract being signed to show that they intended to include any additional provisions in the contract.

When one party in a contract is made aware that the other party has not completely complied with the contract, but chooses not to act on that knowledge, he or she may be considered to have waived any right to enforce that part of the contract, or to have granted a **waiver**. In an insurance contract, the insurer often includes a non-waiver provision that states that no one may waive a provision in the contract except an officer of the company. A policyholder should read a contract carefully to verify that what the agent promised is included in the contract. However, even with this non-waiver provision, a dispute may be settled in the policyholder's favor if the court rules that the agent waived the policyholder's noncompliance. An agent is considered the company under the law of agency.

Waiver and **estoppel** generally are thought of together. If one party relies on the other party's waiver of its right to enforce a part of the contract, the first party is generally prevented (estopped) from enforcing it later. In a property insurance contract, for example, the insured is required to try to minimize subsequent damage when a covered loss occurs. If a tree branch on the insured's property breaks off in a windstorm and breaks the window of someone else's car, the insured is expected to cover the hole to the best of his or her ability to prevent rain, hail, or snow from entering the car through the window frame and causing more damage. If the insured does not do this and more damage is caused with the insurance company paying the claim anyway, the insurer has waived enforcement of that provision. If a similar occurrence happens, the insurance company may be estopped from denying coverage for such additional damage. It is generally estopped from enforcing any provision in the policy it did not enforce the first time. However, if following the first occurrence, the company confirmed with the insured that it would cover the first damage, but would not do it again if he or she did not attempt to reduce subsequent damage, it will not be estopped from enforcement of that provision later.

Contract law also provides for **rescission**: If one party can prove that the other party misrepresented material information in the preparation or negotiation of the insurance contract, the insurance policy may be rescinded.

Reformation is the changing of an existing contract rather than creating a new one. It is done when both parties agree to the change because the new (reformed) contract is what was originally intended. For example: Pat and Les entered into an agreement where Pat was to paint Les's house for a fee of $2,000.When the contract was typed up, it read $2,800. Both Pat and Les agreed that the number needed to be changed, so the contract was rewritten (reformed) to show the correct fee.

Insurance contracts are **conditional** contracts. An insurance company is obligated to pay a claim only when the insured has complied with the conditions of the contract, such as paying the premiums, filing a claim, etc., and when the insured peril results in a loss being sustained. While risk management is much more comprehensive than insurance management, personal insurance management is a critical part of the financial planning relationship. The wide range of insurance products permit individuals to have an insurance program that meets their needs. However, just as with all phases of financial planning, it is not a static part of the plan. It needs to be reviewed and updated. A financial planner schooled in the language of insurance is in a position to help clients not only obtain what they need but also to understand it. There is also a great deal of legal jargon that relates to insurance. Understanding these terms and how they relate to insurance is also valuable in helping clients.

IMPORTANT CONCEPTS

Adverse selection

Components of contracts

Concept of insurance

Concept of indemnity

Defenses against claims of negligence

Function of insurance

Hazard

Insurable risk

Insurance contract terms

Law of Large Numbers

Liability risks

Negligence

Peril

Personal risks

Property risks

Pure risk

Risk

Risk management techniques

Rules of risk management

Speculative risk

QUESTIONS FOR REVIEW

1. Explain the difference between pure risk and speculative risk.

2. Identify and describe the elements of an insurable risk.

3. Differentiate between risk, hazard, and peril.

4. List, explain, and give examples of the five methods of managing risks.

5. Describe the rules of risk management.

6. Explain adverse selection.

7. Describe the different types of negligence and the ways in which insurance may or may not be able to help with the result.

8. List and explain the components of contracts in general and how they apply to insurance contracts.

9. What is the benefit of insurance to the individual?

10. How does probability theory apply to insurance?

11. Are insurance contracts unilateral or bilateral? Explain.

12. What are the types of risks to which individuals may be exposed?

13. Explain the concept of indemnity.

SUGGESTIONS FOR ADDITIONAL READING

Essentials of Risk Management & Insurance, 2nd ed., Emmett J. and Therese M. Vaughan, Wiley, 2003.

Fundamentals of Risk and Insurance, 9th ed., Emmett J. and Therese M. Vaughan, John Wiley & Sons, 2003.

Principles of Risk Management and Insurance, 9th ed., George E. Rejda, Addison Wesley Longman, 2004.

The Tools & Techniques of Life Insurance Planning, 3rd ed., Stephan R. Leimberg and Robert J. Doyle, Jr., National Underwriter, 2004.

CHAPTER TWO

Introduction to Life Insurance

• • •

Until a primary breadwinner dies, no one feels a great desire to talk about life insurance. People will ask family and friends for advice when purchasing a car and then be anxious to show it off, but most people will not even be tempted to mention that they are looking for a new universal life policy.

Life insurance is dollars, purchased for pennies a year, to be delivered at an unknown but particular time in the future. No other financial product can do what it does best: provide a promised amount of cash when it is needed most. Life insurance is an exceptionally versatile tool; a financial planner must understand when and how to use it and recognize the advantages and disadvantages of the different forms. No one kind of policy is best—all have attributes that make them better suited for differing circumstances. As in all areas of financial planning, the planner needs an open mind to be able to understand and use all of the available tools as they are appropriate.

When you finish this chapter, you should be able to:
- Describe the various types and general classifications of life insurance, including the various special life insurance forms
- Identify and explain various life insurance contract provisions and options
- Identify and explain the income- and estate-tax implications of life insurance
- Identify and describe the steps in managing personal risks

MANAGING PERSONAL RISKS

Like all forms of insurance, life insurance is designed to help individuals, families, and businesses with a particular risk: in this case, the risk that an individual's death will leave family members, dependents, employees, or colleagues with a financial burden.

In chapter 1, we introduced the basic principles of risk management. As we begin to study the various risks that individuals face and the accompanying types of insurance that are designed to assist with those risks, keep in mind the following principles:

Establish the Risk Management Objectives

Risk management objectives generally fall into two categories. **Pre-loss objectives** include both cost-effective management of any exposures to loss and reduction of concerns so that an individual can attend to daily living and a business can focus on producing and distributing its product or providing its service.

Post-loss objectives include continuity of everyday life or business operations and continued income or earning stability.

Gather Information to Identify Exposures to Loss

When assessing the potential losses brought on by the death of a family member or breadwinner, a financial planner or insurance expert might use checklists, questionnaires, and financial statements. For other types of loss, the identification of possible exposures might also include inspecting the home, plant, equipment, and general layout of operations on-site and examining operation flowcharts.

Analyze and Evaluate the Exposures to Loss

The most severe risks, those that can cause a financial catastrophe for the individual, need to be addressed first. A severe potential loss—often called a *critical risk*—needs to be insured, or financial preparations need to be made for dealing with it. Next are *important risks*, those that would not be financially catastrophic but would probably require borrowing money to cover. Last come risks that might be called *unimportant or minor risks*: those that can be handled out of current income or assets without much concern. Financially, it is generally more important to get life insurance policies for primary breadwinners than for dependents. In general, the frequency and severity of potential losses should be examined as detailed in chapter 1.

Develop a Plan to Achieve the Objectives

After analyzing the exposures to loss, it is important to identify the alternative techniques available for handling the important or serious loss exposures and select the appropriate technique or techniques to recommend.

Implement the Plan

If your client will not follow through to this step, he or she should not waste time on the first four. Once the exposures have been identified and the plan created, it is time to put it into place.

Review the Plan

No part of financial planning is static. While insurance against personal risks may not need to be reviewed comprehensively every six months, it does need to be reviewed on a regular basis to ensure new risks are managed and known risk management plans are kept current.

GENERAL TYPES OF LIFE INSURANCE

Life insurance is available in a number of different forms, each designed to meet the needs and desires of various consumers and to provide varying levels of security. While the two major categories are *term* and *permanent*, there are many variations of each.

The one thing common to all is that they provide a cash benefit when the insured dies—a **death benefit**. The face amount of a life insurance policy is the stated death benefit, and with a term insurance policy it is typically the total death benefit, but a planner should be aware that the final death benefit check is not likely to be for the face amount of the policy. With some permanent policies, the death benefit could be the face amount plus certain clearly defined additional benefits, or the basic death benefit might be modified by dividend values. Additionally, most companies pay interest on the death benefit from the date of death until the date the death claim is processed and paid, and refund any unearned premiums held as of the insured's date of death. All insurance policies will reduce death benefits by any premiums due, and permanent forms of insurance will reduce the benefit by any outstanding policy loans and interest due on those loans.

Term Insurance

Most of the life insurance in force in the United States is term insurance—insurance that provides death benefits to a beneficiary if the insured dies within the term of the policy. Sometimes called pure insurance or temporary insurance, term life insurance is best suited for temporary needs. Early term life insurance policies had increasing annual premiums. Annually renewable term (ART) or yearly renewable term (YRT) policies are still available, but in recent years, term policies with premiums that are level for a number of years have become the predominant form. There are a number of variations.

Yearly Renewable or Annually Renewable Term (YRT or ART)

Since the premium is adjusted annually, YRT insurance typically has the lowest first-year premium. Technically, the policy renews every year, with most renewals being automatic, but the number of renewals is limited: Few policies renew past age 65 and virtually none renew past age 70. The death benefit most often stays the same throughout the life of the policy, and each year the policy renews at a new premium. Most ART or YRT policies have a current premium and a usually much higher guaranteed premium. The guaranteed premium provides the insurer the flexibility of being able to raise the current premium to a supportable level if mortality rates or expenses increase too much or if interest rates fall too much. The current premium enables the company to remain competitive.

Re-Entry Term

This is a renewal method rather than a specific form of term insurance. Periodically (typically every five years), the insured may choose to be re-underwritten. Underwriting is the process of determining if a person is an acceptable risk. If he or she is still in the same risk classification, a new, lower current premium is charged: the same premium charged for new insurance applicants. This helps keep policies in force by giving the lowest-risk individuals the opportunity to lower their premiums instead of looking at other companies. These policies also reduce adverse selection: The insurance company has a chance to reevaluate insureds, granting good rates if warranted. If the insured does not apply for or qualify for the re-entry rates, he or she will have substantially increased premiums. These increased premiums may be a multiple of the previous rate and may even be the guaranteed maximum rate, which can be rather high. Policies that do not have re-entry provisions will likely have slightly higher premiums initially, but for those who develop a health problem, they will end up being much less than if they had to re-qualify.

Level Premium Term

Many companies offer term insurance with a guaranteed level premium for up to 10 years, generally with a level death benefit, though few policies permit death benefits beyond age 65. Some companies do sell policies with projected level premiums for 20 or 30 years, but few actually guarantee premiums for more than 10 years, since doing so requires substantially larger reserves. Regulation XXX, promulgated by the National Association of Insurance Commissioners (NAIC) to ensure solvency for companies in the low-cost term insurance "wars" that went on for years, forces the premium on policies with a long-term level premium to be much higher than for policies with only a 10-year guarantee. A few policies can be converted to permanent insurance any time before age 65, most for only a few years after the policy is purchased.

In-Depth: Participating and Nonparticipating Policies

Mutual life insurance companies are owned by the policyholders and pay out part of their profits to the policyholders as policy dividends. A policy earning dividends is a participating policy. The policy owners "participate" in the profits of the company. Most traditional permanent and term life and disability policies sold by mutual companies are participating policies: Since the policyholders own the company, they receive the dividends. However, some companies that are owned by stockholders also sell participating policies.

Dividends are not guaranteed, but they are an important part of the equation in determining the true cost of coverage for a client. Dividends paid on participating insurance policies are quite different from dividends paid on stock. Insurance policy dividends are treated as a return of premium and are therefore not treated as taxable income. This is covered in more depth later in this chapter.

Owners of participating policies often pay a premium that is in excess of the amount that the insurer needs to pay for anticipated claims and expenses. If the claims and administrative expenses in a given year are as expected or lower, the company generally elects to pay a dividend to the policyholders. If the claims or administrative costs for the year were higher than expected, the company might pay a lower dividend or elect not to pay a dividend at all. This flexibility can be used to help stabilize the cash flows of a mutual insurance company and ensure its financial stability.

Participating policies can respond to changes in the economy. When interest rates were high in the late 1970s and early 1980s, participating policies were in a position to keep up with the changing interest rates, whereas nonparticipating policies (policies that did not pay dividends) did not have that capability. Policyholders were less likely to be locked into very low interest earnings from their policies. During those years, with short-term interest rates exceeding 10 percent, many of the nonparticipating policies that had been sold with guaranteed interest rates of 2.5 percent to 3.5 percent were replaced with participating policies, universal life policies, and other forms of permanent insurance that could have their returns adjusted if the economic conditions warranted. It was the high interest rates of those years that spawned the demand for universal life insurance policies.

Decreasing Term

With this form of term insurance, sometimes called disappearing term, the death benefit decreases over the life of the policy while the premium usually remains level. These policies are usually limited to 30 years or less. Though it is generally sold as mortgage insurance, most of these policies have straight-line reductions in coverage rather than mirroring the decrease of a mortgage balance. Decreasing term is sometimes sold as a rider with a "whole life" permanent policy to provide income to a family as well as an up-front lump sum benefit when a breadwinner dies. The biggest advantage of this form is that the premiums are relatively low and they are level. The biggest disadvantage is that the level of coverage decreases while needs often increase over the early years of a young family's life.

Changes in the Term Insurance Market

The "term wars" mentioned above began in the late 1970s. It was started when reserve requirements were changed and grew as mortality rates fell. The term wars got its name from the actions of insurance companies that were reducing their term insurance rates to levels that were, in some cases, less than half of what they were before the wars started. Term rates stayed low for about 25 years.

In 2004 the term insurance market began to change significantly. Regulation XXX finally took hold, and insurers were finding that reserve requirements were much higher than those maintained previously. In addition, the reinsurance market changed. Certain insurers do not write policies on individuals directly; they have agreements with insurance companies, reinsurers, that they will accept a certain amount of risk for policies the retail companies are writing. These reinsurance companies began to increase their rates and tighten the rules under which they would accept risk. These factors, along with protracted low interest rates and a stock market that was down for a number of years, all affected the actuarial numbers. In 2004, after many years of continually decreasing term insurance rates, the rates began to rise. Additionally, conversion privileges, mentioned above and further discussed later in this chapter, began a trend to be less generous. These changes all work to make the financial backing of term insurance policies more secure and to reduce the opportunities for adverse selection.

Permanent Insurance

Permanent insurance is designed to last for life. It also has a number of variations, but these are generally in one of two categories: traditional and universal life.

Traditional, or fixed, forms of permanent insurance can be either participating or nonparticipating. A participating policy earns dividends. Nonparticipating policies may have no method of adjusting costs or benefits or may be interest-adjusted or excess-interest forms—two forms used with nonparticipating policies to make them responsive to economic changes. However, since the mid 1980s, few traditional, permanent, nonparticipating policies have been sold which do not include some method of crediting excess interest. Traditional permanent insurance includes whole life, limited pay life, graded premium life, and a hybrid form of permanent and term that has as many names as there are companies offering it. The second form is **universal life**, technically named "flexible premium adjustable life" (not to be confused with an uncommon form of traditional permanent insurance called adjustable life).

In-Depth: Term Insurance Issues

Unfortunately, many people view term insurance as a commodity: The lower the premium, the better. Treating a product as a commodity makes sense when it is indistinguishable from any other version. However, this is not the case with term insurance unless the need is unquestionably short and no riders are purchased with the policy.

Although some agents and planners suggest that it is relatively unimportant to find the best term insurance provider since there is a high probability that the insurance will be replaced after a few years if a lower premium becomes available, there are good reasons not to do this. First, if the insured becomes too great a risk to get a new policy, he or she may be stuck with an inferior policy. There are also provisions in a policy that start whenever a new policy is purchased—among others, the incontestability and suicide clauses begin when a new policy is issued (see below for more on the standard life insurance contract clauses).

Moreover, there is the issue of excessive applications. Most insurance companies use one of the relatively few reinsurance companies to assume part or all of the risk of large amounts of insurance they sell. With life insurance, as with other forms

(continued on next page)

(continued from previous page)

of insurance, if individuals apply to replace insurance too often, the insurance companies and reinsurance companies may decline to issue new coverage. The problem with reinsurance companies has become exacerbated due to the changes discussed above. After all, if an applicant is replacing a five-year-old term policy and has a history of replacing one every five years, the insurance company does not particularly want him or her as a policyholder. The cost of selling a policy generally exceeds the first-year premium, but in another five years, the migratory policyholder will either drop the new insurer for another company or end up as an impaired risk on their books. And if the companies decline to sell a new policy, the policyholder, again, may be stuck with an inferior policy.

What is "inferior"? As you know from reading about the various types of term policies, renewal provisions can make a big difference among policies, possibly leaving the policyholder with very high premiums if the renewal provisions are poorly considered. Another distinct difference is in variations in the disability waiver of premium rider (discussed in depth in the discussion of life insurance contracts below). Only a few companies permit conversion to a permanent policy and continue to waive the new higher premium when a term policy insured becomes disabled, and some companies are more generous in defining "disability" than others.

Conversion privileges should also be considered: The lowest premium policies around may only be renewable for three to ten years with no conversion privilege. Some policies permit conversion to permanent insurance for only the first five years. Some will permit conversion up to the policy anniversary nearest the insured's 65th birthday, although, as mentioned previously, these provisions are becoming scarcer. What form of insurance is available when conversion is desired? What riders, if any, can follow the term policy to the conversion policy?

Finally, in some instances, a policyholder may find it necessary or expedient to keep a policy for longer than originally intended. Therefore, potential purchasers and their financial planners should be very careful to choose an insurer with excellent financial strength and a policy that will provide flexibility to meet long-term needs.

Traditional Permanent Insurance

Whole life is the basic form of traditional permanent insurance with a guaranteed death benefit, guaranteed premium, and a guaranteed cash value. Generally, the policyholder pays premiums and continues benefits until the insured reaches age 100, at which time the policy endows (meaning the face amount of the policy and guaranteed cash value are the same) and the face amount of the policy is paid to the policy owner. As life expectancy has increased, some companies are using endowment dates beyond age 100. This effectively reduces premiums, since cash values have more years to accumulate to the level of the death benefit. A type of variation of whole life is limited-pay life. A limited-pay life policy operates in much the same way as a whole life policy, but the premium paying period is limited to a specified number of years. One of the most common variations of limited-pay life is a **life paid up at 65** policy: a whole life policy with level premiums slightly increased so that they stop at age 65 while the face amount is guaranteed to last until endowment at age 100. At some ages it is still possible to purchase a **20-pay life** policy, which is similar to life paid up at 65 except that premiums end 20 years after the issue date of the policy while the death benefit continues.

Graded premium life is a traditional form with a relatively low initial premium that increases each year for five to seven years. When it levels out, it is typically higher than the whole life premium that would have been charged at the beginning of the policy's life, but lower than the premium payable for a whole life policy taken out at the end of the increasing premium period. It is designed to allow individuals who want permanent insurance to ease into the full permanent insurance premium.

The final variation is a hybrid participating policy with various names. Companies have used a variety of names for this hybrid policy including Economatic, Econolife, ExtraLife, Extra Special Life, Economaster, or enhanced whole life, among others. The base policy is whole life with an additional death benefit made up of a combination of term insurance and paid-up dividend additions (see the dividend options below). Its design is such that, over time, the additional death benefit is made up completely of paid-up dividend additions. It is designed to be a level death benefit policy. Only companies with participating policies have this form: It was created to provide a permanent policy with a premium between 20 and 30 percent lower than an equal amount of whole life insurance. Some companies have expanded this concept to allow applicants and their agents to develop their own mix of whole life base policies with the term and dividend additions.

Universal Life

Named by marketing mavens who touted it as the only necessary life insurance product, **universal life** is a flexible form of permanent insurance that has many uses. It also has disadvantages. Again, it is technically known as "flexible premium adjustable life."

Universal life (UL) can have fixed or variable interest:

- **Fixed interest forms** most often include a minimum guaranteed interest rate and guaranteed maximum mortality (life expectancy) charges. They credit any available excess interest to the accumulation account of the policy. Excess interest arises out of the investment experience of the insurer. It often reflects relatively current market rates of return. With fixed forms of insurance, the cash values and accumulation accounts are part of the company's general assets. If the company becomes insolvent—relatively few have—it creates a problem for owners of fixed policies. The term "fixed" does not mean that the interest rate does not change. Rather, it means that the policy accumulation fund earns interest based on some measure of return. The measure may be based on the company's portfolio return on its investments or on a fluctuating interest rate that may be found in the *Wall Street Journal*. The return may be based on a combination of factors and is not based on returns on equities.

- **Variable forms**, called **variable universal life**, have the same guaranteed maximum mortality charge, but no guaranteed minimum return. The growth of the accumulation account is completely dependent on the return earned by the separate, mutual-fund-like accounts in which the accumulated funds are invested. These separate accounts give variable forms an advantage: They are separate from the assets of the company and are not accessible to general creditors of the company. Variable UL policies are a combination of insurance and a security, so both the federal government and the states regulate them. Any agent who sells them must have a securities license in addition to a life insurance license. While most policy owners of variable universal life put all of their account assets in equities, there is generally a fixed interest account or money market account available for times when they do not want their money in more volatile equities.

There are also two death benefit options for UL:

- **Type A, or type 1, level death benefit**: This death benefit is the face amount of the policy. The mortality charges are based on the net amount at risk, and the net amount at risk is the face amount of the policy minus the accumulation fund.

- **Type B, or type 2, increasing death benefit**: With these policies, the death benefit is equal to the face amount *plus* the accumulation fund. This means that the monthly mortality charges are based on the face amount of the policy every year. This requires a greater fund to keep the policy in force.

With universal life, the premium is not fixed or tied to the face amount except in the first year. Premiums are paid into an accumulation fund. Each month the mortality charges, rider charges, and expenses are taken from the accumulation fund. Except for the first year when the minimum premium is specified, the premium is quite flexible. There is a minimum premium that is required to keep the policy in force only when the accumulation fund is close to zero. There is a maximum premium allowable so that the policy does not become a modified endowment contract (this will be discussed later).

It is important to recognize the specific differences between universal life and variable universal life. While the general operation and structure of the two forms is practically identical, there are significant differences. One factor that is important for a planner to know is that, with most companies, due to the complexity of variable universal life—the administrative costs are slightly higher than for universal life. Table 2.1 compares the two types of policies.

Table 2.1 Comparison of Universal Life and Variable Universal Life Insurance

	Universal Life	**Variable Universal Life**
Accumulation Account	Assets of insurer	Separate accounts
General Nature of Policy	Insurance contract	Insurance contract and security
Return	Guaranteed minimum	No guarantees unless in a guaranteed account
Taxed as	Life insurance	Life insurance
License of Seller	Life agent	Life agent and Registered Representative
Sold by	Computer-generated illustration	Computer-generated illustration and prospectus
Client risk tolerance	Low risk	Moderate to high risk

* An illustration is a multi-page document that shows the cash flow and operation of a particular insurance policy.

In the explanations above there was mention of the accumulation account or accumulation fund. As shown below, the policy essentially has two sides: accumulation and benefits. The accumulation fund is the reserves used to support the policy. In the early years of the policy, the surrender value is less than the accumulation fund. Over time the insurance company will recover the costs of writing the insurance and the accumulation fund may eventually equal the surrender value. The other side of the policy is the benefits. How they work together is described after Table 2.1.

In summary: The policy owner pays a premium to the insurance company. Usually, a small percentage and/or a flat fee is charged per premium as a processing fee. The balance of the premium is added to the accumulation account. If it is fixed, it goes into the cash accumulation account, and interest is credited to the accumulation account monthly. If it is variable, the money goes into the separate accounts chosen by the policy owner, and the account fluctuates with the separate account results. Each month, the company reduces the accumulation account by the mortality, rider, and expense charges. Mortality charges are the policy holder's share of the cost of current death claims. Riders are additional coverages that might be added to the policy such as a benefit that waives the premium if the insured is disabled, or an accidental death benefit. The expense charges cover the administrative costs of maintaining all policy records and running the company. By identifying these charges, the policy is said to be transparent.

Each year the policy owner receives a statement that details the operation of the policy for the year. The death benefit of the policy can always be lowered if the insured's needs change. To increase the death benefit or to change from a level death benefit to an increasing death benefit, the insured must prove insurability.

When using the fixed interest form of UL, it is possible to build a cash accumulation value that is guaranteed to keep the policy in force to a specified age. Some variable UL policies have a guaranteed return fund, but generally it is not sound advice to use this fund in a variable UL policy for the long run, since most variable UL policies have higher expense charges due to the greater complexity of the product.

The primary disadvantage of UL is also its primary advantage: its exceptional flexibility. Some owners of UL policies have difficulties because of the way the policy was sold to them and because they expect life insurance to defy economics. There is no direct link between paying a premium and keeping the policy in force. As long as there are sufficient funds in the accumulation account to pay the current monthly charges, the policy will stay in force. It is only when the funds are depleted that policy owners receive notice that a premium must be paid. Since most people pay personal life insurance policy premiums through the use of an automatic withdrawal from their checking account, this problem is unlikely to affect them.

For those who receive premium notices, the notice shows the planned premium and the required premium. With adequate cash in the policy, there is no required premium. This means that the policy owner must make a decision every time a premium notice arrives. It also means that if the policy owner forgets to pay the premium, there may be no second notice or notice of a late premium. Failing to adequately fund a UL policy leads to it becoming underfunded, usually entailing substantially higher premiums in the future in order to continue permanent coverage. The alternative is that the policy owner pays the minimum required premium each time a premium notice arrives, essentially making the policy a fairly expensive form of term insurance—expensive because of the premium charge and the fact that administrative charges for UL policies are much higher than for simple term policies.

Many people choose UL because an agent shows them an illustration—a computer-generated ledger sheet—that shows the policy will have a lower premium than a whole life policy. A source of misunderstanding arises from the fact that some parts of the illustration are dependent on an assumption that may be selected by the agent or the client—for example, the investment return or an underwriting classification. Additionally, other factors such as mortality rates and expenses are typically illustrated at the current rates rather than the maximum contractual rates.

However, to guarantee that a UL policy will stay in force for the life of the insured at a level premium, a premium similar to or higher than a whole life premium must usually be paid. Some companies offer a UL policy that is guaranteed to never lapse if a certain premium is paid, regardless of what happens to the economy and mortality rates. These policies typically have premiums comparable to or higher than whole life policies of the same face amount.

Thus, UL is a good policy for many purposes. Its flexibility makes it fit many situations, but the agent or planner who recommends it needs to stay in touch with the policy owner to help him or her maintain the contract.

Adjustable Life Insurance

Adjustable life is an uncommon form of insurance. It operates a little like universal life insurance and very much like whole life. At the initial purchase of the policy, the applicant chooses the death benefit and the premium. After determining the amounts for these two options, the nonforfeiture values are calculated based on these choices. As the years pass, the policy owner can elect to increase the death benefit (with proof of insurability), change the premium, or both. He or she can also reduce them. Any changes result in new calculations and a new nonforfeiture table. This procedure is more complex than making similar changes with a UL policy. Dividends paid on these policies are used in different ways as well. Only two or three companies sell this policy form, and each company's version is unique. Adjustable life insurance is considered an excellent form of permanent insurance, but it is much more difficult to explain to consumers than some of the more common types and is therefore not offered by many companies.

Special Forms of Life Insurance

In addition to the more common forms of insurance, there are a number of uncommon or specialized forms. These will not show up often, but you may discover circumstances that call for their use. An analogy: Not many people have a set of Torx screwdrivers, but when faced with a Torx-head screw, nothing else will work.

Mortgage Term Life Policies

Decreasing term insurance has been used for generations to cover mortgages. As pointed out before, however, one of the biggest problems it has is that the decrease in coverage is typically straight line. Mortgages are not straight line. Straight-line amortization is when the principal of a loan decreases by the same amount every payment period. While this would be nice, it would require much higher payments in the early years since the same amount of interest would be due with the initial payment.

A few companies actually offer a decreasing term policy that is designed to coincide with, or at least approximate, the actual interest rate charged on a home mortgage. The rate of decrease in coverage closely follows that of the declining balance of a mortgage. It is important to remember, though, that the policy is not tied to the mortgage. It is merely a life insurance policy purchased for the purpose of paying off the mortgage if the insured dies during its term.

Nationally, most people move every seven years or so. When they move, they often spend more on the next home, and the new mortgage is likely to have a different interest rate with the balance no longer matching the mortgage life insurance policy previously purchased. With a larger loan that probably extends more years than the balance of the old loan and an existing policy that is decreasing faster than the new mortgage, the insured may end up with a significant mismatch. Another potential problem arises if the homeowner takes a second mortgage or a mortgage line of credit. This product looks good at the outset but is not particularly practical. Additionally, as interest rates fell to very low levels through 2004, millions of homeowners refinanced. Often the refinancing included paying off other bills or borrowing extra for one reason or another. While the lower interest rates often reduced the monthly payments being made by these borrowers, the total debt may well have increased.

The purchase of this policy presupposes that separate insurance policies are purchased for each separate insurance need. As you will learn later in this text, that is not a particularly good approach to insurance buying.

Joint Mortgage Term Insurance

This is just a natural extension of the previous form. It is a decreasing term policy that pays when either of the insureds dies. Since two-income couples are more common than single income couples, when decreasing term insurance is desired to cover a mortgage, this makes sense. It does, however, have all of the drawbacks of the single life form.

Survivorship Life

Insuring two people with one policy does make sense sometimes, and not just for mortgages. This version of permanent life insurance is typically purchased by an irrevocable life insurance trust and insures a husband and wife. The most common use is to provide estate liquidity. When wealthy individuals die, there is often an estate tax payable. This can be delayed until after the death of the surviving partner. A survivorship life policy recognizes this and provides the death benefit when the taxes must be paid. If the policy is in an irrevocable trust, the death benefit may be kept out of both estates.

Family Policies

There are a number of policies that have been put together as a package to be marketed to families. For the most part, these policy forms can be created by merely adding various riders to base policies and were far more popular before the advent of universal life with its substantial flexibility. Most companies offering these forms attach a unique name to each type. Few major companies offer them today.

Family Income Policy

This is most commonly a base whole life policy with a decreasing term rider that is set up to pay income in addition to a lump sum. Marketed to young families, the decreasing term portion provides an income from the date of death to a point in time measured from the issue date of the policy.

For example, Mark, age 28, purchases a family income policy. The policy will pay a lump sum of $25,000 when Mark dies, plus it will pay a $1,500 monthly income to his wife from his date of death to the anniversary date nearest what would have been his 48th birthday. If he dies a week after the policy is issued, the income will last 20 years. If he dies 10 years from now, the income will last 10 years. If he dies after the 20th anniversary of the policy, only the $25,000 will be payable. While the term portion of the policy is set up to pay an income, the beneficiary can usually choose to receive a lump sum instead. Since the number of years of income that is paid by the policy decreases over time, the premium for this policy stays level.

The **family income rider** is a rider that can be attached to a base permanent policy that accomplishes the same thing as the family income policy. The premium for this rider typically stays level and often ends a year before the coverage ends.

Family Maintenance Policy

This is a variation of the family income policy. The family maintenance policy still has a base policy that pays a stated amount at the death of the insured. Instead of a decreasing term portion to the policy, it has a level term portion that is designed to pay an income to the surviving family members for a specified number of years after the death of the insured. In Mark's situation above, if he died with the term portion of the policy still in effect, the family would get the $1,500 monthly income for the number of years specified in the contract. This might be 10, 15, or 20 years. Since the income portion of this policy will last for the specified number of years regardless of when the insured dies, it typically has attributes of level death benefit term insurance. It may only be kept on the policy until the insured reaches a certain age, typically age 45, and the premium increases periodically or is substantially higher at the outset than on the family income policy.

Family Protection Policy

This form is a package deal to insure everyone in the family. They are typically sold in "units": A unit may be $20,000 on the spouse with the highest income, $10,000 on the other spouse, and $5,000 on each of the children. Coverage for the wage earner with the highest income is usually whole life and coverage for the rest of the family is most often term. Most of these policies permit the children to convert their coverage to a personally owned permanent policy when they turn 21, 23, or 25 (depending on the company) without evidence of insurability. Some allow the children to convert to a policy five times the amount of their coverage under the family plan and include a guaranteed insurability rider.

Variable Life Insurance

This is the early form of variable insurance products, operating more as a whole life policy than a universal life policy. It has a fixed premium. While it does not have a guaranteed minimum cash value or interest rate, it does guarantee that if the premiums are continuously paid, the policy will not lapse, regardless of what happens to the accumulation values. Most of the early policies had a "take it or leave it" structure. There was no choice as to what investment mix was used though some eventually permitted limited choices. The fixed premium is typically higher than a whole life policy with the same death benefit.

Whole Life Variations

Whole life insurance lends itself well to variations that meet various needs. Again, these were more popular before the advent of universal life. With their unique guarantees, though, they still have a place in the market.

Modified Whole Life

This term is defined in two distinct ways. The first, and oldest, definition of modified whole life is as an automatically converting term policy, typically a level term insurance for five years that converts to whole life. Why have a policy that automatically converts? What happens if the insured cannot afford to convert it? When people fully understand insurance, most want permanent insurance as a part of their total protection. These policies are often sold to college seniors who cannot afford much but who expect to be able to afford permanent coverage five years after graduation.

Assume a 21-year-old male, nonsmoker, wants to buy a $50,000 policy. He cannot afford whole life now but eventually wants to buy a whole life policy. A $50,000 term policy may cost him $8.93 per month, but whole life will cost $27.41. Assuming he converts the term to whole life in five years, the whole life premium would be $32.94 per month. If he buys the modified whole life instead, his current premium will be $9.87 per month, jumping to $30.30 when the policy converts. He will save $2.64 per month for the rest of his life, and the cash values and dividends will likely be comparable to, or better than, a whole life policy purchased at the end of the five-year period.

The other definition of modified whole life relates to guaranteed issue whole life. For people who have been turned down for life insurance, a few companies offer a modified whole life policy. That name can be deceiving, and other companies have the same product and call it modified benefit whole life insurance. In this form, the policy is issued with a key feature. Typically the only benefit available during the first two years of the policy's existence is a return of the premiums. After that time, the policy may provide the full face amount of coverage, or it may gradually begin to provide a benefit above the premiums paid, rising up to the face amount a number of years down the road. There is no standard form of this coverage, so each product offered must be carefully evaluated.

Single Premium Life Insurance

A single premium policy is any form of permanent insurance that has a one-time lump sum premium that is adequate to fund it for life. After the Tax Reform Act of 1986, some insurance companies aggressively marketed single premium policies as a tax shelter: As growth within life insurance policies is tax deferred, individuals would put large sums of money into these policies and then make partial surrenders or policy loans that were income tax-free transactions, as long as the policy matured at death. To prevent this perceived abuse, Congress created modified endowment contracts (MECs, discussed below). Every single premium life policy sold after June 21, 1988, is an MEC.

Single premium life still has its uses. It does permit individuals to put lump sums of money that are generating unneeded taxable income into a life insurance policy. If it ultimately matures as a death benefit, all of the growth will be income tax-free.

At least two companies have turned single premium life into a long-term care product. Their policies provide that if the insured is confined in a long-term care facility, the policy will pay up to 2 percent of the death benefit each month to reimburse the cost of the facility. The reimbursement for a chronically ill patient is an accelerated death benefit, and to the extent it reimburses actual costs of care, the payments are income tax-free. (This is discussed further in chapter 8.) If it is never used for this purpose, the face amount is paid out as an income tax-free death benefit.

Juvenile Insurance

Although no longer available in its original form, many adults have these policies. Juvenile insurance was a life paid up at 65 policy with a relatively high premium while the children were young. Typically when they reached age 25, the death benefit quintupled and the premium stayed the same. When Congress created laws to define life insurance, these policies did not qualify, so today insurance for children is essentially the same product as that used for adults.

Insurance for children serves a few important purposes. First, it ensures that the child can have insurance to carry into adulthood. Changes in health have made it impossible for some young adults to purchase life insurance, so a guaranteed insurability rider that a person can use as an adult is often tied to these policies. A **rider** is an additional benefit attached to the primary policy. Premiums for children are quite low. Remember that whole life policies generally endow at age 100. A child has many more years to accumulate the necessary cash value, and the mortality costs are minimal. Since cash values of life insurance and annuities are often not included in the assets of parents or children when applying for federal and state education financial aid, this may provide a reasonable place to build values for education. Finally, the death of a child, as frightening as the thought is, can be made worse by the financial strain of having to pay thousands of dollars in final expenses.

However, insurance for children should be purchased only after adequate insurance is in place on the lives of the parents.

Responses to Participating Policies

At the end of the 1970s, three factors conspired to spell disaster for older nonparticipating policies:

- Interest rates were climbing: Money market funds in 1979 were paying 9 percent.
- The life insurance industry began to widely recognize the different mortality rates between smokers and nonsmokers.
- The calculation for policy reserve requirements required by the various states changed, permitting new policies to have lower premiums.

It did not take long for agents to recognize that by using an IRC § 1035 exchange (described later in this chapter) from old nonpar (nonparticipating) policies to a new participating nonsmoker policy, insureds could often double their insurance protection, increase their long-term cash values, and decrease their premiums. Nonpar policies were replaced almost as quickly as they were found. The companies that did not have participating policies needed to design policies that could compete. Universal life was one such policy. Others are briefly described below. Be aware that while it may appear from the outside that insurance product availability is fairly stable, the market is constantly changing. Some of the following products are no longer being sold, however a planner may often find them in client insurance portfolios.

Indeterminate Premium Life

This comes in both term and permanent forms, the permanent form essentially being whole life, with both policies having a guaranteed maximum premium. The whole life version has a guaranteed cash value as well. Where participating policies adjust the return to policyholders through dividends, this policy periodically adjusts the premiums based on changes in the economy, reduced expenses, and mortality savings.

Interest Sensitive Whole Life

This is more of a change in dividend structure to one that recognizes short-term interest rates rather than medium-term rates. The greatest criticism of this form is that while it enables insurers to compete in high interest times, it does not often treat existing policyholders very well. These policies are typically designed and illustrated to attract new insureds who are drawn by high interest rates, but when interest rates are up, the earnings are often used to support new sales rather than pay existing policyholders their full share.

> **NEED TO KNOW:**
> **CHOOSING THE RIGHT POLICY**
>
> There is no single form of life insurance that is best. Every form, including the special forms, has its place. The choice may be obvious when gathering facts about a client, or you may need to help the client choose between several workable options. Keep in mind that some clients will want only to provide a specific benefit with their life insurance. If one of the special forms fits best, use it. The right policy that is not in force is worth a lot less than the wrong policy that is in force. If you believe that a certain product best fits your clients' needs but it is clear that they want a different one and will not buy the one you suggest, do not fight with the clients. If they obtain additional life insurance, it is more than they had previously.
>
> Remember, if your client dies without adequate insurance, and his or her survivors believe it is because you could not agree on the policy type to be used, you may be faced with a lawsuit. The critical factor for a financial planner is to keep an open mind. Use all of the tools in the toolbox. Also, keep good notes about recommendations you make and the client's response to those recommendations.

Current-Assumption Whole Life

This is an uncommon combination form of insurance. It has attributes of whole life and UL. The initial premium and death benefit are fixed. However, after a specified period of time, such as five years, the investment experience, expenses, and mortality experience of that block of business is reviewed and the death benefit and/or premium is recalculated. It is unbundled like UL in that annual reports show what amount is growing and how much has been charged for mortality and expenses (unless the expenses are included in the mortality charges). The policy does have a guaranteed minimum cash value like a traditional whole life and fixed premiums and death benefit for specified periods. While the insurer may change the death benefit at the review anniversaries, it generally may not reduce the death benefit below the original face amount.

Low-Load and No-Load Life Insurance

This is a relatively new innovation. Just as the public and fee-only advisors have pushed for no-load mutual funds, they have also pushed for no- or low-load life insurance. Certain companies, such as USAA and TIAA-CREF, have offered low- and/or no-load life insurance to their members for a number of years, but it has been for only 10 to 15 years that these new forms have been available to the general public.

These policies are generally sold by fee-only advisors who charge a fee for obtaining them for clients. Theoretically, with no commissions being paid, these policies should all easily outperform loaded policies. This is often not the case: If the fee charged for obtaining the insurance is included in the comparison, as it should be, the case for low-load and no-load life insurance weakens considerably. Additionally, be aware that some low-load or no-load policies have surrender charges that affect their competitiveness. At a minimum, permanent no-load life insurance should have lower premiums and greater cash values than comparable full-load policies. In the first five years or so, the cash values should increase by at least 10 percent more than loaded policies as well.

Also remember that, when it comes to income tax issues for no-load and/or low-load life insurance, the fees paid to obtain the policies are not part of the income tax basis of the policies. With a traditional load policy, the entire base premium is part of the basis.

LIFE INSURANCE CONTRACTS

This section defines the various provisions of insurance contracts, including common clauses, settlement options, nonforfeiture options, and optional policy riders. Some provisions are common among all life insurance policies and some appear only in certain types of insurance.

General Provisions

Entire Contract

This clause states that the policy, including the attached application, is the whole contract. There are no other documents or oral understandings that control it except as required by law.

Ownership

Life insurance is financial property. It must have one or more owners. At inception, the owner must be someone with an insurable interest in the insured: This could be the insured, a parent, spouse, former spouse (by court order), business partner, a trust, or someone else entirely. The owner can later transfer the contract, in whole or in part, to another person. However, the transfer is only effective if the insurance company is notified in writing. Ownership can be transferred absolutely (completely) or collaterally (temporarily). The various rights and privileges of the policy (discussed later) can be transferred separately.

Beneficiary

The beneficiary or beneficiaries are named in the application. The beneficiary receives the death benefits following the death of the insured. The owner may change the beneficiary unless a prior designation was made irrevocable—meaning the named beneficiary cannot be changed without agreement by that beneficiary. Any change must be in writing and submitted to the insurance company to be effective. Whenever there is more than one beneficiary in any class of beneficiaries (primary and secondary are separate classes), the presumption is that benefits are paid per capita to those surviving the insured in the first class of surviving beneficiaries. This means that if there are three primary beneficiaries and one of them dies before the insured, the other two will each receive half of the proceeds. (See the discussion on beneficiary issues later in this chapter.) As long as one of the primary beneficiaries survives the insured, without an election by the insured prior to death, all secondary beneficiaries receive nothing.

Incontestability Clause

For the protection of the insurance company and the owner, this clause gives the insurance company two years during the life of the insured to discover any information about the insured that would have affected issuance of the policy. "Two years during the life of the insured" is an important statement. If the insured dies before the two-year period has elapsed, the company may take more time to investigate. If the company finds information that was known by the insured before the date of the application that would have changed its underwriting decision, it has the right to void the contract. If the information is found after the two years, the policy stays in force. In some jurisdictions, even fraud is not justification to void the contract after this two years.

Misstatement of Age

If a death certificate submitted with a death claim shows that the insured was older or younger than stated in the application, the death benefit will be adjusted to the amount the premium would have purchased had the true age been known. This may result in either an increase or decrease in coverage.

Grace Period

When a premium is received after the due date, the policy lapses. However, this fairly standard provision provides that as long as the premium is received within the grace period (usually 30 days from the due date) it will be accepted and the policy will continue as if the premium was paid on time. If the insured dies within that 30-day period without having paid the premium, the prorated premium due will be taken from the death benefit and the balance of the death benefit will be paid to the beneficiary.

Reinstatement

If the grace period expires, the policy lapses. The reinstatement provision permits the owner, if insurable interest still exists and if the insured is still insurable, to reinstate a policy that has lapsed for nonpayment of premium. Reinstatement is not permitted if a policy was surrendered for its cash value. Generally, reinstatement is automatic if a request is submitted with the premium within 30 days of the end of the grace period. Later reinstatements generally require repayment of all policy loans and interest due in addition to proof of insurability.

Suicide

If someone contemplating suicide were permitted to purchase a life insurance policy shortly before his or her death, and the company was forced to pay the death claim, adverse selection would be the obvious result. In most states, if the insured commits suicide within the first two years after the policy date, the insurance company will only refund the cumulative premiums plus interest. If the insured commits suicide after the first two years of the policy, the full death benefit is paid. Two states have a one-year suicide clause, and one state has no suicide clause. In the absence of a suicide clause, the state assumes the insurance company will rely on the incontestable clause (see above) and will have to prove that the suicide was contemplated when the policy application was submitted.

Aviation and War

These were common policy provisions at one time, eliminating coverage for any aviation-related death or death due to war or an act of war. However, few if any policies currently issued have these provisions for the basic death benefit. Some policies do exclude accidental death benefits and some exclude waiver of premium for disabilities caused by war or acts of war.

Changes in Death Benefit

While not part of a specific provision, owners of permanent policies are generally permitted to have the death benefit reduced. With traditional forms, the policy is reissued with the same policy date and a lower death benefit as well as a proportionately lower premium. To increase the death benefit, a new policy must be purchased. Universal life policies generally permit increases in the basic death benefit with proof of insurability. Since mortality charges are based on current age, and UL premiums are not based on the age when the policy was first issued, there is no other limiting factor in changing the death benefit. This is one reason that UL is a more flexible product. As long as the insured stays insurable, the policy can be increased without issuing a completely new policy.

Common Disaster Clause

A common disaster clause may prevent the death benefits from being paid to the estate of a beneficiary who dies at the same time as or shortly after the insured. Many states have similar provisions in their probate codes and similar provisions are often included in wills.

Conversion

The conversion privilege applies to term insurance only. It permits the owner of a term policy to convert it from term to permanent insurance. This provision may vary substantially from policy to policy. Many term insurance policies severely limit the conversion privilege. They may permit conversion only in the first 10 or fewer years. A very few permit conversion as late as the policy anniversary nearest the insured's 65th birthday. A few contracts permit continuation of the disability waiver of premium rider on the new policy, even if premiums are being waived under the terms of the rider. More generous provisions, not surprisingly, result in higher premiums. But under the right circumstances, the higher premiums return substantial value. In discussing term insurance options with clients, a planner benefits from knowing that term premiums of today are substantially lower than they were 30 years ago. In some cases they are less than half of what they once were. All things being relative, it may be worth a slightly higher premium to have a superior conversion provision.

Policy Loan Provisions

Permanent policies permit owners to borrow from the insurance company using the policy as collateral. This clause describes that right. Some companies offer a fixed loan rate; some offer a variable rate. Participating policies that offer the variable rate typically pay dividends as though no loans exist, even when there is a loan. Participating policies with fixed loan rates may pay different dividends when there are loans.

Collateral Assignment

The owner may make a collateral assignment, essentially using the policy as collateral. This is often done in a business setting. A policy loan is actually a loan from the insurance company using the policy values as collateral for that loan. The Small Business Administration (SBA) generally requires an assignment of life insurance when an applicant takes an SBA loan.

Automatic Premium Loan

This provision exists to prevent unintended lapses. If the insured has a traditional policy with cash value, at expiration of the grace period (assuming the premium has not yet been paid), the company automatically lends the owner the premium, using the cash value of the policy as collateral. In general, this provision is included in traditional policies. However, the applicant can request this provision not be operable. The request may be made on the application or subsequent to the issue of the policy. However, if the policy was ever included in an employer-sponsored retirement plan, this provision will not be operable unless added after distribution of the policy from the plan. This is one of the key items to check when doing a policy audit for a client.

Dividend Options

Dividends are paid to policy owners as a share in the surplus earnings of the insurance company. There are a number of ways dividends can be used. Policies may offer up to five dividend options. Dividends are paid on the policy anniversary date each year.

Cash

The dividend is paid to the owner in cash. Until the point in time when the cumulative dividends paid exceed the cumulative premiums paid, they are considered a return of premium and are income tax-free. Cumulative dividends in excess of cumulative premiums paid are considered ordinary income.

Premium Reduction

With this option, the dividend is used to reduce the current premium. This option is generally not available to those paying premiums via monthly direct transfer from a bank account. Many companies also permit the owner to apply the dividend to any interest due or principal of a policy loan. Taxation of dividends being used in this way is the same as if they are paid in cash.

While some may be tempted to state that using the dividends to pay interest due or to reduce the amount of a policy loan are additional dividend options, these uses of dividends are merely extensions of the cash and/or reduction options.

Accumulate at Interest

For this option, the insurance company holds on to the funds and pays interest on the accumulated funds. The dividends remain income tax-free as indicated above, but the earned interest is taxed as ordinary income. This is similar to a savings account.

Paid-Up Dividend Additions

This is the most commonly used option. The annual dividend is used to purchase small amounts of paid-up permanent insurance (no future premiums due). They typically have a cash value equal to the dividend paid. The paid-up additions also pay dividends. All growth in the cash value of these additions, as with the basic policy, is income tax-deferred and becomes income tax-free if the policy matures as a death benefit. This option is not available with term insurance.

Fifth Dividend Option

Actually called the "fifth dividend option," this must be used in combination with one of the above options. Part of the dividend is used to purchase one-year term insurance in the amount of the guaranteed cash value of the policy. Since the amount of money required to purchase one year term insurance equal to the guaranteed cash value of the policy in the early years is very low, any balance of the dividend is applied to the other identified dividend options. This makes the basic death benefit of the policy equal to the face amount plus the guaranteed cash value. However, in later years, the dividends may not be adequate to purchase term insurance equal to the guaranteed cash value. This happens because the guaranteed cash value becomes substantial as the insured gets older and the cost of pure protection increases. If that occurs, most companies offer the insured the opportunity to pay the difference. Most companies also permit conversion of this term insurance to whole life if done before the policy anniversary nearest the insured's 65th birthday.

Nonforfeiture Options

Sometimes a traditional form of permanent life insurance is no longer wanted in its original form or not wanted at all. If this time comes, the policyholder has three choices. To support permanent insurance policies, insurance companies have reserves assigned to the policies as a corporate liability.

The policy refers to these reserves as the nonforfeiture or value, and it has nonforfeiture options that essentially state that the owner does not forfeit these cash values if he or she no longer wants to pay for the policy. Again, the option chosen should be based on the needs of the owner.

Lump Sum

Upon surrender of the policy, the most common choice, not surprisingly, is a lump sum payable in cash. The standard nonforfeiture laws require that the surrender value be made available in cash. However, the law also permits a company to delay or postpone payment of a policy's cash value for a period of up to six months after surrender of the policy. These laws were put in place during the Great Depression to help insurance companies avoid insolvency. This option of the company has rarely been used. The lump sum can alternatively be applied to any of the settlement options discussed below.

Reduced Paid-Up Insurance

This option permits the owner to have a policy with a lower death benefit and zero premiums. Instead of taking the surrender value in cash, the policy owner may choose to receive an amount of paid-up life insurance smaller than the face amount of the original policy. The cash value of the new, smaller policy is typically the same as the surrender value that had been available as a lump sum. If the policy was a participating policy, the paid-up policy will also be participating. This is the choice when the policy owner wants some amount of insurance for as long as the insured lives. If dividends have been used to purchase paid-up dividend additions, the amount of insurance purchased that way will be added to the guaranteed reduced paid up amount.

Extended Term Insurance

What if the policy owner wants the full amount of insurance but does not want to pay more premiums? The amount of the extended term insurance is the same as the face amount of the original policy, but the period of coverage will be for a limited period of time. The purpose of this option is to maintain the full amount of insurance for some period of time without any premiums payable. On a 10-year-old whole life policy, the extended term might last 12 to 25 years, depending on the age of the insured at issue. The nonforfeiture options page in a policy may show something like 13 years and 184 days as the period of extended term protection. The specification of an exact time frame assumes the policy will be surrendered for extended term insurance on the policy anniversary. If the decision is made at any other time, the period of years and days will be adjusted appropriately.

Life Insurance Policy Settlement Options

Many lottery winners spend and/or lose all of their winnings within a short time of their wins. The same too often happens to life insurance beneficiaries who receive a single large payment and are inundated with offers of "assistance" with investing and managing the life insurance proceeds. When an individual dies, it may be more important that the survivor's overall needs are met than it is to get a great return on the invested proceeds.

The choice of settlement option(s) should be based on the needs of the individual(s) receiving the money. Life insurance is often purchased to replace income, pay off debts, fund education, and provide for needs that are not necessarily immediate. There is a risk that a large single sum of money will instead be squandered. While not investing the proceeds in the highest possible return investment until six months after the death is not a life-changing problem, losing tens of thousands of dollars through careless spending while trying to figure out what to do can be financially devastating. The best recommendation a financial planner can make to a client who has received a large sum of money as a death benefit from life insurance is to wait.

Whether a life insurance policy is surrendered, endows, or matures as a death claim, there are a number of ways the proceeds can be paid. The most obvious, and most common, is as a lump sum of cash, which may not be the best choice for reasons discussed above. Another is the **interest-only option:** The insurance company typically sends a check to the beneficiary each quarter for the interest on the total amount, keeping other options listed below available.

In general, the entire death benefit does not have to be applied to a single option. A portion can be paid in a lump sum to cover cash needs and investment goals while a portion is directed to an income option. Some of it can be left to continue to earn interest until further decisions are made. If the lump sum is taken from the policy immediately after the death of an insured, annuities may be purchased to provide similar benefits, but the cost of the annuity may be higher than if the beneficiary takes advantage of the choices guaranteed in the policy. It is relevant that the settlement options available through the contractual guarantees in the policy are available to the beneficiaries upon the death of the insured and to the policy owner if he or she chooses to terminate the policy and have the cash value distributed.

There are, however, a number of other settlement options. The next two listed below provide either a specified number of payments or a specified dollar amount for each payment. The rest provide for income throughout the beneficiary's life.

Specified Amount of Income

The recipient may tell the insurance company how much income is needed each month. Using current interest rates or those guaranteed in the policy, if higher, the insurance company will tell the recipient how long the payments will continue.

Specified Number of Payments

The recipient may tell the insurance company how long he or she wants the payments to last. The company then calculates the amount of each payment.

Straight Life Income

Under this option, the proceeds of the policy are paid to the beneficiary for his or her life, with the amount based on average life expectancy. The beneficiary receives a specified amount for as long as he or she lives, but nothing is paid to a beneficiary's estate after his or her death. This option provides the largest monthly benefit per $1,000 of proceeds of any of the life income options because some recipients will receive benefits for only a few years or maybe just a few months. There is normally no guaranteed minimum payout.

In-Depth: Beneficiary Issues

To illustrate the complications that can arise from poorly drafted beneficiary designations, suppose a beneficiary designation read as follows: "In the event of my death, I name my spouse as primary beneficiary. In the circumstance that she dies prior to my own death, I name the children born of this marriage as secondary beneficiaries of my life insurance." It is not hard to imagine a circumstance in which this beneficiary designation could cause a dispute. In today's world of complex estate planning, divorce, remarriage, and children in the home representing multiple combinations of parents, this common beneficiary arrangement can be much less than satisfactory. Start with the spouse: If he or she is not named specifically, as in the example above, and there was a different spouse when the policy was purchased than there is now, and no change of beneficiary was made subsequent to the second marriage, who gets the money? It will likely be the current spouse. However, what happens if the second spouse dies prior to the death of the insured and the person who was the spouse when the policy was purchased is still living? Because this eventuality was not clearly stated in the policy, a court visit might be required to settle it.

Consider the following situation: Jack married Jill when they were 21. Two children followed: Jerry and Jessica. Jill hated being married, felt unfulfilled, and left. She moved to Alaska and worked on a fishing boat. The kids were with Jack. Steve and Sue also got married at 21 and had two children: Sally and Seth. Steve felt the world closing in on him and took off. He led fishing tours up the back bay of Biloxi, Mississippi. Their kids stayed with Sue. Jack and Sue met at a PTA meeting, dated for a while, realized they both disliked fishing, got married, and had one child together: Pat. The family was perfect. The kids did not fight any more than expected, Jack and Sue were very much in love, and everything was fine.

What would happen if the above beneficiary designation were on a policy owned by Jack on Jack's own life? If Jack died first and Sue won a possible fight with Jill and got all of the money, so far so good. However, at Sue's subsequent death, Jerry and Jessica might get nothing. In fact, if Sue remarried and named her new spouse the beneficiary in her will, it is possible none of the kids would get anything. If Sue died first, things might really get messy when Jack dies.

Let us look at the potential claims:

Pat: According to the wording of the above beneficiary agreement, Pat gets it all. Jerry, Jessica, Sally, and Seth would get nothing because none of them were "children born of this marriage."

Jill, Jack's first wife: If the policy was taken out when Jack was married to Jill and no changes were made to the beneficiary agreement, Jill might argue that she should get the money. This would be based on the fact that she was the spouse at the time the designation was made.

(continued on next page)

(continued from previous page)

Jerry and Jessica: A representative for Jerry and Jessica could argue that they were the intended beneficiaries because they were the children intended by the beneficiary arrangement when the policy was purchased. There is merit to all of the claims. By the time the courts get done with it, there may be nothing for anyone.

Now suppose the kids are grown, married, and have grandchildren that Jack and Sue love. Unfortunately, Sue died suddenly at age 67, leaving the five children and 12 grandchildren to mourn. Jack changed his beneficiary arrangement to read: "My children and stepchildren, to include Jerry, Jessica, Sally, Seth, and Pat, otherwise to their children." Sally, however, died shortly thereafter. After a year of mourning, Jack died in his sleep.

Unfortunately for Sally's children, Grandpa Jack accidentally disinherited them. Because he did not state otherwise, his beneficiary agreement is interpreted to read his children and stepchildren, per capita. This means that each surviving child gets an equal share of the estate: Since Sally died before Jack, her share went to her siblings. If Jack had wanted Sally's share to go to her children, he needed to add one of three statements to his beneficiary agreement. If, following the names of the five children, he had added "per stirpes," "by right of representation," or "by line of descent," Sally's share would have gone to her children.

Some advisors attempt to comply with the specific wishes of a client who wants to specify the amount each beneficiary is to get. This is generally not recommended. At least one beneficiary should receive the balance of any benefits payable. As discussed early in this chapter, few policies pay out exactly the face amount of the policy. If a policy owner were to leave $25,000 each to four beneficiaries of a $100,000 policy, there may be money left over with no one to receive it, except an estate, or there may not be enough to go around if there is a policy loan or the premium was late when Jack died.

Beneficiary arrangements for life insurance are contractual. They are not affected by and cannot be changed by wording in a will or trust. One of a planner's first orders of business when it comes to life insurance, including group policies, is to review the beneficiary agreements and find out how those agreements match what the policy owner wants to happen.

Life Income with Period Certain

This option ensures a minimum payout. The beneficiary is paid a life income for as long as he or she lives, with a guaranteed minimum number of payments to be made, regardless of how long he or she lives. The recipient's beneficiary may receive some payments if the primary beneficiary fails to outlive the period certain. Typical periods certain would be 10 or 20 years.

Life Income with Refund

Rather than specify a minimum number of payments, this option ensures distribution of the principal: The beneficiary is paid a life income for as long as he or she lives. If the amount of the principal death benefit has not been paid out by the time the beneficiary dies, the remainder of the proceeds will be paid to his or her beneficiary in a lump sum or continued installments.

Joint-and-Survivor Income

Sometimes there is a desire for income to last as long as either of two people live. This option provides for two payees. After the death of one payee, the payments continue until the death of the second payee. The amount paid to the second payee may be the same as that paid while both were alive, or the installment payment may be reduced. When benefits are payable based on two lives, the monthly income is reduced. If the full benefit, called *joint and full survivor*, is paid as long as either person lives, the monthly income is the lowest since the full amount will be paid as long as either remains alive. Alternatives might be *joint and one-half survivor* or *joint and two-thirds survivor*. The higher the benefit to the survivor, the lower the initial monthly income. This option is usually ideal for a retired married couple with no other source of income.

Life Insurance Policy Riders

Riders are additional benefits or endorsements that may be added to an insurance policy. They may amend the policy, add benefits, increase or decrease benefits, waive a condition, or modify the original contract in some specific way. The terms rider and endorsement are synonymous. The following are the typical riders available for life insurance policies.

Disability Waiver of Premium

This rider waives the premium for the insured if he or she meets the rider's definition of disabled. For a whole life policy, the annual premium is waived by the insurer. It continues to be waived during the insured's *total disability* as this term is defined in the rider. The waiver provision normally takes effect once the insured has been disabled for six months. However, the waiver is generally retroactive to the date of disability. After the six months have elapsed, the company generally makes a refund of six months' premiums. Additionally, with a traditional form of permanent insurance, the cash values, excess interest, and/or dividends are treated the same as if the policy owner were paying the regular premium.

Most universal life insurance policies have a different approach with this rider. For these policies, waiver applies only to the monthly charges for mortality, riders, and expenses. Any accumulated values are left to grow, but other than earnings, nothing is added to those values. Although it is not common, some companies do offer a waiver of planned premiums (the average premiums actually paid) for UL. With this approach the policy continues to operate as a premium paying UL policy. If the average premium was high, the policy is likely to grow and become quite valuable. However, if the average premium was low, it is entirely possible that any accumulated values will deplete. Rather than permit the policy to lapse while the insured is disabled, the insurance company will revert the rider to one that pays the monthly charges—effectively altering the policy to a term insurance policy. And more currently, some companies have added a third option. This option permits the applicant to specify the amount of the premium to be paid by the rider if the insured becomes disabled in accordance with the definition in the policy.

Payor Death or Disability

This is an important rider to have available when someone other than the insured is paying the premiums on a life insurance policy. If the premium-paying person dies or becomes disabled according to the terms of the rider, the premiums on the policy will be waived as they would be under the waiver of premium rider that applies to the insured. This rider is most commonly used on policies issued on the lives of children. When this rider is requested, the insurability of the payor must be proven as well as that of the proposed insured.

Presumptive Disability

Some companies have a presumptive disability provision included with the waiver of premium provision. **Presumptive disability clauses** usually state that if the insured loses both hands, both feet, one of each, or the sight in both eyes or hearing in both ears, the insurance company will waive the premium, regardless of the ability of the insured to continue working. A few companies include loss of speech, but that is not common.

The wording of this provision can make a significant difference in whether the benefit is available. Some policies will specify that the loss of hands or feet must be by severance or must be total and irrevocable. Others merely say the insured must suffer a loss of use of the hands or feet or one of each, and the benefit will continue as long as the loss continues. Using the first definition, you might be in a wheelchair for life without being considered to have a presumptive disability. The other would cover the premium as long as you must use the wheelchair, even if you returned to the same job at the same pay.

Accidental Death Benefit (ADB)

In the past, this was often called **double indemnity**. Historically this provision doubled the death proceeds payable if death resulted solely from an accident and occurred within 90 days of the accident. For large face-amount life insurance policies, the accidental death benefit (ADB) is typically limited in amount. The provision is not applicable after some maximum age, often age 70. The insured/policy owner should not assume that his or her life insurance death benefits will include the ADB. Most people do not die as the result of accidents, so this benefit is generally not very expensive. Financial planners generally do not recommend this coverage because it is difficult to foresee a circumstance in which a person's insurance need will be greater if he or she dies as the result of an accident instead of a sudden heart attack. Also, if a life support system extends a person's life beyond a 90-day period, the extra ADB is not paid. Brain death does not count: It is the date on the death certificate that determines whether the benefit is payable. Recent court cases may change how planners view this coverage. While there is no logical reason to purchase it, there have been cases where an advisor was successfully sued for not recommending it.

Wording is also important. Some policies use the term "accidental death" while some older policies use the term "death by accidental means." An **accidental death** is one that results from an accident, regardless of what the person was doing when the accident occurred. The **accidental means** clause is very different: If the insured was doing something intended, and that activity was the proximate cause of death, it is not covered. If an individual decided to go mountain climbing and died because an anchor gave way or a rope slipped, a benefit would be paid under the accidental death definition but not under the accidental means definition. This is because he or she was mountain climbing intentionally, and the activity was the proximate cause of the death. While most courts hold that either definition should pay, the lawsuit will cost time, money, and emotional trauma. If an older policy is found with this provision, it may be wise to write to the company and ask for clarification of the circumstances under which the benefit would not be paid.

Accidental Death & Dismemberment (AD&D)

This is a variation of the ADB above. It includes benefits for dismemberment. This rider is found more often with group insurance and with mail order offers. The face amount of the rider is called the **principal amount**. Benefits vary, but the following is representative:

Table 2.2

Cause of Loss	Benefit Payable (% of the principal amount)
Accidental loss of life	100%
Loss of both feet or both hands*	100%
Loss of one hand or one foot*	50%
Loss of sight in both eyes**	50%
Loss of hearing in both ears**	50%
Loss of sight in one eye**	25%
Loss of hearing in one ear**	25%

* loss must be by severance at or above the ankle or wrist
** loss must be total and permanent

Additionally, if the plan paid a 25 percent benefit following the loss of the sight of one eye and the insured then lost both feet, only the balance of the principal amount would be paid in most cases.

Guaranteed Insurability

Guaranteed insurability, sometimes called a **purchase option**, permits the insured, at periodic intervals, to purchase specific amounts of additional life insurance without evidence of insurability. The amount obtainable at each specified anniversary is limited by the insurance company and is shown in the policy. The options to purchase additional coverage may be obtained after the policyholder reaches a certain age, marries, or has a child. The most common amount in the past was the face amount of the base policy. However, over the years, as policy sizes have increased, the maximum amount of each option is often limited to amounts such as $25,000 or $50,000. Most companies that offer this rider limit the number of options to seven or fewer. If a policy owner wants to exercise an option following a marriage, the birth of a child or the adoption of a child, the next normal option may be advanced. If the normal option is advanced and used because of one of the above reasons, the normal option will not be available at its normal time. Only one option can be advanced at a time. There is no requirement to advance a purchase option. If the opportunity to advance an option is not used, that option will be available at its normal time.

For example, Jose has a policy with the guaranteed insurability rider. He had the option to purchase additional $50,000 policies every three years between ages 21 and 42. At age 24 he exercises the normal option. At 25 he marries and advances the option that would normally be available at age 27. However, at age 26 his first child is born. Since he already advanced the age 27 option and the normal option date has not passed, he may not advance the age 30 option date. However, if his child was born while he was 27, and after the policy anniversary date closest to age 27, he could advance the age 30 option.

Why have this rider? Why pay extra now to have the option to buy more insurance in the future? The answer is simple. In front of every person is an invisible line of insurability. On the other side of the line the individual is not insurable at standard premiums. He or she may not be insurable at all. Being insurable is not a prerequisite for needing insurance, only for being able to buy it on a favorable basis. This rider guarantees insurability. It guarantees that the insured can increase life insurance coverage at whatever rate classification was used on the original policy. If waiver of premium exists on the original policy, it may generally be included with the new policies as well. Changes in insurability can arise for health reasons or occupational reasons.

Spendthrift

This provision is included to prevent the designated beneficiary from having the right to commute, alienate, or assign his or her potential interest in the policy proceeds. The beneficiary has no right to any benefit from the policy until the insured dies. The only potential control is if the owner named him or her as an irrevocable beneficiary. Even then, there is no access until the beneficiary outlives the insured. The effect of this provision can be used with the settlement options to prevent the beneficiary's spendthrift propensities from depleting the life insurance death benefits. The owner may specify how the proceeds will be paid and withhold any right of the beneficiary to commute (cash in) the balance of the proceeds. It is important to note that the protection is only effective for the period of time the funds are held by the insurance company. The protection no longer applies after the funds are paid to the beneficiary. An alternative that is generally recommended by planners, insurance agents and lawyers is naming a trust as the beneficiary, with the trustee having control of the money for the benefit of the spendthrift beneficiary.

INCOME AND ESTATE TAX IMPLICATIONS OF LIFE INSURANCE

Section 101(a) of the Internal Revenue Code (IRC) provides that the death benefits of a life insurance policy are income tax-free unless they fall under one of the exceptions. Another tax benefit is the tax deferral of the inside buildup of the cash value of the policy. In general, policy loans are also not taxable events. However, when a policy is surrendered for its cash value or a withdrawal is made, any amount received that is in excess of the tax basis (cumulative premiums paid for the base policy, less any dividends received) is considered ordinary income in the year in which it is received. IRC Section 1035 permits qualifying exchanges (discussed below) that will continue the deferral of taxes when a life insurance policy is exchanged for another life insurance policy or an annuity.

What is Life Insurance?

The Internal Revenue Code (IRC) Section 7702(a) defines life insurance, and if a policy, issued or changed after June 30, 1985, does not meet this definition of life insurance, it is not accorded the tax benefits generally afforded life insurance. The IRC outlines two tests to determine if a given policy meets the definition of a life insurance policy:

- **The cash value accumulation test:** The most that can be paid into a policy is an amount that would be the "net single premium" to pay up the policy. This rule is used to determine how much cash can be put into a policy when the goal is to accumulate as much "cash value" as possible. Essentially, the death benefit must be at least 140 percent of the cash value up until the insured individual turns 40. This percentage reduces 1 percent per year for each year over age 40 and cannot drop below 105 percent.

- **The guideline premium and corridor test:** This is a two-pronged test that first defines the maximum premium that can go into a policy at any given point in time. It then compares the cash value to the death benefit. There are limits as to the percentage of the death benefit that the cash value can be. As this test generally is applied to universal life type policies, the death benefit generally increases automatically if the cash value increases, so that the policy will continue to qualify as life insurance. If a policy fails to qualify as life insurance, the death benefit in excess of the policy basis is taxed as ordinary income and the growth in the policy, to the extent that it exceeds the cumulative premiums paid, is taxable as ordinary income as it is earned.

This particular rule resulted in the elimination of a number of policies that existed prior to its enactment. Juvenile policies that started with a low face amount that quintupled when the child reached adulthood, with no change in premium, failed this test. A policy that was often sold to fund education or a wedding, 20 pay life, also failed this test and was lost to the market.

From a practical perspective, no insurance company will allow a policy to be sold that does not qualify as life insurance unless the applicant signs a statement that clearly explains the ramifications of accepting the policy.

Modified Endowment Contracts

The above tests used to define life insurance were created because of perceived abuses of the tax benefits of life insurance policies. Congress, not yet satisfied, and in the face of continued perceived abuses, created modified endowment contracts (MECs). An MEC is not a form of insurance; it is created when an insurance company issues a policy that qualifies as life insurance under the above tests, yet runs afoul of the MEC rules. It is any policy that has failed the **7-pay test**. According to the Internal Revenue Code, a policy fails the 7-pay test "if the accumulated amount paid under the contract at any time during the first seven contract years exceeds the sum of the net level premiums which would have been paid on or before such time if the contract provided for paid-up future benefits after the payment of 7 level annual premiums."[1]

---

[1] The U.S. Code, Title 26, Subtitle F, Chapter 79, Section 7702A

As you might imagine, the 7-pay test is fairly complex. When the law was passed, it took insurance companies months to figure out what it meant. The test determines what amount, called a **net-level premium**, would be needed each year to provide paid-up future benefits at the end of the first seven years of the contract. If in any of the first seven years the cumulative total premiums exceed the amount permitted under this test, the policy becomes an MEC, and if a correction of this error is not made in the same calendar year, it is irreversible. In other words, if the net-level premium is $1,000, the policy owner may not pay more than $1,000 in any of the first seven years. If the policy becomes an MEC, the death benefit remains income tax-free, but to the extent that the policy cash value exceeds the premiums paid, loans and withdrawals are taxed as ordinary income. Additionally, if the owner is under age 59 1/2, there is a 10 percent penalty tax on any taxable portion of the loan or withdrawal. If that portion of the loan is repaid, it is considered to be an addition to the basis in the policy. Even if the repayment is made in the same year it does not eliminate the income or penalty tax. Even on surrender, if the owner is under age 59 1/2 there is a 10 percent penalty tax on any taxable gain in the policy.

If a policy undergoes a material change in any year, the 7-pay test must once again be passed. The most typical material changes are increases in the death benefit or the addition of riders. It can also be due to a Section 1035 exchange and would be effective for conversion of term insurance.

Exceptions to Income Tax-Free Death Benefits

Transfer for Value

A portion of the death benefits from a life insurance policy will generally be taxable if there has been a transfer for value. In general, when a life insurance policy is transferred from one owner to another for "valuable consideration," a transfer for value has occurred. If a transfer for value occurs, the death benefit, minus the amounts paid for the policy, including premiums paid subsequent to the transfer, is taxable as ordinary income. Certain transfers for value do not receive this tax treatment. (Valuable consideration is a legal term that means that something of value is received in exchange for something else. The "something" may be money, a promise, or some other property.)

Exceptions to the Transfer for Value Rule

A transfer for value does not cause any taxes on the death benefit if it falls under one of the following exceptions:

- A transfer to the insured
- A transfer to a business partner of the insured or a partnership in which the insured is a partner (partner here means a partner in a partnership form of business)
- A transfer to a corporation in which the insured is an officer or shareholder
- A transfer where the basis for the new owner is the same as the basis of the original owner (typically a gift of a policy from an insured to his or her spouse, children, or a trust) One situation where this exception exists is when a corporation is the owner and beneficiary of a life insurance contract. At the insured's death, the gain in the policy may result in an alternative minimum tax for the corporation. The details of the alternative minimum tax are beyond the scope of this course.

Taxation of Dividends

The IRS takes the position that dividends paid on insurance policies are a return of excess premium. Thus, when a policy owner receives policy dividends, those dividends are income tax-free. However, at the time when the cumulative dividends paid exceed the cumulative premiums paid for the base policy (excluding rider premiums), the excess is reportable as ordinary income for tax purposes. Dividends used to purchase paid-up dividend additions are not taxable unless and until the policy is surrendered, regardless of the amount paid.

Withdrawals and Loans

Universal life and variable universal life policies generally permit owners to withdraw part of the accumulated funds without surrendering the policy. As long as the policy qualifies as life insurance and is not an MEC, it is taxed on a first-in, first-out method. This means that as long as the withdrawals do not exceed the cumulative premiums paid (less the charges for riders), withdrawals are considered removal of the basis in the policy and are not subject to income tax. With regard to loans from UL, VUL or traditional life insurance policies, those policies that qualify as life insurance and are not MECs do not result in taxable income.

IRC Section 1035 Exchange

Under Internal Revenue Code (IRC) Section 1035, a life insurance policy may be exchanged for another life insurance policy or an annuity contract with no adverse income tax consequences. Section 1035 also allows tax-free exchanges of annuities for other annuities. This is not an elimination of taxes that may ultimately be paid. As long as the rules are met, there are no taxes created because of the exchange. The funds must be transferred company to company, not through the hands of the policy owner. The basis in the original policy is added to any premiums paid after the exchange and reduced by any excludable dividends received after the exchange to form the basis in the new policy. By adjusting the basis in the new policy in this manner, the tax on the gain is delayed rather than forgiven. If the policy owner were to surrender one policy and purchase a new one with the surrender value of the first policy, that would be outside the rules. If the first policy had a surrender value greater than the cumulative premiums paid, taxes would be due on the gain from the sale. If the first policy had a surrender value that was less than the cumulative premiums paid, the basis in the new policy would not reflect the premiums paid for the first policy, potentially increasing any taxes due if the second policy is surrendered. The Section 1035 rules avoid these potential problems.

Moreover, the new policy cannot have a later maturity date than the original policy: An endowment at age 65 may not be exchanged for a whole life policy that endows at age 100. The new policy must cover the same insured(s) or annuitant(s). Generally, if it remains likely that the government will be able to collect taxes within essentially the same time frame, the exchange is acceptable. If the potential for taxation is reduced, delayed, or eliminated, the exchange will not, most likely, be permitted on a tax-free basis.

Specifically, the law provides that no gain (or loss) is recognized on any of the following types of exchanges:

- A life insurance contract for another life insurance contract (one in which the face amount or death benefit is not ordinarily payable in full during the insured's life)

- A life insurance contract for an endowment contract (one that depends in part on the life expectancy of the insured but that may be payable in full in a single payment during the insured's lifetime)

- An ordinary life insurance contract for an annuity

- An endowment contract for another endowment contract which provides for regular payments beginning at a date not later than the date payments would have begun under the contract exchanged

- An endowment contract for an annuity contract

- An annuity contract for an annuity contract

Estate Taxation of Life Insurance

If an insured owns a policy on his or her life, when he or she dies, the death benefit will be included in the estate when determining if any estate taxes are due. This is the situation if there is "any incident of ownership" in the policy. An incident of ownership can be any right. The right to borrow, the right to change the beneficiary, the right to cancel the policy, the right to approve a beneficiary change, even the right to prevent the current owner from transferring the policy to someone else, would keep the policy in the insured's estate. If the insured had an incident of ownership within three years of death, the proceeds of the policy will be included in his or her estate.

To avoid the unintentional application of this three-year rule, it is recommended that the insured never hold an incident of ownership. An individual, other than the insured, or irrevocable life-insurance trust should be the initial applicant and owner of the insurance on the insured. The trust should be an irrevocable life insurance trust (ILIT), one that prevents the insured from having any incident of ownership. Even if a policy is purchased on someone's life by another party, e.g., a spouse, child, or trust, the proceeds may still be included in his or her estate if they are payable to or for the benefit of his or her estate. If a trust, even an ILIT, owns a life insurance policy and the trust is required to use the proceeds for expenses or taxes of the estate at the insured's death, the death benefit will be included in the insured's estate. However, if the trust is simply permitted, and not required, to use the proceeds for those purposes, the proceeds will not be included in the insured's estate, regardless of whether it uses the proceeds for those purposes. If Congress makes the elimination of the estate tax permanent, this will be a moot point after 2010 or whenever that law actually takes effect.

Gift Taxation of Life Insurance

If one individual gives a life insurance policy to another or to a trust, there is a potential gift tax. The value of the policy for gift tax purposes is generally the interpolated terminal reserve. The **interpolated terminal reserve**, a value provided by the insurer, is fairly close to the cash value of the policy.

If there are three parties—an insured, a separate policy owner, and a third person who is the beneficiary—the death of the insured causes a taxable gift of the death benefits from the policyholder to the beneficiary. If this exceeds $11,000 (in 2005), a gift tax return must be filed.

If a gifted policy includes a policy loan where the amount of the loan exceeds the basis of the policy, the assumption of the loan by the transferee is deemed to be valuable consideration which results in the transfer being considered a sale rather than a gift by the government. A transferee's basis is the greater of the transferor's basis or consideration paid (loan assumed). Since the loan is greater than the basis, the transfer for value rule is triggered. The solution to this problem is to repay part of the loan so that the loan amount is lower than basis before the transfer is made.

IMPORTANT CONCEPTS

Accidental death and dismemberment (AD&D)

Accidental death benefit (ADB)

Annually (or Yearly) renewable term

Automatic premium loan

Beneficiary(ies)

Common disaster clause

Death benefit

Disability waiver of premium

Dividend options

Entire contract clause

Family policies

Fixed policies

Grace period

Guaranteed insurability

Incontestable clause

Indeterminate premium life

Juvenile life

Level term

Life insurance definition

Low-load and no-load life insurance

Misstatement of age

Modified endowment contract (MEC)

Modified whole life

Mortgage term life

Nonforfeiture options

Participating policies

Payor death or disability rider

Permanent insurance

Policy assignment

Policy conversion

Policy ownership

Presumptive disability

Re-entry term

Reinstatement

Rider

Risk management process

Section 1035 exchange

Settlement options

Single premium life

Spendthrift clause

Suicide clause

Survivorship whole life

Taxation of life insurance

Term insurance

Type 1 (or A) or Type 2 (or B) death benefits

Universal life

Variable life

Variable universal life

Whole life insurance

QUESTIONS FOR REVIEW

1. Explain why the face amount of a policy is likely to be different than the payment made by the insurance company following the death of an insured.

2. Describe the primary attributes of permanent insurance.

3. Describe three types of term insurance.

4. Explain the difference between type 1 and type 2 death benefits of universal life policies and how this difference affects the amount of premiums payable.

5. What are the benefits of variable life insurance products?

6. Describe the two forms of policy assignment.

7. List and describe the dividend options.

8. List and describe settlement options.

9. List and describe the nonforfeiture options.

10. Discuss the income taxation of life insurance.

SUGGESTIONS FOR ADDITIONAL READING:

Fundamentals of Risk and Insurance, 9th ed., Emmett J. and Therese M. Vaughan, John Wiley & Sons, 2003.

Introduction to Risk Management and Insurance, 8th ed., Mark Dorfman, Prentice Hall, 2004.

Life and Health Insurance, Kenneth Black, Jr. and Harold Skipper, Prentice Hall, 2000.

Principles of Risk Management and Insurance, 9th ed., George E. Rejda, Addison Wesley Longman, 2004.

Tax Facts 2005, National Underwriter, 2005.

The Tools & Techniques of Life Insurance Planning, 3rd ed., Stephan R. Leimberg and Robert J. Doyle, Jr., National Underwriter, 2004.

The Tools & Techniques of Risk Management & Insurance, Stephan R. Leimberg, Donald J. Riggin, Albert J. Howard, James W. Kallman, and Donald L. Schmidt, National Underwriter, 2002.

CHAPTER THREE

Life Insurance Needs Analysis

• • •

People die every day, and life insurance companies pay out billions of dollars a year in death benefits. For most families, the death benefit will only meet their needs for a short while. There are many reasons families do not have enough life insurance: The money to buy it is not there, or the insured cannot purchase sufficient coverage because of poor health. In many cases, the importance of having adequate life insurance is not important enough to move its purchase up the list of priorities. But for many families, the problem is that they do not understand how much coverage is needed.

While businesses might purchase life insurance on a key employee for a number of reasons, most individuals have only one reason for buying life insurance: love. It is rare for individuals to purchase life insurance on their own lives unless they love someone who will benefit from the policy—someone whose future they are willing to ensure in spite of the other things that could be purchased with the dollars required for the premium.

How much life insurance is enough? How much is too much? How does an individual know how much to buy? This chapter will review a number of methods used to determine the amount of life insurance needed and will examine in depth the most widely accepted method of analyzing life insurance needs.

When you complete this chapter you should be able to:
- Explain the concept of human life value and the rules of thumb for determining life insurance needs
- Explain the steps necessary for life insurance needs analysis
- Determine an individual's life insurance needs based on given client data

DETERMINING THE NEED: GENERAL METHODS

One of the most frustrating aspects of financial planning is that most planners, at some time, will feel that they care more about a client's dependents than the client does. Some clients are so focused on their own needs and success that they do not seem to care about the members of their household. The planner's job is to determine what the client wants to provide and help him or her do that. However it may be necessary first to ensure that the client is aware of his or her obligations. This can make a significant difference in the lives of a client's family. It has been said in many ways—whether or not a person applies for life insurance, someone will pay for it. The family of someone who dies without life insurance will surely pay a high price for the failure of the deceased to buy life insurance.

While some clients want to provide everything for their dependents, there will be others who say "my spouse was doing fine before I came along and will just start over again if I die." This does not mean that the client does not love his or her spouse. The client may not fully understand how much a spouse has come to depend on his or her income, may be afraid to talk about death, may have negative feelings about life insurance, or may simply have other plans for his or her money. There is also the superstition factor: For some reason, people believe that if you prepare for rain by taking an umbrella, it will not rain, but if you prepare for death by buying life insurance, you are inviting death.

Normally, the purchase of life insurance is made out of a genuine concern for one's survivors. The individual who purchases life insurance must be willing to give up some income or assets today to provide his or her survivors with financial support in the future. Recommending life insurance requires a similar degree of concern. A planner's clients want juicy recommendations on how to make a fortune with their investments, not reminders that they will die someday and that they have an obligation to continue to provide for their survivors. The physician, true to his or her oath, tells a patient what the patient needs to hear, even if it is not what the patient wants to hear. A financial planner has the same obligation.

When determining life insurance needs, it is important to know what a client wants for his or her survivors. During the fact-finding meeting, one question can tell the planner a lot. After asking about existing insurance, the planner may ask why it was purchased and pursue the answer by asking if there is anything else the client wants it to provide.

Certified Financial Planner Board of Standards, Inc. points out in one of the Financial Planning Practice Standards that not all financial planning engagements need to be comprehensive. Some may be for specific, limited purposes. If that is the sort of engagement, and a question about life insurance comes up, the response may be: "I have plenty of life insurance." A useful response to that, from the financial planner's point of view, is: "For what?" That response may bring a blank stare. The planner should attempt to determine why the client bought it and what he or she expects it to provide. It is important for the client to know what it will and will not provide. For someone earning $50,000 a year, $200,000 seems like a lot of money. But how long would that amount last if he or she had to stop working and live on this sum? Considered in this perspective, its magnitude changes dramatically.

Human Life Value

What is a human life worth? The carbon and water that make up a substantial portion of the human body are not worth much, but that is not the question. The modern concept of human life value, introduced by Solomon S.Huebner[1], is based on an individual's earning capacity as it relates to survivors—the present value of an individual's earnings (and potential earnings) on which dependents rely.

Assume that a 35-year-old individual currently nets $60,000 in earnings annually—one-third of that is used for his or her own support, and the rest ($40,000) goes to support the family. It is reasonable to expect that this individual's income will increase over time at some average rate. The adviser uses this information to determine the present value of the income that would be lost. This is also the amount of money needed at the individual's death so that it can be invested and used to replace the lost income. Additionally, the calculation takes into consideration how long this income would be expected to continue.

This calculation is known as the present value of an annuity due (PVAD). In the example above, $40,000 is the initial payment. The years to retirement is the number of years, and the inflation-adjusted interest rate using assumed investment return and inflation rates is the interest rate.

Calculating the PVAD would result in the lump sum required to replace the lost income. That figure is the individual's human life value. While fairly straightforward, this can create a problem: A strict adherence to this definition means that an individual who dies with no one dependent on his or her income has a human life value of zero.

Remember, this is a measure of value relative to those who will suffer a financial loss due to the death of the subject individual. It is not an absolute measure of someone's worth.

Rules of Thumb

Related to human life value, some agents, advisers, and authors attempt to use relatively simple rules of thumb for determining life insurance needs. Though these rules have been around for a while, new rules arrive regularly.

One of the more common rules of thumb is to use simple **multiples of income**: Five to ten times annual income is often quoted as adequate for determining a client's insurance

NEED TO KNOW: THE CITIBANK METHOD

In 1976, Citibank devised a chart for determining how much life insurance should be purchased. It was based on providing either 60 percent (survival) or 75 percent (lifestyle maintenance) of pre-death income to survivors. Annual income and the individual's age were the chart variables.

The insurance need was calculated as a multiple of earnings, which ranged from three times annual earnings to 8.5 times annual earnings—as well as an amount (typically one times salary) for final expenses and estate settlement costs. The chart was revised once in the 1980s. Both times it was published in the *Wall Street Journal.*

Strangely, considering its simplicity, the chart did a reasonably good job of identifying the life insurance needs of a primary breadwinner who wanted the typical things for his or her family, but it did not provide for any specific or individualized needs.

---

[1] S.S. Huebner, The Economics of Life Insurance, 3rd ed.; New York: Appleton-Century-Crofts, 1959

needs, though some advisers and agents suggest six times income plus one times income per dependent. No one seems to know where these numbers came from, but they seem to come up with a reasonable sounding number that is sometimes close to the life insurance need calculated in a much more precise and detailed analysis for a particular set of client wants. However, no serious financial planning professional should rely solely on any rule of thumb, because to do so would ignore the individual client's unique goals, resources, risk tolerances, investment constraints, and family situation.

Another simplified approach is the **straight income approach**. An insurance agent or adviser using this approach would ask how much income the individual's spouse would need annually and then determine what kind of interest the spouse could conservatively earn on that money for the next 20, 30, 40, or 50 years. If the client's spouse would need $40,000 per year and could earn an average of 5 percent, the agent would simply divide the income need by the interest rate. In this case, $40,000/.05 = $800,000.

With that amount of insurance, the spouse could receive $40,000 a year forever if he or she earned 5 percent on the lump sum. Is this exactly how the money will be handled when the client dies? Probably not, but the amount was easy to calculate and explain. For some clients, an amount that is easy to calculate and explain is exactly what they want.

Other rules of thumb include the consideration of existing debt and final expenses and may even include funds for a child's education, a wedding, a specific bequest, etc. These amounts are added to a multiple of earnings-five being a popular starting place.

While these methods can be helpful, it is important to remember that they generalize the need. Most clients want to believe that their situation, needs, and desires are unique to them. As a financial planner, you know (or will find out) that what most clients want for their survivors is really quite similar to what other clients want although there is a lot of room for differences. The rules of thumb and quick and easy methods also do not lead an adviser to ask what the survivors may want or need. It is normal for a client to want to know that the plan has addressed his or her wants and needs.

If an individual obtained five times his or her annual income as a death benefit and all of it was invested with a net return of 5 percent, it would provide only about 40 percent of pre-death income for 20 years. This would not include final expenses, education, or the elimination of a mortgage or other debts. While it is much better than not having that sum, it is easy to see that it could be inadequate.

LIFE INSURANCE NEEDS ANALYSIS

From the foregoing discussion of human life value and rules of thumb, the shortcomings should be obvious: These methods do not account for the specific situations of individual families—liquid assets that might replace the need for some insurance, extensive debt, a mortgage, children's educational goals, etc. This leads us to the need to develop an approach useful for competent financial planners and insurance agents: **life insurance needs analysis**.

This process enumerates specific needs, determines the amount of money that is needed to fund each, and combines those funding needs with existing assets that would be available at death. This process could be called the "cash needs at death analysis," but that does not sound very attractive. The term "life insurance needs analysis" is the accepted name of the approach, and an unfortunate term. The word "needs" implies the minimum amount required. Few people want to provide their survivors the minimum amount required for their survival. Have clients focus on what they want for their family, not what the survivors will need. The process shows how much money needs to be available to provide for survivors and then subtracts the assets that are already available. This leaves a balance, and life insurance is the only way to make up this balance if the individual dies before having time to accumulate it.

NEED TO KNOW: THE TIME VALUE OF MONEY

Life insurance needs analysis recognizes the time value of money. When working with young families, it is difficult for them to "remember" how much things used to cost. They have heard stories from their parents, and it is important that they recognize that the decisions made today may have a direct effect on the lives of those they love for decades. Thirty years ago a brand new Volvo station wagon sold for $5,000. Today a Volvo wagon has a price tag over six times that amount. Family health insurance back then was less than $50 per month; it is a bit higher now.

The one thing that is not included in such calculations is the possibility of human frailties. A surviving spouse may choose to run away from the situation by taking a long, and expensive, trip. He or she may choose to splurge on a car, home remodeling project, or wardrobe that puts a significant dent in the money left for other purposes. Some planners encourage clients to include an **adjustment fund**– a lump sum of money that is there for the survivor to use in any way to help them get through the grieving process. The only way to ensure that the money is used only for its intended purposes is to have it paid to a trust that is limited in how it may disburse the funds. The issue of fund disbursement is related to estate planning and is beyond the scope of this text.

Like any forecasting tool, life insurance needs analysis relies on a set of assumptions about inflation, rates of return, earning power, and a number of other variables. As any planner knows, the one thing you can assure your clients about these numbers is that they will never be completely accurate. However, they must make sense and be reasonable. It can be difficult for new planners to acknowledge that they cannot foresee future events or predict anything accurately when projecting financial needs 30, 40, or 50 years into the future. However, the greatest financial or economic minds were unable to predict with any accuracy the movements of the economy over the last 20 years, or for any other time frame. The fact that the numbers will most certainly be inaccurate is irrelevant. What is relevant is that the approach to life insurance needs analysis that is used is sound. If the assumptions used are correct, the answers will be correct.

Over the last 20 years, inflation in the United States has ranged from below 2 percent to over 10 percent; short-term money rates have ranged from under 1 percent to over 16 percent; and stocks had the longest bull market in history, not slowing down until the spring of 2000, when the market took an extended turn downward from which it had not recovered in the first quarter of 2005. Experts disagree constantly about averages for inflation or investment returns.

A client, based on his or her own investing history, may want to assume a 12 percent average return on invested dollars for the next 40 years. However, if that individual dies, the survivors may not have the skills or the intestinal fortitude to invest aggressively enough for the death benefit to last 40 years.

Predictions are most valuable when they are solidly based on what we currently know. They should be logical and supportable, giving clients a reasonable target. The numbers should not be set in stone, and the periodic review of the client's financial plan is a good time to revisit the insurance plan: Assets, liabilities, goals, needs, and projections will change as time passes. While the life insurance needs probably will not disappear, they are almost certain to change as well.

The magnitude of these changes in prices may well be repeated over the next 30 years, a time frame easily encompassed in the life insurance planning of clients in their fifties. When dealing with clients in their 40s and 50s, many of them may remember when they were living on less than their current income tax bill. To ignore inflation and the time value of money in the calculation of life insurance needs is to do a great disservice to clients and to open the door to a lawsuit.

The Process

Step One: Gather Information

The first step of the process is the information-gathering stage. If this has already been done carefully and completely as part of the overall financial planning process, the client should already be aware of the necessary insurance.

Step Two: Identify Available Assets

Available assets are those assets that are already liquid or are likely to be sold after the death of a client. Most of this information can come from the financial statements that were prepared as part of the planning process, and for the most part, liquid assets and those that would likely be available for liquidation are included in available assets. Life insurance proceeds may be included at this stage or later—the ultimate effect is the same. Some planners prefer to incorporate current retirement funds; others prefer to include them when the calculation for retirement income needs is done. Ask the clients which assets are to be kept and which ones will likely be liquidated. If there is a valuable collection that no one in the family wants that may be sold or given away, the planner should determine this. Remember when doing this, however, that the insurance or recovery value of a collection or item may be more than double its value as a liquidated asset.

Step Three: Identify Liabilities

Step three logically follows step two—liabilities to be paid off at death are determined. Some clients will want to pay off a mortgage while others will prefer to provide income to continue payments. Terms of the debt agreement may control this choice.

It is important to understand what the client wants paid off at death. This is also where specific bequests would be listed. Unique needs might be listed here, such as funding a special needs trust for a child, a wedding fund, a gift to help children purchase a home, final expenses, etc.

Step Four: Determine Adequacy of Assets

Step four is simply subtracting the liabilities and immediate cash needs from the liquid assets to determine if what is available is adequate to cover all of the expected immediate cash needs. Any surplus will be carried forward to step nine as assets available to cover other needs while any deficit will be carried forward to step nine as additionally needed funds.

Step Five: Income for Dependency

The first need calculated is for income during the years that there are dependent children—an immediate income need.

NEED TO KNOW: MAKING CALCULATIONS

When doing life insurance needs calculations, the assumption is that the individual to be insured will die soon. While this may not be likely, no one has a guarantee that he or she will wake up in the morning. When someone is doing time value of money calculations, it may make the calculations easier to think about when the survivors need the money. If the primary breadwinner died tonight, would the family need the money now, or a year from now? The obvious answer is they need it now.

Because the need is "now," all life insurance needs calculations are done in the Begin mode on a calculator. It is presumed that readers are familiar with time value of money calculations, so keystrokes will not be provided for the example below.

Start with the income desired for the family if a client dies, but avoid the word need: Need implies "minimum daily requirement." The typical client does not want his or her family to simply scrape by from day to day. Maybe the process should be called "life insurance *wants* analysis."

Once the desired income is identified, subtract from that other sources of income. These may include the surviving spouse's income, child support, trust income, or Social Security benefits for dependent children (discussed later in the chapter). The net amount is then treated as the payment in the calculation of a present value of an annuity due (PVAD). Most planners will assume the income is needed until the children graduate from college. Anyone who has, or had, children who are in college knows that just because they are not home does not mean they cost any less to support, even if college costs are covered. Some planners and clients want this period to end when the children are 18, and a few clients will assume that it does not end until the child has completed a Ph.D. Remember, it is the client's plan. Another issue is the boomerang generation: Many empty nesters today are finding their children are moving back home. With any luck, the children are contributing to the household rather than taking from it at that time, but nothing is certain. Some clients may want to plan for this possibility.

Social Security benefits may be available to dependents of individuals fully insured by the Social Security system. Benefits for a child are paid monthly until the child is 18. There is also a monthly benefit available to the parent of a surviving child. This benefit is paid until the youngest child turns 16. This "parent of a surviving child" benefit is reduced if that individual is working and earning more than a fairly low level of income ($12,000 in 2005). Many computer-based life insurance needs analysis programs integrate these benefits if requested. Including this payment adds a great deal of complexity to the calculation, but if a client wants to include it, the planner should do so.

Step Six: Education Funding

Most financial planning clients will want to provide something for the secondary and/or post-secondary education of their children. This calculation requires an estimate of higher education costs today, the average inflation rate for education funding, and an average investment return. The range of college expenses goes from practically nothing in some states for the first two years at a junior college to over $30,000 per year. Tuition alone can run from about $1,500 per year to over $20,000. That does not include room and board, books, fees, or miscellaneous expenses. So how does a client pick a starting number? In one sense, it does not matter: Any number is better than no number, and many, if not most, parents are not prepared for the full cost of a college education. If the clients have no idea where to start, use a state university as an example, or if they have Ivy League aspirations for their children, look for those costs. Many insurance and financial planning software packages have college cost figures included, and there are online databases that provide information on college costs.

Whatever number is chosen in today's costs is inflated to the year the child begins college. Then a PVAD is calculated using that inflated annual cost as the initial payment. The PVAD is the lump sum needed when the child is ready to start college, so it must be discounted back to today to determine how much money would have to be set aside today to pay for the schooling. Many planners prefer to use a college-cost inflation rate that is higher than the general inflation rate assumption, because college costs have been rising at a higher rate for the past several decades. This is the method most often used by testing organizations such as Certified Financial Planner Board of Standards™.

An alternative approach is to multiply the annual cost of education by the number of years the child is expected to be in college, inflate that number to the year the child begins school and discount it back to today. The resulting number will be quite different. Since none of the inputs are likely to be exactly correct, which method to use in practice is not a critical issue. What is important is that clients plan for something.

Step Seven: Funding Income in the Blackout Period

The **blackout period** is the time between the youngest child leaving home and the surviving spouse's qualification for Social Security and/or other retirement benefits. It is called the blackout period because there are no potential Social Security benefits during those years. It is the period of time between the availability of the benefits that exist because there are dependent children at home and the retirement of the surviving spouse. When it ends is partially up to the client. Some will assume the surviving spouse will retire at 60; others may have him or her working until death. For years, the assumption was that the surviving spouse would retire at age 65. That became the "normal" retirement age in 1935, when the Social Security system was created. Now, depending on the age of the client, the "normal" retirement date for Social Security is between ages 65 and 67. Many retirement plans still use age 65 as the norm. It can safely be presumed that as more people realize that full Social Security benefits—if there are any—do not begin until this new "normal" retirement age, more people will delay retirement. Most people assume that it will take less money to maintain a lifestyle when the children are no longer dependent in any way.

It is relatively unimportant from the planner's point of view when the client wants the blackout period to begin. It can start when the children turn 18 or graduate from high school or when they graduate from college. The important thing is that it be the same time as when the dependency period ends in step four.

The difficult question to answer is "when will the children no longer be dependent?" Over the last 25 to 30 years, housing prices have more than quadrupled, and starting incomes in most fields have not kept up. Getting into a first home is much more difficult than it used to be. Many parents today help their children with a down payment to make their first home affordable. Many empty nesters are finding that children are returning home to save money so that they can afford a new car or save for a down payment for a home. Demographics are changing, and they may change the time frame used for the blackout period. The decision should be left to the client, with guidance from the planner.

The calculation is based on either the total desired income (what a family needs to maintain its lifestyle) or the specific amount of income to be provided (e.g., $4,000 a month). Some clients may want to provide enough income to cover all living expenses so that any money earned by the survivor is extra. Ultimately, it is the client's plan, and the planner must ask enough questions to determine what the client wants. A planner should ask for whichever number is chosen to be in current dollars and verify the inflation rate and investment return to be used. If a total income goal is chosen, it is first reduced by the expected income of the surviving spouse and any other income that may be received (such as from a trust or a charitable income annuity), exclusive of income from estate assets. Once the net annual income need is identified, that amount is inflated to the year it is expected to begin. Next, the PVAD of the flow of income is calculated for the years of the blackout period.

The calculated PVAD is the lump sum required at the beginning of the blackout period. Since that amount is not needed until the blackout years begin, it must be discounted back to today at the identified investment rate of return. The result is a lump sum that is adequate—assuming the insured dies next week—to provide the additional income needed by the surviving spouse from the time the children leave home to the time of retirement if invested at the specified interest rate and inflation averages the assumed rate.

Step Eight: Retirement Funding

This step can be handled in a number of ways. Various decisions and assumptions have to be made: Will the client want to provide anything specifically for the survivor's retirement years? Is it the intent of the client and/or the beneficiary to keep all existing retirement funds segregated and available only for retirement? If the client wants to provide something for the survivors, is it to be a percentage of current income or a specific dollar amount to augment whatever the surviving spouse will have?

Should the calculation be based on today's dollars? When will retirement begin and how long will the surviving spouse live? While the answers to these questions are speculative, they must be answered by the client. It is the job of the planner to help clients understand the importance of the decisions and how they may affect their loved one at that time in his or her life.

Starting at the end of the list, the conservative approach is to assume the earliest possible retirement age. This may require extra calculations if some sources of retirement income will not be available at the projected date of retirement.

Part of this discussion will involve Social Security benefits for most clients. Some clients will want to assume full Social Security benefits while some want to ignore Social Security benefits. A good place to get an estimate of future benefits is from the annual Social Security statement received by each person paying into the system. Most of the commercial insurance and financial planning software programs include Social Security calculations.

While these calculations are not difficult, knowing exactly what needs to be calculated can be. It is for this reason that it is very important to understand what is being accomplished in each step. Merely memorizing the calculations for each step will not provide that understanding. If current retirement funds are to be considered part of the liquidity for funding general needs, including retirement income needs, those funds cannot also be considered available to provide a specific amount of retirement income. For example, Henry and Winnie currently have $200,000 in various retirement plans, split evenly between them. With no additional contributions, this money is expected to grow enough so that at retirement it will provide approximately $1,800 per month in today's dollars. Normally, the step seven calculation includes subtracting expected retirement income and Social Security payments from any desired income. So, after calculating the amount of money required today to provide the difference in the desired income, assume that the total needed today if Henry dies is $375,000. The $200,000 is subtracted in an effort to show the additional funds needed. By subtracting the $200,000, the $1,800 is recognized as part of the ultimate retirement benefit. However, when the planner determines the liquid assets that are available to meet any needs in step two, if the $200,000 was included and used to pay off a mortgage or fund education, it will not be available for retirement. This is because the money that would have provided $1,800 for retirement is now being used in the calculation to provide funds for general needs. In other words, if the $200,000 is there to provide $1,800 per month, it cannot be used for something else and still provide the monthly income.

Once the decision is made, a process similar to step seven is followed. If the desired goal is a target income, reduce it by the expected other sources of income. If the only number available is the expected retirement income, just subtract that amount from the desired income rather than subtracting the current lump sum value from the total present amount needed. Inflate that amount to the year of retirement if it has not already been inflated. Using that number as the payment, calculate the PVAD of the flow of income to the projected date of death. This date is, of course, a bit more difficult to determine. Clients have some idea as to when they expect their children to leave home and their spouses to retire. Few people have clear expectations about when they will die.

Normal life expectancy at age 65 is about 20 years. For this reason, when a client has no idea what age to use, most experts use age 85—some planners use age 95 as a more conservative estimate. The difference in the need for most clients will not be particularly large because the calculation covers so many years and is typically many years in the future. When working with clients, planners find that this is a good topic for discussion. What is their family history? Did all of a spouse's parents and grandparents die before reaching 70 or live to 100? In most cases, it will be a mixed history. Again, this is the client's plan, and the client must be comfortable with the assumptions.

Once the PVAD has been calculated, that is the amount of money that must be available to provide the inflation—adjusted income flow when retirement starts. Again, that lump sum—and it may be quite large—is then discounted back to today to determine the amount of money that would be set aside for funding this need if the client dies soon

Step Nine: Adding It Up

The ninth step is to add together all of the needs determined in steps four through eight. Add to that amount any emergency fund that the client wants in place, assuming it was not included earlier in the process. From that total, subtract any excess assets from step four that can be used to offset any of these needs.

The remaining amount is the total amount of money that must be added to the client's estate to meet all of the client's needs for his or her survivors. This result is often a much larger amount than the client had ever considered. Generally, the client's first reaction is to say that it is too much. The planner will then want to ask, "Which of the survivor benefits do you want to reduce or eliminate?" The fact-finding interview provides all of the information used in these calculations. If a planner has verified these goals and desires of the client before showing the calculations and obtains the client's assurance that these are his or her desired goals, there can be little argument that this is a reasonable number. Some planners are hesitant to show this level of need for fear of appearing to pressure the client into obtaining a lot of insurance. Some planners do not show the full need for coverage, out of fear it will take too much discretionary income and leave too little for investing. However, if the client has been honest, all of the pressure comes from his or her own goals. And, as stated before, without a solid foundation, the financial plan is unstable.

This approach takes into consideration inflation, investment returns, other sources of income, and the client's desire to provide for the specific needs of those he or she loves. The number calculated may be adequate if the assumptions used are close to reality; it may be overly generous if the assumptions are too conservative; and it may be woefully inadequate if the assumptions used were too aggressive. As with any financial plan, the life insurance plan must be reviewed periodically.

Life Insurance Needs Determination: The West Family

Analyze the following client information to calculate the amount of life insurance needed for Jeff West.

Jeff West, 38, is married to Rona West, age 36. They have two children, Mike, age 17, and Madison, age 15. All four are in good health. Jeff and Rona expect both children to attend the state university from which they graduated. They assume each one will begin college at age 18 and graduate four years later. Current costs are $11,000 a year per student and have historically increased at the rate of 5 percent per year.

Jeff 's take-home pay as an accounting firm's computer operator is $3,500 per month. Rona works as an administrative assistant and earns a net amount of $1,800 per month from a gross monthly income of $2,690. Their current monthly expenses average $4,900 per month. The net worth of the West's family is approximately $185,000. They own $34,000 in liquid assets (more than adequate for an emergency fund of three to six months of fixed and variable expenses), $12,500 in nonliquid assets, and have approximately $107,000 in liabilities. (If Jeff dies, he wants all of the liabilities to be paid off so that Rona can start free of debt.) They put $5,500 into savings annually, including retirement plans. Rona would most likely liquidate the majority of these assets in the event of Jeff's death. (Jeff and Rona consider $15,000 of their liquid assets as their emergency fund.) They have a low tolerance for risk.

Jeff has a $50,000 group term life insurance policy and a $100,000 five-year renewable term policy, which he owns. The Wests have adequate health and major medical coverage to make a last-illness fund unnecessary. They expect minimal estate transfer costs and funeral costs (approximately $7,000). The Wests feel that Social Security will not provide much for their age category, and they would like to assume no Social Security survivor benefits for the family if either dies while the children are still at home. They want to assume only a $500 per month retirement benefit for either one from Social Security. They feel they can obtain an after-tax return of 6 percent on their investments and that inflation will average 3 percent over the long run.

Rona would like to maintain her current lifestyle through retirement if something were to happen to Jeff, although she thinks her needs will be reduced somewhat after the children have completed college. Initially, Jeff wants her to maintain the total household income even though it is a little more than the monthly expenses. The Wests expect that once Mike and Madison graduate from college, Rona's income needs will be two-thirds of the current income level. Furthermore, the retirement benefit under Rona's pension plan at work is projected to provide 55 percent of final income benefit when Rona turns 67. At that point (i.e., at retirement), Rona would like to be able to provide a guaranteed lifetime income for herself that is essentially the same as her pre-retirement income. Based on family history, Rona does not expect to live beyond age 87. Their views on Social Security carry over to retirement planning; they want to assume they will receive no Social Security retirement benefits.

With the above information, calculate the amount of life insurance needed on Jeff West using the life insurance needs determination worksheet provided on the following pages.

Step 1

Gather information from the client.

Step 2

Estimate fair market value of assets owned. Classify assets as "liquid" or "nonliquid."

Assets	Fair Market Value
Liquid	
Money market fund	$ 3,500
Stock	2,000
Mutual funds	26,000
IRA (Jeff's)	2,500
Total Liquid Assets	$34,000 ✓
Nonliquid	
Antique doll collection	$ 7,000
IRA (Rona's)	5,500
Total nonliquid assets	$12,500 ✓

Step 3

Determine liabilities to be paid off if client dies today.

Liabilities	Amount
Mortgage	$87,000
Credit cards	1,800
Auto note (Toyota)	7,950
Auto note (SUV)	10,250
Total liabilities	$107,000

Estimate postmortem expenses.

Postmortem expenses:	
Funeral expenses	$4,000
Probate and estate costs	$3,000
Total postmortem expenses	$7,000
Total of step 3	**$114,000**

Step 4

Determine liquid assets remaining, if any, after subtracting estimated liabilities and postmortem expenses.

Total liquid assets (Step 2)	$34,000
Total available life insurance	$150,000
Total available liquidity	$184,000
Estimated liabilities and postmortem expenses	($114,000)
Total of step 4	**$70,000**

If the total is greater than zero, the amount represents remaining liquid assets after the total liabilities and postmortem expenses are paid. If the total is less than zero, the amount represents the amount of insurance needed for estate liquidity.

Step 5 (For children age 15–22)

Estimate funds needed to provide all dependents with income until youngest child finishes college.

A. Desired monthly income	$5,300
B. Expected monthly after-tax earnings of spouse	$1,800
Expected monthly Social Security benefits	$0
Other monthly benefits	$0
Total	$1,800
C. Step A minus Step B	$3,500
D. Multiply by 12 to arrive at total annual payment	$42,000
E. Serial payment calculation:	
Number of periods	7
Percent inflation	3
Percent after-tax yield	6
Calculate present value of annuity due (PVAD)	
Total amount needed, if any, in step 5	**$ 270,182**

Step 6

Estimate the amount required to provide higher-education funds for the Wests' children.

Children:	Mike (17)	Madison (15)
Number of years until college	1	3
Total cost in today's dollars	$11,000	$11,000
Inflation rate: 5% (inflation adjustment)		
First year costs in future dollars	$11,550	$12,734
Serial payment calculation:		
4 periods		
5% inflation		
6% after-tax yield		
PVAD of education costs	$45,550	$50,219
Discount rate: 6% (after-tax investment return)		
Amount needed per child	$42,972	$42,165
Total amount needed, if any, in step 6	**$85,137**	

Step 7 (For ages 43–67)

Estimate pre-retirement income fund for spouse after youngest child reaches age 22.

A. Desired annual income for surviving spouse	$42,400
B. Expected annual after-tax earnings and benefits of spouse	$21,600
C. Subtract Step B from Step A	$20,800

D. Serial payment adjustment
 	
Inflation calculation:
    number of periods until serial payments begin: 7
    3% inflation
 	
Calculate the future value of the needed income when serial payments begin
	$25,581

E. Serial payment calculation
    number of periods between date when
    youngest child reaches age 22 and retirement: 24
    3% inflation
    6% after-tax yield
 	
Calculate present value of annuity due (PVAD) $450,079
 	
F. Discount calculation:
    number of periods until serial payments begin: 7
    6% after-tax yield	

PVAD **Total amount needed, if any, in step 7**	**$299,328**

Step 8 (for ages 67–87)

Estimate retirement income fund for spouse.

A. Desired annual income for surviving spouse at retirement	$42,400
B. Expected Social Security retirement or other benefits	$23,754
C. Subtract Step B from Step A	$18,646

D. Serial payment adjustment
    Inflation calculation:
    number of periods until retirement: 31
    3% inflation
    Calculate the future value of the needed income when serial payments begin
	$46,616

E. Serial payment calculation:
    number of periods of retirement income: 20
    3% inflation
    6% after-tax yield
    Calculate PVAD of serial payments
	$699,164

F. Discount calculation:
    number of periods until retirement: 31
    6% after-tax yield
    Calculate the PV	

Total amount needed, if any, in step 8	**$114,841**

719,536 (handwritten, next to row E)

118,187 (handwritten, next to Total row)

Step 9

The amount estimated for an emergency fund:	$15,000

Step 10

Determine insurance needs (summary).

A. Add amounts determined by:	
Step 5	$270,182
Step 6	85,137
Step 7	299,328
Step 8	114,841
Step 9	15,000
Total financial needs	**$784,488**
B. Total resources available (remaining liquid assets from Step 4)	70,000
C. Subtract total resources available in Step B from the total actual needs in Step A to determine insurance needed, if any.	
Insurance needed:	$714,488
D. List insurance needed, if any, to provide estate liquidity. (This is the case when the total in Step 4 is negative.)	N/A
E. Add amounts in Steps C and D to determine additional amount of life insurance needed, if any	**$714,488**

[handwritten: 118,187]
[handwritten: 787,834]
[handwritten: 717,834]

Summary of the Life Insurance Needs Analysis

As you have seen, no single need seems to be out of line or extravagant. The totals required for each step of the process do not seem particularly large. It is when the bottom line is reached that the magnitude of the need is exposed. When presenting the analysis to a client, always confirm the goals first. After confirming the goals, show the need, one goal at a time.

During the prior explanation and demonstration of the analysis, it is clear that there is no single correct way to do the calculations. Life insurance can be included in liquid assets at the beginning of the process or show up on the last page. Retirement funds can be included in the liquid assets or on the retirement page, with the caveat that if they are used as part of the survivor's retirement benefits prior to determining the need, they cannot be subtracted from the calculated need. It is important to recognize that if qualified retirement funds are to be used for current needs, the net amount after income taxes is the amount available.

Some clients will want to calculate for the "needs" only while others will want to provide for the lifestyle maintenance. If the plan does not reflect what the client wants, he or she will not likely follow its recommendations. If the amount is too large, the planner has the blueprint and can ask which goals should be eliminated or adjusted. Knowing how to use a financial calculator to do the calculations will permit a planner to make simple adjustments to the analysis.

It is generally better to help clients partially fund the plan than to cut it back so much that they do not feel good about it. Adjustments in the rates of inflation and investment return will make huge changes in the long-term needs. A planner can help a client find the light at the end of the tunnel. The purpose of providing adequate life insurance is peace of mind. If a client feels that he or she will be letting his or her loved ones down, that is not peace of mind.

In-Depth: Capital Consumption Versus Capital Retention

The previous life insurance needs analysis is based on a capital consumption model. If all of the assumptions in the analysis were exactly right, there will be no money left the day Rona West dies. A common joke among seniors is: "Being of sound mind and body, I spent it all." However, when asked, most people do not want to run out of money and do want to leave something to their children and/or grandchildren besides a drawer full of old socks. So the question is sometimes asked about how to ensure that their estate is left for their heirs. This is known as **capital retention**.

An appropriate first question to ask: What does the client want to leave? The most common approach is to assume that the client wants to provide whatever is left at his or her death to the children and/or grandchildren, with the estate providing the income necessary to support the surviving spouse. At the eventual death of the surviving spouse, one choice is to leave the same dollar amount as is in place when the first spouse dies, while the other is to leave the same buying power. The numbers usually help make the decision.

To leave the same amount as is left at the death of the client is easy. Start with the lump sum that is needed to meet all of the family's needs. In the case above, this would be $714,488, the total financial need. Assume that is the amount that will be left to the children at the death of the surviving spouse. In the above case, the spouse is now 36 and the assumed age at death is 87.

That is 51 years. Using the total financial need as a future value, the 51 years as the number of compounding periods, and the client's 6 percent discount rate, the lump sum that would have to be invested at Jeff's death next week to provide $714,488 51 years from now would be $36,593. This number makes it seem silly not to provide it.

However what if the same buying power is desired? To maintain the buying power of the lump sum, the first step is to inflate it to what it would have to be 51 years from now at the client's inflation rate of 3 percent. That number is $3,226,215. Now discount that back to today at 6 percent. This results in a present need of an additional $165,232 of insurance. This is 4.5 times as much as the prior calculation.

Obviously, a client can pick whichever number he or she desires. The process of calculating how much would have to be set aside is the same. Remember, this is life insurance needs analysis, not estate planning. It is beyond the scope of this text to discuss how best to handle the proceeds of this money.

IMPORTANT CONCEPTS

Blackout period

Capital consumption

Capital preservation

Dependency period

Estate liquidity

Human life value

Life insurance needs analysis

Rules of thumb

QUESTIONS FOR REVIEW

1. Describe the variations that may occur in defining the dependency period.

2. Explain the calculations for premature death education funding.

3. Describe the concept and calculation of human life value.

4. Explain why some individuals, in a strict sense, have no human life value.

5. What are the two general reasons that life insurance is purchased? Can you think of any reasons that do not fall in either category?

6. Describe the process of doing a life insurance needs analysis.

7. What are the benefits of doing a full life insurance needs analysis?

8. Discuss the accuracy of the life insurance needs analysis.

9. What does the bottom line figure of the life insurance needs analysis tell you, other than the amount of life insurance to purchase?

10. Describe three rules of thumb that have been used for determining the amount of insurance to purchase and the pros and cons of each.

SUGGESTIONS FOR ADDITIONAL READING

The Economics of Life Insurance, 3th ed., S.S. Huebner, Appleton-Century-Crofts, 1959.

Fundamentals of Risk and Insurance, 9th ed., Emmett J. & Therese M.Vaughan, Wiley, 2003.

Introduction to Risk Management and Insurance, 8th ed., Mark Dorfman, Prentice Hall, 2004.

Life and Health Insurance, Kenneth Black Jr. and Harold Skipper Jr., Prentice Hall, 2000.

Principles of Risk Management and Insurance, 9th edition, George E. Rejda, Addison Wesley, 2004.

Tax Facts 2005, National Underwriter, 2005.

The Tools & Techniques of Life Insurance Planning, 3rd ed., Stephen R. Leimberg and Robert J. Doyle, Jr., National Underwriter, 2004.

CHAPTER FOUR

Life Insurance Policy Selection and Annuities

• • •

Many years ago, David Bernard, CFP®, CLU, a financial adviser I know, said, "The best life insurance policy is the one that is in force when the insured dies." That axiom still holds true. The selection of a life insurance policy from among the many options may seem a daunting task, but the key is to remember the primary role of insurance: to obtain necessary protection. The policy form is not an issue as long as the policy is in force when the client dies and the client will have the necessary insurance at the time of death.

This chapter also looks at ways to ensure income in the event of chronic or terminal illness or following retirement: accelerated death benefits, viatical agreements, and annuities.

When you have completed this chapter, you should be able to:

- Select the most appropriate policy or policies for a given client
- Analyze insurance policies and decide whether to replace a life insurance policy
- Determine when and how specific clients should use accelerated death benefits or viatical settlements
- Identify various types of annuities and compare and contrast them with mutual funds
- Describe the general taxation principles that apply to annuities

SELECTING THE RIGHT POLICY

The key to determining the best product for a client revolves around his or her life insurance selection factors, which should be gathered during the initial interviews. The key life insurance selection factors include:

- Disposable income available for premiums
- Duration of need
- Amount of insurance needed (covered in chapter 3)
- Risk tolerance
- Self-discipline (history of being able to save and/or invest)
- Predisposition toward various forms of insurance

NEED TO KNOW: INSURANCE FORMS

In review, each policy has unique features so before you recommend a policy to fit a client's needs, it is essential to make sure you understand what types of policies are available and what features are included with each type. Take time now to review the various forms as discussed in chapter 2, paying special attention to the concepts listed here:

Adjustable and level death benefits

Adjustable, fixed, single, and variable premiums

Convertible policies

Decreasing and increasing death benefit

Fixed (level) death benefits

Guaranteed premiums

Guaranteed values

Interest sensitive policies

Participating and non-participating policies

Periodically increasing premiums

Permanent and term insurance

Re-entry provisions

The application of many selection factors is clear. A couple with little disposable income and a substantial, temporary need are generally good candidates for term insurance; an individual with a low-risk tolerance and a short-time horizon is not a good candidate for variable products. A person with poor self-discipline, such as a client who is unable to put money into savings and leave it there for emergencies, is not a good candidate for universal life insurance, especially if they will not be paying the premium by automatic bank draft. However, whole life insurance can provide this same individual with a safe place to build an accessible emergency reserve. Other clients are simply predisposed to certain products: There are clients who demand whole life because that is what their parents had, and other clients that simply want the freedom of a short-term term life insurance commitment, believing, and reasonably so, that permanent insurance is similar to owning the insurance while term insurance is more like renting it.

Here are some sample guidelines to determine what policies may be best for a given client:

- Clients who have a high tolerance for risk usually prefer either term or a variable universal life.
- Clients who are unsure about committing to a long-term product or contract (the kind of people who prefer renting to buying) should consider term insurance. Conversely, a client who likes the stability of a long-term contract is better suited for whole life.
- If a client wants to have something to show for his or her money at any given point, whole life or universal life is indicated. Such a client may want to consider

higher cash value forms of whole life or greater contributions to the accumulation account with UL.

- For the client who cannot afford whole life premiums yet, but still wants permanent insurance, either UL, one of the hybrid forms of whole life, or graded premium whole life are good choices.
- For the client who just does not have much money to spend on insurance, term is the appropriate recommendation. If the client really wants a long-term product, term with a long-term conversion privilege rider is probably best.

Most clients will have a variety of long-term and short-term needs. If clients can set aside money in a structured savings program, a mix of term and permanent policies is best. As stated above, term insurance is a good choice for clients who have a high tolerance for risk. These clients are willing to risk running out of protection before they are ready. They risk becoming uninsurable before the premiums on their current policy skyrocket. They are willing to take a risk that conversion will be an option and that they will be able to afford to convert the term insurance at a later time if they find out their insurance needs last well beyond their initial expectations. There is very little long-term certainty with term insurance. Clients focusing their insurance program on term, by making such a choice, should be willing to take the risks inherent in that choice.

In-Depth: Group and Multiperson Coverage

One option offered to some individuals through their employers is **group life**. The vast majority of this coverage is group term insurance. However, some plans offer employees group permanent insurance (usually universal life). The premium for the first $50,000 of group term life insurance death benefits is not taxable to the employee, but some employers offer more than this amount.

Some clients will want to consider a single insurance policy that covers two or more people. Some policies, most commonly UL, are available in a **second to die** form: The death benefit is paid when the second insured person dies. The premium is determined by reference to the joint life expectancy, which is always longer than the life expectancy of any one individual. A few policies waive the premium after the first death. This type of coverage is typically used to finance the estate tax for a married couple since the marital deduction may completely eliminate any tax at the first death.

Similar to the above is insurance on the **first to die**. With this variation, the death benefit is paid when the first insured dies. Some companies permit reissue of a new policy covering remaining insureds without additional proof of insurability. Some companies permit survivor(s) to obtain individually owned insurance following the first death. This type of coverage is typically used to fund a business buy-sell agreement or a mortgage.

Duration of Need

Before making policy recommendations on what type of insurance to purchase, it is critical that the advisor understand how long certain needs will last:

- Term insurance is best for short-term needs (10 years or less).
- Long-term needs (15 years or more) usually require whole life or adequately funded UL.

- Evaluate needs of intermediate length to see if they might last more or less than 15 years: Use a combination of term and permanent policies to meet these needs with the duration of various needs determining the mix.

- If a need is likely to extend beyond the insured's age 65, whole life or adequately funded UL is recommended.

- Business needs, such as buy-sell agreements, should usually be funded with permanent insurance unless the business plan is to terminate or sell the business in a relatively short period of time.

- Any insurance intended for any purpose funded at the natural death of the insured—bequests, trust funds, death taxes, etc.—should be permanent.

In-Depth: Buy Term and Invest the Difference?

Many advisors believe that buying term insurance and investing the difference is the best option. There are numerous flaws in this plan. Theoretically, investing the difference between whole life premiums and term insurance premiums may result in a greater amount of cash at the ultimate death of the insured. Unfortunately, when it comes to human behavior surrounding money, this type of theory rarely works. Few people successfully invest the difference over the long term: They buy term and spend the excess cash someplace else—car payments, a new washing machine, vacation, more dinners out, etc.

Many times, "buy term and invest the difference" is based on the assumption that life insurance is a temporary need and is primarily a method for the accumulation of money. This advice assumes that investing in securities and investing in life insurance have an approximately equal level of risk. However, after the end of the long bull market of the 1990s, most investors understood that a securities investment will not always provide a better return than an investment with a principal that does not decrease. As this text is being revised in early 2005, most investors have not completely recovered from the downward spiral of the stock market that occurred from 2000 through 2003.

The last assumption is that the invested difference will not be touched until the death of the insured. If any of the invested dollars are used before that time, they should be removed from the comparison.

Besides the assumptions mentioned above, many financial planners fail to consider other significant factors when deciding between term and permanent insurance.

For one, the growth of policy values in permanent life insurance is usually fully income-tax deferred. Also, if a policy is surrendered, the premium payments form the basis for determining the taxable gain. However, when the difference (or the amount saved by choosing term insurance) is invested, the basis for determining the taxable gain does not include the premium payments. Additionally, in bankruptcy, certain cash values of life insurance are not accessible by creditors, while other invested assets are accessible.

The beneficiaries seldom, if ever, ask whether the policy was permanent or term. In fact, the vast majority of death claims paid are those where the policy was permanent and the insured was older than 65.

Those advisors who believe that buying term and investing the difference is the best way to buy insurance might want to consider other ways to save money and invest the difference: A Honda Civic instead of an Acura, macaroni and cheese instead of sirloin steak, a bus ticket instead of airfare, an economical minivan instead of a luxury SUV, reading at the library instead of buying materials to read at home, tap water instead of bottled, and one of the biggest money savers would be to make their own coffee. All of these have the potential of saving clients thousands of dollars a year that they can then invest.

(continued on next page)

(continued from previous page)

When the planner is analyzing insurance needs for a client, it is important to obtain insurance that is appropriate for the client's needs. If income from life insurance for survivors is truly a long-term (i.e., lifetime) need, the lowest net cost insurance, and the most stable investment, is permanent insurance.

Some advisers believe that insurance needs disappear when children leave home or the insured retires. The reality is that most insurance needs will change rather than disappear. Life insurance purchased to protect dependents in the case of a premature death may later be suited for maximizing pension plan income, handling unexpected estate liquidity problems, or funding specific bequests. The vast majority of death claims paid involve individuals who die after retirement; no beneficiaries turn down the death benefits because they already have enough money. Many survivors of older clients are disappointed in the amount of insurance payable, believing that the insured should have had (and could have afforded) more coverage.

ANALYZING INSURANCE POLICIES

Once you and your clients understand what form or product is needed, look at specific policies that are available to determine the value of a particular life insurance policy in comparison with others. This section focuses on comparing life insurance policies.

The different methods of comparing policies all have advantages and disadvantages. Keep the following factors in mind. First, no method has been devised for objectively and effectively comparing different forms of insurance: Reasonable comparisons can be made between two term policies, two universal life policies, or two whole life policies, but not between a term policy and a permanent plan. Second, most methods may produce skewed results. Most of the methods require an assumed interest rate, pure insurance rate, or both; since there is no standard assumed rate, there is often the opportunity to use inputs that create the desired outcome. Finally, most of the comparison methods assume the policy will terminate by surrender or lapse, rather than by providing a death benefit: None of the methods assume maturity by the death of the insured, and after all, that is why life insurance is purchased. Comparison methods primarily analyze life insurance as an investment, which is seldom the primary purpose for its purchase: They exclude the death benefit and protection it provides. One additional issue in using comparison methods is that they are imperfect. Assumptions must be made that, in all likelihood, will be different from what actually happens. Small differences between policies should generally be ignored. Too many things can change the value of a policy to ensure that a comprehensive analysis showing policy A to be 2 percent better than policy B will represent the true end result.

Traditional Net Cost Method

For many years, one of the most common methods of analysis was the "net cost" method—a comparison of the cumulative premiums compared to the cash values and dividend values available upon surrender at 10 years, 20 years, and age 65. Considering the limitations of the other methods, this seemed like a workable method of comparison and, in practice, was nearly as good at identifying better policies as the methods currently in use.

Some aggressive experts claim that the method was misleading: It gave the impression that if an insured surrendered the policy after a certain number of years, then the insurance was free, or, at the least, very profitable. These experts are correct, up to a point: This method often showed that the cumulative premiums paid were *less* than the surrender value. No matter how you look at it, that qualifies as a profit—even the IRS thinks so. These experts, however, complain that traditional net cost does not take into consideration the opportunity cost of purchasing the insurance, which is also correct. And these same experts, who are often the same ones who suggest buying term and investing the difference, often fail to point out that the IRS considers the premiums as part of the insured's basis when determining profit, yet does not consider the premiums paid for term insurance as part of the basis when determining the profit of the alternative investment. More contemporary methods of policy comparison derive dollar figures, but remember they are merely indices for comparison purposes and are not absolute values. The amounts derived from traditional net cost comparisons when used as relative values are generally as valid as those derived from more contemporary methods.

NEED TO KNOW: ADEQUATELY FUNDED UL

Universal life is often sold instead of whole life because it can be shown with a lower premium. For someone in their 20s or 30s, the mortality costs will be relatively low for the next 20 years. However, as the individual ages, the mortality charges increase and may eventually exceed the combined premium and the earnings within the policy. When this happens, the accumulation value decreases. As the individual reaches and passes retirement age, the accumulation fund may not be adequate to keep the policy in force unless premiums are increased.

The flexibility of UL is both its advantage and disadvantage. It is easy to skip premium payments in the early years, but that means the policy will require greater increases in premiums later if it is to be maintained as permanent coverage. Unlike whole life, which operates almost on autopilot, UL requires ongoing management and periodic review. Advisors need to keep policyholders apprised of the effects of changing interest rates and premiums. It is a great product if used properly.

There are two more specific problems with the net cost method. The first is related to the time value of money. Some companies delay dividend payments or increases in cash value until the standard years of comparison so they look better at those specific times. This is to the detriment of policyholders who are forced to terminate their policies before the standard comparison years. These early lapses support the higher values in the comparison years.

The second problem is that of illustrated versus actual results with participating policies: Some companies use a dividend rate for sales material that makes their policies look very good over the long run, yet they seldom achieve these dividend illustrations. Other companies, including most of the better companies, consistently meet or exceed their dividend illustrations. Still, agents and policy owners were not prepared when interest rates began to plummet in the late 1980s and dividend rates could not be maintained. Rather, it is prudent to remember that the insurance industry is part of the same economy as all other businesses. Illustrated values prepared in accordance with insurance company guidelines include statements that the numbers are based on current conditions and may change. The language used in policy illustrations points out that dividend values are based on the current scale, are not estimates or projections for future values, and are subject to change. This means that unless the economy stays exactly where it is, the dividends will change.

Interest-Adjusted Cost Indices

The most common comparison analysis used today involves the interest-adjusted indices as defined by the National Association of Insurance Commissioners (NAIC). These indices were adopted by the NAIC in 1976 and their use was recommended to all of the states. While these indices have not been adopted in every state, most insurers provide the two indices with all illustrations.

The first index is the **interest-adjusted surrender cost index** and the second index is the **interest-adjusted net payment index**. Both indices involve four inputs: (1) premiums, (2) cash values, (3) dividends (if it is a participating policy), and (4) a consistent interest rate. These indices also take into consideration the time value of money.

The goal of each index is to allow the consumer to compare relative costs of similar policies. Although each index is stated in dollars, it is an approximate value to be used as an index, based on recognizing when premiums and dividends are paid and when cash values are available year-by-year rather than at set intervals. This approach prevents companies from delaying payment of dividends or increases in cash values to make their illustrations look better than the competition as they might under the traditional net cost method.

> **NEED TO KNOW:**
> **BEFORE THE NUMBERS...**
>
> Before comparing numbers between policies, it is important to review the ratings of the companies under consideration. This topic is covered comprehensively in the upcoming chapter 5

Surrender Cost Index

This index focuses on the cash value and dividends of a policy. As with the traditional net cost method, the index is calculated for specific years (10, 20, and age 65) with the assumption that the policy would be surrendered at that time. As is obvious by its name, it is an index that illustrates the relative value of the policy if it is surrendered at the given times.

Net Payment Index

This index focuses on the payments due under the policy rather than the cash values accumulated within the policy. The index is an indicator of relative payment if a policy is kept beyond a specified time in the future, such as years 10 or 20, or age 65.

A planner needs to recognize that this index is not the true cost of the policy since the index is based on a number of assumptions; it is merely a device to compare one policy with a similar policy. Any policy that pays dividends can effectively adjust the premium or cash values or vary the earnings on the cash accumulation fund. Some advisors have attempted to use these numbers to compare dissimilar policies or to compare a permanent policy with term and investing the difference. These attempts are misleading at best, inappropriate and meaningless at worst.

Problems with Illustrations

Unfortunately, with the advent of personal computers and their wide adoption by insurance agents in the mid to late 1980s, a few agents decided that the company-provided illustrations included too much information; they did not want to confuse their prospects. Company illustrations include guaranteed values as well as values based on current dividend illustrations, when appropriate. As the NAIC and consumers demanded more information, illustrations became rather long since they included extensive information regarding the assurance of any dividend guarantee for the future. Company illustrations progressed and permitted agents to illustrate policies with higher and lower dividend and interest assumptions. This in itself was not bad. The problem was that insurance products are fairly complex and the agent had the job of educating clients so they understood what all the numbers really meant. In the mid-1970s illustrations typically were on a single page; current illustrations might be a dozen pages or more.

Unfortunately, consumers generally focus on what they want to hear: the upside of the illustrations. They may or may not appreciate the downside of these same illustrations. Sometimes, agents, worried they might talk the client out of a sale, did not ensure that prospective insureds fully understood the illustrations. Some agents did not even bother with the "details." A few agents went so far as to use incomplete illustrations, which did not even afford the client the opportunity to fully understand what might happen.

At the same time, the stock market and short-term interest rates were increasing rapidly. Sales people in other areas of financial services decided the premiums going into life insurance were better spent elsewhere. Many of these sales people started to compare the investment aspect of insurance to alternative investments, ignoring the other benefits of insurance and the long-term costs of term insurance. A great deal of disintermediation subsequently occurred. Money was taken out of life insurance policies and reinvested in other, potentially higher earning investments.

To deal with this competition, the insurance industry began to increase dividend illustrations based, to some extent, on the short-term interest rates that had fueled the rampant disintermediation. Universal life and variable universal life featured interest rates that reacted rapidly to the market, so they became quite popular. Realistically, interest rates could not stay high forever. None of the "experts" expected rates to drop so rapidly and so far. Under the rules of economics, dividends had to follow.

While interest rates were still high, insurance companies were directed to change reserve requirements and use updated mortality tables. This allowed insurance companies to illustrate an "improved" premium-paying program—sometimes called a disappearing premium or vanishing premium. Both of these titles, which came from articles about illustrating and selling the concept, were misnomers, and neither one was widely used by insurance companies. Most companies did not name the program. Those who did name the program referred to it as a "premium offset," which is exactly what it was. This program involved using dividends to purchase paid-up dividend additions for 8 to 12 years. At that point, the policy owner could stop paying premiums—if the current dividend projections held. Current dividends would then be used in later years to reduce the premium, and some of the paid-up dividend additions would be surrendered to pay the balance. Based on the dividend scales in use at the time the policies were sold, this worked quite well: The policy owner would never have to pay another premium. Unfortunately, the dividends dropped because of the substantial reduction in interest rates.

Any agent who did not take a conservative stance in developing and explaining the illustrations had therefore done a disservice to his or her clients. The companies emphasized the importance of explaining to clients that the dividend projections depended on the level of interest rates and that, further, changes in the projections would affect the ability of the policy to support itself. When interest rates fell, many policy owners were upset when they received bills after they were told they would not have to pay anything more. Even those who were told about it, and who received complete illustrations stating that the results were based only on the current dividend projections, often remembered things differently. This led to many lawsuits. Insurance buyers "remembered" that they were guaranteed never to have to pay premiums after a certain number of years.

It is likely that very few, if any, buyers of insurance were guaranteed that after 8, 10, or 12 years they would not have to pay premiums. Yet that is how they remembered it. This is a good lesson for all planners. Just because you explain something to a client does not mean he or she will remember it as you intended. Recommendations and projections, including any caveats, should be in writing and initialed by the client, indicating their complete and full understanding at the time. In addition, details of phone conversations and face-to-face meetings should be kept in the client's file.

The Belth Method

Joseph M. Belth, professor emeritus of insurance at Indiana University, has been an outspoken critic of and writer about the insurance industry. In an effort to provide methods of determining the value of life insurance contracts, he developed two methods of evaluating policies. One is the yearly rate of return method, which is beyond the scope of this chapter. His most commonly used method is the yearly price of protection method, discussed here.

The **yearly price of protection method** calculates a cost per thousand for the policy under consideration and compares that amount to a chart: "Belth's Benchmark Price of Insurance."

The process begins with the following formula:

$$YPT = \frac{(P + CVP)\,(1 + i) - (CSV + D)}{(DB - CSV)\,(0.001)}$$

Where:

YPT	=	Yearly price per thousand
P	=	Premium
CVP	=	Cash surrender value previous year
i	=	Net after-tax interest rate
CSV	=	Cash surrender value current year
D	=	Dividend current year
DB	=	Death benefit of policy (face amount)

Step 1: Calculate the accumulated investment (cash surrender value at end of previous year plus current premium) and multiply it by one plus the net after-tax interest rate, an assumed rate.

Step 2: Calculate the year-end surrender value (year end surrender value plus any dividend).

Step 3: Subtract the results of step 2 from step 1.

Step 4: Divide the result of step 3 by the net amount at risk (policy face amount minus the current year's cash value in thousands) times .001. The result is a cost of protection per thousand dollars of insurance.

The purpose of this calculation is to determine the policy with the lowest cost. However, a single calculation does not accomplish this. Some policies will show a low cost some years, but a relatively high cost other years. The entire calculation must be repeated for a span of several years to ensure that the seemingly better priced policy maintains its edge over the long term.

The Belth method serves two functions. One is to compare two life-insurance policies, preferably before the purchase of either one. The second function is to determine if replacement of a policy might be a reasonable option. Remember that the comparison should cover many years.

If a client is considering the replacement of an existing policy, Belth suggests the use of the following benchmark price per thousand:

Table 4.1

Benchmark Price Per Thousand			
Age	Price	Age	Price
Under 30	$1.50	55-59	$15.00
30-34	2.00	60-64	25.00
35-39	3.00	65-69	35.00
40-44	4.00	70-74	50.00
45-49	6.50	75-79	80.00
50-54	10.00	80-84	125.00

Belth recommends that the application of the table should follow these general rules:

- If the calculated price per thousand is less than the benchmark price, replacement is not likely a reasonable option.
- If the calculated price per thousand is between one and two times the benchmark price, it is likely that replacement is not necessary or indicated.
- If the calculated price per thousand is more than two times the benchmark price, replacement is not mandated but should be considered.

Caution is necessary for the following reasons:

- A single calculation may be misleading. It is not necessarily the actual mortality cost that is being calculated; thus, a series of calculations covering a number of years for competing policies is appropriate before any decision is made.
- In the later years of a policy, when the net amount at risk is relatively small, the variations in the price per thousand might fluctuate a great deal and may not be indicative of the policy's relative value.

This method, like most others, fails to consider policy loans and their effect on dividends: These factors can significantly alter the relative value of a given policy. Nor can this method fully calculate the "sunk" costs of the existing policy and the acquisition costs of the new policy. Furthermore, the ratings and financial stability of the companies are not reflected in the Belth method—when comparing policy illustrations, it is common for lower-rated companies to have superior illustrated numbers. However, actual long-term results of the policy are a much better measure. An aggressive insurance company may show better numbers for certain years, but this is typically at the expense of exposing policy owners to a higher risk.

In-Depth: Calculating to Buy Term and Invest the Difference

Two methods have been developed to help clients see the difference between buying a permanent policy and buying a term policy and then investing the difference in a side fund. Before introducing these models, however, it is important to note that a comprehensive and fair comparison is complicated by economics, policy structure, and tax factors that these two methods cannot adequately measure. In many cases, the difference between the cost of term and permanent is spent, not invested.

The two methods take opposite approaches. Both require a series of calculations that involves several fiscal years, typically 20. Both require that a term policy face amount be adjusted to match a permanent policy death benefit that increases with paid-up dividend additions, the side fund growth, or both. Both have the potential disadvantage of being skewed by the choice of term insurance rates and risk being inappropriately presented with unrealistic or noncomparable interest rates. Like other comparison methods, they make the probably erroneous assumption that the policies will be terminated before death. However, both have an uncommon advantage: They can be used to compare two different forms of insurance.

While these methods produce numbers that may be used to evaluate two different policies, the numbers are not absolute returns.

For both methods, outlays for the permanent insurance and the term (or lower premium) policy and investment fund are equated. If the whole life premium is $1,445 and the term policy is $143, the side fund (alternative investment) would be credited with $1,302 as shown in the tables 4.2 and 4.3.

Next, the lower premium term policy's death benefit must be adjusted each year so that the face amount of that policy plus the side fund equals the total death benefit of the higher-premium permanent policy. The nature of the policies usually prevents this from being an option, making the illustration a fictitious one.

Over the years, the total death benefit (face amount plus dividends or side fund) should be the same, so the cash accumulation fund of the permanent policy can be compared to the side fund to see which performed better for the client.

Any differences in premium are accumulated at an assumed interest rate.

The **cash accumulation method** does permit comparisons of whole life with term insurance. Three factors, however, substantially affect the results: the chosen interest rate (the most critical), the term rates shown, and the whole life rates shown. A person who wants to show whole life in the best light possible will choose a very high quality whole life or a very aggressive whole life illustration and compare it to a relatively expensive term policy and use a very low interest rate. A person who wants to prove that term is better may show unrealistically low term rates, a poorly designed whole life policy, and/or high interest rates. This makes the method subjective rather than objective.

Some consider the only fair comparison to be one that uses comparable interest rates to those reasonably expected in the permanent policy; meanwhile, others take the position that the interest rate used should reflect the average return the client earns on his or her investments. A third group professes that it is best to use an interest rate that reflects the average return on all of the client's assets, including depreciating assets.

It is also worth noting that the entire comparison is based on an unlikely scenario: The comparison requires the term policy to be reduced incrementally so that the total available death benefit of the policies being compared remains the same. While some term policies now permit reduction of coverage as often as annually, most still restrict how much the policy can be reduced. After all, large policies usually have a lower cost per thousand than smaller policies. Most insurance policies also have a fixed policy fee, so that if all other factors stayed the same, reducing a term policy death benefit by 50 percent will not cut the premium in half.

When a term policy is reduced incrementally so that the total available death benefit of the policies being compared remains the same, this frees up money for the side fund that would not otherwise be available. The scenario unrealistically assumes that the side fund will remain untouched until the death of the insured.

(continued on next page)

(continued from previous page)

The other approach, the **Linton yield** method calculates the return necessary to equal the return of the permanent life insurance under the assumption that the death benefits and annual outlay are both the same for the evaluation period.

The difference between the Linton yield method and the cash accumulation method is that the permanent policy values are initially shown, and the term rates are then input with the difference available for the side fund. The cash value of the permanent policy is also shown for the last year of the comparison period, e.g., year 20. Finally, the rate of return necessary for the side fund to accumulate to that amount is then calculated—a fairly time consuming calculation.

Table 4.2

				CASH ACCUMULATION METHOD				
				Ordinary Life (OL) versus Yearly Renewable Term (YRT)				
				$100,000 face value for age 35 male nonsmoker				
Year	OL Prem.	YRT Prem.	Diff. in Prem.	Side Fund at 6.00%	OL Surrend. Value	YRT Face Amount	YRT Plus Side Fund	OL with Paid-up Ads
1	$1,445	$143	$1,302	$1,380	$0	$98,630	$100,010	$100,010
2	1,445	144	1,301	2,842	175	97,269	100,111	100,111
3	1,445	148	1,297	4,388	1,670	95,921	100,309	100,309
4	1,445	154	1,291	6,020	3,324	94,828	100,848	100,848
5	1,445	162	1,283	7,741	5,167	94,076	101,817	101,817
6	1,445	173	1,272	9,554	7,189	93,677	103,231	103,231
7	1,445	187	1,258	11,460	9,435	93,645	105,105	105,105
8	1,445	206	1,239	13,461	11,986	93,997	107,458	107,458
9	1,445	229	1,216	15,557	14,768	94,759	110,316	110,316
10	1,445	257	1,188	17,750	17,898	95,928	113,678	113,678
11	1,445	292	1,153	20,037	21,243	97,574	117,611	117,611
12	1,445	332	1,113	22,420	25,007	99,636	122,056	122,056
13	1,445	381	1,064	24,893	29,147	102,164	127,057	127,057
14	1,445	439	1,006	27,453	33,634	105,216	132,669	132,669
15	1,445	507	938	30,094	38,579	108,809	138,903	138,903
16	1,445	589	856	32,807	44,126	113,014	145,821	145,821
17	1,445	685	760	35,582	50,167	117,872	153,454	153,454
18	1,445	797	648	38,403	56,913	123,410	161,813	161,813
19	1,445	929	516	41,254	64,238	129,808	171,062	171,062
20	1,445	1,084	361	44,112	72,295	137,047	181,159	181,159

From *Tools and Techniqes of Life Insurance Planning*, National Underwriter. Used by permission.

This table assumes that dividends are used to purchase paid-up additions and unambiguously identifies the whole life policy as the superior strategy for years 10 and beyond.

Table 4.3

	**20-YEAR LINTON YIELD** **Ordinary Life (OL) versus Yearly Renewable Term (YRT)** **$100,000 face value for age 35 male nonsmoker**

Year	OL Prem.	YRT Prem.	Diff in Prem.	Side Fund at 9.696%	OL Surrend. Value	YRT Face Amount	YRT Plus Side Fund	OL with Paid-up Ads
1	$1,445	$143	$1,302	$1,428	$3	$98,582	$100,010	$100,010
2	1,445	144	1,301	2,994	175	97,117	100,111	100,111
3	1,445	147	1,298	4,708	1,670	95,601	100,309	100,309
4	1,445	153	1,292	6,582	3,324	94,266	100,848	100,848
5	1,445	160	1,285	8,630	5,167	93,187	101,817	101,817
6	1,445	171	1,274	10,864	7,189	92,367	103,231	103,231
7	1,445	184	1,261	13,301	9,435	91,804	105,105	105,105
8	1,445	200	1,245	15,956	11,986	91,502	107,458	107,458
9	1,445	221	1,224	18,846	14,768	91,470	110,316	110,316
10	1,445	246	1,199	21,988	17,898	91,690	113,678	113,678
11	1,445	276	1,169	25,403	21,243	92,208	117,611	117,611
12	1,445	310	1,135	29,112	25,007	92,944	122,056	122,056
13	1,445	350	1,095	33,135	29,147	93,922	127,057	127,057
14	1,445	397	1,048	37,498	33,634	95,171	132,669	132,669
15	1,445	451	994	42,225	38,579	96,678	138,903	138,903
16	1,445	513	932	47,341	44,126	98,480	145,821	145,821
17	1,445	584	861	52,875	50,167	100,579	153,454	153,454
18	1,445	665	780	58,857	56,913	102,956	161,813	161,813
19	1,445	757	688	65,319	64,238	105,743	171,062	171,062
20	1,445	861	584	72,293	72,295	108,866	181,159	181,159

From *Tools and Techniqes of Life Insurance Planning*, National Underwriter. Used by permission.

This table assumes that dividends are used to purchase paid-up additions. The difference between the OL premiums and the YRT premiums is invested at 9.696 percent in the side fund. The side fund virtually equals the cash value in year 20.

The Linton Yield Method

Another method used to compare policies is the Linton yield method. It is, in some eyes, the inverse of the interest-adjusted indices calculations. In the interest-adjusted indices calculations, the interest rate is identified and remains the same throughout the calculations. With the Linton yield, it is the interest rate itself that is being calculated.

This approach suffers from the same potential problems as the cash accumulation method. That is, the term rates assumed will have a substantial effect on the outcome of the calculations. This leaves the method open to manipulation. Some insurance companies offer a term product that is available to only about 5 percent of applicants. It is for nonsmokers who are in exceptionally good health. Using these rates for an average client would provide misleading results, showing a very low return on the permanent policy. On the other hand, some companies offer relatively expensive term policies because that is not the market they seek. Using uncommonly high term insurance rates will make the permanent policy appear to have an unrealistically high return. It is important, however, to take into consideration what a client would want in a term policy. If he or she wants a policy that permits conversion to age 65, an excellent disability waiver or a premium benefit, and a company with impeccable finances, the policy will not be the lowest-cost policy on the market. The use of a very low-cost term in the Linton yield calculations for this client would also be misleading.

The Linton yield is touted as one method that can be used to compare different types of policies. However, it is critical that the same term rates be used for comparing policies. Although this method does come up with a return that is required to make an outside account equal the return realized by a permanent life insurance policy, it is still to be used as an index for comparison rather than as an absolute interest rate. Table 4.3 shows the result of the calculations, demonstrating how different interest rates can be used to determine how much must be earned in an outside account to equal the ultimate benefit of the policy. (This is in comparison to Table 4.2 where the cash accumulation method assumes a constant 6 percent return.) Fortunately, insurance software applications will take care of this highly iterative process.

LIFE INSURANCE POLICY REPLACEMENT

Financial planners and insurance agents want to know what single formula will guide them to the best policy available; nevertheless, there is no magic formula to uncover the absolute best policy. With 20/20 hindsight, the future will reveal which policy would have been the best. Remember what was said before: "The best policy is the one that is in force when the insured dies."

It is seldom in the best interest of a client to replace an existing, in-force policy. Under certain circumstances a policy is inappropriate or simply a bad policy, but this is uncommon. The easiest way to determine when to replace a life insurance policy is, instead, to first ask, "When should I *not* replace a policy?"

Although a financial planner may come across a handful of policies that are simply a poor value throughout his or her career (such as most policies sold by mail, some founder's policies, or healthy persons with guaranteed-issue policies), few policies are inherently good or bad. Any planner who naively takes the position that all policies of any one type (such as whole life, UL, or term) are "bad" does not serve his or her clients well: Indeed, by doing so, the planner probably has failed to meet the objectivity and integrity standards of CFP Board's Code of Ethics. All major forms of insurance have clients and situations that they fit best, and no specific insurance form has total returns that are guaranteed (as we will see in the discussion of the demutualization of mutual companies in chapter 5).

The following issues should be considered when evaluating an existing policy for the purpose of potential replacement.

- The policy's relative value
- The issuing company's ratings
- The appropriateness of the policy form for the needs of the client
- The future ability of the client to afford adequate insurance
- The cost of starting over
- Any possible changes in a client's insurability
- Any possible effect of new contestability and suicide clauses
- The amount of insurance relative to total need
- The client's risk tolerance
- Any other contractual limitations
- Any other legal limitations placed on the individual

NEED TO KNOW: FOUNDER'S POLICIES

A few companies sold founder's policies when they first began operations in order to establish a certain level of insurance— the level generally required to be in force to enter the business.

Some founder's policies are quite good. Others are terrible. When looking at a founder's policy, or any policy for that matter, look to the guarantees, the dividend or excess interest history, and any other language that may not be common. The poorer policies generally have guaranteed cash values that are very low, providing the company the likelihood of substantial profit from every policy whether they are lapsed or stay in force.

Relative value refers to the value of the policy when compared to others: If another policy is clearly a better value, then replacement should be considered. Company ratings are discussed in chapter 5.

The appropriateness of a policy determines whether this policy is the best policy for the client, as discussed earlier in this chapter—likewise with the client's ability to afford the insurance.

Costs of replacement include beginning again with new suicide and contestable clauses. Other contractual limitations that might affect the decision would be the availability of a conversion privilege, definitions of disability or presumptive disability associated with the waiver of premium clause, whether or not the policy is participating, existence of guaranteed premiums, etc. Remember, many of these factors may simply indicate a client needs more insurance, not a different policy: In most cases it makes more sense to add additional insurance than to replace the existing policy. A legal limitation may arise in a separation or divorce decree, which may prohibit changing any existing insurance.

Note: Under no circumstance should one policy be allowed to lapse before a replacement policy has been issued and put in force.

ACCELERATED DEATH BENEFITS AND VIATICAL SETTLEMENTS

The 1980s brought international attention to AIDS: At the time, life expectancy for those infected was very short, and treatment was experimental (rarely covered by health insurance) and extremely expensive. Many of the victims had previously purchased life insurance, but needed funds to cover treatment and ensure quality of life in their remaining years. This need gave rise to the increased use of viatical[1] agreements and the creation of accelerated death benefits, a source of income for terminal patients that, meeting certain requirements, may also be free of federal income tax.

Planners should note that accelerated death benefits and viatical settlements are not the only alternatives open to a terminally or chronically ill policyholder. He or she can also borrow against the cash values of the policy, surrender the policy to the insurance company, or borrow funds from a third party. These options would reduce the policy's death benefit by the amount received, plus any interest due, but would leave the balance of the death benefit in force.

Viatical Agreements

Viatication is the sale of a life insurance policy by a terminally ill person to an investor or investment group. Viatication is an option when a terminally ill insured does not need his or her life insurance, needs cash now,

---

NEED TO KNOW: DISCLOSURE AND THE NAIC MODEL REPLACEMENT REGULATION

Licensed agents must provide certain disclosure information in virtually all states whenever a replacement of life insurance or an annuity is recommended. Many states have enacted the updated NAIC Model Replacement Regulation, adopted by the NAIC in 2000 to provide consistent guidelines regarding the timing of disclosure information and what this information should be.

The newest version requires the agent and applicant to sign a statement regarding replacement. The statement is to be signed even if there is no replacement. This must be submitted with the application. The model suggests disclosure should occur whenever a policy is being replaced or a new one is being financed from the values in an existing policy. For each replacement policy, the replacing company must provide a 30-day free preview to the buyer, with the right to obtain a full refund if the purchase is subsequently cancelled. The company that issued the original policy must be notified in writing about the proposed replacement. The replacing company may not require the suicide clause to start again, and if it is the same company writing the new policy, the contestable period may not begin again. If requested, the replacing agent must also provide the company being replaced with a copy of any illustrations used. No later than at the time the application is signed, the agent must present and read a statement about the replacement to the client. The statement must include details about the policies being replaced. After having the client either read the application or sign that he or she does not want to read it or have it read, both the agent and applicant must sign the form, which must then be submitted with the application. Over the objections of industry representatives, if a registered representative proposes to replace life insurance with investments, neither a disclosure nor statements about the loss of protection is required by law

---

[1] A viatical agreement is a contract to sell an insurance policy to an investor. The policy owner generally receives more than he or she would if the policy is surrendered.

or has more insurance than his or her heirs will probably need when he or she dies. The process is simple: An independent third-party company (regularly engaged in that business, licensed by the particular state, or controlled by Internal Revenue Code requirements) purchases the life insurance policy of the insured person who has a terminal illness or disease. Typically, the insured receives a lump-sum payment ranging from 50 to 80 percent of the policy's face value; alternatively, the insured may elect to receive periodic payments. The third-party purchaser, as the new owner of the policy, then names itself as the beneficiary, continues to pay any required premiums, and collects the policy's death benefit when the insured dies. Purchasers generally require the life expectancy of the insured to be two years or less. As long as the insured meets the requirements of the Health Insurance Portability and Accountability Act of 1996 (HIPAA) legislation of 1996 (terminally ill with a life expectancy of two years or less), the proceeds will be free of federal income tax. However, even though these proceeds are free of income tax, they will be counted as part of the individual's assets and may affect eligibility for certain government programs.

At the death of the insured, all of the gain realized by the viatical buyer (death benefit minus amounts paid, including subsequent premiums, for the policy) is taxed as ordinary income. Viatical companies typically use the following rules to determine eligibility:

- The insured has owned the policy for at least two years to ensure the contestability period has elapsed.
- The current beneficiary must sign a release or a waiver to clear up any potential problems with irrevocable beneficiary designations.
- The insured must be terminally ill—some companies require a life expectancy of two years or less while others may buy a policy even if life expectancy is four years.
- The insured must sign a release allowing the viatical settlement provider access to his or her medical records to provide it assurance of the life expectancy.

Accelerated Death Benefits

Another source of funds for terminally or chronically ill individuals is accelerated death benefits. If the IRS rules are met, these benefits will also be free of income tax. Many insurance companies have added this benefit to existing life insurance policies and have even begun to include it on all new policies. This provision typically provides that if you are terminally ill, usually with a life expectancy of one year or less, the company will pay out a portion of the death benefit, reserving the balance for when the insured dies. The most common amount paid under these circumstances is 50 percent, generally paid in monthly increments so that it remains income tax-free. Some companies treat this as they would a policy loan, reducing the death benefit by the amount of the payment and charging interest, while others merely reduce the death benefit by the amount of the payment. This is sometimes called a living-needs benefit, an acceleration-of-life insurance benefit, an accelerated benefit rider, or a living-payout option.

The main advantage of these options is that terminally ill or seriously chronically ill insureds can obtain advances of policy death benefits free of income taxes and use them for a variety of personal purposes. On the other hand, the receipt of accelerated death benefits reduces the face amount of the insured's policy, which can be a problem if there are surviving dependents. It is currently unclear whether creditors of the insured can attach these payments for unpaid medical bills, special care, or other personal debts.

HIPAA Definitions and Rules

A **terminally ill individual** is one who has been certified by a physician as having a condition that can reasonably be expected to result in death within 24 months of certification, even if the insured actually lives longer than 24 months. The amount that can be excluded from income is not limited.

A **chronically ill individual** is one who has been certified by a licensed health care practitioner as being unable to perform (without help) at least two activities of daily living (i.e., eating, toileting, transferring, bathing, dressing, and continence) for a period of at least 90 days due to a loss of functional capacity. It is also possible to certify someone as chronically ill if this person requires substantial supervision for protection from threats to health and safety due to severe cognitive impairment. A person cannot be considered both terminally ill and chronically ill.

In order to be income tax-free, payments to chronically ill individuals must be reimbursements for the costs of qualified long-term care services (specifically defined) provided for the insured and not compensated for by insurance or otherwise. As a result, to maintain the income tax-free nature of the payments, chronically ill individuals do not have the discretion to use accelerated benefits or viatical settlements in whatever manner they desire, as most terminally ill insureds do. Also, there are limits on the amount of tax-free periodic payments made to chronically ill individuals based on a per diem allowance indexed annually for inflation. The amount may be the greater of the per diem amount or the actual expenses incurred.

Neither modified endowment contract policies nor payments made to someone other than the insured under a key person policy or other business policy are eligible for favorable tax treatment.

NEED TO KNOW: ACCELERATED PAYMENTS AND TAXATION

As you read earlier in the text, in most cases, the proceeds of a life insurance policy are excluded from the recipient's gross income. However, since accelerated benefits and viatical settlements are paid to the insured during his or her life, they are not payable by reason of the insured's death. As a result, when this issue first arose, it appeared that the proceeds would be subject to income tax. HIPAA has specifically excluded most accelerated payments and viatical settlements from gross income by defining them as being paid "by reason of the death of the insured." However, HIPAA spells out very specific requirements for obtaining this tax treatment.

Viatical settlement companies are subject to what is known as the "transfer-for-value rule" involving the sale or transfer of life insurance for valuable consideration. As a result, the policy proceeds a company receives on the death of the insured on an accelerated death benefit type policy are taxable at ordinary income rates less the sum of the amounts paid to acquire the policy and to maintain the policy. This will be further discussed in chapter 20.

ANNUITIES

Most families buy life insurance to protect against the risk of a person dying too soon. But what about the opposite problem? What happens if a person outlives his or her sources of income? Annuities are designed to meet this need: They provide tax-deferred retirement income. That is their primary purpose. Secondarily, they provide a method of accumulating money needed for retirement funds. An annuity is the only contract designed to continue to pay if the annuitant lives too long.

Annuities come in various forms:

Immediate and Deferred

Immediate annuities initiate periodic payments at the next distribution increment after purchase: If the income is to be received monthly, the first payment will be made one month from the date of purchase or at the first occurrence of the chosen date of distribution. If the distribution is to be made quarterly, the first payment will occur three months after the purchase. When payments are scheduled to begin later, usually much later, the annuity is called a **deferred annuity**.

Single, Fixed, or Flexible Premium

Some individuals put a single lump sum into an annuity. This is usually the case when the purpose is to convert cash sitting in some other account into a regular monthly income or when an individual receives a lump sum of money that he or she wants to use for retirement. By investing in an annuity, the money grows income-tax-deferred. All immediate annuities are single premium annuities. While quite uncommon today, a planner may also come across a **fixed premium annuity**, an annuity purchased with consistent periodic premium deposits. The purchaser of the annuity agrees to make the same periodic payment or cease making payments altogether. **Flexible premium annuities** allow the annuity purchaser to make contributions of varying amounts whenever he or she wants. Some have minor restrictions, such as permitting only one payment per month or limiting the range of contributions.

Fixed, Variable, and Equity Indexed

A **fixed annuity** is one that earns a specified rate of interest, generally a guaranteed minimum such as 3.5 percent annually, for a certain number of years during the accumulation period, after which the interest rate may be changed, but still remains subject to the guaranteed minimum. A **variable annuity** has a number of separate accounts for the investment options of the annuity purchase payments—some have only a few options while others may have 20 or more.

However, all variable annuities are generally invested in a portfolio of stocks or other market-sensitive investment vehicles. The investment options are held in separate accounts and, while they may mirror certain mutual funds, they are kept separate from any existing fund.

Equity indexed annuities are relatively new, fitting between fixed and variable annuities. Their accumulation accounts are tied to an investment index, most commonly the Standard & Poor's 500. Interestingly, since they use the S&P 500 as an index but do not directly fluctuate with the market, they are not considered securities. These annuities are very popular with those who want to share in the upside of the stock market without worrying about the downside and generally have a minimum guaranteed rate of return over a specified period of time, usually seven years. Additionally, they are credited with excess interest based on the index used. However, if the S&P 500 increases 20 percent in a year, the annuity will seldom be credited with that total amount of excess interest.

Some equity-indexed annuities, but not all, have a maximum amount of interest that will be credited in a single year. Generally, the annuity pays a percentage of the increase of the index that is used, 80 percent for example. So if the S&P 500 increases by 10 percent in a year, the annuity is credited with 8 percent. The way earnings are credited also varies.

Some credit the greater of the guaranteed interest rate or the indexed return at the end of a specified number of years—commonly seven years. In the interim, it makes no difference what the index does.

Others adjust the base each year based on the greater of the guaranteed interest rate or the indexed increase. This second method permits the annuity owner to benefit from an increase in the index that may occur in some years but not over a period of several years.

An Ever Changing Market

The above described forms of annuities are the most common forms. However, the annuity market is quite large, and companies introduce new variations on a regular basis. Unless an individual is working full time in the annuities market, he or she is not likely to know what is available. To be competitive, each company puts its own version of an annuity together. Asking lots of questions to ensure a good understanding of each product is critical. Some are better suited for a given individual than others. It is not uncommon for a single company to offer a half dozen or more different annuities.

Surrender Charges

With most annuities sold today, 100 percent of the purchase payment is credited to the accumulation account(s). However, it does cost the insurance company something to sell the annuities and establish the funding vehicles. To cover these expenses and to encourage stability of the invested funds, insurance companies include surrender charges for early termination of an annuity. These charges may be as high as 10 percent of the purchase payment and last as long as 10 years. Typically, single premium annuities have surrender charges that apply for fewer years than those of flexible premium annuities. Most surrender charges reflect annually-reducing percentages over the period of time they apply. In many cases, the surrender charges are waived if the distribution is taken because of death, disability, or annuitization. A handful of companies impose a surrender charge if the funds are taken out in any manner other than through annuitization.

Administrative Charges

Most insurance companies that issue annuities impose an annual administrative charge for maintaining the annuity. With fixed annuities this is usually a flat fee, such as $30 annually. With variable annuities, it is a percentage of the value of the separate accounts plus an annual charge. In some cases, there is a sales charge against all payments made to an annuity.

Distribution Options

Annuity payment options are essentially the same as the settlement options offered with life insurance policies. A **straight life annuity**, also called a pure life annuity, provides a monthly income for as long as the annuitant lives and provides the highest lifetime monthly income. However, the payments terminate at the death of the annuitant. This could be after a few payments or after decades of payments. A few companies offer a refund if the annuitant dies shortly after payments begin; each of those contracts is unique and must be reviewed to determine the specific provisions. In the past, the decision to purchase a straight life annuity was irrevocable. Today, some companies offer a right of commutation. The annuitant is given the right to convert future payments to a lump sum. The right has limits, but it is still better to have limited rights of this type than none.

A period certain guarantee ensures that payments will continue for a specified number of years, even if the annuitant does not live that long. The payout guarantee is typically 10 or 20 years and is usually described as "10 years certain and continuous," meaning that the payments will be made for at least 10 years, but will continue beyond that date if the annuitant is still living. Some companies merely continue the scheduled payments while others may offer a beneficiary a commuted single value for remaining payments.

The **specified income** option allows the owner to set payments at a specified amount. The insurance company will calculate the number of payments to be made and tell the owner. The **specified payment period** is the reverse of the specified income option: The owner specifies the number of payments to be made over a number of years or months, and the insurance company determines the payment to be made at each distribution.

The various options for payments being made on two lives are also available. As with life insurance options, if there is more than one life covered under a pure life annuity, the payments will be smaller than if only one life is used. This is due to the increased likelihood of a longer payout.

Payments may be fixed or variable. In the past, only fixed payments were available. The upside of this was that annuitants always knew what they were going to get, which, for most seniors, is very important. However, there was no recognition of inflation. Some companies offer a **variable payout**, which is a fluctuating payment that adjusts with the value of the underlying investment in the annuity. There is no single method of operating variable payouts on annuities, so each company's offering must be evaluated. More recently, a few companies have built inflation benefits into their policies. The monthly payment increases annually to reflect, usually a predetermined, rate of increase. Of course this means that the initial monthly payment will be lower than with a straight life annuity with a fixed payment.

If the company that issued the annuity does not provide competitive payments, or is not a particularly strong company financially, annuity owners may make an IRC Section 1035 exchange into a different annuity during the accumulation phase. If this is contemplated, all costs of purchasing a new annuity must be considered.

Death Benefit

A portion of the earnings of most fixed annuities and most variable annuities is reserved by the insurance company as a mortality charge. Most annuities guarantee that if the annuitant dies before the scheduled maturity date of the annuity, the beneficiary will receive the greater of the accumulation value or the amount deposited in the annuity. During the long-standing bull market, many people saw no reason to have this benefit, but once the post 1990s recession occurred, few people complained.

In-Depth: Annuities and Mutual Funds

Arguments persist regarding the relative value of annuities and mutual funds, but comparisons are only really appropriate between mutual funds and variable annuities, not between mutual funds and fixed or equity-indexed annuities.

Mutual funds are separate entities in which individuals purchase and sell shares. These entities generally buy and sell the various securities in which they are authorized to invest. Whenever a fund buys and sells investments, there may be a taxable event that passes through to the owner of the fund shares. If the owner of the fund shares decides to change funds, any gain or loss on the sale of the shares is a taxable event resulting in a net gain or loss. With most funds, the fund-share owner may buy or sell shares at his or her discretion.

Other than expected gains or losses, there are no other tax issues surrounding the purchase or sale of mutual funds. Fund shares are included in the owner's estate just as any other owned assets. Currently, if the owner of mutual fund shares dies, his or her heirs receive an adjusted basis in the shares: The new value is equal to the fair market value on the day the shareowner died.

Taxation of gains and losses are in accordance with the rules for capital gains and losses.

Ownership of mutual funds is much like that of any other asset: It may be held in one name, joint tenancy with rights of survivorship, tenants in common, or by a non-person such as a trust.

(continued on next page)

(continued from previous page)

Mutual funds do not have beneficiary designations, so the nature of the ownership, the owner's will, or the state's laws of intestacy control the transfer of ownership at death. If not held in joint ownership, they are generally included in the probate estate of the owner.

Each year that an individual owns a mutual fund, that individual will probably have to pay income taxes arising from fund ownership. These taxes will arise from several sources including dividends and interest payments received by the fund from the underlying investments and capital gains realized on the sale of some of the underlying investments. Taxable income can even arise from a fund that is losing value.

Variable annuities are different in many respects. One of the most obvious similarities is that the investments within the annuity look and act much like mutual funds. Some are in fact mirror images of existing funds. They are, however, separate accounts, dedicated to the annuity.

Annuities have a death benefit, which guarantees heirs that the amount invested is the minimum that will be received if the annuitant dies during the accumulation period. All earnings within the annuity are fully income-tax deferred until taken out of the annuity. If the owner chooses to move from one separate account to another, gains remain income-tax deferred. If the owner decides to move the funds from one annuity to a different one, Internal Revenue Code (IRC) Section 1035 permits this exchange while retaining the income tax deferral.

Ownership of annuities is generally the same as for other assets, but they usually also feature a named beneficiary. This designation provides for transfer of the asset outside of probate as long as the beneficiary is not the estate of the owner. If a corporation owns an annuity there is no tax deferral.

Taxation of Annuities

The primary purpose of annuities is to provide a retirement income that will last as long as the recipient lives. No other investment product has that guarantee. To encourage the use of annuities in planning for retirement, the Internal Revenue Code (IRC) provides that the growth of the assets is income tax-deferred (see sidebar). Because of abuses when interest rates were quite high, the income taxation of annuities has changed somewhat over the years.

Generally, non-periodic distributions from an annuity are now taxed on the last-in, first-out (LIFO) method. This means that if the annuity values exceed the amount invested, any loans or withdrawals from the annuity will be considered ordinary income for tax purposes to the extent the accumulated funds exceed the investment. As with modified endowment contracts, if the annuity owner is under age 59 1/2, there is also a 10 percent excise tax on any distribution subject to income tax.

The penalty is not assessed if a distribution is due to the death or disability of the taxpayer. Additionally, if the payout from the annuity is set up on a periodic basis where distributions are to be essentially equal payments for the life of the annuitant, there is no penalty even if they begin before he or she reaches age 59 1/2.

When an annuity is liquidated through the use of level periodic payments, known as "annuitization," a portion of each payment is free from taxation. The portion that is not taxable is called the exclusion amount. This is calculated by dividing the amount invested (the tax basis) by the amount that is expected to be paid out over the life expectancy of the annuitant. This result is known as the exclusion ratio. When each annuity payment is made, the amount of payment is multiplied by the applicable exclusion ratio. The resulting portion of the payment is considered a return of basis and is not taxed. However, the remaining balance is taxed. If the payments are to last over the lifetime of the annuitant, when the accumulated, excluded payments add up to the owner's basis, then 100 percent of each subsequent payment is subject to taxation.

To illustrate this concept, let us look at an example. Sam bought a fixed deferred annuity several years ago for a single premium of $100,000. On January 1, he learned that his account value had reached $200,000, and he decided to annuitize this amount, electing a straight life annuity.

His annuity issuer informed him that he will receive monthly payments of $1,666.67. Sam consulted the applicable IRS table and found that his life expectancy is 20 years. To determine the amount of his payments that will be excluded from income, Sam computes the following exclusion ratio: $100,000 (basis) / $1,667 x 12 mo. x 20 years = .25. Therefore, for the first 20 years, 25 percent of Sam's benefits will be excluded from income tax. After 20 years, assuming Sam is still alive and receiving payments, the entire benefit amount will be taxable income because he will have recovered his entire basis.

Corporate-owned annuities are taxed differently: Any increase in the accumulated value of an annuity owned by a corporation that is in excess of the basis in the contract must be reported as income every year [IRC § 72(u)].

When an annuity owner dies and the annuity values are distributed, the gain in the contract is taxed as ordinary income, assuming no prior distributions were made. There is no step-up in basis as would normally be the case since any annuity payments are considered as "income in respect of a decedent" (or IRD). If the annuity starting date has already occurred, the remaining value must be distributed at least as fast as if the annuitant was still living. If the annuity starting date has not yet been reached, the value must be distributed within five years of the owner's death. However, if the annuity is transferred to the spouse of the annuitant, it can continue to be income tax-deferred and is not subject to the normal date-of-death distribution rules.

IMPORTANT CONCEPTS

Accelerated death benefits	Interest-adjusted cost indices
Adequately funded UL	Linton yield methods
Annuitant	NAIC model replacement regulation
Annuities	Net payment cost index
Belth method	Period certain guaranteed distribution
Benchmark price per thousand	Pure life annuity
Cash accumulation method	Second to die
Chronically ill (under HIPAA)	Single premium
Deferred	Specified income
Disclosure	Specified payment period
Equity indexed	Surrender charges
First to die	Taxation of annuities
Fixed interest	Terminally ill (under HIPAA)
Fixed premium	Traditional net cost method
Flexible premium	Variable
Group life	Viatical settlement

QUESTIONS FOR REVIEW

1. What are the key considerations when determining the appropriate policy for a client?

2. What is meant by "adequately funded UL?"

3. Identify typical insurance needs and client profile characteristics and then suggest which different forms of insurance are the most appropriate.

4. Describe the difference between the traditional net cost method of policy comparison and the interest-adjusted comparison methods.

5. What is the appropriate use of the Belth method in evaluating life insurance policies?

6. Under what circumstances would it be inappropriate to replace an existing life insurance policy?

7. When is it appropriate for an insured to seek a viatical settlement or accelerated death benefits?

8. Briefly describe the three general forms of personally owned annuities.

9. What are the differences between variable annuities and mutual funds?

10. Describe the income taxation of annuities.

SUGGESTIONS FOR ADDITIONAL READING

Fundamentals of Risk and Insurance, 9th ed., Emmett J. and Therese M. Vaughan, Wiley, 2003.

Introduction to Risk Management and Insurance, 8th ed., Mark Dorfman, Prentice Hall, 2004.

Life and Health Insurance, 13th ed., Skipper and Black, Prentice Hall, 2000.

Life Insurance: A Consumer's Handbook, 2nd ed., Joseph M. Belth, Indiana UP, 1985.

Principles of Risk Management and Insurance, 9th ed., George E. Rejda, Addison Wesley, 2004.

Tax Facts 2005, National Underwriter, 2005.

The Tools & Techniques of Life Insurance Planning, 3rd ed., Stephan R. Leimberg and Robert J. Doyle, Jr., National Underwriter, 2004.

CHAPTER FIVE

Life Insurance Company Selection

• • •

The United States regulates the insurance industry far more than it does most other industries in the country. Many organizations watch and analyze the insurance industry because its success is critical for the country's business, the economy as a whole, and the financial security of families, making it the justified target of extensive scrutiny.

Generally insurance is regulated by the states. Under the McCarran-Ferguson Act (Public Law 15), which was passed in 1945, Congress made it clear that insurance was to be regulated by the states as long as the states did it adequately. Every state has a structure for the regulation of insurance, most commonly under the direction of an insurance commissioner. An insurance commissioner typically oversees insurance regulation. Some commissioners are elected while others are appointed. These regulators determine whether all insurance companies operating in the state meet the requirements of that state. For companies that are domiciled (based) in the state, the commissioner determines whether they are meeting the requirements to be domiciled there. Companies that are domiciled outside the state are called foreign companies, and companies that are domiciled outside the United States are called alien companies. The commissioner grants permission to foreign companies to sell their products in the state if they meet specified financial requirements. The only control the commissioner has over alien companies is control over their sales representatives because it is the insurance commission that grants licenses to insurance sales representatives.

States often require that certain language be included in policies issued in that state to residents of the state. An example is the language used in the suicide clause of life insurance policies. Two states mandate that the suicide exclusion be only one year while nearly all other states permit a two-year exclusion.

The commissioners of the states created an organization for the purpose of coordinating regulation to the extent reasonable. The organization is the National Association of Insurance Commissioners (NAIC). The NAIC promulgates model legislation that the organization encourages states to adopt. The model legislation is generally in the form of regulations to be applied to the financial stability of insurers and to the regulation of sales agents. Each commissioner may or may not encourage his or her state legislature to adopt the recommendations.

The NAIC created an accreditation program in 1989 as a way to show federal legislators that the states were doing an adequate job of regulation. The goal was to create solvency standards for insurers as well as a method of determining if a company was not financially sound. When a company is not meeting the solvency requirements, there are a number of steps spelled out to ensure that the company's finances improve or the company will be taken over by the commissioner to ensure a smooth transition for policyholders as the company is liquidated.

In general, the state insurance commissioners license insurers and insurance sales representatives, examine insurers for solvency, oversee rehabilitation of companies that are not financially sound, regulate insurance rates through various means, and investigate complaints from consumers who are having problems with insurers. If a planner's client is having difficulty resolving a dispute with his or her insurer, a call or letter to the insurance commissioner's office often speeds things along.

Because insurance is tightly regulated and strictly overseen, it would seem reasonable to assume that all insurance companies are equally safe and that they all provide essentially the same products, but this is not so. Many of the regulations and oversight focus on solvency, and as long as an insurance company is not involved in false advertising, fraudulent claims practices, or other illegal activities, they are given fairly wide latitude to manage their products, services, and prices as they wish.

There are approximately 3,000 property/casualty and over 1,100 life/health insurance companies operating in the United States today. With so many companies to choose from, how does a financial planner or insurance agent determine whether a specific company is a reasonable source for insurance? This chapter will provide guidance.

When you complete this chapter you will be able to:
- Identify key factors in choosing a life insurance company and agency
- Understand how life insurance companies are structured
- Compare the various rating organizations and understand their ratings

CHOOSING IN A COMPETITIVE MARKET

The insurance industry is sometimes accused of price fixing and anti-competitive practices; this has been especially so since the substantial increase in the cost of health care plans. While the industry does have a partial exemption from antitrust law, the purpose of this exemption is to ensure that insurance companies can exchange raw claims data, which makes it possible for them to better estimate expected claims. There are three factors that determine the competitiveness of the insurance industry in the United States: (1) the number of competitors and the percentage of the market that the largest competitors control, (2) the ease of entry into the industry, and (3) the shifts in market share among companies.

There are over 1,100 legal reserve life insurance companies in the United States.[1] When you compare that to the small number of automobile or computer manufacturers (two other highly competitive industries), there are sufficient life insurance companies to consider the industry competitive. It has also proven relatively easy to enter the life insurance industry. There were 649 companies in 1950, 1,441 by 1960, and 1,746 by 1975. Toward the end of a period of high interest rates, the number of companies grew to its highest in 1988-2,343. Since then, the number of companies has declined for a number of reasons, but the numbers demonstrate that while it is not easy to succeed longer term, establishing a company initially is not a problem.

> **NEED TO KNOW: INSURANCE PRICE**
>
> While competition occurs in regard to the quality of a company's products and services, a more significant factor in determining a company's competitiveness is price. Insurance companies all price their products using the same set of costs:
>
> - Acquisition expense
> - Administrative expense (overhead)
> - Losses and loss adjustment expense (claims)
> - Taxes
> - Profit (surplus) and contingencies
>
> To compete on price, a company must be as good as other companies in most of these five areas and better in one or more. Some companies are known for stringent underwriting and reducing their losses and loss adjustment expenses. If all other expenses are in line with that of other companies, these low-claims companies can charge less and still make a reasonable profit.

Finally, while the oldest and largest companies write the most insurance, no single company controls even 10 percent of the market, and there have even been changes in market share among the top companies.

Several other indicators also reflect how the insurance market is competitive. The insurance industry is not able to control supply, prices, or profits. If one company decides to sell less of a certain product, others are more than willing to fill the breach. If a company increases prices without having an offsetting benefit, it will lose sales and market share. Companies that do not operate efficiently are now closing their doors. From the late 1980s through the early 1990s, over 1,000 life insurance companies left the industry.[2] These closures occurred because the companies were riding the crest of high interest rates and operated as if the earnings on their investments could keep them in business regardless of expenses and claims, and because they were in a competitive industry where profits are not guaranteed. Some companies became insolvent; others were purchased by larger companies.

But now that we know the market is indeed very competitive, how does an advisor help a client select a company?

---

[1] A legal reserve life insurance company is a company that is subject to state insurance codes that require maintenance of minimum reserves.

[2] Figures as of 1999 derived from the American Council of Life Insurers.

Financial Stability

The primary measure most planners use when evaluating insurance companies is financial strength. Only after identifying adequately sound companies should a planner then compare insurance products. Ratings of financial strength are best obtained from the five primary established rating organizations: A.M. Best, Standard & Poor's, Moody's, Fitch Ratings, and Weiss Research. The ratings from these companies are not infallible, and different rating companies may view the same company quite differently. When combined with other sources of information, these company ratings can be very helpful and are generally accepted as the best information available.

Care should be exercised when examining these ratings: Some organizations do extensive evaluations of company records and interview key people within the company while others use only public information. A high rating from one organization does not necessarily mean top ratings from the others. An often-suggested guideline is to first recommend insurance companies that have one of the top three ratings from at least three of these organizations.

The table below shows the top six ratings from the primary rating agencies. The number next to the bottom is the total number of ratings available. The bottom line shows the lowest rating given

Table 5.1

	A.M. Best	Standard & Poor's	Moody's	Fitch Ratings	Weiss Research
Highest Rating	A++	AAA	Aaa	AAA	A+
2nd	A+	AA+	Aa1	AA+	A
3rd	A	AA	Aa2	AA	A-
4th	A-	AA-	Aa3	AA-	B+
5th	B++	A+	A1	A+	B
6th	B+	A	A2	A	B-
# of Ratings	15	22	19	19	15
Lowest Rating	F	D	C	CCC-	F

As is obvious from the chart, the rankings can be confusing. For example, a rating of A can put a company anywhere in the rating order from second to sixth, depending on which organization is giving the rating. If an insurance company touts itself as being rated A+, it is important to understand which organization's ratings it is citing.

One exception to the focus on financial strength and stability is for clients purchasing variable life insurance products. Some advisors believe an insurance company's financial stability is not as important with variable policies as it is with traditional policies. Why? A company's general assets support traditional policies. Variable policies are built on separate accounts in investment vehicles that support only those policies and are not subject to the claims of the company's other creditors.

In Depth: The Ratings Organizations

As discussed above, different organizations use different standards when evaluating companies and giving ratings. What follows is a brief summary of the methods organizations use.

A.M. Best

Financial Strength Rating: an opinion of an insurer's financial strength and ability to meet ongoing obligations to policyholders.

Debt Rating: an opinion for the credit marketplace as to the issuer's ability to meet its financial obligations, when due, to security holders.

Best's does a comprehensive study with information provided by the insurer as well as with public information. If a company has not been rated by Best's, it assigns a "not rated" classification to it.

Fitch

Insurer Financial Strength Rating: an overall assessment of the financial strength and security of an insurance company.

Fixed Income Security Rating: ratings of senior and subordinated debt securities, commercial paper programs, and various forms of preferred stock issued by both insurance operating companies and holding companies, including surplus notes, insurance contract-backed notes programs, and insurance-linked securitizations.

Fitch does a comprehensive analysis that includes obtaining information from the company being rated.

Moody's

Credit Rating: a measure of financial strength and an opinion on the ability of a company to repay punctually their senior policyholder claims.

Debt Rating: a company's abilities to meet its obligations to repay interest and principal on outstanding obligations to fixed-income investors, including guaranteed investment contract (GIC) investors.

Moody's obtains information from the company being rated as well as public information.

Standard & Poor's

Financial Strength Rating: a rating of debt issues and preferred stock.

Standard & Poor's first analyzes public information and then obtains additional information from the company being rated.

Weiss Research

Financial Safety Rating: assessment of an insurer's future financial stability.

Weiss completes its analysis from public information only.

Risk-Based Capital (RBC) Ratio

Another factor advisors might consider is the risk-based capital (RBC) ratio. The NAIC developed the RBC ratio as a method to measure the minimum amount of capital—determined by the size and degree of risk taken by the insurer—that an insurance company needs to adequately support its overall operations. There are currently four major categories of risk used to determine the overall RBC ratio:

Asset Risk: This measures an asset's potential default of principal, interest, or fluctuation in its market value as a result of changes in the market.

Credit Risk: This measures the default risk on payments that are due from policyholders, re-insurers, or creditors.

Underwriting Risk: This measures the risk that arises from underestimating the liabilities from insurance business already written or due to inadequately pricing current or prospective business in the underwriting process.

Off-Balance Sheet Risk: This measures the risk due to excessive rates of growth, contingent liabilities, or other items that are not reflected on the balance sheet.

Once these risk calculations are complete, the company determines an RBC level. This level is reported to the insurance commissioner of the state in which the insurance company is domiciled. If the RBC level is too low, there are a number of degrees of intervention measures that regulators may pursue. These are as follows:

At the **company action RBC level**, the company submits to the commissioner a statement that shows what the company believes is the cause of the problem and a plan for a remedy.

At the **regulatory action RBC level**, which occurs when the capital is too low to qualify for the company action level or if the company fails to submit its RBC report to the commissioner in a timely manner, the commissioner will direct the company to submit a plan to correct the problem. The commissioner may then perform any examination or analysis he or she deems appropriate and issue an order as to what actions the company must take to remedy the problem.

The **authorized control RBC level** is next. An insurer may be subject to this authorized control if it fails to satisfactorily respond to a corrective order by the commissioner or if the commissioner has rejected a challenge by the company of a corrective order. The commissioner may choose to take control of the insurance company.

The final level of intervention is the **mandatory control RBC level**. If the company's RBC report shows that its capital is below the mandatory control level, or if the commissioner notifies the company that it has dropped to the mandatory control level with no challenge by the company, the commissioner is then obligated to take control of the company.

The RBC ratios were not intended for use by the public in the evaluation of a company. Instead, they were created for the use of regulators only. However, some of this information is public knowledge, and third parties have published RBC ratios for many insurance companies.

The use of the RBC ratio clearly has an effect on the amount of risk insurers accept with invested dollars. Between 1993 and 2003, life insurer assets grew at an average rate of 5.6 percent per year while investment in stocks by those companies grew only 2.1 percent per year. In 2003 the stock investments of life insurers in their general accounts was only 3.6 percent of aggregate assets while bonds were nearly 74 percent. There was more money invested in policy loans than in stock.[3]

Demutualization and Mutual Holding Companies

For many years, most individuals purchased insurance from mutual companies because as owners they did not have to share profits with shareholders, and virtually all of the policy comparison methods showed mutual companies having the best products. Profits went into surplus or were paid out as dividends. A lower net cost for the insurance was the common result. Most of the 10 largest life insurance companies had historically been mutual companies. These companies became large in part because they were mutual companies, and their illustrations and actual results generally showed the best value for premiums paid. This has now changed.

With the deregulation of the financial services industry, it has become increasingly important for insurance companies to expand their offerings to compete and maintain market share. To accomplish this, companies need a great deal of capital. Since policyholders own mutual companies, they are not able to raise funds from the sale of stock—all of their capital must necessarily come from company operations.

Because of this, a number of mutual companies have decided to change their structure. Some have chosen full **demutualization**, converting a mutual company to a stock company. When companies demutualize, it seems reasonable that all of the initial stock would be put in the hands of the existing policyholders; but this has not been the case, leading to a heated national debate regarding demutualization. With a full demutualization, policyholders often get some stock or cash, but in many conversions, company officers and senior management get disproportionately large amounts of stock. The debate gets more heated when mutual holding companies are considered.

A **mutual holding company** is a mutual company that owns other companies, including the original insurance company that is now a stock company. However, nothing requires the stock companies within the holding company to declare dividends. The stockholders of the other companies in the mutual holding have a direct conflict of interest with the owners of the mutual holding company.

---

[3]Life Insurance Fact Book, 2004; American Council of Life Insurers

This debate is likely to continue for many years, and only the future will tell whether mutual holding companies are a reasonable approach for the benefit of both the companies and the policyholders.

In the meantime, when choosing an insurance company, it is reasonable to seek out any available information about whether or not a company plans to demutualize, and if so, into what form.

In Depth: Ugly Surprises

Two insurance company bankruptcies in the 1990s shook the industry. One large eastern mutual company with an impeccable history had made some bad real estate deals and managed to hide its problems until it was on the verge of collapse. Within a period of a few weeks, the problems surfaced, and the company asked its state insurance commissioner to take over the operation of the company as it had become insolvent.

Many in the industry were shocked by this collapse. All insureds had their policies picked up by other insurers and no policyholder lost any value in his or her policies. Future dividends, however, were lower than previously illustrated.

The second company failure was a "high-flying" company that had managed to hide what were considered by some to be flagrant attempts to create unsustainable value. The company had sold many large annuities used to fund corporate retirement benefits. With its apparent high returns, the company-created system in which insurance operations money was invested began to collapse, causing the company to also suffer. For the first time, many annuitants lost significant portions of their benefits. This company had worked very hard to lure agents with promises of high commissions and generous payouts for clients—generally higher than any other company in the market. Some agents chose to sell the products that looked good on paper while more careful agents wondered how a company operating in the same market as all of the other insurance companies could possibly be making enough money to pay high commissions and high interest on annuities. Many large corporations also believed in the company and used its products to fund pensions as a money saving move.

Both companies had performed well for a number of years and most of the rating organizations gave them high marks.

One rating company, which was still rather new at rating insurance companies, gave them a low rating, but it also rated more than half of the companies it reviewed as being in poor financial condition. So ratings alone would have suggested that either of these companies would have been good choices.

Insurance Marketplace Standards Association (IMSA)

In the early 1980s, the insurance industry suffered from severe disintermediation: the activity of moving money from one financial institution to another, generally moving the money from low-interest secure accounts to higher-risk, higher-return accounts. Through the use of policy loans, policy owners borrowed substantial portions of the companies' reserves at 6 to 8 percent and invested that money in money market funds paying 12 percent or more, as well as making other investments.

Earnings on short-term money were so high that the insurance industry was having a difficult time selling enough insurance. It was not because of the lack of need of insurance, but because other financial institutions were very successful at convincing the public that insurance was fundamentally an investment, and not a very good one at that. Insurance companies responded by raising dividends and selling more universal life insurance with high interest rates for the purpose of illustration.

Because the insurance industry had such a strong history of always meeting its dividend illustrations and a reputation for making good on promises, policy owners were dismayed when interest rates ultimately fell and the insurance companies could no longer pay the high dividends or interest that had been shown in their illustrations. It did not matter that the illustrations explicitly stated that those high rates were not guaranteed—people still expected them to hold up. When they did not, the insurance industry got a black eye. Many people lost respect for and trust in an industry that had provided financial security for generations.

The industry realized that it needed to regain public confidence. The goal was to show the public that the industry and its representatives operated in an ethical manner and to encourage ethical behavior by agents and companies. To that end, the insurance industry created the Insurance Marketplace Standards Association (IMSA). The IMSA has since promulgated its six principles of ethical conduct for the marketing of life insurance, long-term care insurance, and annuity products. Membership is voluntary, but is by no means only perfunctory in nature. Rather, member companies must complete a self-assessment and then subject themselves to an external assessment. It is also not enough to merely subscribe to the IMSA principles; the company must put in place procedures to ensure that those principles are indeed followed.

While over 200 insurance companies have qualified to use the IMSA logo, it is still a small percentage of the total number of companies. As noted above, there are over 1,100 life insurance companies in the United States. Failure to be a member of IMSA is not an indication that a company intends to act unethically, but membership does imply that a company is committed to actively pursuing ethical marketing practices. Fortunately, according to the IMSA, the membership represents over 60 percent of the market share of life insurance sales in the United States.

This is clearly one credential that is worth consideration in the selection of an insurance company.

General Company Information

A company's size and age are other useful bits of information to consider. A small company operating for only a few years may be as well managed as a large, well established one, but should still be viewed with special care because it may not have the stable asset base of a long-established company.

A company's primary line of business and policy size also provide important information. Generally, a company selling only life insurance, with a substantial portion of permanent insurance, will have better financial stability than a company offering many product lines.

This is because permanent life insurance tends to be the line of insurance that is most predictable. A company dealing mostly with term insurance may be less stable because the price of term insurance is so competitive and it is viewed as a commodity by many people. Further, even with increased reserve requirements under Regulation XXX, adopted in 2000, the reserves for term life insurance are substantially less than for traditional permanent life insurance.

Companies writing primarily term insurance often only have a few cents in assets for each thousand dollars of insurance issued, and the amounts of insurance on individual lives tends to be relatively high. Conversely, companies with a substantial portion of their life insurance issued in permanent form have many dollars in assets for each thousand dollars of insurance issued with the average policy size being much smaller. The problems with the profitability of health insurance should steer agents and planners away from companies heavily involved in that market (unless they are among the few in that market that are profitable).

A company's lapse ratios and policy persistency are two more important factors. The lapse ratio is the percentage of policies that are cancelled or that lapse due to nonpayment of premium, typically in the first 13 months after the date of issue; policy persistency is a measure of the longevity of policies. Some experts believe that life companies should be examined carefully if their lapse ratios exceed 11 percent and if their policy persistency is less than 87 percent. It is generally accepted that it costs an insurance company at least 120 percent of the first year premium to put a new policy in force.

Since most lapses happen early in a policy's existence, a high lapse ratio may make profitability difficult. The most profitable policies are most often those that remain in force for a long time, even when they ultimately mature as a death claim.

Ultimate Insurance Need

Another factor planners should consider before advising is how much insurance the client will ultimately need. These long-term needs should play a role in determining which companies to consider.

Anyone with Internet access or an email address has likely received offers for low prices on term insurance. As we have discussed earlier, term insurance is an excellent choice for short-term life insurance needs while permanent insurance is the best choice for longer-term goals.

> **NEED TO KNOW:**
> **IMSA'S PRINCIPLES AND CODE OF ETHICAL MARKET CONDUCT**
>
> The following, taken from the IMSA website (http://www.imsaethics.org/), are the principles to which each member company must adhere:
>
> 1. To conduct business according to high standards of honesty and fairness and to render that service to its customers which, in the same circumstances, it would apply to or demand for itself.
> 2. To provide competent and customer-focused sales and service.
> 3. To engage in active and fair competition.
> 4. To provide advertising and sales materials that are clear as to purpose and honest and fair as to content.
> 5. To provide for fair and expeditious handling of customer complaints and disputes.
> 6. To maintain a system of supervision and review that is reasonably designed to achieve compliance with these Principles of Ethical Market Conduct.
>
> Further discussion of these principles may be found on the IMSA website.

Young couples generally cannot afford all of the permanent insurance they need or want, which makes the initial purchase of term insurance a reasonable option. However, if the insurance buyers do not think ahead, the company supplying their term insurance may not have the kind of permanent insurance they want or may not have a competitive permanent policy. If the insured subsequently wants to convert all—or even a portion—of the term insurance to permanent coverage in the future, the conversion can only be done with the products from that company. Selecting a different company's product means the replacement rules generally do *not* apply: The insured will have to medically qualify for the new permanent policy, and the suicide and contestable clauses will begin anew.

Another issue is that some low-cost term policies have rather restrictive conversion privileges. The policy may require that any conversion take place before the policy is seven or ten years old and also may require an all-or-nothing conversion. Some companies will not issue a term policy for less than $250,000 and will not permit the rewriting of a policy to a lower amount. This means that a policy owner who may have a $300,000 term policy could only convert $50,000 or all of it to permanent insurance if he or she wanted to maintain the full $300,000 of coverage. If only $100,000 was converted, the company may not permit retention of a $200,000 policy.

Riders

Finally, available riders may also affect the choice of company. One of the more important riders for a client to consider is the disability waiver of premium rider. As discussed in chapter 2, the language of this rider can make a substantial difference in whether and how the policy is paid for if the client is disabled. The attached presumptive disability clauses are also important: If an individual had a stroke but recovered all of his or her pre-stroke abilities except for the ability to speak, one company would recognize that as a presumptive disability while another would not. An individual who is paralyzed from the waist down would qualify under the presumptive disability clause of some policies and not with others.

Another important rider to consider is the guaranteed insurability (purchase option) rider. The terms of the rider will differ, and if this is an important feature to your client, it should be considered in the purchase decision.

Finally, another rider that is being offered more and more by companies is an accelerated benefit clause. For a client who has witnessed the financial problems of terminal or chronic illness near the end of life, this benefit may be very important.

Agents and Agencies

Not all that long ago, the only source of insurance was from agents who had an agency affiliation with an insurance company. Even today, working with an established agency ensures that there are a number of people who can provide assistance and support when a client needs it. More and more companies are using toll-free numbers for policyholder support services—a more cost efficient method of helping policy owners, and much less personal. If personal attention is important to a client, the choice of company may be dictated to some extent by its agency or the agents available to sell its products. Keep in mind that while personal service may be the method used by a company today, it may change to a toll free number next week. Alternatively, an individual may use an insurance broker, who will represent him or her rather than the company.

The legal doctrine of agency is a powerful tool. An agent, unlike a broker, is the legal representative of the company. If someone with an agency relationship with his or her company tells you the company will do something, the company is bound by those words unless and until it counters the statement. If a property/liability agent says you are covered, then you are covered unless and until the company says otherwise. However, for the vast majority of situations, it makes little difference because circumstances rarely lead to claim situations where the legal relationship between the licensed insurance representative and the company is a factor. Life insurance agents are not given the power to "bind" the coverage of a life insurance policy.

While "captive agents" (agents permitted to sell only the products of that one company) are common with property and liability companies, few life insurance companies still exclusively use such agents. Most agents also have brokerage agreements with other companies so that they can provide the best products for their clients. Some agencies also develop relationships with other companies to make it easier for their agents to serve clients. Interestingly, a single licensed agent may be responsible to different parties depending on his or her role. The agent is responsible primarily to a company for which he or she is licensed as an agent, and responsible primarily to the client—in the same sales relationship—when operating as a broker. The majority of agents work to find the best product for each client. The product chosen will determine who the sales representative legally represents in the transaction.

Some clients may prefer non-captive agents, but these clients should be aware of the problem of quotas: Insurance companies may require that an agent maintain a certain sales quota in order to continue to sell products for that company. Anytime there is a quota, there is the possibility that an agent will recommend a specific company's product because of the quota and not because of the quality of the product. While many life insurance companies do not have production quotas, they do require a certain level of production for increased commissions, expense allowances, and convention qualifications. This is not to say that the insurance sold to meet these quotas will be inferior or overpriced, but the agent is definitely under pressure to offer only those products if he or she wants to continue to represent that company. To avoid these issues, most agents will choose a few companies that have good products covering virtually all of their clients' potential needs. Therefore, the insurance agent is not unlike any other salesperson, except that life insurance sales representatives generally have more flexibility than other salespeople in offering products because of their ability to have brokerage contracts with several companies.

Agents vs. Producers

In recent years, many states have ceased issuing agent and broker licenses to insurance sales people and started issuing producer's licenses. In the past, an insurance representative typically became affiliated with a particular company and became an agent of that company. He or she then tested to obtain an agent's license to be able to sell insurance. After a specified number of years of experience, he or she could apply for a broker's license, and only then could obtain a brokerage agreement with other insurers. With the producer's license, each sales representative is free to affiliate with whichever companies he or she desires. The agreement with that company will define whether it is an agency or brokerage relationship. The benefit of this is that even new agents may obtain insurance for their clients from many companies. The downside is that the lack of experience or the desire to make money fast may lead these new agents to companies that pay sales people well and do not provide the best products. Insurance companies that do not have their own sales force, that rely on brokers to sell their products, pay higher commissions and additional overrides to compensate the sales people for the added administrative work they will have to provide. Inexperienced agents may not know what this additional work entails and are often not prepared for it, to the detriment of their clients.

Binding Authority

As mentioned above, a property/liability agent may obligate the company to provide coverage by telling a client that the coverage is in place. This may be done with a phone call, and the coverage exists with no application having been signed, and in some cases with existing clients, the first premium not having been paid. The authority to obligate the company is called "binding" authority. With life insurance, agents may accept an application for insurance with a payment for the first premium, and all the agent can provide is a contingent receipt or temporary insurance receipt. This receipt states that once the applicant has submitted all information called for by underwriting requirements, the coverage is in place, up to a specified limit, if the policy will be issued on a standard basis with the information provided. The only real benefit is that nothing that happens to the applicant after the underwriting information has been submitted will come into play. So, if (1) an applicant submits all underwriting information (application, medical information, authorization forms, etc.) along with the first payment, and then dies four days later of something that is completely unrelated to any prior medical history, and if (2) the company, based on the information received, would have issued the policy, then the company will pay the claim. Many agents who have been in the business for a number of years have had the experience of having a prospect or client agree to buy insurance and then die before a prepaid application is submitted.

Fraternal Societies

Most students are aware of stock companies and mutual companies: Stock companies are owned by shareholders, much like any other corporation that has shareholders, and mutual companies are owned by the policyholders.

However, there is one other rather large segment of the insurance industry that, by its nature, limits its potential liability.

This segment is made up of fraternal societies. These are essentially mutual insurance companies that focus on a specific market. Policy owners must have some common connection.

Some fraternal societies sell only to members of a specific religious denomination. Some sell only to those who are, or were, in the U.S. armed forces (and their dependents). There is at least one that limits its market to approximately 51 percent of the population by selling only to women. By limiting the group to which the company sells, it may be able to get a better overall underwriting result. For example, the companies that insure only those who are or were in the armed forces know that these individuals learned self-discipline at one time and are likely to be in good physical health while on active duty. By having a common tie among all insureds, their marketing and products can therefore be better tailored. Because of the limited market and the connections among all eligible members, the use of organizational publications, and the support of the group's leaders permits very focused marketing. For those fraternals that use agents, lists of prospects available from the organization, and relative ease of access to them justifies lower commissions and further reduces the cost of selling the products. Few stock or mutual companies, by comparison, can come close to providing equivalent coverage for the same or lower premium.

A company dealing with only one population group—for example, active military and veterans— may not need to use field agents; it can use telephone agents who respond to member queries. It can send out mailings, with marketing and sales costs remaining quite low since it does not market to everyone. If a company has a product that a client wants, but he or she does not qualify as a member of the group to which the company is permitted to sell, the purchase decision now becomes relatively simple.

Fraternal societies may only market and sell to the population they serve. They are typically nonprofit organizations. These should not be confused with the products of other companies that are sold through various associations, where the association is merely the marketing medium and not the policy-issuing entity. A good example of this latter situation is the AARP, a membership organization that serves individuals over 50. The organization sells many products, and it is not the producer of those products. It uses the sale of products as an income source.

Underwriting

When choosing a company, people seldom think about underwriting. This can be a very important factor, and it may be quite difficult to learn much about it. Company A may have exceptionally good products, and it may also have very tight underwriting. This means that the company only accepts applicants who have or are likely to have a lower incidence of claims than the overall market. Some companies specialize in "hard to write" cases. This may mean insuring a driver who has had a number of tickets and a couple of accidents in the last five years. It could mean someone who is seeking life or disability income insurance and who has a condition or occupation that might result in a declination of coverage with some companies. Some companies do cursory initial underwriting and put language in the contract that permits post-claim underwriting. This is the worst form of underwriting from the perspective of the insured. The company can decide not to pay the claim even after receiving premiums for months or years. It is all spelled out in the contract, and most people do not remember it, or more likely, bought the policy through the mail and never read it.

Whenever a client's history is not clean in an area where insurance is sought, it is a good idea to find a specialist who works in the area of finding that type of insurance for "impaired" risks. People experienced in finding this coverage know which companies are likely to accept the individual and how to present the case for the best result. There is nothing surreptitious about it. However, knowing what the companies are looking for and disclosing all of the right information usually helps. An important reason to follow this approach is that once a person is declined for coverage by one company, it becomes far more difficult to get the coverage anywhere else.

WHEN THERE IS NO CHOICE

There are circumstances where there is no choice, or only a limited choice as to the insurance company. When it comes to group life insurance, the employer's choice is the choice, and that may be dictated by the health plan chosen. If a retirement plan permits the purchase of life insurance or an annuity as one of the investment options, the plan sponsor makes the choice rather than the participant. For credit life or disability insurance that is used to cover credit cards or loans, the card issuer or lender chooses the insurance company from among the few companies that offer that product.

Even when purchasing personal insurance, an individual who is an impaired risk because of occupation, medical condition, or history may have severely restricted options.

An important part of the decision process is investigating if there are any circumstances that impact the ability of an individual to obtain desired life or disability insurance coverage.

There is little point spending an inordinate amount of time reviewing insurance company ratings, dividend histories, or the like if an individual's ability to obtain insurance is impaired.

Looking for the best offer from a company that is reasonably sound and will offer a policy now becomes more important than finding the best overall company. Once a person has been rated or declined for insurance, it becomes more difficult to make future insurance purchases.

There are insurance agencies that specialize in impaired risk cases and who may be able to find a company that will otherwise issue the insurance. Periodically, individuals may want to purchase credit life or disability insurance. Some of the companies offering that coverage may refuse insurance to someone who has been declined but may not turn away those who have merely been rated. These forms of insurance are typically expensive and some adverse selection is not a problem.

Finding the right company, or the best company, typically requires the use of different parameters for different clients, depending on their needs and ability to qualify for the insurance coverage.

IMPORTANT CONCEPTS

Agent

Broker

Capital stock company

Comparative/relative ratings

Competitive industry

Demutualization

Fraternal society

Implications of company size

IMSA

Mutual company

Mutual holding company

Producer's license

Rating companies

RBC ratio

QUESTIONS FOR REVIEW

1. Discuss key factors in the selection of a life insurance company.

2. Do you believe the insurance industry in the United States is competitive? Explain why or why not.

3. Describe the attributes of a mutual life insurance company and any benefits it may have for policy owners.

4. Describe the attributes of a capital stock life insurance company and any benefits it may have for policy owners.

5. Describe the attributes of a fraternal society life insurance company and any benefits it may have for policy owners.

6. Discuss the effect demutualization has on owners of mutual insurance company policies.

7. Identify the primary providers of insurance company ratings. How does knowing the company ratings help one choose an insurance company?

8. State a rule to follow regarding the use of insurance company ratings and justify it.

9. What is the IMSA? How can it help one select an insurance company?

10. Explain what the RBC ratio is and its proper application.

SUGGESTIONS FOR ADDITIONAL READING

The Economics of Life Insurance, 3rd ed., S.S. Huebner, Appleton-Century-Crofts, 1959.

Fundamentals of Risk and Insurance, 9th ed., Emmett J. & Therese M. Vaughan, Wiley, 2003.

Introduction to Risk Management and Insurance, 8th ed., Mark Dorfman, Prentice Hall, 2004.

Life and Health Insurance, 13th ed., Kenneth Black Jr. and Harold Skipper Jr., Prentice Hall, 2000.

Life Insurance Fact Book 2005; American Council of Life Insurers.

Principles of Risk Management and Insurance, 9th ed., George E. Rejda, Addison Wesley, 2004.

The Tools & Techniques of Life Insurance Planning, 3rd ed., Stephan R. Leimberg and Robert J. Doyle, Jr., National Underwriter, 2004.

The Tools & Techniques of Risk Management & Insurance, Stephan R. Leimberg, Donald J. Riggin, Albert J. Howard, James W. Kallman, and Donald L. Schmidt, National Underwriter, 2002.

Individual Health Care Plans: Medical Expense Coverage

• • •

Health care is expensive. An MRI costs in the vicinity of $1,000; minor surgery with an overnight stay in the hospital can run $10,000; and prescriptions can easily cost $20 per day. Even an office visit to the doctor can cost $50 to $150 (after all, the doctor may be paying $100,000 a year in malpractice insurance). Debating the numerous causes of high health care costs will not help your clients: A single illness or injury has the potential of creating severe financial problems for a person without a health care plan.

Most individuals in the United States today who have health care plans have them through their employers. However, as more and more people become self-employed, the high cost of health care plans has led to many employers dropping or reducing the benefit levels in the plans they provide for employees, and there have always been those who have their own health care plans.

When you have completed this chapter, you should be able to:
- Understand key terms used in the health insurance industry
- Identify the general types of health insurance available for individuals
- Determine the appropriate medical expense coverage for an individual, given a specific client situation
- Calculate the amount paid by the insurer and covered person under an indemnity health care plan
- Identify the tax implications for different health care plans

BASIC HEALTH INSURANCE TERMS

In reality, life exposes every individual, at any time, to the same general health risks: illness and injury. Actual perils and hazards may vary by age, location, fitness level, or family background, and it is even possible for a person to live a long life with no injury more serious than a sunburn and no illness more serious than a cold. It is also possible to live a long life without cancer, cardiovascular problems, diabetes, hypertension, or any other serious medical problem. After all, the human body is an exceptional machine: It is self-healing, durable, and adaptive. However, it is also, in many ways, complicated and fragile—and fixing it can be costly. Health insurance is one tool that your clients have available to help them manage health risks and their financial impact.

This text assumes that every reader has had some experience with some form of health care plan. Before getting into too much detail about health care plans, there are a number of terms and definitions that are important. Students may want to refer back to these terms periodically as each is important in understanding the various health care plans under which individuals may be covered.

Adverse Selection

This concept from chapter 1 is very important for health insurance. People who expect to use medical services are the most likely to want health insurance, and people who do not expect to use it do not want to spend a lot of money on something they believe will have little value.

When people who are most likely to submit a claim are the only ones seeking out coverage, adverse selection is the norm. Remember, the concept of insurance is that a group or individual trades a relatively small, known amount—the premium—in return for assurance that a particular loss will not destroy them financially.

Any Willing Provider

This refers to legislation that has been passed in some states in response to complaints by some health care providers. When some providers who were excluded from certain plans lost patients, these providers demanded to be allowed to be included on the approved list. Therefore, this legislation generally states that if a provider is willing to accept the lower compensation and any other terms of the health care plan, it must be accepted into the plan as an approved provider.

Unfortunately, this makes managed care more expensive. Managed care plans lower costs by contracting with a limited number of health care providers. Since the health care provider is one of only a few approved under such a plan, the provider can be assured of an adequate number of referrals to justify acceptance of the lower compensation. Similarly, the insurance company underwriting the plan saves money since it is paying only a limited number of providers to see many patients rather than many providers to see only a few patients. As the number of approved providers increases, so do the costs of the plan.

Breakpoint, Cap, or Stop-Loss Limit

The breakpoint, stop-loss limit, or cap is the maximum out-of-pocket share of covered expenses for which the covered person is financially responsible. After this amount has been reached, the insurance company typically pays 100 percent of covered charges up to the policy's maximum benefit.

There are various ways these terms may be applied, and it is critical for a planner to determine which definition applies. Here are some examples of how a $5,000 stop-loss and a $300 deductible might be interpreted:

- The covered individual pays the deductible and 20 percent of all other expenses until the total of his or her out-of-pocket payments equals $5,000. The total out of pocket is, therefore, $5,000 for covered expenses.
- The covered individual pays the deductible and then pays 20 percent of all covered expenses until his or her out-of-pocket payments equal the deductible plus $5,000. Therefore, the total out of pocket costs are $5,300 for covered expenses.
- The covered individual pays the deductible plus 20 percent of the next $5,000 of covered expenses—therefore, totaling out-of-pocket expenses of only $1,300.

Capitation

When an individual chooses a primary care provider (PCP) under certain managed care plans, that PCP is paid a specific amount (usually monthly), whether or not any services are provided. This amount is called capitation and is in lieu of the regular fees for medical care.

The provider will likely lose money on a sick individual who needs weekly visits, but once that individual is well and only needs infrequent care, the provider will probably make money. Conversely, some covered persons may use little or no services while the PCP still receives monthly income from the health care plan for them.

Coinsurance

Under coinsurance, the plan provider and covered person share the cost of covered medical expenses after the deductible has been met. Expenses are split by a predetermined percentage—the individual most commonly pays 20 percent while the provider pays 80 percent. This is expressed as "80/20 coinsurance." See "Breakpoint, Cap, or Stop-Loss Limit" above.

Co-Payment

Under most managed care plans, the covered individual pays a fixed charge each time he or she meets with a provider or fills a covered prescription. Typical provider co-pays are $15 to $40 per visit, with prescription co-pays ranging from $5 to $50. There may be different co-payments for urgent care clinics, emergency room visits, specialist office visits, and/or hospital admittance.

Cost Containment

Everyone wants the best care he or she can get, but the cost of providing that health care is increasing at a rate well in excess of the rate of inflation. Cost containment is the effort by plan providers to control costs so that premiums do not become completely unaffordable. Cost containment includes plan exclusions, limitations, deductibles, capitation, coinsurance, co-payments, and efforts to implement less-expensive-to-administer plans.

Covered Expenses

Health care plans provide medical care for illness and injury, but no plan covers every expense. Excluded expenses often include charges that are above a certain schedule of payments for particular procedures, expenses covered under another plan, expenses associated with experimental medicine, or expenses not incurred in accordance with generally accepted medical procedures. Only covered expenses apply toward deductibles and coinsurance calculations. See "Exclusions" below. This is one of the most important concepts to remember. An example of a problem might be when a covered person receiving acupuncture from his or her internist finds out that acupuncture is covered only when given by someone with a specific accreditation in that form of care. The competence of the internist is not of concern, if he or she does not have the particular accreditation, that service will not be covered.

Covered Person

An individual who is covered by a health care plan is a covered person. Some plans use the terms "subscriber," "participant," and "member." Since insurance companies are not the sole providers of health care plans, such terms are often preferred to the term "insured."

Deductible

Some health care plans require each covered individual to retain a certain portion of the health care expense risk in the form of a deductible. When a covered person receives covered care, he or she pays the first expenses of the year out of pocket until his or her deductible is met (most health plans use an annual deductible). Once covered medical expenses equal the deductible, further expenses then qualify for the co-insurance cost sharing. For example, the covered person will pay 20 percent of all bills for expenses incurred until the breakpoint or stop-loss limit has been reached. There are usually separate individual and family deductibles, both of which will be further explained in the discussion of traditional indemnity health care plans. Some health plans work like property and liability insurance and have a per cause deductible, such as $50 to $100 for each illness or injury. A per cause deductible is like a co-payment except that it is part of a traditional indemnity plan. It is important to remember that only payments for covered expenses apply toward meeting the deductible.

In recent years, many plans have adopted both deductibles and co-pays. With these plans, the deductibles often apply to certain types of care, such as care from a specialist, and do not apply to PCP visits. There may also be a deductible on prescription benefits.

Exclusions

Health care plans typically exclude some procedures, therapies, and medications to keep costs under control. If every medical procedure were covered, the cost of health care plans would be substantially higher than it is. Every health care plan should be reviewed to determine exactly what forms of health care are excluded. Typical exclusions would include:

- Drug therapies not approved by the FDA
- Drugs that are not included in the company's formulary
- Experimental therapies or surgery
- Specified high-cost treatments that do not usually have a good outcome
- Some forms of alternative medicine
- Treatment by certain providers (such as chiropractors or physical therapists outside of a hospital clinic)
- Expenses covered under other plans such as workers compensation plans
- Elective surgery, especially cosmetic, that are not related to an accident or illness
- Treatment for intentionally self-inflicted injuries
- Personal comfort items, such as private room, separate phone or TV charges

Formulary

The formulary is the list of drugs that the company will cover with its prescription benefit. In some cases, other drugs are covered, but require a higher co-payment or deductible.

Gatekeeper

Many health care plans use primary care physicians (PCPs)—usually a general or family practitioner, an internist, or a pediatrician. PCPs are known as gatekeepers because they require covered persons to obtain a referral before seeing a specialist. If the PCP does not believe a specialist is needed, the plan may not pay for any visits should the covered person still seek a specialist's advice.

Health Plan Employer Data and Information Set (HEDIS)

A list of performance measures that the National Committee for Quality Assurance (NCQA) uses in the accreditation process for health care plans. More information on HEDIS is available in the Publications section of the NCQA website (www.ncqa.org).

Health Savings Account (HSA)

A health savings account is a trust account associated with a high-deductible health care plan (HDHC) that permits an individual or family to set aside money on a pre-tax basis for the purpose of paying qualified medical expenses. These is an updated version of medical savings accounts.

High-Deductible Health Care Plan (HDHC)

A high-deductible health care plan is a health care plan with a high deductible, the minimum amount being determined by whether it is for use with a medical savings account or a health savings account.

Indemnity

The basic principles of indemnity are covered in chapter 1: An insured individual will be made financially whole when a loss is due to a covered risk. Traditional indemnity insurance reimburses the covered individual for covered expenses as outlined in the insurance contract.

However, there are a number of other policies, often in the form of hospitalization policies or "dread disease" policies that also call themselves indemnity policies. They pay a specified amount for each day an individual stays in the hospital because of a specified illness or condition with the "benefit" payable from $100 to $300 per day, regardless of the actual expenses or the extent to which other plans pay for the care received.

Insured

Technically, a person can only be an insured under a plan offered by an insurance company, and most HMOs are not technically insurance companies. See "Covered Person" above.

Limitations

Not only do most plans exclude certain treatments, but most also have limitations. In some cases, limitations have been imposed because of past abuse. In other cases they have been imposed because an objective method of determining outcomes or progress is difficult or impossible to establish. In still other cases, it is merely for cost containment. A common list of limitations may include:

- Physical therapy: No more than 15 visits in a calendar year and only when provided in a hospital clinic
- Chiropractic care: Only 50 percent of the cost is covered for no more than 26 visits per calendar year
- Mental disorders: Only covers the first $50 per visit for outpatient treatment with a limit of no more than 26 visits per calendar year

Managed Care

In a managed care plan, each covered individual must choose a primary care physician. The plan charges a co-pay for each office visit and generally emphasizes preventative care.

Medicaid

Individuals below certain state-specific standards in income and assets generally qualify to receive Medicaid, a form of government-subsidized health insurance. Medicaid is funded by federal and state governments and is administered by each state. Medicaid is essentially medical welfare.

Medical Savings Accounts

A medical savings account (MSA) is a tax-deferred bank or savings account used in combination with a high-deductible health care plan. This account is designed as an alternative for individuals and/or families to fund health care expenses and medical insurance. Contributions to the plan are made with pre-tax dollars if paid through an employer, or deductible dollars if paid by an individual, and distributions from the plan are not included in gross income if used to pay for qualified medical expenses. This form of account has essentially been replaced by HSAs, see above.

Medicare

Medicare is health care for those over age 65, people of any age with kidney failure, and certain other disabled individuals.

National Committee for Quality Assurance (NCQA)

This is a private, independent, non-profit organization that has accredited managed care plans since its founding in 1993. NCQA provides report cards to help plan buyers better understand the quality of a plan being considered. According to the NCQA website, they have evaluated managed care plans representing over 75 percent of all individuals covered by managed care.

Pre-Certification

Pre-certification is a form of cost containment requiring the covered individual's physician to submit a request for specified treatments. The plan administrator may accept the request as made, suggest alternative treatment, or require a concurring second opinion before approving the treatment. Most surgeries must be pre-certified under plans that include any pre-certification requirement, and the approval often limits the number of days of hospitalization. If additional expenses are required, they must be requested as needed.

Preexisting Condition

A preexisting condition is any illness or injury for which treatment was received prior to a specific date. Generally, group health care plans have a preexisting conditions clause that may last no more than 12 months. Typically, any condition that was diagnosed or for which treatment has previously been received within the 90 days prior to being covered under the plan will not be covered until the individual has been covered for 12 months. State law may shorten this time frame. Some individual plans may extend the preexisting conditions clause to many years in the past. Variations of a preexisting clause may include any illness for which symptoms were experienced within a specified period prior to the time an individual was covered by the plan. This language excludes conditions and illnesses that were not diagnosed. There are a number of variations in the wording of these provisions. It is important to know exactly what it says.

Primary Care Physician (PCP)

Managed care plans generally use PCPs. This is usually an internist, family practitioner, pediatrician, general practitioner, or obstetrician/gynecologist. The covered individual chooses the PCP from a list of approved PCPs. The control the PCP has over an individual's care varies from plan to plan. Some require the PCP to approve any treatment by any other provider and some require a written referral. Other plans give more control to the covered individual.

Provider

A provider is any individual, organization, or institution that provides health care services. It may be a physician, physical therapist, nurse practitioner, hospital, clinic, etc.

Self-Funded Plan

Self-funded plans are employee benefit plans that are funded directly by an employer. Rather than have a commercial plan as the primary coverage, the employer designs a plan and funds for expected claims. These plans typically have a relatively low-cost, high-deductible plan underlying them that pays claims when the self-funded plan has paid out a specified level of benefits. Self-funded plans may be administered by a company employee or a third-party administrator. This is risk retention by the employer for most of the health care plan payments. It is only done by large employers.

Stop-Loss Limit

See "breakpoint."

Third-Party Administrator (TPA)

A TPA is usually a small company that manages various employee benefit plans for employers. The TPA may manage a commercial health care plan for a group of employers that are too small to obtain the type of coverage they want or may manage a plan for a single employer. The plan may be a health care plan, disability income plan, or some other employee benefit. The advantage of using a TPA is having a disinterested third party interpret the plan benefits rather than a coworker who may lack objectivity in granting or denying claims.

Usual Customary and Reasonable (UCR)

Indemnity plans do not automatically pay every bill that is sent. After ascertaining that the treatment is covered, the claims representative looks at a schedule the company maintains to ensure that the charge is reasonable. The company researches the market to determine the customary charge for this service in the particular geographic area and insures that it is the usual charge made by that provider. This review may result in a lower overall reimbursement.

GROUP AND INDIVIDUAL PLANS

While most students are familiar with group insurance plans (indeed, most are probably covered by group insurance), there are several areas in which group and individual plans differ: price, coverage, and underwriting.

Price

Adverse selection ensures that individual plans are generally more expensive than group plans. With group plans, the risk is spread out over the entire group: The vast majority of group plans are subsidized by an employer and the majority of employees have the coverage, even if they are quite healthy. Self-employed individuals who perceive themselves to have few health risks often choose not to have individual health care coverage—those who are in low-risk categories are likely to avoid insurance expenses altogether. However, those who plan to make regular visits to a physician, such as a young couple with children, know a plan will save them money and expect to use it regularly. This means there is a natural adverse selection that must be compensated for with higher premiums.

Coverage

The extent to which coverage varies between group and individual plans depends on the type of plan. An individual managed care plan may have higher co-payments for visits and prescriptions, but coverage will typically be the same for most health care concerns. Such plans may, however, limit or exclude coverage for maternity, mental or nervous disorders, and other types of treatment that tend to be aggravated by adverse selection. State laws often mandate inclusion of these benefits in group plans.

Indemnity (major medical) plans often limit coverage to a much greater extent: The lifetime maximum benefit is often reduced; there are often limits or exclusions that seldom appear in group plans; and very high deductibles are available. A group indemnity plan might have a deductible of $500, but individual plans might offer a similar plan for similar premiums for deductibles of $1,000 to $2,500. These high deductibles reduce the cost of insurance substantially, since only serious medical problems will result in a claim. The advent of HSAs along with the required HDHC plans has increased the likelihood that group plans will make high deductible options available.

One area of coverage that often is of great concern is that of maternity benefits. In many individual policies, except in states where it is mandated, maternity benefits are excluded or very limited. As the risk of pregnancy is largely under the control of the covered person, maternity benefits are ripe for adverse selection.

This is another area where there have been many changes over the past few years. Self-funded plans provided by employers do not fall under many state mandates and may exclude coverage that is required when a commercial plan is in place. In addition, most states have some requirements regarding individual health care plans. So it is possible that an individual plan will have benefits that are superior to a group self-funded plan.

Underwriting

Most group insurance plans are put in place on a guaranteed issue basis: The employer signs up for the plan, and any employee who applies when first eligible will automatically be covered.

With individual health care plans this is not the case. When an individual applies for health insurance he or she may be turned down or may have specific benefits or health conditions excluded. This does not mean, however, that he or she cannot get a health care plan. Some states mandate that individuals who apply for a health care plan must be covered. The rules vary from state to state. There are circumstances where individuals may obtain health care plans without underwriting if it is done within 62 days of leaving a group plan.

HEALTH CARE PLANS FOR INDIVIDUALS

Many types of health care plans have been offered to individuals over the years. Some are uncommon, but most look much like plans offered to groups. The cost of health care plans is one of the reasons there are so many variations and options. Options for individuals include traditional (indemnity) plans, medical savings accounts (MSAs), health savings accounts (HSAs), managed care, temporary insurance, Medicare (and Medicare Advantage), and some specialized types of plans with very limited benefits.

Traditional Plans

Plans that fall in this very general category are true indemnity or fee for service plans. These are generally sold by insurance companies, and are set up to reimburse insured individuals for expenses incurred. There are four general categories of expenses covered under these policies:

- Hospital expense coverage
- Surgical expense coverage
- Physician's expense coverage
- Major medical coverage

The first three categories of expenses might be covered in separate policies or in a package; the fourth category is a single policy with all three previous types of coverage. The vast majority are sold as a package or a single major medical plan.

Hospital Expense Coverage

This type of policy comes in one of three forms. The first provides for expenses related to hospitalization (room charges, prescriptions, hospital services, etc.) up to a specified amount. The second, started by Blue Cross as a hospital service benefit, provides for hospitalization up to a certain number of days without a limit on cost. The third form, misnamed a **hospital indemnity policy**, provides a specified payment for each day the insured is hospitalized, usually with a set maximum number of days. In some states, the coverage under this type of contract is spelled out in state statutes.

Surgical Expense Coverage

This policy is designed to reimburse the insured for costs associated with surgery, with the general exclusion of the physician's charges and hospital charges not directly related to the surgery. This policy covers expenses incurred in the pre-operative area, the operating room, and the post-operative area, as well as surgical supplies. Blue Shield is a common form of coverage for surgical services and physicians' charges that is sold separately in some parts of the country. Like Blue Cross, it is a service plan, covering the services of a physician and covered surgery, not any specific dollar value. In some states, the coverage under this type of contract is spelled out in state statutes.

Physician's Expense Coverage

These policies generally limit the amount payable for each visit to a relatively small amount, and may also limit the number of visits per year. Medicare Part B is an example of this form of coverage. Medicare Part A pays for hospital expenses but does not pay for anything outside of the hospital or any physician charges, even when in the hospital. Private plans may cover all or part of the usual, customary, and reasonable (UCR) rates. Medicare pays 80 percent of the Medicare approved rates, which are based on the UCR charges made for each type of physician visit in the geographic area of the covered individual.

Major Medical Coverage

The problem with the above three forms of insurance is that an individual would have to purchase all three to have coverage for the most common health risks. This is a real disadvantage for both policyholders and insurance companies, since, among other problems, it is often quite difficult to predict out-of-pocket expenses. Therefore, while the three previous separate types of coverage may still be available, they are not currently very common.

Rather, the major medical policy has become much more popular as it combines all three types of benefits (hospital, surgical, and physician expense coverage). These plans have a deductible, co-insurance, a stop-loss limit, and a few exclusions or limitations. This form of coverage was the norm for nearly 50 years, with most plans relying on the UCR standards to determine how much they will reimburse. "Expected" expenses, such as routine physical exams, immunizations, and well baby care, are generally not covered as those expenses are controlled by the insured and, thus, are inappropriate to include in a health insurance plan covering only more significant risks. Likewise, these plans routinely exclude elective and cosmetic surgery unless a procedure is needed to repair damage from a covered accident or illness.

Individuals insured under these plans are often billed by their providers, submit claims to the insurance company, and are reimbursed for expenses incurred. They can use any licensed provider with some providers submitting the bill first to the insurance company and then billing them for any portion left unpaid or not covered. If the provider charges more than the insurance plan's UCR estimation, the insured typically has to pay the difference in addition to any portion of the bill applied to a deductible or coinsurance.

Medical Savings Accounts

Medical savings accounts (MSA), called Archer medical savings accounts, were created as a way for individuals to put money away on a pre-tax basis for the purpose of paying eligible medical expenses. When combined with a high-deductible health care (HDHC) plan, they are a relatively low-cost alternative to low-deductible major medical plans. MSAs, and the HDHC plans purchased with them are the epitome of health "insurance." This method of covering health care expenses is exactly what insurance is about. They are made up of a qualified tax-deferred bank or savings account combined with a relatively low-premium/high-deductible insurance policy. Individuals and/or families are encouraged to invest the premium savings in a medical savings account by making tax-deductible contributions to the MSA. Medical expenses are then paid out of the account until the deductible is reached, or it runs out of funds. Unused balances in the account may be accumulated year to year. The underlying insurance is used only for those years when medical expenses exceed the deductible. The MSA program was started in 1997 as an experimental program for only a four-year period or until the number of accounts reached 750,000; however, Congress extended the ability to establish an MSA through 2005 or the time when the numerical limit is reached, whichever comes first.

Anyone who is self-employed or an employee of an employer with 50 or fewer employees is eligible to choose an MSA as an alternative to the more common ways of paying for health care. For the self-employed individual and others, purchasing the high-deductible insurance policy and making a permitted contribution establishes the MSA. The permitted contributions are 65 percent of the individual's deductible and 75 percent of the individual and family deductible. Health expenditures for qualified medical expenses from the MSA account are distributed income tax-free and accumulated balances earn interest, which is also tax-free if used for medical expenses.

The following table shows the range of acceptable deductibles for plans to qualify as high-deductible health care plans in 2005. Additionally, it shows the maximum annual out-of-pocket expenses that are acceptable for a high-deductible health plan.

Type of Coverage	Minimum Annual Deductible	Maximum Annual Deductible	Maximum Annual Out-of-Pocket Expenses
Self only	$1,750	$2,650	$3,500
Family	$3,500	$5,250	$6,450

MSA plans for families generally have individual deductibles that are less than the family deductible but higher than the lowest acceptable deductible under a self-only plan.

Income tax deductible contributions to the MSA are limited to 75 percent of the maximum deductible for a family plan. The acceptable medical expenses, including policy premiums, that can be paid for with funds in the MSA are quite extensive. Visit the Internal Revenue Service website at www.irs.gov and search for "medical savings account" to learn more about the details of these plans.

Health Savings Accounts

An important provision in the Medicare Prescription Drug Improvement and Modernization Act of 2003, signed by President George W. Bush on December 8, 2003, is that it expanded the former medical savings accounts into new and innovative health savings accounts (HSAs) effective January 1, 2004. Individuals are eligible to contribute to an HSA if they (1) have a qualified high-deductible health plan, (2) are not eligible for Medicare or are under 65, (3) are not covered under another health care plan, and (4) cannot be claimed as a dependent on another person's tax return. For individual policies, a qualified health plan is one that has a minimum deductible of $1,000 and a $5,115 out-of-pocket expense maximum (for 2005, indexed annually). For family policies, a qualified health plan must have a minimum family deductible of $2,050 and a $10,250 out-of-pocket expense maximum (for 2005, indexed annually). Preventative care services are not subject to the deductible. Policies with out-of-network dollar requirements do not take those particular requirements into consideration when determining the deductible or the out-of-pocket maximums.

HSA plans are designed to help individuals save for qualified medical and retiree health expenses on a tax-free basis. Individuals may contribute the lesser of the health plan deductible or $2,650 (for 2005, indexed annually). For family coverage, the account holder may contribute the lesser of the health plan deductible or $5,250 (for 2005, indexed annually). Individuals ages 55 to 64 may make additional catch-up contributions of up to $600 in 2005, increasing by $100 per year to $1,000 annually in 2009 and thereafter. A married couple can make two catch-up contributions as long as both spouses are at least 55 years old. HSA contributions must be coordinated with MSA contributions: the HSA contribution limitations are decreased by any contributions to an MSA and/or employer contributions to the HSA. There are no income limits for individuals claiming the deduction for HSA contributions. The HSA contribution deduction is an above-the-line adjustment to gross income, so it is not dependent on whether the taxpayer itemizes deductions, and it is not subject to any phase-out.

Contributions may be made by individuals, family members, and employers; contributions are tax deductible even if, as indicated previously, the account beneficiary does not itemize deductions. Employer contributions are made on a pre-tax basis and are not taxable to the employee. Employers will be allowed to offer HSAs through a cafeteria (Section 125) plan. Investment earnings accrue tax-free. HSA distributions are tax-free if they are used to pay for qualified medical expenses. In fact, as long as the distributions are used to pay for qualified medical expenses, they will never be taxed—not before they are contributed, not while they are in the account, and not when they are withdrawn. Qualified expenses include amounts paid for "medical care" as defined in IRC Section 213(d), such as deductibles and co-payments under a health plan, as well as expenses not covered under a health plan (that is, vision care, dental care, over-the-counter medications, and so on). Health insurance premiums generally are not qualifying medical expenses for HSA purposes, but HSAs can reimburse premiums for COBRA continuation coverage, for qualified long-term care insurance, for health coverage while unemployed, or for health insurance (other than a Medicare supplemental policy) covering Medicare-eligible HSA beneficiaries. Once individuals turn 65 and become eligible for Medicare, they can draw on their HSA account tax-free to pay their share of the program's medical premiums and co-pays.

Distributions made for any purpose other than medical care are subject to income tax and a 10 percent penalty. The 10 percent penalty is waived in the case of death or disability; it is also waived for distributions made by individuals age 65 and older. Upon death of the account holder, HSA ownership may transfer to the account holder's spouse on a tax-free basis. If the account is left to any other heir(s), it is subject to income tax but not the 10 percent penalty.

One significant advantage of an HSA over a flexible spending account is that unspent funds in an HSA can be rolled over on a year-to-year basis. With a flexible spending account, funds unspent by March 15th of the following year are lost. This feature of HSAs permits those account holders who remain healthy and do not incur significant medical expenses to build up a cash fund to cover medical expenses when they are older. In addition, HSAs are portable; they stay with a person when changing jobs or health insurance coverage. On the other hand, the advantage of a flexible spending account is that it can be funded so that medical expenses over and above the amount of the deductible can be paid on a pre-tax basis. Comparing the two from a practical viewpoint, the HSA is most beneficial for very healthy individuals who have low annual medical costs; however, the FSA is most beneficial to those who have expected annual medical costs that exceed the deductible.

HSAs are currently funded through bank accounts or mutual funds. It is anticipated that health insurers will also offer these accounts. The employer, the employee, or both can contribute to an HSA. The party or parties contributing to the HSA is (are) entitled to the income tax deduction. When employers offer both options, it will be possible to have both an HSA and a flexible savings account (FSA), but the owner will not be permitted to use funds in both accounts to pay the same expenses. It would seem appropriate to use the FSA account first—until it is exhausted—and then use the HSA account.

The main disadvantage of HSAs is that a participant must forego comprehensive health insurance coverage and instead enroll in a plan with a high deductible. These plans would appear to offer greater advantage to younger, healthier persons who are unlikely to have large medical bills and can, therefore, allow the savings to accumulate. Upper-income persons may find these plans attractive by switching to high-deductible plans and taking advantage of the tax deductions in their higher tax brackets. Plans established by employers can permit healthy employees to accrue large balances over several years. The downside of this is the potential for adverse selection with more comprehensive plans offered by employers since the healthiest are likely to opt out of the more comprehensive plans.

Finally, rollovers can be accepted into an HSA account from the account beneficiary's MSA account or from another HSA account. Rollover amounts transferred from one account to another must be completed within 60 days, and cannot occur more than once per year.

In a question and answer format, IRS Notice 2004-2 defines HSAs, outlines who is eligible for them, provides information on how to establish them, and describes the basic rules for contributions and withdrawals.

To view the PDF of IRS Notice 2004-2, go to www.irs.gov/ and search for IRS Notice 2004-2.

Managed Care

In the mid-1990s, managed care became the most common form of health care plan, with some of its benefits incorporated into most traditional major medical plans. Managed care plans come in a variety of forms and grew from the belief that preventative care was less expensive than waiting until an illness became serious. Managed care plans generally provide for routine physical exams so that illnesses and conditions can be diagnosed and treated in their early stages.

Managed care introduced the concepts of co-payments (rather than an annual deductible) and the primary care physician (PCP). While the following descriptions may seem quite clear, the lines between various forms of managed care are quite blurred, and there are few, if any, managed care plans that still fit perfectly in the basic definitions.

Health Maintenance Organization

A health maintenance organization (HMO) offers medical services to its members (also called "subscribers") for a monthly fee. While this may appear to be an insurance plan, the provider, seller, and administrator are one and the same—the HMO. Therefore, these organizations are not technically insurance companies since they essentially provide only prepaid medical services.

Generally, the plan offers the services of its own participating physicians and hospital(s) to the plan's members under the terms of the contract. The difference is that members may only use the providers who are a part of the HMO network. If the member chooses to use a nonparticipating physician or hospital, there may not be coverage or the coverage may be severely limited. If a member happens to be outside of the **service area** (the geographic area within which the HMO has providers), the HMO will generally cover only emergency care.

HMOs are generally found in one of three general structures. The simplest form is the **staff model HMO** where all of the network providers are employees of the HMO, working in HMO owned or leased facilities. The second form is a **group/practice model HMO**, with the HMO contracting with groups of providers or with a "practice" made up of a number of providers who are usually spread out geographically within the service area. The individual physicians and other providers are not directly employed by the HMO as an entity. Both staff model and group practice HMOs may be closed-panel plans meaning that subscribers must use doctors and other providers who are either employed by, or are under contract to, the HMO. Under an open-panel plan, outside providers also may be covered, usually upon the referral of a listed provider. The third and final form is the **independent practice association model (IPA) HMO**, in which the HMO maintains contracts with individual providers to deliver care for HMO members. Under the IPA and Group/Practice Models, primary care physicians are generally paid on a capitation basis, and other providers—such as specialists—are paid a negotiated fee for services rendered. Staff HMOs are the most restrictive in nature since only employee provider services are covered. A closed-panel version of a group/practice model or an independent practice association model is slightly less restrictive, and the open-panel versions are the least restrictive of the HMO models.

HMO contracts generally have no annual deductible or coinsurance provision. Usually, there is a nominal co-payment (typically $10 to $35 paid for each office visit), with a larger co-pay for hospital stays or lab tests and x-rays. Every member must choose a participating physician as a primary care physician, and if a visit with a specialist is sought, it must be approved and referred through the primary care physician. This does not appear unreasonable on the surface, but there have been situations where the primary care physician has been given monetary incentives to keep each individual's costs within preset limits. Thus, the PCP's year-end bonus may depend on sending as few HMO members to specialists as possible.

The most frequent complaints about HMOs include the "gatekeeper" physician (PCP), limited choice of providers, limited choice of prescriptions, and a restricted choice of hospitals. Physicians have expressed some frustration about the common practice of limited patient contact for each visit, regardless of the reason for the visit. This may lead to multiple visits when one longer-than-average visit would suffice.

Preferred Provider Organization (PPO)

A PPO is most often operated by a company that acts as an intermediary between health care providers and health care purchasers. Generally, the various providers affiliated with the PPO accept reduced fees in exchange for the benefits of more rapid and certain payment, and for being on the preferred provider list. Most PPOs require covered individuals to choose a primary care physician (PCP). PCPs usually receive a capitation payment for each patient, regardless of the number of visits. The covered individuals generally benefit in that they have little or no paperwork to fill out when they receive care. While most PPOs are sponsored and operated by insurance companies, some are organized by health care providers, large employers, or even HMOs.

As with HMOs, PPOs seek to provide quality care at reduced prices. They also attempt to provide a more flexible program than that offered by HMOs while also featuring more comprehensive coverage than indemnity plans. Some PPOs accomplish more comprehensive coverage by offering a so-called "swing plan." This means that the insured/participant can use the plan as either an indemnity plan or a PPO plan. If the insured/member uses providers on the PPO list of participating physicians, he or she ends up paying the co-pay, usually without having to pay a deductible and/or coinsurance. However, if the insured/member wants to use a nonparticipating doctor, he or she can "swing" to the indemnity side of the plan without being limited to the PPO list. When doing this, a deductible and coinsurance, however, will apply. Such a plan is very flexible in that the insured may choose between the two options at will. If the insured takes advantage of this flexibility, the plan will have a fairly high out of pocket cost, but the insured/participant will nevertheless maintain control. Pure PPOs and HMOs have substantial similarities: Both have a list of physicians and a co-pay, with no deductible. There may or may not be a coinsurance requirement, depending on the contract.

Generally, covered persons have no claim forms to fill out: Non-staff model HMO providers and PPO providers both agree to accept what the plan lists as covered under the contract. There are several potential problems associated with a PPO. First, the participants end up with the worst of both the HMO and indemnity worlds when they obtain some services under the PPO arrangement and some outside of it. The result is that the insured may pay both a deductible and coinsurance for the indemnity-covered services and a co-pay for the PPO-covered services. This can occur when the insured, who is unaware of this problem or is receiving emergency care, receives services from both PPO and non-PPO providers in one procedure. For example, an insured might select a PPO doctor and hospital for surgery and then find that the anesthesiologist was not part of the PPO. These problems do not apply to all PPOs, and some PPOs deal with it differently than others, but one must read the contract to find out for sure.

Another problem is that some PPOs also use HMO-style gatekeeper mechanisms. As with the HMO, when serious conditions arise, the insured must have faith that the PPO providers are competent or accept that he or she will have to pay for someone outside of the approved list of providers. Most PPOs provide preventative care, but it may be more limited than that offered by HMOs.

Exclusive Provider Organization (EPO)

An EPO is generally a self-funded PPO specific to one employer. It typically has the same carrier (an insurance company or a TPA) as a local PPO, but is modified somewhat for the specific employer. If an individual leaves a job and wants to continue the EPO coverage personally, there is the possibility that benefits will not be available if he or she moves out of the area.

Point-of-Service (POS) Plans

Consumer demands and employer desires to keep employees happy also led to a new generation of managed-care plan: the point-of-service (POS) plan. These are often less expensive than PPOs or HMOs and easily accessible for employers to implement, but are uncommon as plans for individuals. The plan gets its name from the nature of its operation.

Individuals covered under the plan may receive health care anywhere they choose. A POS plan has attributes of an HMO, PPO, and indemnity plan each. If providers who work for the plan are used, their services are either fully covered or provided with a very low co-pay (similar to an HMO). If a contracted physician is used, as with a PPO, the plan typically requires a higher co-pay, and some preventative medicine may not be covered. A POS plan choice may also leave the insured with other expenses, such as lab fees. A final option available under a POS plan is to use an unaffiliated provider. When this is done, payment is provided as under an indemnity plan; however, the stop-loss limit may be relatively high, and the coinsurance may be 70/30 or 50/50, rather than the most common 80/20. Where the individual receives his or her care (the "point of service"), in turn, determines how much of the bill will be covered by the plan.

The goal of a POS plan is to provide flexibility for every covered individual. He or she can use any provider, and the provider's relationship with the plan will determine to what extent benefits are paid. Certain choices come at a very low cost, but if the insured wants to use a different provider, that option is also available.

Provider-Sponsored Organizations

In 1997, part of the Balanced Budget Act (BBA) approved a form of Medicare provider that had been used in the private sector for well over a decade. Provider-sponsored organizations (PSOs) are provider-run health care plans that are available to Medicare participants. This is not a lot different from an HMO except that, in this case, it is typically a group of private physicians who band together for the purpose of providing care to a group of Medicare patients. PSO plans operate much like Medicare HMOs in that the plan receives a capitation payment for each enrollee, regardless of the services required. If the PSO can sign up a large group of healthy members, the plan can be quite profitable. If the PSO signs up a large group of not-so-healthy members, it can lose money.

This particular problem is where controversy about PSOs arises. Insurance companies, HMOs, and PPOs must meet certain solvency requirements to remain in business. There is always the possibility, especially with seniors as the group of patients, that there could be a substantial, unforeseen spike in claims. Without adequate reserves, the PSO could collapse. The NAIC and regulated insurers and providers like HMOs take the position that PSOs should be regulated in the same manner. On the other side of the discussion, the American Medical Association and other providers claim that since they are the ones actually providing the services, they can continue to do so even if money becomes tight. This side of the discussion states that providers are assuming a "service risk" rather than an "insurance risk," which means that they can provide services for free—using their own personal resources to stay afloat—until things turn around. The counterargument is that the self-funded approach may work for physicians with substantial personal resources to carry them when they do not receive a paycheck, however that is not likely the case for their support staffs, both administrative and medical. Further, any provider can establish a PSO, so there is no assurance that one would be established by those who can weather a short-term cash flow shortage.

PSOs have expanded to provide services to groups outside of Medicare. This expansion has necessitated state regulation. The Department of Health and Human Services (HHS) conducted a study to determine how states have chosen to regulate PSOs. All of the nine states studied regulate the ways in which PSOs deal with employers, and two extend the ultimate responsibility to the employer rather than having the PSO ultimately responsible for providing the benefits. All of the states studied require some form of licensing. When it comes to Medicare, states apparently have no regulatory authority over companies that provide PSO plans, since Medicare is a federal program.

Significant Changes in the Marketplace

The health care plan marketplace has experienced some considerable changes in the past couple of years. Plans that operated as they did a few years ago appear to be the exception rather than the rule. For a number of reasons, most plans appear to be reducing the benefit for prescription drugs. Deductibles and/or co-pays for drugs have risen sharply. Many PPOs and HMOs have remodeled their plans so that they have co-pays as well as deductibles for certain benefits.

Again, for numerous reasons, the cost of health care plans has risen at a much faster rate than inflation. The advent of HSAs may result in more adverse selection of the more comprehensive plans as the healthiest individuals seek ways to hold down the premiums on their plans.

Another issue that has affected the marketplace is the number of uninsured people. While large numbers of the millions of uninsured are not devastated by uncovered medical bills, more and more people are being financially drained by medical bills for procedures that are more expensive than people assume. This leaves providers with more uncollectible accounts and results in increased charges to the rest of the population who have health care plans.

Not many years ago, physicians in general were opposed to any single-payer plan of health care. As providers hire more and more administrative support staff to handle the submission of claims for the dozens of plans their patients use, many of them have become vocally supportive of a single payer plan. Their reasoning includes the recognition that while they may be paid less for particular care giving, they will have fewer uncovered patients and will be able to substantially reduce the support staff required to obtain payment. This in itself is a significant change.

Temporary Insurance

Sometimes called interim insurance, this type of policy is designed for someone who:

- Recently graduated from school
- Is no longer a dependent under a parent's group coverage
- Is between jobs
- Is waiting for group insurance to start
- Is temporarily or seasonally employed
- Is on strike, has been laid off, or is terminating employment

This insurance is sometimes purchased when continuation of the prior group coverage is considered impractical or unnecessary. It has a single premium and is typically available for periods of one to six months. Most policies are renewable only once and have comprehensive pre-existing conditions exclusions, usually reading: "This plan excludes coverage for any condition for which the insured received a diagnosis and/or treatment within the three year period prior to the date of this contract." For example, if the insured injures his or her knee in a soccer game, subsequent medical problems with that knee will not be covered unless it can be proven that the problem had nothing to do with the earlier injury.

The upside to these plans is that they are relatively inexpensive. The biggest downside is that if necessary treatment is received while under the policy, when the policy is renewed, that condition becomes a preexisting condition. In addition, the list of conditions typically not covered under such a policy is extensive. Therefore, temporary insurance should only be used when no other option is available and the need is truly temporary.

Medicare

Medicare is a federal program provided to all retirees who have paid into the Medicare or Railroad Retirement systems. Additionally, if an individual becomes disabled to the extent that he or she is eligible for Social Security Disability Income, he or she will be eligible to be covered by Medicare after 24 months of receiving Social Security benefits.

Medicare, in its original form called Original Medicare, is divided into two basic parts, Part A and Part B. The government pays for Part A (for those who paid Medicare taxes) hospital coverage, handling the bills for hospital-related costs (excluding physician charges). The covered individual shares the Part B costs: physicians and other out-of-hospital expenses. A physician who agrees to accept a Medicare payment from his or her patients is a participating physician, and has accepted a Medicare assignment. There is a Medicare Part C that is nothing more than a title to indicate that there are alternative forms of Medicare benefits. It is not actually a schedule of benefits like Parts A and B. Beginning in 2006, there will be a Medicare Part D: a prescription drug benefit.

The original Medicare plan, which is a fee-for-service type plan and Medicare Advantage are the two current approaches to providing Medicare benefits. Medicare Advantage was previously called Medicare+Choice and is sometimes referred to as Medicare Part C. Where available, there are three forms of Medicare Advantage: Medicare managed plans, Medicare preferred provider organization plans, and Medicare private fee-for-service plans. Some plans will not be available nationwide due to accessibility of providers.

Original Medicare has numerous deductibles, including those for hospital stays, the first three pints of blood, etc. Additionally, it generally pays for only 80 percent of covered charges, and covered charges and actual charges—the amount the provider bills—are often different. A physician may charge $110 for a procedure, and Medicare may only cover $100 of it. So Medicare pays 80 percent of the $100, or $80. This leaves the insured to pay $30 of the total bill. Medicare pays for prescription drugs while an insured is in the hospital but does not cover any prescriptions when he or she is not hospitalized. There is currently an interim prescription program in place that will be discussed below.

Additionally, covered charges must not exceed "approved charges"—charges Medicare does not consider too high, as determined annually and based on the type of procedure and the geographic location. These amounts are the maximum a provider may charge a patient if the provider accepts Medicare payments, even if the patient is willing to cover additional costs. In an effort to control Medicare costs, current federal law requires that the approved charges actually decrease each year, regardless of the actual cost of providing the service. Thus, many physicians around the country are opting out of accepting Medicare patients because they are losing money treating them. Any planner discussing health plan options with seniors must be prepared to discuss the problems of finding physicians who accept Medicare.

A new benefit was added as of January 2005: a physical exam benefit. This is a one-time physical exam that is available if obtained in the first six months of being covered. It does not cover the cost of lab tests. This benefit is available only to those who initially obtain Part B coverage on January 1, 2005, or later.

Medicare Advantage is a developing part of Medicare. Generally, an individual first obtains Medicare Parts A and B and pays the premium for Part B. Then he or she chooses one of the additional plans in their area. A search engine is available on the Medicare website at www.medicare.gov. Different locales have different providers of these alternate plans. They generally operate as PPOs or HMOs, and they may have no additional cost or they may cost well over an additional $100 per month. Generally, these plans offer more benefits than the Original Medicare plan. One of the biggest differences is that the individual must usually use providers who are part of a particular plan.

Medicare HMOs, also known as **Medicare-risk health maintenance organizations**, are part of the Medicare Advantage program. They have been the fastest growing segment of the Medigap market. A person who is eligible for, and covered by, Medicare may choose to use a Medicare HMO, and many individuals do so because such an option features expanded benefits, including prescription drug coverage, while at the same time keeping costs relatively low. The disadvantages of this option are the strict restrictions regarding which facilities and physicians may be used, and if a covered person travels, the fact that only emergency services will be covered when away from home—nonemergency expenses will generally be out of pocket. Initially, premiums paid by members of Medicare HMOs were very low, ranging from zero to the normal charge for Medicare Part B, but, in recent years, plan providers have found that the premium was far too low to cover expenses, especially with reduced Medicare payments, and they subsequently have substantially raised their premiums or terminated their programs. Additionally, many of the plans across the nation found it fiscally impossible to provide the necessary benefits and terminated their programs, forcing thousands of seniors to seek new plans.

A retiree may not be turned down for either a Medigap policy (discussed below) or a Medicare HMO as long as he or she applies for it within six months of enrolling in Medicare after age 65. Additionally, the law states that preexisting conditions may only be considered for up to six months prior to an application for a late enrollment and that the seller of any Medigap plan must provide the buyer with a Medicare Supplement Buyer's Guide explaining policy revisions.

Prescription Drug Plan

In 2003, Congress passed a prescription drug plan, which will be referred to as Medicare Part D in 2006. Until Part D becomes effective in 2006, seniors on Medicare can choose from many different cards that provide discounts on prescriptions. Program enrollment began in May 2004, and the cards are intended to be used through December 2005 when the drug card program is to be replaced by a prescription benefit, discussed below. Those with an exceptionally low income may also qualify for a $600 credit toward prescription drugs.

Prescription drug discount cards are offered by private companies. If they meet the requirements laid out in the legislation, the cards will be approved by Medicare. Cards that are offered must be available to everyone in the state unless the card is part of a Medicare managed care plan. The company may choose the drugs for which it will offer the discount and the price discount that will be offered. The cards offer a discount only on the drugs on that company's discount drug list, and only at specified pharmacies.

At any time, the companies can either change the drugs listed or their prices. To get a card, an individual must be covered by Medicare and must not have any other prescription benefits except those in a Medigap plan (see below) or that are a part of a Medicare Advantage plan. The limitations about who can get a card seem somewhat contradictory, and each case must be looked at individually. The company offering the card may charge up to $30 to enroll with that card. Individuals may have only one card, and if they did not like the card they got in 2004, they were not allowed to change it—with very few exceptions—until January 2005.

Beginning in January 2006, Medicare participants will have the option of buying prescription coverage. The current view of the plan is that participants who choose to buy the plan would pay varying amounts toward prescription drugs, depending on the plan chosen. This plan would be provided by private insurers and would have a cost that is estimated to be $35 monthly. When this plan goes into effect, it will be called Part D of Medicare. Anyone with a Medigap policy that has prescription benefits prior to 2006 will lose the prescription benefits of the Medigap policy if he or she chooses to participate in Part D of Medicare.

The premiums, deductibles, and other limits will begin increasing in 2007. According to the Congressional Budget Office, between the beginning of this program in 2007 and 2013, the potential out of pocket costs for individuals will go up 78 percent, or an average rate of over 8.5 percent per year.

A planner must be cognizant of the ever changing nature of Medicare plans as his or her clients age. Practically everyone who reaches retirement age will be covered by one Medicare plan or another.

Excellent, comprehensive information about all Medicare plans is available at www.medicare.gov.

Medigap

As mentioned above, Medicare has a number of deductibles and does not currently (as of 2005) provide for any prescription benefits outside of the hospital unless an individual signs up for a discount card (see above). Because of this, many Medicare supplement insurance plans were developed over the years, and while some plans were quite good, others offered very poor coverage. Some individuals would buy multiple policies on the mistaken notion that the combined policies, with Medicare, would also cover every contingency (despite the fact that most policies had "other insurance" clauses preventing this).

To remedy these problems, Congress charged the National Association of Insurance Commissioners (NAIC) to develop standardized Medicare Supplement (or Medigap) plans. There are 10 standard Medicare supplement plans available that were designed by the NAIC in 1990 under the provisions of the Omnibus Budget and Reconciliation Act (OBRA). The 10 plans (A – J, see "In-Depth: Medigap Plans" below) are the only plans available unless the covered individual lives in a state that provided guidelines, before OBRA, on what a Medicare Supplement plan must include. The only states to use their own plan designs are Massachusetts, Minnesota, and Wisconsin. Insureds may be sold only one plan, and if an agent recommends a different plan, the consumer must sign a statement that he or she will terminate the old plan.

In-Depth: Medigap Plans

Originally called Medicare Supplements, Medigap policies have been around for many years to provide for the many deductibles and costs of medical care that are not covered by Medicare parts A or B. These are limited to use with the Original Medicare plan. The following table details Medigap plans A – J. Plans F and J have high-deductible options (discussed below). As would be expected, plans that provide more benefits have a higher cost. Since insurance companies offer the same ten plans, the differences are limited to premium and service. Not all insurers that provide Medigap plans offer all variations.

Benefits	Plan A	Plan B	Plan C	Plan D	Plan E	Plan F	Plan G	Plan H	Plan I	Plan J
Basic Benefits Package	✔	✔	✔	✔	✔	✔	✔	✔	✔	✔
Skilled Nursing Care			✔	✔	✔	✔	✔	✔	✔	✔
Part A Deductible		✔	✔	✔	✔	✔	✔	✔	✔	✔
Part B Deductible			✔			✔				4
Excess Doctor's Charges						100%	80%		100%	100%
Foreign Travel			✔	✔	✔	✔	✔	✔	✔	✔
At-Home Recovery				✔			✔		✔	✔
Prescription Drugs								✔	✔	✔
Preventative Screening					✔					✔

Basic Benefits Package: This benefit, part of any Medigap plan, covers the Part A coinsurance amount ($228 per day in 2005, the amount normally payable by the individual) for days 61 through 90 of hospital stay in each Medicare benefit period. In addition, such a package may also be used to cover individual's share of days 91 through 150 of a hospital stay ($456 per day in 2005) for each of Medicare's 60 lifetime reserve days that may be used only once. After all Medicare hospital benefits are exhausted, the package then covers 100 percent of the Medicare Part A eligible hospital expenses. Coverage is limited to a maximum of 365 days of additional inpatient hospital care during the policyholder's lifetime with the policyholder responsible for payment when Medigap hospital benefits are exhausted. The package also covers the reasonable cost of the first three pints of blood or equivalent quantities of packed red blood cells per year under Medicare Parts A and B unless this blood is replaced. Note that plans F and J have a high deductible option that exists to reduce the monthly premium of the plan. There is a $1,690 annual deductible of expenses that the insured must pay prior to the Medigap plan paying anything. Depending on the source of the plan, the reduction of the premium may be greater or less than the additional deductible. Obviously this package is most appropriate for generally healthy individuals.

Finally, the package covers the coinsurance amount for Part B services (generally 20 percent of Medicare-approved amount) after a $110 annual deductible is met.

Skilled Nursing Care: In 2005, this benefit covers the coinsurance amount of $114 per day for days 21 through 100 of skilled nursing care per benefit period.

Medicare Part A Deductible: This benefit covers the inpatient deductible at $912 per benefit period (in 2005) for the first 60 days.

Medicare Part B Deductible: This benefit covers the $110 Part B deductible per calendar year (in 2005).

Excess Doctor's Charges: This benefit covers up to 100 percent of excess charges made by a physician, limited by the amount Medicare will permit a physician to charge for various procedures and treatments. However, if the physician charges more than the government-dictated amount, he or she will be prohibited from receiving any Medicare reimbursement.

Foreign Travel: For individuals covered under Medicare who want to travel, Medigap plans with this benefit pay 80 percent of covered charges for medically necessary emergency care in a foreign country, after a $250 deductible.

At-Home Recovery: Coverage for at-home recovery provides a benefit of up to $40 each visit and a maximum of $1,600 per year for short-term, at-home assistance with activities of daily living for those recovering from an illness, injury, or surgery.

Prescription Drugs: The cost of prescription drugs is one of the biggest problems for those on Medicare. This benefit provides coverage for 50 percent of the cost of prescription drugs up to the maximum specified in the plan per year after the policyholder meets a $250 per year deductible. Beginning in 2006, when Medicare Part D goes into effect, any person with a Medigap policy who elects Medicare Part D will lose the Medigap prescription benefits. Theoretically this should lower the Medigap premium, helping to offset the cost of Medicare Part D coverage.

Preventative Screening: The benefit for preventative medical care pays up to $120 per year for such a physical examination, serum cholesterol screening, hearing tests, diabetes screening, and a thyroid function test.

Medigap Select: A policy that requires insureds to use specified providers is called a Medigap Select policy. It still qualifies as a Medigap plan. Policies that specify which providers may be used generally have lower premiums than policies that have no limitations.

Long-Term Care

Medicare does not provide any substantial benefit for long-term care. However, if an individual is confined to a long-term care facility for skilled nursing care following a hospitalization, and has the prospect of having his or her condition improve, Medicare will pay essentially all costs for up to 20 days of confinement and will participate in the payment for the next 80 days after a substantial deductible ($114 per day in 2005). The individual must be in a Medicare-approved facility and must be confined within 30 days of at least a three-day hospital confinement for the same condition. If a bed is not available within that 30-day period in the facility, the benefits will not be paid. Individual long-term care insurance, including the limited use of Medicare and Medigap for long-term care, is further discussed in chapter 8.

Other Individual Plans

Other plans are frequently offered for sale from a variety of sources. Because of the limited scope of most of these plans, many financial advisers believe they are not a good value for the premium and may provide little other than a false sense of security.

Hospital Indemnity Plan

These plans are generally sold door to door, through the mail, via the Internet, and by a few insurance agents. They promise to pay a specified amount for each day the insured spends in the hospital. Most have comprehensive pre-existing condition exclusions. While called "indemnity plans," they have little to do with indemnity since they pay a specified amount regardless of the expenses incurred.

General daily room rates in hospitals are in the range of $1,000 while the typical benefit of these policies is around only $300 per day. Additionally, in today's health care marketplace, it is only the seriously ill or injured who spend more than a few days in the hospital.

Dread Disease Policy

This type of plan is much like the hospital indemnity plan. It promises to pay a specified amount if the insured develops one or more of a list of diseases or conditions. Some pay a daily amount when hospitalized for these diseases or conditions while others pay based on a "principal sum." An example of the "principal sum payment":

Dread Disease Policy	
Principal Sum $50,000	
Condition	Amount Payable
Cancer*	$50,000
Cancer**	$25,000
Heart attack	$50,000
Crohn's Disease	$10,000
Stroke	$50,000
* Cancer requiring chemotherapy and radiation therapy.	
** Other cancers	

The list included with a particular policy is usually far more comprehensive than the above example.

Nevertheless, you should note, that this is very much like a gambling policy: If you get the right disease or condition, you receive a substantial reimbursement; if not, you receive nothing. Therefore, most clients are much better served by a comprehensive health care plan and disability income insurance.

Accidental Death and Dismemberment Plan (AD&D)

Another type of plan often sold through the mail or the Internet to individuals is AD&D insurance, as covered in chapter 2. These policies are generally quite inexpensive because they seldom pay a benefit—relatively few people lose limbs or die in accidents. Again, these plans are poor substitutes for a health care plan, disability income insurance, and life insurance.

WHICH PLAN?

Determining which plan is best for an individual is not particularly easy. It will depend on how much he or she can afford and the type of medical expenses that are expected.

NEED TO KNOW: MEDICARE ADVANTAGE – FORMERLY MEDICARE+CHOICE

The Taxpayer Relief Act of 1997 introduced Medicare+Choice plans (pronounced "Medicare plus choice"). In 2003 the name of this program was changed to Medicare Advantage, effective in 2004. This was an effort to provide more choices to those covered by Medicare. Until passage of this law, those who were eligible for Medicare could choose only from the regular Medicare program with its deductibles and coinsurance payments, with or without a Medicare supplement (Medigap), or they could opt for a Medicare HMO. With the issuance of regulations, recipients may now choose from:

- Original Medicare program (with or without a Medigap Policy)
- Medicare Managed Care Plans
- Medicare Preferred Provider Organization Plans
- Medicare Private Fee-for-Service Plans

The details of these varied options are beyond the scope of this text. Two excellent sources of information on Medicare are All About Medicare and Social Security Manual, published annually by The National Underwriter Company as well as www.medicare.gov.

For a retired individual or couple over age 65, Medicare is the starting place, though all of the Medigap options need to be considered. If they do not travel or want a very comprehensive plan, an HMO might be best. If travel is a big part of their lives, a supplement that covers them while traveling is a valuable option.

Younger, single clients will want to protect against catastrophic losses, but might figure that physicals and minor emergencies may be covered out of pocket, especially if they can keep their premiums down. For them a major medical plan with a high deductible ($1,500 to $3,000 per year) is probably best. A couple with small children, however, will have to decide (based on the health of the children and family history) whether a major medical plan with a lower premium but higher coinsurance payments (and deductible) will ultimately cost less than a managed care plan with a higher premium and lower co-payments.

There are other factors to consider as well: If a person believes in chiropractic care, be sure that it is covered under the plan. If a female client does not plan to become pregnant, do not be concerned about whether maternity is covered. A client in excellent health probably should not worry about prescription benefits.

Finally, to some extent the choice will be limited to those plans available in your state and area and their cost. Investigating the available plans and discussing the pros and cons of each, with the individual's health history in mind, is the best way to determine the most advantageous plan.

Leaving Group Coverage

Sometimes people quit their jobs. Sometimes they get fired, laid off, downsized, or otherwise informed that their employment is coming to an end. In any case, since most people have health care coverage through their employers, it is important to understand what options are available while transitioning to individual coverage. Two federal laws come into play: the Consolidated Omnibus Budget Reconciliation Act (COBRA) of 1985 and the Health Insurance Portability and Accountability Act (HIPAA) of 1996.

COBRA permits an individual to continue his or her group health care plan for a period of 18 to 36 months, depending on which one of several so-called "triggering events" applies. However, COBRA is only transitional coverage until the individual is covered under a different group policy or purchases an individual policy. COBRA will not apply if the company goes out of business.

HIPAA, as its name implies, makes health care portable, in a sense. When an individual has been covered under a health care plan and has met any waiting period or preexisting conditions clause, he or she cannot be required to complete another preexisting conditions clause as long as new insurance is purchased or put in place within 62 days of coverage under a prior plan.

These two laws will be discussed in more detail later in this text.

NEED TO KNOW: INSURANCE FOR CHILDREN

Every state has been charged with providing access to health insurance for otherwise uninsured children. The rules in each state are a little different, but such insurance is generally available for those who cannot afford coverage for the whole family. Over the past few years, some states have had such financial troubles that they have limited the number of children who are actually covered.

NEED TO KNOW: WHEN A CLIENT IS UNINSURABLE

Sometimes a planner will run across a client who has no health insurance and is uninsurable. This does not necessarily mean the individual is at death's door: He or she may merely have an unpredictable condition, such as muscular dystrophy.

When a client is uninsurable, there are usually alternatives to pursue. The best option is to find employment where health insurance is one of the benefits. If that is not possible, many states have health insurance for the uninsurable. In some cases, the state mandates that any insurer that sells health care plans in the state must accept all applicants for a particular plan.

Typically the individual must apply for an individual policy and show the state that he or she was turned down by private companies. These plans are usually comprehensive major medical plans and normally cost a bit more than commercially available plans.

In Depth: Calculating Major Medical Benefits

Planning for possible medical expenses under a major medical plan requires calculating the level of benefit to be paid. While the specifics will vary from plan to plan, we will consider two examples here, one example involving only an individual and the second a family.

Bob Smith is covered by a major medical insurance plan with a $500 deductible and co-insurance of 80/20 of the $5,000 beyond his deductible. His plan limits chiropractic care to 50% of up to $80 per treatment.

In the past year, Bob has had the flu, injured his shoulder, and had several visits to the chiropractor for back treatment. Here are his bills over the past year and how they were handled.

(continued on next page)

(continued from previous page)

Date	Reason	Charge	To Deductible	Bob Pays	Insurance Pays
1/18	Flu	$56	$56	$56	0
3/27	Shoulder	$180	$180	$180	0
4/06	MRI	$985	$264	$408.20	$576.80
4/08	Physical Therapy	$88	0	$17.60	$70.40
4/15	Chiropractor	$125	0	$85.00	$40.00
4/22	Chiropractor	$125	0	$85.00	$40.00
11/14	Dermatologist	$90	0	$18	$72.00
TOTALS		$1649.00	$500	$849.80	$799.20

The first $500 of expenses was applied to the deductible. Bob had to pay all of those expenses out of pocket. $264 of the $985 for the MRI was applied to the deductible, so the amount subject to the coinsurance is $721. Bob pays the $264 plus 20 percent of the $721. The insurance company pays 80 percent of the $721. Bob's plan places no limitations on physical therapy, so it is covered 80 percent by the insurance company and 20 percent by Bob. The chiropractic care is only covered at 50 percent of the first $80 per visit. So the insurance company will pay only $40 for each visit. Bob pays the other 50 percent of the $80 and all of any charge in excess of that amount, and the dermatologist fee is covered 80/20.

The second example introduces the family deductible. There are two methods of defining a family deductible: One sets the deductible at a multiple (such as two or three) of the individual deductible; the second requires two or three family members to satisfy their individual deductibles in order for the family deductible to be met.

The Stone family has a plan with a family deductible that is "three individual deductibles" of $200. The Juarez family has a deductible that is "three times the individual deductible" of $200. There are five members in each family, each with the same medical expenses through the last year for purposes of illustration.

Family Member	Amount of Claim/Date	Stone Family (Three Individual Deductibles) Cumulative Deductible	Juarez Family (Three times the individual deductible) Cumulative Deductible
Mother	$150 January	1 member with partial deductible	$150
Father	$175 February	2 members with partial deductible	$325
Child 1	$175 April	3 members with partial deductibles	$500
Child 2	$185 July	4 members with partial deductibles	$600 family meets deductible. $85 of bill is applied to coinsurance
Child 3	$100 September	5 members with partial deductibles	All family bills now applied to coinsurance

No one in the Stone family has yet met the individual deductible, and not until three individuals incur additional covered expenses will the family deductible be met. However, once any individual in the Stone family meets his or her individual deductible, future covered expenses for that individual within the same calendar year will be applied to the coinsurance percentage or be paid in full (depending on the cumulative amount). It is also important to remember that the date of treatment is the date that determines how a specific claim will be paid. The family cannot wait until three people have enough bills to cover their deductibles and then submit them all so that they too will be subject to the coinsurance only.

The Juarez family, on the other hand, has met the family deductible even though none of them have yet met their individual deductible. If one of them had bills that were in excess of $200, only the first $200 would apply toward the family deductible. The rest would then be applied to the coinsurance amount.

TAXATION OF HEALTH PLANS

When discussing the taxation of health care plans, there are three issues to be considered:

- Taxation of health insurance premiums
- Taxation of payments made for health care expenses
- Taxation of benefits paid or reimbursed

Premiums on health care plans are deductible with certain restrictions. Generally, the premiums are deductible if the insured itemizes deductions on his or her tax return. Premiums are deductible on IRS Form 1040 Schedule A to the extent that total medical expenses including the insurance premiums exceed 7.5 percent of adjusted gross income. Beginning in the year 2003, self-employed individuals who do not have a subsidized health insurance plan may deduct all of their premiums in arriving at adjusted gross income on the front of the IRS form 1040 without the 7.5 percent requirement. Premiums paid by an employer are deductible by the employer as an ordinary and necessary business expense and are not taxable to the employee.

Payments made by an individual for health care, even for care that is not covered under a health care plan, are deductible on Schedule A of his or her Form 1040, but only to the extent that these expenses are not reimbursed and then only if exceeding the 7.5 percent floor. The types of expenses that are deductible include remodeling a home if it was required because of a medical condition, massage therapy if a physician recommends it as part of treatment, installation of an exercise-designed swimming pool needed for continuous physical therapy, or an elevator in a multistory home if a physician states that the insured is not to climb stairs.

If an individual takes a deduction in one year for unreimbursed medical expenses and is reimbursed the next year, he or she must then report the reimbursement as income.

Any benefit payments made by the insurance company that pay for or reimburse an insured for medical care are not reportable as income. If payments are made that exceed the cost of the health care, that amount will be considered ordinary income and is taxable.

Health Care Plan Needs Analysis

Unlike life insurance needs analysis, the analysis of a client's needs in the health care area is far more complex, and any advice can be considered inappropriate in a given set of circumstances. Simply stated, the conservative planner will always recommend a comprehensive health care plan. While this protects the client from potentially devastating health care costs, such comprehensive coverage usually means a fairly high monthly payment.

The first issue to review is whether the client has a group plan available. While it is clear there are exceptions, the vast majority of group plans provide a greater level of benefits at a lower monthly cost to the insured than individual plans. As discussed above, the last couple of years have seen significant changes in the design of health care plans. Some group plans have dropped prescription benefits altogether, and others have eliminated many previously covered services. To some extent, as mentioned above, there is some movement back to the concept of health insurance rather than comprehensive health care plans. While HSAs may have lower premiums, the potential cost of deductibles and other out of pocket costs may substantially exceed those of a group plan with a higher premium.

The client's particular circumstances also affect choices. A single male with no adverse medical history will generally believe that he does not need to spend anything on health care plan premiums. A young single female will most often recognize the need to have health care coverage. However if she must pay the full premium, she may consider that fee too high relative to the few costs she might expect to have in a given year. Not wanting health care coverage or not wanting to pay for health care coverage comes, in part, from the belief that health care plans are supposed to pay for all medical costs, rather than, as health insurance, covering only the unexpected claims. If a person perceives a plan as being there to cover an annual exam, a visit for a cold and other minor things and he or she has not used any of those services for a couple of years, then they question why they would want to pay for it anyway. If they recognize that at any time they may face a $10,000 or $50,000 pile of medical bills, then a health care plan makes more sense. So the second consideration is to determine how much in the way of medical expenses the client can handle without a plan.

A person with $10,000 of liquidity may feel they can handle any medical expenses up to $10,000. That is a good place to start a discussion. A health care plan with a $5,000 or $10,000 deductible will cost substantially less than a plan with a $500 deductible. For these people, the health savings accounts discussed above may make a great deal of sense.

If a person has a chronic condition that requires periodic doctor visits and regular prescriptions, the picture changes. A chronic condition may be as simple as allergies, mild asthma, nondisabling arthritis, lower back pain, high cholesterol, high triglycerides, or high blood pressure. All of these, with reasonable treatment, can permit individuals to lead normal lives. However, they are usually taking prescriptions which can cost hundreds of dollars a month, with or without a prescription plan, and require one or two physician visits a year. This can mean thousands of dollars a year in expenses for fairly routine health maintenance. For this person, a more comprehensive plan with lower co-pays and/or deductibles may make more sense.

Next are families. A young couple that is incapable of having children and that has no plans for adoption is not concerned about maternity benefits or benefits for children. However, if they are merely "taking precautions" to prevent pregnancy, anything other than complete abstinence is not guaranteed to avoid it. Normal prenatal care and childbirth costs thousands of dollars. Complications can add thousands more. For people who do not have access to a group plan, maternity coverage will be either very expensive or not available. In the past, maternity costs were generally not covered unless there were complications, since pregnancy is usually elective. This lack of coverage makes sense given the concept of insurance. State and federal mandates have changed that for group health care plans, and so people expect it to be covered.

Once children are on the scene, the picture changes again. In many cities, a child may not attend school until his or her parents can prove the child has had certain immunizations and often a required physical as well. Prior to adolescence, male children seem to be genetically required to do something that necessitates sutures. One or more visits to the emergency room should not be ruled out. When a family has children it is time to look at prior expenses. Do the children stay very healthy all year? Do they tend to get various illnesses in different seasons? Do they have allergies? Do they play contact sports like soccer, hockey, or football?

When there is more than one choice of plan through an employer, the planner should determine if the premium savings will be more than offset by higher co-pays and/or deductibles with a lower cost plan, or, based on historical expenses, if the family will still come out ahead with a lower premium, lower benefit plan? Another key factor is whether the family's providers are included in the plan. Economics aside, the first question people ask when presented with a new or different plan is whether "their" doctor is included. Do not believe for a moment that most people will choose a slightly more economical plan over being able to stay with their physician. This consideration is usually most important when it comes to pediatricians and OB/GYNs.

One of the greatest factors in obtaining individual health care coverage is finding a plan that is available and within the budget of the client. Because of the inclination of individual plans to lean toward adverse selection, there are limits as to what plans are available for individuals. For those who are not coming off group plans, the availability of individual coverage is often controlled by state rules. In some states, if you are turned down for individual coverage, you may be eligible for a state-sponsored plan. In some of those states, once you have been on that state-sponsored plan for a year, you may obtain an individual policy with no preexisting conditions exclusions. In other states, you are guaranteed the right to buy a comprehensive health care plan, regardless of prior coverage–typically with some preexisting condition limitations.

This is a constantly changing market, and it is advised that working with an insurance agent or planner who specializes in the individual health care plan market is the best option for providing competent advice. Since each state has its own rules, and those rules are subject to change, it is not reasonable to put a summary of state rules here. A great deal of information about each state's rules is available on the Web. The first place to look would be the website for the State's insurance commissioner.

CAVEAT

Giving advice in the area of health care coverage may be the subject of misunderstandings between a planner and a client. Be careful and read each contract carefully. When a client has questions, help him or her reference the answers in the actual contract. It is important for a client to understand that his or her legal relationship is with the insurer under the terms of the contract and that the planner has no authority either to interpret the contract on the insurer's behalf or to modify its terms. A planner needs to ensure that this caveat is made clear to the client so that he or she does not think that the planner can guarantee how the plan will pay or, indeed, whether a specific benefit is provided at all. With many plans, when a participant calls customer service, even the customer service representative will not guarantee that the information given is correct. Participants are generally told that only the claims department may make an accurate determination, and the folks there are not available.

IMPORTANT CONCEPTS

Accidental death & dismemberment (AD&D) policy

Adverse selection

Any willing provider

Breakpoint

Capitation

Coinsurance

Co-pay

Cost containment

Covered expenses

Covered person

Deductible

Dread disease policy

Exclusions

Formulary

Gatekeeper

Health Savings Accounts (HSAs)

HMO

Hospital indemnity policy

Indemnity

Insured

Limitations

Major medical insurance

Managed care

Medicaid

Medical savings accounts (MSAs)

Medicare

Medicare Advantage

Medicare Parts A, B, C, & D

Medicare Prescription Drug Card

Medicare Prescription Drug Plan

Medicare supplement

Medigap policy

POS

PPO

Pre-certification

Pre-existing condition

Primary care physician (PCP)

Provider

Stop-loss limit

Temporary insurance

Usual, customary, and reasonable (UCR)

QUESTIONS FOR REVIEW

1. What are the health exposures facing individuals that can be addressed with a health care plan?

2. Why is adverse selection more likely with individual health care plans than with group health care plans?

3. What is the difference between coinsurance and co-pays?

4. Why is the term "covered expenses" important, relative to health care plans?

5. Describe the two methods of defining a family deductible and explain when each method might be the best choice.

6. Why do health care plans have exclusions?

7. How might a major medical plan for an individual be different from a plan from the same company that is provided through an employer group?

8. Describe the primary differences between the typical HMO, PPO, and POS plans.

9. Comment on the pros and or cons of hospital indemnity, dread disease, and AD&D plans.

10. Describe the taxation of health care expenses and plan premiums.

11. Describe the various coverages of Medigap policies and how they link to Medicare benefits.

12. Describe the differences between MSAs and HSAs.

SUGGESTIONS FOR ADDITIONAL READING

2005 Mercer Guide to Social Security and Medicare, J. Robert Treanor, et al.

Fundamentals of Risk and Insurance, 9th ed., Emmett J. Vaughan and Therese M. Vaughan, Wiley, 2003.

Introduction to Risk Management and Insurance, 8th ed., Mark Dorfman, Prentice Hall, 2004.

Life and Health Insurance, 13th ed., Kenneth Black Jr. and Harold Skipper Jr, Prentice Hall, 2000.

Principles of Risk Management and Insurance, 9th ed., George E. Rejda, Addison Wesley, 2004.

Risk Management & Insurance, 12th edition., James S. Trieschman, South-Western College Publishing, 2004.

Social Security Manual 2005, Joseph F. Stenken, ed., The National Underwriter Company, 2005.

Social Security and Medicare Answer Book, 2nd edition, David A. Pratt and Sean K. Hornbeck; Supplemented 9/2004

Tax Facts on Insurance & Employee Benefits 2005, National Underwriter.

Individual Health Care Plans: Disability Income Insurance

• • •

Have you ever missed school, work, or a social activity because you were too ill to get out of bed? That day you were totally disabled. Almost all adults have been totally disabled at one or more points in their life. Disability can happen to you and likely has.

For many, disability evokes images of permanent confinement to a bed or wheelchair—a kind of living death. Yet disabilities come in many forms. Temporary conditions may be just as disabling as permanent disabilities. One person's manageable setback may prove disastrous for another.

This chapter focuses on individual disability income insurance policies. Group disability income insurance will be covered later in the text.

When you complete this chapter you will be able to:

- Discuss exposures to disability and differentiate among the various policy definitions
- Identify, describe, and appropriately apply various terms,provisions, and riders used with disability income insurance policies
- Name the provisions that ensure a disability income policy's durability
- Determine the appropriate disability income coverage for an individual given a specific client situation
- Explain some of the underwriting issues specific to disability income insurance

DISABILITY INCOME INSURANCE: THE BASICS

Disabilities can be temporary or permanent, total or partial. For insurance purposes, they can even be presumptive. Any serious disability, permanent or temporary, prevents or reduces the individual's ability to make a living and contribute to his or her household (which may mean providing for it financially or rendering services that would otherwise have to be purchased).

Additionally, time, money, and energy may be spent to care for or assist the disabled individual. More homes are foreclosed on because of disability than premature death. Retraining or rehabilitation may not always be possible, depending on the nature of the disability. Some disabilities will require substantial structural changes to the individual's home—or may require relocation—while others require virtually no changes. Disability can also affect a business when a valuable employee can no longer work or is severely limited in the amount or type of work he or she can do.

Disability income (DI) insurance can mitigate the most devastating loss: the loss of earning power. If a car, home, or another item of personal property is destroyed, it can be replaced. If substantial health care expenses arise, they can eventually be paid. However, if an individual loses the ability to earn a living, his or her financial independence and property are at risk.

NEED TO KNOW: FACTS ABOUT DISABILITY

According to "Commissioner's Individual Disability Table A":

- One in three employees will become disabled for 90 days or more before age 65.

- One in seven employees will be disabled for five years or more before retirement.

- At age 32, a disability of three months or longer before age 65 is six times more likely than death.

According to a 1998 report from the Department of Housing and Urban Development:

- One out of 18 mortgages is not paid due to a disability of the mortgage holder.

- Almost 60 percent of disability claims are denied by the Social Security Administration.

Most disability income insurance is obtained through an employer; however, many people obtain individual policies directly from an insurance company. Many professional associations also offer disability income insurance policies that are either fully underwritten individual policies or association policies.

Individual policies, written for amounts between 60 to 70 percent of the insured's gross income, are issued as a fixed amount of monthly benefits. The amount is limited so that the insured receives slightly less than his or her net income while working—this helps alleviate the moral hazard that might result if the insured received 100 percent.

Benefit periods range from two years until age 65 and, in certain policies, until the end of life. The occupation of the insured is the primary factor in determining the available duration of coverage, the standard premium, and the definitions of disability available.

Financial planning is generally based on income and asset protection and asset accumulation; thus one of the most important forms of voluntarily owned insurance a client can have—from a financial planner's perspective—is disability income insurance. This coverage protects a client from a loss of income. If a client's income stops before adequate assets have been accumulated, whatever planning has taken place will be seriously affected.

Nevertheless, DI insurance is one of the most difficult forms of insurance to obtain. When discussing disability income needs with a client, it is wise to point out that many people who apply for individual disability income insurance do not get the exact policy for which they apply.

Underwriting is very strict. For this reason, some planners and insurance agents do not want to discuss DI with clients for fear they cannot meet their expectations. However, failure to discuss disability income insurance with a client could result in serious professional liability.

Definitions of Disability

The most important part of any DI insurance policy is the language used to define disability. The variations in this single section cover a very broad range: Some definitions are available only to certain individuals while others are available to virtually everyone.

Social Security Definition

The most draconian of definitions for disability comes from the Social Security Administration's (SSA) disability income program: "The inability to engage in any substantial gainful activity by reason of any medically determinable physical or mental impairment which can be expected to result in death or which has lasted or can be expected to last for a continuous period of not less than 12 months." In other words, a physician must attest that not only is the person unable to do the job he or she held when the disabling condition began, but that he or she cannot, considering age, education, and work experience, do any other substantial work that exists in the national economy, regardless of whether such work exists in the individual's geographic location, whether a job vacancy exists, or whether an employer is willing to hire him or her. Under this definition, it is very difficult for anyone to qualify for disability benefits, which is the primary reason clients should not rely on Social Security for disability income protection.

Any Occupation Definition

Within the private insurance industry, the strictest definition in use is any occupation or "any occ," requiring the insured to be "unable to perform the duties pertaining to any gainful occupation" to be considered totally disabled. This definition is most often limited to policies for blue-collar workers. It provides benefits only for insureds who are unable to work in any occupation, despite their qualifications or salary needs, which can seem quite harsh: For example, a construction worker is injured and cannot continue construction work. Assume this worker is physically able to work in another field where the income is one-third or less of his or her prior income. Under this definition, the insurance company does not consider the individual to be disabled, and, accordingly, no benefits will be paid. If the individual applies for 50 jobs and cannot find one, the policy still does not pay because he or she is capable of working, even if unable to find a job.

Modified Any Occupation Definition

The modified any occupation definition is slightly less restrictive. It defines disability as the individual's inability to engage in any occupation for which he or she is reasonably fitted by education, training, experience, and, with some policies, prior economic status. This is a far more generous definition. Individuals in certain occupational classifications that do not qualify for the own occupation definition of disability (discussed below) because of the issuing insurance company's underwriting standards often receive the modified any occupation definition of disability. Using the prior example, if the construction worker was only able to do work that would reduce his or her income by two-thirds or more, benefits would be paid.

Own Occupation Definition

The most liberal definition of disability is referred to as the own occupation definition, or "own occ." This states that the insured is considered totally disabled if he or she is unable to engage in the principal duties of his or her own occupation (the occupation at the time of the disability). This definition is available only to individuals in select occupational classifications.

Generally, the individuals eligible for this definition include professional/technical and managerial personnel who meet certain income and length of employment criteria. For some types of professionals, a few insurance companies have been willing not only to specify that the insured must be able to work in his or her own occupation, but also in his or her own specialty. The insurers issue a letter to this effect, known as a **specialty letter**, with the policy, modifying the policy's terms. However, specialty letters are becoming somewhat rare due to serious adverse selection. When a specialty letter is issued, the results are quite generous. For example, a surgeon would be disabled if he or she were unable to perform surgery even if he or she could train to be a radiologist. Even if his or her income increased, benefits would be paid.

Several companies have tightened the requirements for continuation of own occupation benefits. Typically, the individual must be under the care of a physician and not be gainfully employed. Additionally, a residual benefit allows the individual to take another job without completely eliminating benefits.

Extremely heavy underwriting losses within the disability income insurance industry have made the own occupation definition less common in recent years. More and more professionals who qualify for own occupation disability benefits are less inclined to return to work than in the past. In the early 1980s, it was uncommon for an insurance company to make long-term payments to any claimant under the own occ definition of a policy. Today those claims are quite common. Because of this, few companies will issue policies with this definition. However, there are still thousands of them in force.

Split Definition

Seeking a happy medium, insurance companies have expanded the use of split definition policies, a combination of the own occupation and modified any occupation definitions.

Typically found in group disability income policies, this is becoming more common in individual contracts. Under split-definition policies, disability is defined as the liberal own occupation for a limited time (such as for the first two to five years following the onset of disability) after which the stricter modified any occupation definition takes effect for the duration of the maximum benefit period.

The split definition by its design encourages disabled individuals to become productive. If they become disabled to the extent that they cannot work in their field, then they receive benefits for two to five years. During those years, they can learn new skills and locate acceptable employment so they will be able to earn a living when the own occupation definition ends. If they are capable of working at the end of the own occ period, but choose not to, benefits will generally cease. In contrast, many older own occupation policies allowed capable individuals to choose not to work in a different field and still collect full benefits.

Loss of Income Definition

The own occupation definition has been criticized because situations arise where benefits are payable even though no loss has occurred. For example, the insured may be able to change occupations after the onset of a disability and receive an equal or greater income. This violates the principle of indemnity; thus it creates potential for abuse. While this was practically unheard of 30 years ago, it is not uncommon now.

To address this costly problem, a few insurers (and currently, only a few) have used the loss of income definition to give insureds a less expensive option that still addresses the real concern: losing one's income. This definition of disability is based on the percentage of income loss due to an illness or injury. The insurer compares post-disability income to the pre-disability income; the duties, time on the job, and activities in which the insured is able to engage are no longer significant factors.

If, as a result of injury or sickness, the insured suffers a loss of income, benefits based on that loss are payable regardless of whether the insured returns to work in the same or a related occupation. This definition is obviously not as desirable to those who want to double their income, but it covers the real financial risk at a generally lower premium than the own occupation definition and eliminates simply insuring one's professional ego (own occ has been called "ego insurance"). The loss of income definition is increasing in popularity among insurance companies because it specifically addresses the risk and reduces the moral hazard.

Under the loss of income definition, disability is not defined; therefore one must identify how loss is defined in a particular policy, specifically noting how the time period of the loss of income is defined. It may be based on the date on which the insured is no longer earning an income due to illness or injury (the accrual method) or the date on which any received income drops (the cash method). The latter could be a problem for an insured with substantial receivables as it may delay the beginning of the elimination period by a month or more. For other clients, the accrual method could also be a problem: Benefits end as soon as the insured is able to earn his or her prior income, but there is often a delay between when a person returns to work and when the first paycheck or other income is actually received. Some policies give the insured a choice between the two.

A clear grasp of the loss of income definition and the residual disability benefits (discussed later) is necessary to understand how average earnings are defined—after all, this determines the amount of base income used to identify the percentage reduction in income. Each company has its own method of calculating base income: Some average the two years immediately prior to the onset of the disability; others average the two highest income years among the last five years or use some other formula. Better policies automatically adjust the identified average earnings by the consumer price index or some other factor so that inflation does not erode the buying power of the benefits received.

Policies that use the loss of income definition provide benefits under circumstances when no other policy will: If an insured person faces a progressive disease, such as multiple sclerosis or muscular dystrophy, he or she will be eligible for benefits much sooner than under any other basic policy definition. As the disease (or other disability) progresses, the individual's ability to work decreases, gradually eroding earned income; benefits usually start after the income drops by at least 20 percent. With most other definitions, benefits would not start until the insured could not work at all or until income dropped by at least 80 percent.

There are some circumstances where this definition has little to no value. If the insured is a member of a partnership and entitled to a specific portion of the partnership income, a disability may not reduce his or her income at all or not enough to trigger benefits. In this situation no benefits would be paid.

Someone with this type of business arrangement should seek a policy with a more appropriate definition of disability.

Basic Terms

Following are some basic terms and concepts with special significance to DI.

Earned Income

The amount of disability income insurance available to an individual is based on earned income. Many people assume that their W-2 reflects their earned income. Yet the W-2 lists more than one income: taxable and nontaxable income, among others, as well as the amounts paid by an employer for retirement plans, health insurance, and other benefits. Bonuses and commissions may vary from year to year. Some people, even those with full-time jobs, may bring in additional income through self-employment or freelance work.

If a person becomes incapable of working, all other forms of income may stop as well. For individual insurance policies, all other earned income may be considered insurable income. (Group disability insurance generally covers only the base income paid by that one employer, excluding commissions and bonuses.) Companies vary in what they accept as insurable income, so it is worthwhile to find out the details.

Elimination Period

Sometimes called a waiting period, the elimination period of a disability income insurance policy is essentially a period of risk retention. Its name is derived from the fact that it eliminates claims of a short duration. It is the period of time after the individual meets the definition of disability but before benefits are payable, during which the insured will have to cover his or her own expenses—in effect, the deductible for a disability income policy.

While elimination periods as low as 30 days are often available, many companies are moving to a minimum of 60 or 90 days, and some elimination periods can run as long as 180 or 365 days. Longer elimination periods naturally reduce policy premiums, and the reduction in premiums should be balanced against the length of time a client can manage without income.

Elimination periods also mean that in addition to having a DI policy in force, a client needs to create an emergency fund. Also remember that the benefits do not begin until after the elimination period is over and are paid in arrears. So the first check will not arrive until at least 30 days after the elimination period ends. If there is a 90-day elimination period, the first check, which generally covers disability income for day 91 through day 120, will not come until at least 120 days after the disability begins. Some policies may waive the elimination period for accidental injuries or presumptive disabilities (described below).

Maximum Benefits

This term is used rather loosely. It may apply to the maximum monthly payment or the maximum benefit period.

Maximum Benefit Period

The maximum number of months or years that a policy will pay a benefit is the maximum benefit period. Typically, insureds with higher classifications and lower risk to the insurance company can obtain longer benefit periods. Many professionals may obtain benefit periods lasting until age 65, and in certain contracts, for life. Most individuals in blue-collar and some white-collar occupations are limited to a five-year or shorter benefit period. Obviously, if the benefit period is longer, the premium is higher.

The cause of the disability may affect the length of the benefit period. A few contracts provide lifetime benefits if a disability is caused by an accident while providing much shorter benefits if caused by an illness.

Maximum Monthly Benefit Payment

How much will the insured receive if he or she meets the definition of disability? The maximum monthly benefit, stated in the contract on the declarations page, answers this question. All insurance companies have financial underwriting guidelines (a company-specific table that limits the amount of disability income insurance that may be issued, based on the income of the applicant). Most guidelines are quite similar. The amount of insurance available to an individual is dictated by the desire to reduce moral hazard. However, the amount of benefit various insurers will issue sometimes varies enough to be an important factor in policy selection. Especially when clients have very high incomes, the maximum amount of disability income insurance a company is willing to offer the insured—even where the amount is justified by income—varies substantially by carrier.

The general approach is to permit individuals to receive slightly less than their net after-tax income from working if they become disabled, providing a financial incentive to return to work. Many clients, especially those successfully working with a financial planner, may have sources of unearned income as well as substantial assets. Applications for DI include questions about unearned income and net worth. The intent is to further limit available benefits if the insured would likely remain financially comfortable while unable to work. This is where the experience of an agent can come into play.

Assume Jack Cash receives $35,000 each year in unearned income from his ownership and management of real estate investments. If no further explanation is added to the application, Jack would have his potential benefit level reduced or possibly eliminated. However, an experienced agent would question the client and add that if Jack did not actively manage the property himself, he would have to pay the prevailing rate in the area for property management; thus his earnings would drop to $5,000 per year. Effectively, $30,000 of his investment earnings on the property is earned income. For a number of reasons, he chooses to list it as investment income; however, an underwriter who knows all the facts, when properly presented by the agent, might permit Jack to have substantially higher monthly benefits. There is no intent here to deceive the underwriter; deception would hurt the underwriting process and may result in a declination of coverage. It is important, however, that the underwriter know all pertinent facts while underwriting the application.

When an individually owned DI insurance policy is purchased, the contract states the maximum monthly benefit on the benefits page (declarations page). The benefit payable under the policy can never exceed this amount unless the policy is later modified with the company's permission or through a rider. Additionally, some provisions may be included that can reduce the benefit payable below the amount on the declarations page of the contract. Two such provisions will be discussed below: relation to earnings and coordination of benefits.

The following table gives an example of the level of basic disability income benefits that are available at various income levels from a major insurance company.

Table 7.1

Annual Earned Income	Basic Monthly Indemnity Benefit
$24,000	$700
$30,000	$1,000
$40,000	$1,350
$50,000	$1,900
$60,000	$2,350
$80,000	$3,100
$100,000	$3,800
$150,000	$5,450

From a client's point of view it is interesting that some people have the perception that insurance companies and agents want to sell them more insurance than they need. With disability income insurance, they often find that they are not allowed to purchase as much as they want.

Occupational Class

One of the key determinants in the type of coverage that is available, the amount of coverage available, and the length of the maximum benefit period is the occupational class of the applicant. Each occupation has a relative risk associated with it in addition to the risk of disability because of disease that affects the population as a whole. Additionally, through experience, the insurance companies have recognized that the propensity to file claims is different in various occupations. These differences in claim experience lead to a series of occupational classes. There is no consistent method of naming the classes, and companies disagree about which occupations belong in each class. Classes may be numerically designated, such as 1, 2, 3. They can be alphabetically designated, such as A, B, C. And they may use a combination, such as 1A, 1B, 2A. The goal of the insurers is not to deny legitimate claims, but to keep premiums affordable for the majority of qualified applicants. A high incidence of long-lasting claims results in high premiums.

From the company's perspective, the highest classification is the lowest risk. With one company it may be a Class 1, Class A, Class 1A, or Class 4A. The classifications are meaningless without knowledge of how the company sets up its classes. The highest classification is typically reserved for high-income earners who have little exposure to causes of disability. These folks generally work in a single building in their own offices, and a disability that was severe enough to cause them to not be able to work would be quite serious. At the other end are most often blue-collar workers, people who work with their hands and those who require substantial mobility. They may be exposed to equipment and work sites that are full of potentially disabling risks. The loss of a few fingers or a hand might make them totally disabled from their present line of work.

Some occupations are uninsurable. Self-employed individuals who work out of their home, will find it difficult, if not impossible, to obtain DI insurance when most of the work is done in their home. Massage therapists who do not work in a spa or in another brick-and-mortar business are generally not offered DI insurance. There are many occupations that do not have access to this coverage or who will be offered only minimal benefits with a very strict definition of disability.

The higher the classification, the lower the risk and the lower the cost per $100 of monthly benefits for a specified benefit period. Further, the lower the risk, the more likely it is that the insurer will permit more generous definitions of disability and longer benefit periods. These higher income groups are traditionally more likely to want to return to work as well, further justifying lower premiums and longer benefit periods.

Preexisting Conditions

The reason an insurance company includes a preexisting conditions clause in a DI insurance policy is to protect itself and other insureds from adverse selection. While preexisting conditions clauses in health care plans are fairly consistent, there are substantial differences in their wording in DI insurance contracts.

Some companies use a very favorable definition: Any condition for which the applicant saw a physician, or reasonably should have seen a physician, is considered a preexisting condition. Some older policies will even include terminology that would require the condition to have been specifically diagnosed.

If a problem existed but the applicant had not seen a physician and/or thought that symptoms of the condition were of no consequence, it is not a preexisting condition. Other companies may include language stating that any condition that manifested itself before the application was signed would be excluded as a preexisting condition. This means that if the insured noticed the previously mentioned symptom of the condition, even if he or she thought it was nothing about which to be concerned and had not seen a physician about it, the insurer will exclude it. It could mean that an undiagnosed symptom that had not caused any problems but was not "normal" would lead to an eventual finding of a preexisting condition. Finally, a more conservative company might include language stating that any condition that existed before the application was signed would be excluded. This would mean that if the insured had cancer, muscular dystrophy, or any other condition that had not progressed to a point where symptoms became observable but reasonably would have existed before the application was signed, those conditions would be excluded. This strict definition may seem unfair, but it is in the contract and may be the primary reason a given company has lower premiums or more generous underwriting than other companies.

Presumptive Disability

Many disability income policies include a presumptive disability provision. This provision typically states that the loss of use of two bodily members, the loss of sight in both eyes, or hearing in both ears will be presumed to be total disability, even if the insured continues to work for compensation (a few companies include loss of speech). With some policies, it is presumptive as long as the loss continues. Other policies are a bit stricter and require that the loss be both total and permanent. Occasionally, a severe definition will require that any loss of feet and/or hands must be by severance; others only require the loss of use of the appendages. Paralysis from the waist down is considered presumptive only under the latter definition. If the insured is presumptively disabled, some companies waive the elimination period and begin payment of benefits immediately.

Probation Period

Separate and distinct from the company's elimination period, the probation period is how long the individual policy must be in force before it covers the insured for perils and/or illnesses specified in the contract or not disclosed on the application. This provision is designed to protect the insurance company from covering certain preexisting conditions and other adverse selection situations while still providing the insured with coverage for other potential disabilities. If an insured discloses preexisting conditions on the insurance application and the company does not list or exclude them in the policy, they are usually fully covered. If any preexisting conditions are not disclosed, they are not covered during the probation period and may result in cancellation of the policy, depending on the seriousness of the omission. The probation period typically lasts two years.

It is important to review the contract. It is possible that the contract may state that any condition disclosed in the application will be subject to the probation period.

Riders and Provisions

Since there is no consistency within the industry on what is standard in a contract and what should be attached as a rider, these are listed together.

Change of Occupation

This is a relatively uncommon provision in DI insurance policies. When included, change of occupation permits the insurer to reduce the benefit payable, shorten the benefit period, and/or increase the premium if the insured changes to a higher-risk occupation. The benefit level is usually reduced to the amount the premium paid would have purchased at the higher-risk employment classification. If the insured changes to a lower-risk occupation, the premium is reduced, but the benefit remains the same.

Coordination of Benefits

This provision, common in group disability policies and sometimes included in individual policies, may reduce benefits below the amount shown in the declarations page. The purpose of the clause is to reduce the benefits otherwise payable by any amounts received under Social Security, workers compensation, or other sources of indemnity related to the insured's employment. An individual policy will seldom reduce benefits based on any other individual disability income policy benefits received. This could happen during **post-claim underwriting**, which is when a policy is issued with broad exclusions and little up-front underwriting. Since there is a wide range of possibilities, the planner should read each contract for details.

Many individual policies have a social insurance provision or rider (discussed later) that replaces this provision.

Cost of Living

The advantage of group long-term disability income insurance is that it is generally tied to the employee's earnings. Individually issued DI insurance policies have a specified monthly benefit, and as income changes, these policies do not automatically adjust. Cost-of-living riders generally take two approaches to adjusting benefits: One is before the onset of a disability, and the other is after the onset of a disability.

The most common cost-of-living rider increases the benefit paid after the insured starts collecting benefits. This buffers the loss of purchasing power over the course of a long-term disability.

The insurance contract must be consulted for the details since the approaches used with this form of rider vary greatly. However, one of the most common approaches is to increase the benefit level by the consumer price index (CPI) or a percentage specified in the policy—generally 5 to 7 percent. The rider usually limits the total monthly benefit by setting a maximum amount, most often two to five times the original monthly benefit. The cost-of-living rider is a fairly expensive addition to a disability income insurance policy.

The **front-end cost-of-living rider** is a variation of the cost-of-living rider combined with a guaranteed insurability option, often called the **additional insurance rider** (AIR). This rider automatically increases the policy benefits by 5 percent (or by a percentage determined by an index) each year while the insured is not disabled. Usually at the end of each four- or five-year period, the company does financial underwriting to determine if the insured is eligible to continue to have his or her benefits increase.

In most versions of this rider, if the insured does not accept every increase, or is denied an increase due to inadequate income, no further increases will be allowed. This rider usually has no premium associated with it; however, the policy premium increases each year as the benefit level increases.

A person who seeks the greatest level of protection from the potential loss of purchasing power during a disability should seek out a company offering both types of cost-of-living riders and apply for each of them.

Exclusions

In addition to preexisting conditions, there are a few other standard exclusions in disability income insurance contracts. Those that commonly show up are injuries or illnesses:

- Due to war or an act of war
- Due to pregnancy or childbirth (disability due to complications in pregnancy is covered)
- Due to the insured committing or attempting to commit a felony
- From a period when the insured was incarcerated
- Due to self-inflicted injuries, including those related to or caused by drinking alcoholic beverages and/or illicit use of drugs

A closely related provision that is often included suspends coverage while the insured is on active duty in the military. No premiums are paid for that period of time. When the insured is released from active duty, the policy may be immediately reinstated with no changes.

Facility of Payment Clause

Unlike life insurance, many disability income insurance policies do not have a named beneficiary. Some policies have some death benefits since it is entirely conceivable that an insured person may die with some payment still due. A death benefit may also exist through the inclusion of accidental death and dismemberment coverage in the contract. Additionally, other benefits may be payable following the insured's death.

The facility of payment clause permits the insurer to pay any available death benefit from the policy to any relative by blood or marriage of the insured or to any beneficiary whom the company has approved as entitled to receive the money. This provision usually limits the amount of payment a single individual may receive. It allows the insurer to find an authorized and legitimate payee for a small amount of death benefits.

Guaranteed Insurability

Particularly in a DI insurance policy, any version of this rider is important. DI insurance is one of the most difficult (and important) forms of personal insurance to obtain. Once individuals are approved through underwriting, this rider allows them to increase their coverage in the future, avoiding a potential headache.

The most common form of this rider guarantees the insured the opportunity to increase the benefit amount under the policy or purchase additional policies at specified option dates (time periods in the future), regardless of his or her physical or mental health, or occupation.

A usual requirement to obtain this rider is that the initial policy purchased by the insured must be at least 80 percent of the maximum amount that the insurance company would approve. Option dates are usually specified policy anniversaries with windows of 30 to 90 days on either side. The only limiting factor is financial underwriting. If the insured meets the financial underwriting requirements (i.e., has adequate income to qualify for the new total amount of benefit), he or she may purchase additional coverage. As with life insurance, this is called a purchase option. Whichever underwriting classification was used for the initial policy will normally be used for the additional coverage, even if the insured has changed occupations or has compromised health.

Another version of this rider is sometimes called an **additional insurance rider**. It is similar to an inflation or cost-of-living rider (discussed earlier).

Long-Term Care

One benefit, long-term care insurance, has recently received a great deal of attention after (at least) one major insurance company recognized an opportunity to help its insureds. The company added a new provision to its revised disability income insurance policy: The insured may convert to a long-term care policy without evidence of insurability. As long-term care insurance (covered in chapter 8) becomes more prevalent, this provision will likely become more common. The down side of the current version is that if the individual becomes disabled and lives beyond the disability income benefit period, needing long-term care, there are no additional benefits.

Misstatement of Age

As with life insurance contracts, this provision permits an adjustment in the amount of coverage when the insured has misstated his or her age on the application. Coverage is adjusted to provide the benefit that the premium paid would have purchased if the age had been correct on the application. This provision, in a disability income insurance policy, protects the policyowner when an error is made with respect to the insured's age. It provides an alternative to making the contract voidable. Thus, the clause protects both the insurer and the insured.

Nonoccupational Coverage

Policies excluding occupational disabilities are known as nonoccupational policies. Many insurance companies only sell policies to blue-collar workers that are nonoccupational. These contracts eliminate coverage for work-related injuries or illnesses, which are generally covered by workers compensation insurance, a state mandated coverage. Double payment would only encourage the moral hazards of faking disabilities or being less than honest about recovery. Long-term DI insurance policies written and issued for professionals and other white-collar insureds often provide benefits for both occupational and nonoccupational disabilities, which is reflected in the level of available benefits. For the higher classification applicants, the workers compensation benefits are typically a small percentage of their pre-disability income and are taken into consideration when policies are issued.

Partial Disability

This is one of two provisions included in policies that permit an insured who has qualified for benefits to be able to return to work at a reduced income and still get benefits. A partial disability benefit provision is often included to encourage a return to work. It promises to pay a reduced benefit if the insured can perform some but not all of the important daily duties of his or her occupation.

Alternatively, the disability may not limit what duties the individual can or cannot perform, but may prevent the insured from working a full day. The partial disability benefit is usually 50 percent of the total disability benefit and is usually paid for only a short time, typically a period of six months.

Relation of Earnings to Insurance

When this provision is included, it generally provides that, at the time disability occurs, if the total disability income provided by all policies exceeds the insured's earned income or average earned income for either of the preceding two years (whichever is greater), the income benefits under the policy will be reduced proportionately. The provision, also known as the **average earnings clause**, is designed to protect the insurer from the moral hazard that may exist if the disability benefits payable would exceed the normal income of the insured. Many insurers have been exposed to a moral hazard because some people prefer to receive insurance benefits rather than work. This provision may reduce benefits when an insured's earned income has dropped for reasons other than disability.

Here's an example: A real estate agent had an income in the range of $150,000 a year for over five years. She obtains a disability income insurance policy with a monthly benefit of $6,500 ($78,000/year) if she is disabled. Three years ago the real estate market in her city became depressed. Since a big company was closing its facilities, it was a buyer's market and prices were substantially lower than they had been. Although she was working twice as hard, her income dropped to an average of $60,000 over the three year timeframe. Recently she was injured and unable to work. She met the elimination period and applied for benefits. However, the insurer was not willing to pay her $18,000 a year more than she was earning before the onset of her disability. Using the relation of earnings to insurance clause, her benefit was reduced to $3,500 per month, and she received a substantial premium refund.

Rehabilitation

A fairly common provision, intended to help insureds return to work, is the rehabilitation provision. This extra benefit provides a win-win solution to a disability. While the insured is receiving benefits, either the insured or insurer may suggest that the insurance company help pay for a rehabilitation program. This includes training for a new job or any form of occupational therapy that will help the insured return to work. The insured and the company must mutually agree upon the rehabilitation plan. In most cases, until the extra training or therapy allows the insured to return to work, benefits received are not affected.

Residual Disability

Residual disability benefits are more generous than the partial benefits that follow a total disability claim. Although these benefits are usually paid after total disability, some policies pay benefits prior to total disability under certain circumstances (unique to each policy). These benefits, when paid following total disability, are also designed to allow the insured to return to work without losing all benefits. Rather than a specified percentage of the base policy benefits (as under a partial disability benefit), these benefits are usually paid based on the percentage of lost income. Further, there is often no time limit, other than the contractual benefit period, on the availability of reduced benefits. To keep the relative benefit at an appropriate level, the policies offering it adjust the base income. This means that if the individual's reduced income increases because of inflation, the base income for determining the percentage loss also increases. This prevents the benefits from stopping simply because the insured earns, due to inflation, as much as he or she was making before the onset of the disability.

Here is an example. If a $60,000 income is reduced to $40,000, there is a 33 percent reduction. The insured's residual monthly benefit would be 33 percent of the promised maximum benefit. Assume that the insured receives nominal salary increases each year, so that in the eighth year, she is earning $48,000, or 80 percent of her original income. Normally in this situation, her benefits would stop. However, if the base income of $60,000 were to increase at the inflation rate of, say, 2 percent per year, her eighth year income of $48,000 would only be 68.3 percent of the adjusted base earnings of $70,300 so she would still receive 31.7 percent of her disability income policy benefits.

Social Insurance

Part of the reason available benefits appear to be so low with individual disability income insurance policies is because an insured may qualify for some form of government disability income. This could take the form of Social Security disability income and/or a state provided benefit. If the insured receives these benefits in addition to individual disability income insurance benefits, the combined amount may result in the moral hazard of the insured receiving too much income to encourage him or her to seek rehabilitation.

In Table 7.1, the benefit levels range from about 33 percent to 44 percent of the earned income. While these numbers show what an insured might receive from a policy, it is clear that these benefits would be inadequate. However, if the individual earning $24,000 per year qualified for Social Security disability income, he or she might receive $950 per month from the government. With that amount added to the insurance policy benefit of $700, the total benefit would be $1,650. This is 83 percent of the pre-disability income. This level of income might make the insurance company a little uncomfortable, but not as uncomfortable as if the insured would receive 110 percent of his or her pre-disability income.

Table 7.2 shows the same company with the addition of a third column that shows the total benefit available when a social insurance rider is included.

Table 7.2

Annual Earned Income	Basic Monthly Indemnity Benefit	Total Monthly Indemnity Benefit
$24,000	$700	$1,500
$30,000	$1,000	$1,900
$40,000	$1,350	$2,350
$50,000	$1,900	$2,900
$60,000	$2,350	$3,350
$80,000	$3,100	$4,100
$100,000	$3,800	$4,800
$150,000	$5,450	$6,450

The common application of the rider is that if the insured receives social insurance or workers compensation benefits, the entire social insurance rider amount will be eliminated. Under this rider, the insured must apply for social insurance or workers compensation benefits. The rider will typically continue to pay for the duration of the maximum benefit period unless and until the insured is approved for benefits and receives them. Even if benefits are approved retroactively, few companies will ask the insured to return any benefits paid.

Some companies' social insurance riders are written in such a manner that the reduction in the rider is limited to the rider amount or the actual social insurance benefit received, whichever is lower. If the rider is for an amount that is greater than the benefits received and is reduced only by the amount of benefits received initially, rarely will it be reduced again if social insurance benefits increase while the individual is on claim. However, the amount of social insurance rider available is typically very close to the benefits that will eventually be received.

The primary purpose of social insurance riders is to provide an adequate level of protection to an insured without creating a moral hazard if he or she eventually receives Social Security disability benefits, state benefits, or workers compensation payments. The amount of coverage subject to reduction has a lower premium than the base policy benefit to reflect the probability that at least some claimants will receive social insurance benefits and that the insurer will not continue to pay that part of the benefit.

Waiver of Premium

In a life insurance policy, this provision is almost always an additional rider, but with DI insurance, if this exists at all, it is normally a standard provision in the contract. The provision waives payment of the policy premium whenever the insured qualifies for receipt of disability income benefits from that policy. Some companies include a provision that the elimination period for this benefit is the same as for basic policy benefits or 90 days, whichever is less. This limits the amount of time a disabled individual has to pay premiums. Remarkably, some companies do not waive the premium; they effectively reduce policy benefits by a hidden increase in cost

---

In-Depth: Policy Durability Provisions

Can a policy be cancelled? Can the company change the premiums? These are two of the most common questions asked by policyowners. With knowledge of the various policy continuation provisions, a financial planner can answer these questions.

Cancelable
Even more common in association policies than the optional renewal provision, this language permits the insurer to terminate the coverage at any time. It may permit termination with as little as 30 days' notice.

Conditionally Renewable
A conditionally renewable policy is one that the insurer, under conditions specified in the policy, may choose not to renew. The insured always has the right to cancel, but the insured's right to renewal is limited because, under certain conditions, the insurer may refuse to renew the policy. This is an uncommon provision.

Guaranteed Renewable
A policy that is guaranteed renewable gives the insured the right to continue the disability income policy by the timely payment of premiums to a specified age or for a specified number of years. Additionally, the insurer may not cancel or rewrite any policy provisions to be more restrictive than at the date of issue. The difference between this and noncancelable contracts is that, with this provision, the insurer may increase premiums as long as the increase is done for the entire class of policyowners in which the insured was placed when the policy was issued.

Guaranteed renewable policies generally have lower premiums than noncancelable policies; therefore, a client can get the same level of protection for a lower cost. The vast majority of insurance companies have not yet increased premiums on guaranteed renewable contracts. In some cases, underwriting is not quite as stringent for guaranteed renewable contracts since the company can increase its cash flow on the block of business if claims get too high. The possibility of substantial increases in premiums should not be underestimated; however, current practices must be kept in mind.

Noncancelable
A noncancelable policy not only guarantees that the insurance company may not cancel the policy, it guarantees that the premiums will not change unless scheduled to do so as part of the initial contract. The guarantee states that the insured has the right to renew the disability income policy for a stated number of years or to a stated age with no change to the stated premium in the contract at issue. This does not mean the premium will not change; it means that if a change is going to take place, it will be spelled out in the contract.

(continued on next page)

(continued from previous page)

> **Policy Renewable at the Company's Option (Optionally Renewable)**
> This provision is usually found in association-type plans. The insurance company has the right to cancel the insured's policy at the end of the policy year. The company may not cancel just one insured, but may cancel coverage for all association members covered under the plan. While many associations use disability income insurance as an income-raising program, this is a good form to avoid since it lacks stability. Hundreds of association groups with thousands of insureds have had their association disability income insurance plans cancelled. Sometimes replacement coverage is available from other carriers, and sometimes it is not. In some cases, new carriers accepting the association will provide equivalent coverage for all previously insured members. In many cases new underwriting is required. If an individual is currently receiving benefits, his or her claim will continue to be paid by the canceling company. However, if an insured has suffered a deterioration in health, it may be impossible for him or her to replace the lost coverage. This form is also used in many employer-provided plans. It usually requires a 60- to 90-day notice of the intent not to renew.
>
> **Policy with No Provision**
> These policies are not particularly common; they are usually single-term contracts that do not have to be renewed by the insurer after the term of coverage expires. If there is no language regarding renewal of the policy, the insurer has complete flexibility as to whether to renew or refuse to renew it. In most instances, the insured must apply for new coverage rather than continue coverage through renewal.

Disability Income Insurance-Needs Analysis

As you learned, life insurance needs analysis can become rather complex. With disability income insurance, it is much easier. Look at the net earned income of the individual and his or her expenses. Also look at the availability of unearned income. If unearned income and/or a spouse's income can cover 100 percent of expenses without a reduction in the family's standard of living, then purchasing DI insurance is not critical. However, this is rarely the case. In the vast majority of planning cases, most current earnings are required to maintain the family's lifestyle.

Thus, it is generally advisable for individuals to obtain as much DI insurance as they can. Because of the financial underwriting (discussed earlier), most people find it difficult to make ends meet with the permitted level of benefits. Not only do prior bills continue, additional bills related to the disability often arise. Knowing the rules allows a planner to recognize when and how adequate coverage can be obtained.

Anyone who has attempted to obtain an individual DI insurance policy while covered by a group DI plan knows that very little individual coverage, if any, is available. However, if individual DI insurance is in place prior to a group DI insurance plan, the insured can receive both benefits. Individual policies that do not have a social insurance rider are not typically offset by any other benefits received. There are a few companies who include provisions for the offsetting of other benefits, so review each contract to ensure it does not contain such provisions.

Group benefits are generally offset only by other employer-provided benefits, Social Security disability income, workers compensation payments, and/or any state-provided benefits, and not individual DI insurance benefits. When working with a client who does not have group disability income insurance, it is valuable to let the client know of the unique opportunity that exists.

There are a number of contract provisions and/or riders that warrant comparison when evaluating competing products. Even subtle differences in policies may substantially alter the result of a submitted claim. Some differences are obvious, such as the definition of disability, the length of the elimination period, and the maximum benefit duration. On the surface, these may not appear to mean much, but some companies will offer greater benefits than others. Therefore the differences in the definitions of total disability are very important. The following issues can result in vastly different consequences and must be evaluated relative to the client's circumstances and ability to pay:

- Occupational classification
- Presumptive disability definition
- Partial versus residual disability benefits
- Built-in features versus optional riders
- Cost-of-living adjustments

When evaluating an insurance carrier for a client, the planner should evaluate its:

- Financial stability
- Occupational classification system as related to the client
- Specific products offered
- Benefit levels offered
- Available provisions and riders
- General attitude toward writing disability income coverage
- Underwriting philosophy and standards, specifically related to conditions of the client
- Claims-paying reputation
- Efficiency in processing applications

Most insurance companies offer only one or two forms of disability income insurance policies. Furthermore, they tend to focus on certain markets rather than selling to anyone and everyone. Underwriting philosophies for certain occupational classifications can be substantially different between companies. Some companies focus on the blue-collar and lower level white-collar market. Some focus on professionals and high-income white-collar workers. Many companies that offer the most favorable products use only one definition of disability for all policies, which makes them unsuitable for some clients since certain occupational classifications will not be eligible or the premiums will be noncompetitive.

Underwriting

Insurance companies were very aggressive in the 1980s with their disability income insurance policies. Underwriting was not performed as carefully as it is now. In an effort to court high income professionals, companies offered very generous benefits at relatively low prices.

Until that time, any given company had suffered only a handful of own-occupation claims from various professionals, specifically the medical profession. Physicians had held an elevated place in the public eye, were shown great respect, and, for the most part, had very profitable and enjoyable practices. Several things changed in the late 1980s and the early 1990s.

Managed care plans began questioning decisions made by physicians and started limiting their income. Malpractice lawsuits increased at a rapid pace. The practice of medicine, for many physicians, was not as enjoyable or profitable as it had been. This led to two consequences. In the past, a physician who became disabled worked very hard to modify his or her practice around his or her limitations. Physicians wanted to get back into the practice of medicine as fast as they could. In the new era, that changed. Many physicians decided not to get back into medicine. Because of the wording of their contracts, as long as they could not practice the specialty they had when the disability began, they were entitled to full benefits. Instead of going back into medicine, some chose not to work; others followed different career paths.

> ### NEED TO KNOW: TAXATION OF DISABILITY INCOME INSURANCE
>
> Benefits from individually-owned disability income insurance policies are income-tax free. Premiums are not deductible. For employer-provided policies, any employee contributions are not deductible; however, the portion of benefit payments attributable to employee premium contributions is tax-free. As a result, the portion of DI benefits attributable to employer contributions is taxable as ordinary income to the insured unless the employer's contribution was reported as taxable income by the employee. When the employee reports the premium paid by the employer as income, subsequent benefits are income tax-free.

What had been a rare occurrence with medical professionals in regard to own occ policies became a regular occurrence. Insurance companies lost a great deal of money on that block of business. The result has been even greater restraint in underwriting and occupational classifications. In the earlier years, medical professionals were generally in the highest classification. This gave them the lowest cost per $100 of benefit and the most favorable contract provisions. Today, medical professionals are seldom found in the top two classifications. Careful underwriting by the insurance companies is now critically important in disability income insurance.

Consequently, the occupational classification into which the insured falls is of great importance. Different companies put similar occupations into different classes. Underwriting standards are still generally more liberal for professionals than for blue-collar workers. It is still assumed (not always correctly) that professionals are more motivated to work and have more stable careers. Occupations have shifted a great deal from one classification to another.

Over the past 10 to 15 years, disability income insurance underwriting has become more and more difficult to manage from the point of view of an agent or planner. Since insurance companies lost so much money due to overly generous underwriting and contract terms in the 1980s, this form of insurance is now the most difficult to obtain. Companies tend to specialize in order to focus on a target market. Despite the difficulty of obtaining this form of insurance, it is incumbent upon financial planners to bring up the subject with their clients. Each client should be made aware that obtaining specifically desired coverage is not always possible.

Certain conditions may eliminate any possibility of obtaining coverage or may result in permanent exclusions, including:

- Any treatment for depression prior to application
- Any psychological or psychiatric counseling prior to application
- Back pain
- Knee pain
- History of stroke
- History of heart attack
- Self-employed working from residence
- History of cancer
- Diabetes

These conditions create problems in underwriting. Experienced agents often will know which companies look more favorably on certain conditions. The underwriting process requires a great deal of information and may seem to take an extraordinarily long time. It is still critical that this piece of the personal financial planning puzzle is not missed or ignored.

Here is a real-life example of how strange underwriting can be. Jake and Jolene were traveling on their honeymoon and were in an auto accident. Jack banged his knee rather hard on the steering column, and Jolene was bounced around in the car quite a bit. An ambulance took Jolene to the hospital where her ruptured spleen was removed. Jake eventually had x-rays taken of his knee and, after some physical therapy, eliminated any discomfort. Years later, when Jolene applied for DI insurance, her application was approved the day it reached underwriting. Her ruptured spleen was life-threatening when it happened and, following surgery, posed no disability concern. Jake's application resulted in the underwriter asking for medical records and an exam of his knee before eventually issuing the policy with an exclusion for the knee.

If you learn nothing else from this example, learn this: Do not permit clients to put off applying for DI insurance. Seemingly minor problems can get in the way of having a policy issued.

IMPORTANT CONCEPTS

Additional insurance rider

Any occupation definition

Cancelable

Conditionally renewable

Coordination of benefits clause

Cost-of-living rider

Disability income insurance needs analysis

Earned income

Elimination period

Exclusions

Front-end cost-of-living rider

Guaranteed insurability

Guaranteed renewable

Long-term care provision

Loss of income definition

Maximum benefit period

Maximum monthly benefit payment

Misstatement of age clause

Modified any occupation definition

Noncancelable

Nonoccupational coverage

Occupational classification

Own occupation definition

Partial disability

Policy renewable at the company's option

Policy with no provision

Post-claim underwriting

Preexisting conditions

Presumptive disability

Probation period

Rehabilitation

Relation of earnings to insurance clause

Residual disability

Social Security definition of disability

Specialty letter

Split definition

Waiver of premium

QUESTIONS FOR REVIEW

1. Describe how a specific disability may be worse for one person than for another.

2. If a person wants to be able to replace as much of their income as possible, using both individually owned and group DI, under what circumstances is this possible?

3. Describe the most strict and most generous (desirable) definitions of disability.

4. Explain a split definition of disability that may be found in a DI insurance contract.

5. Explain how the elimination period works and when the first check can be expected relative to the elimination period.

6. Under what circumstances might a preexisting condition be covered immediately under a DI policy.

7. What is the difference between occupational and nonoccupational coverage?

8. Discuss how and why a social insurance rider affects a DI contract.

9. Compare the differences between guaranteed renewable and noncancelable DI policies. Address the advantages of each type.

10. Describe how underwriting for DI is different than for other forms of insurance.

SUGGESTIONS FOR ADDITIONAL READING

2005 Mercer Guide to Social Security and Medicare, 33rd ed., J. Robert Treanor, et al.

The Disability Fact Book, John Hewitt & Associates; 2003/2004

Disability Income Insurance: The Unique Risk, 5th ed, Charles Soule, American College, 1998.

Fundamentals of Risk and Insurance, 9th ed., Emmett J. Vaughan and Therese M. Vaughan, Wiley, 2003.

Introduction to Risk Management and Insurance, 8th ed., Mark Dorfman, Prentice Hall, 2004.

Life and Health Insurance, 13th ed., Kenneth Black Jr. and Harold Skipper Jr., Prentice Hall; 2000

Principles of Risk Management and Insurance, 9th ed., George E. Rejda, Addison Wesley, 2004.

Risk Management & Insurance, 12th ed, James S. Trieschman, Prentice Hall, 2004.

Social Security, Medicare & Government Pensions, 10th ed., Dorothy Matthews Berman and Joseph L. Matthews, NOLO, 2005.

Tax Facts, National Underwriter, 2005.

Tools & Techniques of Financial Planning, 7th ed. Leimberg, Satinsky, Doyle, & Jackson, National Underwriter; 2004.

Individual Health Care Plans: Long-Term Care

• • •

In years past it was common to have many generations living in the same home, or at least in the same town, but technological changes have made Americans more independent: Older Americans often prefer not to live with their children, single parent families are increasingly common, and most married couples both work outside the home. Families are increasingly unlikely to relegate the care of a senior to a daughter (or daughter-in-law). On top of these demographic changes, people are living longer, dramatically increasing the number of Americans needing assistance as they age. Various studies have indicated that between 400 and 600 of every 1,000 Americans eventually will need some level of long-term care.

This chapter will address how to assist clients in preparing themselves for the possibility of needing long-term care.

After reading this chapter you will be able to:
- Describe the various levels of long-term care
- Identify the types of long-term care benefits and their eligibility requirements
- Understand the tax issues surrounding long-term care and "qualified" policies
- Understand how Medicaid and Medigap coverage affect long-term care

WHAT IS LONG-TERM CARE?

Doc just turned 70, and though he has worked as a physician and was a knowledgeable leader in his professional association, and though he holds a pilot's license and is a talented photographer, he is now forgetting such things as where he parks his car or what he said to someone five minutes ago. Right now, he just forgets little things, but his memory is getting worse. His mother had a similar form of "dementia" and had to be confined in a long-term care facility. His wife, who is younger and still working, knows that as long as Doc does not get lost, he can live where he chooses and pretty much do anything he wants, but she has to travel sometimes on business. For peace of mind, she would like to have someone look after him at home while she is away.

The phrase "long-term care" usually brings with it a mental image of a grandparent sitting in a nursing home (or "long-term care facility"), confined to a bed for his or her remaining years. It is important to remember, though, that there are numerous other instances that may fall under the "long-term care" heading: care in a long-term care center, ongoing in-home care, or part-time in-home care, where someone simply looks after an Alzheimer's patient while the patient's family is away. And it is not only seniors who may need help. Because of accidents and illnesses, there are many younger people who need long-term care, even if some of them only need help getting up in the morning, bathing, toileting, and then getting to work. The Government Accounting Office estimates that 40 percent of the 13 million Americans receiving some form of long-term care are between the ages of 18 and 65.

Long-term care (LTC) insurance products have been changing rapidly and drastically as the market has expanded, and insurance companies have developed experience and responded to consumer needs and wants. When early LTC policies were introduced, no company had the necessary claims experience on which to base policy premiums. However, the insurance companies were aware of the potential for substantial losses.

In an effort to deal with this lack of claims history, carriers designed restrictive policies that were derived to a great extent from the provisions required by Medicare, which did have loss experience. The problem with using Medicare as a guideline is highlighted in this quote from *Your Guide for People with Medicare: Choosing Long-Term Care* by the Centers for Medicare and Medicaid Services and the Agency for Healthcare Research and Quality: "Medicare generally does not pay for long-term help with daily activities."

The outcome of these standards was that only a small percentage of individuals needing some form of long-term care ever qualified for policy benefits. The restrictive nature of the policies was enforced by either limiting benefit payments to those made for skilled nursing care or by requiring that some period of skilled nursing care be received before any lower level of care would be covered. Additionally, similar to Medicare requirements, many policies required that admission to a long-term care facility be preceded by a hospitalization of a minimum number of days (generally three). This also cut into the number of claims that would result in benefits under a policy, since only about half of the nursing home admissions were directly from hospitals. Some policies included clauses that restricted benefits to those who had a demonstrably physical cause for their infirmity, effectively excluding one of the most common problems—cognitive impairment. Until relatively recently, Alzheimer's disease could only be proven to exist through an autopsy.

Some insurers wrote policies that permitted post-claim underwriting. Under this practice, the insurer investigated information provided on the application only after a claim was filed. This post-claim underwriting practice sometimes resulted in a retroactive revocation of the policy and a return of only the insured's premiums.

The consumer backlash to these practices made it difficult for the industry to improve its market acceptance, even with much-improved products. A great deal of the bad press that long-term care still receives is a result of these older policies now maturing into claims, though many insurance companies have offered updates to existing policies without adding underwriting requirements.

Activities of Daily Living

Both the customers and the insurance industry were poorly served by claims based solely on specific conditions a covered person may or may not have, and by 1996, the industry had shifted its focus to the capabilities of the covered individual and adopted the activities-of-daily-living (ADL) concept. However, each company was creating its own list of essential daily activities (also called ADLs), and each policy had to be evaluated to determine which activities were measured. The federal government, under the Health Insurance Portability and Accountability Act of 1996 (HIPAA), undertook to create a more consistent ADL standard. HIPAA, based on the definitions being used by the insurance industry, created a list of six ADLs:

- Eating
- Toileting
- Transferring
- Bathing
- Dressing
- Continence

In some policies, toileting and continence are combined into one.

Generally, under LTC policies sold today, an individual who needs "substantial assistance" with two of the six ADLs described above will qualify for long-term care benefits. "Substantial assistance" is defined as either "hands-on assistance" or "standby assistance." In addition to the ADLs, a trigger of cognitive impairment or dementia is included. The advantage of the use of ADLs is the essential objectivity of the measures. While there are gray areas, if a person cannot get out of bed and get to a chair, he or she needs substantial help in transferring. If the individual needs help getting food into his or her mouth, that individual meets the eating ADL. A person who can get into a bathtub but cannot get out without help, needs help bathing. When it comes to cognitive impairment, the person may be perfectly able to do all of the ADLs but may not remember to do them without being reminded. Or he or she could wander away from home and be totally lost one block away. These levels of cognitive impairment also qualify the individual for benefits.

The specific circumstance that causes a long-term care benefit to be paid is generally referred to as a **benefit trigger** or **qualification trigger**. Some older policies still use the prior hospitalization requirement found in Medicare rules, but prior to HIPAA a number of states made the hospitalization requirement illegal. These laws are generally still on the books in those states to negate that requirement in any contracts still in existence that were sold with that provision. Some used, and a few still use, a doctor to certify the need for such care. This practice is known as the **medical necessity trigger**.

Qualified Policies

Passed in 1996, after years of debate, HIPAA addresses a number of issues surrounding LTC insurance, including the outlining of the required provisions of a qualified LTC policy and the establishment of the benefits of such a policy being qualified. Under HIPAA, a qualified policy may use either five or six ADLs (listed above), must provide benefits to an insured if he or she needs substantial assistance with two of them, and must include cognitive impairment as a benefit trigger. All forms of dementia must be covered. Additionally, an LTC policy must include a provision that if a policy lapses because of a missed premium caused by cognitive impairment, the insured or a representative of the insured must be permitted to reinstate the policy. HIPAA does not permit a medical necessity trigger in a qualified policy, so other than with cognitive impairment, the need for confinement or care is no longer in the hands of a physician without reference to ADLs. Another requirement included in HIPAA is a provision that provides nonforfeiture benefits.

These benefits may be used when a policy owner defaults on the payment of premiums. The available nonforfeiture options are limited to reduced paid-up insurance, extended term insurance, a reduced benefit period, or other similar approved offerings. Cash as a nonforfeiture option is not permitted. Also, a qualified LTC policy must be at least guaranteed renewable. This ensures that the insurance company may not cancel the policy and may only increase the premium if it does so for an entire class of insureds, not just for an individual because of his or her use of the benefits. LTC contracts may be noncancelable, meaning they have a fixed, guaranteed level premium; however because of the lack of adequate claims experience with this type of contract, no insurer currently sells a policy with that provision. Finally, the policy must conform to specified portions of the National Association of Insurance Commissioners' long-term care insurance model regulation. While no current policies are non-cancellable, a number of companies offer limited payment policies. An example of this would be a company that will permit an insured to pay 150% of the premium for 10 years and then never pay any other premiums to have the policy last their lifetime.

Generally, many planners believe that the primary benefit of a qualified policy is income-tax savings. HIPAA established the above requirements, among other reasons, to identify policies for which all or a portion of their premiums would be deductible as a medical expense from income for tax purposes. Additionally, benefits received of up to $240 (2005) per day or the actual cost of long-term care, whichever is higher, are income tax-free if paid by qualified policies. Because of this potential income-tax benefit, the HIPAA requirements have essentially become the standard LTC policy structure.

It is important to remember, though, that LTC premiums are deductible only as a medical expense; i.e., they are deductible only to the extent they exceed 7.5 percent of the individual's adjusted gross income. This means they will not result in an actual deduction for most insureds until after retirement, at which point many insureds will not have enough deductions to justify filing a Schedule A (Itemized Deductions) form with their income tax return. Thus, the primary benefit is that the benefits are income tax-free. Remember though, that at least some LTC benefits received, whether from qualified or nonqualified policies, are likely to be used for reimbursement for medical care received and therefore are not subject to income tax anyway. It is important that a planner work with the income tax advisor of a client regarding this issue—further discussion of these tax issues is beyond the scope of this text.

Sources of LTC Policies

A number of sources may provide long-term care coverage, including:

- Individual long-term care insurance policies
- Group long-term care insurance policies (or a mass-marketed, or sponsored, plan), usually from an employer or association
- Life insurance policy riders
- Specialized life insurance policies
- Disability income insurance policy riders or options
- Continuing care retirement communities (see below)
- Health maintenance organizations

The most obvious and common source of coverage is an individual policy from an insurance company. Long-term care contracts are written specifically to address long-term care needs, and insurance company contracts are generally the most flexible in design and provide the broadest range of benefit choices. Likewise, group LTC plans are becoming more common, though participation in the plans, when offered, is not very high, with better-educated employees between the ages of 40 and 60 typically expressing the most interest. Group LTC is very attractive to some employees because it is often guaranteed issue and frequently permits employees to purchase benefits for spouses (and sometimes for parents). However, the plans offered are usually package plans without too many options for the buyer. Importantly, most group LTC plans are also portable. Once the policy is issued, the insured can take it when leaving the employer.

LTC Through Life Insurance

Recently, life insurance policies have also become able to provide LTC benefits, usually through accelerated death benefits provided under a long-term care rider. Until HIPAA passed, state law often prohibited accelerated death benefits, and there was a serious risk that the accelerated benefits would be taxed as a surrender of cash value from a policy, with any gain over the cumulative premiums considered as ordinary income. One popular rider providing long-term care coverage, known as a **living benefits rider**, accelerates payment of the death benefit only if the insured contracts a terminal disease, generally one of several specified in the policy. Over the last five years or so, companies have been adding more generous living benefit riders, encouraged by the passage of HIPAA. Under HIPAA, if accelerated death benefits are received as reimbursement for terminal illness expenses, they are treated as death benefits for income tax purposes.

If the individual is chronically ill, defined as needing substantial assistance with two of five or six ADLs or protection due to cognitive impairment, those benefits, to the extent they pay for care not otherwise reimbursed or paid for by other insurance, are income tax-free up to $240 per day (in 2005) or the actual cost, if higher. These accelerated death benefits are, for the most part, not the best way to provide long-term coverage as a person may need a substantial amount of long-term care without having a terminal illness.

A few life insurance companies have developed policy riders that are designed specifically to provide LTC coverage. These typically pay a portion of the policy's death benefit (or net amount at risk, depending on the rider's wording) up to a specified percentage of the total death benefit. The payment is usually made on a monthly basis during the insured's life if he or she requires LTC. They commonly pay 2 percent of the policy's death benefit each month for up to 50 months. It is important that clients know that these payments reduce the remaining policy death benefit and cash value by the amount of any payments made.

A fairly uncommon insurance company product is a single premium life insurance policy that is designed specifically to provide long-term care benefits if the need arises. These policies, being single premium policies, are modified endowment contracts, or MECs. However since they are sold to individuals who plan to use them for either long-term care benefits or have them result in a death benefit, the limitations of MECs are of no concern. By design, the benefits would be paid as reimbursement for expenses that arise due to a chronic problem and would be income tax-free. If the insured does not need the benefits for long-term care, the policy is ultimately paid as a death benefit, which also is normally income tax-free.

LTC Through Disability Insurance

At least one company offers a disability income insurance policy that converts to a long-term care policy. While this option requires no underwriting, the conversion does not come until retirement, so if the individual becomes disabled prior to the retirement date, he or she would receive disability benefits according to the contract terms but would not receive any long-term care benefits, even if he or she continued to receive long-term care after the disability income benefits stopped.

There is no guarantee that long-term care needs occur only after normal retirement age. At least combining these two coverages is a logical option, even if it has its flaws.

Other Sources of LTC Coverage

HMOs are also occasionally sources of LTC plans, generally operated under waivers from federal regulations and typically extensions of Medicare and Medicaid, both as a service to their members and as a way of providing a multi-life discount. Most HMOs provide skilled nursing care and home health care, but they are unlikely to cover custodial care. In some states, HMOs providing long-term care benefits are at risk of losing nonprofit status because they are no longer serving just as a health care provider. Similarly, Blue Cross/Blue Shield plans may offer individual long-term care insurance, usually similar to plans offered by life and health insurers. However, some plans base the benefit payments on a percentage of the total charges up to a specified maximum rather than having a fixed payment.

One other source of long-term care plans of which most people are not aware, is a group of long-term care providers, **continuing care retirement communities** (CCRCs). These organizations offer care and housing, primarily to seniors, for a substantial one-time payment upon entry followed by monthly maintenance payments thereafter. Usually, individuals are initially independent but will have someone close by in case of problems. As their needs increase, the available services are increased (normally with attendant increases in the monthly fees). More details on CCRCs are available in the next section of this chapter.

By obtaining long-term care coverage through the CCRC, the individual is protected from excessively increased costs if his or her needs increase while residing in the "community." However, a long-term care contract with a CCRC is rarely transferable or refundable. If an individual decides he or she does not want to use that particular "community," any lump sum paid to get in is often forfeited and future care will not be available through any facility within the "community." It is also easy to imagine situations that could create serious problems: the financial insolvency of the CCRC, a change in its management, dissatisfaction with the standard of care, etc. There are a number of ways CCRCs operate, so it is imperative to fully review the details of a particular one before committing to it.

LEVELS AND LOCATIONS OF CARE

Karl had severe back pain, and after months of trying to diagnose the problem, his physician discovered an infection in his spinal cord. For a while, he could not walk at all. Now, after receiving care in a long-term care facility, he simply needs 30 minutes of physical therapy when he wakes in the morning. While he has some difficulty walking throughout the day, he can generally do whatever he wants as long as he gets this therapy in the morning, and he no longer needs full-time care.

Long-term care comes in many forms. The categories of care available generally depend on where the care is delivered.

Long-Term Care Facilities

Long-term care facilities can provide the highest level of care and are designed for full-time residency by the individual. There are three general levels of care provided in a long-term care facility: skilled nursing care, intermediate care, and custodial care.

Skilled nursing care refers to the 24-hours-a-day, seven-days-a-week availability of a registered nurse who operates under a physician's supervision.

Intermediate care care is less intensive nursing or rehabilitative care, often not requiring 24-hour availability of a registered nurse or physician, though a registered nurse and physician are typically on call at all times.

Custodial Care Care is generally care that is not medical in nature but is necessary for the health of the individual. This includes assistance with such things as bathing, transferring (moving from bed to chair), eating, toileting, etc. This level of care is generally where the ADLs come into play.

Home Health Care

An individual who is recovering from an illness or injury can typically receive a certain amount of care at home, covered by his or her health plan or, sometimes, Medicare. However, Medicare and health insurance will generally cease to provide payment once the purpose of the home health care becomes maintenance rather than therapy (leading to recuperation or improvement).

Many LTC policies today provide home-health-care benefits. The individual usually must not be in such a condition that he or she needs 24-hour care, but as long as there are legitimate needs for assistance with ADLs, the policy will pay benefits.

Adult Day Care

Closely related to home care is another fairly recent long-term option. Adult day care is for those adults who are fine as long as there is someone around who can keep an eye on them, remind them to eat, etc. Many of these individuals live with family members who are employed outside of the home. Adult day care offers activities, companionship, and someone to make sure individuals do not harm themselves or get lost. A number of LTC policies also cover this type of care, which is far less expensive than home care or confinement in an LTC facility.

Assisted Living

Assisted living facilities are one of the more recent developments in long-term care. These facilities typically provide private apartments for the individual and sometimes for couples. Some are single buildings while others are entire communities. These are for individuals who may be able to provide most of what they need on a day-to-day basis but sometimes need additional help with certain activities. A basic contract often provides an apartment-type setting with limited cooking facilities. The facility generally provides most meals in a common dining room. Other levels of care are provided as needed, and the charge for them is separate. Until an individual meets the requirements for receiving long-term care benefits, the cost is completely borne by the resident.

While the costs may not initially be paid by the LTC policy, the advantage of an assisted living facility is that an individual does not have to be moved to a new location as his or her physical or mental dependence increases. Some assisted living facilities provide all levels of care while others do not. Most do not offer skilled nursing care.

Continuing Care Retirement Communities

Quite similar to some assisted living facilities, continuing care retirement communities (known as CCRCs) provide an even broader range of residence options. These communities often have separate houses or townhome-type buildings that are the first stop for residents. The communities also have buildings that are more apartment-like and ones that provide various levels of care. Generally, new residents must pay a substantial one-time "buy-in" followed by monthly maintenance payments. Residents are generally assured of space in the facilities as they require higher levels of assistance or care, eliminating one serious problem faced by individuals who need placement in a long-term care facility. However, outside of a CCRC, when the time comes to find a room, the search can sometimes be long and difficult. As with assisted living facilities, unless and until a resident meets the requirement of his or her LTC contract to receive benefits, the policy does not cover any of these costs.

Nursing Homes

Nursing homes are residential facilities. In the past, the general view of long-term care was confinement in a nursing home. This created visions of despair and room after room of old people who were incapable of providing anything for themselves.

There are people in nursing homes who need extensive custodial care and are truly incapable of caring for any of their own needs. At the other extreme are people who do not quite qualify for assisted living in that they do need some nursing care periodically, and more care than may be available at an assisted living facility. Other than this need, they may be quite active.

Nursing homes generally do not have individual living units in which there are cooking facilities or multiple rooms. With all of the options available for long-term care, nursing homes are typically the last stop, but not always. The residents normally require some level of custodial care and often need some nursing care as well. It is the need for custodial care that usually results in an individual's transfer to a nursing home.

There are many younger residents with various conditions that require them to be in nursing homes. Some may be lifelong residents and others only temporary. This is often the case for indigent young adults who are confined because they can only receive the needed care through Medicaid if they live in a nursing home. A young person with multiple sclerosis may be confined to a nursing facility until she or he has stabilized enough to be more independent.

BUYING LONG-TERM CARE POLICIES

Many people are concerned with the cost of long-term care (LTC) insurance. It is important to compare the cost with the potential benefit. A policy that pays $3,000 per month for three years has a potential payout of $108,000. If an individual purchases this amount of benefit in his or her late 50s, the premium may be about $500 to $800 per year. At that rate, it would take 22.5 to 36 years to pay premiums equal to six months of benefits. Even if the time value of money is considered, and assuming the client achieves an after tax return of 5 percent on money that would otherwise be expended for premium payments, an individual paying $800 per year for LTC coverage would still require 15.45 years of premium payments to equal six months of benefits. It would take nearly 42 years of premium payments to accumulate enough for a full three years of benefits.

Long-term care insurance is generally purchased to cover a certain dollar amount per day. Costs for long-term care can vary widely between different geographic areas of the country as well as within a single community. While the average cost of LTC in one community may be $125 to $180 per day ($3,150 to $5,400 per month, or $45,000 to $64,800 per year), some "exclusive" facilities charge well in excess of $250 per day. A few LTC facilities that are perceived to be better than most can cost over $100,000 per year.

The amounts of coverage available generally range from $50 to over $300 per day, with most falling between $50 and $200. Life insurance policy riders, however, typically have benefit amounts stated in terms of a percentage of the policy's face amount. The most common percentage is 2 percent of the face amount payable for each month of qualifying need.

However, some life insurance policy riders state their benefit in terms of a percentage of the net amount at risk. This could potentially reduce the available benefits substantially. If the rider is sold to a relatively young client, it would most likely be used when he or she is much older and has built up a substantial cash value. If this were the case, the net amount at risk would be relatively small.

A client should choose the benefit amount with some regard to the current cost of long-term care in his or her geographic location, or in the area in which the client anticipates that he or she would be if long-term care becomes a necessity. If a couple buys LTC insurance, the dynamics are different than if a single individual purchases it. With a couple, the needed amount of coverage should be fairly close to the expected cost of care. Household expenses for the nonconfined person will not decrease much if the other is confined. However, when the insured is single, virtually all other living expenses cease with the exception of health care costs while he or she is confined. Income and/or assets that were used for food, entertainment, rent, house payments, utilities, etc., are generally freed up if there is a permanent confinement.

However, since there may be many years that elapse between the time of purchase and the time of claim, the use of an inflation rider is strongly encouraged.

One popular premium payment option is a limited payment plan. Many companies offer a plan such as this, with a ten-pay plan being the most common. The way it works is that the policy owner pays an increased premium for a limited number of years and the plan is then considered "paid-up." At least one program charges 150 percent of the annual premium for ten years. The biggest advantage is that even if the insurer increases premiums after that ten year period for other policies, the "paid-up" policies will not be charged anything additional. Some insurers are surprised at the positive response by consumers to this approach.

Long-Term Care: Needs Analysis

The first question that comes to mind for most people is whether or not they will need LTC insurance. If such a need is determined, they should then ask how much coverage should they get and then they should determine whether they can afford it.

At the beginning of this chapter, the determination of the need itself was discussed. While it is not assured that someone will follow in the footsteps of his or her parents and grandparents, the family medical history is a good place to start when determining the need. If an individual's family history shows a propensity for long life with some of those years being spent in a nursing home or needing other forms of long-term care, then it may be an easy decision. On the other hand, people today are likely to live longer than their ancestors. The people who are typically considering buying LTC insurance today may have parents who are only in their 60s or 70s and may well be a long way from needing long-term care.

Then there is the financial viewpoint. If an individual considering this question has substantial income producing assets and if that income is more than adequate to cover the cost of long-term care, there are two choices. The first choice is to retain the risk. The second is to insure against it anyway. The following was related by an LTC specialist. She had a client who was quite well off and wanted to purchase LTC insurance. When asked why, since her estate could easily pay for any needs, the woman candidly said that she did not want to be in her room in a long-term care facility listening to her children in the hall arguing about how much of her estate was being used up to pay for her care.

The next question regards how much would be needed if it is to be purchased. This may actually require some research. In one metropolitan area in 2004, the average daily rate for respected nursing homes was $160. One nursing home that was particularly desired by one ethnic group had a daily rate in excess of $200, 25 percent above the average. Clients need to be aware of the available care options, which include average costs, as well as the current cost of facilities they might be most interested in using.

The discussion earlier in the chapter addressed a single individual versus a married couple. Those issues are also quite real, and they make decision making even more complex. What we do not know is what the real cost will be in the future. We can look at historical increases in cost, and that will give us some idea of the cost. However, just as the life insurance needs analysis is based on assumptions that are certain to be wrong, any inflation of cost rate that is chosen for this purpose is likely to be wrong. The advantage of using an inflation rider that increases the coverage each year is that it is fairly likely to come somewhat close to the amount of the need sometime in the future, assuming that the need today was covered in today's dollars.

Related to this is the length of benefits to be obtained. The average stay in a nursing home is about three years, a figure that includes the length of stays for nursing home residents who die within a few days or weeks of admission as well as people who stay 15 to 20 years. A couple of states have plans that provide state supported long-term care up to the number of years the individual paid for them, without any requirement to pay it back. This program was a short lived exception given to those states in regard to Medicaid rules. There does not seem to be much of a push to expand this program.

Can people afford LTC coverage? This is a difficult question. This coverage, which people think about in terms of a daily benefit, can seem expensive. If a couple in their early 50s obtains a plan for $150 per day and their monthly premium is over $250 a month for lifetime benefits, that seems expensive. However, if one of them spends three years in a nursing home, then they could receive about $160,000 of benefits, not including the inflated benefits provided by the policy, which is equal to about 640 months of premiums (That is over 53 years). If the benefit level increases 5 percent per year and the one who needs care is confined 35 years from now, the daily benefit would be $827.40, and three years of benefits would be over $900,000.

This brings up an important point. Someone in his or her 50s today will not likely need benefits for 30 years or more. Long-term care costs have risen 5 to 7 percent per year for a number of years. At 5 percent, the $150 per day cost today will increase to $827 per day 35 years from now. Does a client believe his or her estate will be able to handle that daily cost in the future?

Policy Provisions

One critical issue in selecting long-term care insurance is the length of the waiting or elimination period. As with disability income insurance, the elimination period is the number of days following certification of eligibility before the insurance company will cover the insured costs. Common elimination periods are 30, 60, 90, and 180 days, and the longer the elimination period, the lower the premium. However, when searching for low premiums, it is important to consider how long the individual's assets can carry the $3,000 to $8,000 per month before the insurance starts paying.

When a policy is issued, it typically is written to provide a specific daily benefit for a specified number of years or for life. The most common options for length of coverage are two to six years, and lifetime (or unlimited). The average stay in a long-term care facility is three years, and most companies offer a three-year benefit period.

As with mortality and morbidity tables, statistics are poor predictors for specific individuals. It is difficult to foresee a circumstance in which a financial planner would recommend anything other than a lifetime benefit period. However, the cost of lifetime benefits is generally much higher than for plans with limited benefits, and some clients will not want to purchase any plan that will cost a lot without any assurance of receiving benefits.

Policies that are issued with a specified number of years use one of two methods: The first pays a set amount per day for up to the policy period while the second approach provides a pool of money to be used for the costs of care, with the latter approach offering a couple of variations. For some, the company will pay up to the promised daily benefit, but if the actual cost is less, the benefit is extended. Other plans will pay actual costs for however long a set pool of money lasts. The pool of money is calculated by multiplying the daily benefit by the number of days of coverage. So a $150 daily benefit for three years would be 3 × 365 × 150 = 1,095 days × $150 = $164,250. If the actual cost is $175 per day, the benefits will last about 938 days. If the actual cost was $140 per day, the benefits would last 1,173 days.

One provision that is not universal is **waiver of premium**. While it might seem logical that a person receiving benefits would not have to continue payment of premiums, it is not always true for LTC policies. The policy often requires the insured to pay premiums for a certain number of months following certification of need before the premium is waived. Some companies will reimburse the insured for those premiums; others will not.

There is almost always a **spousal discount** if both husband and wife purchase policies from the same company. The discounts can be from 10 to 50 percent. The 10 percent discount usually applies to both policies and the 50 percent discount typically applies to the policy on the younger of the two.

Virtually all LTC policies cover confinement in an LTC facility, but most individuals want benefits provided for in-home care. Some policies will pay 50 percent of the facility benefit for home care, while other policies pay the full daily benefit amount. An uncommon policy, but one that is available, is a home care policy with an LTC facility rider attached. Unless a policy specifies adult day care as a benefit, it is not likely to cover that type of care. If the company representative says it is covered, it may be advisable to get something in writing from the insurance company that describes the specifics of coverage. There are also a number of specialized benefits that may be available with LTC coverage.

Bed Reservation

As more and more people require space in long-term care facilities, it is possible for a person who must be hospitalized to lose his or her bed in the LTC facility. This provision continues to pay for the bed for a limited period of time so that a short hospital stay does not cause the individual's family to begin a new search for a needed LTC bed.

Cost of Living

Another provision that is not always included is a cost-of-living benefit. The most common benefit rider increases benefits once the insured is receiving benefits, and the cost-of-living rider commonly provides a percentage increase-usually 5 percent or the increase in the consumer price index, whichever is less. There are variations on this form of the rider, so reviewing each company's explanation is important. Some companies offer a rider that increases the coverage prior to a claim, which is a much better option, and usually expensive. With some companies, the premium increases each time the coverage increases and for others, the premium is shown to be level for the life of the contract. Do remember that these contracts are guaranteed renewable, so the company can increase the premium for an entire class of policies, even if the initial illustration shows a level premium. For most people, the cost of long-term care will increase more between the time they purchase their coverage and the time they enter a care facility than between the time they enter a facility and the date they leave.

Equipment

Insurers have realized that many people do better and need less attention when they are permitted to stay at home. With that realization, some companies provide money for specialized equipment for use in the home so that qualified insureds can remain there.

Family Caregiver

This benefit provides payment to a primary caregiver in the home. The early plans that provided for home health care as an alternative to inpatient care, limited payment to individuals who were not related to the individual needing care. A number of policies have since made it possible for a family member who is qualified, as defined by the carrier, to receive payment for providing the care that would otherwise be provided by outsiders.

Health Care Coordinator

As a response to accusations that the industry deals with LTC as it deals with acute care under health care plans, some companies have developed managed long-term care. The companies provide for a health care coordinator (someone who works with the patient and family to determine the best method of obtaining care). Insurers generally give this coordinator substantial power to create obligations for the company.

Personal Care Advocate

A number of companies are now paying for a personal care advocate, an individual who will provide an objective evaluation of the care being received. This gives family members additional support to arrange for better care if their loved one is not being treated properly.

Respite Care

When family members are caring for a person, the toll on those caregivers can be quite high. Much like children, some individuals needing long-term care must be watched constantly. They can be very demanding and often need a great deal of assistance. Many policies provide for payment to an outside caregiver to come in so that the primary caregiver can get a rest. Statistically, the life expectancy of family caregivers is reduced if they do not have adequate rest and support.

Restoration of Benefits

For LTC contracts with benefits limited to a specified number of years, this provision is sometimes included, providing for a complete restoration of full benefits if the individual was previously collecting benefits and then becomes ineligible to receive benefits for a specified number of months because of improved health or abilities. With most policies providing this benefit, the insured must be able to function without qualifying for benefits for six months or longer following a qualifying period.

If he or she is able to meet this requirement, the waiting period will then begin again, and the full limited-year benefit will again be available. For people with lifetime benefits, it is a detriment if the policy requires a second elimination period if they leave long-term care for some period of time. However, most policies do include a provision that does just that. It is important to note that the measure is whether the person qualifies for LTC benefits. If a person uses up three years of benefits and then is cared for at home by family members for a little over six months, benefits will not automatically be restored. The requalification period starts when the individual does not need enough care to qualify for benefits.

Return of Premium

A rider is sometimes offered on a nonqualified policy providing that if no benefits are paid by the policy, the entire premium paid will be returned after a specified number of years or at the death of the insured. In some cases, the excess premium, if invested at a moderate rate of return by the company, will prove favorable for the insured even if benefits are paid. Doing some time value of money calculations with the excess premium is a worthwhile exercise. However, when the return of premium is actually made varies with each contract. Some give a partial refund by reducing any return of premium by the amount of benefits paid.

Shared Benefits

A relatively new type of benefit, this provision provides that if both spouses are covered by LTC insurance from the same company, and one spouse dies, the surviving spouse may use the total benefits that both policies would provide if he or she is confined to a LTC facility. Some state laws prohibit this rider from being attached to a married couple's policies.

Underwriting for Long-Term Care

As noted above, in the early years of long-term care insurance, some companies did full underwriting, and some waited until a claim was submitted. There are still some companies that ask few medical questions on an application, and planners and their clients should assume that there will be post-claim underwriting. Post-claim underwriting is the process of evaluating the health of the individual at the time of the claim with regard to his or her health when the application was submitted. From the company's point of view, this protects it from paying claims that arise from conditions that were known but not disclosed on the application. From the insured's side, this is a disaster waiting to happen.

When people buy LTC policies from companies that do not ask questions until after a claim is submitted, they have a false sense of security and run the risk of leaving themselves without coverage when it is too late to make other plans. Because of this, whenever possible, planners and clients should use a company that relies on comprehensive medical information for underwriting and where misrepresentation by the insured is the only reason a claim can be denied for conditions that existed prior to application for the policy

A word of caution: Many consumer-oriented periodicals write about and analyze long-term care products as well as other insurance policies. These magazines are, unfortunately, sometimes not as objective as trade magazines. Some have been accused of offering conventional wisdom as basic truth. The public in general wants to hear that there is a low-cost method of doing everything. Some periodicals respond to this attitude for the primary purpose of selling magazines. It is important for a planner to know what is being read by clients. It is equally important for that planner to not be swayed by biased consumer-oriented articles.

THE FACES OF LONG-TERM CARE

Most people who walk into a facility where individuals meet the tests for benefits of LTC policies expect to see senior citizens. They do not expect to see people in their 20s, 30s, or any age under 70. But it is not only seniors who may need help. Because of accidents and/or illnesses, there are many younger people who need long-term care. Some of them only need help getting up in the morning, bathing, toileting, and then getting to work. Others need more or less care, but are not capable of meeting all of their own physical needs. Long-term care in one form or another is for them, as are Medicare and Medicaid.

Unfortunately, too many people still believe that Medicare will pay for long-term care. If an individual meets stringent requirements, he or she may receive some benefits from Medicare for limited skilled nursing care—the first 20 days and all but a co-payment (up to $114 per day in 2005) for the next 80 days if an individual meets all of the following requirements:

- Has Medicare Part A and still has available days under the coverage
- Is confined in a Medicare approved skilled nursing facility
- Begins confinement within 30 days of a three-consecutive-day stay in the hospital (even if no beds are available until after the 30 days)
- Has a physician who believes skilled nursing care is needed
- Receives only Medicare-approved services

One exception: A person already in a skilled nursing facility and in need of therapy or treatment for an injury or illness that occurred while he or she was there could be covered by Medicare. Simply stated, Medicare is a health care plan, not a long-term care plan. If the care being received is not necessary because of illness or injury and will not improve the individual's condition, it will not be covered. To receive care in a long-term care facility and to have the stay paid for by Medicare requires meeting all of the above requirements.

A Medigap policy (detailed in chapter 6) may pick up the co-pay for the 80 days that Medicare requires it. Other than this potential and difficult to obtain benefit, Medigap policies do not cover long-term care. The same conditions that would cause Medicare to stop paying also result in Medigap plans terminating coverage. If the treatment is not directly associated with recovery from an illness or injury, no benefits are available.

Medicaid

Medicaid is medical care for the poor and provides both health care and long-term care. It is jointly funded by the federal and state governments and is managed at the state level. In order to qualify for coverage, applicants must meet both an income and asset test as determined by the state.

An applicant's assets are categorized as either exempt or nonexempt for the purposes of Medicaid qualification. One of the principal exempt assets is an applicant's home (including land and adjoining property), regardless of its value, provided it is the person's principal place of residence. For this purpose, an applicant's home is referred to as a homestead and it must be the primary residence of the Medicaid applicant, his or her spouse, his or her minor children, or his or her disabled adult children. However, an applicant's homestead is treated as a resource (nonexempt asset) after the individual has been institutionalized for six months, unless the individual's spouse or minor, disabled, or blind child continues to reside in the home, or it can be shown that the individual may be able to leave the institution and return home. As long as any one of the above resides in the house, then the property is exempt and cannot be considered in evaluating eligibility, regardless of its value. Medicaid cannot force an applicant to sell it or put a lien on the property. Moreover, a house may be transferred without triggering a Medicaid disqualification period if it is transferred to any of the following:

- The community spouse
- A child who is under age 21, blind, or permanently and totally disabled
- The applicant's brother or sister if he or she has lived in the house for at least one year prior to the applicant's admission for care and has an equity interest in the house
- A nondisabled adult child residing in the home and providing care that delayed the applicant's need for care in a medical institution or nursing facility for at least two years
- A trust created solely for the benefit of disabled children of the applicant
- Certain trusts created for a disabled child or grandchild under age 65

A house can lose its homestead exemption if proper planning is not undertaken. If ever the house becomes unoccupied by anyone in the four homestead categories listed above, or if it is transferred to someone not qualifying under the other additional categories just described, it will lose its exemption and may have to be sold to pay for current medical costs and those previously paid by Medicaid.

The amount of money a long-term care facility receives from Medicaid is often less than it receives from private-pay patients, and there are many anecdotal stories of individuals who were initially private-pay patients and, after using up their assets, became Medicaid patients in the same facility, receiving a lower level of care in rooms that were less comfortable.

Whether these are isolated incidents or are indicative of widespread differences in care or not, they do raise questions about the desirability of attempting to qualify for Medicaid paid long-term care for a loved one.

In-Depth: Medicaid Planning

While some question the government's role in paying for long-term care for anyone, most Americans recognize the need to support those who are incapable of taking care of themselves. However, this brings up the very touchy and controversial issue of Medicaid planning.

On one side of the issue are individuals who need LTC and their family members. Most people want to leave an inheritance for their heirs. Spending $36,000 to $100,000 a year for long-term care may easily eliminate any planned bequests. Planners and lawyers are hired by their clients to find ways to keep the money in the family.

On the other side are the taxpayers: Most would at least raise an eyebrow over the government paying tens of thousands of dollars each year for the long-term care of a person so that he or she can leave large sums of money to his or her heirs.

Many feel it is completely inappropriate for those who can afford long-term care to have other taxpayers foot the bill. This puts a strain on the states and on the federal government to provide the benefits and makes it more difficult for those who truly need the help to get it.

This creates a moral dilemma for planners and lawyers who are asked to do Medicaid planning.

Is it morally right to provide advice (even for free) regarding how to transfer assets so that heirs get an inheritance? Is it morally corrupt to ask taxpayers to pay for benefits that the client can afford just to provide an inheritance for those who did not earn it?

Federal criminal law, punishable by a fine of up to $10,000, one year in jail, or both, restricts assisting an individual, for a fee, in the disposition of his or her assets for the purpose of qualifying for Medicaid-paid long-term care. Additionally, if any assets are transferred within 36 months (60 months if the money was transferred into or out of a trust) of application for Medicaid-paid care, a period of ineligibility is calculated beginning with the month following the month of the transfer, with the length of total time of ineligibility based on the amount transferred and the average cost of LTC in the region. If, for example, the average monthly cost of care is $3,000 in the region and $60,000 was transferred, the individual is ineligible for Medicaid coverage for 20 months. The length of time for the period of ineligibility is not limited: If the transfer were for $300,000 in assets, the period would last 100 months.

It is the position of the Justice Department that this law is unenforceable, and the attorneys general under the Bill Clinton and George H. W. Bush administrations have stated they will not enforce it. Laws exist that describe how assets can be transferred for the purpose of removing them from an individual's estate so that he or she can qualify for state-supported long-term care. The attorneys general take the position that telling people how to take advantage of current laws cannot be considered illegal.

IMPORTANT CONCEPTS

Activities of daily living (ADLs)

Adult day care

Assisted living

Bed reservation

Benefit trigger

Cognitive impairment

Continuing care retirement community (CCRC)

Cost-of-living benefit

Custodial care

Family caregiver benefit

Group long-term care

HIPAA qualified policy

Home health care

Intermediate care

Long-term care

LTC benefit levels

LTC elimination periods

Medicaid LTC benefits

Medicaid planning

Medicare skilled nursing care requirements

Nursing home

Medigap coverage

Personal care advocate

Post claim underwriting

Respite care

Restoration of benefits

Return of premium rider

Shared benefits

Skilled nursing care

Sources of LTC coverage

QUESTIONS FOR REVIEW

1. Describe the activities of daily living and their relationship to long-term care insurance.

2. Describe the three basic levels of care provided in long-term care facilities.

3. What are the requirements for Medicare to pay for time spent in a long-term care facility?

4. How is assisted living different than residing in a long-term care facility?

5. What is a continuing care retirement facility and what services are offered?

6. Describe a HIPAA qualified LTC policy.

7. What are the benefits of having a HIPAA qualified policy?

8. What types of benefits are available through LTC policies?

9. Explain how individuals qualify for Medicaid-paid LTC and the pros and cons of using Medicaid to pay for LTC.

SUGGESTIONS FOR ADDITIONAL READING

Ethical Dilemmas in Long-Term Care, 2nd ed., J. Idziak, Simon & Kolz, 2002.

Fundamentals of Risk and Insurance, 9th ed., Emmett J. Vaughan and Therese M. Vaughan, Wiley, 2003.

Introduction to Risk Management and Insurance, 8th ed., Mark Dorfman, Prentice Hall, 2004.

J.K. Lasser's Choosing the Right Long-Term Care Insurance, Ben Lipson, Wiley, 2002.

Life and Health Insurance, 13th ed., Kenneth Black Jr. and Harold Skipper Jr., Prentice Hall, 2000.

Long-Term Care: Your Financial Planning Guide, Phyllis Shelton, Kensington Publishing Corporation, 2003.

Principles of Risk Management and Insurance, 9th ed., George E. Rejda, Addison Wesley, 2004.

Social Security Manual 2005, National Underwriter, 2005.

Tax Facts on Insurance & Employee Benefits 2005, National Underwriter, 2005.

Your Guide for People with Medicare: Choosing Long-Term Care, Centers for Medicare and Medicaid Services & Agency for Healthcare Research and Quality

CHAPTER NINE

Homeowners Insurance

• • •

For most Americans there are only three forms of insurance that are mandatory. The first is usually auto insurance. States require all drivers to be financially responsible for any damage they cause or injuries they inflict on others as a result of automobile ownership.

The second is homeowners insurance, and the third is its close cousin, title insurance. The government does not require either of the latter, but lenders require both, as they want to be assured that if the structure on which they lent a large sum of money is destroyed, damaged, or claimed by someone with a competing interest, they are protected. However, homeowners insurance provides many types of protection in addition to protecting the dwelling. This chapter will introduce you to the various forms of homeowners policies, the coverages and exclusions, and how to calculate claims.

When you complete this chapter you will be able to:
- Identify and describe the various types of coverage under a homeowners policy
- Describe the various forms of homeowners insurance
- Describe the various endorsements to homeowners policy forms
- Explain the various exclusions under homeowners forms
- Identify and describe the limits of policy provisions
- Calculate the amount to be paid on a claim
- Describe the purpose of title insurance

THE FIELD OF PROPERTY AND LIABILITY INSURANCE

Individuals who sell property, liability, and casualty insurance have their own professional designation: chartered property casualty underwriter (CPCU). Along with experience requirements, those individuals take eight courses and pass nationally administered exams to become experts in that field, and to a great extent, subspecialists in the field. The property/casualty field has two general subdivisions: personal lines and commercial lines. The personal lines are the policy forms sold to individuals. The commercial lines are the policy forms sold to organizations. Many personal lines agents will provide packaged policy forms to small organizations but generally do not work with large organizations because of the complexity of the coverages. Agents who sell primarily commercial lines of insurance do not, in most cases, sell personal lines. Within the category of commercial lines agents, there are also specialists who limit their work to certain types of coverage, just as some life and health insurance agents do.

This is an introductory chapter on property and liability insurance. As such, it will not adequately prepare readers to give comprehensive advice to clients. That ability will come with experience, or it may be something most financial planners will leave to specialists—individuals who have earned the CPCU designation or one of the lesser designations. Although students are often asked to make judgments about this type of coverage on exams, these cases are not particularly complex, and you are not expected to be an expert in every aspect of insurance.

PROPERTY AND LIABILITY BASICS

Financial planners are often called upon to review clients' insurance policies. While the declarations page provides a summary of the policy coverage, an effective financial planner needs a basic understanding of the coverages and the ability to determine whether the coverage needs to be examined by an expert. Reviewing a clients' property and casualty insurance policies clearly is within the scope of providing comprehensive financial planning advice. Making specific recommendations is not.

Property and liability insurance policies are complex. Financial planners should know enough about them to recognize common inadequacies in their client's policies that may affect their ability to achieve their financial goals. The material in this book dealing with property and liability insurance is introductory in nature, so the reader must not expect to be an expert when finished. Most financial planners recognize that they best serve their clients by referring them to competent insurance agents who specialize in these areas for implementation and specific advice. Indeed, in many states, it is illegal for anyone who is not a licensed insurance agent or broker to give any advice about insurance for compensation. Any planner who, for a fee, gives inappropriate advice about these forms of insurance may get to find out how good his or her own professional liability insurance is. A good rule for this or any area of financial planning: Know your strengths and call on experts to cover any weaknesses.

This chapter introduces the homeowners forms of property and liability insurance. The policy forms described in this chapter are based on the standard forms as published by the Insurance Services Office (ISO). However, individual states may modify the standard forms introduced here, and companies may alter them further and/or give them unique designations. In most cases, a modified form will still include all that is in these standard forms in addition to some expanded coverage, and possibly some limitations. For some types of coverage, the standard forms are rarely used. National Underwriter publishes the FC&S Bulletins (fire, casualty, and surety) detailing the ISO standard forms of property and liability insurance as well as explanations and comments about them. This is an excellent resource for better understanding the various forms of insurance and their terms. There is another widely used standard set of policies provided through the American Association of Insurance Services (AAIS). These forms are second in use only to the ISO forms. In many respects they are similar, and in some ways they are different. These will not be covered in this text. Just as the ISO forms may be modified because of state law, the AAIS forms may be modified for the same reason. Also, companies may modify the AAIS forms by endorsement.

Terminology

Homeowners insurance and property and liability insurance in general, use a number of terms that are important to know. Understanding this vocabulary will help in understanding both this chapter and those that follow.

Actual Cash Value: The replacement cost minus depreciation.

Blanket Coverage: One insuring agreement covering an entire class of items or structures rather than items or structures being listed individually.

Broad Form: The lower end of homeowners coverage, having a limited list of named perils for which it provides protection.

Dwelling: Rather than use the term house or home, the homeowners series uses the term "dwelling." There are also a series of policy forms called "dwelling forms" that are primarily for non-resident owners.

Endorsement: A rider or attachment to a policy that expands or modifies the coverage.

Floater: A form of protection for property that can be transported, usually applied to valuable personal property. It is one form of endorsement.

Form: Another word for policy type.

Hazard: A condition that increases the chance that a given peril will cause a loss.

Homeowners Policy: A series of policy forms that are designed for resident owners and renters.

Insurable Interest: For an individual to have an insurable interest in any property or liability loss, he or she must actually be in a position to suffer a financial loss if there is a loss of, or damage to, the property insured.

Loss Assessment: The analysis of the extent of a loss.

Loss Settlement: The process of paying a claim or the check that pays the claim. In the policy, it is the section that explains how the loss will be covered.

Open Peril: A more generous coverage level (versus broad form) for homeowners policies, essentially meaning that coverage is provided for all perils not specifically excluded.

Personal Property: All property except real estate and things permanently attached to real estate, including clothes, jewelry, cameras, furniture, rugs (not nailed down), and any other personally owned items.

Peril: A cause of loss such as fire, hail, flood, or explosion (see chapter 1).

Replacement Cost: The amount it would cost to replace the lost item or structure with similar materials and construction methods.

Scheduled property: High-value personal property that is listed and individually insured.

HOMEOWNERS COVERAGE BY SECTION

Before discussing the general forms of coverage, it is important to understand the provisions of the specific sections found in a homeowners policy. Section I of the homeowners policy has four general types of coverage, designated A, B, C, and D, and a fifth section that includes numerous "other" coverages. Section II of the homeowners policy includes coverage E (personal liability), coverage F (medical payments to others), and additional coverages.

Homeowners Section I Coverage

There are four general types of coverage in this section (A-D), as well as "other coverages" and some miscellaneous provisions.

Coverage A—Dwelling

This is the coverage for the structure itself, and the amount of coverage in this section is determined by policy form and the structure being insured. The amount of coverage will be identified on the declarations page of the policy. Unless otherwise stated, this is generally determined on a replacement cost basis.

Coverage B—Other Structures

This provides protection in the amount of 10 percent of the coverage on the dwelling for any other structures/buildings that are on the property and are not attached to the basic dwelling. If 10 percent is not adequate, based on the type and value of other structures, it may generally be increased. Unless otherwise stated, this is generally determined on a replacement cost basis.

Coverage C—Contents

This is often called personal property coverage. This section provides coverage for personal property that is owned by an insured whether the property is at home or anywhere else in the world. The standard limit of coverage is 50 percent of the dwelling coverage amount, and there are some limits on certain classes of personal property such as cash, silverware, and firearms that will be discussed later in this chapter. Unless otherwise stated, this coverage is generally provided on an actual cash value basis (the replacement cost minus depreciation).

Coverage D—Loss of Use

If the dwelling is damaged to the extent that it is not habitable, the insurance company will typically pay up to 10 or 30 percent of the dwelling coverage amount to cover the additional expenses of living in temporary quarters

Other Coverage

The various forms also include other coverages that fall under a general category. These include:

Collapse

An interesting clause, it provides indemnity for losses from a collapse caused by a limited number of specified perils, including:

- Those that apply to personal property
- Hidden decay, unless the owner had prior knowledge of such decay
- Hidden insect or vermin damage, unless the owner had prior knowledge of such damage
- Weight of contents, equipment, animals, or people
- Weight of rain on a roof
- Defects in materials or methods used in construction if the collapse occurs during construction

This list of perils is generally substantially more generous than coverage for the dwelling itself.

Debris Removal

When damage has occurred due to an insured peril, cleanup is often required before repairs can begin. Coverage for cleanup is usually limited to 5 percent of the dwelling coverage.

Financial Loss

Called the "Credit Card, Forgery, and Counterfeit Money" coverage, it provides five different protections:

- Credit card losses
- Unauthorized use of debit cards
- Depositors' forgery
- Counterfeit money coverage
- Defense coverage

The first two protections are generally limited to $1,000 of protection for unauthorized use of the cards regardless of the reason the cards were misused. The depositors' forgery coverage protects the insured from someone forging a check or changing a check written by the insured, usually with a limit that is also $1,000. The same dollar limit generally applies to losses incurred because of receipt of counterfeit currency. Defense coverage provides defense and court costs for any insured involved in a lawsuit dealing with these losses, but will not cover defense costs for an insured found guilty of a criminal offense.

Fire Department Service Charge

This will generally pay up to $500 for a service charge made by a fire department when it is called to protect a home from an insured peril-fire being the most obvious peril.

Glass or Safety Glazing Material

This covers the replacement of broken glass from any cause, unless the dwelling has been vacant for longer than 30 days. If the law requires the use of safety glazing materials (tempered glass), the cost of that material will also be covered, up to the limit of the coverage.

Hail Damage

While not a specific provision included in standard policies, hail damage is often treated differently than other perils in certain parts of the country. In areas prone to hail, where a major hailstorm can damage thousands of homes, the deductible is sometimes specified by the insurer and is generally higher than that for other perils. It may be a stated amount or, alternatively, the greater of the standard deductible or 10 percent of the loss,

Landlord's Furnishings

This would obviously be included in a policy purchased by a renter to cover damage he or she may accidentally cause to a landlord's property, such as appliance or carpet damage.

Loss Assessment Coverage

This provides protection against assessments made by a condominium, corporate, or homeowners association because of its losses to collectively owned property. The limit of protection is generally $1,000. This would not generally include a special assessment because the association wants to fix something that has worn out or shows wear.

Ordinance or Law

Building codes change. A house that is severely damaged or destroyed must meet current building codes when being repaired or rebuilt. Building codes further require that if a structure suffers damage of more than a specified percentage (usually 40 to 50 percent) then repairs cannot be made unless they bring the entire structure up to code. This rider/endorsement typically pays as much as an additional 10 percent to bring the structure up to code. Without it, the insurer is not required to pay the extra amount to bring the structure up to code.

Property Removed

If property is damaged while being removed from a dwelling or away from a dwelling that has been damaged due to a covered peril, this coverage provides payment for the loss. It is in place to protect insureds from being penalized for attempting to minimize damage to personal property that might otherwise be caused by a covered peril.

Reasonable Repairs

One requirement of a policy is that the insured attempt to minimize damage when possible. If an insured incurs expenses in an effort to provide temporary repairs, which will minimize additional damage, the insurance company will reimburse him or her for those expenses under this provision.

Trees, Shrubs, Plants, and Lawns

When these are damaged because of an insured peril causing damage to the dwelling, there is limited coverage to repair or replace these items.

Miscellaneous Provisions for Section I

Homeowners policies have added various provisions over the years to add clarity to the contracts.

Abandonment of Property

This is a very important clause that prevents the insured from abandoning the property and considering it a total loss. In many cases, especially with automobiles as well as with other property, it is up to the insurer to decide if the loss is "total."

Appraisal

This provision is included to specify how disagreements about valuation are to be managed.

Glass Replacement

This limits the payment for safety (tempered) glass to places where it is required by law.

Insurable Interest and Limit of Liability

This is a very important concept to remember. The insurance company will not pay more than the amount of coverage under the policy and will only pay claims to the extent the insured has an interest in the property.

Insured's Duties

This refers to the duties of the insured once a loss has occurred, including:

- Protecting the property from additional damage
- Notifying the insurer of the loss in a timely manner (as well as notifying any others that circumstances require the following: police in the case of theft, credit card company when a card is missing, etc.)
- Preparing an inventory of lost, damaged, or destroyed items to the extent possible
- Cooperating with the insurance company. This means that if the insurance company requests information, the insured is expected to provide it.

Loss Settlement

This explains how claims will be paid, generally pointing out that personal property is covered at actual cash value and that buildings are covered on a replacement cost basis as described elsewhere in the policy.

Loss to Pair or Set Clause

This gives the insurance company a number of options when one item of a pair or set is lost, damaged, or stolen. The company may repair or replace the one item or pay the difference in the actual cash value prior to the loss and after the loss. This clause is included to prevent someone from being paid for a total loss when only a partial loss was suffered while acknowledging that, for example, the loss of one earring may be worth more than one-half of the value of the set. Examples of this are the loss of only one expensive earring in a set or three hand-cast gold chess pieces out of a set of pieces.

Mortgage Clause

This gives any mortgagee (lender) certain rights and responsibilities under the contract. For example, the lender will be notified if the premium is not paid. In most cases, a mortgage agreement gives the lender the right to insure the property and have the borrower pay the premium to the lender.

No Benefit to Bailee

A bailee is a person, business, or organization who is holding a person's property in trust. This clause states that if a bailee has possession of the property and it is damaged or lost, it is the bailee's responsibility to make the insured whole, not the insurer's. Normally, an insured's wardrobe is covered as personal property under the homeowners policy, wherever it is. However, if clothes are taken to the laundry/cleaner's, that business is a bailee: It has taken possession of the property in order to provide a service, and while the clothes are in possession of the cleaner, the cleaner is responsible for their safe return.

Nuclear Hazard Clause

This standard clause excludes any protection under section I of the policy for damage caused by a nuclear reaction, radiation, or radioactive contamination, except for fire caused by a nuclear hazard.

Recovered Property

This explains what happens if previously lost or stolen property is returned. The insured may give up the property to the insurer or may essentially pay back any payments made for the loss to the extent that payment would not have been made. In other words, if the property is returned but damaged, the insured may keep the property and may keep any portion of the payment made that would have covered the damage.

Other Insurance

Just as with health insurance policies, this provision limits the insurer's liability to an appropriate proportion of any losses when the insured has more than one policy that covers the same loss.

Our Option

This gives the insurer the right to repair or replace the insured property instead of writing a check. This can be used to avoid inappropriate or unreasonable cash claim payments. It provides some protection for the insurer that an insured will not decide that the ugly statue given to him or her by aunt Agness might mysteriously get knocked off of a table and destroyed.

Suit Against Us

This limits the insured's right to sue by stating what must be attempted prior to filing a lawsuit and limits the time frame in which a suit may be brought.

Volcanic Eruption Period

If there is more than one volcanic eruption within a 72-hour period, they will all be considered one eruption. This can save the insured multiple deductibles from multiple eruptions, each causing additional damage.

Homeowners Section II Coverages

Section II of a homeowners policy covers personal liability issues and medical payments to others as well as certain other coverages.

Coverage E: Personal Liability

The personal liability section of the homeowners policy is one of the primary reasons even a renter might want one. This coverage states that the insurance company will pay any covered legal liabilities of the insured due to bodily injury or property damage not done intentionally by the insured. The standard limit of liability is $100,000 but can be increased at the option of the insured.

In addition to paying the judgment, the policy may pay for the defense of the insured. However, along with this benefit is the right of the insurer to settle the lawsuit. As will be mentioned again in the chapter on liability insurance, settling a case sometimes has little to do with right or wrong, it is most often just a business decision. If the insurer pays a claim of the maximum amount of the coverage and there is a lawsuit to collect more, no defense is provided.

Probably the most important clause in this section is the definition of the persons who are insured. Insureds include the named insured, any resident relative, any individual under the age of 21 who is under the care of the insured, and students enrolled full time in schools away from the residence who were full-time residents before leaving for school.

Further, if the insured owns any animals or watercraft and someone else has control of either of them and a claim arises due to the actions of the animal or problems with the watercraft, that individual is an insured unless the animal or watercraft was being used in a business. There are two sets of exclusions that apply to personal liability coverage. These will be covered in chapter 11.

Additional Coverages

This is intended to cover a few additional expenses that might arise: first aid costs for someone injured on the premises; the cost of dealing with a claim; payment for property of others that is damaged, lost, or stolen while under the control of the insured but not due to actions of the insured; and loss assessment coverage. If an insured borrows a neighbor's lawnmower and it is stolen out of the insured's garage, this provision will cover it. The claim expenses covered include defense of a claim, interest on any judgment and some other legal costs as well as earnings up to $50 per day. These expenses are in addition to the liability limits.

In-Depth: Provisions Applied to Sections I and II

Assignment: Insurance is a personal contract between the insured and the insurer. The insured does not have the right to assign or transfer the benefits of the contract to anyone else without the written approval of the insurer.

Cancellation Clause: While it is a given that the insured may cancel the policy at any time, the insurer is allowed to cancel it only under certain circumstances and by following the procedures outlined in this clause. There are three general reasons the insurer can cancel the policy: (1) Nonpayment of premiums, but only after giving 10 days written notice; (2) Any reason during the first 60 days after issue or for material misrepresentation by the insured, or if the risk has changed substantially more than 60 days after issue with 30 days written notice; (3) Any reason with policies written for more than one year on the policy anniversary following 30 days written notice.

Concealment of Fraud: This provision protects the insurance company from intentional concealment of relevant information and fraudulent claims by the insured.

Death: The death of the insured does not terminate coverage until legal title has passed to a new owner. The legal representative (or custodian of the property holding it until the representative is appointed) is considered to be an insured under the contract.

Liberalization Clause: This allows the insurance company to modify the contract without approval of the insured as long as it is to the insured's benefit and does not increase the premium.

Nonrenewal: The insurer must give 30 days written notice if it doesn't intend to renew the contract.

Policy Period: Specifies that claims will only be paid if the loss occurs while the policy is in force.

Subrogation: To receive benefits from the insurer for a loss, the insured must assign his or her rights to sue another for the loss. This right of subrogation is limited to the extent he or she received payment from the insurer.

Coverage F: Medical Payments to Others

This covers the medical costs of individuals who are not residents but are on the premises with the permission of the insured and are hurt in an accident. Medical costs may also be paid for individuals away from the premises who suffer injuries requiring medical attention due to the actions of the insured, a condition on the premises, the actions of a residence employee, or the actions of the insureds pet(s). This payment may be paid regardless of liability and is intended to cover those visits to the emergency room necessitated by accidents. This coverage is generally limited to $1,000, which the policyholder can choose to increase.

Severability of Insureds

This means that while all of the potential insureds are covered for their own actions, the insurance company will not be subject to claims for more than the stated amount of coverage for a single occurrence when two or more insureds are involved.

HOMEOWNERS FORMS

There are seven standard ISO forms of homeowners insurance, but all provide one of three general levels of coverage.

Basic or **standard coverage** for specifically named perils provides the least protection. Specifically, it covers damage due to:

- Fire or lightning
- Windstorm or hail
- Vandalism or malicious mischief
- Theft
- Damage from vehicles and aircraft
- Explosion
- Riot or civil commotion
- Glass breakage
- Smoke
- Volcanic eruption

Broad form or **named peril coverage** expands basic coverage to additionally include:

- Building collapse
- Freezing of or accidental discharge of water or steam from internal plumbing; heating or air-conditioning systems or domestic appliances
- Falling objects
- The weight of ice, snow, or sleet
- The rupture or bursting of steam or hot water heating systems

Open perils or **special coverage** covers all risks except those specifically excluded. "Open perils" and "special form" have, for the most part, replaced the use of the term "all risk." Since there are exclusions, the term all risk created confusion and lawsuits.

The standard ISO forms, commonly referred to as forms HO-01 to HO-08, are generally listed as follows. (**Note:** In most states the HO-01 and the HO-05 forms are no longer offered.) Table 9.1 shows a comparison of the various forms and the perils insured against. Below is a more comprehensive description of broad form and open perils coverage. Note: this table applies to one- and two-family dwellings. Different percentages apply on coverages B, C, and D for dwellings with a larger number of units.

Table 9.1

Coverage	Form HO 02	Form HO 03	Form HO 04	Form HO 05	Form HO 06	Form HO 08
Section I	Broad form on structure and contents	Open peril on structure		Open peril on structure		Fire or lightning, windstorm, hail on structure
A: Dwelling	Covered	Covered	Not Covered	Covered	$1,000 base	Covered
B: Other Structures	10% of A	10% of A	Not Covered	10% of A	Included w/ A	10% of A
C: Personal Property	50% of A	50% of A	$6000 minimum	50% of A	$6000 minimum	50% of A
D: Loss of Use	30% of A	30% of A	30% of C	30% of A	30% of C	10% of A
Section II						
E: Personal Liability	Covered	Covered	Covered	Covered	Covered	Covered
F: Medical Payments to Others	Covered	Covered	Covered	Covered	Covered	Covered
Additional Coverages	Covered	Covered	Covered	Covered	Covered	Covered

HO 01 Homeowners 1 Basic Form

The HO-01 basic form policy has fewer perils covered than under a broad form policy. It is available in only a few states and is generally not recommended. Under certain circumstances, it is the only form available.

HO 02 Homeowners 2 Broad Form

The HO-02 policy is another lower cost form of insurance available to homeowners, providing protection to a dwelling and its contents against the limited number of perils listed under broad form coverage. Any losses that are caused by any peril other than those listed are simply not covered. However, if a peril that is not covered results in a peril that is covered, coverage is generally provided by the policy. For example, if an earthquake (not covered) causes a natural gas pipe to rupture and ignite (fire is covered), the loss due to the fire is covered. This can get pretty messy: If the earthquake caused a wall to collapse, which started a fire, the insurer would cover repair of the fire-damaged portion of the home but not the collapsed wall since it was caused by the earthquake.

HO 03 Homeowners 3 Special Form

The HO-03 policy form is the most common homeowners form as it is more comprehensive and offers more protection than HO-01 or HO-02. This form provides open perils coverage on the structure and broad form coverage on the contents. Many companies offer an HO-15 rider, which changes coverage on contents to open perils, essentially offering the same coverage as the HO-05 form, since that form is not available in all states or from all companies.

HO 04 Homeowners 4 Contents or Renters Broad Form

The HO-04 form is generally called a renter's policy as it provides no coverage for the structure (since it is not owned by the insured) but does provide broad form coverage for personal property.

HO 05 Homeowners 5 Comprehensive Form

A policy form that is equivalent to the combination of an HO-03 with an HO-15 rider is the HO-05 form, providing open peril coverage on both the dwelling and its contents.

HO 06 Homeowners 6 Unit-Owners or Condominium Form

For those who own a condominium or co-op, the HO-06 policy provides open perils coverage for the interior part of the structure and broad form coverage of the contents. This is different from the HO 04 since the resident has an ownership interest in the structure.

HO 08 Homeowners 8 Modified Coverage Form

Many old homes were built with methods and materials that would be very expensive to use today. Quite often, the cost to rebuild one of these homes using the same materials and methods would exceed the value of the home on the market. This often happens in older neighborhoods where the price of the homes is depressed relative to the cost of building a new home on the same land. Additionally, in some cases, these homes are more likely to have fires because of the age of the wiring, heating system, and/or construction materials. For this reason, the HO-08 policy was created. Generally, if an older home is destroyed, it is replaced with a *functionally equivalent* building, meaning that if the house that was destroyed was an 1,800-square-foot, three-bedroom home, that is what will be built in its place with modern methods and materials. There is a good chance it will not have the appearance of the original structure.

How Coverage Works

Generally, dwellings are insured on a replacement cost basis. What this means is that if the insured adequately covers the dwelling, any loss will be covered for the amount of the cost of required repairs without any deduction for depreciation. To operate in any other manner would create severe problems for virtually all homeowners. Without this type of coverage, the depreciation on a 25- to 30-year-old home would likely require the insured to cover most of the cost of repairs out of pocket.

The vast majority of losses are not total losses. Even extensive fires typically leave large portions of a home with nothing more than smoke damage. Knowing this reality, many individuals might want to cover only a portion of the value of their home in an effort to save premium dollars. For this reason, to make replacement cost coverage work, every insured who wants damage covered on a replacement cost basis must insure the home for at least 80 percent of the cost to rebuild it. This is called the coinsurance requirement. It is important to remember that this is not 80 percent of the purchase price. Land is not typically considered part of the insured value since there is little that can happen to it in most locations. The location of a home has a significant effect on its value in the marketplace, but probably will not impact the amount of insurance coverage needed. For example, a 1,700-square-foot bungalow in one neighborhood may sell for $225,000 while a similar one in a more desirable neighborhood a mile away might sell for $400,000. However, if they are about the same age and style and consist of the same materials, the insurance coverage will likely cost the same.

Since most claims are not for the full replacement of the home, many homeowners do not insure for the full cost of rebuilding. Also, homeowners who did purchase enough to fully cover the cost of rebuilding but who have not reviewed their coverage in many years may find themselves with less than the 80 percent of the cost of rebuilding. If this occurs, the claim is not paid on a replacement-cost basis. It would be paid for the higher of either: a) the actual cash value (replacement cost minus depreciation of the damaged portion) or b) the proportion of the replacement cost of the loss that the amount of insurance bears to the minimum 80 percent of the replacement cost of the structure.

What does this mean? Determining the replacement cost and then subtracting depreciation from it yields the actual cash value. If you have a structure that would cost $200,000 and its useful life is 40 percent extinguished, then the structure has depreciated 40 percent. So the structure's actual cash value is $200,000 - (.40 x $200,000) = $200,000 - $80,000 = $120,000, which would also be the maximum that would be paid for a total loss, assuming that there is at least $120,000 of coverage. With a few exceptions, the amount paid for a loss will not exceed the amount of coverage. If the loss was only $40,000, the actual cash value of the loss would be $40,000 - (.40 x $40,000) = $40,000 - $16,000 = $24,000. From this amount, subtract the deductible to determine the amount to be paid.

The alternative ("b" above) is calculated this way: The amount of insurance required is 80 percent of the $200,000-or $160,000. If the insured had $150,000 of coverage, that is not enough. The percentage of the loss that is covered is the percentage calculated by dividing the amount of insurance in place by the minimum amount of insurance required: $150,000÷$160,000 = .9375 = 93.75 percent. For a total loss, the amount paid would be the lesser of 93.75% of the loss (.9375 x $200,000 = $187,500) or the amount of insurance. In the example case, $150,000 would be paid. For a partial loss of $40,000, the amount paid would be .9375 x $40,000 or $37,500. Be sure to subtract the deductible from this final number. When the amount of insurance is less than the calculated amount of coverage, the deductible is usually subtracted from the calculated amount of coverage, not from the actual amount of coverage available.

With both examples above, a total loss and a partial loss, the alternative valuation method provides the larger payment. With newer construction and less depreciation, the actual cash value figures may be higher.

An issue that has created some concern is a situation where an insured files a claim for damage to a home, receives the money, and then does not have the repairs completed. One of the changes that has taken place to prevent this from happening is that when the loss exceeds either 5 percent of the amount of insurance or $2,500 only a portion of the money will be paid until the repairs are made. This is often modified to cover the required payments to the contractors as repairs progress. In the past, people would often collect payment for roof repairs required due to hail damage and then not repair the roof. They would subsequently sell the home and find a new buyer who did not realize the roof needed replacement. This is not part of the standard ISO form and is not permitted in every state. The standard ISO form states, under the Loss Payment clause, that once the value of the loss is determined and agreed upon, the insurer has 30 days in which to pay the claim. The Our Option clause may be used by the insurer. This clause says the insurer may pay for the amount of the loss or pay for the repair or replacement. If the insurer chooses the latter, it can state that it will pay for the repair or replacement directly.

When determining value, it is important to remember that the replacement cost of a home is the cost of rebuilding the structure with like kind and quality of materials. It is not based on the retail market value of the home or its loan value or a generic value per square foot. It is based on the type of construction and the number of square feet, with consideration made for any unusually expensive modifications and, to some extent, its location as it relates to construction costs and accessibility of construction materials and equipment.

As long as the insurance in place is at least 80 percent of the replacement cost, partial losses will be covered at replacement cost, with a maximum of the amount of insurance. So, if the insured had enough insurance to cover 90 percent of the replacement cost and the structure was a total loss, the insurer would pay 90 percent of the loss, less the deductible.

In-Depth: Inflation

So what happens as construction costs go up and the insured doesn't think to increase the amount of coverage? A rider called the "inflation guard endorsement" is available. This rider automatically includes quarterly or annual increases in coverage. The purpose of the endorsement is to keep the coverage from falling below the necessary 80 percent level. However, construction costs don't necessarily increase at a stable rate as demand can have a serious effect on costs.

In a disaster area where many homes are damaged or destroyed, the aftermath creates a huge demand for design work, general contractors, skilled labor, unskilled labor, and materials. The basic economic effects of supply and demand do not disappear in the face of a disaster—indeed, they are exacerbated. Those who can afford it will bid up the cost of architects, general contractors, and materials, as well as the labor required to do the work, just to get their home done first. What can be done to protect against this potential problem?

An endorsement is available called "guaranteed replacement cost coverage." As long as the insured has this coverage, endeavors to maintain 100 percent coverage on the replacement cost of the dwelling, and notifies the insurer within 30 days of completion of any changes in the building that would increase its value, a total loss will be covered even if it is more than the amount of insurance. This provision often has limits, such as 15 percent of the expected cost of repair or rebuilding.

Personal Property Losses

Unscheduled personal property coverage is blanket coverage, meaning that all personal property is insured as a class of property instead of being individually listed. For personal property losses, actual cash value is the standard coverage. Clothing would have a value significantly below the cost of replacing it, and many items would be depreciated to nothing because of their age, regardless of their functionality. For the homeowners forms, personal property is covered at 50 percent of the coverage for the dwelling. For HO-04 and HO-06 forms that provide little or no structure coverage, the minimum amount of insurance for personal property is $6,000. While 50 percent is the standard level, some companies automatically issue policies with a higher level of protection, and others generally permit the insured to increase it. For forms 2, 3, and 5, the lowest level, if the insured wants to decrease it, is 40 percent.

Interestingly, personal property owned or used by an insured is covered, including borrowed property. This coverage is also provided when the personal property is anywhere in the world—not just when it is in the residence. However, if the insured has a secondary residence, the personal property located there has coverage limited to 10 percent of the coverage on the dwelling.

The insured may also choose to insure the property of others when it is on the insured's premises, including property of guests or employees of an insured.

Replacement cost coverage on personal property is available as an endorsement to the policy. Generally, there is a provision that states that payment for replacement of any item valued over $500 is paid only if that item is actually replaced. For this specific coverage, there are four classes of items that are not covered for replacement cost under this endorsement.

They include:

- Antiques, fine art, and the like
- Memorabilia, souvenirs, collectors items, and the like
- Property that is not kept in good or working condition
- Obsolete items being stored and not used

It actually makes sense to have these exclusions. The first two, by their nature, are difficult to value. They would be more appropriately covered under a personal property endorsement or inland marine coverage (see definition below) based on appraisals. The second two are obviously not insurable at replacement cost since they are either in poor condition or are not being used. Being able to get paid for the value of new items to replace these would create a moral hazard.

ENDORSEMENTS

It is important that each homeowner have appropriate endorsements/riders/floaters on his or her homeowners policy. Most insurance companies are very good at paying claims. Where most problems occur is with inadequate insurance policies: a policy that drops to below 80 percent coverage of the replacement cost of the home; personal property not covered under the same perils as the structure; no flood insurance when the home is in a flood plane; and hard-to-value items that are not adequately insured, etc.

Inflation Guard

As previously discussed, the inflation guard endorsement automatically increases the amount of insurance each quarter or each year to prevent the coverage from becoming inadequate. Even with this rider, it is incumbent on the insured to periodically review the coverage with his or her insurer to make sure it is adequate. The cost of repairs and rebuilding do not follow the cost of real estate and may increase or decrease at a very different rate than that chosen for the endorsement. The endorsement generally costs nothing, but the policy premiums will automatically be adjusted as the replacement cost increases.

HO-15

There is little question that the perils under the broad form of coverage will cover the vast majority of losses. However, it is still possible to have all personal property lost through destruction of a home and not have it covered. The HO-15 endorsement provides that all personal property, with few exceptions, is covered with open perils coverage. With this rider, personal property is protected from the same perils as the home itself.

Inland Marine and Scheduled Personal Property

Particularly valuable items are normally not adequately covered in a homeowners policy form. There are limits on how much will be paid for various articles of personal property, including cash, precious metals, jewelry, sterling silver, antiques, and art, among others (See the sidebar: "In-Depth: Personal Property Limits"). Anything that is worth more than these limits should be covered with an endorsement to the homeowners form or through a separate policy. Certain of these items can be covered under an **inland marine policy** (essentially insurance for anything that can be moved with relative ease from one place to another) or a floater attached to the homeowners policy that is sometimes called a **scheduled personal property endorsement**. Typically those items that can be appraised and that would have a value above that set in the policy limits would be the items to insure through this method. For items that do not have a readily ascertainable market value, an appraisal is required.

The advantage of a floater or inland marine policy is that the listed property is insured for the appraised value, often with no deductible, for any damage or loss. However, once an item has been listed (scheduled) in a floater or inland marine policy, it is no longer covered under the basic coverage of the homeowners form. For example, if a couple had $5,000 of sterling silverware, they would need to insure it specifically for $5,000. Once it is scheduled for specific coverage, the limit of $2,500 under the homeowner's policy is no longer in place and if they insured the property for only this amount under the floater, that is all they would receive.

In-Depth: Personal Property Limits

Money, bank notes, bullion, coins, medals, etc.	$ 200
Securities, manuscripts, personal records, stamp collections	1,500
Watercraft, including trailers, equipment, and motors	1,500
Other trailers	1,500
Jewelry, furs, precious and semiprecious stones lost by theft	1,500
Firearms and associated equipment lost by theft	2,500
Silverware, goldware, silver plated and gold plated ware, and pewterware if lost by theft	2,500
Business property on the premises	2,500
Business property away from the premises	500
Electrical equipment that can be used with or away from a motor vehicle while in or on a motor vehicle	1,500
Electrical equipment used for business that can be used with or away from a motor vehicle while away from the premises	1,500

It is important to note that these special limits on watches, jewelry, fur, and firearms only apply to loss by theft. Personal property items that are not included in the above list are covered with broad form coverage.

Other Members of Your Household

A recently developed endorsement, this was created in 2000 due to the ever-increasing number of nontraditional families. This covers as an insured an adult resident of the named insured's residence. This is intended to include as an insured another adult living in the home of either gender who is helping to pay expenses or is in a personal relationship with the insured.

Assisted Living Care Coverage

Another relatively new endorsement, this provides both section I and section II coverage for a relative who is necessarily confined to an assisted living facility. There are specific limits of coverage on certain personal property. Additional living expense coverage is provided if the facility becomes uninhabitable. Please note, this does not pay for care of any kind, it is merely an extension of coverage for property of an insured who is living in an assisted living facility.

Nonbuilding Replacement Cost

For a few specific items, replacement cost coverage is available for structures that are not buildings through the endorsement. For fences, mailboxes, light poles, satellite dishes, and swimming pools that are constructed of reinforced masonry, metal fiberglass, or plastic, replacement at cost rather than actual cash value is covered.

Computers

Surprisingly, despite the wide ownership of computers, they are not covered particularly well under a homeowners policy. The biggest problem is power surge damage, which, if resulting from circumstances other than on the premises, will not be covered. This endorsement covers computer equipment on an open peril basis, but the ISO form also includes an exclusion for mechanical breakdown.

Earth Movement

This coverage may be included in the homeowners policy as an endorsement. It typically has a percentage deductible rather than a dollar deductible. Since some areas are more earthquake-prone or sinkhole-prone than others, the premiums for this endorsement will vary widely.

EXCLUSIONS

Virtually all forms of property and liability insurance have long lists of exclusions. Most of these are perfectly logical when evaluated, but the normal reaction for individuals reading these exclusions is to think that the insurance company is trying to avoid liability for just about everything. The truth is quite simple and reasonable, and the exclusions generally exist for one of two reasons: Either the risk is not insurable, as discussed in chapter 1, or the form of insurance being reviewed is not the proper form or part of the proper form to provide the insurance.

For example, personal property is excluded from the dwelling portion of the homeowners forms (coverage A) because it is covered under coverage C. A homeowner who owns a business will find that his or her business equipment has very limited coverage under the homeowners policy because it should be covered under a commercial policy written for the business. The standard forms of insurance are written to cover the most common needs of everyone who purchases the policy. Not everyone has a boat, equally valuable jewelry, or a set of sterling silver flatware; thus, it would not be appropriate for everyone to pay extra premiums to adequately cover certain items of high value owned by a limited number of people. This also requires people with valuable items to obtain a verifiable value for the items prior to insuring them rather than trying to come up with a value after they are gone.

Section I General Exclusions

These exclusions are the common exclusions found in Section I of the homeowners HO-03 and HO-05 policies. Both of these forms provide coverage on an open perils basis, and all perils are covered except those specifically excluded. The broad form and basic form of coverage only cover those perils that are listed, so they generally do not need these exclusions. The identifying numbers given are based on the standard ISO forms.

A.1 Ordinance or Law

As discussed before, if the building codes make the structure more expensive to replace than those in place when it was originally built, the extra cost is not covered unless an endorsement is made to the policy.

A.2 Earth Movement

This can be any form of earth movement, such as earthquakes, mudslides, and sinkholes. Damage caused by the earth movement is not covered. However, this does not exclude coverage for damage caused by fire, explosion, breakage of glass, or theft that may have occurred as a result of the earth movement.

A.3 Water Damage

This not only excludes coverage for floods, it excludes coverage for sewer back-ups and damage caused by any water that enters the home from outside of the structure, whether is it from above or below ground. Like coverage A.2, this does not exclude coverage for losses caused by other perils such as fire, explosion, or theft that may be a result of the water damage. Flood insurance, water backup, and sump discharge or overflow coverage is often available for an additional premium.

A.4 Power Failure

This excludes coverage for losses caused by a power failure that occurs away from the insured residence. If power lines are knocked down in a storm, losses due to that power failure are not covered.

This does not exclude coverage for power failure at the residence. If a tree is hit by lightning and falls across the power line coming into the home, thus knocking out the home's power, losses caused by that power failure will be covered.

A.5 Neglect

Under the terms of the policy, the insured has an obligation to take whatever opportunity is available to minimize further damage or loss following a loss. If he or she fails to make an effort to minimize further losses, the additional loss is not covered. An example would be a large window being broken by a branch breaking off of a tree. If the owner did nothing to attempt to cover the opening and further damage from rain coming in through the window or loss by theft occurred because of that failure, those secondary losses would not be covered.

A.6 War

This exclusion includes war or acts of war (declared or undeclared), insurrections, rebellion, or revolution. The reason for this is that it is likely there would be widespread destruction that could not be handled by the entire insurance industry. Generally it is believed that this clause, with its standard wording, does not apply to terrorist attacks. However, some companies are adding terrorist activity exclusions.

A.7 Nuclear Hazard

Damage caused by nuclear reactions, radiation, or radioactive contamination is not covered, as the owner of the nuclear facility would cover it. However, a fire that is caused by the nuclear hazard would be covered.

A.8 Intentional Loss

This may seem obvious: If someone tries to burn down his or her own home, the insurer will not cover the loss. However, the exclusion extends to other insureds who had nothing to do with the loss.

An example may help: Brad was separated from his spouse; though his name was still on the title of the home and he was still an insured, he no longer lived there. When he intentionally set the house on fire, the intentional loss clause eliminated any coverage, even though Brad no longer lived there and his spouse lost all that she owned. The NAIC adopted a model law in 1998 that eliminates this clause as it relates to innocent co-insureds, remedying the obvious injustice in this situation. The insurer would have the right to seek restitution from Brad, but would have to pay the claim for the loss.

A.9 Government Action

If the government seizes the property, generally due to illegal activities, the insurance company is not liable to the insured for its loss.

B.1-B.3: Current Causation Exclusions

These were added, as was the case with many other exclusions, due to court decisions where the insurers were required to pay for losses for which coverage was never intended.

B.1 excludes loss caused by weather conditions that cause or contribute to an excluded peril. This would apply to heavy rains that lead to a mudslide that damages a home. If the heavy rain itself causes damage to the structure, such as water accumulating on a flat roof and, in turn, causing the roof to collapse, that would be covered.

B.2 excludes losses due to action or inaction; decisions or failure to make decisions by a person, group, organization, or government body. This would include inspectors failing to enforce building codes or a responsible party failing to maintain a dam that collapsed. The loss is caused by the action or inaction of someone other than the insured, and that person or entity is ultimately responsible for the damage.

B.3 excludes loss due to bad, faulty, defective, or inadequate planning, design, maintenance, or materials. Losses directly caused by the foregoing are not covered; however, if any of the foregoing caused a covered peril, that loss would be covered. For example, if a plumber used flawed pipes and joints in plumbing a home, failure of the plumbing would not be covered, but water damage inside the home due to the failure would be covered. Again, the basic loss is due to problems caused by someone other than the insured.

C.1-C.4

These exclude coverage for losses caused by freezing of plumbing or damage to fences, pavement, patios, and other specified items due to freezing and thawing; pressure of water or ice; theft from a building under construction; and vandalism and related losses when a building has been vacant more than 60 days.

C.5 excludes loss due to mold, fungus, or wet rot. However, if these problems arise from gradual, hidden leakage from plumbing or appliances, they are not excluded. A number of nationally publicized cases have caused insurers to reword their exclusion for toxic mold. In the late 1990s, there was a handful of claims for mold in the state of Texas. In 2001 there were hundreds. Accordingly, this has become a much more serious problem.

C.6 includes a list of exclusions on open peril coverage:

- Wear and tear, marring, or deterioration
- Mechanical breakdown, latent defect, inherent vice, or a quality in a property that causes it to damage or destroy itself
- Smog, rust, or other conversion
- Smoke from agricultural smudging or industrial operations
- Discharge, release, or dispersal of contaminants or pollutants, unless caused by one of the named perils which insures personal property

- Settling, cracking, shrinking, bulging, or expansion of pavement, foundation, walls, floors, or ceilings
- Birds, vermin, rodents, or insects
- Animals owned or kept by an insured

The exclusion for mold has been clarified recently because of substantial increases in claims that seem to be running out of control.

If one of the above results in a covered peril causing a loss, that loss is covered. For example, if rodents chew through wires, replacement of the wires is not covered. If the chewed-through wires cause a fire, the damage caused by that fire is covered.

Personal Property Exclusions for Open Peril Coverage

In addition to the section I exclusions for any structures, there are exclusions for personal property, including:

- Breakage of eyeglasses, glassware, statuary, marble, bric-a-brac, porcelain items, and similar fragile items unless caused by a covered peril (in other words, if you drop your favorite antique vase while dusting it, too bad, unless it is covered by a floater)
- Dampness or extremes of temperature, unless the loss is caused directly by rain, snow, sleet, or hail
- Refinishing, renovating, or replacing damaged property other than watches, jewelry, and furs
- Collision, other than collision with a land vehicle; the sinking, swamping, or stranding of watercraft, including their related equipment, trailers, and motors
- Destruction, confiscation, or seizure by a government authority
- Actions or decisions or failure to act or decide by anyone that causes a loss

Theft Exclusions

It may seem inappropriate to exclude any theft losses; however, these do make sense:

- Theft by an insured: A rebellious teen decides to take off and fund his or her travels by stealing and pawning valuable family assets
- Theft from a dwelling that is under construction, including the materials and/or supplies used in the construction, until it is completed and occupied; until the property is occupied, those losses are the responsibility of the builder
- Theft from any rented part of the residence that is rented to someone who is not an insured

- Theft from another property owned by the insured, unless the insured is residing at the other property; that property should have its own coverage
- Theft of watercraft, their related furnishings/equipment, and motors while away from the residence; the risk is substantially greater for theft, so separate insurance is warranted
- Theft of campers and/or trailers that are stolen while away from the insured residence

Other Forms

Besides the forms listed above, several other specialized policy forms are available.

Flood Insurance

One standard exclusion is for floods, including any surface water. In fact, any water that enters the house from the outside, rather than water that is already in the house by way of the plumbing system, is generally excluded. It is clear that many people want coverage to protect them from this type of damage, but flood coverage is fraught with adverse selection and the losses can be too catastrophic for the entire private insurance industry to handle. Because of this, insurance companies on their own do not want to cover these potential losses, though flood insurance is separately available.

The Federal Insurance Administration, under the Federal Emergency Management Agency (FEMA), is in charge of the National Flood Insurance Program (NFIP). Policies are available from the NFIP and private insurers. All flood insurance is reinsured through NFIP.

To be able to obtain flood insurance, an individual must reside in an eligible community. This requires that the community pledges to adopt and enforce land use control measures that guide the development of the community away from flood-prone areas. The amount of coverage is limited to $250,000 for single-family homes (structure) with $100,000 for contents, $500,000 for nonresidential buildings, and $500,000 for contents of nonresidential buildings.

Rates vary based on the risk of each building, and rate maps show the risk in different areas. When the news talks about low-cost loans being available for those wiped out in floods, it generally does not mention that those loans are only available to those who have the insurance.

This is limited to areas known as special **flood hazard areas**; areas very prone to flooding. Homes in those areas are generally required to have the insurance in order to obtain a loan to purchase the home.

Dwelling Coverage

Dwelling coverage is generally for homes that do not qualify for homeowners forms. There are three forms: DP-1, a basic form; DP-2, a broad form; and DP-3, a special open perils form. Residences that have more than two boarders, rental houses, and very old homes that are among those not intended for coverage under the HO series typically use the dwelling forms.

Various coverages that are included in the HO series are excluded, available only as endorsements, or more limited in the DP series.

Mobile Home Coverage

With nearly half of the new homes sold today being mobile homes, there is a significant demand to cover them as dwellings. Historical statistics show that the average loss from a fire in a mobile home is more than ten times the average loss from permanent structures,[1] and they are more prone to weather damage. The coverage for mobile homes is something of a cross between the homeowners series and automobile insurance.

Inland Marine

This type of coverage is very flexible and does many things. Certain items, such as boats, campers, and trailers, have limited coverage under the homeowners forms that is often not effective when the property is away from the residence. Inland marine can provide adequate protection regardless of the location of the property. Certain other items, such as personal all-terrain vehicles, may be completely excluded from homeowners policies and do not fit under the personal auto policy, but inland marine forms can be used to provide coverage. Further, many valuable items are not adequately covered under the homeowners policy, so inland marine coverage can provide adequate protection for these as well. When property is insured under an inland marine policy, it is scheduled or listed individually.

Wedding Presents

Anyone who has been at the bride's home prior to a wedding knows that gifts come in for weeks, sometimes months. These gifts may include china, crystal, sterling silver, and other valuable items. With some fairly obvious exclusions, such as money, notes, bonds, securities, stamps, animals, and vehicles, this policy or floater provides open perils coverage from the date gifts begin to accumulate until, at latest, 90 days following the wedding. The 90 days provides adequate time to obtain proper insurance on the valuable items.

Title Insurance

This is not homeowners insurance, and everyone who borrows money to buy a home pays for it. For most buyers, title to the property is not a problem. However it is possible that the title being transferred in a sale is not clear or that someone else has a legitimate claim against the property. There are many ways this can happen, legally and illegally. If another person or entity can prove ownership, the current resident may be forced to leave without compensation. Title insurance pays for that loss.

An alternative to title insurance is the **Torrens System**, developed by Robert Torrens in Australia, which states that the current purchaser keeps the property. Fees are paid when the property is purchased that go into an insurance fund. If another owner proves an ownership right, the fund pays that person for his or her loss. Laws in place permit the operation of the Torrens System in 15 states, and only Hawaii, Illinois, Massachusetts, and Minnesota have currently implemented them.

---

[1] FEMA analysis of National Fire Protection Association's 1981 National Fire Experience Survey.

HOMEOWNERS INSURANCE NEEDS ANALYSIS

The key to analyzing the needs of a client is to have a clear picture of the client's living situation. In most cases, people purchase their home with a mortgage. When doing so, they are required to have homeowners insurance in place. This leads the individual to seek an insurance agent and get the home covered with a policy that is acceptable to the lender. This will generally be adequate coverage, at least for the structure, for some period of time.

This is an area of specialization, and as mentioned before, giving insurance advice without a proper license in most states is illegal, so care must be taken in what is said. However, there are some issues that can be discussed without giving specific advice.

A planner may not be able to easily determine which policy form is being used since some companies use their own terminology and often modify the standard ISO forms. To determine the type of coverage, review the perils that are insured against. If it is a list of perils, it is a basic or broad form. If it is all perils, unless specifically excluded, then it is open perils coverage. Then look at the levels of coverage for Parts B, C, and D. That will also give some idea as to the plan.

Review the amount of personal property coverage relative to the insurance on the structure. If the structure is insured for $200,000, ask the client if he or she believes all of their personal property can be replaced at the level of coverage provided by the policy. Standard ISO forms cover personal property for up to 50 percent of the amount of insurance on the structure. Some companies use a different percentage. While you are at it, ask if the client has specific coverage on jewelry, fine art, etc. If not, you may point out the limits in the policy and ask if those amounts are adequate.

Compare the value of the home to the amount of coverage. Unless the home is in a low priced area, the market value of the home should exceed the insured value by a substantial sum. With experience, a planner will learn what insurance companies consider adequate coverage for a particular type and size of home. If the amount of coverage seems too low, ask when the client last had the coverage reviewed. As a general rule, ask when the last review was performed and look for an inflation adjustment rider. If there is no rider and the policy has not been reviewed in five years or more, strongly suggest that the client have a review conducted.

If the home has an attached garage, it is likely that the Other Structures coverage is adequate. If it has a detached garage, gazebo, pool house, tool shed, and custom fence, the amount of that coverage should be determined and the client should be asked if that amount is adequate for all of the other structures.

In today's world, many people use a portion of their home for work. They may not take a deduction for that space; however it typically has business equipment and material in it. Coverage under the basic policy for business equipment in the home is very limited. If someone works out of the home, he or she should definitely consider separate coverage for business assets.

Rather than using the analysis to make recommendations for which the planner is seldom qualified, the planner can use it to encourage the client to review his or her coverage to ensure its adequacy. This helps build the credibility of the planner and serves to strengthen the client's financial plan.

IMPORTANT CONCEPTS

Actual cash value	Loss of use coverage
Basic form	Named-peril coverage
Broad form	Neglect exclusion
Concurrent causation	Open perils coverage
Duties of the insured	Ordinance or law coverage
Dwelling policy forms	Other structures coverage
Earth movement exclusion	Pair and set provision
Endorsements	Personal property coverage
Floaters	Power failure exclusion
Flood insurance	Replacement cost coverage
Homeowners forms (HO-01 to HO-08)	Torrens System
Inflation guard	Water damage exclusion

QUESTIONS FOR REVIEW

1. Explain what is meant by "standard ISO forms."

2. How is "actual cash value" different from "replacement cost?"

3. What are the four types of coverage under section I of the homeowners forms? Describe them.

4. What is the result of the ordinance and law provision of a policy? What can be done to change that result?

5. Which coverages are included in section II of the homeowners forms?

6. For what reasons may an insurer cancel a homeowners policy?

7. List the homeowners forms and explain how they differ from one another.

8. Jack's home was struck by lightning, caught fire, and was virtually destroyed with everything in it. He had a standard ISO HO-03 policy with an HO-15 rider and replacement cost coverage for personal property. The house replacement cost is $125,000 and his general personal property was valued at $70,000. When he bought the house eight years ago, he insured it for $90,000 and never changed that amount. Considering the age of the home, it would be considered depreciated by 30 percent. With a $500 deductible for the structure and personal property, how much is the insurance company likely to pay for his loss?

9. Assume that Jack's wife had an heirloom diamond necklace valued at $10,000 that disappeared in the fire. What would the insurer pay for that particular item? If that is not adequate, what could Jack have done to change the result?

10. List five general exclusions from the homeowners policy and explain why they are excluded and how those particular losses can be indemnified.

SUGGESTIONS FOR ADDITIONAL READING

Fundamentals of Risk and Insurance, 9th ed., Emmett J. Vaughan and Therese M. Vaughan, Wiley, 2003.

Homeowners Coverage Guide, 2nd ed., Diane W. Richardson, CPCU, National Underwriter, 2002

How Insurance Works: An Introduction to Property and Liability Insurance, 2nd edition., Barry D. Smith and Eric A. Wiening, American Institute for Chartered Property and Casualty Underwriters, 1994.

Introduction to Risk Management and Insurance, 8th ed., Mark Dorfman, Prentice Hall, 2004.

Principles of Risk Management and Insurance, 9th ed., George E. Rejda, Addison Wesley, 2004.

Property and Liability Principles, 3rd ed., Constance Lutheardt, American Institute forChartered Property and Casualty Underwriters, July 1999.

CHAPTER TEN

Automobile Insurance: The Personal Auto Policy

• • •

There are three forms of insurance that are generally required: Lenders require homeowners and title insurance, as covered in chapter 9 (they may also require physical damage coverage on a leased auto or for an auto that is used as collateral for a loan), and most states require most individuals to have the liability portion of the personal auto policy (PAP)—the portion of the policy that protects others. The states view driving as a privilege that comes with responsibilities, namely the responsibility for damages and injuries an automobile owner inflicts on others. Most drivers will also want additional protection. Financial planners typically find that most clients will need automobile insurance, which has its own distinct issues.

When you have completed this chapter, you will be able to:

- Describe the protections offered to policyholders under a personal automobile policy
- Describe the liability limits shown in the PAP
- Describe the operation of the various methods of claims settlement
- Describe factors that affect policy pricing

THE PERSONAL AUTO POLICY

In one 2001 study, the Insurance Research Council estimated that the percentage of uninsured drivers ranges from 14 percent nationally to 32 percent in Colorado, with Mississippi, South Carolina, Alabama, New Mexico, and California close behind. (These statistics are based on claims submitted.) According to another study, 28 percent of vehicles being driven nationally are uninsured.[1] Various other studies have stated that, in some municipalities, as many as 34 percent of the cars on the road are being driven without insurance. This is in the face of state laws that generally require insurance to be in place for a car to be registered.

The reason so many car owners are able to drive without insurance is that they generally obtain the insurance for the period of time required to obtain their registration and then allow the policy to lapse or they cancel the coverage. Most states do not have a procedure in place to determine if insurance has been cancelled. Additionally, people who choose not to insure generally have a relatively low income and will not be sued because of their lack of assets. On registration renewal forms, often done through the mail, there is usually a statement that is signed that insurance is still in place. For those who do not have it, and who do not intend to buy it, it is simply a matter of failing to tell the truth on the form so that they can maintain current registration for their vehicle.

While many drivers view insurance primarily as a way of protecting their own cars, the greatest financial concern of most financial planning clients should be the liability that can arise from owning and/or driving an automobile. In a single accident, it is possible to cause $50,000 of damage to vehicles and leave a person in need of medical care for the rest of his or her life. The potential liability is the reason 47 states require at least some automobile insurance and the rest have financial responsibility laws requiring drivers to prove they are financially capable of covering a specified amount of damages they may cause.

In the marketplace there are four standard Insurance Services Office (ISO) forms of automobile insurance: the personal auto policy (PAP), family auto policy (FAP), special auto policy (SAP), and basic auto policy (BAP). This chapter will limit itself to the PAP, which is the most widely used form. The PAP, initially created in 1977, provides coverage for liability, medical expenses, and property damage.

The PAP was written to be much easier to read than its predecessors. However, it has many parts, and clients often find it to be rather complicated. A planner's understanding of the basic components will provide the ability to explain coverage to a client. If a client does not have adequate coverage, an informed planner can explain the potential consequences of any shortcomings. When studying this contract, the planner should remember that, as with homeowners forms, there are exclusions to the PAP that at first blush may seem unfair. And as with homeowners contracts, the exclusions are logical in that the coverage excluded is generally better when it is provided under a different type of contract or as a different coverage within the same contract.

---

[1] "What We Know About Uninsured Motorists and How Well We Know What We Know," *Resources for the Future*, 2000.

PAP Coverages

The personal auto policy has four general areas for which it provides protection:

Part A: Liability Insurance

The specifics of negligence and legal liability will be covered in chapter 11, but putting it simply, if the operation or ownership of a motor vehicle causes physical damage or personal injury for which the insured is legally responsible, the owner of the vehicle is responsible for the cost of the damage or injuries. Liability insurance generally will pay all or a portion of these claims.

Part B: Medical Payments Coverage

This coverage pays for medical expenses of the insured owner of the vehicle and his or her family if injuries are suffered as a result of being involved in an accident with the vehicle. It also provides coverage when an insured is struck by an automobile while a pedestrian.

Part C: Uninsured Motorist Coverage

This coverage, when available, is generally sold with underinsured motorist coverage. It is sometimes not available when physical damage coverage is included.

Part D: Physical Damage or Loss Coverage

Loss coverage is coverage for physical damage to your automobile. If the vehicle is stolen or suffers damage, this is the section of the PAP that provides protection. The insuring agreement generally uses the terms "collision" and "other than collision." **Other than collision** coverage is essentially open-perils coverage that excludes collision and a few other specific perils. In the past, the term **comprehensive** was used rather than "other than collision." However, as the term comprehensive implies *everything* and even though policies had exclusions, many lawsuits were filed based on claims that insureds assumed comprehensive meant that everything was covered in spite of the exclusions.

State Requirements for PAP Liability Coverage

Most states have provisions that require drivers to prove financial responsibility before they may drive or to register their automobiles with each state having its own specific requirements. Generally, owners must have insurance or show some other acceptable form of security. Acceptable substitutes for auto liability coverage vary across states but usually require an affidavit of financial responsibility or the posting of a bond.

Interestingly, state requirements for liability coverage are not generally viewed as adequate. Table 10.1 shows the levels of coverage required for the three states with the highest coverage (Alaska, Maine, and North Carolina) and the four states with the lowest (Florida, Oklahoma, Louisiana, and Mississippi).

Table 10.1 National Range of PAP Liability Limits

State	Liability Coverage Limits
Alaska	50/100/25 or 125
Maine	50/100/25
North Carolina	30/60/25
Florida	10/20/10 or 30
Oklahoma/Louisiana	10/20/10
Mississippi	10/20/5

In Alaska, the minimum state coverage provides up to $50,000 for injuries to an individual, with a maximum of $100,000 per accident for injuries and up to $25,000 per accident for property damage. Alternatively an overall limit of $125,000 for liability may be substituted. At the other end of the table, if an individual is injured by a driver who has the minimum insurance in Mississippi, an at-fault driver's minimum insurance will pay only up to $10,000 for the treatment of the injuries of any individual with no more than $20,000 for everyone injured in a single accident and no more than $5,000 toward repairing any damage caused.

This level of coverage would cover only the costs of relatively minor injuries and minor damage to a vehicle. For most serious injuries, $10,000 would not cover the medical treatment received in just the first 24 hours.

Alaska, Maine, and North Carolina are the only three states where the total required liability coverage exceeds $50,000 for a single accident, and there are 23 states in which the minimum amount of liability for all personal injuries in a single accident is less than $50,000. In contrast, all Canadian provinces require a $200,000 (Canadian) liability minimum (with the exception of Quebec, which requires a minimum of $50,000).

What does this mean to a financial planner? It means that if your client has only the state minimum coverage in liability insurance, he or she is likely underinsured. Financial responsibility laws in some states require only that a driver who is involved in an accident show that he or she has the necessary financial resources to accept responsibility for the accident. This applies to all drivers involved in an accident, regardless of fault.

When this is the case, there is no sense of urgency to have insurance unless the state requires proof of financial responsibility before registering a vehicle, as was the normal situation several years ago. Since failure to have insurance prior to an accident was not illegal, the laws that permitted it were sometimes called **free bite laws**, a term borrowed from liability for pet dogs who were not considered vicious until they bit someone. Once a dog is considered vicious, an infraction will often result in its destruction. So therefore, "each dog gets one free bite."

Financial planners are also in an excellent position to dispel a far too common myth. Some people believe the maximum liability they can face is the amount of insurance they have. This is not true. A person can have a policy with a $25,000 per person limit for personal injuries, and if they were an at-fault driver who caused $1 million worth of personal injuries, he or she is personally responsible for everything above the amount of insurance in place.

Insuring Agreement

In the PAP, each part of the policy (A through D) has its own separate and distinct insuring agreement. For example, the insuring agreement for part D states that the insurer will pay for direct and accidental loss to your covered auto or any non-owned auto, including its equipment, minus any applicable deductible shown in the policy declarations.

If there is a loss to more than one of an insured's covered autos or non-owned autos from the same collision, only the highest applicable deductible will apply. If a loss is to a non-owned auto, the coverage will be the broadest coverage applicable to any of your covered autos as shown in the policy declarations.

Losses will be paid when they are caused by collision (if the policy declarations include this coverage) or other than collision (if the policy declarations include this coverage). The physical damage insuring agreement looks like two separate coverages, but it is still considered a single insuring agreement, and some of the greatest confusion arises out of defining collision and other than collision. **Collision** is defined as the impact of the vehicle with another vehicle or object or the total upset of the vehicle: A collision happens when your car runs into something or turns over and coverage applies regardless of fault. If the insured is at fault, it is the insured's coverage that pays for the damage to the insured's vehicle. If there is another party at fault, his or her insurance (or individual funds) is expected to pay for the damage. However, if the at-fault driver does not have insurance or fails to pay for the damages, the insured may collect from his or her company, which then pursues the at-fault driver. The PAP includes a subrogation clause so that the insurer has first right to collect from the at-fault driver if it has paid the claim. When a recovery has been made from the at-fault driver, the insurer must indemnify its insured by paying back the deductible.

> **NEED TO KNOW:**
> **SINGLE LIMIT AND SPLIT LIMIT**
>
> When insurance coverage is listed as in table 10.1 (e.g., "50/100/25") it is called **split-limit liability** because the liability limit is divided among various benefits. If there is a single amount of liability for which the insurer is responsible, it is called **single-limit liability**. For any expenses over and above the insured amounts, the injured parties must sue the other driver and hope there are adequate assets to cover the costs.

The following perils are not considered collisions:

- Breakage of glass
- Contact with a bird or animal
- Damage due to "missiles" (anything that comes flying at the car)
- Earthquake
- Explosion
- Damage due to falling objects
- Fire
- Flood
- Hail
- Malicious mischief or vandalism
- Riot or civil commotion
- Theft or larceny
- Water
- Windstorm

As discussed above, **other than collision** is basically open-perils coverage covering just about everything listed above, except that which is excluded from both coverages (see the sidebar, "Need to Know: General Exclusions").

Why separate the two coverages of collision and other than collision? Some automobile owners want to save money by retaining the risk for other than collision losses but insuring the risk for collision losses. An owner may not worry about theft since he or she believes the car is parked in a safe place, or about other non-collision damage since owners often believe that such damage is only cosmetic—this is especially true when the car already has a few dents, some chipped paint, or small windshield cracks. A financial planner can help the client realize that there are several causes of loss that can be financially devastating without involving a collision with another car: theft from a shopping center parking lot, hitting a deer or cow on the highway, damage from an earthquake or tornado—all of these can total a car. If a person cannot afford to lose his or her car in a collision, he or she probably could not afford to lose it if the garage caught fire.

Some drivers, because of their ages and/or driving records, may find that collision coverage is quite expensive. They are often willing to retain the risk for circumstances where they are at fault, but they do want to be covered if they are not at fault—sometimes the case when the premium for collision is relatively high because of a driver's record or other attributes (as discussed above). As mentioned, collision policies cover a person running into something or the vehicle being upset, both of which rarely happen without carelessness on the part of the driver. If the driver wants to have damage covered from collisions when he or she is not at fault but does not want collision coverage, uninsured/underinsured motorist coverage is usually appropriate.

Many people choose to drop the collision coverage and get only other than collision for older automobiles. Since damage claims are paid on an actual cash value basis, a car worth $2,000 is not worth insuring when the premium for collision coverage may be $500 or more a year. These people are retaining the risk of running into someone or something else but do not want to lose their vehicle to a tree branch falling on it or having hail destroy the exterior. Since this part of the policy will pay for damage to the insured's vehicle if it is involved in an accident and the at-fault driver is uninsured or inadequately insured, insurance companies permit the addition of uninsured and underinsured motorist coverage (discussed later) for that possibility.

In-Depth: Covered Auto

It is always helpful to know how insurers define what they have insured. A "covered auto" is a bit more complex than appears on the surface. The standard ISO PAP defines a covered auto as follows:

- Any vehicle shown in the declarations page of the policy
- A newly acquired auto
- Any trailer the insured owns
- Any auto or trailer the insured does not own but that is used as a temporary subsitute for any other vehicle described in this definition that is out of normal use because of its:
  - breakdown
  - repair
  - servicing
  - loss
  - destruction

However, the fourth part does not apply to physical damage coverage, which is covered under a specific provision of the physical damage insuring agreement.

It is obvious that any vehicle shown on the declarations page of the policy would be covered. A newly acquired vehicle will not show up on the policy immediately, and if purchased on a weekend, it might be difficult or impossible to notify the insurer of the acquisition. Therefore, the policy automatically covers any new vehicle for 14 days. It is important to note that the automatic coverage will apply to new pickups and vans only if they are eligible to be insured under the PAP.

The new vehicle is covered with the most comprehensive coverage in place on any listed automobile. If two other vehicles are listed, one with physical damage coverage and one without it, the new car will have it included. If there is no

---

NEED TO KNOW: GENERAL EXCLUSIONS

There are 14 general exclusions to physical damage coverage, whether collision or other than collision:

- Loss incurred while the vehicle us being used as a livery or public conveyance
- Damage from wear and tear, freezing, mechanical breakdown, electrical breakdown, or road damage to tires
- Damage due to radioactive contamination, war, or rebellion
- Damage to non-permanently installed sound systems
- Damage to other non-installed electronic equipment
- Loss of tapes, records, CDs, or other media
- Destruction or confiscation by a governmental body
- Damage to camper bodies, trailers, or motor homes not listed in the policy
- Damage to non-owned vehicle if it is being driven without reasonable belief it is permitted
- Loss of radar detection devices
- Damage to custom furnishings in a van or truck (except covers, bed liners, and caps installed on a pickup)
- Damage to a non-owned vehicle being used while employed in the automobile business
- Damage to a vehicle in a racing facility for the purpose of racing or practicing for a race
- Loss to a rental car if the rental company is precluded from recovering damages because of the rental agreement or state law

(continued on next page)

(*continued from previous page*)

physical damage coverage on any listed vehicle, the automatic insurance will still include physical damage coverage for four days with a $500 deductible. That should cover even a three-day weekend.

However, if the insured fails to notify the insurer of the acquisition of the new vehicle within the 14-day period, it will not be covered until the insurer is notified. A practical application would be that Sander buys a car on June 10. On June 18, he is involved in a one-car accident. He takes the car in for an estimate and discovers that the accident caused $5,000 worth of damage. On June 27, he calls to notify his insurer of both the purchase of the car and his accident. The coverage on the car started on June 27 because he did not notify the insurer about the purchase by June 24. The damage is not covered. If he had called the insurer on June 18 and notified the company of the purchase and accident, the damage would have been covered even though the insurer did not know about the car until after the accident.

Non-Owned Auto Physical Damage Coverage

An important provision in the physical damage insuring agreement is the physical damage coverage for non-owned vehicles. This extends the broadest coverage the insured has on any automobile to any non-owned vehicle used by or in the possession of the insured or any member of his family. It also means that if the insured owns a vehicle carrying both collision and other-than-collision coverage, the non-owned vehicle would be covered for both these contingencies as well. The ISO standard policy defines a non-owned auto as:

1. Any private passenger automobile, pickup, van, or "trailer" not owned by or furnished or available for regular use by you or any "family member" while in the custody of or being operated by you or any "family member"; or

2. Any automobile or "trailer" you do not own while used as a temporary substitute for "your covered automobile" which is out of normal use because of its:

    - Breakdown
    - Repair
    - Servicing
    - Loss
    - Destruction

An important part of the coverage is that the person operating a non-owned auto must have a reasonable belief that he or she has permission to do so. The coverage of the insured who is driving a non-owned auto is secondary to the coverage of the owner's insurance. If Jack is driving Jill's car (they are still friends after the hill tumbling days) and has an accident (you would think Jill would learn), Jill's insurance pays first, assuming Jill gave Jack permission to drive it. If Jill's insurance is inadequate, then Jack's insurance picks up where Jill's left off.

Uninsured/Underinsured Motorist

Earlier in the chapter, we introduced the issue of uninsured drivers and later discussed the inadequacy of minimum liability coverages. How can a responsible individual be adequately protected from those who do not take their responsibilities seriously?

Assume Lynn is driving a nine-year-old Honda Accord in Mississippi when a careless driver runs a red light and slams into the side of her car, breaking her left arm and leg and causing whiplash to her neck.

Her car is virtually destroyed and will cost $6,500 to replace with the same year, model, and accessories. The other driver has only the minimum insurance, so Lynn is already out $1,500. The ambulance ride to the hospital, surgeries for her arm and leg, neurological tests, and initial treatment over two days in the hospital is $22,000, and Lynn is out another $12,000 for medical expenses before she even begins physical therapy (and she is also likely to suffer neck pain for the rest of her life). Since the other driver had the minimum coverage and no assets, where is the money going to come from to pay for her losses?

Collision coverage will cover the cost of the car and medical expense coverage will help with the medical claims. However, with a car worth only $6,500, she may have decided to drop the collision coverage since she has never caused an accident. In that case, underinsured motorist coverage would pay the difference for both the physical damage to the car and for her medical expenses. If the other driver had no insurance, or was a hit and run driver, uninsured motorist coverage would cover the bills.

Company Cars and Rentals

A potentially serious gap in coverage arises if an auto is "furnished or available for regular use" to an individual—a company car, for example. If the company states that it will provide the vehicle but that the driver must provide the insurance, there is no way for the individual to provide damage insurance. All coverages under the PAP exclude this type of vehicle, and there is a specific exclusion for coverage under the physical damage portion of the PAP. For all but the physical damage coverage, there are endorsements that can be added for a fairly low premium to extend the coverage to a "furnished or available" vehicle, but there is no apparent method of including this vehicle under the physical damage portion of the policy. In this situation, where the company will not provide physical damage insurance on the vehicle, the individual would be wise to turn down the offer.

Another potential problem is long-term car rentals. The exclusion for physical damage does not apply for a short-term rental, but most policies do not specify how long is too long. In court cases, 10 days was found not to be too long while 90 days was long enough for the exclusion to apply. There may still be some confusion: Some policies specifically provide for coverage when a car is being used as a substitute for one that is not available for any of the above-listed reasons, so coverage would clearly be extended for a rental car being used as a substitute for a vehicle that is being repaired. But if the rental car is being used for other reasons, the exclusion may apply because the courts have ruled that a rental car is "made available for the regular use" of the insured.

Other Provisions: Physical Damage Coverage

Physical damage coverage also includes a number of other provisions.

Use of Aftermarket Parts

An ongoing debate exists over the use of aftermarket parts to be used for auto repairs subsequent to an accident. While there is concern about the quality of the parts being used, there is also a concern about the extremely high cost of auto repair, due in large part to the near monopoly that vehicle manufacturers have on replacement parts.

One organization, the Certified Automotive Parts Association (CAPA), exists to ensure that aftermarket parts meet or exceed original parts quality. Most aftermarket parts do not meet CAPA standards, but comparisons appear to indicate that CAPA certified parts are, on average, if not superior to original equipment, at least more consistent. There is a great deal of information on this issue on the CAPA website (www.capacertified.org), including comments about a November 1999 class action lawsuit verdict against State Farm Insurance for $1.464 billion because of the use of aftermarket parts. The 1999 verdict was overturned on first appeal—a decision that may be subject to a later appeal. Many individuals choose to use aftermarket parts for various reasons. Some may consider certain parts, such as batteries and spark plug wires, to be far superior to original equipment manufacturer (OEM) parts. In other cases, such as with oil filters and windshield wiper refills, the parts may be at least equal in quality and much less expensive.

Some policies state that aftermarket parts will be used unless OEM parts are specifically requested by the insured prior to repairs being done.

Limit of Liability

Related to the above statement, the language of the policies often includes "with like kind and quality." This would appear to give the insurance companies the authority to direct the use of replacement parts that meet or exceed the OEM standards, regardless of the manufacturer.

When an insured has an accident, the insurer is obligated to pay the lesser of the actual cash value of the damaged or stolen property, or the cost of repair or replacement of the property with like kind or quality. Further, since 1994, there is a provision that also takes into consideration the depreciation and physical condition of the property under consideration when there is a total loss. The company maintains control as to how the claim will be paid and also the choice of repair and/or replacement.

NEED TO KNOW: VALUE REDUCTION OF VEHICLE

When an auto has been in an accident, even when fully repaired, some states require that the title reflect that information. This generally results in a reduced resale value. Buyers would prefer to buy a given model of car that had never been in an accident. The ISO released the coverage for damage to your auto exclusion endorsement in 1999. This endorsement, when used, excludes benefits for this reduced value. It is a fairly new endorsement, so there is no strong indication as of yet regarding the extent to which insurance companies have adopted it.

Towing and Labor Cost Coverage

For an additional premium, the insurer will cover the cost of towing and labor (charge for hooking up the vehicle) with the maximum limit being $75 per tow. An auto club with additional benefits is a reasonable alternative.

Alternate Transportation Expense

If a covered vehicle is damaged and unavailable for use, the PAP may provide up to $20 per day with a limit of $600 per incident toward the cost of renting a replacement vehicle or taking another form of transportation. The benefit generally begins 24 hours following the time the vehicle is not available for use, except in the case of theft. In the case of theft, the benefit starts 48 hours after the theft occurs and ends when the vehicle is returned and is again available for use by the insured or until the insurer pays for the loss. The daily benefit and maximum amount may sometimes be increased by endorsement and additional premium.

Parts E and F: Policy Conditions

Parts E and F of the policy deal with various provisions of the contract.

Part E: Duties After an Accident or Loss

When a covered loss occurs, the insured has the obvious obligation to notify the insurer of the how, what, when, and where of what happened. Further the policy specifies that the insured must do the following:

- Cooperate with the insurer with any investigation, defense, claim, or settlement
- Send copies of any notices or legal papers connected to the loss to the insurer as soon as possible
- Accede to any physical exam by insurer-selected physicians as often as the insurer reasonably requests, the costs of which are covered by the insurer
- Authorize insurer access to insured's medical records if relevant to the claim
- Submit reasonable proof of loss when requested.

If a vehicle is stolen or if a claim is submitted under the uninsured motorist coverage, a policy report must be made and a copy must be sent to the insurer. If a vehicle is damaged, the insured is expected to take reasonable steps to preclude any further loss. The insurer must be given the opportunity to inspect and/or appraise the damaged property before it is repaired or disposed of.

Part F: General Provisions

Nine general provisions are included with the personal auto policy to clarify and address issues that may arise.

Bankruptcy

Bankruptcy or insolvency of the insured does not invalidate or void the contract. If the insured declares bankruptcy or becomes insolvent in response to a lawsuit, the insurer is still required to meet all of its obligations under the contract.

Changes

Changes in the terms or provisions of the policy cannot be waived or changed unless it is done by endorsement to the policy. This provision also includes any liberalization clause that permits the company to unilaterally change the policy if it is for the benefit of the insured. Changes in premium will occur on the effective date of coverage.

Fraud

Fraud that is perpetrated against the insurer through statements about or conduct surrounding a claim will result in denial of the claim.

Legal Action

The "legal action against us" provision states that the insured may not sue the insurer for breach of contract or for any reason unless he or she has complied with the terms of the contract. If the policy is issued in a state that permits a third party to sue an at-fault driver's insurer, this provision will be invalid for purposes of the third person.

Payment Recovery

The "our right to recover payment" provision requires the insured to subrogate his or her claims against any third party to the extent that he or she was paid by the insurer. It also requires the insured to avoid any action or statements that jeopardize the insurer's ability to be compensated for any losses that it paid which are owed by a third party.

Period and Territory

The "policy period and territory" provision generally states that the policy period is one year from the date of issue and that it is effective for the vehicle in any of the United States, its territories or possessions, and Canada. (Insurance under the standard ISO PAP does not extend into Mexico.) Coverage also extends to the vehicle when it is being transported over water between covered locations.

Termination

Termination of the policy is specified in this provision as anytime at the request of the insured. The insurer may terminate the policy only under certain conditions. If the policy has been in force for less than 60 days, the insurer may terminate it by giving 10 days written notice. After the policy has been in force 60 days or more, it may be terminated only under the following conditions:

- Nonpayment of premium (with 10 days' written notice)
- Upon revocation of the insured's license or that of any resident relative (with 20 days'written notice)
- If the policy was obtained through the use of material misrepresentation

A policy that has been renewed is considered to have been in force 60 days or longer. With these limits in mind, a company may choose not to renew a policy with 20 days written notice.

A renewal is also considered an offer for continuance of the insurance. If the insured does not pay the premium for the renewal, the policy will automatically be cancelled. Since some states have laws that would modify the insurer's right to cancel or fail to renew a policy, this provision is typically superseded by those requirements.

Transfer

The "transfer of policy interest" provision is an assignment clause, or more accurately a nonassignment clause. The insured may not assign his or her rights or duties under the contract without written consent of the company. However, if the named insured dies, coverage is automatically provided for the insured's spouse or estate representative.

Two or More Policies

The "two or more auto policies" provision limits the company's liability arising from a single accident if the insured has two or more policies with the same company. The policy that has the highest limit of coverage will establish the maximum benefit the insurer will pay.

Endorsements

As mentioned above, there are circumstances in which a non-owned policy would normally be excluded from coverage under the PAP. Certain vehicles are excluded from coverage since most insureds do not own them. This may lead to a problem with the definition of a "covered auto."

Sometimes a person does not own an automobile but has one provided for them, so he or she would not have a PAP. These endorsements are specifically designed to fill most of those gaps.

Antique and Classic Auto

Antique and classic autos may be added with the miscellaneous type vehicle endorsement. Antique vehicles that fit in this category must be at least 25 years old and be primarily used for club activities, parades, exhibitions, shows, and similar public interest functions. Classic vehicles must be at least 10 years old and not be limited in their type of use. They also must have higher-than-typical value because of their condition and/or rarity. Because these vehicles may be worth much more than their original value, they usually are insured only for a maximum stated amount. This is different from the scheduled amounts as listed for appraised personal property since if an antique or classic vehicle is stolen or damaged beyond repair; the full amount is not necessarily paid. Instead, the insurer's liability is the *lesser* of:

- The stated amount of coverage shown in the schedule or declarations page of the policy,
- The actual cash value of the stolen or damaged vehicle, or
- The amount necessary to repair or replace the vehicle

Extended Liability

This extends the liability coverage to a vehicle that is made available for the regular use of the insured with the exception of a vehicle used in the garage business. It covers only those named in the endorsement.

Miscellaneous Type Vehicle

Motorcycles, motor scooters, all-terrain vehicles, go-carts, motor homes, etc., can be insured by specialized individual policies or can be added to a standard ISO PAP through the miscellaneous type vehicle endorsement. This includes all of the coverages under a PAP.

The covered auto definition includes newly acquired vehicles that are not yet listed on the contract; when the miscellaneous type vehicle endorsement is added, the covered auto portion of the policy is concurrently endorsed to include newly acquired miscellaneous types of vehicles.

Motor Home

When a motor home is insured under the miscellaneous type vehicle endorsement, the endorsement excludes liability and physical damage coverage on the home when it is rented or leased to others. However, the insured can pay a premium and add back liability coverage on the property with the same endorsement. The amount of this premium varies with the number of weeks per year for which the motor home is rented.

Named Non-Owner

This is not an endorsement to the PAP but is, rather, a separate policy for those times when a PAP is not needed. There are circumstances when an individual borrows a vehicle but has no personal vehicle. This individual would not have a PAP, but may still want insurance whenever driving a borrowed vehicle just in case it is not adequately insured. This coverage is excess coverage to whatever insurance exists on the borrowed auto. For example, if there is an accident and the auto was insured for up to $25,000 for medical expenses for an injured party and the costs were $40,000, the insurance on the auto would pay the first $25,000 and, if the named non-owner policy had a limit of $40,000 or more, it would pay the difference. If the named non-owner policy had a limit of $25,000, it would pay nothing. This special form covers only individuals named in the policy.

Snowmobile

This endorsement specifically covers issues surrounding snowmobiles. It eliminates coverage for any snowmobile rented or leased to another and excludes coverage whenever the snowmobile is used in any racing event.

BUYING AUTO INSURANCE

It is frustrating for good drivers to pay a lot for auto insurance, but adequate insurance coverage is a part of effective risk management. Most drivers can handle a $500 deductible if there is damage to a car, but having major repairs done for thousands of dollars is often difficult. If a car is totaled with a deductible payment still due, the driver could be forced to survive without a car.

Furthermore, if a driver causes an accident and someone is injured, the medical expenses along with any damages for the lost income of the victim may leave the at-fault driver financially devastated.

Liability Insurance

From the view of risk management, this is the most important coverage. While few people are deliberately negligent with another person's property or person, when accidents happen, they can be quite expensive. Since property damage and personal injuries can result in substantial expenses, the potential loss to the individual who is at fault can be quite sizable. The table showing liability limits illustrated that the state with the largest level of benefits still provides only $50,000 for losses suffered by any individual. Most states require less than half of that amount.

According to the Insurance Services Office, Inc., to increase liability coverage by a factor of 10, from $50,000 per individual to $500,000 per individual, only a 24 percent increase in premium is required. It is only an 11 percent premium increase to move from $50,000 to $100,000 per individual. To move from $25,000 per person coverage to $500,000 coverage is only a 47 percent increase in premium compared to a 1,975 percent increase in coverage.

Most claims are for small amounts, but one large claim can wipe out a driver's financial security. A relatively slight increase in the cost of coverage may operate to minimize that risk.

Medical Payments Coverage

When discussing health insurance, specific-cause type insurance was discouraged since it only provides benefits under certain circumstances. So it would seem that medical payments coverage makes little sense to have as long as adequate health insurance is in place. However, medical payments coverage provides benefits that many health care plans do not provide: Medical payments coverage covers the medical expenses of passengers in the insured's vehicle—a valuable benefit since these passengers may be uninsured, and the coverage can be used to replace any lost income or to pay funeral expenses on their behalf. Finally, not only does the coverage apply when an insured is in the vehicle, but it also applies when a family member of the named insured is a pedestrian or riding a bicycle. The cost of the coverage is also relatively low considering the possible benefit to be received.

NEED TO KNOW: BANKRUPTCY

Some people will encourage bankruptcy as a legitimate method of dealing with the maintenance of inadequate insurance, but this creates a lose-lose situation: The injured party is left with medical bills, property damage, and lost income, and the at-fault driver is left with few assets, very poor credit, and the knowledge of the severe hardship he or she has caused another person. A financial planner has an obligation to help his or her clients be financially responsible. Maintaining inadequate insurance with the attitude that if they get sued they will just file for bankruptcy is not responsible. Further, 2005 Congressional legislation made it more difficult to obtain financial relief through bankruptcy.

Physical Damage Coverage

Basic risk management comes into the picture again here. If the loss of the vehicle would create a financial problem for the insured, physical damage coverage makes sense. However, if the car is financed and is used as collateral for any loan, the lender will probably require such coverage even if the insured would not otherwise incur such an expense. As discussed earlier in the chapter, if the car's value is low because of its age, the cost of insuring it against physical damage may be too much to justify.

Cost of Insurance

While some companies advertise great customer service or some other intangible attribute, most clients will want to find the most reliable auto insurance company with the lowest premiums.

Premiums are affected by many factors. Insurers may set premiums based on the selectivity of the insureds who are accepted; some companies will modify the terms of the contract to make it more restrictive. Some have been accused of underpaying claims or making it difficult to collect legitimate claims, and others may cut back on customer service to save money or lower their prices merely because of economies of scale. One national company ran an extensive ad campaign that solely focused on the strength of its customer service.

However, there are generally several variables that universally affect the insurance premium amounts. Some are related to the owner/driver of the auto being insured, while others are based on the location of the vehicle, the vehicle insured, and/or the deductible to be incurred.

Age and Sex of Driver

Single male drivers under the age of 25 are the highest risk category, so their premiums are the highest. Some savings are available if a young driver has taken approved driver training, maintained a B or 3.0 grade average or better, is in the upper 20 percent of his or her class, is on the dean's list or honor roll, or has received other equivalent recognition. A young driver away from home at school and at a minimum distance—typically 100 miles—can also earn a discount if the car stays home. Generally, most insurance companies will honor only two discounts of all those available to any one driver.

Claim History

The propensity of an individual to submit a lot of small claims may affect the premium or renewal of a policy. This is not generally a publicized topic, but many insurance company claims representatives will tell insureds that the submission of small claims may work against them.

Deductibles

As discussed above, higher deductibles result in lower premiums.

Discounts

There are various discounts offered by most auto insurance companies, including:

- Safe driver
- Nonsmoker or nondrinker
- Carpool
- Antitheft devices
- Antilock brakes
- Multi-vehicle

Driver History

Poor drivers—those with many citations for violating traffic laws or who have caused accidents—generally pay higher premiums and run the risk of having their insurance cancelled. If an insured is clearly not at fault in an accident, the insured's premiums will usually not be affected.

Location

Where a vehicle is located is critical. Whenever a consumer publication shows comparative premiums for auto insurance, it lists various cities. The incidence of theft, accidents, and duration of typical commutes affect the claims history of these cities. Within cities there are areas with different claims histories. How the vehicle is stored may also affect the cost. A vehicle kept in a garage when at home is safer than one parked on the street. Additionally, lawyers in some parts of the country become involved in auto accident claims far more often than in other parts of the country, thus increasing the cost to the insurance companies even if it provides no greater benefit to the overall class of insureds.

Type and Number of Vehicles

High performance autos and sports cars are frequently driven at high speeds, resulting in more (and more dangerous) accidents. Sport utility vehicles, because of their size, can inflict more damage than smaller autos and also tip over more easily. Certain vehicles seem to be prime targets for thieves. These vehicles cost more to insure.

The number of vehicles in a household also affects premiums, although most companies offer a multiple-vehicle discount.

Vehicle History

Based on claims history, certain vehicles suffer greater damage in accidents than others. The physical damage portion of the policy will cost more when this is the case.

Vehicle Use

An auto used for pleasure costs less to insure than one driven to work daily. Low annual mileage generally results in lower premiums. Long commutes to work—15 miles or more—and/or use of the auto for business can also increase the amount of the premium.

In-Depth: High-Risk Drivers

Single male drivers under the age of 25 are among the most likely to be involved in an accident. Additionally, there are drivers who have poor driving records. Because of comparatively high claims, these groups often find it difficult to obtain auto insurance. When it is available, it is usually quite expensive.

Insuring poor risks leads to adverse selection because the expected claims are high. State law, on the other hand, requires all vehicles on the road to be insured, and states have a vested interest in making certain all drivers are insured, whether companies want to provide this insurance or not. To avoid having the government sell insurance directly—an unpopular possibility for the insurance industry—companies created alternate approaches to insuring bad drivers.

The most common approach is the **automobile insurance plan**. Generally, eligible drivers are those who have been turned down for auto insurance in the last 60 days. Upon application, this high-risk driver is assigned to one of the various insurers that writes auto insurance in the state. Each insurance company is expected to accept a proportionate number of these drivers based on the percentage of that state's market that each insurance company has. In some states, this program is open to any driver. In other states, certain habitual offenders are prevented from obtaining coverage through any other means. These plans provide liability insurance, and some of the plans offer other coverage as well—physical damage coverage and no-fault benefits in those states mandating it. These plans are generally given the name of **assigned risk plans**.

A few states use the **joint underwriting associations** approach. With these plans, a few companies administer the insurance policies for high-risk drivers. When claims occur, all companies writing auto insurance in the state share in the losses.

The opposite approach, called **reinsurance pools**, is used in some states. Under this program, all insurers in the state accept bad drivers. When a driver is identified as being in the "bad driver" group, his or her name is included on a pool list. All premiums received from this driver are included in the pool, which pays all claims related to those identified as high-risk drivers. The insured benefits with this approach since no one can tell by the name of the insurer whether he or she is a bad driver.

There are some drivers who have such dismal driving records that they do not qualify for any of the above plans. For these road hazards, there are a few companies, referred to as **distress risk companies**, that specialize in high-risk drivers. The policies available are usually quite expensive and have more limited coverage than those available under other insurance methods.

Unfortunately, the long-term result is that good drivers subsidize bad drivers. If bad drivers had to pay premiums to completely cover their expected claims, they would likely not be able to afford the insurance and many more of them would drive without it.

MAKING CLAIMS

Individuals who live in only one state for all of their driving years generally believe claims are handled the same everywhere. There are actually a variety of ways that claims are handled. One is essentially adversarial while others are less so.

Traditional System

The traditional method of handling automobile claims is through the tort system: One driver is generally found to be at fault in an accident. The at-fault driver's insurance carrier is obligated to pay for the losses suffered by the other parties to the accident, which means that an injured party might not receive any payment for losses or might receive only partial payment if the at-fault driver has no insurance or inadequate assets, or if the loss is too small to justify the use of a lawyer.

There are those who claim the traditional system makes the amount received from the at-fault driver more a function of a lawyer's skill than the merits of the case, and this approach can make the claims process quite lengthy if the insured's carrier chooses to deny liability or attempts to offer payment that is much lower than the loss. When a court's judgment is reasonable, keeping a percentage of the payment as a contingency fee usually compensates the lawyer for the injured party. However, this may well leave the client with less than what he or she believes is adequate compensation for injury.

No-Fault System

To speed up the process and reduce the adversarial nature of claims, some states established no-fault auto insurance laws. Under no-fault laws, the insured's insurer pays for his or her losses first. Then the insurance company generally seeks reimbursement from the at-fault driver and his or her insurer. There are three forms of no-fault coverage. While all three are called no-fault programs, only the first eliminates the need for blame. To successfully sue someone, blame must be placed, even if in some cases it is difficult or impossible to determine where.

Pure No-Fault

Under this form, the insured may not sue the other driver nor the other driver's insurer. This approach has been advocated for years, but has never been adopted in any state.

Modified No-Fault

This approach permits a lawsuit only when a statutory threshold is surpassed. The threshold may be either a dollar amount of physical injuries or a verbal threshold, such as death, serious injury, or disfigurement. Generally a suit is limited to losses that exceed the amount paid by the insured's own insurer.

Expanded No-Fault

Sometimes called expanded first-party coverage, this allows the injured individual to sue the other driver and his or her insurer regardless of the amount received from his or her own company.

In 2003, Colorado moved from being a no-fault state to having tort coverage. The theory was that it would save drivers a substantial amount of money on premiums each year. The actual result has been less than expected. Claims typically take longer to settle, and the premium savings have been less than many insureds expected. A reduction of about 27 percent is touted as the average savings. However that figure does not include any medical benefits coverage. Those who included medical benefits coverage had less than a 15 percent reduction. Some individuals had savings of single digit percentages and others had increases in premiums. The biggest savings went to those with the minimum coverage, which is often inadequate. The lowest reduction, or even increases went to those who had 100/300/50 coverage, usually considered adequate coverage. The other side of the issue is that only a quarter of insured's chose to have medical benefits, so hospitals have found that their uncollectible billings due to treatment of those in auto accidents are up substantially.

In-Depth: What is an Accident?

The term "accident" is used to describe an event where there is a collision or the rollover of a vehicle. This is an accepted, but often misleading, term. Virtually every "accident" is avoidable. Each one is the result of carelessness and/or poor choices of at least one driver. People use the term "accident" to avoid responsibility for their own choices.

Someone who slides down an icy hill, regardless of the condition of the road, made choices that led to the loss of control. The choices may be conscious or unconscious. That driver may not have adequate snow tires or chains on his or her vehicle. Knowing that the particular hill may be dangerous in icy weather, the choice was made to travel that way anyway. Other choices that lead to unnecessary problems include eating, drinking or smoking while driving; talking on a phone or to another person while driving; listening to the radio, changing tapes or CDs, fiddling with temperature controls, reading, or watching for an address or street name all affect the ability of the driver. Whenever a driver is behind the wheel of a moving vehicle, any other activity reduces his or her ability to make good decisions about his or her driving.

A Virginia study showed that the leading cause of accidents was rubbernecking—looking at other accidents. Driver fatigue and looking at scenery were next, followed by adjusting the radio or CD player and talking on the phone. In all, 90 percent of accidents were related to being distracted by things that did not have to be done while driving.[2] With the exception of insects or animals entering the vehicle and unexpected medical problems, most of the last 10 percent were also due to such chosen distractions as reading and adjusting vehicle controls. Fortunately, insurers do not deny payments because of poor judgment or carelessness.

---

[2] Cathryn Conroy, "Unexpected! No. 1 Driving Distraction," Netscape Network News, March 24, 2003

IMPORTANT CONCEPTS

Auto liability insurance

Collision

Comprehensive

Medical payments coverage

Miscellaneous type vehicle endorsement

Named non-owner coverage

No-fault claims settlement

Non-owned auto

Other than collision

Personal auto policy (PAP)

Physical damage coverage

Split-limit liability

Traditional claim settlement

Underinsured motorist coverage

Uninsured motorist coverage

QUESTIONS FOR REVIEW

1. Explain the differences and similarities between collision, other than collision, and comprehensive physical damage coverage.

2. Describe a "covered auto."

3. What are the three forms of no-fault claims settlement, and how are they different?

4. Explain how split limit liability is illustrated and operates.

5. What does "of like kind and quality" mean, and how has that term become controversial?

6. What are the duties of the insured following an insured loss?

7. How does bankruptcy of the insured following an accident caused by the insured affect the obligations of the insurer?

8. Over what geographic area does an ISO PAP provide coverage?

9. Under what circumstances can an insurer terminate a policy or refuse to renew it?

10. Discuss five factors that affect premiums for the PAP.

SUGGESTIONS FOR ADDITIONAL READING:

Fundamentals of Risk and Insurance, 9th ed., Emmett J. Vaughan and Therese M. Vaughan, Wiley, 2003.

How Insurance Works: An Introduction to Property and Liability Insurance, 2nd ed., Barry D. Smith and Eric A. Wiening, American Institute for Chartered Property and Casualty Underwriters, 1994.

Introduction to Risk Management and Insurance, 8th ed., Mark Dorfman, Prentice Hall, 2004.

Personal Auto Coverage Guide: Interpretation and Analysis, 2nd ed., David D. Thamann and Michael K. McCracken, National Underwriter, 2005

Principles of Risk Management and Insurance, 9th ed., George E. Rejda, Addison Wesley, 2004.

Property and Liability Principles, 3rd ed., Constance Lutheardt, American Institute for Chartered Property and Casualty Underwriters, 1999.

CHAPTER ELEVEN

Personal and Professional Liability Insurance

• • •

Few days pass without news of a large settlement of a lawsuit in which one party claims to have been legally wronged by another party. When people suffer physical, emotional, or fiscal harm because of another's actions, they want to be compensated. Liability means that if someone causes a loss, he or she may be legally obligated to compensate the injured party. Since liability risks can be so great, basic risk management dictates that transfer of that risk is generally the most logical option.

This chapter covers the legal concept of liability, personal liability insurance, the products used for high levels of protection, umbrella liability, and professional liability insurance.

When you have completed this chapter you will be able to:

- Understand and discuss negligence and legal liability
- Describe and explain personal liability insurance
- Understand and explain the forms of professional liability insurance
- Describe the application and availability of umbrella liability insurance

LEGAL LIABILITY

Before discussing the different types of liability insurance, it is important to review and expand on the basic principles of liability introduced in chapter 1. If one person causes another person to suffer a loss, the person causing the loss may be liable for compensating the injured party for that loss. While this liability may arise out of the commission of either a tort or a breach of contract, this chapter is concerned primarily with torts (see "Need to Know: Private and Public Wrongs").

Simply suffering a loss does not mean that someone is liable for it, even if that loss is caused by a person's actions or failure to act. Generally, liability occurs only if all of the following three tests are met:

- There was a breach of a duty owed to the injured party
- Actual damage or loss happened
- The proximate cause of the loss or damage was the breach of duty

Negligence

The first test to determine liability is breach of duty, and a leading cause of breach of duty is negligence. Most policies limit insurable liability to that caused by unintentional negligence.

To determine whether or not an action was negligent, the courts generally look to the **prudent man rule:** The law assumes that a certain level of care is expected of a prudent person, and negligence is the breach of this duty. The ideal prudent person always pays attention to and considers all the risks involved in any activity, exercising an appropriate level of care in everything he or she says, writes, or does—a high standard of conduct. However, just because, in hindsight, a different action would have resulted in a better outcome, the law does not require an individual to accept liability if the action taken was reasonable at the time. Note that the course of a lawsuit may be determined not by the person's intention in committing the act but by other people's perceptions of the action as determined by a jury of an individual's peers. Some other factors that may contribute to a finding of negligence are discussed below.

Absolute Liability

Absolute liability, or **strict liability**, means that liability exists by virtue of the circumstances, even if all actions taken were reasonable. It sounds rather odd that one party can do everything right and still be found liable for damages, but certain conditions and activities are inherently hazardous and therefore, the person engaging in them assumes responsibility for any damage or injury that may result. For example, if Stan stores explosives on his property or provides a sanctuary for wild animals, he will be liable for harm or damage that occurs if an animal attacks a neighbor or an explosion occurs, even if the injured party contributed to the harm.

Workers compensation laws generally impose absolute liability on employers for on-the-job injuries, even if employee violations of company rules cause the injury.

Negligence Per Se

In addition to the prudent man rule, legislatures have passed laws to protect specific classes of individuals. Negligence per se means "negligence in itself." Anyone violating a law meant to protect members of a particular class is liable if he or she harms a member of that class. For example, a disabled customer may sue Hermann's Department Store because she was injured in a fall in the store's non-ADA compliant restroom. Since the ADA (Americans with Disabilities Act) protects the disabled and the fall resulted from noncompliance, Hermann's Department Store was negligent per se.

Res Ipsa Loquitur

Translated from Latin, *res ipsa loquitur* means "the thing speaks for itself." In short, the injury or loss would not have occurred if the individual had not been negligent. This reverses the burden of proof, requiring the individual accused of being negligent to prove his or her innocence. If a tree service team is trimming a tree that has limbs overhanging the street and does not make an effort to warn oncoming drivers or redirect traffic, they will likely be found liable if a limb falls and damages a passing car.

For *res ipsa loquitur* to apply, three conditions must generally exist:

- The harm or damage would not likely occur if there were no negligence.
- The cause of the harm or damage must be under the exclusive control of the defendant.
- The injured person must not have contributed to his or her injuries in any way other than being present when the incident occurred.

NEED TO KNOW: PRIVATE AND PUBLIC WRONGS

A tort is a private wrong arising out of actions that are not necessarily illegal but still cause another to suffer a loss.

Criminal wrongs are public wrongs: activities that are against the law. While the government can prosecute a person who violates criminal law, the injured party of a tortious act must take the initiative to file a lawsuit. It is possible for the same act to be criminal and tortious. An individual who commits an armed robbery not only violates criminal laws, but also causes financial and possibly physical and emotional harm.

Thus, the robber would not only be prosecuted for the crime, but the victim could also sue for the tortious harm committed. If the robber was guilty of violating the law, the injured party could claim he or she was negligent as a matter of law, as stated in chapter 1.

Liability insurance will not insure individuals against claims caused by their criminal acts. The robber mentioned above might have a million dollars of liability insurance, but the insurer will not pay any claim to the victim since the harm that was done occurred as a result of a criminal act. Any payments would have to come from the assets and/or income of the robber.

While it may seem that the victim is being punished by this failure to provide protection, it is actually the robber. The person who committed the wrong is obligated to compensate the victim.

In-Depth: Obligations and Duties

As discussed in chapter 1, a property owner is legally obligated to different types of visitors in different ways. A person who enters another's property with no right to do so and without the owner's consent is a **trespasser**, and the only duty generally owed to an adult trespasser is to avoid intentional injury to him or her. An owner who becomes aware of an adult trespasser must use ordinary care to avoid doing harm.

A person who comes onto the property for his or her own benefit, but with the owner's presumed approval or permission, is a **licensee**. This class may include door-to-door sales people or someone passing out fliers. It also includes individuals invited to another part of the property, such as someone who is hired to replace a garage door but wanders into the kitchen for a glass of water. Additionally, if the owner knows that a trespasser regularly comes onto the property and does not tell the trespasser to stop, the owner gives **implied consent** for the trespass and is obliged to treat the trespasser as a licensee. To avoid this increased potential for liability, the owner should inform the trespasser that he or she is not welcome and/or post "no trespassing" signs. The property owner is obligated not to cause intentional harm to a licensee and must also warn or take steps to protect the licensee from known dangers that may not be obvious, such as a vicious dog or an unmarked open well.

An **invitee** is one who has been invited onto the owner's property for some purpose that is of benefit to the owner. Invited businesspersons, friends, or delivery people are invitees, and if the property is a business, so are customers, members, employees, etc. Those who provide wanted services but who have not had a specific invitation (mail carriers, delivery service employees, suppliers) are also invitees. The owner must not only avoid intentionally harming an invitee but also must find any unsafe conditions and either make them safe or provide adequate warning of their presence.

A special, increased level of responsibility exists when children enter a property. The property owner is obliged to determine if children are on his or her property and to protect them from their own carelessness, as the law generally assumes that children often act without the prudence of an adult. It does not matter if they otherwise qualify as trespassers, licensees, or invitees. Also of special concern are **attractive nuisances**: any object to which children are drawn, in spite of inherent dangers that may exist, and on or about which they might be injured. A climbing tree, a swimming pool, or an accessible train engine might be attractive nuisances. If a child is injured on an attractive nuisance, there is a high probability that the property owner will be held liable unless he or she had taken steps to prevent children from having access.

Vicarious Liability

Also referred to as imputed liability, this arises when one party is liable for the actions of another party as based on a common law principle: *respondeat superior*, or "let the master answer." A principal is liable for the acts of his or her agent. An employer is responsible for the acts of employees, even if they are not acting in a manner approved by the employer, as long as they are acting as employees (and not on their own time).

On the other hand, parents are not automatically liable for their children's acts. For a parent to be liable, he or she would have to act negligently, either by providing inadequate supervision or by **negligent entrustment**—permitting the child to have control of such dangerous items as guns, knives, explosives, or the family car. A parent who owns a gun and does not take appropriate measures to keep it out of children's hands may be found negligent if a child injures or kills someone with it. Some states have passed specific legislation that makes parents liable for certain acts committed by their children.

It is also possible for one adult to be considered negligent because of the acts of another adult. For instance, Joe loans his car to Dirk knowing that Dirk is a reckless driver who has lost his license. If Dirk hits Bill's car, negligent entrustment dictates that Joe could be found liable for damages. The same would apply if Joe knew that Dirk never had a license or had been drinking. If Dirk let Joe use Bill's lawnmower knowing Dirk's yard was full of rocks and other debris that was likely to damage the mower, Bill could hold Dirk liable under the same principle.

Damages

Before someone can be liable for damages, some form of damage must occur, so the second step in determining liability is to verify damages. If no harm is done, no claim can be made.

Not only must there be proof that damage has occurred, but there also must be an estimate of the dollar amount of those damages, which is often quite difficult to ascertain. There are generally three categories of damages for which a person may be held liable:

Special Damages

Special damages are those for which a dollar value is easily ascertainable. If Catherine accidentally damages Jeff's designer lamp, the special damages would be the cost of restoring or replacing it.

If Matt borrows and unintentionally damages Michele's business laptop, the special damages could include the cost of repairing or replacing the machine, the cost of redoing any lost work, and the lost revenue from her business. Liability insurance will generally cover these types of damages.

NEED TO KNOW: WHO CANNOT BE NEGLIGENT

Not everyone may be held liable when something goes wrong. The first consideration is whether the person had a duty to act but failed to take action or took inappropriate action. However, there are those who do not have a duty to act.

Government Bodies

Governments have a certain level of immunity from lawsuits. Essentially, the government must give its permission to be sued, and the extent to which it does varies by jurisdiction. However, even where a government body is immune, its employees generally are liable when carrying out their duties. If a street cleaner negligently damages a private automobile while on duty, the city may be immune but the employee may be held personally liable.

Infants and Children

Before a certain age, called "the age of reason," it is presumed that a child cannot understand the difference between right and wrong or the consequences of his or her actions. In some states, this may be as early as age seven. After this age, children can be legally liable for their acts, though the degree of care that is expected of a child is generally different from that expected of an adult.

Mentally Incompetent

A mentally incompetent person is generally considered to be in the same class as an infant, without the capacity to make reasonable choices. However, if a mentally incompetent person is capable of exercising a reasonable degree of care, he or she may be held liable.

General Damages

General damages are subjective. These include mental anguish, pain and suffering, disfigurement, and/or loss of consortium. The problems with general damages are obvious: How does one put a figure on pain and suffering? For that matter, how does one measure pain and suffering? What does $5,000 worth of mental anguish look like? Liability insurance will usually cover general damages.

Punitive Damages

This type of damage is meant to punish the offender, or "teach a lesson." Punitive damage requires proof of gross negligence or willful intent to cause harm, and always raises the question of how much of a punitive award is too much: Is it right to award such heavy punitive damages in a workers compensation case that the company is forced to close the plant, costing all the employees their jobs? After some highly publicized court decisions carried punitive damages to the extreme, they have become a controversial issue, and some states limit punitive damages. Liability insurance will generally *not* pay punitive damages.

Collateral Source Rule

The collateral source rule dictates that the foresight of an injured party should not absolve the liable party from paying for damages.

Simply because the victim of a negligent act has a health care plan that covers medical expenses and a disability income policy that pays for lost income does not mean that the party causing the loss should not have to pay for it.

A **tort feasor** (a person who commits a wrong) cannot be absolved from having damages reduced because the injured party recovered expenses or lost income from another source. Even if the health care plan has already paid for all or some of the injured party's medical bills, the health care company may choose to subrogate the injured party's claim until it has been repaid, since those medical bills are now the liability of the person causing the injury.

Joint and Several Liability

This principle means that if two or more parties were negligent, an injured party can sue both parties or either one individually. The negligent party with the money (the party with the deeper pockets) can be forced to pay the entire claim, regardless of the percentage of responsibility.

**NEED TO KNOW:
DEATH AND BANKRUPTCY**

What happens to a liability claim if the liable party files for bankruptcy or either party dies? Just how far does the continuity of liability extend?

In the past, common law generally stated that if a party dies—either the injured party or the one who is liable for the loss—the obligation no longer exists. If Brian were to seriously hurt Barbara, Brian would owe Barbara a great deal of money for medical expenses, lost income, etc. However, if, under the common law doctrine, Brian killed Barbara, nothing would be owed to Barbara, though Brian might still face criminal charges. Many states now have laws providing for survival of tort actions that override this. Under these laws, if either party dies, any obligation that was agreed to or adjudicated continues, and heirs are able to sue for their loss.

Bankruptcy, on the other hand, will result in different outcomes based on the facts of the case. Generally, the injured party will not receive all that is due. Either the liability will be partially paid through liquidation of the tort feasor's assets or a reduced judgment will be paid through the courts. However, if the liability resulted from a willful or malicious tort, bankruptcy will not discharge the debt even if the tort feasor has to pay for the loss from earnings throughout the rest of his or her life.

However, since 1986, approximately two-thirds of the states have either modified or abolished the joint and several liability doctrine, usually replacing it with a method of splitting liability according to the percentage of fault.

Proximate Cause

The final test to determine liability requires a link between the negligence (or other breach of duty) and the damages. It must be shown that the negligence was the proximate cause of the damage—that if negligence had not occurred, the loss would not have occurred. This often is the case when there is an unbroken chain of events that began with the claimed negligence.

The chain of events may include an **intervening cause** that exacerbates or magnifies the negligent act, but the intervening cause generally must have been foreseeable.

For example, Bill put his rather large pet boa constrictor in a cardboard box in his back yard while he was painting in his house. When it rained later in the day (an intervening cause), the box became soft and the snake got out. It slithered through the fence into the neighbor's yard and terrified Bill's neighbor Dirk, who ran through a glass sliding door, suffering severe cuts.

The intervening cause of rain, which made the box soggy, was foreseeable—Bill needed only to listen to a weather report or look out the window periodically. If he had not left the snake in a cardboard box in the rain, the problem would not have occurred; therefore, Bill will probably be held liable for the neighbor's injuries.

Defenses for Negligence

After a number of widely publicized cases, including the famous McDonald's coffee lawsuit of 1994, some people believe our courts perpetuate the notion that whenever something bad happens to someone, someone else should be held responsible for it. For the most part, however, individuals are legally responsible for their own actions. Even in lawsuits, juries may amend or reject damages if the plaintiff had a hand in his or her own loss.

There are a number of specific defenses to claims of negligence that may be effective even if the defendant is negligent.

Assumption of Risk

Certain activities are inherently risky: Skiing, skydiving, handling explosives, using power tools, and even attending stock car races and rock concerts are among the activities that have some level of associated risk. A participant in these activities assumes a certain level of risk, and if a potentially foreseeable injury occurs, the injured party must accept some or all of the responsibility. Courts have even found that an individual riding in a vehicle with a driver known to be negligent or intoxicated has assumed the risk of continuing in a known dangerous situation unless he or she protests and/or attempts to get out.

Assumption of risk is often the first defense in a medical malpractice lawsuit. People who undergo medical procedures generally receive counseling on all possible complications and outcomes and sign a statement acknowledging that they are aware of the risks.

In-Depth: Last Clear Chance

As discussed in chapter 1, if a property owner does not take a last clear chance to warn someone of danger, the owner may be liable for any injury or damage. An individual who takes the last clear chance may use it as a defense; if he or she does not, not only is this defense not available but the owner may be found wholly negligent and barred from using the contributory negligence defense. Two examples follow.

Jackson owns a rather large rural plot of land, which contains a number of abandoned vertical mine shafts. He has numerous signs around the property and at every hole in the fence warning of hazardous conditions and dangerous open mines. He even has signs posted around each of the open mines. He is working on the fence one day when a young man drives up in an all-terrain vehicle (ATV) and asks how he is doing. In addition to saying he is fine and that it is a hot day, Jackson points to one of the signs and tells the driver that the area is dangerous, as it has many open mines and driving into one can be fatal. As people have been driving their ATVs all over his property for years, but seldom when he is there, he then just goes about his business. Later, he hears some yelling from a few hundred yards away and finds that the young man's ATV has fallen into one of the mineshafts. The man jumped off just before the ATV tipped over the edge and fell in. Jackson took the last clear chance to warn the driver of the hazards and will be able to use this defense.

On the other hand, Star turned left onto a one-way street going the wrong way while Carlisle was driving in the right direction on that street and had the opportunity to see Star's car from more than a block away. In total confusion, Star stopped and was thinking about what to do next. Carlisle had more than enough time to stop or change lanes but was not paying attention and collided with Star's car, leaving 30 feet of skid marks. Since Carlisle had more than enough time to avoid the collision, even though Star was heading the wrong way on a one-way street, Carlisle will likely be found liable for failing to take a last clear chance to avoid the collision.

Injured Party's Negligence

In some cases, the injured party voluntarily took part in a hazardous activity and directly contributed to the injury. The level of participation might be quite minimal or it could be substantial. If Lynn is taking a walk in the park and sneezes as she passes Alexander's dog, scaring the dog into biting her, she had very little to do with her injury. However, if Joe is punched while trying to break up Billy and Stan's fistfight, knowing they were larger than he, he was very much involved in his injuries. One of two methods may apply to the injured party's negligence, depending on the jurisdiction: contributory negligence or comparative negligence.

Contributory Negligence

This is a harsh rule: If the injured person contributed in any way to his or her injuries, there is no obligation for payment by the individual accused of negligence. Because the law is so harsh, it is seldom permitted in its pure form, and courts often ignore minor negligence on the part of the injured party. This defense may not be used for intentional torts or when there is strict liability.

Comparative Negligence

This method bases awards on the percentage of negligence on both sides. There are two general rules used to determine who pays what when the injured party has a hand in his or her own loss. The **pure rule** states that the party accused of negligence must pay a portion of the loss based on his or her part of the responsibility for the loss. The **Wisconsin Rule**, also referred to as the **50 percent rule**, holds that a party who is less than 50 percent responsible does not have to pay, and the other party must pay only his or her portion of the loss. If one party is 25 percent at fault and the other is 75 percent at fault, the latter must pay 75 percent of the loss to the other party, but the former pays nothing. How is the percentage of responsibility determined? Generally it is subjective. There is no easy way to make this determination.

COMPREHENSIVE PERSONAL LIABILITY INSURANCE

As you can see from our discussion, everyday life presents most of us with the risk of being legally responsible for the infliction of physical, emotional, or financial losses on others. A visitor to your home could trip on a sprinkler head or hose in the yard, slip on a polished floor or loose rug, or be cut by a glass that was chipped in the dishwasher. A neighbor's child could get hit in the head by a swing.

The legally ideal "prudent man" might have dealt with the risks in various ways: marking sprinkler heads with colorful flags, putting down traction strips on the polished floor to provide better traction, nailing down loose rugs, inspecting every piece of glassware, and closely supervising all visiting children. Not a particularly pleasant way to live, but our legal system presumes that failure to do these things is negligent behavior. Personal liability insurance is one remedy to living in constant fear of a lawsuit.

Comprehensive personal liability (CPL) coverage provides for damages payable due to an insured's negligence that results in bodily injury or property damage (as long as those damages are covered by the policy). As mentioned in chapters 9 and 10, liability coverage is an integral part of homeowners and automobile insurance, so why would someone need a separate CPL policy?

Some individuals may not need homeowners or auto insurance, but that does not remove their need for liability insurance. Others may need substantial liability protection above what their other insurance provides. For example, an affluent securities professional renting in New York City and who does not own a car may, nevertheless, require liability insurance to protect himself from sizeable financial loss.

Liability Coverage

The insured refers to the named insured and any member of his or her household who is a relative or minor under his or her care. Coverage also extends to others who, with the insured's permission, have control of his or her animals or watercraft and cause damage. An insured's child who is at college but still maintains the insured's residence as his or her weekend and/or vacation home would also be covered.

Medical Expenses

If someone is visiting the insured with the insured's permission and is injured on the premises, the liability policy will cover the medical expenses. This would include injuries to any invitee or licensee. The covered damages include the medical expenses of others (including funeral expenses) for up to three years following the injury if it is caused by any of the following:

- A condition of the insured premises, even if not on the premises
- A condition on the roads or walkways adjoining the premises
- The actions of an insured or an animal owned by an insured

Neither fault nor negligence is an issue. Note that this coverage does not include injuries to an insured, with the exception of resident employees. A resident employee would be covered if he or she is injured on or off the premises while acting as an employee.

Additional Coverages

Personal liability insurance provides various additional protections for the insured.

Claims Expense

Expenses related to a claim, including those of or related to a lawsuit defense, and up to $50 per day of lost earnings will be paid in addition to the limit of liability under the policy. The insurance company will pay only for legal defense by a lawyer of its choosing. If the client wants to choose the lawyer, the insurer may or may not agree to pay. Insurance company funded defense is completely impersonal: If the insurer believes it will pay less by defending the case, it will defend; if it believes it can settle the case for less than it might otherwise have to pay for defense or damages, it will settle. The insured has no say in the decision.

Damage to Property of Others

If an insured damages another person's personal property and if the property is not covered under section I of a homeowners policy, the CPL provision (sometimes called a **good neighbor provision**) will cover it, even when the insured is not liable. The maximum claim is generally $1,000. If Dana borrows Lynn's outdoor grill and ruins it by leaving it on high for too long, this provision will pay up to $1,000 for a new grill. There are generally some specific exclusions to this coverage, detailed in the discussion of exclusions below.

First Aid

If there are first aid costs incurred for a covered injury under the policy, they will be paid in addition to the limits of liability of the policy.

Loss Assessment Coverage

If a member of a homeowners or condominium association is assessed for his or her share of the association's legal liability, the policy will pay that assessment if the liability would be covered by the homeowners policy form. The amount of the benefit is limited to $1,000 but can be increased by endorsement.

Policy Conditions

The comprehensive personal liability policy, as well as section II of the homeowners policy, has a number of provisions that are typically included for the purpose of clarity.

Bankruptcy of the Insured

Following the same provision related to other parts of a homeowners policy, if the insured files for bankruptcy to reduce or avoid his or her obligations under a court-ordered settlement, the insurance company's obligations under the same settlement are not affected. If Jeff was found liable for $1 million and had only $500,000 of insurance, the insurance company would only have to pay its $500,000, even if Jeff filed for bankruptcy and ultimately only had to pay $100,000 out of his own pocket because his assets were collateral for other debts.

Duties After a Loss

The insured has an obligation to cooperate with the insurance company whenever an insured loss occurs. First, he or she must notify the insurance company of the loss, provide any reasonable information, give names of witnesses if available, provide copies of any legal documents related to the loss, attend any related trials if requested to, and cooperate in any settlement discussions. Additionally, the insured may not make or promise any payment or make admissions of guilt that might obligate the insurance company.

Limit of Liability

Regardless of the number of people involved, the maximum amount payable under a policy is the amount stated on the declarations page of the contract—it is not multiplied by the number of people claiming to have suffered a loss or by the number of insureds. It is also critical to remember that the policy's liability limit is not the limit of potential damages. Many people believe, incorrectly, that if they have a $400,000 estate, a liability policy of $500,000 will protect it. That policy will provide protection up to the first $500,000 for which an insured may be liable, but if an insured is liable for $1 million, the insurance will pay its $500,000 obligation and the insured will be responsible for paying the other half, possibly losing the estate and still having $100,000 in debts.

Other Insurance

This clause states that the liability insurance is excess over any other existing insurance under which a claim can be made, with the exception of umbrella liability insurance (discussed below) or any "excess coverage" policies written specifically as such. Excess coverage only pays when other coverage is exhausted.

Severability of Insureds

This provision clarifies how the insurance is applied. While each insured is covered for his or her acts, the coverage does not extend between insureds. If the same policy covers Tom and Michele and should he damage her property, she may not sue him and expect the insurer to pay.

Suit Against Us

As with virtually all other insurance contracts, the insured may not sue the insurance company for failure to pay a claim if he or she did not comply with the duties after the loss in an attempt to settle the claim. Further, a person who files a claim against an insured may not sue the insurer unless and until the insured is found to be liable, either by the courts or by agreement with the insurer.

Exclusions

There are two general types of exclusions: those that exclude coverage for both liability and medical payments (these generally involve vehicles of some sort) and those that exclude coverage for liability only. There are also some particular exclusions to claims for medical payments to others and damages to the property of others.

Vehicle Exclusions

The personal liability policy does provide some protection for unregistered vehicles that would not be covered by a personal auto policy, including:

- Unregistered motor vehicles that are in storage, such as those that are inoperable
- Vehicles that are on the insured's property but belong to others
- Vehicles used in service on the insured's property, such as riding lawnmowers
- Motor vehicles designed and used to assist the handicapped, but only when either being used for this purpose or remaining parked
- Unmodified golf carts when on a golf course or being driven on streets in a private housing area in which the insured lives and on which they are permitted

Any vehicle that would be covered under the personal auto policy rather than a CPL policy (such as any vehicle that would normally be registered for use on the roads) is, obviously, excluded. While there have been attempts to get around this exclusion, they have generally been unsuccessful.

Other types of vehicles are excluded as detailed below. They are excluded both from medical coverage as well as from liability coverage.

Aircraft

Since few people own or rent aircraft, this exclusion eliminates coverage of any owned or rented aircraft that carries people or cargo. Coverage for hang gliders and ultralights is also excluded. Model/hobby aircraft are not excluded.

Hovercraft

There was confusion as to whether a hovercraft, which moves while being lifted off of the surface by large propellers, was excluded, so they are now excluded specifically.

Watercraft

While small boats are relatively common, especially in some locales, and therefore are covered by a personal auto policy (PAP), larger boats are relatively uncommon and generally excluded. The following three classes of boats are excluded specifically from coverage under the unmodified personal liability insurance policy:

- Inboard/outboard motorboats having more than 50 horsepower, whether owned by or rented by the insured
- Sailing vessels longer than 26 feet that are owned or rented by the insured
- Any outboard motorboat or boat with a motor with greater than 25 horsepower if it was owned by the insured at the inception of the policy and was not listed on the application or reported to the insurer in some other manner

Liability-Only Exclusions

The following exclusions apply only to liability claims, not to medical payments.

Assessments and Contractual Liability

These are covered under part II of the homeowners forms by property insurance rather than liability insurance.

Business Activities

The standard ISO form defines business as "a trade, profession, or occupation engaged in on a full-time, part-time, or occasional basis." It also means "any other activity engaged in for money or other compensation." Four types of activity are excluded from the definition of "business" and are therefore covered:

- Uncompensated volunteer work
- Uncompensated day care
- Home day care for a relative of the insured
- Any other business activity for which compensation was less than or equal to $2,000 in the 12 months prior to inception of the policy

The definition of "business" is sufficiently broad to include the rental activities of an insured. The rental activities exceptions to the business exclusion provides coverage for either the occasional rental of an insured's residence or the rental of part of the residence as an office, a school, a studio, or a private garage.

Finally, it is also possible to add business coverage through an endorsement to the liability portion of the homeowners form for certain types of business, such as an office, studio, or school run in the home, or a home day care. If the type of home-based business is not eligible for coverage under a homeowners form, it should be covered under a professional or commercial liability policy.

Communicable Disease

A disease transferred to another by an insured is excluded.

Controlled Substance

Liability that may arise from the sale, use, manufacture, delivery, transfer, or possession of a controlled substance, as defined by federal Food and Drug Law, is excluded.

Damage to Own Property

The insured may not collect for damage to his or her own property under a liability policy. Personal property should be covered under the property damage portion of a homeowners policy.

Insured Persons

Injuries to insured persons are also excluded since an insured cannot be liable to him- or herself. Covering one's own injuries and illnesses and the expenses related to them is the role of health insurance, DI, and long-term care policies.

Intentional Injury

Liability policies universally exclude harm or damage done intentionally because the transfer of this risk is against public policy. The exclusion extends to unintended results of intentional acts: If Dirk became angry with his neighbor Pat and put roofing nails at the end of Pat's driveway, damages to vehicles of other drivers would not be covered by his CPL policy because he intentionally did something to cause damage. That the wrong people suffered is irrelevant.

It is important to note that this generally applies only to acts deliberately intended to harm others: If Dirk was grilling hamburgers, which would be an intentional act, and Joe, his guest, burned his hand on the grill, that is not an intentional injury. If Dirk grabbed Joe's hand and put it on the grill, it would be.

Libel and Slander

Slander (verbal defamation) and libel (written defamation) are not normally covered under the personal liability portion of a CPL policy.

Molestation or Abuse

Any sexual molestation or abuse claims against an insured are excluded.

Nuclear Incidents

The policy excludes property damage or injury coverage for anyone who is insured under a nuclear energy liability policy. While most people would not normally acquire such a policy, each nuclear facility has liability insurance that covers anyone who might be sued because of a nuclear incident.

Professional Liability

Professional activities, such as those performed by a financial professional, physician, or lawyer, are more appropriately covered under a professional liability policy.

Rented To/In Care Of

Property that is rented to or in the care, custody, or control of the insured is excluded from liability coverage, since it is covered under the property-coverage section of the homeowners policy. However, if the property is damaged by fire, smoke, or explosion that is not caused by illegal activity but is the responsibility of the insured, it will be covered.

Uninsured Premises

This might occur if an individual owns or rents a residence but chooses to have a comprehensive personal liability policy with nothing for the structure or contents. Section I of a homeowners form contains a long list of what constitutes an insured premises. If the insured has property that is not on this list, such as a residence that was owned or rented but not listed when the policy was issued, then it would not be insured.

War

This section excludes damage or loss arising from war, civil war, rebellion, revolution, insurrection, or similar conflicts. This has not traditionally excluded terrorism, but a terrorism exclusion is being included in some policies, typically identifying it as an illegal activity which is not insured. Keep in mind that this is liability insurance: An insured's unintentional participation in these activities in one way or another would be required for a claim to be considered.

Workers Compensation

Workers compensation and other statutory benefits are excluded, including injuries to any person eligible for workers compensation benefits. This exclusion does not apply to injuries to an on-site employee who is not covered by workers compensation. The policy will automatically cover two full-time household employees, such as a maid or other domestic employee, but additional employees must be covered with an increased premium.

Medical Payments Exclusions

In addition to other exclusions, medical payments for others will not cover resident employees who are away from the premises and are not acting in the capacity of an employee. Workers on the property who are covered by workers compensation or any non-occupational disability or occupational disease law benefits are also not covered. Persons who reside on the premises are also excluded, including boarders, family members, renters of a unit on the premises, or roommates.

Damage to Property of Others Exclusions

There are four general exclusions for this coverage: business pursuits, uninsured locations, and vehicles; intentional damage; losses covered under section I of the policy; and owned or rented property.

Business Pursuits, Uninsured Locations, and Vehicles

This exclusion covers three areas: damage caused to property of others through the business pursuits of the insured, any harm or damage that arises out of the use of uninsured premises, and damage or injury caused by the use of any vehicle that normally would be registered.

Intentional Damage

This is a somewhat obvious exclusion that applies to any insured 13 years old or older. Without this provision, people could ask their neighbors to destroy things for them that they no longer wanted or for which they wanted a replacement. When a child under 13 intentionally destroys another's property, the maximum liability coverage is generally $1,000.

Losses Covered Under Section I

This exclusion denies coverage for any damage that should already be covered under section I of a homeowners policy. The exclusion is only from this part of the policy, not the entire policy. Property that would not be covered under section I may well be covered under this section.

Owned or Rented Property

This is another obvious standard exclusion: If the individual owns or is renting the property, it should be covered under part I of a homeowners policy.

Endorsements

There are several endorsements that may be added to a CPL.

Homeowners Pollution Endorsement

This is primarily designed for homeowners who use liquid fuel (heating oil) to heat their homes. Federal and state environmental organizations generally are charged with locating a leak of heating oil or other pollutants and having the responsible party repair it and clean up any seepage or damage. Standard coverage is limited to $10,000 for losses caused by liquid fuel leaking from a storage tank. Those who use large quantities of fuel and more conservative homeowners may choose to increase the limit.

Personal Injury Liability Endorsement

As discussed in this chapter, physical and emotional harm related to bodily injury are covered under personal liability insurance. However, nonphysical harm to others, such as libel, slander, false arrest, violations of privacy, or defamation of character, are not normally covered. For an extra premium, this endorsement extends coverage to these "personal injuries." There are still certain reasonable exclusions:

- Liability accepted via a contract
- Any act that is known by the insured to be a violation of the law
- Personal injuries to employees of an insured
- Business pursuits (this is a personal liability policy, not a business liability policy)
- Injuries that arise out of civic or public activities of the insured

Premises Rented to Others

This coverage extends liability protection to portions of an insured's property that are rented to others, or the entire property if it is rented to others.

Watercraft and Snowmobile Endorsements

If coverage for these types of assets against damage is sought through endorsements to another policy, it is a good idea to endorse the liability policy to cover them as well. If a separate policy is purchased to cover damage to these items, that policy is the most appropriate place to attach liability coverage.

PROFESSIONAL LIABILITY INSURANCE

One of the standard exclusions found in both personal liability and property insurance policies is business pursuits. Within limits, some coverage can be provided through endorsements to personal policies. However, for professional liability, separate coverage is always necessary.

Most businesses can obtain commercial insurance, which includes various coverages under the liability portions, but these policies do not generally cover professional liability. When negligence in the practice of a person's profession may inflict physical or fiscal harm on clients using the services, that person will be liable for damages. Professionals, therefore, need professional liability coverage.

Interestingly, professional liability insurance usually does not exclude intentional acts. Since professionals intentionally do their jobs, if intentional acts were excluded, the purpose of the insurance would cease to exist. Professionals may opt for or recommend a course of action that turns out to be damaging. A lawyer might deliberately choose language for a contract that ends up damaging the client; a surgeon might perform a type of surgery that injures his patient in some unforeseen way. If the policy excluded these intentional acts, these professionals would not be able to do their jobs and survive financially. As long as the action taken was reasonable under the known circumstances, the professional is covered.

Like all forms of insurance, professional liability insurance is a business. A policy usually requires the insured to notify the insurer if a lawsuit is filed or if he or she believes one might be filed. As with claims coverage on CPLs, the insurer chooses the defense lawyer for the insured, and if the insurer believes that a settlement might cost less than a defense, a settlement will be offered. This will occur even if there is no evidence that the insured made any kind of error, or if it appears that the plaintiff may be completely at fault—it is purely a financial decision. The emotional toll on the professional is not considered in what is essentially a purely financial decision on the part of the insurance company. Personal injury lawyers know this, which gives rise to lawsuits being filed merely to obtain whatever settlement is offered.

The tort system in most states permits judges to require the losing party to pay the winning party's legal fees. However, judges are hesitant to impose this even when there is little or no evidence of any wrongdoing, which lessens its effectiveness as a deterrent to frivolous litigation. As long as the U.S. tort system permits individuals to sue anyone for just about anything, professional liability insurance is a critically important product.

Occurrence Versus Claims-Made Forms

Professional liability policies are written as either occurrence forms or claims-made forms. An **occurrence form** pays claims for actions that led to a loss if the policy was in force when the action took place. For example, assume that in 1998, a self-proclaimed financial planner told his financially conservative clients to purchase a certain dot-com stock with 80 percent of their investment dollars.

In 2000, when these stocks started to suffer a decline in price, he told them to hang on, that they were assured of great returns so long as they did not panic. In late 2001, they sued the financial planner when they realized that their concerns were ignored. The planner had RSM Insurance Inc.'s occurrence form of professional liability insurance from 1995 until 2000, when he changed to PDL Insurance Corp. Since the advice that resulted in the loss occurred while he was insured by RSM, RSM covers the claim.

The alternate approach, **claims made**, provides protection if the policy is in force when the claim is made, regardless of when the action that caused the loss occurred. In the above case, assuming the planner had a claims-made form, the claim was made while the planner was insured by PDL, so PDL would be responsible for the claim. Claims-made forms are currently the most common, since some claims may arise 10 to 20 years after the action that gave rise to the claim. Some insurers that sold professional liability insurance that long ago may no longer exist, and many of those that do have little in the way of reserves to handle claims that long after the fact. Additionally, the amount of coverage a professional would have had 20 years ago is likely much less than he or she would have in place today.

With occurrence forms of insurance, for a professional error made as early as 1985, when premiums were based on lower costs and smaller court settlements, an insurer might have to defend a claim and/or pay damages as late as 2005, a time when court settlements have increased substantially and defense costs have more than doubled. When this happens, the occurrence form is said to have **long-tail coverage**.

Errors and Omissions Insurance

A professional with a business that can result primarily in the infliction of financial losses will purchase a form of professional liability insurance called errors and omissions (E&O) insurance.

Financial planners, accountants, insurance agents, and lawyers are among those who purchase E&O insurance. Coverage is typically designed for each profession, and there are no standard forms of E&O insurance.

Malpractice Insurance

Malpractice insurance is generally for professionals who may cause physical harm, such as physicians, chiropractors, morticians, barbers, opticians, and dentists. Like E&O policies, each company designs its own—there are no standard forms. There are dozens of different forms designed for specialties within general categories.

For many years, certain professionals, specifically physicians, were given veto power over the right of a malpractice insurance carrier to settle a claim rather than fight it. Because of the high cost of defending a lawsuit, however, most insurers have now eliminated this option.

Coverage for both E&O and malpractice insurance is not usually limited to physical or fiscal harm and may include libel, slander, false imprisonment, or mental anguish.

UMBRELLA LIABILITY INSURANCE

There may be situations for which the basic CPL policy, homeowners policy, or PAP are not adequate when compared to the net worth of a client and the size of lawsuits against people in similar circumstances. So in today's litigious world, many people want more protection than the typical policy provides. The amount of liability insurance available under a PAP or homeowners series policy is somewhat limited. Therefore, rather than separately increase coverage on these policies, clients are often better served if they obtain an umbrella liability policy, sometimes referred to as **catastrophe liability insurance**.

A typical umbrella policy will usually have a liability limit of $1 million or more. Generally, the person seeking the coverage must have a specified level of coverage under both homeowners and auto policies with those policies both being from the same company—the one from which they also want to obtain the umbrella policy. Most insurers require the underlying liability insurance to be at least $300,000, but there is no standard amount.

While boosting liability coverage on a PAP, homeowners, or CPL policy increases the coverage for that policy alone, an umbrella liability policy not only increases the coverage for those policies, it also broadens it. Umbrella policies provide coverage for some risks excluded in basic liability coverage, most commonly libel and slander, and may include other items not covered by a CPL, such as personal injury claims and blanket contractual liability claims. Since each firm designs its own policy, the specifics must be reviewed with the individual company.

Umbrella policies are also excess policies: They pay when the underlying coverage limits are used up. If an insured gets sued and the claim falls under the insured's homeowners or auto policy, that policy will pay first, with the umbrella policy picking up any difference to the limit of its liability. For example, if a base policy has $300,000 of coverage and the umbrella policy covers up to $1 million, the maximum that will be paid out between them will be $1 million.

As mentioned, though, the umbrella policy broadens the coverage under the base policy, so even if the original liability insurance would not have covered the liability, the entire $1 million is still available. When the umbrella policy is the only coverage for a claim, it has its own deductible, which may be as high as $10,000 or as low as $250. Typically, as long as a liability claim is covered by the base policy, the base policy is effectively the deductible for the umbrella policy.

Umbrella coverage is generally inexpensive. A $1 million level of coverage will likely cost less than $200 per year; however, premiums will vary because of a number of factors, including occupation and location. It is not uncommon for high net worth people to have between $3 million and $5 million of umbrella liability insurance.

In-Depth: Policy Language

Why do insurance policies include so much detailed information, and why are they so confusing?

Historically the insurance industry as a whole has treated its insureds fairly. The language of insurance policies has been an evolutionary process; early policies were relatively short and the meaning was not often contested. As years passed, more and more insureds sued insurance companies in an effort to extend the coverage beyond what was written in the policies and contemplated in the calculation of premiums. Individuals with CPL policies attempted to expand coverage to automobile liability in the absence of an auto insurance policy, insureds attempted to claim losses caused by other insureds on the same policy, etc.

Many of these lawsuits became catalysts for the insurance companies to clarify the policies. Changes in terminology, additional exclusions, and expanded lists of covered losses were the result. It is this confusing language that makes it important for financial planners to understand the various forms of insurance, and in the absence of becoming an insurance expert, to develop relationships with those who are.

Exclusions

While broad in coverage, the umbrella liability policy does have some exclusions. If watercraft, aircraft, professional services, or business pursuits are covered by some underlying insurance, they will also be covered by the umbrella policy; if they are not, they will not be covered by the umbrella policy. As expected, any act by an insured or at the request or direction of the insured that is intended to cause property damage or inflict personal injury will not be covered. And, of course, damage to property of an insured is also excluded.

WHY LIABILITY?

This is a litigious society. Our legal system, with all of the good it does, does little to discourage individuals from seeking to blame others for any loss they suffer. The mere existence of liability insurance may have exacerbated the problem, but the fact remains that the cost of defending oneself against a claim of liability can be very high. The activities of daily life and business expose everyone to potential claims of liability. A clumsy guest tripping over a doorjamb or sprinkler head can result in injury for which a homeowner or renter may be held liable. Calling someone an idiot in a public place, even if it is in a private conversation with another person, might give rise to a claim of slander. Sending an email to someone expressing the same sentiment may lead to a claim of libel. For these reasons, it is essential for a financial planner to understand the liability risks of his or her clients. Financial planners must sometimes be bearers of unpleasant news. Telling a client that he or she needs to review existing liability coverage falls under this category, but it is critical for your client's fiscal peace of mind.

LIABILITY INSURANCE: NEEDS ANALYSIS

Because everyone is a potential target for a liability lawsuit, appropriate liability coverage is clearly part of a sound financial plan. Much like other forms of property and liability insurance, knowing the situation and point of view of the client is the basis for ensuring that adequate coverage is in place. For the same reasons, a planner who is not licensed properly may not make specific recommendations as to appropriate coverage. However, a planner does need to be aware of the general issues surrounding liability coverage and how it might affect a client so that recommendations to have the client meet with a qualified insurance advisor are made when appropriate.

For example: Jim is divorced. The vast majority of his net worth was tied up in his home, which is now owned by his ex-wife. He rents his condo, and all of his invested assets are now in his qualified retirement plans. An analysis he had performed determined that his retirement plans will give him a fairly comfortable retirement. He also knows that in most cases, those funds would not be available to pay a liability claim. Jim does not want any more liability insurance than he must have on both his automobile and renters insurance. Jim is probably adequately covered as far as his legal obligations are concerned. His attitude is that it is not likely anyone will sue him since he has nothing for them to get. The first question normally asked by a lawyer representing a plaintiff in a liability lawsuit is for information on existing liability insurance policies held by the defendant. While some may feel that Jim lacks a strong sense of morality, as a practical matter his conclusions about his liability coverage are probably correct.

Karen, on the other hand, as a specialized medical technician, owns her own home, has some money in an emergency fund and some invested outside her retirement plans. While her professional liability concerns are covered through her job, she is concerned about losing what she has worked hard to acquire. As a minimum, maximizing the amount of liability insurance on her auto and homeowners policies is probably a good idea. While this may amount to a maximum of $300,000, she may feel that it is inadequate, based on stories she has read about liability lawsuits. Since a $1 million umbrella policy is not particularly expensive, she may want to consider having it.

In the professional world, there are typically only a few insurers that sell policies for a given profession. Most professionals are more concerned with obtaining the coverage than shopping for the best price or service. In some fields, the professional must work a certain minimum number of hours or earn a minimum amount of income before the coverage is even available.

A planner who works with a lot of people in a particular profession would provide a great service by determining all of the companies that offer professional liability insurance to that group.

The exposure of a particular person to liability lawsuits is somewhat affected by the amount of interaction they have with others. Someone who drives many places, especially in areas with which they are not familiar, is exposed to making more driving mistakes that may lead to accidents. A person who has many guests in his or her home clearly has a greater risk than someone who rarely entertains. In most states an individual who serves alcoholic beverages to guests in their home may be held liable for a guest's subsequent actions that cause harm to others.[1] Since a person throwing a lot of parties does not necessarily know if a guest is too drunk to drive safely, the host would be wise to have adequate liability insurance. A "soccer mom" who transports a number of children to games or other activities increases her exposure by having children other than her own in her vehicle. It is a nice thought that friends do not sue friends but, when it comes to large sums of money, friendship, in some cases, has a price.

Most clients will go through life without being sued. However, many lawsuits arise out of situations that do not seem to warrant them, and being the defendant in a lawsuit is stressful enough without being concerned about losing all that one has. While a typical planner will not be an insurance expert, this is another area of exposure that can destroy all other financial plans if not adequately addressed. It is part of the foundation discussed in chapter 1—part of the subterranean structure that keeps the rest of the plan working.

[1]The Insurance Information Institute Fact Book, 2004

IMPORTANT CONCEPTS

Absolute liability

Assumption of risk

Attractive nuisance

Business pursuits

Care, custody, and control exclusion

Claims-made form

Collateral source rule

Comparative negligence

Comprehensive personal liability

Contributory negligence

Errors and omissions insurance

First aid expense

General damages

Intentional tort

Invitee

Last clear chance

Legal expenses

Licensee

Long-tail coverage

Loss assessment coverage

Malpractice insurance

Negligence

Negligence per se

Negligent entrustment

Occurrence form

Personal injury liability

Professional liability

Proximate cause

Punitive damages

Res ipsa loquitur

Respondeat superior

Special damages

Tort

Trespasser

Umbrella policy

Vicarious liability

QUESTIONS FOR REVIEW

1. What is the relationship between a tort and liability?

2. What three things have to be present for liability to arise out of negligence?

3. Define and give examples of:

   • absolute liability

   • negligence per se

   • *res ipsa loquitur*

4. Explain the defenses against a claim of negligence.

5. What happens if a person who has been found liable for negligence dies? What happens if the person files for bankruptcy?

6. What are the exclusions to the comprehensive personal liability policy (CPL)?

7. For whom will the medical-payments-to-others coverage not pay for medical care?

8. What are the pros and cons to occurrence forms and claims-made forms of professional liability insurance?

9. Discuss both sides of the issue of permitting a professional the authority to allow an insurer to settle a claim or require the insurer to defend the claim.

10. What are the advantages of obtaining umbrella liability insurance over merely increasing the liability coverage on a PAP or homeowners policy?

SUGGESTIONS FOR ADDITIONAL READING

Fundamentals of Risk and Insurance, 9th ed., Emmett J.Vaughan & Therese M.Vaughan,Wiley, 2003.

How Insurance Works: An Introduction to Property and Liability Insurance, 2nd ed., Barry D. Smith and Eric A. Wiening, American Institute for Chartered Property and Casualty Underwriters, 1994.

The Insurance Information Institution Fact Book 2004, Insurance Information Institute, 2004.

Introduction to Risk Management and Insurance, 8th ed., Mark Dorfman, Prentice Hall, 2004.

Personal Umbrella Coverage Guide, National Underwriter, 2003.

Principles of Risk Management and Insurance, 9th ed., George E. Rejda, Addison Wesley, 2004.

Property and Liability Insurance Principles, 3rd ed., Constance Lutheardt, American Institute for Chartered Property and Casualty Underwriters, 1999.

CHAPTER TWELVE

Commercial Insurance Lines

• • •

Just like individuals, businesses need to protect their assets and earnings, but these needs are often far more complex. Businesses often need more general lines of insurance than would be available for individuals, and these are generally called commercial lines. While property and liability agents in most states are licensed to sell all lines of property and liability insurance, many agents choose to avoid commercial lines because of the breadth of the field and the complexity of available coverages. Failure to provide adequate recommendations for insurance to businesses can result in the loss of the business.

When you have completed this chapter, you will be able to:

- Identify and describe seven classes of business property and liability insurance
- Explain the difference between direct damage property insurance coverage and indirect loss coverage
- Describe the general nature of the various coverages available to businesses

GENERAL INTRODUCTION TO COMMERCIAL LINES

Individuals own most businesses, and under certain circumstances, individuals who operate as sole proprietors will have some commercial insurance. It is not surprising that in working with individual clients, a planner will come across certain commercial insurance issues worth noting. This is an area fraught with potential liability for a financial planner. As commercial lines of insurance differ from the individual lines covered in prior chapters, it is very helpful for a planner to have an appreciation of the risks faced by business owners and a basic understanding of the various forms of coverage.

There are seven general lines of commercial insurance. Each is somewhat broad and not necessarily consistent from one type of business to the next:

- Commercial property insurance
- Boiler and machinery insurance
- Transportation insurance
- Crime insurance
- Commercial liability insurance
- Commercial automobile insurance
- Workers compensation and employer liability insurance

Commercial Property Insurance

Commercial lines of property insurance are broken down into subcategories because businesses operate in so many different ways. It is beyond the scope of this text to detail each form, but readers should be aware of the wide range of coverages:

- CP 00 10 Building and Personal Property Coverage Form
- CP 00 15 Glass Coverage Form
- CP 00 17 Condominium Association Coverage Form
- CP 00 18 Condominium Commercial Unit Owner's Coverage Form
- CP 00 20 Builder's Risk Coverage Form
- CP 00 30 Business Income Coverage (and Extra Expense) Form
- CP 00 32 Business Income Coverage (Without Extra Expense) Form
- CP 0040 Legal Liability Coverage Form
- CP 00 50 Extra Expense Coverage Form
- CP 00 60 Leasehold Interest Coverage Form
- CP 00 70 Mortgage Holder's Errors and Omissions Coverage Form
- CP 00 80 Tobacco Sales Warehouses Coverage Form

When looking at these forms, it is apparent that some are for direct losses, such as glass coverage, and some are for indirect losses, such as the extra expense form. These forms are put together with one of the relatively standard "causes of loss" forms. This simple list begins to show the complexity of the commercial lines of property insurance. By adding a form that specifies the perils for which the benefits are to be provided when a loss occurs, policies can be more closely aligned with the needs of each specific business.

The more common forms of commercial property insurance are detailed below.

Building and Personal Property Coverage

Homeowners generally live in the homes they own, so logically a homeowners form of insurance covers the building and personal property. A business may or may not occupy a building it owns, or conversely, own the building it occupies. Since business owners and occupants are often different, the building and personal property (BPP) coverage form provides coverage for the building, personal property, or both, depending on the needs of the business. It can also cover tenant improvements, which is not part of a homeowners policy.

There are several distinct coverages that set BPP forms apart from homeowners policies:

Functional Building Valuation

This specific endorsement recognizes that if a given building is destroyed, new building methods and technology may make it possible to build a functionally equivalent building for less money. The new building will generally be in the architectural style of the original, but the new methods and/or materials help reduce the cost of rebuilding and the cost of insurance.

Functional Personal Property Valuation (Other Than Stock)

Similar to the coverage above, if there are personal property items (desks, bookcases, chairs, industrial signs, etc.) that can be replaced with less expensive models that can perform the same function, using this coverage option will reduce the cost of insurance. If the insured property is damaged or destroyed and not replaced, the limit of the benefit is the *lesser* of the amount of insurance coverage, the market value of the specific property, or the actual cash value.

NEED TO KNOW: MONOLINE TO PORTFOLIO TRANSITION

In years past, business owners bought monoline insurance, meaning they were forced to purchase each type of coverage separately, creating paperwork nightmares and administrative problems.

In the very early years, companies often did not write more than one or two lines of insurance, so businesses had to buy different coverages from different companies, each negotiated and paid separately, with differing procedures for filing claims. A business needing 5 of the 12 listed lines of coverage would have to deal with five complete contracts just for property insurance.

The situation improved when insurance companies began to write multiple lines of commercial insurance and created **portfolio programs**, combining multiple coverages in a single policy to reduce the number of policies a single business needs to manage. Not only does a final policy include the appropriate coverages from the above list and the causes of loss form, it includes one of the standard policy declarations forms, one of the common policy conditions forms, a commercial property declarations form, and a commercial property conditions form. While this may seem overly complex, it is obviously done to make things much easier and less complex than the prior method.

Manufacturer's Selling Price

Something that would obviously not be included in a homeowners policy is coverage for the profit margin on destroyed products that are ready to ship. Without this endorsement, the coverage for this inventory would be actual cash value. Only manufacturers can have this coverage. Wholesalers and retailers are not eligible for it since they can usually replace the stock easily.

Newly Acquired Buildings

Some businesses build extra buildings or buy buildings as part of the business. Rather than getting coverage lined up in advance, additional buildings are automatically covered up to $250,000. (Higher limits are available.) This is similar to the provision in the personal auto policy that automatically covers a newly obtained vehicle.

Non-Owned Detached Trailers

Manufacturing and retail businesses often have goods delivered in towed trailers. In some cases, these trailers are left at the business to be unloaded as needed by the business employees. If the business is obligated to pay for damage to the trailers that occurs while they are parked at the business, this provision covers up to $5,000 in damages.

Spoilage

When perishable goods are used by a business in preparation of their final product or as products themselves, the value can be significant. If there is a breakdown of a mechanical or electrical system, contamination of the goods, or a power outage that causes a loss of the perishable goods, this provision covers the loss.

Glass Coverage

Typical building coverage forms severely restrict the amount that will be paid for glass breakage. Common limits are $100 per plate with a limit of $500 per occurrence. A 4-foot-by- 8-foot plate may cost more than $300, not including the costs of delivery or installation. For a business with 30 feet of front windows, each standing 6 feet high, $500 would not go far in covering the cost of replacing them. Plate glass coverage is scheduled[1] coverage. The windows to be insured are listed. If there is any etching, lettering, or the like, these are covered only if they are specifically insured as well.

Condominium Association Coverage

Condominium associations are generally responsible for the structure of the building and all common areas. Condominium association agreements generally require each unit holder to insure the interior of his or her unit. To the extent that the agreement requires unit owners to insure the property, the condominium association coverage form excludes it.

---

[1]Scheduled coverage is coverage that is specific in regard to what is covered. Non scheduled coverage is general in nature. Insuring a building is general coverage that protects damage to walls, floors, ceilings, doors, standard windows, etc. Scheduled coverage, as in this case, covers limited items, such as the plate glass windows, which are far more expensive to replace than typical windows.

In-Depth: Building & Personal Property Alternatives

The previous section describes the traditional BPP, a commercial property form similar to homeowners insurance, covering specified property for a specified amount and requiring the coverage to be 100 percent of the value of the property in order to get complete replacement costs. There are two alternatives to the traditional BPP.

Blanket Insurance

Suppose Jackson Coffee Express (JCE) owns 22 drive-up coffee kiosks in grocery and hotel parking lots. These are in addition to two warehouse/roasting facilities that the company owns. The warehouse/roasting buildings would cost $100,000 each to replace while each kiosk would cost $20,000 to replace. The total replacement value of the buildings is $640,000. With traditional coverage, if JCE wanted enough insurance to replace any structure if it was destroyed, it would have to buy a total of $640,000 of insurance.

Blanket insurance, which permits complete replacement cost coverage with only 90 percent of the value insured, is appropriate when a business has a number of buildings in geographically diverse locations. The primary advantage is the reduced amount of coverage required. With blanket coverage, JCE would only need $576,000. Under the blanket policy, even with the reduced total amount of insurance, if any one structure was destroyed, it would be covered at 100 percent. This works because of the geographic diversity. Regardless of the peril that causes the loss, it is a virtual certainty that not all of the facilities would be destroyed at the same time.

Reporting Form

Retail and manufacturing businesses have a constant flow of materials and merchandise in and out of the operations. For some, the flow is rather steady, with the value of inventory staying relatively static. For others, changing levels of inventory due to seasonal or other differences could easily find them paying for more insurance than they need at some times or being very much underinsured at other times. For large operations, the fluctuations may be in the millions of dollars. To be able to adjust the level of insurance needed, as needed, could potentially save a lot of premium dollars.

This form is established by determining the maximum coverage that would be needed during a year, for example $1 million. The business then "reports" changes in the inventory monthly or quarterly, which results in an adjustment of the premium as required. It is critical for the business to keep this valuation current. The policy includes a **full-value reporting clause** that is often called the "honesty clause." If by chance the company reports the value as $300,000 when it is actually $500,000, and a loss occurs, the loss is covered at only 60 percent (300,000/500,000). This occurs even if the maximum value for the year is pegged at $1 million. The clause means that the policy has a 100 percent coinsurance requirement, but it can be adjusted as often as monthly.

Builder's Risk Coverage

When a builder is erecting a building, since it is not a complete building while under construction, the value changes as construction progresses. Because a BPP policy will not provide protection for the value of the property at appropriate levels throughout construction, the builder's risk form is generally best for insuring these buildings.

The premium for a builder's risk policy is based on 55 percent of the final value of the building. Coverage terminates when the structure is complete, but the policy owner may be permitted to change it to a reporting form (see "In-Depth: BPP Alternatives"). The building owner, the general contractor, or one of the subcontractors may apply for this coverage as they all have an insurable interest in the building.

Business Income Coverage

Business income forms cover indirect income losses due to business interruptions caused by property loss and may be written with or without extra expense coverage. The goal is to insure that, for the estimated time it would take for an interruption to run its course and for the business to be up and running again, the business will be able to meet expenses. These policies include coinsurance provisions that require 50 to 100 percent coverage for the 12 months' income being insured, depending on circumstances. If the nature of the business is such that resumption of operations would likely take over a year, a 125 percent coinsurance clause can be used. Coverage can include the loss of rental value during the interruption. Expenses that will not continue during an interruption are not covered. The insured may also choose not to insure the payroll for "rank-and-file" workers in order to keep premiums low.

Whether the business income policy includes coverage for extra expenses or not, the policy provides certain extra expenses. (Extra expenses are those that would not have been incurred if a covered loss had not occurred, including the cost of a temporary location, relocation expenses, and the cost to equip the space until the business is able to move back in to its old space or find adequate replacement space.) If the policy form is "without extra expense," it will still cover extra expenses that are made to reduce the loss but the cumulative payments made will not exceed the amount of coverage. When the business income policy includes extra expense coverage, the policy pays for extra expenses required to keep the business operating, even if it does not reduce the loss.

Extra Expense Coverage

Some businesses are not in a position to have business interrupted, even if the facility in which they work is damaged or destroyed. These businesses, such as a stock brokerage firm or bank, may be forced out of their regular offices but will have to set up shop, at least temporarily, somewhere else, sometimes in temporary facilities that can be put together and made operational in a few days. For these businesses, business interruption insurance is not necessary, but they do need to be indemnified for what might be the substantial cost of moving to, setting up, and operating in a new space. There are a number of options regarding what percentage of the whole benefit can be received each month. This may vary based on the business's anticipated needs and the period of operation in the temporary space.

Leasehold Interest Coverage

In times of a slow economy and in areas with too much commercial space for the market, businesses are generally able to negotiate very favorable long-term lease agreements. Leases such as this may have a provision that cancels the lease if the property is damaged to the point that the tenant would have to move out. Assume the tenant has a lease for $2,500 per month, and the commercial real estate market has changed so that equivalent space would now cost $3,500. If the business had to leave because of a fire or other damage, this coverage would pay the discounted (present) value of the difference between current market rent and the rent payable under the current favorable lease for the balance of the original lease period. The amount of coverage decreases each month since that portion of the lease has ended. For example, if the lease rate was for three years, the effective amount of insurance would be a 36-month benefit. If the damage occurred with 19 months to go on the lease, it would become a 19-month benefit.

In-Depth: Contingent Business Interruption Endorsements

The foregoing are all coverages that provide payment when there is a loss to property owned, occupied, or controlled by businesses. However, many businesses rely on other businesses to operate. In certain circumstances, these other businesses are critical and irreplaceable, or only replaceable at substantial cost. It may sound odd, but when the property of a supporting business is damaged so that the supporting company cannot provide the critical support, the insured company's policy will pay for a loss of income due to the damage if it includes this endorsement.

This endorsement generally insures the following four types of property:

Contributing Property
This would be a business that is either the sole supplier or one of a very limited number of suppliers that can provide critical materials for the insured company's continued operation.

Leader Property
In a large mall, the big stores, called "anchors," are often the key to the success of the smaller stores. The anchors draw customers who then visit the smaller stores. Similarly, a restaurant or gym near an office building may find that most of its customers come from that building. If an anchor store in a strip mall or an office building near a restaurant suffers severe damage, the smaller businesses may suffer substantial reductions of income.

Manufacturing Property
This business would be the sole supplier or one of very few suppliers of the merchandise sold by the insured business.

Recipient Property
The insured company may have a very limited market for its output. A recipient property would be that of a business that was the primary buyer of the insured's output.

Other Indirect Loss Forms

Businesses can suffer many types of indirect losses. The following are brief descriptions of the two special forms used to cover those types not fully covered by the above policies. Each has provisions that increase or decrease payments, but the full details are beyond the scope of this text.

Business Interruption Insurance

Simply stated, this form pays the ongoing expenses and replaces the profits that are lost when a business cannot operate due to property damage. It is most often written as an indemnity policy but can be written as a valued form. Two business interruption forms are available under the portfolio program: business income coverage (and extra expense) and business income coverage (without extra expense). Under either form, coinsurance is required ranging from 50 percent to 100 percent of the insured's annual earnings for the 12-month period of the policy. If the insured's business is interrupted, payment is made for the loss of business income, defined as the net profit that would have been earned (including or excluding rental income if elected by the insured) and the necessary expenses that continue during the period of restoration. The definition of business income may be modified to delete or limit coverage on ordinary payroll (generally, the payroll for rank-and-file workers) if the insured does not wish to collect for this expense in the event of interruption.

The so-called "without extra expense" coverage includes those expenses designed to reduce loss (e.g., to resume operations or otherwise reduce the amount of the business interruption loss). Under the so-called "and extra expense" form of coverage, payments are made for expenses incurred to continue operations whether or not such expenses reduce the business interruption loss. The entire amount of insurance is payable under the "and extra expense" form for either business interruption or extra expense.

In addition, there is a type of coverage known as the **extra expense only form** that provides payment for expenses above normal costs when such expenses are incurred to continue operations after damage to the premises by an insured peril. This type of coverage does not provide payment for lost profits.

Rain/Weather Insurance

Rain insurance is another form of loss of income insurance. It is purchased by businesses that sponsor or operate outdoor events that would be adversely affected if bad weather occurs on the day of the event. This coverage does not cover property damage. It can be written to provide a payment for loss of expenses or income, or extra expenses required to continue with the event.

Contracts may or may not specify the amount of rain that must fall before payment will be made. Hail, sleet, and snow are generally included as covered perils. Some companies that provide the product offer a relatively standard form while others have their own unique forms. The coverage generally must be in place at least seven days prior to the event and, once in place, may not be cancelled by either party.

Other uses have been found for this policy type. Certain businesses and cities may insure against excessive snowfall that might result in budget-busting snow removal expenses. Some retail businesses, as a sales motivator, offer customers a 100 percent refund if a certain depth of snow or amount of rain occurs on a specified date. For example, a jeweler may offer a 100 percent refund on the purchase price of jewelry bought during October if there is at least six inches of new snow on Super Bowl Sunday in the local city.

NEED TO KNOW: FLOOD INSURANCE

Commercial flood insurance is similar, in some respects, to residential flood insurance. There are, however some significant differences. The amount of flood insurance available for commercial property is higher, $500,000 under the regular program and $100,000 for an emergency program ($150,000 in Alaska, Hawaii, Guam, and the U.S. Virgin Islands). If other insurance covers part of the loss, the National Flood Insurance Program (NFIP) coverage only pays a proportionate share, and then only if the full amount of available insurance is purchased.

Boiler and Machinery Insurance and Breakdown Protection Coverage

This is a very specialized area of insurance that actually serves as more of an inspection program than insurance. It grew out of companies that inspected boilers and machinery and guaranteed the continued safe operation of the equipment for a specified period of time if all recommended repairs and maintenance were completed. This was very important to early companies that relied on boilers for heat and power generation. An exploding boiler could take a whole building with it, and heavy machinery can cause substantial damage or be very expensive to repair if not maintained properly.

The ISO form name was changed to breakdown protection coverage in 2000. There are 10 coverages under this form that may be included when the policy is purchased, six relating to direct damage and four to indirect damage:

- Property damage
- Expediting expenses
- Business income and extra expense or extra expense only
- Spoilage
- Utility interruption
- Newly acquired premises
- Ordinance or law coverage
- Errors and omissions
- Brands and labels
- Contingent business income and extra expense or extra expense only

An in-depth discussion of these coverages is beyond the scope of this text, but the reader should be aware of the breadth of the coverages available under this one general form. As the effect of each of these perils is different for different types of businesses, the mix of coverages included and the amount of each effectively makes every policy unique.

Financial planners should also be aware of one uncommon provision included in boiler and machinery policies: The insurer may suspend coverage if any of the insured items is found to be in dangerous condition. The suspension is effective immediately upon the insured's receipt of notice, and the company will only lift it by endorsement to the policy. This means that the insurer will take an active role in making sure that all insured equipment is well maintained.

Transportation Coverage

Unlike a homeowners policy, a commercial property policy does not cover property that is taken off of the business premises. This means that when a business ships its products, additional insurance is needed to protect against loss during transit. There are two general insurance forms that are used: ocean marine and inland marine. Depending on the contract for purchase of the items, the shipper or the recipient may obtain this coverage.

Ocean Marine Insurance

Ocean marine policies protect property that is involved in oceanic transportation. There are four basic sub forms. Ocean marine policies are valued policies: The amount payable when a loss occurs is stated in the contract. Generally, there is 100 percent coinsurance.

Cargo Insurance

This insures the cargo of a ship against damage, destruction, or loss.

Freight Insurance

This insurance is not what it sounds like. This is a loss of income policy that pays a ship owner for lost income if the ship is lost and does not finish a voyage.

Hull Insurance

This insures against the loss of the ship itself and includes property liability coverage in the form of a **running-down clause** in case the ship runs into another vessel.

Protection and Indemnity

As part of the ocean marine form, this coverage protects the ship owner from lost income or lawsuits that are a result of the negligence of his or her agents.

Averages

Ocean marine contracts use the word "average" to mean partial loss. If a policy deals with a **particular average**, it limits coverage if the loss is under a certain percentage, such as 5 percent—a loss equal to or exceeding 5 percent would be fully covered.

A **general average** means that everyone who was involved in the operation shares in the loss of any party whose goods were lost in an effort to bring the operation to a successful close.

For example, if goods belonging to Carlin Imports were on the deck of the *Princess Minnow* when she hit rough seas and her crew tossed the Carlin goods overboard to prevent the ship from capsizing, Carlin Imports, all other companies with goods on the ship, and the *Princess Minnow's* owner(s) would share in payment for the lost goods.

Inland Marine Insurance

Inland marine insurance is generally for any items that are being shipped other than on the ocean, but also refers to various miscellaneous forms of coverage that have nothing to do with goods in transit. The various forms can be divided into controlled and uncontrolled forms.

Controlled forms are those that are essentially standardized by the rating bureaus and part of the ISO portfolio program. **Uncontrolled forms** are unique to a specific insurer and may be written in what is called a manuscript format that permits modification for each insured.

There are six general classes of inland marine insurance:

Bailee Forms

This insures goods being held by a business for the benefit of customers. Dry cleaners and storage companies are considered bailees.

Business Floater Forms

This class covers personal property that is subject to loss related to its being transported, such as equipment used at a construction site. It does not include property owned by the business that is being held for sale, but would apply to property that is for sale that is being sold on consignment.

Dealers Forms

These are unusual in that they cover merchandise not only while it is being transported but also while it is in a dealer's store. It is generally limited to certain classes of merchandise, such as cameras, jewelry, coins and stamps, furs, and musical instruments.

Means of Transportation Forms

These forms provide protection for a conglomeration of seemingly unrelated properties, including broadcast towers, rolling stock (the company's cars, trucks, rail cars, etc.), bridges, power lines, and pipelines. The single thread that connects them is that they are all involved in the transportation of goods (electricity as well as radio and TV shows are products).

Transportation Forms

These forms are written to protect goods that are being transported by a common carrier (a transportation company that holds itself out for hire to the general public), a contract carrier (a transportation company under contract to transport goods for a specific company), or a business's own vehicles. It covers the goods while they are being transported by road, rail, or air. This form of insurance can cover certain valuable items when they are sent via registered mail.

NEED TO KNOW: SPECIAL CAUSE OF LOSS

There are generally two types of losses caused by dishonesty: losses from employees and losses from crime.

General property insurance often includes some level of protection against crimes, but there are some exclusions or substantial limits on losses. Because of this, when this type of coverage is appropriate, a special cause of loss form is used—a type of coverage with some similarities to professional liability insurance. There are two general approaches used to determine when a loss is covered: loss sustained and loss discovery.

For example, if the manager walks into the business one morning and the office door is kicked in and the safe broken open, any loss sustained from that incident will be covered by either approach since the loss was discovered essentially at the same time it occurred. It is when losses occur over time—employee theft of merchandise, someone outside the business tapping into the company's power supply or long distance, etc.—that they vary.

Loss sustained coverage covers losses that are sustained and are discovered during the period of time the policy is in place. Sometimes there is a one-year tail of coverage for discovery of the loss. **Loss discovery coverage** covers losses discovered while the policy is in place, regardless of when the losses took place.

Miscellaneous Forms

This is, as expected, a catch-all category for unrelated forms of insurance. These forms might provide protection against the loss of accounts receivable if records—including electronic data processing equipment and related software—are lost or damaged, making them impossible to collect. They might provide **manufacturers output coverage**, which is a different form of property coverage protecting goods in transit only when they are not on the businesses property, or they might provide **valuable papers insurance** (maps, various types of recording media, drawings, titles and deeds, manuscripts, etc.) that is written on a valued basis or a blanket basis, covering the papers at actual cash value.

Crime Insurance

In 2000, the ISO put together an updated commercial crime program. It affected 11 coverage forms, all three causes of loss forms, 24 coverage endorsements, and a number of schedule endorsements. The complete details of the program are beyond the scope of this text, but the following may be of interest to financial planners.

With all of the forms, there are only three basic crime policies:

- Commercial crime policies
- Employee theft and forgery policies
- Government crime policies

These policies use either the loss-sustained or discovery approaches to determine when a loss has occurred and is covered by insurance (see sidebar, "Need to Know: Special Cause of Loss"). The International Risk Management Institute (IRMI) generally has substantial information on the various ISO forms on its website: www.irmi.com.

Employee Crime Coverage

Employee crime coverage is called a fidelity bond. These fidelity bonds protect insured companies from employee dishonesty that results in the loss of cash, securities, or any other property due to embezzlement, forgery, fraud, or theft by a bonded employee. The face amount of the bond is the limit of liability of the insurance company. That dollar amount is called the bond penalty. Fidelity bonds come in both the loss-sustained form and the discovery form and may also be either schedule or blanket bonds.

A **schedule bond** covers only named individuals or positions. This unusual approach means that if a person leaves a specific job within the company where a fidelity bond was required, his or her replacement is automatically covered. Conversely, a **blanket bond** covers all employees, and new employees are covered automatically.

There are some reasonable exclusions from employee crime coverage.

- Theft by an insured, partner, or member—the company or owner is insured against employee dishonesty, not its own
- Theft by any employee except under employee theft—this sounds odd, but if an employee steals while acting as a customer rather than an employee, it is not covered by this policy
- Indirect loss—this policy only covers the actual losses
- Legal expenses—this coverage is only for the loss itself
- War, nuclear hazards, government authority—these seem to be universal exclusions, but are not likely to give rise to losses caused by employees

There are also exclusions limited to the employee theft coverage.

Cancellation as to Any Employee

This automatically excludes from future coverage any employee found to have committed a dishonest act. This takes effect as soon as an insured partner, officer, director, or trustee becomes aware of current or prior acts of dishonesty of an employee. This is one reason some people with prior convictions are turned down for jobs where there may be an opportunity for them to steal from the employer.

Employee Cancelled Under Prior Insurance

This exclusion eliminates coverage for loss caused by an employee of the insured (or of a predecessor employer) for whom similar insurance was canceled and not reinstated.

Inventory Shortage Exclusion

A company may not submit a claim just because inventory losses appear. It must be shown that an employee is responsible.

Non-Employee Crime Coverages

Non-employee crimes generally take the form of burglary, robbery, or theft. Burglary is stealing from a closed business while robbery is stealing from an open business through the use of force, violence, or threat of violence. Theft encompasses burglary and robbery as well as other forms of theft. Fidelity losses, due to employees, are excluded.

Commercial Liability Insurance

Just like individuals, businesses face the potential for substantial liability claims—perhaps even more so as businesses are believed to have deep pockets and are often targeted when someone is looking for a wealthy party to sue after suffering a loss. A "deep pocket" is a person or business that is perceived to have a great deal of money and/or insurance from which a plaintiff and his or her lawyer(s) can obtain a substantial benefit.

There are three general areas of potential liability.

- Employer's liability (including workers compensation, covered later in this chapter)
- Automobile liability (covered later in this chapter)
- General liability

General Liability

There are a number of areas that may be a source of general liability for a business:

Conduct of Business Operations: : A business could be liable if an employee harms someone or damages the property of others during business operations on or off of the premises.

Contingent Liability: If a business uses an independent contractor, any losses caused by the work of that independent contractor might become the responsibility of the business if the contracted work was illegal, inherently dangerous, or done under the supervision of the business. This is called "contingent liability" since it is contingent on damages caused by the activities of others.

Contractual Liability: This arises when the business in question has agreed, by contractual agreement, to accept responsibility for the negligent actions of another party.

Ownership and Maintenance of the Premises: A condition of the property of a business could cause injury or property damage.

Product Liability: People are quite inventive in the ways they misuse products. This coverage protects the insured business from injuries sustained by the proper or improper use of its products as well as any negligence in its manufacture or design. Often combined with product liability is **completed operations liability.** This is liability arising from the finished work of a business—remodeling, customization work, installations, etc.

Miscellaneous Exposures: Differing business situations give rise to potential liabilities that need to be covered.

Commercial General Liability Coverage

The commercial general liability program (CGL) is part of the portfolio program and is used to cover the general liability exposures faced by most businesses. It is sold in both claims-made and occurrence forms, similar to professional liability insurance. Even though insurers may find themselves facing claims decades after a policy has terminated, occurrence forms are still the most popular CGL forms. There are fifteen exclusions, most of which are quite logical, and in some circumstances endorsements can be used to provide coverage that would otherwise be excluded.

Most exclusions are in place because the liability is best covered by other specific forms. The exclusions include:

- **Pollution:** This excludes coverage for clean-up, property damage, or personal injury caused by the release of pollutants, even if the discharge of pollutants was sudden and accidental.
- **Product Recall:** If a company has a product that is recalled because of a defect, coverage for that is excluded. Other policies are specifically designed to cover this.
- **Workers Compensation:** This is covered under workers compensation insurance.
- **Contractual Assumptions:** In most cases, if the business agrees to perform under the terms of the contract, the CGL policy will not pay them if they do not do it.
- **Liquor Liability:** There is a specific policy for this purpose.
- **Damage to the insured's product:** If a business's product causes damage, the damage caused by the product will be covered but not the damage to the product itself, e.g., if the company makes an air tank and it explodes, causing damage to a buyer's garage, damage to the garage is covered but not damage to the tank.

Miscellaneous Coverage

The various standard packages are designed for the needs of most businesses. However, there are a number of coverages that are specifically needed by only some businesses, including:

Directors and Officers Errors and Omissions Insurance

Anyone who is a director or officer of any business is responsible for the overall management and operation of the firm, meaning other parties can bring suit for mismanagement. This can apply to both for-profit and nonprofit concerns. From a financial planner's perspective, this may be one of the most important forms of liability insurance. Any client who is a director or officer of a business, religious institution, non-profit organization, or even a homeowners association should be protected by this coverage, and if the coverage is not in place, it might be prudent to resign from the position.

Liquor Liability Coverage

Businesses that sell liquor often come under "dram shop" laws. These dram shop liquor liability laws hold the proprietor responsible if a patron drinks too much and injures someone shortly after leaving the business. In many cases, this liability extends to nonprofit organizations that sponsor parties or fund-raisers where liquor is provided. This coverage provides protection against lawsuits that arise out of the serving or selling of liquor. There are only seven states that have neither statutes nor court cases that hold alcoholic beverage servers liable.[2]

Pension Fiduciary Liability

Anyone given authority over the investments and management of pension funds holds a high level of liability. This liability is required by the Employee Retirement Income Security Act (ERISA) of 1974. In some cases, this coverage extends to employee benefits beyond the pension plan.

---

[2]The Insurance Information Institute Fact Book, 2004; Insurance Information Institute

Pollution Liability Insurance

This is one source of coverage for potential liability arising out of the release of pollutants.

Underground Storage Tank Liability

This is obviously one of those coverages that affect relatively few businesses. However with the financial responsibility regulations promulgated by the EPA, it is an important coverage for any business that has an underground tank that contains any pollutant.

Bailee Liability

Whenever a business takes possession of a customer's property for the purpose of providing a service, the business is a **bailee**. The person leaving the property is a **bailor**, and the process, called a **bailment** is created when a customer drops off his or her laundry for cleaning, leaves a car for maintenance or repair, etc. The responsibility of the bailee exists even without negligence. The level of responsibility varies with the type of bailment.

NEED TO KNOW: WAIVING LIABILITY

Jack drove his new Lexus up to the door of the restaurant, handed the keys to the valet and walked in. When his car was returned after dinner, there was a long scratch on the driver's side of the car.

When he angrily pointed it out to the valet and restaurant manager, they pointed to the back of the valet receipt that stated they were not responsible for damage to the vehicle or its contents.

Fortunately for Jack, most courts will not permit bailees to absolve themselves of responsibility.

They may be able to limit their liability, but the receipt did not address limitations. Jack will likely be able to collect for the full cost of repair of the damage.

A **gratuitous bailment for the benefit of the bailor**, such as Erika leaving her dog with neighbor Kendra over a weekend to ensure the dog will be fed, etc., requires little care as the benefit is all for the bailor.

A **gratuitous bailment for the benefit of the bailee**, such as when Catherine loans Jeff her chainsaw so that he can cut firewood, requires extraordinary care of the property.

A **mutual benefit bailment** is where both parties gain from the transaction. One party receives a product or service and the other gets paid for providing that benefit. The auto repair shop will accept the bailment of the customer's vehicle for the purpose of repairing it. The bailee expects to be paid for the work.

Excess Liability Insurance

Excess liability insurance comes in three forms. The most commonly known is the umbrella form, but following-form excess liability policies and the combination forms are also available.

The **following-form liability policy** is merely an extension of underlying coverage, essentially incorporating all of the terms and conditions of the base policy.

The **combination umbrella and following-form excess coverage** combines the umbrella and following-form policies. The following-form excess portion covers some parts of the underlying liability coverage while the umbrella form covers other parts. The policy may also provide coverage on an occurrence or on a claims-made basis.

Commercial umbrella liability policies are much like the personal liability umbrella forms, providing excess coverage for the underlying policies. Likewise, they are also more comprehensive, meaning that some liabilities that are not covered under the base coverages are covered under the umbrella policy. However, they do typically have "corridor" deductibles, often $10,000 or more, for those items not covered by the underlying policies. As with personal umbrella policies, there is a minimum of underlying coverage required. Unlike the personal umbrella policy, defense costs may be included in the total indemnity benefit or might be in addition to the level of indemnity provided by the policy.

In-Depth: The High Cost of Modern Liability

Everyone is paying for a general lack of common sense. Laundry irons come with labels that read "do not iron clothes on body." Electric hair dryers are labeled "do not use in bath tub, or while sleeping." A child's superman costume reads:

"Wearing of this garment does not enable you to fly." How about the warning on a box of nails that says swallowing them may cause irritation, and the ever popular sign on golf carts: "Not for highway use." There is only one reason these statements are on these products: Someone did these things and sued the manufacturer when there was the inevitable injury.

According to the Insurance Institute, in 1971 the average product liability award was under $200,000. By 2000 the average, without punitive damages, was $1.8 million. According to Tillinghast, an actuarial consulting firm, in 1950 tort costs averaged about $12 per citizen of the US; in 1970 it was $68; and in 1980 it was $188. In 2002, tort costs were $809 for every US citizen. Furthermore, with these skyrocketing costs, the individuals who actually suffered a loss only received 45 percent of the payments. Adjusted for inflation, that is a 4.34 percent annual increase in the cost per person. If not adjusted for inflation, it is an 8.43 percent average annual increase.

The cost of liability insurance has been rising to cover the increasing costs of litigation and settlements. These costs are passed on to consumers. When a fast food chain pays damages to a clumsy customer because the customer spilled hot coffee and got burned, everyone pays.

According to the Insurance Institute, the cost of liability losses in business today costs the average family of four almost three weeks' income.

Commercial Automobile Insurance

The type of insurance purchased to cover a business-owned automobile is generally one of four commercial forms. For a sole proprietor, his or her auto, used in business, may well be covered by the personal auto policy. The four general commercial forms of automobile insurance are:

- Business auto coverage form
- Garage coverage form
- Truckers coverage form
- Motor carriers coverage form

Business Auto Coverage

The first part of this insuring agreement sounds much like the PAP, but it also includes provision for the cleanup of pollutants caused by an accident, when required by a governmental entity, as long as there is bodily injury or property damage concurrent with the spillage. (In other words, this policy does not simply cover any careless spilling of pollutants.)

Another big difference is in the definition of a covered auto. The PAP definition is complete in the policy. For the BAC, there are nine classes of autos from which the insured chooses so that the coverage applies to those autos the business needs to have insured. There are special endorsements to provide liability coverage for employees who drive employer-owned cars but who have no personally owned vehicle, for limited coverage when company cars are driven in Mexico, for when an employee rents a car under the company name, and for when employees other than the designated driver are in the vehicle or driving the vehicle.

Garage Coverage Form

For insurance purposes, certain businesses are called garages. These would include repair shops, service stations, car sales businesses, and public parking lots. In most of these cases, the business takes control of the vehicles at some point and becomes a bailee. This leaves them open to claims of property damage and liability; thus, they need insurance.

Truckers Coverage Form

This is more a modification of the business auto policy than it is a new form. It provides coverage for a trucking business for the trucks it owns as well as any it leases. Insureds include the company and owner-operators of trucks leased to the company while they are carrying loads for the company. An endorsed form is available for owner-operators when they are driving their tractor without a trailer (bobtailing) or pulling an empty trailer (deadheading).

Motor Carrier Coverage Form

This is similar to truckers coverage in many ways, but it is more flexible in its coverage and can be used in situations both where truckers coverage may be used and where a truckers coverage form is not appropriate, such as by truckers who carry both exempt and non-exempt commodities—a designation based on the existence or non-existence of regulations controlling the transportation of the specific commodities. Motor carrier coverage forms are the only ones that can be used by a trucker carrying both exempt and non-exempt loads.

Employer's Liability

Workers compensation insurance was established to create absolute liability whenever an employee is injured on the job. There is no necessity to prove who was at fault, either completely or partially. As long as the loss was suffered on the job, related medical expenses and lost income benefits are paid. One of the primary purposes of the workers compensation laws was to eliminate the need for employees to sue the employer to receive compensation for injuries that occurred on the job; it also eliminates blame or responsibility for the loss in the determination of the amount payable.

However, in some circumstances, employers must defend themselves against lawsuits that ask for additional compensation. These problems emphasize the need for **employer's liability insurance** to provide for defense against these suits and cover any additional compensation.

Generally, these policies have limits of $100,000 per incident and $100,000 per employee for an occupational disease, with a $500,000 aggregate limit for any single occupational disease. Employer's liability insurance is helpful in a number of situations. If an employee is injured on the job, many states permit the employee's spouse to sue the employer for losses he or she suffers as a result of the spouse's loss. Then there are **third-party over suits**, which allow an employee's injury to be blamed on a third party who is either another employee or someone with a business relationship to the employer. When the injured employee sues that third party, the third party then sues the employer claiming it is at least partly the employer's fault due to the employer's negligence. The **dual capacity situation** arises when an employee may be injured while in a capacity of someone other than that of an employee, e.g., an employee who is using a company product at home. State law might bar the employee from suing the employer as an employee but would not prevent a lawsuit from the individual as a consumer of the employer's product.

Package Policies

In reading about homeowners policies, it is easy to see the advantage of having multiple coverages included in a single policy, and commercial insurance providers finally came around to the advantages of packaging commercial policies. There are two generally used package programs for commercial lines of insurance: the **commercial package policy** (CPP) and the **business owners policy** (BOP).

The CPP includes commercial property, liability, and auto insurance. This permits a great savings in paper, provision duplication, and confusion, as well as reduced administrative and billing costs. The BOP is very similar, but is geared to the needs of smaller businesses.

From the foregoing discussion, it is easy to see how complex the commercial lines of property and liability insurance can become. For many small business owners, the business owner's policy is adequate, and many multi-line insurance agents will sell that policy. But even with small businesses, there may be special needs that only an expert will see or know how to handle. Insurance is one of those business expenses that most owners do not particularly like, but being without it can bring any business to a quick and painful end.

IMPORTANT CONCEPTS

Bailee's liability form

Blanket insurance

Business auto coverage form

Business owners policy (BOP)

Claims-made form

Commercial general liability policy (CGL)

Commercial umbrella policy

Condominium association coverage form

Dram shop liquor liability laws

Builders risk coverage

Business income coverage with
    extra expense

Business income coverage without
    extra expense

Discovery period

Employee dishonesty coverage

Employer's liability

Independent contractor coverage

Indirect property loss

Inland marine

Leader property

National flood insurance program

Occurrence form

Ocean marine

Portfolio program

Product liability

Reporting form

Workers compensation

QUESTIONS FOR REVIEW

1. Why are there commercial lines of insurance?

2. What is the benefit of portfolio policies over monoline policies?

3. Identify and describe at least five coverages that are included in commercial property insurance that are not in a homeowners policy.

4. What is the difference between blanket coverage and reporting-form coverage?

5. What are the uses for rain/weather insurance?

6. Briefly describe the four major classes of ocean marine insurance.

7. What are the six classes of inland marine insurance?

8. Explain how companies insure against dishonesty.

9. What is the most common form of employer's liability insurance and why does it exist?

10. What are the liability risks faced by a business that are generally not faced by individuals?

SUGGESTIONS FOR ADDITIONAL READING

BOP Businessowners Policy Coverage Guide Interpretation and Analysis, 2nd ed., George Krauss, National Underwriter, 2002.

Commercial Property Coverage Guide: Interpretation and Analysis, 2nd ed., Bruce J. Hillman and Michael K. McCraken, National Underwriter, 2001.

Fundamentals of Risk and Insurance, 9th ed., Emmett J. Vaughan and Therese M. Vaughan, Wiley, 2003.

The Insurance Information Institute Fact Book 2005, Insurance Information Institute, 2005

Introduction to Risk Management and Insurance, 8th ed.,Mark Dorfman, Prentice Hall, 2004.

Principles of Risk Management and Insurance, 9th ed., George E. Rejda, Addison Wesley, 2004.

Risk Management & Insurance, 12th ed., James S. Trieschman, South-Western, 2004.

The Tools & Techniques of Risk Management & Insurance, Stephan R. Leimberg, Donald J. Riggin, et al, 2002.

Introduction to Employee Benefits and Group Insurance

• • •

There was a time when an employee's only benefit was his or her compensation, and it has been less than 100 years since employee benefits of any kind have been widely available. Of course, there were companies in the early part of the twentieth century that provided employees with some benefits in addition to their wages, but they were the exception. This chapter is an introduction to the wide variety of employee benefits that exist in the workplace today.

When you have completed this chapter, you will be able to:

- List the private insurance and retirement plans made available to employees
- List payments made to employees for time not worked, cash payments made to employees other than wages or salary, and other employee benefits and services
- Identify and briefly describe legally required social insurance payments made on behalf of employees
- Describe how group insurance differs from individual policies
- Explain the effect of the Employee Retirement Income Security Act of 1974, as amended, on employee benefit and insurance plans
- Recognize the value of employee benefits planning

THE BASICS OF EMPLOYEE BENEFITS

What constitutes an employee benefit?

While this seems like a simple question, not everyone agrees with a single definition. Do benefits include all benefits and services, other than wages for time worked, that are provided in whole or in part by an employer for the benefit of employees? What about payments that are required by law, such as Social Security contributions, workers compensation protection, and unemployment compensation insurance?

While understanding employee benefits is particularly important in working with clients who own businesses, financial planners should also help other clients understand the value of employee benefits. This is especially true if a client is considering self-employment or has been offered a consulting contract. If a client decides to become self-employed, lost benefits may need to be replaced.

To fully understand both the extent of the payments in excess of salaries or wages that employers will need to make as well as the range of benefits an individual might receive from his or her employer, this text will use a very broad definition of benefits that includes all of the following:

- Legally required benefits
- Private insurance and retirement benefits
- Payment for time not worked
- Additional cash payments
- Services Provided

Legally Required Benefits

While these payments are legally required, they are still payments made for the benefit of employees. These programs include:

- Social Security tax
- Medicare tax
- Workers compensation insurance
- Unemployment compensation insurance
- Temporary disability insurance (in some states)
- Family and medical leave

Social Security and Medicare are federal programs covering the majority of workers in the United States. Employers match what employees pay into these programs. Every state requires employers to provide unemployment compensation and workers compensation insurance, though some states allow employers to purchase workers compensation insurance from private insurers instead of from the state itself. A few states have a temporary disability insurance program to which employers (and, in some cases, employees) must contribute.

Though employers are not required to pay employees for family and medical leave, federal law requires most employers to provide unpaid leave for up to 12 weeks for maternity/paternity leave and certain other family-related needs.

In-Depth: Employee Satisfaction

Management texts often divide benefits into two categories: satisfiers and dissatisfiers.

When an employee benefit is unexpected and desirable, it is a **satisfier**. It makes employees happy, and they generally feel that receiving that particular benefit or group of benefits is an indication that their employer appreciates them. Employees who perceive benefits as satisfiers are generally pleased with them and with their employers. For many years, every employee benefit was a satisfier, since most employees had never previously had benefits.

When an expected benefit is not offered, or if it is less than expected, the benefit is a **dissatisfier**. If an employer offers a comprehensive health care plan and then either increases the employee's share of the premium or reduces the benefits in the plan, employees often become dissatisfied. This can take place even when the benefit is better than that offered by most other employers.

Of course, different employees may see the same benefit from completely different points of view. Darlene, a new employee with Tidmore Studios, recently came from Birmingham Western, where the health care plan cost her $200 per month. A similar plan at Tidmore only charges employees $120 per month, so she is satisfied with this benefit. Chuck has been with Tidmore Studios for eight years and knows that four months ago they had to increase the employee's share of the health care plan from $75 to $120 per month, so he is dissatisfied with this benefit.

Companies may have a difficult time understanding how employees view a benefits package. For example: Carlin Imports buys The McCall Southern Company so that it can expand into a new market. Carlin Imports is based in a state where employee benefits are not particularly generous, so their benefits package satisfies home office employees. However, when the same benefits package is explained to the McCall Southern employees, they see only that they will be paying more for a health plan that doesn't provide as much, will get fewer vacation days and holidays, will be working under a new sick leave plan that is not as generous, etc. It may take a while before Carlin Imports' managers understand why their newly acquired employees are also newly dissatisfied employees.

As this example points out, the perception of the plan by employees is important: Employees who believe they are important in the eyes of management generally perform better than those who do not feel appreciated. For this reason, some employers work hard to educate their employees about the advantages of their benefits package. Most employers invest between 35 and 60 percent of an employee's wage or salary in employee benefit programs, amounting to an average of 42.3 percent of the total payroll[1]—a substantial sum.

Of course, some benefits neither satisfy nor dissatisfy. Most employees know that Social Security and Medicare are required by law, so an employer would have difficulty convincing employees that these were important incentives.

---

[1] 1 U.S. Chamber of Commerce, news release, 21 January 2004

Private Insurance and Retirement Benefits

When two friends compare their employee benefits, they are usually thinking of insurance programs and retirement plans, which may include:

- Health care plan
- Dental care plan
- Vision/hearing plan
- Retirement plan
- Life insurance
- Disability income insurance
- Liability insurance
- Long-term care insurance

Health care plans, including dental and vision plans, are quite common. Unless an employer pays 100 percent or nearly 100 percent of the cost (or a plan provides little coverage or is completely absent), employees will not likely initially consider these satisfiers or dissatisfiers. Because of the rising costs of health care plans in the past few years, employers are often forced to choose among three unpopular options: making employees pay more, reducing benefits, or terminating the plan. Most employers are now requiring employees to pay a greater share of the cost and, as a result, many employees are becoming dissatisfied.

Retirement plans have changed a great deal over the past decade or so, and employees still expect to see some sort of a plan. Life insurance is nearly universal as a benefit and is relatively inexpensive. Disability income insurance, both short- and long-term, provides important benefits, and most employees do not understand them. Long-term care insurance is a relatively new benefit and seldom purchased by young employees. Liability insurance also is generally provided for employees who interact with the public and therefore are potential targets of lawsuits for the work they are doing for the company.

Later in this chapter we will discuss how group insurance differs from individual coverage.

Payment for Time Not Worked

Most employees do not think much about the time for which they get paid when they are not at work. However, employers are making a substantial investment in employees when they provide these benefits. These benefits may include:

- Paid vacation
- Paid holidays
- Sick leave
- Sabbatical leave
- Bereavement leave

- Jury duty
- Reserve duty
- Maternity/parental leave

These benefits may be required by law; however, some of them do little more than anger a few employees while having no particularly positive effect on the rest. Some employees may resent parental or family leave since they are not likely to use it; or some may feel that they are being cheated for being honest about sick leave when other colleagues routinely take "mental health days."

Employees generally expect paid vacation time, and it is a good idea to give them a break. However, an employer with 50 employees who each have two weeks of vacation per year spends approximately two average annual salaries for zero productivity. The same could be said for paid holidays: Most companies will grant anywhere from 5 to 11 days, with some offering additional floating holidays. Similar to vacation, sabbatical leaves are common for college instructors, clergy members, and members of certain other professions. These are typically paid leaves of six months to one year that often require that the individual be involved in research, study, or training during that time.

Sick leave is an important benefit, but employees often abuse it, regularly taking "mental health days"- in essence vacation days that are winked at by some managers, frowned upon by others. Some companies pay employees for excess unused sick leave after they accumulate a certain number of days or hours, in order to reward lack of abuse. For those companies that have a "use it or lose it" sick leave plan, honest employees without current medical problems may be angry because they don't get any benefit from the plan, especially when they see other employees using their allotted sick days as just additional days off work.

When an employee experiences a death in either his or her immediate or extended family, most employers grant a certain number of paid days for the employee to travel and attend funeral services for the deceased. Ordinarily, the employer requires the family relationship between the employee and the deceased to be reasonably close before this benefit is provided. Some companies are quite generous with this benefit, and others are quite stingy.

Most states require employers to permit employees to participate in jury duty. Employers usually are not required to pay employees for that time; however, most will grant employees paid leave since those courts that do pay jurors generally pay very little. In some cases, employers expect employees to turn over any payment made for jury duty.

Federal law requires employers to release employees for required active duty when they are members of the military reserves. Like jury duty, payment is not required. Many employers will pay the difference between what the individual earns while on active duty with the military and his or her regular income.

While the law requires employers to allow unpaid leave for maternity or other parental needs, many employers provide paid leave and/or allow leave periods for longer than the law mandates. This applies to all employees who are parents, male or female. Giving employees the opportunity to spend time with a newborn or ill child usually means that they are less distracted and better rested when they return to work.

Additional Cash Payments

Many companies grant additional payments beyond base compensation, including:

- Bonuses
- Education reimbursement programs
- Moving expense reimbursement
- Profit-sharing payments
- Suggestion awards
- Savings/thrift plans

Many companies give annual bonuses to employees when they have had profitable years. The amount may be based on individual merit or departmental successes or may be given at the discretion of a manager. In some cases, everyone gets the same bonus; in others, it is determined by base income. Profit sharing is sometimes tied to retirement plans, but it may also be a current cash payment. Suggestion awards encourage employees to improve company products and processes by rewarding them for savings and/or making money for the company. They can help create loyalty and encourage other employees to work to make the company more profitable, putting into action common HR statements that employees are the company's most important assets and that the company's employees are a team.

Education reimbursement programs encourage employees to improve their skills and become more valuable to the company. Employees recruited from other parts of the country or who are transferred may receive moving expenses. There may be recruiting bonuses when an employee refers someone to the company who is eventually hired to take a position that is difficult to fill.

Savings or thrift plans are most often part of qualified retirement plans, encouraging employees to plan for retirement by matching their retirement plan contributions. If a matching program is available to a client, a financial planner has a great opportunity to help the client see the exceptional benefit of maximizing the employer's contribution to his or her retirement plan.

Services Provided

There are many benefits for which employers pay; however the amount spent may not be obvious to the employees. These include:

- Subsidized cafeterias
- Recreation facilities
- Wellness programs

- Retirement counseling
- Financial counseling
- Clothing/uniform allowances
- Daycare centers or allowances
- Adoption assistance
- Employee assistance programs
- Transportation benefits (commuting and parking)

Employees who have subsidized cafeterias can often eat there for less than it costs to brown-bag. A subsidized cafeteria saves employees money, promotes connections among the employees, and often saves everyone time, making working lunches easy.

Exercise and shower facilities provide a convenient and money-saving alternative to joining a gym. Wellness programs may include newsletters and consultations, often offered through the health care plan provider.

Many people do not seek out financial planning or retirement planning because they do not know where to start. When employers make these services available, they encourage fiscal prudence and help employees gain control over and take responsibility for their financial lives.

Some companies that require a uniform either give employees the clothes or offer an allowance for clothes that are specifically used at work. This helps the individual maintain his or her personal wardrobe with whatever money he or she budgets for clothing.

Day care centers and adoption assistance are efforts to be family friendly and recruit individuals who either have or are planning for families. These benefits have become important as more women have entered the workforce and more men have taken a more active family role. Magazines for parents and professional women often rank top companies according to the type of family benefits they offer–a high rank or positive review gives the company an edge in recruiting and retaining employees. However, regardless of whether or not employees use these benefits, the message that the company understands the outside stresses of family life is often appreciated and can boost general morale.

Some companies offer employee assistance programs that provide confidential help in personal areas, such as substance abuse counseling, stress management, crisis intervention, and marital or family counseling. While these programs generally do not provide comprehensive, long-term help, they give employees a starting place and provide referrals for more in-depth assistance.

In-Depth: Commonality of Benefits

The U.S. Department of Labor's Bureau of Labor Statistics periodically compiles a survey of employee benefits. This survey provides information about many employee benefits by occupation, full vs part-time workers, union vs nonunion, manufacturing vs service companies, business size, income levels and geographic areas. Dozens of tables are available for review at the Bureau's website: http://www.bls.gov/ncs/ebs/ The most current information was gathered in a 2003 National Compensation Survey of private industry.

Some BLS tables cover all workers while others cover only those workers who have access to certain benefits. Covering all workers means that it includes workers who are self employed and those in businesses with very few employees and no benefits of any kind.

This table shows figures for all workers in private industry. The numbers represent the percentage of employees who have the various benefits listed. By itself the table is interesting. In searching the BLS archive information it becomes enlightening. In 1995, 77% of employees in medium and large private companies were covered by a medical care plan, including 75% of those in service occupations. In small private industry companies surveyed in 1994, 66% of all employees, including 57% of service occupation employees had a medical care plan.

Table 13.1: Commonality of Benefits in Large Companies

Type of Program	All Employees	White Collar Employees	Blue Collar Employees	Service Occupations
Insurance				
Medical care	53%	58%	61%	25%
Dental care	36	42	38	18
Vision care	21	24	23	11
Life	47	54	50	25
Disability benefits				
Short-term disability income	37	40	44	20
Long-term disability income	28	40	20	10
Retirement				
Defined benefit plans	20	22	24	7
Defined contribution plans	40	51	38	16
Paid time off				
Holidays	79	86	85	54
Vacation	79	84	84	61
Jury duty leave	70	79	69	46
Military leave	50	59	46	34
Other benefits				
Child care assistance	14	20	8	8
Adoption assistance	9	13	6	2
Long-term care insurance	11	16	7	4
Travel accident insurance	15			
Subsidized commuting	5	7	4	2

GROUP INSURANCE

Insurance is one of the most common types of employee benefits. Group insurance is a single contract that provides an insurance benefit to a group of individuals who have a common bond that is for purposes other than obtaining insurance–most commonly, a group of employees.

Usually a single payment is made to the insurer by the organization that brought the individuals together.

Members of an association such as a labor union, a religious organization, or a trade group for freelance professionals, may receive group insurance, since their association is for noninsurance purposes. While this is usually permitted, the nature of the group may make it difficult or impossible to find an insurance carrier willing to offer a policy. Policies offered to these groups are often association plans that are actually individual plans with a discount for having a common list of benefits.

There are four basic areas in which group insurance differs markedly from individual insurance: the contract, premium determination, underwriting, and regulation.

Contracts

With individual insurance policies, the contract is between the insured and the insurance company. There is very little negotiation, and virtually all contracts are in a standard format with standard benefits. With group insurance, the contract is between the organization that represents the group and the insurance company. The individuals do not have a copy of the group insurance contract, usually just a certificate of coverage.

Individual contracts generally permit applicants to choose from various options. With health insurance, it might be a choice of deductibles or co-pay amounts, or whether maternity coverage is included. Life insurance applicants may choose to include disability waiver of premium, accidental death benefit, purchase option, and the form of the policy itself. Disability income insurance policies give choices in the area of elimination period, definition of disability, purchase option, and monthly benefit.

However, group insurance does not offer the individual much in the way of choices. Employers work with the insurance companies and/or plan administrators to design the plans, but the nature of group insurance is such that there is little difference among companies offering benefits from the same insurance carriers.

Typically, participation requirements state that a certain percentage of employees must be covered by the plan in order to reduce adverse selection since people who are most likely to submit a claim are those who most want insurance. The most common requirement is 75 percent participation. When a plan is completely paid for by the employer, 100 percent participation is required, and the premiums are generally the lowest per person. This is because adverse selection has been virtually eliminated.

Premiums

When an individual applies for insurance, the insurance company looks at the age, sex, health, and history of the individual and puts him or her into a general classification. The classification determines the premium for his or her insurance. Those in a particular classification group pay the same premium. Most insurance companies consider that group a "class" of insureds. For example, 39-year-old male nonsmokers in average physical condition comprise one "class" of insureds.

In addition, one of the primary concerns of insurance companies is adverse selection. For example, if it were possible to purchase homeowners insurance during or after a fire—and to be covered retroactively under this insurance—would anyone ever purchase it before a fire? If this type of coverage were the norm, insurance premiums would be slightly higher than the amount of insurance purchased, which is not how insurance policies function. Instead, classes of insureds are identified and premiums for that group are determined.

With group insurance, the process of determining a premium is often different. Large group premiums are normally based on the claims experience of the group that is being insured–the insurance company or plan provider uses past claims to estimate future claims, factoring in inflation. Rare claims, such as those for liver transplants, are not assumed for the following year. This is called **experience rating**, which means that the group as a whole pays the amount of the expected benefits plus the administrative cost of paying the claims as they come due and an additional amount to provide a reasonable profit to the insurer.

Since most group insurance is offered through employers, the total premiums paid need to be enough to pay all of the claims. This could be viewed as a pool of funds that will be distributed to those who need it and not as insurance; but to the individual employee, this is insurance. Each employee pays a small amount toward the pool, and the employer makes up the balance. If an employee has thousands of dollars in medical expenses, all or most of them are covered by the plan.

Some groups are too small to have their premium determined by past claims. They are put into groups of small employers, typically in the same or a similar industry, and the premiums are based on the expected claims of the group as a whole.

Groups that are experience rated are often in a position to use a self-funded plan rather than insurance. Since this reading merely introduces employee benefit programs, self-funded plans are discussed in more depth later in the book.

Underwriting

This is where employee benefits most differ from individual plans. When an individual applies for insurance, the insurance company looks at his or her specific age, health history, and any other relevant information for the purpose of evaluating the risk. This process, called underwriting, is used to put the individual into the proper class so that the right premium is charged. With groups, it is done a bit differently.

For a group contract, the company gathers group information-age, sex, marital status, type of work done, claims history, etc.—individuals are seldom asked many questions unless the group is small. For small groups, the most important factors are usually the average age of the employees, the type of industry, the type of work performed, the average income of employees, the gender makeup, and past claims history. You may wonder if this is just experience rating again. Although the experience-rating method is effective for large groups, the vast majority of businesses in this country are small businesses with less than 50 employees–groups too small to use experience ratings. One heart bypass surgery would skew the premiums significantly.

Underwriters evaluate the likelihood and magnitude of claims from the group as a whole rather than as individuals. The advantage of group underwriting is that the insurer can better evaluate the risk and minimize adverse selection. It reduces the cost of underwriting and therefore permits the insurer to provide the same amount of coverage for less money. For employees, the advantage of group underwriting is that it permits individuals with health problems to obtain life insurance at standard premiums rather than pay extra, as well as allowing individuals to obtain disability income insurance and health insurance when they have a condition that would otherwise prevent it or make it difficult and expensive.

Regulation of Employee Benefits and Group Insurance

Employee benefits and group insurance are affected by a number of federal laws and regulations, including:

- ADEA (Age Discrimination in Employment Act)
- COBRA (Consolidated Omnibus Budget Reconciliation Act)
- ERISA (Employee Retirement Income Security Act)
- FMLA (Family and Medical Leave Act)
- HIPAA (Health Insurance Portability and Accountability Act)
- HMOA (Health Maintenance Organization Act)
- IRC (Internal Revenue Code)
- MHPA (Mental Health Parity Act)
- NMHPA (Newborns' and Mothers' Health Protection Act)
- PDA (Pregnancy Discrimination Act)
- PL-15 (McCarran-Ferguson Act)
- SSA (Social Security Act)
- WHCRA (Women's Health and Cancer Rights Act)

Many states also have regulations that affect employee and group insurance or other benefits. Most states have instituted certain mandated coverage for health care plans, and this can be one of the most confusing areas of state law. One state may require that alternative medicine be covered under a group health plan, while another will mandate no variation in coverage for physical therapy or chiropractic care. These may also include having maternity benefits treated as any illness, treatment for expanded mental and nervous disorders, fertility/infertility treatments, transplants, well-baby care, and others. These mandates generally follow a public outcry for additional benefits to be included. Unfortunately, every mandate has a cost attached, and that cost is reflected in the premiums.

State laws and regulations of group insurance are often far more specific than federal laws and regulations. For example, state law may define eligible groups. To be eligible, a group must exist for a purpose other than buying insurance and must also be formed for the long-term (rather than for a temporary project); or an eligible group may be required to be of a minimum size. States may limit benefits for certain types of insurance. Some states provide benefits to disabled workers in addition to any Social Security disability benefits; these disability benefits affect the benefits available through employer-sponsored plans. All states also charge a premium tax. Some states charge the tax only to insurance companies located outside the state, while others tax all companies.

COBRA and HIPAA, discussed in greater detail in chapter 14, increase group insurance costs. COBRA permits a person to extend his or her health care plan when leaving an employer, though there is typically adverse selection when this happens. Very healthy people, especially the young, often choose to go bare (without coverage) while looking for a new job. Anyone with a medical condition will be certain to continue coverage under COBRA.

HIPAA allows an individual who changes employers to start over with a new group health care plan without having to prove insurability or wait for preexisting conditions to be covered. However, some individuals will leave one job when they or a member of their family have used up all of the benefits available under a health care plan. The prior employer's plan premiums will be affected by the extensive benefits paid, even though the individual who used those benefits is gone. The new employer's plan will be affected as this new insured begins to incur large medical bills.

These laws do serve an important purpose, but it is important to remember that there is a cost associated with regulations.

Employee Retirement Income Security Act of 1974 (ERISA)

In 1974, Congress passed the most sweeping legislation that dealt with employee benefit plans, and everyone who had been in the employee benefit field found themselves at a completely new starting point. Originally called the Pension Reform Act, it is more widely known as the Employee Retirement Income Security Act (ERISA), and it has affected every employee benefit plan selected by employers. ERISA was also the law that created individual retirement accounts (IRAs). This text does not discuss in depth the topic of retirement plans. The reader is referred to retirement planning texts that address this topic in detail.

Prior to passage of ERISA, many employer-based "employee benefit" programs were heavily weighted toward management. In many cases, management employees received generous benefits, especially in the area of retirement planning, and rank-and-file employees got very little, if anything. The primary purpose of ERISA was to eliminate or at least reduce discrimination, so that employee benefit plans might truly benefit all employees.

ERISA affected health care plans, sick pay and disability income plans, vacation benefits, daycare benefits, education reimbursements and scholarships, holiday pay, and even apprenticeship and training programs.

For an employer and employees to benefit from the most favorable income tax rules surrounding employee benefits, they must meet the requirements of ERISA and its many amendments. If they meet these rules, the plans are said to be **qualified plans**. Individuals working in the financial services industry will hear and deal with qualified plans a great deal.

In general, qualified plans must not discriminate too much in favor of highly paid employees, managers, or owners. While certain types of extra benefits for higher-level employees may be included, by and large, the plan must treat all employees fairly for it to be qualified

Employee Benefit Planning

Financial planners may be called upon to help clients with employee benefit planning. The potential number of employee benefit choices can be daunting. Because there seem to be so many options, situations may arise where a client does not know what to do.

Many clients will have few choices. Their employers may provide the following benefits: employer-sponsored health plan, group life insurance plan, group dental insurance plan, and some form of group disability income insurance. The choices for these clients may be limited to who in their families will be covered under the health plan and whether or not to accept the dental plan.

However, some clients will have additional choices that are more complex, such as the ability to buy additional group life insurance or to increase the percentage of income replaced by a long-term disability plan. There may also be more than one health plan from which to choose. In addition, the employer might provide a 401(k) retirement plan and offer to match contributions made by the employee, so the employee must then decide how much to contribute to the plan.

In addition to some basic benefits, employee-benefit packages may include long-term care, life insurance for dependents, public transportation discounts, child care, flexible spending accounts, and more, as described earlier in this chapter.

Some benefits just come with the job. Others require the employee to make a decision. All too often, the choices must be made either relatively soon after the employee starts the job or at annual intervals during an "open enrollment" period—a time where employees can make changes in their plans without risking losing benefits or having to prove insurability.

Some employee benefits, such as an appropriate health care plan, are critical, while others, such as a dread disease policy, are not particularly useful. The number of choices can be overwhelming. A financial planner can help a client evaluate each option in relation to the overall plan.

As you progress through the chapters on employee benefits, it is suggested that you think about how each benefit might fit in a client's overall financial plan. Risk management, from chapter 1, comes into play here. What is the best way for a client to deal with the risks that are addressed by each employee benefit? It's also important to recognize that the mere fact that certain benefits are available may eliminate the possibility of using a different tool. For example, if an employee has group long-term disability insurance available, it is likely that he or she will be denied that coverage on an individual basis.

Financial planning is a multi-faceted practice. Helping clients get the most out of their employee benefits package is an important part of the whole.

IMPORTANT CONCEPTS

Additional cash payments

Adverse selection

Costs of regulation

Dissatisfier

Eligible group

Employee Retirement Income Security
    Act (ERISA)

Employee benefit planning

Federal group legislation

Group underwriting

Insurance benefits

Legally required benefits

Participation requirements

Payment for provided services

Payment for time not worked

Qualified plans

Satisfier

Group contracts

State mandates

Group premium determination

QUESTIONS FOR REVIEW

1. How do employee benefits satisfy or dissatisfy employees?

2. List legally required employee benefits.

3. List at least seven employee benefits involving insurance.

4. List at least seven employee benefits that provide payment for time not worked.

5. What are at least six types of cash payments that may be made to employees that are separate from their basic wages or salary?

6. What are at least eight services that employers may provide in lieu of cash payments?

7. What are the five most common employee benefits for medium and large businesses?

8. How are group insurance contracts different from individual insurance contracts?

9. What type of state regulation affects employee benefits?

10. What is the purpose of the Employee Retirement Income Security Act of 1974?

SUGGESTIONS FOR ADDITIONAL READING

Benefits Facts 2005, National Underwriter, 2005.

Employee Benefits, 7th ed., Burton T. Beam, Jr. and John J. McFadden, Dearborn, 2005.

Fundamentals of Risk and Insurance, 9th ed., Emmett J. Vaughan and Therese M. Vaughan, Wiley, 2003.

Introduction to Risk Management and Insurance, 8th ed., Mark Dorfman, Prentice Hall, 2004.

Life and Health Insurance, 13th ed., Skipper and Black, Prentice Hall, 2000.

Principles of Risk Management and Insurance, 9th ed., George E. Rejda and Addison Wesley, 2004.

Tax Facts 2005, National Underwriter, 2005.

The Tools & Techniques of Employee Benefit and Retirement Planning, 9th ed., by Stephan R. Leimberg and John J. McFadden, National Underwriter, 2005.

Group Life, Medical, and Disability

• • •

When asked about their employee benefits, most people respond that they have life insurance, health care, and possibly disability income insurance—all among the most common forms of employee group benefits, even if there are many variations. A planner should be able to help clients understand their coverage.

When you have completed this chapter, you will be able to:

- Describe group life insurance options and identify its various types and available supplemental coverages
- Describe the various types and related provisions of group medical plans and explain how COBRA and HIPAA apply to them
- Describe the various types and related provisions of group disability income policies
- Describe the income tax implications of group life, medical, and disability policies

GROUP LIFE INSURANCE

This section introduces a range of group life issues, including:

- Benefit levels
- Insurability requirements
- Beneficiary designations
- Conversion
- Assignments
- Ownership
- Settlement options
- Claims
- Common provisions
- Termination
- Continuation of coverage
- Accelerated death benefits
- Additional benefits (dependent life coverage, AD&D, and supplemental life insurance)

We will also look at unique features of group permanent life policies and income taxation of group life insurance.

Benefit Levels

Group life insurance is generally offered in a few limited ways: either as a multiple of salary, with one or two times salary being the most common—or as a flat amount for all employees, typically $50,000 (an amount derived from tax law). Plans can be quite flexible in determining the amount of coverage per employee—tying the amount to longevity, income, rank within the company as determined by a position schedule, or a combination of these factors—as long as they do not discriminate too much in favor of highly compensated individuals. To control costs, most plans provide a reduction of the benefit level for employees who work beyond age 65, commonly occurring at five-year increments starting at age 60 or after retirement if benefits are extended beyond retirement.

Employers pay either for all or for a limited level of benefits. In most circumstances, employers will pay for group term life insurance up to $50,000 of death benefit. The reason for this amount is discussed below. Employees may be given the option of having more insurance if they are willing to pay for it at the group rates.

Insurability

Except in the case of a very small group, an employee who signs up for group life when it is first offered usually does not have to prove insurability; but if he or she declines the first offer and then decides to accept the coverage, the insurer may require proof of insurability. The initial amount of coverage is generally provided on a guaranteed issue basis.

Some insurers may require simplified health questionnaires to obtain insurance beyond the initial amount offered, a process called **simplified underwriting**. With this procedure, employees can obtain additional insurance at standard rates when their general health might not permit them to do so with an individual policy.

Beneficiary Designation

Employees must name a beneficiary to receive the benefits of any group life insurance, just as they do for individually owned policies; the employer may not be the beneficiary. While there is typically only a small line for this on the application, the employee may use more comprehensive designations, including secondary or tertiary beneficiaries. The beneficiary can be the estate of the insured, and the designation can be very specific when there are multiple beneficiaries in the same class.

As with personal life insurance, it is important to keep group life insurance beneficiary agreements current. A change in a will does not change beneficiary arrangements on group insurance any more than it does for individual life insurance, except when the insured's estate is the beneficiary. Unfortunately, just as with individually owned life insurance, that choice of beneficiary turns a non-probate asset into a probate asset, available to any creditor of the insured and/or his estate.

Conversion

The term "conversion" applies only to the change of one form of insurance to another. When a person leaves a job, often he or she is not in the position of being able to afford a new permanent insurance policy. Conversion privileges are common in group term life contracts, permitting the insured to convert all or a portion of the group term insurance into a specified form of permanent insurance policy offered by the insurer (either whole life or universal life, depending on the company). Generally, the conversion privilege is available for 30 to 60 days following the date the employee is no longer eligible to be insured under the group policy and rarely permits the inclusion of a disability waiver of premium.

When available, the conversion is a guaranteed benefit, and most experts agree that applying for a fully underwritten policy may be the better route, as the inexpensive disability waiver of premium rider is a valuable benefit. Because of this, when insureds seek to convert group life insurance, the agents may, depending on the individual's insurability, encourage them to apply for new insurance rather than take advantage of the conversion. With a new policy, not only is the individual able to add a disability waiver of premium rider, dividend scales on fully underwritten policies are usually better, and most agents will be paid a slightly higher commission. This means the agent has an incentive to make a greater effort in helping the employee get a better quality policy.

Additionally, the value of a new policy for qualified applicants is usually higher. As for those who convert, rather than obtain new insurance, they generally do it for one reason: They will not qualify for new insurance at standard rates, and this is the only way they can obtain life insurance without paying extra.

Conversion tends to create a class of insureds with a greater-than-average risk of claims, resulting in adverse selection. Converted policies are generally kept as a block of business separate from other life insurance policies because of the adverse selection of this group, which is the reason dividends for participating policies that were conversions from group life insurance, will be lower than for fully underwritten policies. If the policy is UL, the mortality charges are often higher.

When a group term life policy is converted, the employer incurs a charge for the conversion because of the substantial increase in expected mortality of converted policies. With group permanent insurance, there is no conversion privilege, though there may be an opportunity to change ownership, so that the individual has complete ownership of his or her policy when separated from the employer.

Assignment

A group life insurance policy can usually be assigned. Assignments are considered to be effective only if recorded by the insurance company. An assignment can be temporary for meeting financial or legal obligations, or absolute, requiring a transfer of ownership. In a temporary assignment, called a collateral assignment, the policy is assigned to the lender as collateral to the extent that the policy owner owes money. This is the same as assigning a car to a lender until the car loan is paid off. An absolute assignment is a complete transfer of ownership. A word of caution: Some lenders demand that the beneficiary agreement be changed naming the lender as the beneficiary rather than having the borrower execute a collateral assignment. If this happens, and the language of the beneficiary agreement is not very specific, it is possible that the lender will remain the beneficiary long after the debt has been repaid. If the beneficiary agreement has not been changed, there may be no legal remedy for legitimate heirs to recover death benefits paid to the lender. Additionally, once the debt is paid, a release of assignment should be obtained from the lender and submitted to the insurer.

Ownership

In most cases, the employee is the owner of the death benefit, even though the employer is the owner of the contract. Some individuals might want to transfer ownership to another person or a trust for estate-planning purposes. However this may not be permitted under the master contract.

Settlement Options

Group life insurance has the same settlement options available to beneficiaries as individual policies have, including lump sum, an interest option, installments for a fixed period, installments of a fixed amount, or life income.

Claims

As with all other life insurance, death claims are simple to handle: A short claim form and a copy of a death certificate are all that are needed. Before a claim is submitted, it is always a good idea to consult with a financial planner or life insurance agent as to how the proceeds should be taken. Under some circumstances, one or more of the settlement options may be better choices than a lump sum. If the beneficiary takes a lump sum and later decides that he or she prefers another option, there will be additional costs for obtaining them, and it is possible the terms of the option will not be as favorable. Little is lost by leaving the life insurance proceeds with the insurance company until decisions have been made regarding the use of the money.

Common Provisions

Grace period, entire contract, incontestability, and misstatement of age clauses operate similarly to those in individual contracts. Because the incontestability clause is affected by state law, it is usually applied according to the state of domicile of the business, which may be different from the state in which the insured lives and/or works. The entire contract clause is modified a bit because the individual does not get a copy of the contract. For this reason, some courts have found that descriptive pamphlets received by the insured employee may be considered controlling over the contract itself.

Termination

This is one provision that is significantly different for group life insurance as compared to individual policies. While individual life insurance policies can be terminated only by the policy owner, either the insurance company or the employer may terminate group life insurance policies. The insurance company can terminate the policy for cause, or with 31 days' notice without cause. The employer can cancel the policy at any time.

If a group contract is cancelled by either the employer or the insurer, most insurance carriers will not permit conversion of group term life insurance. The primary reason is the increased adverse selection and the insurance company's subsequent inability to charge the employer for the conversion.

NEED TO KNOW: PORTABILITY OF GROUP LIFE

Generally speaking, group term life insurance policies are not portable. There are a few insurers that offer a contract that can be continued as individual term life if a covered employee leaves the group, but these contracts are uncommon.

Conversion is typically the only way to take the coverage with you. Group term life does not come under the provisions of COBRA.

Continuation of Coverage

There are two ways group term life is continued after the employee is no longer employed: conversion and retirement death benefits. The conversion provision was discussed earlier in this chapter.

Postretirement death benefits are not particularly common with group term life. Some large companies provide a reduced benefit to retired employees. Those plans are typically the result of collective bargaining. One plan provides for premiums to be paid while the coverage continues. This requires some faith by the retirees that the company will continue to exist. In another approach, known as retired lives reserve, the company prefunds the death benefits. This went out of favor in the 1980s because of restrictive tax laws, although some such plans still exist.

Accelerated Death Benefits

Changes in the insurance market have found many group plans adding accelerated death benefits, and many companies have even added these provisions to existing contracts at no additional cost. While the specifics vary, if an insured employee is diagnosed with a terminal illness that is expected to result in death within 12 months, suffers from certain illnesses such as AIDS or Alzheimer's disease, has had a stroke, or is confined to a long-term care facility, the plan will pay from 25 to 100 percent of the death benefit while the insured is still alive. Most pay up to 50 percent.

If the employee fully recovers and returns to work, the group life benefit is permanently reduced by the benefits paid. Federal tax law specifies under what circumstances these payments are treated as income tax-free payments as described in chapter 4.

Additional Benefits

Some group life contracts offer other benefits. The most common are dependent life, accidental death and dismemberment benefits, and supplemental life insurance.

Dependent Life

Dependent life insurance usually comes as a package deal. The spouse is covered at 50 percent of the amount of the employee's coverage, and children are covered for $2,000 to $5,000. The levels of permitted coverage vary. This is often an elective benefit paid for by the employee. If there is a conversion privilege for dependent life, it is usually limited to the spouse, unless state law requires that all dependent insurance be convertible. Some plans will permit the insured employee to add a spouse or children only.

AD&D

Accidental death and dismemberment (AD&D) is one of the most common—and to some, the most gruesome—forms of insurance. These are generally sold in conjunction with the group life insurance plan, however they are technically not part of the group life plan under IRC § 79 (discussed below). Group contracts tend to have the most restrictive provisions for accidental death and are typically the only place you will find dismemberment coverage. For an accidental death claim to be paid, usually the death must be completely accidental: That is, if the insured is doing something that is inherently dangerous, such as skydiving, and has a fatal accident, it may not be covered, since the dangerous activity that caused his or her death was undertaken voluntarily. This topic was covered in the chapter 2 discussion on the difference between accidental death and death by accidental means. As also discussed, some courts will not enforce that strict definition.

For more information on AD&D benefits, see chapter 2.

> **NEED TO KNOW: SUPPLEMENTAL GROUP LIFE**
>
> Many companies will permit employees to obtain additional life insurance coverage at group term rates. It is often limited to a multiple of salary and/or a maximum benefit. The employee often pays for the entire amount above $50,000, but sometimes the employer pays a portion of it. With larger companies, the additional insurance is often available on a guaranteed issue basis. In smaller companies, the insured must prove insurability.

Taxation of Group Life Insurance

To maximize income tax benefits of group life insurance, the group life insurance plan must meet the requirements of IRC § 79. The rules are as follows:

1. The plan must provide a general death benefit, one that is paid regardless of the cause of death. It will still have a suicide clause. This means that accidental death benefits or travel accident coverage is not part of the plan. (Note: This does not mean the employers do not offer accidental death or travel accident benefits, only that these benefits are not involved in a discussion about the taxation of group life insurance.) In addition, life insurance that is part of a qualified retirement plan does not qualify.

2. It must be a plan that is provided for an identifiable group of employees as part of their compensation. The group may be all salaried or hourly employees, normally including only full-time employees. It may be only for employees who have been with the company for at least six months or it may even be limited to a particular division or department. It may not include non-employee shareholders or be a group limited to shareholder employees.

3. The policy may be carried directly or indirectly by the employer. This generally means that the employer is paying at least part of the premium.

4. The formula used to determine who receives a particular level of coverage must preclude individual selection. It can be based on age, years of employment, compensation or even by position, as long as it would be reasonable for a nonshareholder employee to qualify for that position.

As long as the plan is not discriminatory for the benefit of highly compensated employees and meets the rest of the IRC § 79 requirements, premiums paid by the employer for up to $50,000 of group term life insurance death benefit for each employee are deductible by the employer and not considered income to the employee. To the extent that the employer pays premiums for life insurance benefits above $50,000 per employee, the value of the benefits, as calculated with IRC-provided rates from *Uniform Premiums for $1,000 of Group Term Life Insurance Protection* (Table 14.1), is considered taxable income to the employee. In simpler terms, if the employer pays for more than $50,000 of group term life insurance for an employee, the employee must report the economic benefit of the extra insurance as income. Death benefits are generally income-tax free under the same rules—IRC § 101(a)—used for individually owned life insurance. For dependent life insurance, premiums for death benefits of up to $2,000 per dependent can be paid for by the employer on an income-tax-free basis as a *de minimis* fringe benefit. In laymen's terms, de minimis means that it is not a big deal; it is a low cost benefit.

The taxable rates are calculated on a monthly basis. The following table is found in Treasury Regulations §1.79-3(d)(2).

Table 14.1: Uniform Premiums for $1,000 of Group Term Life Insurance Protection

Five-Year Age Bracket	Cost Per $1,000 of Protection, Per Month
Under 25	$0.05
25-29	.06
30-34	.08
35-39	.09
40-44	.10
45-49	.15
50-54	.23
55-59	.43
60-64	.66
65-69	$1.27
70 and above	$2.06

*The age of the employee is his or her attained age at the end of the taxable year.
(Applicable to group term life insurance provided after 6/30/1999)*

If the employee pays a portion of the premium for group life insurance above $50,000, that amount is subtracted from the amount that would otherwise be considered income.

For example, Jim, a 41-year-old employee, has $100,000 of group term life insurance. The employer pays the entire premium for the first $50,000, and the employee pays $2.00 per month for the balance. The amount of insurance above $50,000 is $50,000. The uniform premium rate is $.10 per thousand, so the monthly amount for the $50,000 of excess coverage is $.10 x 50 = $5.00. Since Jim pays $2.00 per month, the premium the employer must report as taxable income to Jim is $5.00 – $2.00 = $3.00 per month, or $36.00 per year.

Group Permanent Insurance

Most group permanent policies operate essentially as individual policies with simplified underwriting, group billing, and some savings in administrative costs. Some large groups have no underwriting but require a certain percentage of employees to participate. When an employee leaves or retires, this type of group policy usually stays in force as an individual policy.

Continuing the policy is not a conversion, since the coverage is already permanent. Other plans may be set up as a master contract where the insureds receive only a certificate of coverage, but an employee who terminates or retires usually can continue the coverage on the same basis as it was issued. In this case, it may remain part of the master contract, or it may change to an individual contract of the same type with premiums paid directly to the insurance company.

In either case, if the employee does not wish to keep the policy, it can be terminated for its surrender value, or the surrender value can be put into an annuity using the settlement options outlined in the policy or the master contract. Employees insured under a master contract who leave the group do not have the option to convert the policy to a different form of permanent insurance.

Group permanent life insurance plans make it easy for individuals to add permanent insurance to their portfolio, but there are some disadvantages. With simplified underwriting (or no underwriting), there is an increased chance of adverse selection for employees who leave, though not quite as much as with group term life. For this reason, the policies of terminated and retired employees are generally treated as a separate class, so this entire group pays for any adverse selection. Additionally, since there is no longer group billing, often the expense charges on these policies will be higher if they are UL policies.

Very large groups tend to be experience rated, even for group life insurance. If the group has an unusually high number of deaths, all employees under the plan will have increased mortality charges.

There are a number of forms of this uncommon benefit, as explained below:

Group Ordinary Life Insurance

This is essentially a whole-life policy. The employer typically pays the term portion of the premium for up to $50,000 of coverage, and the employee pays the rest. Any portion of the premium paid by the employer above the term cost of the first $50,000 of coverage is taxed as income to the employee.

Group Paid-Up Life Insurance

With this rare policy, the employer or employee purchases small amounts of paid-up life insurance each year that the employee is with the company, with the goal of having it completely replace the group term amount by retirement. Some plans provide reduced benefits if an employee leaves before retirement, while others do not.

Group Universal Life Insurance

Much like individual universal life, group universal life most often entails the employer paying the term portion of the premium and the employee paying any additional amounts. In some cases, the employee pays the entire premium, and the plan is completely elective.

Retired Lives Reserve

Generally, employers may take a deduction for group term life insurance premiums paid on behalf of active employees. With retired lives reserve, the employer makes tax-deductible contributions to a trust that is used to pay for insurance on retired employees. This policy was more popular a number of years ago.

In-Depth: Group Life and the Financial Plan

Today's college graduates are expected to have an average of seven different jobs by the time they retire. Since group life insurance offerings vary widely among employers, are not generally available to sole proprietors, and are not generally portable, planners must warn clients against relying on group life insurance for their primary coverage, and any additional AD&D benefits should never be counted on since they are unlikely to be paid. That said, any client that is an impaired risk for life insurance should obtain as much group life as possible, especially if group permanent life insurance is available.

If (or when) an impaired risk client leaves the employer, converting to permanent insurance or changing a group permanent policy to an individual policy should definitely be considered.

Never assume that a young client will be healthy enough in the future to buy individual insurance when and if the group insurance is no longer available. Practically every planner and insurance agent has a story about a client who became uninsurable or died while waiting for the right time to buy individually owned life insurance.

GROUP HEALTH CARE

In the early years of health insurance, policies operated in the way they were meant to— covering unexpected medical expenses and paying providers for care given only when an insured person was ill or injured. Managed care, on the other hand, attempted to provide comprehensive health care, providing preventative care as well as care for the sick or injured.

Over time, people wanted their medical plans to cover all health care-related expenses, leading to the dominance of today's comprehensive care plans.

In this chapter, as well as in chapter 13, we discuss many forms of medical plans. Just as with the individual plans detailed in chapter 6, some operate as insurance and others as prepaid health care.

As planners work with clients, they find that almost no plans are a pure form of any one structure. As we move through the first decade of the twenty-first century, this is becoming more and more true. Practitioners in the field are finding that nearly every plan is unique. The public and employers have demanded choices, and even some HMOs today permit members to seek certain treatment outside the organization with some level of coverage. This chapter gives you a solid base with which you will be able to read a client's group health care plan booklet and be able to understand and explain the coverage to the client.

It is critical, however, for a planner to ensure that each client understands that only the health care plan provider can tell them what is and is not covered. Planners should state directly that their understanding is nothing more than opinion, and that the client should verify it through company customer service representatives. No planner wants an unhappy client pointing a finger and accusing him of saying something was covered and then finding out it is not.

Group Health Care Terms

In addition to the terms discussed in chapters 6 and 13, here are some terms that may be referred to in relation to group health care plans.

Coordination of Benefits

Policies have a provision that prevents people from collecting more from insurance companies than the cost of the medical care provided. It is acceptable to be reimbursed 100 percent but not more, and excess payments are considered taxable income to the recipient. When both adult members of a household are covered by medical insurance through their respective employers, each person's own coverage is primary for him or her. Coverage for dependent children can be more complex. Two factors are commonly used in determining which plan will be used as primary coverage for the children: the parents' gender or birth date. Some plans default to the insured male's policy for primary coverage for dependent children. Other plans determine primary coverage by defaulting to the insured whose birth date falls first in the year, or who is the oldest. This can be confusing if the plans use different coordination of benefits clauses and the female's birth date comes before the male's. When there are two plans in a household, the insureds typically have to obtain duplicate copies of bills and submit them to the secondary company with a copy of the statement of benefits received from the primary carrier.

Cost Containment and Cost Shifting

In an attempt to control costs and keep health care plans reasonably priced, plans have provisions that are designed to limit certain expenses or shift them to the insured. This has been made more difficult by the demands put on health care plans by employers, the public, and various laws. In chapter 1, you learned a basic concept of insurance: True insurance does not pay for expected losses. However, many expenses that we now rely on health care plans to cover, such as preventative care and maternity care, are in fact expected in the sense that they can be scheduled and anticipated. If we had true health insurance, these would not be covered at all. With pregnancy, for example, only complications would be covered.

In health care plans, some of the cost-containment provisions include limits on the amount that will be paid for certain types of care, such as chiropractic visits, psychological counseling, or physical therapy. These are also known as maximum-benefit provisions.

Cost shifting also occurs through the use of deductibles, co-pays, and coinsurance. Whenever there is a limit to what the insurance company will spend for a given treatment, the insurer perceives it as cost containment, a method of shifting more of the cost to consumers. Some cost-containment provisions deal only with attempting to reduce unnecessary expenses. The mandatory second surgical opinion is an effort to ensure that the patient is certain that a surgery, an expensive health care procedure, is necessary and appropriate. A voluntary approach for obtaining second surgical opinions, under which a covered person can seek a second opinion with the cost borne by the medical expense plan, is often used. Some plans provide larger benefits for a covered person who has obtained a second opinion, even if it does not agree with the first. More and more plans are requiring mandatory second opinions that frequently apply only to a specified list of procedures. In contrast to voluntary provisions, mandatory provisions generally specify that benefits be paid at a reduced level if surgery is performed either without a second opinion or contrary to the final opinion. If two opinions differ, a third may be required or requested, depending on the contract.

In some cases treatment can be effectively handled on an outpatient basis, rather than inpatient. In years past, it was standard procedure to admit patients to the hospital at least 24 hours before surgery to run various tests and to control the diet and activities of the patient.

The practice of preadmission testing has all but eliminated this tradition and has saved insurance companies—and those paying premiums—millions of dollars each year. Similarly, long stays in the hospital for relatively routine procedures are a thing of the past. Surgeries that used to require a five- to seven-day hospital stay are done on an outpatient basis or a 23-hour hold.

There is also an area of cost shifting not directly related to commercial insurance: Medicare, as a cost control measure, annually reduces what it pays providers for various services and treatment. However, since costs are not lowered, private pay patients, those with health care plans, and those paying bills by themselves are left to pay higher prices. Medicare's reduction of payments has shifted some costs to other patients. Patients who pay their own bills and who do not actively negotiate with providers typically pay the highest prices. Negotiations, especially when the individual is willing to pay at the time of service, will typically result in a substantial reduction of the charges.

Experience Rating and Underwriting

As stated throughout this text, insurance companies do not magically supply people with money. They must collect enough in premiums and investment returns to pay all claims and all of their administrative and sales costs, plus a profit or contribution to surplus, in order to stay in business.

With group insurance plans for large groups, the insurance companies evaluate the business' prior claims to determine the future premiums. If a company with 200 employees had $1.2 million in claims in the prior year, the insurance company knows that it will take an average premium of $500 per month per employee to pay that amount of claims. The company will also look at the specific claims— in particular those that were high for an individual. If one individual in the company had $200,000 in claims for a medical condition that normally occurs in one out of every 5,000 people, the insurance company will not assume a recurrence of that claim. Conversely, if the company had no big claims of a type expected to occur in one out of every hundred people, they may factor in an expectation of those claims. This evaluation is called experience rating.

However, the greatest weight is generally given to actual claims. If in one group there are an uncommonly high number of employees and/or dependents who suffer from an ongoing condition that is expensive to treat, the group will be expected to pay for it. If the condition is such that it is treated and is not likely to recur, the insurance company looks at the statistical probability that a large number of employees and/or dependents in that group will have the condition in a subsequent year. Large groups are charged a small additional amount to cover very uncommon, expensive claims. Added to the expected claims is the cost of administration of the group.

The foregoing is how the premiums are generally determined, which is part of the underwriting process for groups. Insurers evaluate the group as a whole, including the ages, gender, number of women of childbearing age, the number of employees with dependents, and the historical claims. Sometimes, especially with smaller companies, there is no claim history because the underwriting process is being done for the first time. In this case, the other information carries much more weight. Each factor tells the insurer something about expected claims. Except for very small employer groups, the coverage is offered on a guaranteed issue basis when employees initially become eligible. Most states require that all providers of health plans offer basic and standard plans, on a guaranteed issue basis, to small groups. Readers should check with a group insurance expert or their state's insurance commission to find out if this is the case in their state.

Once the group is underwritten as a whole, no employee can be turned down unless he or she chooses not to be covered when first eligible and later decides to enroll. So from the employee's point of view, there seems to be no underwriting. Their only concern would be the preexisting conditions clause.

Late Enrollees

When an employee waits until after the initial enrollment period, usually he or she must provide full medical information in an application in order to obtain coverage. This is the case when the employee has not had any other coverage. However, if the reason the employee declined coverage at the time of initial enrollment was that he or she was covered under his or her spouse's group coverage, and that coverage is now terminated, the employee may then be a late enrollee with the same guaranteed coverage as if he or she enrolled at the first opportunity. If an individual is covered under his or her own group plan and that coverage ceases, the individual may generally be added to his or her spouse's plan with no underwriting.

Additionally, some large groups have **open-enrollment periods**, generally occurring annually, in which employees may join any plan offered by the employer or change plans if more than one is offered. The rules surrounding late enrollment help to minimize adverse selection.

Group Plans

Just as in chapter 6, the term "health care plan" is used in lieu of the term health insurance. This is because most HMOs as well as some other managed care plans are sponsored and operated not by insurance companies but rather by separate corporations that provide health care and collect payments to cover these costs. It is worth noting that most PPOs not run by insurance companies will have insurance companies administer their plans to protect themselves against exceptionally high claims. So-called self-insured plans are often administered by insurance companies or third-party administrators and, while practically all claims are paid from funds set aside by the employer, they also have insurance to protect them against excessive claims.

Coordination with Medicare

When employees work beyond age 65, they are generally given the choice of continuing insurance coverage through their group plan or switching to Medicare alone. Since Medicare does have significant limits to its benefits, most choose to keep the company health plan in addition to having Medicare. In that case, the company plan is primary, with Medicare being secondary. What this means to the employee and his or her dependents is that the health care plan pays first, then a claim must be submitted to Medicare for any benefits it may pay.

Eligibility

Under the laws of most states, there is a requirement that only groups put together for purposes other than obtaining insurance may purchase group insurance. Most employers will spell out which employees and officers are eligible to be covered and when. Frequently there is a waiting period before any benefits are provided.

With large companies, the employer has some flexibility as to who will or will not be eligible for coverage. With small plans, it is common to see limitations that require employees to be working at least 30 to 32 hours per week to be eligible for benefits. With some large employers, benefits will be offered to employees working as few as 20 hours per week. When an industry is having a difficult time finding qualified employees, the employers tend to offer more benefits and make it easier to qualify for those benefits, in order to attract qualified employees or prevent other companies from luring them away.

Certain employees can be excluded; typically they are seasonal or part-time employees, or those covered through collective bargaining. One practically universal requirement is that the employee must be actively at work for the coverage to begin. This means that an employee out on sick leave will not be covered until he or she returns to work, even if the waiting period (also known as a probationary period) has expired.

Eligibility for group benefits varies among employers. Typically, with large employers, new employees are eligible for most benefits on the first of the month following the date of hire.

Others may make employees eligible on the first of the month following 30 days of employment.

Some companies use a probationary period of 90 days, hiring the person on a temporary basis for 90 days and offering a regular position after that time. In such cases, the person may be eligible to receive benefits immediately upon becoming a full-time employee. Eligibility for different employee benefits may occur at varying times. It is not uncommon for employees to be required to wait a year before participating in a retirement plan, even when they begin receiving life insurance and health care benefits shortly after their date of employment.

Groups and Associations

State law generally defines groups for the purpose of obtaining group benefit plans, usually as two or more individuals who are associated for purposes other than obtaining group insurance.

Planners may come across plans that are aimed at sole proprietorships—individuals who are self-employed and work alone—but advertised as group health plans. In these plans, the only eligibility requirement to apply for the coverage is to be a member of an association of self-employed businesspeople; dues may be $25 per year, which includes a newsletter that provides some generic information about being self-employed. While these plans may be called group insurance, they are more like association plans, with individual applications for coverage and complete underwriting of every applicant.

Multiple Employer Plans

Also known as multi-employer plans (MEPs) and multiple employer trusts (METs), these employee benefit plans are typically established to provide health care plans to small employers.

The plan or trust works with an insurance company to put together a package that normally includes group life and health insurance, providing few variations. The benefit to small employers is that they are able to offer health care plans that are similar to those found at other larger employers. The benefit to the insurance company is the reduced adverse selection, since one insured plan will be geographically diverse and have a large number of participants. Some of these plans will have simplified underwriting or be guaranteed issue, with no individual underwriting.

Participation Requirements

If an employer pays 100 percent of the premium for employee health care, life, or disability income insurance plans, ordinarily, there will be 100 percent participation. From the insurance company's point of view, this eliminates any potential adverse selection. However, when employees pay a portion of the premium, they have the right to opt out of the coverage.

Insurance companies and others offering health care plans want to avoid adverse selection as much as possible. To this end, they require a certain percentage of employees to be covered under the plan—in most cases, 75 percent. Those who do not count against the participation limits are those who are covered as dependents under a spouse's or parent's plan.

Third-Party Administrator

Most insurance companies are not interested in marketing to small groups with fewer than 25 to 50 employees, even when MEPs are an option. This created an opportunity for small companies to put together a health care plan they can market to (and sometimes administer for) small groups of two or more. They do not offer many choices; often two or three variations are all that are available.

Either the vendors or those who establish the MEPs/METs administer the plans, which involves installing the plan, handling claims, and in many cases, doing the underwriting. These vendors also provide the sales support for the insurance agents who sell the plans. When the insurance company does not administer the plan, those who do are called third-party administrators (TPAs), the first two parties being the insured business and the insurance company.

The TPA also negotiates with the insurance company that underwrites the plans. If the insurance company decides to stop covering these plans, the TPA attempts to find another insurance company to accept the risk.

The insurance company experience rates the risk of all of the small groups as a whole, not individually. Generally, since the TPA is an added layer in the process, small groups pay more for their plans than do larger employers.

Another important function of TPAs is to administer self-funded plans. When a large employer wants to directly fund a health care plan rather than use an insurance company, it often does not want to be the party that determines which claims are paid and which are not.

Using a TPA brings a neutral participant to the decision-making process. Further, it adds the expertise required for proper claims administration.

Consumer-Directed Plans

In the past couple of years there has been a move toward the use of a new variation of health care plans called consumer-directed plans, starting with the medical savings accounts combined with high-deductible health plans (HDHPs) and moving to the health savings accounts and their HDHPs. As of January 1, 2005, a number of large employers were expected to make these plans an option for employees. At publication of this text, it is too early to know how many employers did provide this option. These plans are getting a lot of exposure, but unfortunately, not enough explanation. Reading the popular press and seeing news accounts of these plans gives one the impression that they are the greatest form of health care plan ever.

Planners do need to be aware of the benefits and detriments of the plans. The discussion in chapter 6 provides those perspectives.

Group Plan Changes

With the continued slow economy through 2004, and continually increasing health care costs, more and more employer-sponsored plans are being modified to include deductibles as well as co-payments. This combination was extremely rare only a few years ago.

The variations seem endless. With some plans, there is a separate deductible for prescriptions only. For others, there is a deductible for all medical care and then co-payments for the cost of doctor visits after the deductible has been met. There are different co-pays for different providers. There may be one co-payment for the primary care physician and one that is double that amount for specialists. Some plans have a substantial co-pay for an emergency room visit that may or may not be reduced or eliminated if the insured is admitted to the hospital. Almost any combination can be found in a plan today.

In addition to the changes in plan structure, there are changes regarding which providers can be used or how much will be paid toward different providers. Employers are also asking employees to pay a higher percentage of the cost. As family coverage reaches $1,000 per month, employers are faced with difficult decisions. More changes are likely to take place over the next few years. There may be a complete upheaval, changing the way healthcare is provided in this country.

COBRA

In 1986 Congress passed the Consolidated Omnibus Budget Reconciliation Act (COBRA), sometimes called the Continuation Health Law, as an amendment to ERISA, specifically to provide individuals the right to continue their group health care plans when they leave an employer. Before this law was passed, the only option was conversion to an individual policy that was generally more expensive and had fewer benefits.

COBRA provisions give most former employees, retirees, spouses, and dependent children the right to temporary continuation of health coverage at group rates. This coverage is only available in specific instances. Those who take advantage of this usually find that continued group coverage is more expensive than health coverage for active employees, since the employer no longer pays part of the premium. Additionally, the employer may charge the individual up to 2 percent of the premium as an administrative charge. However, this option is usually less expensive than comparable individual health coverage.

In general, the law covers group health plans maintained by employers with 20 or more employees in the prior year. These 20 employees may be full- or part-time, and the measurement is whether there are 20 employees on more than 50 percent of the typical business days of the year. It applies to plans in the private sector and those sponsored by state and local governments. Federal government employees and employees of certain church-related organizations are not subject to the act. There is a comparable law in place for federal employees.

When companies have plans that are subject to ERISA and COBRA, the laws affect who is eligible and which plans come under the laws, but not which benefits must be offered, how much the employer must pay, or whether an employer must offer plans. The laws do require certain reporting and nondiscrimination testing and outline the rules that control how employees become eligible for benefits. The laws outline the fiduciary standards that must be met by the plan administrator to ensure that it is for the benefit of employees.

The following benefits are affected by COBRA:
- Inpatient and outpatient hospital care
- Physician care
- Surgery and other major medical benefits
- Prescription drugs
- Any other medical benefits, such as dental and vision care

COBRA does not affect life insurance and disability income insurance.

COBRA Eligibility

Three elements are measured for the determination of qualifying for COBRA benefits: plans, beneficiaries, and qualifying events.

Plan Criteria

Plans that include the above-mentioned benefits and are offered by employers with 20 or more employees on more than 50 percent of the working days in the previous calendar year are subject to COBRA. The term "employees" includes all full- and part-time employees, as well as agents, independent contractors, and directors if they are eligible to participate in a group health plan.

Beneficiary Criteria

Usually a qualified beneficiary is any individual covered by a group health plan on the day before a qualifying event. The qualified beneficiary may be an employee, his or her spouse and dependent children, and in certain cases a retired employee as well as his or her spouse and dependent children.

Qualifying Events

"Qualifying events" are those types of events that would cause an individual to lose health coverage if it were not for COBRA continuation opportunities. The specific qualifying event will determine who the qualified beneficiaries are and the required number of months that a plan must offer the health coverage to them under COBRA. The following are qualifying events.

For the employee:
- Voluntary or involuntary termination of employment for reasons other than gross misconduct

- Reduction in the number of hours of employment
- Termination because of disability

For spouses:
- Termination of the covered employee's employment for any reason other than gross misconduct
- Reduction in the hours worked by the covered employee
- Covered employee becomes entitled to Medicare
- Divorce or legal separation of the covered employee
- Death of the covered employee

For dependent children:
- Same as for the spouse
- Loss of "dependent child" status under the plan rules

Coverage begins on the date of a qualifying event and generally ends when:
- The last day of maximum coverage is reached
- Premiums are not paid on a timely basis
- The employer ceases to maintain any group health plan
- Coverage is obtained with another employer group health plan that does not contain any exclusion or limitation with respect to any pre-existing condition of such beneficiary
- The beneficiary is entitled to Medicare benefits

In-Depth: Periods of Coverage

The following table details how long coverage lasts after a COBRA qualifying event.

Qualifying Events	Beneficiary	Coverage
Termination or reduced hours	Employee, spouse, or dependent child	18 months
Employee entitled to Medicare, divorce or legal separation, or death of covered employee	Spouse or dependent child	36 months
Loss of "dependent child" status	Dependent child	36 months
Disability*	Qualified beneficiary	29 months

*If a qualified beneficiary becomes disabled during the first 60 days of the COBRA continuation coverage, benefit eligibility is extended to 29 months if benefits would otherwise have been limited to 18 months. Three conditions must be met: the the employee was terminated or had hours reduced; disability began within 60 days of the qualifying event; and notification of the disability is made within 60 days of the determination of the qualifying disability and before the end of the 18 months.

Specific COBRA Notices

When a qualifying event occurs, employers, qualified beneficiaries, and plan administrators all have specific notice requirements to meet.

Employers

The employer must notify the plan administrator within 30 days after an employee's death, termination, reduced hours of employment, entitlement to Medicare, or notice of bankruptcy proceedings of the employer.

Administrators

Upon notification of a qualifying event, the plan administrator/employer must automatically provide a notice to the employee and his or her family members of their election rights. The notice must be provided in person or by first-class mail within 14 days of receiving information that a qualifying event has occurred. However, if the employer continues to pay for the benefits, the notice by the plan administrator may be delayed until the employer ceases to do so.

Beneficiaries

A qualified beneficiary must notify the plan administrator/employer within 60 days after a divorce or legal separation, or a child's ceasing to be covered as a dependent under the plan rules.

COBRA Election

Each qualified beneficiary has a 60-day period to elect whether to continue coverage. This period is measured from the later of the coverage loss date or the date the notice to elect COBRA coverage is sent. If elected, COBRA coverage is retroactive to the date coverage was lost and is paid for by the qualified beneficiary.

A covered employee or his or her spouse may elect COBRA coverage on behalf of any other qualified beneficiary. A parent or legal guardian may elect for the benefit of a minor child.

A waiver of coverage may be revoked by or on behalf of a qualified beneficiary prior to the end of the election period. A beneficiary may then reinstate coverage, and the plan only needs to provide continuation coverage beginning on the date the waiver is revoked. This prevents a person from going without coverage for up to 59 days and then starting the COBRA extension of coverage.

Covered Benefits

The benefits provided under COBRA extended coverage are identical to those received immediately before qualifying for continuation coverage.

For example, an employee may have medical, hospitalization, dental, vision, and prescription benefits under single or multiple plans maintained by the employer. If a qualifying event occurs, that individual has the right to elect to continue coverage under any or all of the health plans.

If a plan provides core and non-core benefits, qualified beneficiaries normally may elect either the entire package or just core benefits. Individuals do not have to be given the option to elect just the non-core benefits, unless the plan comprised only those benefits before the qualifying event.

Non-core benefits are typically vision and dental services, except where they are mandated by law, in which case they become core benefits. Core benefits include all benefits other than vision and dental services received by an employee.

If the benefits under the plan for active employees change, that change may apply to qualified beneficiaries. Beneficiaries also may be permitted to change coverage during periods of open enrollment by the plan.

Prior to COBRA, many health care plans permitted separating employees to convert to an individual health care policy. Some plans still allow beneficiaries to convert group health coverage to an individual contract. However, if this option is available from the plan extended under COBRA, the beneficiary must be permitted to enroll in a conversion health plan within 180 days before COBRA coverage ends. The premium for these individual group plans is generally higher than the group rate, and the coverage is typically not as comprehensive.

However, the conversion option is not available if the beneficiary allows the COBRA coverage to end before reaching the maximum period of entitlement.

Employer Bankruptcy

If an employer becomes insolvent and files for bankruptcy, the health care plan, and COBRA coverage may or may not be affected. If the company files for Chapter 11, reorganization bankruptcy, there may be no effect on existing employees or those under COBRA. If the filing is for Chapter 7, liquidation, the plan, including COBRA coverage, is likely to terminate.

Health Insurance Portability and Accountability Act (HIPAA)

Congress passed HIPAA in 1996 with two purposes. The one known by most people is the purpose of providing portability of health care benefits, which is not as obvious as it might initially appear. Prior to HIPAA, those who wanted to change jobs were concerned that if they left one employer and continued health care under COBRA, when they accepted new health benefits they would have to keep the COBRA plan for six months to a year to ensure coverage of any preexisting condition. Additionally, claim paperwork had to be provided to both plan administrators, and it often took months to get claims paid correctly. This could cost individuals and families thousands of dollars, and individuals often chose not to change jobs because of this potential expense. The problem was called "job lock": Individuals were locked into a specific job, or at least locked to a specific employer. HIPAA effectively ended these problems.

The second purpose of HIPAA was administrative: Congress designed it to standardize record keeping and provide greater security of an individual's personal health information. Virtually everyone who has visited a medical provider since this portion of HIPAA went into effect has been asked to read and sign a number of documents related to HIPAA disclosure, giving the providers the right to share a patient's medical information with others when it is necessary. Individuals have likely seen changes in the way their pharmacies operate as well. The administrative side of HIPAA has significantly increased the volume of paper, files, and administrative costs.

HIPAA also modified COBRA, adding children born while COBRA coverage is in effect as qualified beneficiaries.

Preexisting Conditions Clause

HIPAA also added standardization to preexisting conditions clauses in group health care plans. Because of HIPAA, preexisting conditions clauses for group health care plans may not exceed 12 months for a new employee who signs up for the plan at the first opportunity. For late enrollees to the plan, the preexisting conditions clause may not exceed 18 months. As with the rest of the law, these limitations apply to groups that have as few as two active participants.

HIPAA generally overrides state law, but the state law prevails if it is more beneficial to the insured. If the state permits a maximum preexisting conditions clause of less than 12 months, then that is the limitation for the plan. When it comes to portability, if state law requires a new plan to exempt an individual from the preexisting conditions clause because he or she had six months of creditable coverage, then that is as far back as the plan can look.

Portability

This is the most important aspect of HIPAA for most individuals. It does not mean that a person covered under a specific health care plan can continue that plan if he or she changes jobs, but the law's provisions lessen or eliminate the effects of a preexisting conditions clause under new coverage.

If a person has been covered under an individual policy, an employer-based group plan, an HMO, Medicare, or Medicaid, he or she is said to have **creditable coverage.** This is a critical factor in the application of the portability rules. If the individual has 12 months or more of creditable coverage, without a lapse of coverage of *longer* than 62 days, he or she will be able to sign up for the new coverage without being subject to the preexisting conditions clause. If the creditable coverage is for eight months, he or she will only be subject to a maximum preexisting conditions clause of four months.

When leaving a group, HMO, or other type of plan, the insured must be sure to request a certificate of creditable coverage. Typically one certificate will cover an employee and his or her family. Some providers of the certificates will provide one for each covered family member. If a dependent child loses his or her coverage, he or she is eligible to continue insurance under COBRA and should obtain a certificate of creditable coverage to avoid a preexisting-conditions clause when taking a job with benefits. Generally employers or plan administrators will automatically provide this certificate.

It is not necessary to show creditable coverage for more than 12 months, and the creditable service does not have to have been under a single plan. If it requires multiple certificates, that is acceptable.

Taxation of Group Health Care Plans

Premiums paid by the employer for employee health care plans are tax deductible by the employer and are not considered taxable income to the employee. Employees may deduct their portion of the premium in addition to any unreimbursed health care expenses, to the extent that the combined expenses exceed 7.5 percent of their adjusted gross income, assuming they itemize their deductions.

All payments made by the plan to providers or to reimburse the employee for health care expenses incurred are not considered income for tax purposes. If an employee takes a deduction in one year for unreimbursed medical expenses and receives reimbursement for those same expenses in a subsequent year, he or she must report the reimbursement as income. In many companies the employees are offered an IRC §125 cafeteria plan. With this plan, the employee directs the employer to reduce his or her income to pay the employee's share of the health care plan premium. When this occurs, the employee's payment is made on a before-tax basis, never reporting that amount as income. These types of plans will be discussed in greater detail in chapter 15.

General Notes

It is important for financial planners to understand both sides of the health care cost discussion. As a nation, we decry the increasing cost of health care coverage; it is expensive and premiums are rising faster than inflation. However, at the same time, we demand more services, better technology, and more thorough treatment. We want to see physicians rather than physician assistants. We want better and faster access to new drugs and procedures with promising results, and the right to sue when those drugs and procedures do not perform as hoped. Physicians in certain specialties, even those who have never been sued, may pay over $200,000 a year in premiums for malpractice insurance, often paid for by the first $100 per hour of every billed hour of patient time. All of this ultimately drives up the cost of health care.

The group medical benefits industry is constantly changing, and there are so many options and variations that many insurance agents do not sell it, or even maintain the ability to evaluate existing and alternatively offered coverage, but instead leave recommendations regarding which plan to seek to specialists. A financial planner who does not focus on this industry would be wise to follow that track.

With the rising cost of health care plans, there may be significant changes in the not-too distant future. Keeping up with those changes will take a concerted effort.

GROUP DISABILITY INCOME INSURANCE

Most individuals who have any kind of disability income insurance have group coverage. While there are some similarities, there are significant differences between personally owned disability insurance and group disability insurance.

There are two general forms of group disability income insurance: short-term and long-term.

Short-Term Disability Income Policies

These are generally available only through employer-based plans. Short-term disability (STD) income insurance policies may have elimination periods as short as seven days for illness and one day for injury.

More commonly the elimination period is one to two weeks, with some consideration being given to the sick leave benefits offered by the employer. Benefits are limited to anywhere from 90 days to 104 weeks. The benefit is a percentage of income, and generally has a relatively low maximum weekly amount, such as $500 to $800 per week. The definition of disability for STD income insurance plans is typically that of total disability, but it may merely state that if the individual is sick or injured and cannot work, benefits will be paid. This is a fairly liberal definition and one that is not unrealistic, due to the nature of the STD income insurance providing benefits for only a short time. There are few, if any, extra provisions included with STD income insurance plans.

Long-Term Disability Income Policies

These policies (abbreviated LTD) typically have elimination periods of 30 to 180 days, but may be longer if they are used in conjunction with an STD income insurance plan. In such cases, the benefit period of the STD income insurance plan becomes the elimination period for the LTD income insurance plan. The benefits are also based on a percentage of income, but this is monthly income rather than weekly. The maximum monthly income that a plan will cover may be as high as $10,000 to $15,000, and the insured income is generally limited to base salary or wages, excluding bonuses and/or commissions.

Benefits may last from five years to the employee's normal retirement age. The definitions of disability range from total disability to own occupation (see chapter 7). Quite often, group plans begin with an own occupation definition for two to five years and then change to a modified own occupation definition. Many group LTD income insurance plans include provisions for rehabilitation and partial disability.

Underwriting

The underwriting for group disability income policies is done on a group basis, similar to that for group health insurance. Individuals who apply for it when it is first offered generally have it issued without medical underwriting. In some cases, group disability income policies will have a preexisting conditions clause. In others, mostly large groups, they will not. In all cases, the employee must be at work for the policy to take effect.

Non-Occupational

Some disabling conditions are caused by accidents that occur on the job and would normally be covered by workers compensation. Group disability income insurance policies are either nonoccupational coverage or are offset by any workers compensation payments made, which means that they pay no or partial benefits if the accident or illness occurs on the job.

Group and Individual

When an employee has group disability income insurance coverage, he or she is usually precluded from obtaining an individual policy. Insurance companies are concerned about individuals having too much disability income insurance. A person who can have his or her full income while disabled would not be as likely to want to get back to work as one who had only 60 or 70 percent of the predisability income. Too much disability income insurance leads to malingering and affects all policyholders adversely.

There is a downside: Group disability income insurance is rarely portable. If an individual develops a condition that increases his or her chances of being disabled and then leaves a job where there was group disability income insurance, he or she will likely be unable to obtain individual coverage, as underwriting for individual policies is stringent. Relatively minor issues, such as having sustained a knee or back injury, or having undergone psychological counseling, may result in an exclusion of coverage or a rejection of the application.

Definitions of Disability

As with individual policies, the definitions of disability can vary quite a bit. For the low-risk classes of insureds, individual policies may have much more liberal definitions. The own occupation definition for individual policies may require that the insured be unable to perform important job functions, while a group policy may require that the insured be unable to do each and every function of the job. There are numerous definitions of own-occupation coverage. The specific wording of a policy and questioning of the insurance company are necessary to fully understand how they are applied.

The typical group LTD income insurance policy is own-occupation for two to five years and then modified any occupation.

The modified any-occupation coverage typically states that the insured is considered totally disabled if he or she cannot work at an occupation for which he or she is suited by education, training, and/or experience. This essentially means that if the employee had certain skills and was earning an income of $50,000/year, he or she will still be considered disabled if the only work that can be done is unskilled work paying $20,000 per year.

Somewhat related to definitions of disability is a provision often included in group disability income contracts. To encourage employees to return to work, some insurance companies will pay for rehabilitation programs that are expected to speed up the recovery process. Benefits are continued through the rehabilitation program so that the process itself does not reduce their income as their abilities increase.

While most individual policies have a presumptive disability provision, many group policies do not. When this provision is included in group contracts, it generally has the most restrictive provisions, as detailed in chapter 7.

Offsets

Some individual policies have a provision that pays an additional amount unless and until social insurance such as Social Security disability income benefits are paid. Virtually all group policy benefits are reduced by payments received from Social Security disability income benefits, workers compensation, state benefits, or any other payments made by the employer.

However, group policies usually have a provision stating that they will pay at least $50 per month, even if the other sources pay an amount that exceeds the policy benefit.

This reduction of disability income insurance payments generally applies to retirement benefits as well. So if an individual is disabled, begins receiving disability income insurance benefits, and then chooses to retire, the retirement benefits may eliminate the disability income benefits. Rather than have an offset for workers compensation payments, many group policies exclude benefits for on-the-job disabilities, even if workers compensation payments might be much lower than the insurance policy benefits. Rarely does a group disability income insurance policy reduce its benefits because of payments made by an individually owned policy.

As with individual policies, group policies generally exclude benefits for intentionally self-inflicted disabilities or disabilities that arise out of illegal activities.

Return-to-Work Provisions

Some group policies permit an individual to return to work without the fear of starting another elimination period if they find after a few days or weeks that they are not capable of working. These provisions vary widely. Typically, they consider periods of disability for the same problem that are not separated by more than 30 days to six months to be the same disability. Although these provisions can be beneficial if the benefits last until retirement age, they are not as helpful to the insureds if the benefits last only a few years.

Alternate Short-Term Benefits

Group disability insurance plans are one way that employers provide payments to disabled employees. Another way to deal with short-term disabilities is through salary continuation plans, also known as sick-leave plans. The most important thing for a business to know when using an uninsured plan is that it must be in writing and be communicated to the employees before any benefits are paid. If it is not, the IRS may treat the payment as a nondeductible gift or dividend from the employer to an employee/stockholder.

Sick-Pay Salary Continuation Plans

Disability income insurance policies are typically part of a sick-pay salary continuation plan. This type of salary continuation plan is among the few types of employee benefits where discrimination is permitted. They are covered by IRC § 105. It is permissible to provide this benefit only to top management, or to continue a sick or injured manager's salary longer than that of a line worker. Because of the potential expense of such plans, these plans are generally limited by the length of time an individual's salary will be continued if he or she is unable to work.

Planning Considerations

Disability income insurance is one of the most important forms of insurance for working clients. It is also the most difficult to get underwritten on an individual basis. It is important that clients understand what is covered and what is not. With this form of insurance, there are no bargain policies, and there are no black-and-white rules.

Each individual's situation dictates what is best. However, few disabled individuals ever think their benefits are adequate. It is important for clients to understand the term "disabled." If a person is hurt or sick and cannot work for a few hours, days, or weeks, he or she is disabled.

A migraine headache or the flu can be disabling under the right circumstances. Anyone who is unable to function for a day due to illness or injury is disabled for that day—not permanently, but totally. With that in mind, you may be better able to help your clients understand the necessity for adequate disability income protection.

There are a few things a planner can do in the area of planning, relative to disability income insurance. The most important action is to not avoid discussions about it. Disability income insurance is far more likely to create a claim prior to age 65 than is life insurance. While it is true that most clients will not be able to purchase an individual disability income insurance policy if group coverage is in place, there are times that it may be possible.

As mentioned earlier, typical group LTD income insurance plans cover base salary only, usually excluding commissions and bonuses. But for many individuals, these constitute a substantial portion of their annual income. Some people may have a second job or work independently in their spare time. All of these sources of income, as long as it is earned income, are used to determine how much in disability benefits they may be permitted to purchase. If a client has a base salary of $30,000 annually, which is insured, but also receives an average of $40,000 in commissions and bonuses from the same employer, he or she probably has only $18,000 in annual LTD income insurance benefits but may be eligible to have over $40,000 in benefits when combined with individual coverage.

Another way an individual may more easily obtain adequate coverage is to have a disability income insurance policy purchased before he or she is eligible for a group plan. Once the individual policy is in place, it cannot be cancelled except for fraud, nonpayment of premiums, or misstatements made on the application. When he or she becomes eligible for group LTD income insurance, the existence of the individual policy does not affect group benefits. If he or she becomes disabled and meets the definitions of disability, benefits will be paid by both the group plan and the individual policy. This is the case even if the cumulative total exceeds his or her prior income.

Taxation of Disability Income Insurance

Benefits received from a group disability income insurance policy under which the employer pays 100 percent of the premiums are considered taxable income to the employee. Further, the benefits received for the first six months of disability are also subject to FICA taxes. If the employee pays a portion of the premium, the benefits that are paid on account of that payment are income tax-free. If, for example, the employee pays 40 percent of the premium for the LTD income insurance coverage, 40 percent of the benefit would be income tax free and also not subject to FICA taxes for the first six months. Some companies have attempted to get around this issue by having the employee reimburse the employer for the premiums paid at the end of the year if there was a claim, or by having the employer reimburse the employee at the end of the year if there was not a claim. The IRS now looks at the last three years of the employer's financial records to determine who—the employee or the employer—actually paid the premiums.

There are disability income insurance experts who claim that if the documentation is done carefully, the employee's contribution can be attributed to the first six months of benefits.

This would make the benefits paid in the first six months of disability free of income and FICA taxes. Subsequent benefits would be subject to income taxes. Most disabilities are relatively short, so this would provide income tax-free benefits for most disabilities. This approach should not be undertaken without the advice and guidance of a disability income insurance specialist and a competent tax advisor. Apparently, the required paper trail is extensive and must be complete.

IMPORTANT CONCEPTS

Accelerated death benefits

COBRA

Conversion

Coordination of benefits

Cost containment

Cost shifting

Employee benefits eligibility

Experience rating

Group eligibility

Group health care plans

Group life beneficiary options

Group life insurance

Group LTD offsets

Group permanent life insurance

HIPAA

IRC uniform premiums

LTD income insurance

Multi-employer plan (MEP)

Multiple employer trust (MET)

Qualified beneficiary

Qualifying event

STD income insurance

Supplemental group life

Tax-free group life insurance

Taxation of group benefits

Termination of group insurance contracts

Third-party administrator (TPA)

QUESTIONS FOR REVIEW

1. What is the primary benefit of COBRA to individual employees and how does it operate?

2. What is the primary benefit of HIPAA to individual employees and how does it operate?

3. What is the significance of employers paying only for $50,000 of group term life insurance for an individual employee?

4. What happens in relation to group term life insurance when an employee terminates employment?

5. What is the income tax status of group life insurance proceeds if the employer paid the premiums on a tax-deductible basis?

6. What is the basis of determining premiums for group health care plans for large employers?

7. What is different for an employee who signs up when he or she is first eligible for group life insurance, a health care plan, and group long-term disability insurance, and an employee who signs up nine months later?

8. Under what circumstances might an individual have to report a medical expense reimbursement as taxable income?

9. What are the differences between group short-term disability income insurance and group long-term disability income insurance?

10. If an employee becomes disabled and qualifies for group LTD benefits, what might reduce those benefits while he or she is still totally disabled?

SUGGESTIONS FOR ADDITIONAL READING

Employee Benefits, 7th ed., Burton T. Beam, Jr. and John J. McFadden, Dearborn, 2005.

Fundamentals of Risk and Insurance, 9th ed., Emmett J. Vaughan and Therese M. Vaughan, Wiley, 2003.

Introduction to Risk Management and Insurance, 8th ed., Mark Dorfman, Prentice Hall, 2004.

Life and Health Insurance, 13th ed., Kenneth Black Jr. and Harold Skipper Jr., Prentice Hall, 2000.

Principles of Risk Management and Insurance, 9th ed., George E. Rejda, Addison Wesley, 2004.

Risk Management & Insurance, 12th ed., James S. Trieschman, South-Western College, 2004.

Social Security Manual 2005, National Underwriter, 2005.

Social Security, Medicare & Government Pensions 10th ed., Dorothy Matthews Berman and Joseph L. Matthews, NOLO, 2005.

Tax Facts 2005, National Underwriter, 2005.

CHAPTER FIFTEEN

Other Insurance Benefits: Cafeteria Plans, FSAs, and Group Dental

• • •

In the prior discussion of satisfiers and dissatisfiers, we discovered that a benefit that may satisfy one person may dissatisfy another. This discrepancy sometimes happens when a company pays more for one employee's benefits than for those of another, which is one issue addressed by the development of cafeteria plans.

Other employees may be concerned about the deductibility of premiums, medical costs, and other expenses. Flexible spending arrangements (FSAs), often called flexible spending accounts, permit a virtual 100 percent deduction for certain premiums and expenses. And beginning in 2004, all employers were permitted to establish high-deductible health plans (HDHPs) in conjunction with health savings accounts (HSAs) or health reimbursement arrangements (HRAs).

After reading this chapter, you will be able to:

- Describe the general structure and operation of cafeteria plans
- Explain the general structure and operation of flexible spending arrangements (FSAs) and identify the specific benefits that can be included
- Explain the taxation of benefits in cafeteria plans and FSAs
- Explain how cafeteria plans and FSAs meet employee and employer needs
- Explain the general rules surrounding cafeteria plans
- Explain the general rules surrounding FSAs
- Describe group health savings accounts, health reimbursement arrangements, and high-deductible health plans
- Describe the differences among and operation of various group dental plans
- Briefly describe group long-term care and group property and liability insurance

CAFETERIA PLANS

John and Luis both work for the Corporate Corporation Company (CCC). John is 31 and single (never married) and has no children. Luis is 31, married, and has two children. CCC offers a health care plan to all employees and pays 85 percent of the entire premium, whether it is individual or family coverage. CCC also offers a long-term disability income insurance (LTD) plan that covers 50 percent of the employee's base salary. Employees are permitted to elect and pay for additional disability coverage of up to an additional 20 percent of their salary. CCC also pays for group life insurance equal to three times each employee's annual salary. There is also dental coverage, for which CCC pays 50 percent of the cost for employees and dependents.

John and Luis work in the same department and have similar titles and responsibilities. They are paid the same, and when it comes to the health care and dental plans, they each pay their portion of the premiums. In regard to the disability plan, the amount they are asked to pay for the additional coverage is also the same. Luis is pretty happy with the entire package. John becomes more and more unhappy with it every time he thinks about it. Why?

The premium for John's health care plan is $170 each month, for which he pays $25.50 and CCC pays $144.50. For his dental coverage, the monthly premium is $11.00 for which he pays $5.50, the same as CCC. A friend of his in human resources told him that the premiums for family coverage for the health plan and dental plan are $885.00 and $26.00 respectively. For John's health care and dental benefits, CCC is paying a total of $150.00. For Luis, CCC is paying $774.35, which is $624.35 more than it is paying for John's benefits. When it comes to the extra disability income benefits, John and Luis pay the same amount, and the company is paying for a lot of life insurance that John feels he just does not need right now.

Luis does not even think about this situation, but John is really irritated about it because he feels cheated. He is doing the same job as Luis, and essentially, in his mind, getting paid $624.35 per month—or almost $7,500 per year—less. When the numbers are laid out like this, few can argue with John. The other view is that Luis must pay much more out-of-pocket each month for his health care and dental plans. No one wins when there is a disagreement about the fairness of such benefit packages.

The idea for cafeteria plans arose from these types of disagreements, with the goal of making employee benefits more equal. Cafeteria plans essentially permit employees to choose those benefits in which they find value and allow them to use benefit dollars provided by the employer to best meet their particular needs.

Rules

There are some basic rules that apply to cafeteria plans. First, the plan must offer a cash benefit that would generally be taxable to the employee as compensation. Second, there must be one or more qualified benefits available that would not be taxable to the employee if paid for by the employer. The plan must be offered to employees in such a manner that it does not discriminate in favor of highly compensated employees. Generally, cafeteria plans work best in large businesses but are sometimes found with companies that have 20 or fewer employees.

There is a **safe harbor test** that requires that the employees covered under the plan be classified in a manner that precludes discrimination for highly compensated employees (an officer, a highly compensated employee, a shareholder of 5 percent or more of the business, or a spouse or dependent of any of the first three). In addition, all employees must be covered under the plan no later than the beginning of the plan year following their completion of three years of employment. Discrimination is measured based on the amount of contribution, as well as the benefits offered.

If the plan is found to be discriminatory, the benefits remain nontaxable to most employees, and become taxable to highly compensated employees. To add to the confusion, each benefit included in the cafeteria plan is separately tested for nondiscrimination.

The nondiscrimination requirements arose out of ERISA, and IRC § 125 is the controlling section of the Internal Revenue Code. Even though employees receive current benefits from their employers, this section of the code makes an exception to the **doctrine of constructive receipt**. Without this exception, the value of all of the benefits would be considered income to the employees. This exception applies only to those benefits that would otherwise be income-tax-free, such as health care plans, STD income insurance and LTD income insurance plans, the first $50,000 of group term life insurance, dental and vision plans, and the like. Unlike MSAs (listed below), contributions to an HSA may be made for employees through a cafeteria plan. There are a number of benefits that cannot be offered on an income tax-free basis through a cafeteria plan. These include:

- Contributions to an IRC § 106(b) medical savings account
- IRC § 117 scholarships and fellowships
- IRC § 127 educational assistance program payments
- Employee discounts (of company products or merchandise) or such no-additional-cost benefits as free standby tickets for airline employees and any other IRC § 132 benefits, such as transportation or parking benefits.
- Retirement benefits other than money directed to a 401(k) plan
- Long-term care plans

Types of Plans

There are three approaches used in the operation of cafeteria plans. The first is most commonly found in very large companies and is sometimes called a two-level or two-tiered method, giving all employees a basic package of benefits. This might include health care, dental, short-term disability income insurance, a basic amount of life insurance, and some LTD income insurance coverage. Each employee then receives a monthly sum or "credits" that can be used to pay for other benefits, such as family coverage. This sum may be the same amount for all employees or it may be based on a formula that considers years of employment or another nondiscriminatory measure. The benefits purchased by this extra amount may be additional life insurance, a vision plan, additional LTD income insurance coverage, an upgrade to a more expensive health care plan, child care, and possibly additional vacation days. If cash is elected instead of qualified benefits, such cash payments are taxable income to the employee. A separate cafeteria plan in the form of an FSA can be used to repay the employee for any out-of-pocket medical costs, such as deductibles or co-payments. The government has expanded the list of expenses for which reimbursement can be made to include many more items such as over the counter drugs.

The second approach is that employees are given a monthly amount or "credits," and they choose the benefits that they want from a "menu" of benefits offered by the employer, thereby providing great flexibility.

The third approach is the least common, but it is easier to administer than the other plans. This method offers two or three set packages of benefits available to all employees, which reduces costs and administration time by reducing options. The employer's contribution is essentially the same for all employees, and the choice of plans establishes how much the employee will be contributing.

Making Changes

Generally, an employee may not make any changes to the elections made in regard to a cafeteria plan until the next plan year. However, changes may be permitted when there is a "change in family status." When any of the following occurs during a plan year, employees are permitted to make certain changes in their elections.

- Marriage, divorce, or legal separation of the participant
- Death of a spouse, child, or of the participant
- Birth or adoption of a child (being pregnant during the plan year does not constitute a change in family status)
- Termination of employment (the employee's or his or her spouse's)
- Obtaining employment (the employee's or his or her spouse's)
- Change in employment status, either the employee's or his or her spouse's (i.e., from part- to full-time, or vice versa)
- Significant change in health coverage attributable to spouse's employment

Income Tax Issues

Generally, as stated, contributions by the employer that are made to pay for qualified employee benefits within a cafeteria plan are deductible by the employer and are not reportable by employees as income. Money that is put into the plan to be used at the discretion of the employee within the structure of the plan is also income tax-free to the employee and deductible by the employer, unless the employee chooses to take unexpended funds in the form of cash or other benefits that would normally not be income tax-free If the employee chooses this option, the money is still deductible to the employer but becomes taxable as earned income by the employee. If the employee uses these funds to purchase extra group term life insurance so that the total amount exceeds $50,000, the employee will have to report the economic value of that excess term life insurance as taxable income. The option of taking cash is not a requirement and may not be available.

FLEXIBLE SPENDING ACCOUNTS (FSA)

FSAs, also known as flexible spending accounts, are a special form of cafeteria plan funded typically with employee salary reductions, allowing employees to pay for certain expenses with before-tax rather than after-tax dollars—specifically, unreimbursed medical and dental expenses and child care. Coverage of these expenses may be part of an employer's cafeteria plan package. If there are both medical and child care expenses to be paid, they are generally established in separate accounts since each type of account has different limits.

Consider Luis from the example discussed in the cafeteria plans section. With two children, Luis and his wife find that they have, on the average, two provider co-pays of $20 each, every month. Additionally, their monthly share of prescriptions is $60. Two members of the family wear glasses, and on the average, they spend a total of $150 per year on glasses and eye exams beyond what the vision plan covers. Their share of unreimbursed dental plan expenses adds up to $200 per year. That totals $1,550 of expected expenses each year that would be paid for with after-tax dollars if Luis did not have an FSA. Additionally, Luis's wife works part-time and spends $60 per week on child care, with an annual expense of $3,000.

Assume that Luis and his wife are in a 28-percent tax bracket. If they had to pay these medical costs on an after-tax basis, they would have to earn $2,409 (taxes on income at 28 percent plus 7.65 percent FICA taxes) to net the $1,550 in expenses. If Luis reduces his salary by $129.17 each month, putting that amount in the FSA, the plan will pay them back for those expenses, and they will save $859 a year in income and FICA taxes. If they put $250 per month into the child care FSA, they will save an additional $1,070 in taxes, for a total of $1,929 that can be spent on other family needs. The downside is that Luis's income for Social Security purposes is less, so he might consider putting this tax savings into retirement savings to compensate for a potentially lower Social Security retirement benefit.

Planning note: Some people complain because any money left in the plan more than two and a half months after the year in which the contribution is made is lost. For Luis and his wife, if he leaves anything less than $1,929 in the plan, he comes out ahead. Even if there were $50 to $100 left in the plan, Luis would still be more than a thousand dollars ahead by using the FSA

Note that if the employee's income is higher than the Social Security wage base so that not all of it is subject to Social Security taxes, only income taxes and those taxes that apply to Medicare would be reduced.

Here are specific expenses that may be covered by the child care FSA. Eligible expenses can be full-time day care, after-school day care, the tuition and fees for private preschool or kindergarten, even day camps or the cost of a housekeeper who is also a sitter for children under the age of 13 (though not for a sitter who is under the age of 19 or who is a dependent of the taxpayer for tax purposes). Under the FSA, Luis can reduce his salary up to $5,000 per year ($2,500 if he and his wife file separately), to pay for child care. The tax savings on these expenses can be almost $1,800 when considering the taxes they would have paid in a 28 percent income tax bracket and FICA.

If this $1,800 were put into a Coverdell Education Savings Account each year for 10 years at 5 percent and then compounded for another five years at the same 5 percent, the couple would have over $30,000 saved toward the education of their children, merely from the income tax savings from the FSA. This is $30,000 worth of education funds that were created just by the reduction of taxes. While this is a simplified illustration, it is clear that this plan can be quite valuable.

Rules

As with any cafeteria plan, an FSA must not discriminate in favor of highly compensated employees. There is a limit of $5,000 for child care, and no limit to the amount (other than the employee's income) that can be withheld for health care expenses. However, most employers limit the amount that may be withheld for health care expenses to ensure that the plan does not discriminate. If highly paid employees all deferred large amounts of their income for medical expenses and few regular employees did so, the plan would likely be found to be discriminatory.

Only health care expenses and dependent care expenses can be reimbursed out of FSA accounts. If expenses in the year plus two and a half months after the end of the year, are not adequate to use up the amounts withheld, the remainder is forfeited.

The employee must decide on the amount of the salary reduction in the calendar year prior to the year in which it is to take effect and must then provide a written election for that reduction (see sample enrollment form below). The amounts for health-care-related expenses and those for dependent care are tracked separately and must be shown as separate amounts on the election form.

The entire amount of the projected annual contributions must be available at the beginning of the calendar year for all employees. So, if an employee is scheduled to put $100 per month into the plan, the full $1,200 is available to reimburse the employee for covered expenses incurred in January. If the employee leaves during the year, he or she is not required to complete making the monthly contributions or to repay any portion of the benefits paid that were not yet contributed. If the employee has paid more into the plan than has been paid out at the time he or she leaves, qualifying expenses incurred after separation may still be reimbursed up to the amount actually contributed. While the amount for child care expenses may have been chosen because of the expected monthly cost to the family, a change in plans for the child may result in more expenses early in the year. The entire account may be used for child care expenses in the first month if the expenses were actually incurred then.

The maximum amount permitted for dependent care is $5,000 annually ($2,500 if the parents are married, filing separately). Even if there is money left in the health care account at the end of the year, it cannot be used for dependent care, and dependent care money may not be used for health care expenses. Again, any funds not used by the end of two and a half months after the end of the calendar year are forfeited.

Illustration 15.1: Sample Enrollment Form

Corporate Corp., Co.
Flexible Spending Account (FSA)
2007 Enrollment Form

Each employee must complete and submit this form no later than December 31, 2006.

Employee Name: _____ SSAN: _____

( ) No, I do not want to participate in the CCC FSA plan for 2007. I understand that I will not be permitted to enroll in the plan after 12/31/06 for the 2007 plan year.

( ) Yes, I want to participate in the CCC FSA plan for 2007. Effective as of 1/1/07 I authorize CCC to reduce my annual income through equal reductions in each pay period, in the following amount(s):

Amount to be allocated for health care expenses. . . . .$_____

Amount to be allocated for dependent care expenses ($5,000 maximum) . . . . . . $_____

Total. . . . .$_____

- I understand that the amounts selected for health care expenses and dependent care expenses are separate and that each amount may only be used for the specified purpose.

- I understand that I cannot stop, increase, or decrease this salary reduction amount at any time during 2007 unless I experience a "life event" as outlined in federal regulations.

- I understand that if I do not have adequate expenses by March 15, 2008 to use all of the money in the FSA, any remaining balance will be forfeited.

- I have received a printed explanation of the Flexible Spending Account. I understand that my employer is not responsible for any income tax liabilities that may arise as a result of my participation in the plan.

_____   _____

Your Signature / Date

Forfeited Deferrals

Funds that are forfeited when an employee fails to use them during the allotted time may not go directly to the employer. However, they can be used to defray administrative expenses of the plan. Other ERISA-permitted uses of forfeited money in the FSA include protection of the underwriting integrity of the plan or reallocation of contributions in the following plan year.

Protection of the underwriting integrity may include repayment to the plan for distributions that were made in excess of contributions. This could be the result of employees terminating their employment during the year after having received reimbursements from the FSA without having paid in an equivalent amount. Reallocations must be done on a per-capita basis for all plan participants. They may not be done based on income, contributions, or any other factor that is discriminatory.

Receipt of FSA Funds

There are two general methods for employees to access FSA funds. The most common is that periodically, employees submit a request for reimbursement. With large companies, employees may generally submit them at any time. Alternatively, to manage the administrative costs, smaller companies may limit employees to paperwork submissions at certain times each month or possibly only once per quarter. Larger employers may alternatively choose to issue credit/debit cards that may be used only for qualified expenses. This can save the employee and employer time and expense. The general rule is that expenses incurred during the year are eligible for reimbursement from funds contributed in the same year. On May 18, 2005 the Treasury Department announced a relaxation of this "use-it-or-lose-it" rule that limited reimbursements in this way. The new guidance is that there is a two and a half month "grace period" in which expenses occurring in that time frame may be reimbursed from funds remaining in the FSA at the end of the prior year. Now, as of March 16th of each year, any money contributed in the prior year that is left in the FSA, is forfeited. Interestingly, during the funding year, an employee may be reimbursed an amount that is greater than the year-to-date contributions. Assume Susan Smith agrees to reduce her salary by $125 per month ($1,500 for the year) for medical expenses. Also assume that in early February, her son broke his leg and chipped a tooth in a pick-up basketball game. The emergency room co-pay plus the dental expenses add up to $425 that was not covered by her health care and/or dental plans. She has contributed only the first $125 of her annual contribution.

Logically it seems that she could only get reimbursed $125 now, $125 after her contribution in February, etc. until she had paid in enough to cover all of the costs. In fact, the IRS has stated that the employee may ask for, and expect to receive, the full amount to cover actual annual expenses, even though the year has not ended and the contributions have not been made. If Susan were to leave her employer before she had contributed enough to cover the expenses for which she had been reimbursed, the employer must cover the difference.

However, this statement by the IRS is based on Proposed Treasury Regulation § 1.125-2, A- 7(b)(2). This means that if an employer does not abide by this rule, there is little the IRS can do about it. The employer would not currently be subject to any fines or disciplinary action.

Mid-Year Changes

Generally, employees may not change their salary reduction agreement, up or down, or terminate it during the plan year. However, if they experience a **life event**, they may make a change. Among the qualifying life events are marriage, divorce, birth or adoption of a child, death of a spouse or child, and the loss of a spouse's job.

If an employer chooses to offer an FSA, it does not have to offer both health and childcare reimbursement options.

GENERAL NOTES

In many cases with cafeteria plans, married employees with children realize that the employer's contribution is not enough to pay for all of the requested benefits. In many cases, it may not be enough to cover the costs for single employees. When an FSA is included in a cafeteria plan, it is used to reimburse the employee for out-of-pocket medical and child care expenses, other than plan premiums, on a pre-tax basis. The employer may set up a separate plan that permits employees to pay their share of premiums with pre-tax dollars.

Benefit Funding

Generally, group benefit plans are offered to employees on a **contributory** basis where the employee pays some portion of the cost or on a **noncontributory** basis where the employer pays the entire cost. It is where the plan is contributory that an FSA is most beneficial to the employees. Planners generally should recommend that an employee use an FSA to pay his or her part of such medical expenses as deductibles, co-pays, and other expenses not covered by the health care plan, including the cost of over-the-counter drugs. There is no good reason for an employee not to take advantage of this option. It is the only way that the entire employee's contribution toward health care, dental care, and child care can be made with pre-tax dollars.

In traditional plans, the employer engages an insurance company and/or health care plan companies to provide various benefit coverages. The alternative to the traditional approach is to use a self-funded plan. From the employer's point of view, the self-funded plan has some risks associated with it and may be appropriate only for certain types of benefit plans. Cafeteria plans and FSAs can be offered with both traditional methods of funding these employee benefit plans and with self-funded plans.

Health Savings Accounts, Health Reimbursement Arrangements, and High-Deductible Health Plans

Health savings accounts (HSAs) and high-deductible health plans (HDHPs) were discussed at length in chapter 6. There is no difference in the plans established by individuals and those established for employees by their employers. Health reimbursement arrangements (HRAs) are different from HSAs in that all of the contributions are made by the employer. Unused HRA funds can be carried over into future years. Self-employed individuals may not establish HRAs. The funding of HRAs may not be part of any deferred compensation plan.

An employer may make contributions to an employee's HSA and pay all or a portion of the premium for the affiliated HDHP. Employers may make HSAs and HDHPs one of the choices among a number of choices for employee health plan options. A more generous choice would be an HRA and HDHP. These are called consumer- or employee-directed plans. Since the employee is responsible for a much greater share of the medical expenses than under other contemporary plans, it is assumed that the employees will be more selective as to what health care is sought and from whom. Since the premiums are typically much lower for HDHPs than for other plans, employers prefer employees to use them. It is possible for an employer to spend less per employee and have the employee think he or she is getting more. If the employer pays only 65 percent of the premium for a more common plan and pays 85 percent of the premium for an HDHP, it is likely spending less, and since the employee's portion is so much less, he or she may assume the employer is paying more. Further, as the cost of these plans goes up, the dollar increase for employers will be less since the base plan cost less before the increase.

Employers may not offer an HSA and an FSA to the same employees. If an employee had an HSA in conjunction with an HDHP and then becomes covered under a new plan that is not an HDHP, he or she may participate in an FSA and use any funds in the HSA as long as distributions from the HSA are not taken to cover the same expenses reimbursed by the FSA. The HSA funds may continue to grow on a tax-free basis while the employee uses the FSA funds. Contributions may not be made to both, regardless of when they were established. However, an HRA and FSA may be offered concurrently.

One major difference between FSAs and an HRA or HSA is that all of the funds that will be contributed to an FSA in a given year are available to cover reimbursable expenses at any time of the year, regardless of the amount paid in to that date. With HRAs and HSAs, reimbursement is limited to contributions made. As long as the employee was covered by the plan when the expenses were incurred, he or she may apply for reimbursement when the funds become available.

NEED TO KNOW: GROUP PROPERTY AND LIABILITY

Very few companies offer group property and liability insurance. It is, in most cases, nothing more than group billing for individual policies. There is really no significant benefit to obtaining this type of coverage in this manner other than having the premium deducted directly from the employee's paycheck, meaning the payment is rarely, if ever, late.

GROUP DENTAL COVERAGE

One of the most widely offered employee benefits is coverage for dental care. In the early years of dental care plans, virtually all of the plans were insured plans of the indemnity type. Over the years, dental plans have changed alongside health care plans.

Indemnity Plans

As with indemnity-type health care plans, the insured person must first pay the dentist and then seek reimbursement, unless the dentist's office will submit the claim directly to the insurer. The major problem with pure indemnity-type dental plans is that they can be fairly expensive if a person does not get regular check-ups and cleanings when a visit to the dentist is necessary. Soon after the establishment of dental insurance plans, preventative care became a standard component. This type of care, through these modified indemnity plans, generally either has very low deductibles and coinsurance or is paid in full. The primary reason for the change was to get insureds to the dentist on a regular basis, generally preventing or reducing the seriousness and related costs of dental problems.

Incentives

Some plans added incentives for regular visits to the dentist. Incentive-based plans often provide for graduated payments, depending on how regularly the insured visits the dentist.

For example, preventative benefits are covered at 70 percent during the first year, at 80 percent in the second year (if you go at least once every 12 months), and at 100 percent in the third year. If you neglect to visit your dentist for one year, you start this process over. From the insurance company and employer perspective, the goal is to keep costs down by encouraging good dental care and catching any problems before they become serious and expensive to treat. A few plans even provide increased coverage for major dental care if preventative care visits are made twice each year.

Managed Dental Care Plans

Employers also use the managed dental care plan as another approach to reduce costs. Using managed health care as a model, many insurance companies and employers believe that by specifying which dental clinics can be used, costs can be kept down. Some managed dental plans only provide benefits if you visit participating dentists. Some operate as dental HMOs where the premium payments are sent directly to the provider of the service. Others operate more like PPO plans with a list of otherwise unaffiliated dental offices.

Sources of Dental Care Coverage

Some insurance companies that offer health care plans also offer dental plans. When the same insurance company provides both plans, it is called an **integrated plan**. Some integrated plans are more integrated than others. A few plans actually have combined the dental and health care deductibles; most do not. Probationary periods for dental plans are typically the same as for medical expense plans.

Companies that specialize in dental care coverage provide the majority of dental plans offered. The family of Delta Dental care plans is probably the largest. There may be local dental service plans, managed-care-type plans, or modified indemnity plans. In some locations, Blue Cross and Blue Shield still offers dental care benefits. Some large employers may choose to self-fund their dental care benefits. For most of the expenses, such as the preventative care benefits, the plans operate as prepaid care. If the employer pays for the plan directly, it saves money by not having to provide a profit to an insurance company or a dental HMO. This makes self-funding of the plan attractive to large employers.

Variation of Benefits

Some plans, often called "basic plans," offer no orthodontic benefits at all. Some plans offer them only to dependent children, and still others offer them to all covered members.

Orthodontic benefits are usually limited in amount and rarely exceed 50 percent of the ultimate cost. Some employers will offer plans with two levels of benefits: the basic plan with limited or no coverage for certain types of care, such as orthodontia, partial and full plates, and caps; and the advanced plan, which covers these benefits to a much greater extent.

Employers that offer both often require employees to be under the basic plan for at least one year before becoming eligible to receive benefits from the more advanced plan. This reduces adverse selection for the most expensive dental treatments.

Most plans today require a predetermination of benefits for specified dental procedures to make sure the dentist and the individual receiving the treatment know how much the plan will cover and how much will be paid by the insured. In general, the predetermination of benefits provision, also known as pre-certification or prior authorization, applies only in non-emergency situations and when a dentist's charge for a course of treatment exceeds a specified amount (varying from $200 to $300). If an employee fails to obtain a **predetermination of benefits**, he or she will still receive a benefit, but neither the dentist nor the covered person will know in advance what services will be covered or how much will be paid for those services.

While all plans will cover two cleanings per year, some only cover one exam by the dentist each year. With some plans, each visit must be at least six months after the prior visit (not five months and 29 days).With other plans the exact timing is not critical, but only two visits for cleanings per year will be covered. X-ray coverage is also a variable. Some plans will cover full x-rays as often as every two years. Others limit coverage to once each three to five years, with partial x-rays being covered within shorter time frames.

The amounts paid for various procedures may also vary. Some plans will pay 50 percent for crowns without a deductible; others will pay 50 percent after a deductible. Most plans that cover orthodontia will pay a limited amount of the potential benefit for each year of treatment. Others will pay it out as a percentage of the total cost until it is used up, without regard to the time involved. Orthodontia typically is covered to a maximum benefit of $1,000 to $2,500.

Exclusions

All dental care plans have certain exclusions. Some plans exclude certain treatments, such as injuries to the mouth, because they should be covered under a health care plan. Other exclusions may include:

- Cosmetic procedures
- Replacement of dentures or prosthetic devices
- Services related to occupational injuries, which are generally covered by workers compensation insurance
- Some services that started before the date of coverage or problems that predated the start of coverage
- Services provided after the termination of employment

As with group health care plans, the insured has no control over the continuation of the coverage. Generally the employer can terminate the plan at any time, and the insurer may generally terminate the plan with 30 days' notice. Fortunately, if the insured leaves the employer in the middle of expensive, covered dental care, the plan may be continued under a COBRA extension with the full premium plus, possibly, a two-percent administrative charge, payable by the employee.

In-Depth: Group Long-Term Care Insurance

This form of insurance is making a slow entry into the employee benefit market. It provides a much needed benefit, and one that most people do not think about until they have parents who need long-term care or until they themselves begin to think about it in their 50s or 60s. While this type of coverage does not fall under HIPAA or COBRA for continuation of coverage after leaving the employer, these contracts are often individual contracts paid through group billing and can be taken by the employee when he or she leaves. The greatest advantage to group long-term care plans is that they will sometimes permit the employee to purchase coverage for a parent, as well s a spouse. The premiums may appear to be high, but if you have a three-year benefit that pays $150 per day, the potential payout could be $164,000. Chapter 8 provides more information on long-term-care plans.

IMPORTANT CONCEPTS

Cafeteria plans

Flexible spending arrangements or accounts (FSA)

FSA childcare expense limits

FSA enrollment limitations

Forfeited deferrals

Group dental care plans

Group HSAs, HRAs, and HDHPs

Group long-term care plans

Life events

Safe harbor test

Types of cafeteria plans

QUESTIONS FOR REVIEW

1. What is a cafeteria plan?

2. What is a flexible spending account?

3. What is the income taxation of group life insurance provided inside of a cafeteria plan?

4. If Bob and Sylvia Starch are married and file their income tax returns separately, what is the maximum amount that Sylvia can have withheld from her annual salary for child-care expenses?

5. How often can an employee change his or her salary reduction agreement in the year in which it is effective?

6. What is the latest date for an employee to submit his or her salary reduction agreement for an FSA?

7. What is the maximum salary reduction permitted for payment of health care expenses?

8. What happens if the employee's childcare and/or health care expense accounts have unexpended funds remaining at the end of the plan year?

9. What effect does choosing an HDHP with an HSA normally have on an employee's FSA during an open enrollment period for employer-sponsored plans?

10. How do cafeteria plans operate?

11. What percentage of a company's employees is typically enrolled in a noncontributory plan?

12. What is the primary difference between an HSA and an HRA?

SUGGESTIONS FOR ADDITIONAL READING

Employee Benefits, 7th ed., Burton T. Beam, Jr. and John J. McFadden, Dearborn, 2005.

ERISA FACTS 2005; Frank Bitzer and Nicholas Ferrigno, Jr.; National Underwriter, 2005

Fundamentals of Risk and Insurance, 9th ed., Emmett J. Vaughan and Therese M. Vaughan, Wiley, 2003.

Introduction to Risk Management and Insurance, 8th ed., Mark Dorfman, Prentice Hall, 2004.

Life and Health Insurance, 13th ed., Kenneth Black Jr. and Harold Skipper Jr, Prentice Hall, 2000.

Principles of Risk Management and Insurance, 9th ed., George E. Rejda, Addison Wesley, 2004.

Risk Management & Insurance, 12th ed., James S. Trieschman, South-Western College, 2004.

Social Security Manual 2005, National Underwriter, 2005.

Social Security, Medicare & Government Pensions, 10th ed., Dorothy Matthews Berman and Joseph L. Matthews, NOLO, 2005.

Tax Facts 2005, National Underwriter, 2005.

Tools and Techniques of Employee Benefit and Retirement Planning, 9th ed., Stephan J. Leimberg and John J. McFadden, National Underwriter, 2005.

CHAPTER SIXTEEN

Non-Insurance Benefits and Benefits Taxation

• • •

As described in chapter 13, employee benefits come in many forms. The previous chapters looked at group insurance and insurance-style benefits. This chapter looks at several other types of benefits, some that are not particularly common and some that are fairly widespread.

When you have completed this chapter, you will be able to:

- Describe the various types of pay for time not worked
- Explain the purpose and operation of personal time off (PTO) plans
- Describe the purpose and operation of the Family Medical Leave Act (FMLA)
- Describe the tax treatment of meals and lodging furnished for the convenience of the employer
- Describe the operation of an education assistance plan, a dependent care assistance plan, and a qualified adoption assistance plan
- Describe the basic provisions of a 501(c)(9) trust or voluntary employees' beneficiary association (VEBA) as a funding vehicle for the employee benefits offered to members
- Compare and contrast no-additional-cost services, qualified employee discounts, working condition fringes, and de minimis fringe benefits
- Describe the basic provisions of a severance plan
- Analyze a given client's employee benefit package to determine its adequacy
- Describe various sick pay plans
- Describe the operation of qualified transportation fringes, qualified moving expense reimbursement, qualified retirement planning services, and qualified tuition reduction plans
- Describe the tax treatment of other fringe benefits, including golden parachutes, employee achievement awards, employee assistance plans, financial planning and legal services plans, wellness programs, athletic facilities, and holiday bonuses

PAY FOR TIME NOT WORKED

Among the most common benefits are payments for time not worked: time off when an employee is disabled due to sickness or injury as well as time for rest or relaxation away from work. Employees generally take it for granted that the employer will offer time off. However, these may still be satisfiers or dissatisfiers, depending on employee perceptions. For example, Carmen and Darnel both start new jobs with Carlin Imports, which offers nine paid holidays. Carmen's previous company only offered six paid holidays, so she is quite satisfied with the benefit. Darnel's previous company, however, offered 12 paid holidays, so he is somewhat dissatisfied with the loss of holiday time.

Disability Due to Sickness or Injury

Employees may miss as little as a day or two of work, for sickness or injury, to as much as several weeks, due to a more serious illness or injury. Employers deal with such temporary absences from work in several ways, including sick pay, short-term disability income insurance, or long-term disability income insurance.

Note the use of the term *disability* above and below. A disability may exist for a day or for a lifetime. Any physical or mental condition that results in a person being unable to work is a disability. People outside of the financial services industry use the term "disability" to mean lifetime incapacity. There is a wide range of levels of disability along with varying time frames. A migraine headache often results in total disability for the period of time it takes for it to pass. Recognizing the true meaning of this term is a good way to emphasize the value of these benefits.

Sick-Pay or Sick-Leave Plans

Most people who have ever had a full-time job have received the employee benefit that permits them to take a day off with pay when they are sick or injured. This type of sick-pay or sick-leave plan (also known as a salary continuation plan) is fully funded by the employer. Such plans are uninsured and generally fully replace lost income for a limited period of time, starting on the first day of disability. Such a benefit is usually for a broad group of employees but can be for selected executives only, or it can be structured as a plan with more favorable benefits for executives. This is one benefit plan that can exhibit significant discrimination. Employers typically provide employees with printed information describing various employee benefits, such as vacations, holidays, and sick days.

Historically, sick-pay or sick-leave plans were informal and at the discretion of the employer. Often such plans were not in writing and were administered in a very informal manner. A high-ranking manager who was well liked might be paid his full salary while being out for two or three weeks following a surgical procedure. A lower-level or less popular manager might only get three or four days of pay in a similar situation. This informal system proved problematic, but not because of discriminatory practices, which would be acceptable with this type of plan since it is not a qualified plan under the Internal Revenue Code. Rather, it caused an income tax issue for other reasons. Sick-leave payments are considered part of an employee's compensation and are tax-deductible by the employer and taxable to the employee, subject to the reasonable compensation requirement. However, if the sick-leave plan is not formalized (i.e., adopted in the minutes of the corporation and articulated in writing), the IRS may determine that the payments are not earned income but rather gifts or dividends (if the employee is a shareholder). Gifts of this magnitude and dividends are not tax-deductible. Accordingly, to preserve the income tax deduction, a noninsured sick-leave plan needs to be in writing and communicated to all employees. It also needs to define who is eligible and to specify what benefits are provided. Failure to formalize a sick-leave plan can have the additional unfavorable result of increasing the likelihood of lawsuits by persons not receiving benefits.

Sick-leave plans come in several varieties. Most plans pay 100 percent of an employee's regular compensation. Some plans provide a reduced level of payment after an initial period of full pay. Most plans credit each employee with a certain amount of sick leave each year (e.g., 10 days). Some plans allow "carryover" of benefits to a later year. For example, where an employee is credited with 10 days of sick leave in the current year but uses only 5 days in that year, the plan may allow the employee to carry over the 5 unused days to the next year, thus making 15 days available in the subsequent year. Typically, employees can accumulate sick leave up to a maximum amount, which is rarely more than six months. Moreover, the number of days that can be used in any year may be limited.

When there is a cap or limit, some employers permit excess sick days to lapse so that once an employee has accumulated more than the maximum limit of sick days, he or she forfeits any additional earned sick days. In this type of plan, employees may feel that this punishes those who remain healthy and/or who do not abuse the available sick days. Some employers that cap the number of sick days will pay employees once each year for accumulated sick days in excess of the maximum permitted. The payment is often made at a rate of one half of the employee's current daily compensation per excess sick day.

With regard to eligibility, most plans require a one- to three-month probationary period before benefits are payable and, as discussed earlier, benefits may be offered only to certain classes of employees (e.g., top management or nonunion employees). Other plans credit an employee with one day of sick leave for each month of service, or a certain number of hours of sick leave for each week worked. Others adjust the duration of benefits based on an employee's length of service. In addition, such plans may be coordinated with workers compensation insurance benefits to pay a total of 100 percent of an employee's regular pay.

One of the potential disadvantages of sick-leave plans is that employees may come to believe that they are entitled to take advantage of such sick days and, as a result, abuse the benefit. To limit such abuse, some employers require a physician's certificate if an employee's absence from work is longer than one week. Of course, there are a few employers that do not permit a carryover of sick days and actually encourage employees to take all sick days, as "wellness" days, even if they do not get sick or injured..

Short-Term Disability Income Insurance

When a company has a short-term disability income insurance plan for its employees, all of the basic provisions present in a sick-leave plan are provided under the policy. The policy spells out eligibility, benefits, qualifications, exclusions, and the benefit-application process. This approach, aimed at longer periods of illness or recovery from illness or injury, was discussed in chapter 14. Obviously, short-term disability income insurance is more appropriate for treatment and recovery from a heart attack or cancer than for a mild case of the flu. Short-term disability income insurance plans usually provide benefits that replace only a portion of an employee's lost income and often contain a waiting period before benefits start, particularly for sickness. The typical waiting period for short-term disability income plans is one week. Some begin the first day for injuries.

If an employee's disability continues for an extended period of time, both the sick-leave plan and the short-term disability income insurance plan may pay benefits up to their respective limits. At this point, long-term disability income insurance benefits, as discussed in chapters 7 and 14, will normally become effective.

There are employers that provide sick days and only long-term disability income insurance plans. For employees of these employers, there is often a shortfall of sick days before the LTD begins. As an example, someone may have accumulated 30 days of sick leave that are used up with an extended illness or disability. If the LTD plan benefits do not start for 60 days, there is a 30 day period of no income. Some employers provide a sick leave bank for employees to use only after using all of their sick days or after taking a specified amount of personal time off (see below) for an illness or injury. The days in this bank can sometimes be given to other employees who have serious medical conditions or need additional family leave.

Paid Holidays

Companies most often give employees between six and twelve paid holidays per year. When there are only six, they are typically national holidays that virtually everyone gets off. As the number of paid holidays increases, lesser national holidays are included and days like the day after Thanksgiving, Christmas Eve, and the employee's birthday are added. Often, when a company's business is such that it cannot close for those days, those hourly employees who work are paid one-and-a-half to two-and-a-half times their normal compensation. Businesses such as hospitals that must stay open all of the time typically use a personal time off (PTO) program instead, as discussed below.

The typical six paid holidays are:

- New Year's Day
- Memorial Day
- Fourth of July
- Labor Day
- Thanksgiving
- Christmas

Beyond these basic holidays, employers often add others, such as:

- Martin Luther King Jr.'s Birthday
- President's Day (or Washington and Lincoln's birthdays)
- Good Friday
- Columbus Day
- Veterans' Day
- Friday after Thanksgiving
- Christmas Eve
- New Year's Eve
- Employee birthdays
- State holidays
- Floating holidays

In-Depth: Put It in Writing

To avoid questions about the deductibility of premiums and the taxability of benefits, a sick pay plan must be in writing, generally providing information that protects the company from IRS problems and that reduces the chance that an employee will sue the company for discrimination. Not only must the plan be in writing to accomplish these goals, it also must be communicated to the employees. Without putting the plan in writing, the IRS may take the position that an employee who is paid for not working is receiving a non-deductible gift from the employer.

The plan must spell out who is eligible to receive benefits—usually only permanent full-time employees. It is quite common to require an employee to have been working for 3 months or 90 days before becoming eligible for payment for time off due to illness or injury. Additionally, the employee must be at work on the day the plan takes effect.

The plan must provide a clear explanation of the number of days and how they are earned, which may appear as a text description or in a table. The sick-day accumulation rules (discussed above) must also be included.

If the plan excludes certain illnesses or injuries, such as injuries incurred while under the influence of illegal drugs, these exclusions will be spelled out in the plan. If benefits are to be reduced by any other payments, such as group disability insurance, workers compensation insurance, or Social Security Disability Income (SSDI) payments, the plan must also spell that out.

Vacation Days

In addition to paid holidays, most employers realize that people cannot work all of the time—or at least do not want to. In general, it is healthy for people to get away from work, and breaks usually improve productivity. To accomplish this, employers offer to pay employees for a certain number of days that they choose to take off: vacation days.

Some people want their vacation days one at a time. Some plan carefully in order to make a two-day vacation into a four- or five-day weekend. Others want one or two weeks all at once to take a long trip

NEED TO KNOW: HYBRID HOLIDAY/VACATION

Some employers have season-sensitive workloads or find that at certain times of the year, they have so many employees who want time off that they cannot operate efficiently. Rather than tell many employees that they cannot have that time off, the company may close for a week or so. This is typically paid time off that is in addition to other holidays and vacation days.

or work on a big personal project. Most vacation plans offered by employers are very flexible. Vacation plans may provide that vacation days are earned over time, for example one day for every 30 days worked. Some companies give new employees one or two weeks vacation for their first year, but require them to be on the job for a certain amount of time before any days can be taken. Most employers reward longevity with increasing vacation time as employees' years of service increase.

Everyone knows people who so love what they do that they practically never take any vacation. This can create a problem for employers because the company budget includes vacation time. Another type of employee is the one who is not comfortable leaving the job, even for a deserved vacation, for fear that he or she will miss something important or will be perceived as not carrying his or her load. When this happens, it is typically the company culture that brings it about.

The company assumes people will take vacation during the year and continue to receive their normal income. Additionally, most companies will buy back any unused vacation time when an employee leaves. If an employee accumulates a year's worth of unused vacation time and then decides to leave, the year's salary that would have to be paid would clearly be a burden for the company. Also, many of the unused vacation days were awarded when the employee was earning much less. Another potential problem is that certain retirement plans calculate the benefit paid based on the years an employee has been with a company. Funding for those plans is based on projections of when employees are likely to retire and the number of years they will have with the company when they do retire. An employee who accumulates an extra year's worth of vacation may be able to use that to increase his or her retirement benefits as well. This could result in an employee leaving the job a year before retirement, collecting all income and benefits, and leaving the employer to fund the retirement program as well, while getting no productivity out of the individual.

To help make these problems manageable, employers use a variety of approaches. The most straightforward is to require that employees use or lose their allocated days of vacation each year. These employers do not permit a carry-over of any unused vacation days, even if the employee's manager did not allow employees to take their requested days. Other employers will permit a limited carry-over of unused days, perhaps five days. This may be five days per year, which still permits a fairly large accumulation over time, or a maximum of five days can be carried into the next year, after which they are lost if not used. Still other employers limit the number of days that can be accumulated. After that limit is reached, some will have a program where additional days just disappear; others will pay the employee for the additional days. The amount paid will vary from one quarter of a day's pay to a full day's pay for each excess day. Most employers prefer that employees take their vacation days, so this last option is not particularly common.

Personal Time Off (PTO) Plans

In an effort to deal with many problems and issues that arise when dealing with sick days, vacations, and paid holidays, especially in businesses that are open all of the time (24/7), the concept of personal time off (PTO) was developed.

PTO plan employees generally accrue one PTO hour for each specified number of hours worked. These hours generally apply to holidays, vacations, and, often, sick leave. In most cases, even when a business closes for a holiday, employees' PTO accounts are charged for those hours. In some cases other leaves, such as funeral leave, are also included in the PTO plan. Their pay statements typically keep a running total of PTO hours earned and used.

Those who are new to PTO plans often assume that personal time off is equivalent to vacation time, but plans usually do not operate that way. Accumulated PTO hours are, in most cases, also used for holidays and often for certain sick days. Additionally, some businesses, when the budget is stretched too thin, will require employees to take off a certain number of days using PTO hours so that the employer will not have as big a liability on its books for unused PTO. Also, a business that must be open 365 days a year may sometimes require non-essential employees to take various holidays off, charging their PTO hours for those days.

When the plans are instituted, it is rare that the total PTO hours granted in a year would provide fewer than the previous combined paid holidays and vacation days offered by the employer. The total is often greater when short-term sick leave is included.

The greatest advantage of PTO plans from the employee's point of view is that he or she is given complete flexibility as to how to take available paid time off without any concern about stretching the truth regarding the use of sick days. They do not have to worry about funeral leave being different than a vacation day or floating holiday. An employee with children who get all of the expected childhood illnesses can use his or her time to care for the children. For those who rarely take a sick day, they get the same number of paid days off. Employees must be careful, however, that they do not expend all their hours on vacations. If an employer grants 10 holidays, the employee must budget 80 of his or her PTO hours for those days or face a negative PTO balance or cut in pay (depending on the details of the plan). The same thing could happen if an employee uses all of his PTO hours for vacation and holidays and then becomes ill.

Employers benefit from PTO plans as well. Keeping track of one plan is administratively less expensive than keeping track of vacation and sick days separately. If a budget is very tight, employers may require every employee to take a certain number of PTO days off when their department or the entire business is experiencing a slow time. Budgeting is generally better since it is hard to know exactly how many sick days will actually be used.

For an employer, the potential down sides of a PTO plan are no different than those of more traditional plans. It may have to pay a departing employee for any unused days. It may also find employees using up all of their PTO days and needing more time for an illness. One other problem is

If sick leave is part of the PTO, as mentioned above, employees use these hours when they become ill. When PTO is an adjunct to sick days, an employee typically must use a certain number of consecutive PTO hours before the sick days kick in. This approach permits the employer to have a better handle on the cost of time off and eliminates employee use of the "mental health day"—usually a euphemism for taking sick leave instead of vacation days if employees just do not feel like working that day. This practice is very costly to employers and puts excess pressure on coworkers who have to make up the work for the malingerer.

that the employer may have little warning of an impending FMLA (Family Medical Leave Act – covered later in this chapter) leave that would be provided if an employee started using many sick days.

Other Personal Time Off With Pay

Many employers also provide some or all of these other forms of paid leave:

Family Leave

Family leave comes in two different forms, either of which may be with or without pay. The first is extra time off for extended vacations, honeymoons, or education and is usually limited to certain employees (e.g. employees with long tenure) at a specified level in the management hierarchy, or in some other specific group.

The second form allows employees to deal with medical issues such as the birth or adoption of a child or the extended illness of a family member. The federal Family and Medical Leave Act (FMLA), which is covered more extensively later in the chapter, mandates unpaid leave for these reasons, though employers may choose to provide at least some of the time as paid leave.

Bereavement Leave

A typical bereavement leave benefit generally provides up to five days off for the death of a parent, spouse, child, or other relative living in the employee's household. There are many variations of this benefit.

Jury Duty

While in most jurisdictions the law requires employers to release employees for jury duty, it does not require that they be paid for that time. However, since most jury duty pay is so minimal, most employers do pay for the time taken to fulfill this civic duty.

National Guard/Military Reserve Duty

Generally, the law requires that employees be given time off to meet their military obligations. However, the law does not require the employer to pay them for that time away from work. Many employers will pay the difference between what the individual earns from the military and their regular income if their regular income is higher than military pay.

Sabbaticals

Most commonly found in educational institutions, but not limited to them, a sabbatical leave with pay is often granted to individuals who have provided a certain number of years of service. This leave may be from three months to a year in length and often has a requirement that some sort of research or education be undertaken in conjunction with the leave.

FAMILY AND MEDICAL LEAVE ACT: FMLA

Before 1993, if an employee needed to take extra time off, the employee took the chance that his or her job would not be there when it was time to go back to work. The employee might require extra time due to a serious illness, either the employee's own or that of a member of the employee's family. The employee might also feel the need for more maternity leave than was available through vacation days and sick days. That changed with the passing of the Family and Medical Leave Act (FMLA).

The law applies to private employers, nonprofit organizations, and government entities, including Congress, that has more than 50 employees within 75 miles of the main facility of the employer. An employer is required to comply with the law if it has more than 50 employees, including part-time employees and employees on unpaid leaves of absence, for a minimum of 20 weeks during the current or preceding year.

Generally, under the law, an employee must be permitted to take up to 12 weeks of unpaid leave in a 12-month period for the birth or adoption of a child or because of a serious health condition of the employee or the employee's spouse, child, or parent.

The employer chooses how to measure the 12-month period, but that choice must apply to all employees. An employer's FMLA coverage can be based on a calendar year, any consecutive 12-month period, the 12-month period beginning the date the employee's leave begins, or a moving 12-month period that ends with the employee's last unpaid leave day. The only time the chosen method might not apply to all employees is if an employer has operations in more than one state and at least one of the states specifies how the 12-month period is determined.

> **NEED TO KNOW:**
> **EXEMPT AND NONEXEMPT**
>
> An employee's status as exempt or nonexempt is determined by the application of employment laws. Generally, employment laws are aimed at protecting hourly workers. Most salaried workers are exempt from the protection of these employment laws, which is not necessarily a negative thing. Salaried employees are paid a salary to get a job done. Whether they get the job done in 30 hours one week or 60 hours the next, their salary is the same either way. It is common for exempt employees to take a half-day off and not be charged any vacation time or PTO hours. A nonexempt employee will be charged vacation time or PTO hours if he or she leaves even one hour early or arrives one hour late. A nonexempt employee also gets paid extra for any extra hours worked, including overtime. Most salaried positions are exempt while hourly positions are nonexempt.

To comply with the law, employers must provide a written family-leave policy. It must include the following:

- Eligibility requirements
- Certification requirements to show need for leave
- Employee's rights after the end of the leave
- Employer's rights if the employee quits at the end of the leave

Moreover, the employer must post a notice explaining the FMLA.

The leave does not have to be 12 consecutive weeks. A good example of this might be for an employee who has used all sick and vacation days for cancer surgery and must still have chemotherapy treatments. The employee may take a week after each treatment to recover from the treatment. He or she may then be able to work until the next treatment. When an employee requests that family-leave days not be consecutive, approval must be obtained from the employer, and the employer is under no obligation to grant it.

If the employee still has accrued paid leave, either sick or vacation days, the employer can require that those days be taken first. Also, if the employer believes that a leave by one of the individuals who is in the group of the highest paid 10 percent of employees would result in a substantial and grievous injury to the employer, permission for the leave can be denied.

An employee may be required by the employer to provide 30 days notice of any foreseeable FMLA leave and to provide the necessary physician certification. This would apply to maternity leave, adoption, and planned medical procedures. The notice and certification are not requirements of the law. They are required at the employer's discretion.

The only benefit that the employer must make available to the employee who is on FMLA leave is the health benefit plan. This is provided on the same basis as if the employee was working, so if the employee normally pays a portion of the premium, that is still the employee's obligation, subject to a 30-day grace period. If the employee quits at the end of the leave, the employer has a legal right to collect any premiums due from the employee. This is tempered in that the right exists unless there is a continuation of the problem that gave rise to the request for leave; the onset of a new health condition that affects the employee, his or her spouse, child, or parent; or if there are other circumstances beyond the employee's control—in other words, if it would be difficult for the employer to collect.

Ultimately, when the employee returns at the end of a qualified leave, the employer is obligated to provide the employee with the same job or an equivalent job and the right to regain any benefits enjoyed prior to the leave, without having to meet any requalification requirements. Of course, if the reason for the leave leaves the employee with any limitations, then the employer must deal with the Americans with Disabilities Act (ADA) to ensure the employee is given reasonable accommodation to be able to work.

In some cases, states have passed laws which are even more stringent than the FMLA and in those cases employers must comply with those laws as well as with the FMLA.

STATUTORY FRINGE BENEFITS

Fringe benefits received as compensation for services rendered are includible in the gross income of an employee or other service performer, unless the benefits are specifically excludable under one or more provisions of the Internal Revenue Code (IRC). Normally, the amount includible by the employee is the fair market value of the fringe benefit, minus: 1) the amount, if any, paid for the benefit by the employee and 2) the amount, if any, that is specifically excluded from gross income under a provision of the IRC. Also, note that the requirements for deductibility of compensation, in general, apply to fringe benefits as well. Therefore, fringe benefits must be provided for services performed and must be reasonable in amount when combined with all other compensation for the individual.

The more common types of statutory fringe benefits include group-term life insurance (discussed in chapter 14), split-dollar life insurance (discussed in chapter 20), medical, accident, and disability benefits (discussed in chapter 14), meals and lodging furnished for the convenience of the employer, education assistance plans, group dependent care assistance plans, qualified adoption assistance plans, IRC Section 132 and 117(d) fringe benefits (including no-additional-cost services, qualified employee discounts, working condition fringes, *de minimis* fringe benefits, qualified transportation fringes, qualified moving expense reimbursements, qualified retirement planning services, and qualified tuition reductions, discussed in this chapter).

> **NEED TO KNOW: CONSTRUCTIVE RECEIPT**
>
> If the funds are set aside for an individual and not accessible by the employer's creditors, the individual has constructively received them, and they will be taxed immediately, even if they are not to be paid for years. If the individual is leaving the company and is given a choice of how to take the pay, it is all taxable as a single payment, even if taken over a number of years because the individual had the option of taking it as a single payment. If the agreement is to pay the individual an amount equal to one year's income, payable over a two-year period, and that is the only option, he or she will report it as income received.

Meals and Lodging Furnished for the Convenience of the Employer

In those cases where an employer provides an executive or other employee, his or her spouse, or his or her dependents with meals and lodging, it can be an extremely valuable fringe benefit if it can be excluded from the employee's gross income. And, unlike many of the other tax-free fringe benefits discussed in this chapter, meals and lodging can, in some cases, be provided in a discriminatory manner.

In order to qualify for this tax-free treatment, several requirements must be met. First, in the case of meals, the meals must be furnished on the business premises of the employer. Second, in the case of lodging, the employee must be required to accept the lodging on the business premises of the employer as a condition of his or her employment. Third, the meals and/or lodging must be provided "for the convenience of the employer." In general, only meals and lodging furnished to employees "in kind" are excludable. Also, they must be furnished directly to the employee. As a result, cash allowances or employer reimbursements for meals and lodging purchased by employees are not excludable. However, supper money or other sporadic meal reimbursements are excludable.

In some cases, employees are charged a fixed and unvarying amount for meals and/or lodging furnished for the employer's convenience on the business premises. In these cases, the amount charged can be excluded from the employee's gross income only if the employee is required to make the payment whether he or she accepts or rejects the meals (or lodging). It does not matter whether the employee pays the fixed charge out of his or her stated compensation or directly. But the exclusion is not permitted where the employee is charged a varying amount or can decline to take some of the meals.

When it is said that meals and/or lodging must be furnished "for the convenience of the employer" it means they must be furnished for a "substantial noncompensatory business reason." In other words, the employer must have a good business reason for providing the meals and/or lodging other than giving the employees more pay. Such a determination is based on the surrounding facts and circumstances. In general, an employee's meals, furnished before or after hours, are not for the employer's convenience (except for restaurant or food service employees). Meals furnished on nonworking days are not excludable as a general rule. However, if meals are furnished to the employee in lodging on the employer's premises that the employee is required to accept as a condition of employment, the value of meals furnished at any time is excludable. Examples of situations where meals may qualify for the exclusion are 1) where there are insufficient eating facilities near the place of employment, or 2) where the peak workload period occurs during the normal lunch hour.

The meaning of "on the employer's business premises" should be clear; however, it has been the source of considerable IRS-taxpayer litigation. The U.S. Tax Court has held that the term "business premises" should mean either the living quarters that constitute an integral part of the employer's business property, or premises on which the company conducts some of its business activities. The Sixth Circuit Court of Appeals held that the employer's business premises are the locations where either the employee performs a significant portion of his or her duties or the locations where the employer conducts a significant portion of its business.

When it is said that lodging must be accepted as a "condition of employment" in order to be excludable, it is meant that the employee must be required to accept the lodging in order to enable him or her to properly perform the duties of his or her employment. This requirement will be considered satisfied in cases where the employee must be available for duty at all times or where the employee cannot perform the services required of him or her unless he or she is furnished the lodging. Accordingly, if the employee has the option of accepting or rejecting the lodging, no exclusion will be allowed. The exclusion test may be satisfied if the employer-furnished lodging provides important benefits or advantages to the employer or otherwise facilitates job performance. Hence, it is not necessary to show that the employee's duties would be impossible to perform without the provision of the lodging.

A simple example is a firefighter. While he or she may live only 15 minutes away from the fire station, one of the requirements of being on duty is to reside at the fire station. This is so that response time can be measured in seconds from the sounding of the alarm to being ready to leave the fire station.

Education Assistance Programs

A second common non-insurance benefit is education assistance, most commonly reimbursement for education expenses incurred by employees when improving job skills and knowledge. Some companies offer benefits when the education is unrelated to the job, and some go even further to offer education assistance to children or dependents of employees.

The payment can cover tuition, fees, books, equipment, and supplies, and the employer may pay directly for the course instead of offering reimbursement. The course does not have to be job-related, but if it involves sports, games, or hobbies, it must be related to the employer's business or be required as part of a degree program. Qualified courses can be taken at any educational level.

If the education assistance program is set up properly and reimburses employees for improving job-related skills, the benefits are generally income tax free. Beyond specified limits, all benefits are taxable as earned income. Generally, IRC §127 permits an employer to make payments up to $5,250 (currently) annually to an employee as reimbursement for qualified education expenses on an income-tax-free basis. As with other benefit programs that have income tax benefits, it must not discriminate, and it must be in writing before any course is undertaken. Annual reporting is required to ensure nondiscrimination. Not more than 5 percent of the amounts paid or incurred by the employer for educational assistance during the year may be provided to shareholders or owners of the business each of whom (on any day of the year) owns directly or indirectly more than 5 percent of the business (the concentration test). As an added benefit, the plan can provide income-tax-free benefits to prior employees, such as retired, laid-off, or disabled employees. If there are any tools or supplies that become property of the employee upon completion of the course, any payment made for those items is not income tax free. The same is true for meals, transportation, and lodging.

While this is an excellent benefit that tells employees that the employer cares about them and their growth, the downside of these programs is that the employer may be funding the education of an employee who will want to leave as soon as he or she is qualified for a better job. Employers generally deal with this issue by providing growth opportunities within the company as employees become better educated.

Dependent Care Assistance Plans

Societal and workforce changes often bring about the need for additional types of employee benefits. A dependent care assistance plan is one such type of benefit. Such a plan can take one of two forms. It can reimburse employees for daycare and other dependent care expenses or, alternatively, it can provide an actual daycare center or similar arrangement. If structured correctly, the expenses paid by the employer are tax deductible as compensation under IRC Section 162 and nontaxable to employees under IRC Section 129. Such a plan can be fully or partially funded through employee salary reductions under a flexible spending account (FSA) discussed in chapter 15.

Qualifying dependent care assistance expenses must be for care alone, not for education above the kindergarten level. The following items qualify as care:

- Full preschool and kindergarten expenses (full tuition and fees for these programs)
- After-school programs for children under 13
- Summer camp for children under 13 (however, expenses for overnight summer camp do not qualify)
- Cost of a housekeeper/sitter for children or other dependents cared for at home (the taxpayer must report the correct name, address and taxpayer identification number of the care provider on his or her tax return)

IRC Section 129 contains several nondiscrimination rules for such plans. For example:

- Eligibility, contributions, and benefits must not discriminate in favor of highly compensated employees or their dependents
- No more than 25 percent of the benefits may be provided to the class of employees composed of persons who own more than a 5 percent interest in the employer
- Eligible employees must receive reasonable notice of the availability of benefits and the terms of the plan
- An annual statement must be provided by January 31 of the following year to each employee showing the amounts paid or expenses incurred by the employer for the employee's benefit in the current year
- The average benefit provided to non-highly compensated employees must be at least 55 percent of the average benefit provided to highly compensated employees

However, an employer is permitted to exclude employees who (1) are under age 21, (2) have not completed one year of service, or (3) are covered by a collective-bargaining unit that has bargained for dependent-care benefits. Failure to comply with these nondiscrimination rules makes plan benefits taxable, but only to highly compensated participants.

In order to obtain the aforementioned income tax benefits, assistance under such plans is limited to (1) a child under 13 for whom the employee-taxpayer is entitled to take a dependency deduction on his or her income tax return or (2) a taxpayer's dependent or spouse who is physically or mentally unable to care for him- or herself. The amount that may be excluded with respect to dependent care services provided during a taxable year is currently limited to $5,000 ($2,500 for a married person filing a separate return). Further, the value of dependent care assistance in excess of the exclusion limit must be included in gross income in the taxable year in which the dependent care services are provided (even if payment for those services is made in another year). These limits apply to the employee, not to each child.

Moreover, the amount excludable under IRC Section 129 cannot exceed (1) the earned income of an unmarried employee or (2) in the case of an employee who is married, the lesser of the employee's earned income or the earned income of the employee's spouse. However, earned income may be imputed for spouses who are physically or mentally incapable of caring for themselves or who are full-time students. No exclusion is permitted to the extent that employer dependent care assistance payments are made (1) to an individual who qualifies as an income tax dependent of the employee or his or her spouse; or (2) to a child of the employee under age 19 as of the close of the taxable year.

Dependent care assistance programs must be in writing but need not be funded in order to qualify for the previously discussed income tax benefits.

Qualified Adoption Assistance Plans

While natural parents have long enjoyed the benefits made available to them for maternity and child birth expenses, adoptive parents have historically not received such benefits. Under IRC Section 137(a), gross income of an employee does not include amounts paid or expenses incurred by the employee's employer for qualified adoption expenses in connection with the adoption of a child by the employee where the amounts are furnished under an adoption assistance program.

Qualified adoption expenses include reasonable and necessary adoption fees, court costs, attorney's fees, and other expenses which are (1) directly related to, and the principal purpose of which is for, the legal adoption of a qualified child by the employee; (2) not incurred in violation of state or federal law or in carrying out any surrogate parenting arrangement; and (3) not incurred in connection with the adoption of a child of the employee's spouse. An eligible child is any individual who is less than 18 years old, who is physically or mentally incapable of caring for him- or herself, or who is a child with special needs, as specifically defined.

In the case of foreign adoptions, no exclusion is allowed until the adoption becomes final (in the event it is finalized, adoption expenses incurred before that event can be taken into account.) Also, married couples must file joint income tax returns to get the exclusion, and the name, age, and taxpayer identification number of the child must be placed on the employee's return.

The maximum amount excludable for all taxable years on account of the adoption of a child by an employee cannot exceed $10,000 (adjusted for inflation annually beginning in 2003; the amount for tax year 2005 is $10,630). The exclusion is a per-child limit. The excludable amount for any taxable year is phased out ratably for employees with adjusted gross income of from $150,000 to $190,000 (adjusted upward for inflation beginning in 2003—the 2004 inflation-adjusted range is $155,860 to $195,860).

As is the case with dependent care assistance plans and other similar plans, an adoption assistance plan must be in writing and operated for the exclusive benefit of the employer's employees. Further, the plan must meet requirements similar to the nondiscrimination and eligibility rules, the concentration test, and the plan notification rules that apply under IRC Section 127(b) to education assistance plans discussed earlier.

IRC Section 132 and 117(d) Fringe Benefits

In the Tax Reform Act of 1984, Congress codified the tax treatment of a number of miscellaneous fringe benefits whose tax treatment prior to that time had been uncertain or unclear and based only on the vagaries of administrative and judicial law. Congress enacted IRC Sections 132 and 117(d) to provide statutory treatment of these miscellaneous fringe benefits. The following types of fringe benefits are (under appropriate circumstances) excludable from gross income:

1. No-additional-cost services
2. Qualified employee discounts
3. Working condition fringes
4. *De minimis* fringe benefits
5. Qualified transportation fringes
6. Qualified moving expense reimbursements
7. Qualified retirement planning services
8. Qualified tuition reductions

If the above miscellaneous fringe benefits are excludable for income tax purposes, they are also excludable for FICA and FUTA tax purposes. The employer will ordinarily be permitted to take a tax deduction for the cost to the employer of providing these fringe benefits rather than for the value of such benefits to the employee.

No-Additional-Cost Services

Employers in many service industries provide their employees with free or discounted services. Examples include excess airline, bus, or train tickets, unused hotel rooms, or telephone services provided free or at a reduced price. The cost of these services is not considered to be taxable income to employees, if the following rules are observed:

- The services must be provided in a nondiscriminatory manner, not favoring highly compensated employees. If such services are provided in a manner that discriminates in favor of highly compensated employees, only the nonhighly compensated employees will be permitted to exclude the benefits.

- The employer cannot incur any substantial additional cost or lost revenue in providing the services, determined without regard to what the employee pays for the service. Therefore, any reimbursement by an employee for the cost of providing the service does not affect the determination of whether the employer incurs substantial additional cost.

- The services must be provided in the employer's line of business in which the employee actually works.

Such a no-additional-cost service must be offered for sale to nonemployee customers in the ordinary course of the employer's line of business in which the employee is performing services.

Qualified Employee Discounts

Many manufacturing and retailing businesses offer discounts on their products or merchandise to employees. Just as with no-additional-cost services, the discounts must be made available on a nondiscriminatory basis on goods or services ordinarily sold to the public in the employer's line of business in which the employee works. For discounts on qualified property, the discount cannot exceed the gross profit percentage on the normal public selling price. However, unlike no-additional-cost services described previously and any other IRS Section 132 fringe benefits, the term "customer" includes employee customers for purposes of the qualified employee discount exclusion. The effect of this rule is to reduce the excludable qualified employee discount amount since the price at which qualified property and services are sold to employees negatively affects the overall normal price of the qualified property on which the allowable discounts are computed. In general, an employer must determine the gross profit percentage on the basis of all property offered to customers (including employees) in each separate line of business.

For services, the tax-free discount cannot exceed 20 percent of the normal public selling price. If the discount exceeds 20 percent, the excess is subject to income taxes.

Working Condition Fringes

Where an employer provides property or services to an employee, the fair market value of such property or services is not taxable to the employee to the extent the costs of such property or services would be deductible by the employee under IRC Section 162 or 167 (without regard to the normal two percent of adjusted gross income limitation) as an employee business expense, if the employee paid for the property or services. In order to be treated as tax-free to the employee, the expenses must be ordinary or necessary under Section 162 and related to or associated with the active conduct of the employer's trade or business as required under IRC Section 274(a). This would apply to uniforms or other equipment employees are required to have on the job that becomes their personal property.

The normal nondiscrimination rules for fringe benefits do not apply to working condition fringes. Also, a cash payment made by an employer to an employee will not qualify as a working condition fringe unless the employer requires the employee to (1) use the payment for expenses in connection with a specific or prearranged activity or undertaking for which a deduction is allowable under IRC Sections 162 or 167; (2) verify that the payment is actually used for such expenses; and (3) return to the employer any part of the payment not so used.

A classic example of a working condition fringe is an employee's use of a company car or airplane for valid business purposes. The use of company vehicles and airplanes for personal purposes is not excludable. Moreover, employer-provided transportation must meet all of the requirements for excludability as a working condition fringe benefit in order to be excludable. To illustrate how employee use of a company vehicle is treated for income tax purposes, let us examine the following example:

Example: An employer provides an employee with a car for the entire year. Assume that the value of the use of the car is $6,000. If the employee drives the car 10,000 miles for the employer's business purposes and 2,000 miles for personal use, the working condition fringe benefit that is excludable would be $5,000 (10,000 /12,000 x $6,000). The other $1,000 would not be excludable.

Instead of excluding the value of a working condition fringe benefit with respect to an automobile, an employer may use what is known as the lease valuation rule of IRS Regulation 1.61-21 to include in an employee's gross income the entire annual lease value of the automobile. In this case, the employee can take a miscellaneous itemized deduction (subject to the two percent of AGI limitation) on his or her tax return for the business-related use of the automobile.

Other examples of working condition fringes include payment of bar association dues by a law firm, employer payment of club dues to provide membership in a club to an employee for business purposes only or provision of travel allowances for the spouse or other companion of an employee on a business trip for the employer (if not treated by the employer as deductible compensation payments), the subscription cost of business-related periodicals, and the value of fringes provided for an employee's safety, where necessary, including a bodyguard, a car and driver, or a car designed for security where such a need is demonstrated. Also, job placement assistance provided by a worker's employer can be excluded as a working condition fringe benefit if the employer obtains a "substantial business benefit" from providing the job placement assistance to the workers. A substantial business benefit is obtained by the employer if the job placement assistance is established to promote a positive corporate image, maintain employee morale, avoid wrongful termination suits, foster a positive work atmosphere, and/or help attract quality employees. Of course, the exclusion is not available if the employee can elect to receive cash or other taxable benefits in place of the job placement assistance.

Example: An employer-provided service that is not considered to be a working condition fringe benefit is employer-provided tax preparation for employees.

De minimis Fringe Benefits

Under IRC Section 132(e)(1), the value of any property that (after taking into account the frequency with which similar fringes are provided by the employer) has such a small value that accounting for it would be "unreasonable or administratively impractical" is considered to be excludable as a *de minimis* fringe benefit. The fringes that qualify for exclusion as *de minimis* fringe benefits are ones that otherwise would be includible in gross income. Generally, the less frequent an item is furnished and the lower the value of an item furnished to employees, the more likely the item can be excluded as a *de minimis* fringe benefit.

Examples of *de minimis* fringe benefits include:

1. The occasional typing of a letter by a company secretary
2. Occasional personal use of employer copying machines

3. Infrequent use of the employer's automobile

4. Certain holiday gifts or property with a low market value, such as a holiday turkey given to employees

The electronic filing of an employee's individual income tax return by the employer and the provision of income tax preparation services by volunteers on the employer's premises, but not (as discussed earlier) payments by an employer to an income tax preparer for services provided in preparing an employee's income tax return, are considered *de minimis* fringe benefits.

De minimis fringe benefits also include the operation by the employer of any eating facility (either owned or leased by the employer) for employees if the facility is located on or near the business premises of the employer and the revenue derived from the facility normally equals or exceeds the direct operating costs of the facility. The meals furnished at the facility must be provided during or immediately before or after the employees' working hours. For this purpose, beginning in 1998, an employee entitled under IRC Section 119 (Meals and Lodging Furnished for the Convenience of the Employer) to exclude the value of a meal provided at the eating facility will be treated as having paid an amount for that meal equal to the direct operating costs of the facility attributable to that meal. In addition, if more than one half of employees to whom meals are provided by an employer on the employer's business premises are provided for the convenience of the employer, then all of the meals furnished by the employer on its business premises to employees will be regarded as furnished for the convenience of the employer. Cash reimbursement of an employee's meal expenses is included in gross income. If meals are furnished for the convenience of the employer, they must be furnished for substantial noncompensatory business reasons (such as having the employee on call) rather than as additional compensation.

As discussed earlier in this chapter, lodging furnished to employees by an employer, a spouse, or dependents for the employer's convenience is not includible in the employee's gross income if, in the case of lodging, the employee is required to accept the lodging on the employer's business premises as a condition of employment.

Qualified Transportation Fringes

Under IRC Section 132(f)(1), the following fringe benefits are excludable as qualified transportation fringes:

1. Transportation of the employee in a commuter highway vehicle between the employee's residence and place of employment (excludable up to $105 per month in 2005)

2. Any transit pass provided to an employee (excludable up to $105 per month in 2005) (This limit is a combined limit with number 1 above.)

3. Qualified employee parking (excludable up to $200 per month in 2005, adjusted annually for inflation) provided on or near the business premises of the employer or on or near a location from which the employee commutes to work by mass transit, in a commuter highway vehicle, or by carpool. Does not apply to parking on or near property used by the employee for residential purposes.

Beginning in 1998, an employer may offer an employee a choice of one or more qualified transportation benefits or the cash equivalent without loss of the exclusion. The amount is includible if the cash option is chosen.

Qualified Moving Expense Reimbursement

Some companies help pay the moving expenses for employees who take jobs with different offices located far from their current job site. Others will help pay moving expenses to attract new employees. Some companies desire employees to be flexible and capable of working in any of the company's geographically diverse sites. Covering moving expenses helps ease transitions. Employers do not have to withhold taxes from reimbursements for expenses that it reasonably believes will be deductible by the employee. Taxes must be withheld for any reimbursements for non-deductible expenses.

For moving expenses to be deductible, the employee's new workplace must be at least 50 miles farther from the employee's previous home than the employee's former workplace, and the employee must work full time for at least 39 weeks for the business during the twelve months following the move. Discrimination testing is not a problem. A business can cover moving expenses differently for different employees, or can even provide it for only one employee.

Expenses that are deductible under IRC Section 217 include packing and/or crating and moving household goods and personal effects. Personal effects may include pets and personal automobiles. The cost of connecting and disconnecting utilities may also be covered as well as storage and insurance costs incurred within the 30 days after moving from the original residence but before moving into the new one. Also deductible is $.15 per mile for travel to the new home (2005) if using the employee's personal vehicle. The cost of meals consumed during travel is not deductible. Generally, any expenses not listed above will not be deductible by the employee. Reimbursements in excess of the amount deductible under IRC Section 217 are taxable to the employee. Some employers pay employees a taxable bonus to cover the income taxes payable on these other nondeductible moving expense reimbursements.

Moving expenses are not considered a welfare benefit plan and do not come under the requirements of ERISA or require any special reporting by the employer.

The employer's moving expense reimbursement plan must meet the following requirements:
1. Under the moving expense reimbursement plan, advances, allowances, or reimbursements must be provided only for deductible moving expenses incurred by the employee.
2. The plan must require the employee to substantiate the expenses to the employer, unless the expenses are of a type for which substantiation is not required.
3. Advancements or reimbursements in excess of substantiated expenses covered under the plan must be required to be returned to the employer.

Qualified Retirement Planning Services

Beginning in 2002, the value of qualified retirement planning services provided to employees is excludable. Qualified retirement planning services are defined as any retirement planning advice or information that is provided to an employee and his or her spouse by an employer maintaining a qualified employer plan. However, the exclusion is not available to highly compensated employees unless the retirement planning services are available on substantially the same terms to each member of the group of employees normally provided education and information regarding the employer's qualified retirement plan.

Qualified employer plans include the typical qualified plans offered by employers, including 401(k) plans, SIMPLE plans, defined benefit pension plans, and others. The exclusion is not limited to information concerning the qualified plan, and therefore, for example, applies to advice and information about retirement income planning for an employee and his or her spouse and how the employer's plan fits into the employee's overall retirement income plan. The exclusion does not apply to other services that may be related to retirement planning, such as tax preparation, accounting, legal, or brokerage services.

Qualified Tuition Reduction Plans

A qualified tuition reduction plan is not taxable to the recipient under IRC Section 117(d). The term "qualified tuition reduction" means the amount of any tuition reduction provided to an employee of an educational institution for education at that institution below the graduate level. For example, employees of a college would not be taxed if they were permitted to take one undergraduate class at no cost. A special rule applies to graduate students who are teaching or are research assistants at the educational institution where they are enrolled. They are entitled to exclude the value of tuition reductions they receive on account of their teaching and research activities. The exclusion does not apply to amounts received which represent payment for teaching, research, or other services by the students required as a condition for receiving the qualified tuition reduction.

OTHER FRINGE BENEFITS

In addition to the many benefits already discussed in this chapter and in previous chapters, employers often provide other benefits. We will discuss some of these additional benefits below.

Severance Pay Plans

When certain employees leave a company, they receive a severance package. This will certainly include either a lump sum cash payment or a continuation of income for a specified number of months. Since this is compensation to an individual for services rendered, it is deductible by the employer and treated as earned income by the employee, assuming that it meets the reasonable compensation test. Executives with companies generally negotiate severance pay prior to starting work. Plans established in this manner are not subject to the Employee Retirement Income Security Act (ERISA) reporting and can be different for each individual considered. Some employers choose to do an ERISA filing as a safety precaution. These plans may also come under non-qualified deferred compensation rules that are discussed in chapter 17.

For a plan that is available to a wider group of employees to avoid coming under ERISA as a pension plan, it must meet the following requirements:

- Receipt is not contingent on retirement.
- Total payments may not exceed two times the individual's final annual salary.
- Payments must generally be completed within 24 months of separation. For certain programs it may be the later of 25 months after separation from employment or 24 months after the employee reaches normal retirement age.

Meeting all of these requirements will make the plan a welfare benefit plan.

Welfare Benefit Trusts and VEBAs

Another way for an employer to provide employees with life insurance, health and accident benefits, and other fringe benefits is the welfare benefit plan, of which the most common form is the voluntary employee benefit association (VEBA). Under a VEBA or other welfare benefit plan, the employer makes contributions to the plan which, in turn, pays benefits to employee-participants according to the terms of the plan. A VEBA must meet certain statutory and regulatory requirements and nondiscrimination standards as well as the rules governing taxation of employees under the plans and the deductibility of employer contributions to the VEBA. Consequently, a VEBA is a method of advance funding of certain employee benefits.

First, a VEBA is a tax-exempt organization that provides for the payment of life, sick, accident, or similar benefits to the members of the VEBA and/or their dependents. No part of the net earnings can inure (other than through the payment of permitted benefits) to the benefit of any private shareholder or individual. In order to retain its tax-exempt status, a VEBA must satisfy the following four basic requirements:

1. The organization must be an association of employees.
2. The membership in the association is voluntary.
3. Substantially all of the VEBA's operations are to provide for the payment of life, sick, accident, or other benefits to its members and/or their dependents or beneficiaries.
4. As mentioned previously, no part of the net earnings of the association can inure (other than through the payment of permitted benefits) to the benefit of any private shareholder or individual.

The membership of a VEBA must consist of individuals who are entitled to participate because they are employees and whose eligibility for membership (according to IRS Reg.§ 1.501(c)(9)-2(a)) is defined by objective standards constituting a "common employment-related bond" between the individuals. Membership in a VEBA that is open to all employees of a particular employer would satisfy the guidelines. Membership is considered voluntary if an affirmative act is required on the part of an employee to become a member or if membership is required of all employees, if the employees do not incur a detriment (such as deductions from pay) as a result of membership in the VEBA.

In addition, a VEBA cannot be controlled by an employer. Instead, it must be controlled by its membership, an independent trustee or trustees (such as a bank), or trustees or other fiduciaries at least some of whom are designated by, or on behalf of, the membership. A VEBA may be established as a nonprofit corporation or a tax-exempt trust. This permits the VEBA to avoid paying income tax on its net earnings.

The following benefits do not qualify for payment by a VEBA:

1. Paying commuting expenses
2. Providing accident or homeowner's insurance benefits for damage to property
3. Providing malpractice insurance
4. Providing loans to members except in times of distress
5. Providing savings facilities to members
6. Paying any benefit similar to a pension or annuity at the time of voluntary or mandatory retirement
7. Paying any benefit similar to that provided by a stock bonus or profit-sharing plan

The Tax Reform Act of 1984 (TRA '84) established statutory coverage and benefits nondiscrimination standards for VEBAs. They are similar to the standards applicable to other employee benefits, such as those for medical reimbursement plans. A VEBA is nondiscriminatory only if 1) each class of benefits is made available to a classification of employees set forth in the plan and is found by the IRS to not favor the highly compensated, and 2) each class of benefits is not provided in a manner that discriminates in favor of highly compensated employees. Certain employees may be excluded from consideration, including those who 1) have not attained the age of 21; 2) have not completed three years of service with the employer; 3) work less than half-time; 4) are included in a collective bargaining unit, or 5) are nonresident aliens.

With regard to the taxation of VEBA benefits, the taxation of each particular benefit received is based on the taxation rules applicable to that benefit under the IRC. If employer contributions to a welfare benefit plan qualify as ordinary and necessary expenses, they are deductible under IRC Section 419 in the year paid into the VEBA to the extent the contributions do not exceed the "qualified cost" of the welfare benefit fund for the fund's taxable year that relates to the employer's taxable year. In other words, employer contributions are deductible if they are actuarially reasonable and designated to fund the benefits provided through the VEBA. Employer contributions in excess of the amount deductible under Section 419 can be carried over to later taxable years, assuming they are deductible to begin with. Employer premium payments or other funding deposits to the VEBA are generally not taxable to employees. As a result, such payments are treated the same as they would be if there was no VEBA and the employer maintained the plan without a VEBA.

Some of the advantages of a VEBA to an employer include:

1. The acceleration of the deductibility of employee benefit costs by pre-funding those costs
2. The added security for all covered employees by placing funding amounts in trust, for the exclusive benefit of employees, beyond the reach of corporate creditors, and not subject to reversion to the employer

These advantages are offset by a few disadvantages, including:

1. The relative complexity and cost of installing and administering them. They are generally not for small employers unless they use a vendor of "packaged" plans.
2. The loss of some degree of control over plan design, investments, and, to some extent, tax consequences because of the practical necessity of using a multiple-employer plan
3. The effective prohibition of reversion of assets to the employer

Golden Parachutes

In light of the recent increase in the number of corporate takeovers, executives and other key employees have negotiated contracts requiring their employer to make large cash and/or property payments to them in the event of a successful takeover. Such payments are known as golden parachute payments and are often used as a defense against such takeovers by obligating the acquiring corporation to make the required payments. However, they often have the effect of reducing resistance to a takeover by certain key employees who would receive large payments after the takeover is completed. The term comes from the fact that senior executives generally lose their jobs when their company is taken over. The golden parachute provides a soft financial landing when this happens.

Under IRC Section 280G(a), excess golden parachute payments made to "disqualified individuals" are not deductible. Moreover, under IRC Section 4999, the recipients of excess golden parachute payments are subject to a nondeductible 20 percent excise tax on the excess and the employer must deduct and withhold the excise tax from payments made to an employee. At the same time, excess parachute payments are also fully taxable to the recipient and are subject to FICA and FUTA taxes. To make matters even worse, the usual $1 million deduction limitation on an executive's compensation is reduced by the amount of that executive's excess parachute payments.

A "disqualified individual," for golden parachute payment purposes, is any individual who is an employee or independent contractor of the corporation and is, with respect to the corporation, a shareholder, officer or highly compensated individual. A shareholder is anyone who owns stock of a corporation with a fair market value that exceeds one percent of the fair market value of the outstanding shares of all classes of stock of the corporation. For golden parachute purposes, a highly compensated individual is an individual who is a member of the group which consists of the lesser of (a) the highest paid one percent of the employees of the corporation, or (b) the highest paid 250 employees of the corporation, unless that individual's annualized compensation is less than the amount determined under IRC Section 414(q)(1)(B)(1) (the alternative highly compensated individual test used for many other benefit purposes).

A parachute payment is compensation to or for the benefit of a disqualified individual if:

1. The payment is contingent on a change in the ownership or effective control of the corporation or in the ownership of a substantial portion of the assets of the corporation, and

2. The aggregate present value of the payments in the nature of compensation to the individual which are contingent on the change equals or exceeds an amount equal to three times the individual's base amount. The base amount is the individual's annualized includible compensation for the most recent five taxable years.

The amount treated as a parachute payment can be reduced by (1) the portion of the payment that the taxpayer establishes is reasonable compensation for personal services to be rendered on or after the date of the takeover and (2) the portion of the payment which the taxpayer proves is reasonable compensation for services actually rendered by the taxpayer before the change in ownership or control occurs.

Employee Achievement Awards

Under IRC Section 274(j), an employer may deduct the cost of an employee achievement award up to $400 for all "nonqualified plan awards." The employer's deduction for the cost of "qualified plan awards" made to a particular employee is limited to $1,600 per year, taking into account all other qualified and nonqualified awards made to that employee during the tax year.

An employee achievement award is an item of tangible personal property awarded to an employee as part of a meaningful presentation for length of service or safety achievement under circumstances that do not create a significant likelihood of disguised compensation.

A qualified plan award is an employee achievement award provided under an established written plan or program that does not discriminate in favor of highly compensated employees as to eligibility or benefits. An employee achievement award is not a qualified plan award if the average cost of all employee achievement awards exceeds $400. Calculation of the average cost includes the entire cost of all qualified plan awards, ignoring employee achievement awards of nominal value.

A length of service award will not qualify if it is received during the employee's first five years of service or if the employee has received a length of service award (other than an award excludable as a *de minimis* fringe benefit, discussed previously) during the year or within the last four years. An award will not be considered a safety achievement award if made to a manager, administrator, clerical employee, or other professional employee or if, during the tax year, awards for safety achievement previously had been made to more than 10 percent of the employees, excluding managers, administrators, clerical employees, or other professional employees.

Employee Assistance Programs

As the trend toward fostering wellness in the workplace continues, an increasing number of employers are establishing employee-assistance programs (EAP), which are designed to help employees with certain personal problems, such as treatment for alcohol or drug abuse; counseling for mental problems and stress; counseling for family and marital problems; financial, legal, and tax advice; referrals for child care or eldercare; and crisis intervention. Studies have shown that proper treatment of these problems is very cost-effective and leads to a reduction in hospital costs, disability claims, the number of sick days, and absenteeism.

Traditionally, employee-assistance programs have used job performance as the basis for employer concern. Typically, no attempt is made by the employee's supervisor to diagnose the specific problem. Several employee-assistance programs act as the gatekeeper for mental health and substance-abuse services. As long as the treatment is for the purpose of alleviating medical conditions, including mental illness, an employee has no taxable income. If the treatment is for a non-medical condition, the employee will have taxable income as the result of employer payments.

Financial Planning Programs

Companies have begun to offer financial planning for executives. Although these leaders are often competent at planning the financial strategies for their organizations, they often focus on their business and leave their personal finances unanalyzed and unmanaged. This benefit may also be offered to lower-level employees on a reduced scale and is often found where there are programs for pre-retirement counseling, another employer sponsored benefit.

Financial planning programs provided for specific individuals are deductible by the employer as long as the employee's overall compensation is reasonable. The employee also must report the amount of any fees paid to a financial planning firm or other professional on the employee's behalf as income. However, an employee may be able to take miscellaneous itemized deductions for certain services relating to tax and investment advice. Services that the employer provides to executives on an individual basis also result in taxable income. Programs provided to employees in general via newsletters, seminars, or group meetings are not taxable to the employees.

Legal Services Plans: Prepaid Legal Services Plans

While still uncommon, over the last 15 to 20 years, legal benefit plans have been developed to address the problems average citizens face when it comes to legal issues, such as covering expenses and finding a lawyer that will help when needed. Prepaid legal expense plans do just that. A participating law firm or group of law firms generally accepts a level monthly payment and provides certain legal services at no additional charge or at substantially reduced charges to covered employees. This often includes drafting or updating wills, writing letters to creditors or businesses that have not lived up to their obligations, reviewing contracts, and providing general legal advice. The expenses of the plan are deductible to the employer. If the plan is funded in advance, the amount of deductible advance funding is limited to approximately the benefits provided during the taxable year plus administrative expenses. Under such pre-funded plans (i.e., where the employer pays a group legal plan payment to a plan provider), the employee is taxed on his or her share of the cost at the time the employer pays it (assuming the employee is fully vested in the benefit at that time). The benefits should then be received tax-free. If, on the other hand, the employer pays for benefits out of current revenues as employees receive benefits, the employee is taxed on the value of benefits as they are received.

There are a number of variations in legal expense plans, and they are not all available throughout the country. Some provide only access to a legal firm with discounted fees, while others provide substantial services with no additional fees and other services at reduced fees. All have some exclusions, a quite common one being that the plan will not provide benefits that may be used in a dispute with the employer. The advantage these plans provide is that when an employer sponsors the plan and sends a sizeable check to the law firm each month, the individual's small piece of business may be given more attention than it might otherwise receive. After all, if too many plan members complain about bad service, the plan may well change law firms. Some law firms specialize in this type of practice and realize the importance of every call.

Much like variations in health care plans, benefits may be provided on a scheduled basis with a certain amount available for certain benefits—sometimes shown through a limited list of services that are provided. Alternatively, benefits may be comprehensive, providing all necessary legal services, except those that are excluded or limited, such as audits by the IRS, contingent fee cases or class action suits, and actions arising out of the employee's separate business transactions. A third approach might be called an indemnity plan: It reimburses employees for qualified legal expenses. These plans generally have a dollar limit for a given legal service, a maximum hourly rate, or a maximum annual benefit.

Most plans will provide the following services at a minimum:

- Preparation of a simple will for the employee and his or her spouse
- Preparation and/or review of deeds, powers-of-attorney, and other routine legal documents
- General legal consultations and advice on practically any legal matter
- Adoption proceedings
- Juvenile proceedings
- Domestic law work (divorce, separation, and child custody)
- Personal bankruptcy
- Defense of civil and criminal matters (commonly limited)

Prepaid plans are more common than indemnity-type plans. In a prepayment plan there is no direct expenditure by employees. Employees are required to obtain covered services from specified groups of lawyers employed by or under contract with the plan.

Holiday Bonuses

Many companies offer a holiday bonus in the form of cash or other personal property. Cash is typically subject to income tax, but other types of personal property generally are not, as long as their value is small. This type of gift is included in the $1,600 allowance (see "Employee Achievement Awards") a company can give in awards and gifts each year to an employee without the employee incurring a tax liability.

Wellness Programs

Some employers offer seminars on many topics related to healthy living, mental and physical well-being, exercise, and others. Some provide exercise equipment and some large companies have a full-time staff in a health facility. On a periodic basis, some companies send a wellness newsletter. Additionally, some companies offer a discount on the employee's share of the health insurance premium if the employee and spouse attend some of these seminars or programs. Medical screening programs may be provided on the company property, or the company can use the resources of other organizations. And lifestyle management programs, such as smoking cessation and weight loss clinics, may be offered at company expense or subsidized by the company.

Unless the cost of providing lifestyle management programs is *de minimis*, participation will probably result in taxation to employees. The costs of programs that promote general health, such as programs for smoking cessation or weight control, are not considered medical expenses. While the cost of providing these programs to employees is deductible by the employer, an employee will incur taxable income unless the purpose of the program is to alleviate a specific medical problem. There is one exception to this general rule: Employees incur no taxable income as a result of being provided with or using athletic facilities that are located on the employer's premises.

Athletic Facilities

In the situation where an employer provides the use of an on-premises athletic facility to its employees, such use is not taxable to the employees. An on-premises athletic facility is any gym or athletic facility located on the premises of the employer, operated by the employer, and substantially all the use of which is by employees of the employer, their spouses, and their dependent children.

The facility does not have to be located on the employer's business premises but it must be located on premises owned and operated by the employer and cannot be a facility for residential use, such as a resort. Qualifying facilities include gyms, swimming pools, tennis courts, golf courses, and running and bicycle paths.

The athletic facilities exclusion does not apply to any membership in an athletic facility (including health clubs or country clubs) unless the facility is owned or leased and operated by the employer and used substantially by the employer's employees.

INCOME TAX RAMIFICATIONS OF EMPLOYEE BENEFITS

We have attempted to describe the income tax implications of each employee benefit as it is discussed. However, it should be added that in the area of employee benefits, all compensation to an individual is considered, including benefits, under IRC Section 162 to determine if his or her compensation is reasonable. If it is not reasonable, the business may not deduct the payments, and the employee still must report it as income. "Reasonable compensation" is also not addressed directly by the code. This limiting language does not mean an employee cannot be paid $1 million in salary plus other benefits. If a comparable position in other comparable companies earns that level of income, or it is clear that attracting a capable person to that position requires an income at that level, it is reasonable. On the other hand, if the child of a senior partner were being paid $100,000 a year to be mailroom clerk, the courts would deem him or her to be receiving unreasonable compensation.

The code also uses the terms "ordinary and necessary" to describe those items that are deductible, but it does not define either term. Instead, federal courts are left to interpret the intent and apply it to a particular set of facts. "Ordinary" has generally been held by the courts to mean "normal, common, and accepted under the circumstances by the business community" while "necessary" means "appropriate and helpful." Taken together, the legal consensus is that "ordinary and necessary" refers to the purpose for which an expense is incurred.

Nondiscrimination

For some of the benefits discussed above and throughout the text, there are special nondiscrimination rules. Wherever these rules exist, they are for the purpose of making sure a business does not favor highly compensated employees with extra benefits while ignoring other employees.

For certain benefits, there is a definition of highly compensated employees that applies under IRC § 414(q)(1). For these benefits, employees meeting either of the following are considered highly compensated employees:

- The employee currently owns 5 percent or more of the firm, or did in the last year.
- The employee received employment compensation in the preceding year from the employer in an amount over $95,000 (for 2005), indexed for inflation, and, if the employer elects, was among the top 20 percent of employees by compensation for the preceding year.

Seemingly just to keep things confusing, this definition is different from the definition used to determine highly compensated employees for other benefits.

It is clear that those who provide advice to employers regarding employee benefit plans must be specialists.

NON-INSURANCE BENEFITS AND FINANCIAL PLANNING

Sound financial planning is more than dealing with the money coming in and going out; it requires taking advantage of ways to save money and maximize one's resources. This chapter has pointed out that employee benefits may extend well beyond the basics of a health plan, group life insurance, and a retirement plan. The employee benefit package offered by a given employer may be quite comprehensive. Financial planners have ample opportunity to point out to clients the value of benefits that too many employees take for granted—even though the cost to the employer can run from 30 to 70 percent of an employee's salary. Planners need to help their clients reap the maximum advantage from their employee benefit plans.

IMPORTANT CONCEPTS

Adoption assistance plans (qualified)

Athletic facilities

De minimis fringe benefits

Dependent care assistance plans

Education assistance programs

Employee achievement awards

Employee assistance programs

Employee discounts (qualified)

Exempt and non-exempt employees

Family and Medical Leave Act of 1993 (FMLA)

Financial planning programs

Golden parachute plans

Highly compensated employee

Holiday bonuses

IRC §132 fringe benefits

IRC §162

Jury duty

Legal services plans: prepaid legal services plans

Meals and lodging furnished for the convenience of the employer

Moving expense reimbursement (qualified)

National Guard/Reserve duty

No-additional-cost services

Pay for time not worked

Personal time off (PTO) plans

Reasonable compensation

Retirement planning services (qualified)

Sabbaticals

Severance pay plans

Sick-pay or sick-leave plans

Transportation fringes (qualified)

Tuition reduction plans (qualified)

Voluntary employees' beneficiary association (VEBA)

Welfare benefit trust

Wellness programs

Working condition fringes

January : Fundamentals
February : Investments
March : Income tax
July : Retirement
Sept : Estate

November 2008

QUESTIONS FOR CONSIDERATION

1. What is the purpose of IRC §162 and how does it relate to employee benefits?

2. How does a sick-pay or sick-leave plan generally operate?

3. What is accomplished by putting a sick pay plan in writing?

4. How does a typical PTO plan operate?

5. What problems are solved by the use of a PTO plan?

6. What is the difference between exempt and non-exempt employees?

7. What is the test for determining if moving expense reimbursements are income-tax-free to an employee?

8. What limits are there on employer-provided transportation and/or parking benefits?

9. What is the purpose of the FMLA?

10. Under what circumstances can an employer deny the request of an employee for leave under the FMLA?

11. What basic requirements must be met for meals and lodging to be received free of income tax by an employee?

12. What is the income tax treatment of an education assistance plan, a dependent care assistance plan, and a qualified adoption assistance plan?

13. What is meant by a "no-additional-cost service" to employees?

14. What constitutes a qualified employee discount?

15. Give examples of a working condition fringe.

16. What constitutes a *de minimis* fringe benefit?

17. What types of moving expenses qualify for tax-free reimbursement?

18. What is the definition of qualified retirement planning services?

19. What is the primary income tax advantage of a VEBA?

20. How does a prepaid legal services plan operate and what are the income tax advantages of such a plan?

SUGGESTIONS FOR FURTHER READING

Benefits Facts 2005, National Underwriter, 2005

Employee Benefits, 7th ed., Burton T. Beam, Jr., John J. McFadden, Dearborn Financial Publishing, Inc., 2005.

ERISA Facts 2005, National Underwriter, 2005

Fundamentals of Risk and Insurance, 9th ed., Emmett J. Vaughan and Therese M. Vaughan, Wiley, 2003.

Tax Facts On Insurance & Employee Benefits 2005, National Underwriter, 2005.

The Tools and Techniques of Employee Benefit and Retirement Planning, 9th ed., Stephan R. Leimberg and John J. McFadden, National Underwriter, 2005.

CHAPTER SEVENTEEN

Nonqualified Deferred Compensation

• • •

Corporate leaders—those who can successfully develop and share a vision for the future of a company—are sought by every business that hopes to survive and grow in a changing economy. As part of the effort to attract and retain these leaders, companies use creative executive benefit packages. This chapter introduces these benefit packages, focusing on nonqualified deferred compensation. Other executive benefits will be discussed in the following chapters.

When you have completed this chapter, you will be able to:

- Describe the general characteristics and advantages of nonqualified deferred compensation plans and compare them with qualified plans
- Describe the doctrines of economic benefit, constructive receipt, and substantial risk of forfeiture as they pertain to the taxation of nonqualified deferred compensation
- Describe the various methods of informal funding of nonqualified deferred compensation plans
- Compare and contrast the various types of nonqualified deferred compensation plans

EXECUTIVE BENEFIT ALTERNATIVES

Some executives are interested only in salary or stock options, while others require a comprehensive package of benefits. Employers want to supply whatever benefits are necessary to recruit and retain these executives, but are concerned about providing these incentives for an executive who may leave shortly thereafter. Some companies offer benefits outright, while others only do so with strings attached. These benefits might include:

Additional Medical Reimbursement Benefits

Most health care plans limit certain types of treatments, have co-pays or deductibles, and may exclude certain treatments. Medical reimbursement benefits for selected executives may pay for all of these otherwise out-of-pocket expenses.

Cash Bonus and Incentive Plans

These plans can take many forms. They are typically tied to the success of the business. They may require that the executive remain with the company for a specified number of years.

Corporate Loans to Executives

Under IRC Section 7872, if an employer loans an employee more than $10,000 at less than the applicable federal rate (AFR), the employer is deemed to have paid additional compensation to the employee equal to the foregone interest (difference between AFR interest and interest actually collected from the employee). Moreover, if one of the principal purposes of the loan is the avoidance of federal tax, Section 7872 applies to any employer-employee loan, regardless of amount. The amount treated as additional compensation is taxable to the employee and deductible by the employer as compensation under IRC Section 162. This same amount is also treated as a payment of imputed nondeductible personal interest (unless it can be classified as investment interest) that is includible in the gross income of the employer. There are four exceptions to the rule requiring recognition of foregone interest: (1) loans made available to the general public at the same below market rate; (2) loans without significant tax effect on either the employer or employee; (3) loans under $10,000, unless the principal purpose is the avoidance of federal tax; and (4) an exception for employee relocation loans, under very specific conditions.

Excess Disability Income Benefits

Standard disability income insurance plans will seldom provide benefits in excess of $15,000 per month. Although this would be a substantial sum for most employees, for an executive who is earning a substantial salary, this may represent a significant reduction. Highly paid executives generally negotiate for additional disability coverage.

Life Insurance

This is one of the most common benefits, and it can be offered in a number of different ways, beyond typical group term life insurance. For executives, some sort of permanent (cash value) protection is prevalent. We discuss death benefit only and split-dollar life insurance in chapter 20.

Nonqualified Deferred Compensation

Generally these plans require the executive to remain with the company for a specified number of years in order to receive additional income either during later years of employment or in retirement. Nonqualified deferred compensation is discussed in detail in this chapter.

Restricted Stock or Other Property

This benefit is similar to stock options, except that actual stock or some other property is given to the executive (with restrictions on its sale) rather than options to buy stock at a specified price at a future date. Restricted stock is discussed in chapter 19.

Severance Pay

This benefit includes the so-called golden parachute plans discussed in chapter 16.

Stock Options

Stock options provide the right to purchase stock for a stated price at some time in the future, expecting the executive's efforts to cause the price of the stock to increase. This benefit provides a new executive with an ownership stake in the company that will become valuable only if he or she is successful in increasing the value of the company. They are granted as tax-qualified (or incentive) stock options or as nonqualified stock options. These benefits are covered in chapter 18.

Other Fringe Benefits

The list of miscellaneous fringe benefits offered to executives is typically considerable, including access to a company jet, the executive dining room, chauffeur services, professional financial and estate planning, tax planning, vacation planning services, and education assistance for the executive's children.

NONQUALIFIED DEFERRED COMPENSATION

Simply stated, a nonqualified deferred compensation plan is compensation that is not qualified for the tax-favored status under the requirements of the Internal Revenue Code (IRC), nor under ERISA, as such a plan discriminates for the benefit of specified employees. In attempting to adequately compensate executives and other key employees, employers are limited by the relatively severe requirements for qualified deferred compensation plans, including the maximum contributions that can be made to, and benefits that can be paid from, such plans. Tax-favored employee benefits must

TAX FAVORED BENEFITS are nondiscriminatory.

generally be nondiscriminatory in their application. This may be a good approach for the vast majority of employees, but it means that highly compensated employees receive relatively lower benefits.

While the Economic Growth and Tax Relief Reconciliation Act of 2001 (EGTRRA) increased (1) the maximum dollar contribution (or annual addition) percentage for defined contribution plans to the lesser of (a) 100 percent of compensation or (b) $42,000 (in 2005) and (2) the maximum dollar benefit under defined benefit plans to $170,000 (in 2005, adjusted for inflation annually), such maximums are still relatively small compared to the total amount of compensation paid to some executives and owner-employees. Moreover, under a 401(k) qualified retirement plan, the most an employee under age 50 can defer in any one year is scheduled to gradually increase to $15,000 in 2006. This means that the under-age 50 employee making $75,000 can defer $15,000 in 2006, or 20 percent of his or her income, while the CEO making $350,000 can still defer only this same $15,000, or only 4.3 percent of his or her income. When a long-term employee's retirement benefit from a qualified retirement plan is combined with Social Security benefits, he or she may receive 60 percent or more of his or her pre-retirement income, but a CEO might receive only 25 percent.

Even with a $210,000 maximum amount of employee compensation that can be taken into account (in 2005) in determining permissible contributions to qualified plans, nonqualified plans hold more attraction to highly compensated employees looking for greater retirement income than can be received from qualified plans. Nonqualified plans also are not subject to the vesting and minimum coverage rules applicable to qualified plans.

Nonqualified deferred compensation plans serve other purposes as well. An employer may want to provide retirement benefits for selected employees without having to incur the high cost of providing a retirement plan for all employees. Or the employer may want to provide tax-deferred compensation for certain employees that is different than what is offered to other employees. Some employers use nonqualified deferred compensation as a recruiting tool as well as a way to reward and retain executives. For closely held corporations, such compensation may be the only way to recruit highly skilled leaders who will not be receiving any ownership interest in the business. Finally, the highly compensated employee may want to defer receipt of some income until some point in the future, due to his or her current, high income tax bracket (though this has been somewhat mitigated by reduction in the maximum individual income tax bracket to 35 percent).

Comparison With Qualified Plans

In spite of the limitations discussed in the previous section, qualified deferred compensation plans offer five major tax benefits over nonqualified plans:

1. Deferral of income recognition for the employee until amounts are actually received under the plan

2. Exemption of contributions into (except for elective deferral employee contributions) and distributions from qualified plans from FICA and FUTA taxes

3. Tax-deferred accumulation of earnings on employer and employee contributions to the qualified plan

4. Favorable tax treatment of distributions from qualified plans in certain cases

5. A current deduction, within limits, for employer contributions to qualified deferred compensation plans

Nonqualified plans offer only one of these tax advantages. If properly structured, a nonqualified plan can provide a deferral of income to the recipient-employee (i.e., the employee will not be taxed until he or she receives or has a nonforfeitable right to receive the income). However, the employer does not receive a tax deduction until the employee includes the compensation in gross income.

While qualified plans provide the five major tax benefits just discussed, they come at a fairly high price. In order to receive such benefits, such plans must satisfy an array of nondiscrimination requirements including the following:

1. They must cover a large percentage of the rank and file employees (i.e., those who are not highly compensated under IRC Sections 401 and 410.

2. They are subject to rules which not only limit the deferral of income, but also require minimum funding of benefits (in the case of defined benefit plans) and put a ceiling on employer contributions (in the case of defined contribution plans) under IRC Sections 401, 412, and 415.

3. They must provide for the vesting of employer contributions and earnings on contributions over specified minimum time periods under IRC Section 411.

4. They must make distributions to participants in accordance with restrictions that limit the timing and the amount of the distributions under IRC Sections 401 and 403.

In addition, qualified deferred compensation plans are subject to the fiduciary, reporting and disclosure requirements, as well as other requirements of Title I of the Employee Retirement Income Security Act of 1974 (ERISA). These requirements can significantly increase the cost of maintaining qualified plans for rank-and-file employees.

Nonqualified plans do not have to meet these requirements. Therefore, they can be designed in a more flexible manner so as to provide the particular benefits that are desirable in specific circumstances. For example, a nonqualified plan allows coverage of any group of employees or even a single employee, without any nondiscrimination requirements. Moreover, it can provide an unlimited benefit to any one employee (subject only to the "reasonable compensation" requirement for deductibility). Finally, as discussed previously, it can provide different benefit amounts for different employees, on different terms and conditions.

Nonqualified plans are subject to a minimum of regulatory requirements, such as reporting and disclosure, fiduciary, and funding requirements. In addition, an employer can use such plans to create a disincentive for key employees to leave the employer by designing a vesting schedule and termination contingencies (e.g., terminating employment before retirement, misconduct, or going to work for a competitor) that discourage such early departure.

In addition, it is possible to provide some degree of security for the executive through informal financing arrangements (discussed later in this chapter), while keeping such funds available for corporate purposes at all times.

On the other hand, nonqualified deferred compensation plans carry some disadvantages, including (1) delay in the employer's tax deduction until the income is taxable to the employee; (2) lack of security to the executive who must rely only on the unsecured promise of the employer to pay the benefit; (3) lack of confidentiality due to the possible need for disclosure of such plans on the employer's financial statements; and (4) inability of S corporations and partnerships to take full advantage of such plans.

Design of Nonqualified Plans

From the standpoint of the employee, typically the most important advantage under nonqualified plans is the deferral of income recognition. This assumes that the employee will pay less income tax by having the amounts paid to him or her at some future time when he or she expects to be subject to a lower marginal income tax rate. This may not necessarily turn out to be the case, as income is subjected to inflation. However, the reduction of individual marginal tax rates by the 2001 and 2003 Tax Acts may tend to support this assumption. Moreover, if the employee expects to have higher cash flow needs in the future or needs that will not be met after retirement by Social Security and other retirement income, deferral of a portion of current compensation may make sense.

An additional issue for an employee is to receive interest or to have the deferred amounts invested in some manner so that the deferred amount will be increased by some rate of return. However, if the employer invests such amounts to produce a rate of return, the employer is taxed on the income earned unless the amounts are invested in tax-exempt securities.

Other employee concerns include (1) receiving nonqualified deferred compensation as a retirement supplement to their maximum qualified plan benefits and (2) the ability of the employer to pay the deferred amounts in the future. With regard to the latter concern, any attempt to fund the payment of the deferred amounts or provide the employee with security on the deferred amounts may result in the loss of deferral for income tax recognition purposes. We will discuss this later in the chapter.

From the employer's position, nonqualified deferred compensation can serve to attract and retain key employees by (1) substituting for qualified plan benefits lost to the employee as a result of a job change; (2) permitting certain employees to share in profits to reward superior performance; (3) permitting companies with temporary cash flow problems to offer a larger compensation package for recruiting purposes; and (4) retaining key employees for years into the future by making deferred compensation that is payable to them forfeitable unless they remain employed with the employer for a specific period of time (so-called "golden handcuffs"). In addition, an employer can use nonqualified plans to induce certain employees to take early retirement by supplementing their possibly reduced qualified plan benefits with nonqualified deferred compensation.

Types of Nonqualified Plans

The most popular forms of nonqualified plans include excess benefit plans, supplemental executive retirement plans (SERPs), salary continuation plans, top hat plans, deferred compensation arrangements, restricted stock plans, incentive bonus plans (performance unit plans and phantom stock), stock appreciation rights, and nonqualified stock options. Nonqualified stock options will be discussed in chapter 18. Restricted stock plans, incentive bonus plans, and stock appreciation rights will be discussed in chapter 19.

Excess Benefit Plans

The sole purpose of an excess benefit plan is to provide benefits that exceed the maximum benefit payable by a qualified retirement plan. For example, the maximum benefit under a defined benefit plan is only $170,000 per year in 2005 (adjusted for inflation) and this amount must be actuarially reduced if the employee takes early retirement.

Supplemental Executive Retirement Plans (SERPs)

The benefits payable under a SERP are usually provided in a form similar to defined benefit pension plans (that is, an annuity beginning at retirement and continuing for the remainder of the employee's life). This benefit can be stated as a specified dollar amount or as a percentage of the final year's compensation. It can also be based on the employee's qualified retirement plan benefit and Social Security benefits.

Salary Continuation Plans

Under a salary continuation plan, the employer agrees to continue payment of all or a percentage of the employee's salary in the event of the employee's death or disability for a specified period of years or upon separation from service.

Top Hat Plans

Under ERISA, a top hat plan is an unfunded, nonqualified deferred compensation plan that is "maintained by an employer primarily for the purpose of compensation for a select group of management or highly compensated employees". Under such a plan, the participants must have, by virtue of their position or compensation level, the ability to affect or substantially influence the design and operation of their deferred compensation plan. If top hat plans meet certain requirements, they can be eligible for an alternative method of compliance with the reporting and disclosure requirements of Title I of ERISA. Under this alternative method of compliance, the employer need only provide a statement that the employer maintains a top hat plan or plans, indicate the number of such plans, and provide the number of participants in each plan. Such a plan is not subject to the participation and vesting, funding, fiduciary responsibility, and termination insurance requirements of ERISA.

Deferred Compensation Arrangements

Deferred compensation arrangements, or salary reduction plans, permit the employee to defer receipt of some of his or her current compensation. The amounts deferred are payable at some future time, typically increased by interest.

Important Tax Factors Affecting Nonqualified Deferred Compensation

Great care must be exercised by the employer in designing nonqualified deferred compensation plans to avoid the tax pitfalls presented by such tax doctrines as the constructive receipt doctrine, the economic benefit doctrine, and the substantial risk of forfeiture rules under IRC Section 83.

Constructive Receipt Doctrine

Under IRS Reg. § 1.451-2, income is considered "constructively received" by the taxpayer "in the taxable year during which it is credited to his account, set apart for him, or otherwise made available so that he may draw upon it at any time or so that he could have drawn upon it during the taxable year if notice of intention to withdraw had been given." However, if the taxpayer's control over the receipt of the income is subject to substantial limitations or restrictions (known as a substantial risk of forfeiture, discussed later in this chapter), it is not considered constructively received. Correspondingly, simply crediting a bonus to employees on the employer's books does not constitute receipt if the bonus is not available to employees until some future date. Alternatively, if the employee has unfettered control of the income, it is considered constructively received no matter when the employee chooses to exercise his or her control. In general, a deferred compensation arrangement will be honored by the IRS unless the arrangement is a sham transaction that permits the employee to defer income recognition while simultaneously allowing access to the deferred amounts.

In Revenue Ruling 60-31, the IRS provides the principles under which it will permit the deferral of income recognition under deferred compensation arrangements. The ruling distinguishes between (1) a mere contractual right to receive income at a future date, not evidenced by any type of security and (2) cases in which the employee had the right to receive the compensation income, but instead had it put into trust or escrow for him or her or held on demand by the employer until a future tax year. Under this ruling, a "mere promise to pay, not represented by notes or secured in any way, is not regarded as a receipt of income within the intendment of the cash receipts and disbursements method…". Accordingly, the recognition of compensation can be deferred if the employer and employee enter into a contract to defer a certain amount or percentage of compensation *before the income is earned* (that is, before the services are performed) and the employer does no more than make a basic bookkeeping entry of the liability to pay the deferred amount in the future. Moreover, the employee's future right to the compensation does not have to be subject to a substantial risk of forfeiture and the employer can credit the deferred amount with interest.

Economic Benefit Doctrine

It is important to distinguish between the constructive receipt doctrine and the economic benefit doctrine, as they are often confused. The constructive receipt doctrine indicates *when* income is taxable. The economic benefit doctrine defines *what* constitutes income. The economic benefit doctrine applies where an economic benefit is currently conferred on a taxpayer even though there may be no right and no opportunity on the taxpayer's part to receive the money currently. In general, the economic benefit doctrine will apply to a nonqualified deferred compensation plan that: (1) provides to the employee rights to the employer's property that are in some way superior to those of the employer's general creditors, (2) permits the employee to assign or otherwise anticipate the income before it is due, or (3) conveys some other immediate economic benefit on the employee. What this means is that if funds placed into a nonqualified plan remain subject to the rights of the employer's creditors or if the employee does not have a vested right to those funds, the economic benefit should not apply. Another form of economic benefit is when the employer provides a current benefit to an employee that may not be in the form of cash, but nevertheless has a fair market value measured in dollars. An employee who is provided group life insurance of $250,000 would have the value (the economic benefit) of the amount over $50,000 reported as income.

Substantial Risk of Forfeiture

One of the keys to deferring the recognition of compensation is to make certain that the employee's right to the property is subject to a substantial risk of forfeiture under IRC Section 83. The IRS regulations state that a substantial risk of forfeiture exists where rights in the transferred property are conditioned, directly or indirectly, upon (1) the future performance (or refraining from performance) of substantial services by any person, or (2) the occurrence of a condition related to a purpose of the transfer, and the possibility of forfeiture is substantial if the condition is not satisfied. In Revenue Procedure 71-19, the IRS states "that a substantial forfeiture provision will not be considered to exist unless its conditions impose on the employee a significant limitation on duty which will require a meaningful effort on the part of the employee to fulfill and there is a definite possibility that the event which will cause the forfeiture could occur."

The most common type of condition to be satisfied in the case of nonqualified deferred compensation plans is that the employee remain employed and perform significant services for the employer for a specified minimum period of time. Requirements that the property be returned if the employee is discharged for cause or for committing a crime will not be considered a substantial risk of forfeiture.

Other Tax Issues

In addition to income taxes when payments are actually or constructively received by the executive, payments made to survivors may be considered so-called "income in respect of a decedent"— essentially taxable income. The details of these rules are beyond the scope of this text, but a financial planner should alert clients about this possibility.

Moreover, amounts deferred under nonqualified deferred compensation plans are included as wages for FICA and FUTA (federal unemployment tax) tax purposes in the later of: (1) the year in which the services are performed; or (2) the year in which there is no substantial risk of forfeiture of the amounts. As a practical matter, since an executive receiving a deferred compensation package is likely to have other earned income well in excess of the maximum amount subject to the Social Security portion of FICA, only the Medicare tax of 1.45 percent probably will be applicable.

Effect of Funding and/or Securing Nonqualified Plans

In terms of the income tax consequences associated with nonqualified deferred compensation plans, there are basically four classifications of nonqualified plans—unfunded, unsecured plans; unfunded, secured plans; funded, unsecured plans; and funded, secured plans. We will discuss the income tax consequences of each of these classifications.

Unfunded, Unsecured Plans

Such a plan will result in the deferral of income recognition until the compensation is actually paid to the employee. The constructive receipt doctrine does not apply because the employee does not have control over or a right to receive the compensation until the time specified in the contract. Neither does the economic benefit doctrine apply because the employer has only made a bookkeeping entry, a mere promise to pay the amount in the future. Even investment earnings (such as interest) may be credited to the base amount of compensation deferred simply as a bookkeeping entry or the employer may segregate and invest the amount of compensation deferred. As long as the assets remain subject to the claims of the employer's creditors, the employee will not be taxed on the deferred amounts until they are received.

Unfunded, unsecured plans have certain disadvantages. First, if the employer credits the employee's deferred amount with interest, the right of the employee to receive the deferred compensation is an employer liability which increases in amount yearly. Second, the employer's obligation may have to be paid when the employee is no longer performing services for the employer and thereby not helping to produce the funds needed to pay the deferred compensation. Finally, the employee runs the risk that the employer will become financially unable to meet the contractual obligation to pay the deferred compensation at the scheduled future dates of payment. Employees who have deferred compensation under unfunded, unsecured plans are only general creditors, and if the employer becomes bankrupt, the employee may collect nothing or, at best, a small percentage of the amount promised to be paid.

Unfunded, Secured Plans

This type of plan has to walk a fine line between providing some security to the employee and running afoul of the constructive receipt or economic benefit doctrines. Some of the methods that can be used to "secure" the deferred compensation payments include the following:

1. Life insurance
2. Reserve funds
3. Revocable trusts
4. Vesting trusts

5. Rabbi trusts

6. Third-party guarantees, and

7. Surety bonds and deferred compensation insurance

An employer can retain ownership of **life insurance** on the life of the employee with the employer as the beneficiary. This conveys no property interest to the employee and therefore he or she does not have to recognize income under either the constructive receipt or economic benefit doctrines. However, in this situation, the employer is not allowed a deduction for the premiums paid on the life insurance. Except under very limited circumstances, the employer also may not deduct interest paid on any loans from these life insurance policies. This method of "funding" is generally advantageous to the employer, except where the employer becomes insolvent before all benefits have been paid to the employee. The life insurance policy would be considered an unsecured asset and can be attached by the employer's creditors in bankruptcy.

Care must be exercised not to place the life insurance in trust or escrow for unconditional payment to the employee, since such an action would trigger the economic benefit doctrine and cause immediate taxation to the employee of the cash value and additional premiums as paid. Also, immediate taxation would result under a trust arrangement unless the employee's rights under the trust are subject to a substantial risk of forfeiture.

Another method of "securing" the employer's promise to pay is to have the employer establish a **reserve fund** invested in a portfolio of securities or other assets. Since the fund is the employer's general asset, it remains subject to the claims of the firm's general creditors thus avoiding the applicability of the economic benefit doctrine.

Also, the employer could set up a **revocable trust** for the benefit of the employees involved in the plan. The trust assets will be treated for tax purposes as those of the employer, since the employer retains the right to revoke the trust. Consequently, the employer is taxable on the earnings of the trust.

Another security device is a **vesting trust** under which the employer contributes to such a trust but the employee's right to the amounts accumulated in the trust does not vest in the employee until the occurrence of specific events, such as termination of employment, attainment of a certain age, retirement from the employer, or upon a change in ownership or control of the employer. Usually, the deferred compensation is paid to the employee when his or her rights to the compensation vest. Therefore, it is not necessary that the assets of the trust be subject to the claims of the general creditors of the employer. Employees are not taxed on their vested interest until those interests become transferable or are no longer subject to a substantial risk of forfeiture. The economic benefit doctrine will not apply because the employee does not have a current cash equivalent right, and the constructive receipt doctrine should not come into play because the employee first needs to vest.

If the vesting trust is revocable, the employer will be taxed on the income of the trust. The employer can deduct its contributions to the trust only to the extent that the amounts are taxable to the employees in the year of receipt and as long as a separate account is maintained for each participant.

A **rabbi trust** is an arrangement under which the employer places assets into an irrevocable trust to "secure" the payment of promised deferred compensation to selected employees. The trust agreement normally states that the assets placed in the trust will remain subject to the claims of the employer's general creditors in the event of insolvency or bankruptcy. The trust agreement cannot grant the employees vested ownership rights in the trust assets before they receive the deferred compensation payments. This type of trust takes its name from the first IRS letter ruling that approved deferral of compensation for a rabbi under such an arrangement. The IRS has developed, for use by employers, model rabbi trust agreements that almost guarantee a favorable ruling allowing deferral of compensation.

Since the assets of a rabbi trust remain subject to the claims of the employer's general creditors, the economic benefit doctrine is not applicable and employees will not be taxed until they actually receive the promised compensation. Also, the constructive receipt doctrine should not apply because the employee cannot receive the compensation until some future time. However, the employer will be taxable on the income of the trust. Separate accounts for each employee need not be maintained in a rabbi trust as a condition for getting the tax deduction when paying the benefits.

Another approach to "secure" the deferred compensation to the employee is to use a **third-party guarantee**. Under this method, a third party guarantees the employer's promise to pay deferred compensation in the event that the employer is unable to pay. Such guarantees may come from a shareholder of the employer, a related corporation, or may be in the form of an irrevocable bank letter of credit issued in favor of the employee. As long as the guarantor's obligation is not evidenced by notes or secured in any manner, the existence of the guarantee should not trigger recognition of income to the employee before actual receipt of the income.

A final method to "secure" the employer's promise to pay the deferred compensation is for the employee to purchase a **financial surety bond** from an independent insurance company. The surety bond insures payments under the nonqualified plan if, for any reason, the employer is unable to make the payments. It is essential under this option that the executive pay the premium for the bond without being reimbursed by the employer. The IRS has held that the purchase of a surety bond is similar to the purchase of a life insurance policy and does not create a current property right or change the employee's rights to the deferred compensation.

Funded, Unsecured Plans

Funding the deferred compensation payments will reduce the risk to the employee that the promised amounts will not be paid and provides a source for the employer to make the required payments. However, under a funded plan, the employee is currently taxable on the funded amounts under the economic benefit doctrine unless (1) the employer retains ownership of the assets used for the funding, (2) those assets remain subject to the claims of the employer's creditors, or (3) the rights of the employee to the deferred compensation are subject to a substantial risk of forfeiture.

Funded, Secured Plans

If a plan is both funded and secured it will ordinarily trigger the immediate recognition of income unless the employee's right to the deferred compensation is subject to a substantial risk of forfeiture under IRC Section 83.

An important type of funded and secured plan is a **secular trust**. Such a trust is a funded, irrevocable trust whose assets are beyond the reach of the employer's creditors. Consequently, there is no deferral of income recognition. Such trusts became popular when there was a meaningful differential between the top corporate tax rates and those for individuals. Secular trusts have become less favored because the corporate tax deduction is generally less valuable than the tax cost to the employee of not having deferral of income recognition. The top corporate and individual income tax rates are currently both 35 percent. In addition, secular trusts are subject to double taxation (to the trust on its earnings and to the highly compensated participant).

Just for clarification, the terms "funded" and "unfunded" are not defined in terms of whether the employer sets aside funds to pay the future promised benefits under a NQDC plan. Under the regulations, a "funded" plan is one where money is set aside in a manner that prevents it being used for any purpose other than paying the future benefits. The employee is effectively vested in the money, unless it is subject to a substantial risk of forfeiture. An "unfunded" plan exists even if the employer sets aside money for the purpose of paying the future benefits as long as the money is available to its general creditors in the case of the company's insolvency. When money is set aside to provide for the future benefits in a "funded" plan, the plan is said to be formally funded. In an "unfunded" plan, it is said to be informally funded.

Effect of the American Jobs Creation Act of 2004 on NQDC

On October 22, 2004, the president signed into law the American Jobs Creation Act of 2004. This new law created a new section 409A of the Internal Revenue Code which specifically addresses deferred compensation requirements. The new requirements include restrictions on:

- When a participant may make an initial deferral election
- The earliest date a participant may receive a distribution
- The ability to accelerate distributions
- A participant's ability to make a subsequent election that delays the time of distribution or changes the form of distribution
- The use of offshore rabbi trusts as well as immediate taxation of plans that provide for funding or increased security of deferred compensation assets triggered by a change in the employer's financial health (even if the assets remain subject to the claims of the employer's creditors)

The new tax law makes clear that rabbi trusts, commonly used deferred compensation arrangements where life insurance is used as the funding vehicle, are within the law. The Internal Revenue Service was expected to provide guidance on the new legislation within 60 days of enactment. On December 20, 2004 the Treasury Department issued IRS Notice 2005-1 that provides initial guidance regarding the transition to the new rules. Existing plans were given until December 31, 2005 to revise the agreements to comply with the new rules. It also provided guidance regarding reporting requirements under the new Code section.

IMPORTANT CONCEPTS

Constructive receipt doctrine

Deferred compensation arrangement (or salary reduction plan)

Economic benefit doctrine

Excess benefit plan

Formal funding

Informal funding

Nonqualified deferred compensation

Rabbi trust

Reserve fund

Salary continuation plan

Salary reduction plan (or deferred compensation arrangement)

Secular trust

Substantial risk of forfeiture

Supplemental executive retirement plan (SERP)

QUESTIONS FOR REVIEW

1. What are the general characteristics of a nonqualified deferred compensation plan?

2. How is a nonqualified plan different from a qualified plan?

3. What are the advantages of a nonqualified deferred compensation plan from the point of view of the employer?

4. What are the advantages of a nonqualified deferred compensation plan from the point of view of the employee?

5. How is constructive receipt different from economic benefit?

6. How do the various methods of informal funding operate?

7. What is the primary benefit of a rabbi trust used to fund a nonqualified deferred compensation plan, and how does it avoid the applicability of the constructive receipt and economic benefit doctrines?

8. What are the ramifications of using a secular trust to fund a nonqualified deferred compensation plan?

SUGGESTIONS FOR ADDITIONAL READING

Comprehensive Deferred Compensation: A Complete Guide to Nonqualified Deferred Compensation, National Underwriter, 1997.

Employee Benefits, 7th ed., Burton T. Beam and John J. McFadden, Jr., Real Estate Education Company, 2005.

Nonqualified Deferred Compensation Answer Book; 4th Ed., Michael P. Connors and Henry A. Smith III, Aspen, 2002.

Pension Planning: Pensions, Profit-Sharing, and Other Deferred Compensation Plans, 9th ed. Allen, Melone, and Rosenbloom, McGraw-Hill/Irwin, 2002 .

Tax Facts On Insurance & Employee Benefits 2005, National Underwriter, 2005

The Tools and Techniques of Employee Benefit and Retirement Planning, 9th ed., Stephan R. Leimberg and John J. McFadden, National Underwriter, 2005.

CHAPTER EIGHTEEN

Equity-Based Compensation: Stock Options and Stock Purchase Plans

• • •

During the late 1980s and most of the 1990s, the United States had a stock market that, even at its worst, refused to decline for more than a few months at a time. In times of low inflation and economic growth, attracting and retaining executives and other skilled employees often required offering them equity (or ownership) in the business. Executives and other employees enjoyed reaping some of the benefits of making the company successful. Equity-based compensation is still a viable method of offering employees an opportunity to share in their employer's future financial success. In addition to benefiting the employer, many of these stock arrangements provide tax advantages to the executive by deferring what would otherwise be currently taxable compensation, and converting ordinary income into capital gains.

This chapter continues the discussion of additional compensation for highly paid employees. In addition, it includes information on stock purchase plans that may be available to *all* employees.

When you have completed this chapter you will be able to:

- Describe the provisions of nonqualified stock options, incentive stock options, and employee stock purchase plans
- Describe the tax treatment of various types of equity-based compensation
- Describe the circumstances under which it would be appropriate to use each form of equity-based compensation
- Compare and contrast nonqualified stock options and incentive stock options

EQUITY-BASED COMPENSATION

Employers and executives often want to have compensation based on the company's financial performance. By paying the executive part of his or her compensation in stock, there is a direct correlation between total compensation and success of the business overall.

Of course, the employer must be willing to accept additional owners. While this will not be an issue for a large publicly traded corporation, it can be a major decision for a family-owned or closely held business (which typically does not want additional owners).

The employer can also use equity-based incentives to discourage an employee from leaving his or her current place of employment. Accordingly, stock options may be tailored to be withdrawn in this event.

Stock Options

In general, a stock option is a right granted by an employer corporation to its employee that allows the employee to purchase the employer's stock at a fixed price for a stated period of time. The price at which the stock will be sold to the employee (known as the exercise price) is either its fair market value at the time the option is granted or a value substantially below it. The option is merely the right to purchase stock; it is not stock itself. If the employee expects the stock to appreciate in value, he or she will consider this a benefit. There are two general approaches to the granting of stock options to executives. One is simply called a stock option plan for executives. It is nonstatutory and therefore is not "qualified" within the meaning of IRC Sections 421-424, meaning it is not afforded any favorable tax treatment. This type of stock option is referred to as a nonqualified stock option (NQSO). The other type is called an incentive stock option (ISO) and does have certain tax benefits if established correctly.

Another common part of an executive's compensation consists of restricted stock or some other corporate security. Restricted stock is stock in the company that cannot be sold or transferred to another person until a specified date. Employers typically use these restrictions as incentives for the executive to remain with the company. Since the executive or other key employee cannot benefit immediately from this form of compensation, it is generally structured to defer any income tax liability for the employee. Subsequently, any deduction by the employer is also deferred. Restricted stock is discussed in chapter 19.

Nonqualified (or Nonstatutory) Stock Options (NQSOs)

A nonqualified stock option is an offer by an employer corporation to sell its stock to its employee at some future date at a price that is specified today, usually today's market value of the stock.

NQSOs are taxed under IRC Section 83, which provides that property transferred in connection with the performance of services will be taxed in the year in which the property either becomes transferable or is no longer subject to a substantial risk of forfeiture (discussed in chapter 17). The amount of gain taxable to the employee is the excess of the fair market value of the stock on the date that it first becomes transferable or free of the substantial risk of forfeiture over the amount paid for the stock (the exercise price). Accordingly, on the date the option is granted, there is generally no taxable income reportable by the employee, *unless the option has a readily ascertainable fair market value at the time of grant.* Having a readily ascertainable fair market value generally means that the option must be actively traded on an established market. However, even if the option is not traded on an established market, it can still be considered to have a readily ascertainable fair market value if:

1. The option is immediately exercisable
2. The option is transferable and free of restriction which would constitute a substantial risk of forfeiture; and
3. The option has a readily ascertainable fair market value, as determined under IRS Regulation § 1.83-7(b)(3)

Most of the time, NQSOs will not satisfy all of these conditions, because (1) either the option's exercise price equals the fair market value of the stock at the date of grant, (2) there is no established market value for the option (such markets do not generally exist for five- and ten-year options), (3) the options are not transferable, or (4) the right to exercise the options is conditioned upon the future performance of services by the employee. As a result, in the majority of cases, the employee will be taxed at the date of exercise on the difference, or spread, between the market value of the stock on the exercise date and the option's exercise price. This income is treated as ordinary income taxed at the employee's highest tax bracket and is subject to withholding tax. The stock's holding period, for purposes of determining long-term capital gains, begins with the exercise date. The employee's tax basis in the stock, for purposes of determining ultimate capital gain or loss, includes the amount paid for the option (if any), the exercise price paid, and the amount of ordinary income recognized upon the exercise of the option.

In the event that the options have a readily ascertainable market value, the excess of the value of the option over the cost, if any, is taxed as ordinary income at the date of grant. In such a case, the employee realizes no further income at the exercise date and the employee's holding period for the stock begins on the grant date, not the exercise date. In these circumstances, the employee's tax basis in the stock includes the exercise price plus the amount paid for the NQSO (if any) plus the income recognized at the grant date.

The employer corporation's tax deduction must match the amount included in income by the employee and the employer must include such amount on the employee's Form W-2. Such income is subject to income tax withholding, FICA taxes, and FUTA taxes.

Here is an example with and without a readily ascertainable value for the option. Carlin Imports grants stock options to CEO Dee X. McCall as part of her compensation. The options give Dee the right to purchase 1,000 shares of Carlin stock at $50 per share (or $50,000) no earlier than eight years from the date of the grant. Dee purchases the stock at the earliest date, and its value at that time is $150 per share (or $150,000 total).

Scenario 1: The stock is traded on the American Stock Exchange at $50 per share on the date of the grant. Dee may not transfer the option, which is also not separately traded on an established exchange. When Dee purchases the stock, her basis is the $50,000 she paid for the shares plus any amount paid for the option (usually none) plus the $100,000 bargain element. She must report this excess value of the stock ($100,000) as ordinary income at the time of exercising the option. The employer also gets a $100,000 deduction at that time. So, while Dee pays $50,000 plus the tax on $100,000, her total basis now becomes $150,000 in the event of a subsequent sale of the stock. Her holding period for determining subsequent capital gain begins on the exercise date.

Scenario 2: The difference between this and scenario 1 is that the option has a determinable value at the date of the grant and is also separately traded on an established exchange. Since the option does have a readily ascertainable market value, Dee must currently report the value of the options as earned income at the date of grant. The employer also gets an immediate deduction for that same amount. The advantage here is that when Dee exercises the option to buy the stock, her basis is $50,000 plus the value of the options included in income at the grant date plus any amount paid for the options (usually none), but she does not have to report any ordinary income at that time. She will only have to report a capital gain (the difference between the sale price of the stock and her basis) when she sells the stock. Her holding period for determining subsequent capital gain begins on the grant date.

From the executive's point of view, there is no downside risk when there is no income reported upon the granting of the options. If the stock goes up in value, he or she can purchase it at a discount. If the stock goes down in value, the options become worthless, but the executive has not lost anything out of pocket. However, if the stock options were separately transferable, he or she would have to report their value as income. If the options are not sold and subsequently become worthless, then he or she is out the taxes paid on the reported value of the options.

Incentive Stock Options (ISOs)

The incentive stock option (ISO), also known as a qualified stock option plan, is one form of statutory stock option that provides favorable income tax treatment for the employee if certain requirements are met. Unlike the NQSO, the ISO does not result in ordinary income recognition either at the grant date or the exercise date. Instead, all of the potential income is treated as capital gain and is not recognized until the stock is disposed of by the employee. However, the executive may be subject to the alternative minimum tax when exercising the option. For those unfamiliar with the alternative minimum tax (AMT), it is a separate method of determining income tax devised to ensure that at least a minimum amount of tax is paid by high-income taxpayers who reap large tax savings by making use of certain tax deductions, exemptions, losses and credits. Without the AMT, some of these taxpayers might be able to escape income taxation entirely. In essence, the AMT functions as a recapture mechanism, reclaiming some of the tax breaks primarily available to high-income taxpayers, and represents an attempt to maintain tax equity. In recent years, the AMT has tended to extend itself to even middle-income taxpayers who take advantage of certain tax breaks.

The specific requirements that must be met by ISOs under IRC § 422, include the following:

1. ISOs must be issued pursuant to a written plan approved by shareholders within twelve months of board adoption that specifies the total number of shares to be issued and the employees, or class of employees, eligible to receive the options.

2. ISOs must be granted within ten years from the date of adoption of the plan (or shareholder approval, if earlier).

3. ISOs may be granted only to employees and must be exercised by the employee either during employment or within three months of termination of employment.

4. ISOs cannot be transferable by the employee, except by will or the laws of descent and distribution, and must be exercisable only by the employee during his or her lifetime.

5. The option price must be equal to, or exceed, the fair market value of the stock on the date of the grant.

6. The maximum term of an ISO cannot be longer than ten years from the date of the grant.

7. All shares acquired from the exercise of ISOs must be held for two years from the date of the grant and one year from the date of the transfer of such shares (exercise date).

8. ISOs may not be granted to an individual who owns more than ten percent of the total combined voting power of all classes of stock of the employer corporation, or its parent or subsidiary corporation. However, this rule will not apply if, at the time the option is granted, (a) the option price is at least 110 percent of the fair market value of the stock subject to the option, and (b) the option is not exercisable after five years from the date the option was granted; and

9. The maximum aggregate value of the stock (determined as of the grant date) which is first *exercisable* during any one calendar year may not exceed $100,000 for any employee. Thus, for example, an ISO award could permit acquisition of up to $500,000 worth of stock if it provided that the options were exercisable in five installments, each of which becomes exercisable in a different year and does not exceed $100,000.

If all of the above requirements are met, the employee will not recognize any taxable income at either the grant date or the exercise date. When the employee disposes of the stock acquired, the difference between the selling price and the exercise price is treated as long-term capital gain, since the required holding period of the stock is at least one year from the exercise date. However, for alternative minimum tax (AMT) purposes, an ISO is essentially treated as if it were an NQSO. The spread between the ISO exercise price and the market value of the stock on the date the rights become freely transferable, or no longer subject to a substantial risk of forfeiture, (normally the exercise date) is treated as a positive adjustment item (i.e., recognized as income for AMT purposes). Accordingly, if the employee is subject to AMT in the year he or she exercises an ISO, the deferral benefit is lost. For AMT purposes, the positive adjustment item (addition to AMT income) reverses in the year the stock is sold and becomes a negative adjustment item (subtraction from AMT income).

The employer must follow the same matching concept as with NQSOs and therefore has no tax deduction at either the grant date or exercise date, since the employee reports no income at those times under an ISO. In fact, even if the employee is subject to the AMT for the year in which the ISOs are exercised, the employer is not entitled to either a regular income tax or AMT deduction. However, if the employee makes a disqualifying disposition (fails to hold the stock for two years from the date of grant and one year from the date of exercise, discussed later) and therefore recognizes income in a particular year, the employer is allowed a deduction for an equal amount in that same year.

Here are examples of the income tax treatment afforded to NQSOs and ISOs.

Example 1: First assume that on May 25, 2004, when its stock was selling at $15 per share, X Co. granted *nonqualified stock options* to Mr. Catterson to purchase 1,000 shares of X Co. stock at $15 after one year of employment. On the grant date, the NQSOs had no readily ascertainable market value. (Note that the option price may be below the market value of the stock. It has been set equal to the stock price for the purpose of making a comparison with an ISO, discussed next). The options were exercisable anytime after May 25, 2005, and before May 25, 2016. Mr. Catterson exercised his options on October 16, 2005, when the X Co. stock was selling for $22. He sold the shares on June 12, 2006 for $25 per share.

Result: Mr. Catterson recognizes no taxable income on the grant date of the options. He recognizes $7,000 of ordinary compensation income on October 16, 2005, when he exercises the options [($22 - $15) x 1,000]. X Co. will be allowed a deduction of the same $7,000 for its taxable year which contains December 31, 2005, Mr. Catterson's year-end. Mr. Catterson will also recognize a $3,000 short-term capital gain upon the sale of the stock on June 12, 2006, since his holding period was less than twelve months (October 16, 2005 - June 12, 2006).

Example 2: Now assume that on May 25, 2004, when its stock was selling at $15 per share, X Co. granted *incentive stock options* to Mr. Catterson to purchase 1,000 shares of X Co. stock at $15 after one year of employment. The options were exercisable anytime between May 25, 2005 and May 24, 2014. (Note that the option price must equal the market value of the stock on the grant date, and the option period may not exceed 10 years.) Mr. Catterson exercised his options on October 16, 2006 when the stock was selling for $22. He sold the shares on June 12, 2008, for $25 per share.

Result: Mr. Catterson recognizes no taxable income on the grant date, nor does he recognize any on the exercise date. Because Mr. Catterson has met the required holding period for the stock (two years from May 25, 2004, and one year from October 16, 2006), he recognizes a long-term capital gain in 2008 from the sale of the stock totaling $10,000 [($25 - $15) x 1,000]. X Co. is not allowed any deduction in connection with the ISOs, since no ordinary income was recognized by Mr. Catterson.

For AMT purposes, however, the $7,000 spread between the exercise price and the market value of the stock on the date his right to purchase the stock becomes freely transferable or is no longer subject to a substantial risk of forfeiture (October 16, 2006, the exercise date) is treated as a positive adjustment for AMT purposes. This positive adjustment is taxed at the special AMT rate provided under IRC Section 55(b)(3) (usually 15 percent). This adjustment item reverses and becomes a negative adjustment item for AMT purposes in the year the stock is sold.

Comparison of NQSOs and ISOs

The table below compares the tax treatment of the NQSO and the ISO in the examples presented earlier with a $15 option price:

Income Recognized

Date	Market Price	NQSO	ISO
Grant date	$15	None	None
Exercise date	$22	$7,000 ordinary income	None (However, the $7,000 is an AMT positive adjustment)
Sale of stock	$25	$3,000 short-term	$10,000 long-term capital gain ($3,000 for AMT purposes, i.e., a $7,000 negative adjustment)

[handwritten annotation: — 15% tax rate]

It should be clear from the table above that the ISO allows the employee to postpone the recognition of any income (except for AMT purposes) until the ultimate disposition of the stock. Moreover, all of the income is treated as long-term capital gain. If an employee plans to hold the stock for a long period of time, postponement of the payment of tax under an ISO would be an attractive feature. Of even greater importance, however, is the taxation of all income with an ISO (for regular tax purposes) at the maximum long-term capital gains rate of 15 percent. With an NQSO, the portion of the income taxed as ordinary income could conceivably be taxed at the maximum 35 percent rate. The favorable character and timing of income recognized under an ISO probably outweigh an ISO's inherent restrictions.

[handwritten annotation: Required holding pd.]

As discussed previously, if the employee does not hold the stock acquired from the exercise of an ISO for the required holding period (two years from the grant date and one year from the exercise date), the gain, up to the spread at the exercise date, will be treated as compensation income and, accordingly, taxed at ordinary income rates. Any excess gain will be treated as capital gain. As a result, an early disposition disqualifies the ISO and treats the transaction as if it were a NQSO, with the exception of the date of income recognition. Such a disposition is known as a **disqualifying disposition**.

If the sales price of the stock sold in a disqualifying disposition is less than its fair market value on the exercise date, but more than its exercise price, the amount of ordinary income is limited to the amount of gain. The employer is allowed a deduction for the same amount. If the sales price of the stock sold in a disqualifying disposition is less than the exercise price, the employee recognizes a capital loss and the employer is not entitled to any deduction.

General Considerations

In the case of ISOs, the employer incurs little or no out-of-pocket cost. The only real cost to the employer is that it no longer has the opportunity to sell the stock to the public.

However, the employer gets no deduction for the option at any time. Unlike nonstatutory options, incentive stock options (ISOs) must meet the requirements of IRC § 422, which are somewhat technical and complex. Also, unlike nonstatutory options, the ISO price must be at least equal to the current market value of the stock at the date of grant. Accordingly, there is no possibility of a built-in gain.

Many Internet-based companies have provided stock ownership opportunities to employees as a low-cost recruitment method. The hope of both the employees and the company is that the business will do very well. In that case, the employees, who typically accept smaller incomes than they might otherwise be offered, receive substantial rewards for being there from the beginning. For example, some dot-coms made their employee-owners wealthy. Unfortunately, this has not always been the case. The restrictions on the stock prevented employees from selling any stock before its value had entirely disappeared.

So a question arises as to who should consider stock as part of a compensation package. Typically, the individual who is offered stock should be one who is paid adequately for his or her position without the stock. The individual being offered the stock must then determine whether the company either is promising enough that the stock will be a valuable asset or has a good chance to become a valuable asset. A publicly held company typically has years of history and some stability. A start-up company has no history, so the person accepting the stock is putting his or her faith in the product or service offered by the company and its ability to deliver it competitively and profitably. There is no simple answer.

EMPLOYEE STOCK PURCHASE PLAN

In theory, owners of a business are more interested in its success than the employees. Few would argue that major shareholders of a business are interested in its success, even more so if they were the founders of the business and/or key employees. The theory has been expanded to the point where some believe that any employee who owns stock in his or her employer, and is therefore an owner of the company, will be more interested in the success of the company than if he or she were merely an employee. It is probable that some employees feel this way, while others feel it is merely a ploy to make them work harder or give their hard-earned money back to the company on the hope that the stock will go up in value. Given these motivations, employee stock purchase plans were implemented some 40 years ago.

Basic Characteristics

Employee stock purchase plans (ESPP) are governed by IRC § 423. They are arrangements under which all full-time employees meeting certain eligibility requirements are allowed to buy stock in their employer's corporation, usually at a discount. Technically, such stock purchase plans, like ISOs, are considered a form of statutory stock option. Under this plan, an employer may not discriminate in favor of "key employees" (as defined in the tax code) by granting only some the right to buy employer stock. Therefore, such a plan appeals primarily to an employer who wants to provide the right to buy employer stock as a general benefit of employment to all employees. In turn, management may believe that employee stock ownership will act as an incentive and improve employee performance.

Generally, to participate in such an employee stock purchase plan, employees agree to have a percentage of their income or a specific dollar amount of their income deducted from each paycheck. Such money is typically accumulated over a period of months, with a prevailing accumulation period of as short as six months but as long as 27 months. At the end of the accumulation period, the employee's funds are used to purchase shares of the employer's stock. The price is typically 85 percent of the lesser of the price at the beginning of the accumulation period or at the end of the accumulation period.

Definition of an ESPP

The term "employee stock purchase plan" means a plan which meets the following requirements:

1. the plan grants options only to employees of the employer corporation or of its parent or subsidiary corporation to purchase stock in any such corporation;

2. the plan is approved by the stockholders of the granting corporation within 12 months before or after the date such plan is adopted;

3. the terms of the plan cannot grant an option to any employee if, immediately after the option is granted, he or she owns 5 percent or more of the total combined voting power or value of all classes of stock of the employer corporation or of its parent or subsidiary corporation. For this purpose, stock which the employee may purchase under outstanding options is treated as stock already owned by the employee.

4. options must be granted to all employees of the employer except the following:
   a. employees who have been employed less than 2 years.
   b. part-time employees (20 hours or less per week)
   c. seasonal employees who work 5 months or less per calendar year
   d. highly compensated employees (within the meaning of IRC § 414(q))*

5. all employees granted options shall have the same rights and privileges, except that the amount of stock which may be purchased by any employee may bear a uniform relationship to the total compensation, or the basic or regular rate of compensation, of employees, and the plan may provide that no employee may purchase more than a maximum amount of stock.

6. the option price must not be less than the lesser of:
   a. 85 percent of the fair market value of the stock on the grant date, or
   b. 85 percent of the fair market value of the stock on the exercise date

7. such option cannot be exercised after the expiration of:
   a. 5 years from the grant date if, under the terms of the plan, the option price is to be not less than 85 percent of the fair market value of such stock at the exercise date, or
   b. 27 months from the grant date, if the option price cannot be determined in the manner described in 7(a).

8. no employee may be granted an option to buy more than $25,000 per year (determined at the grant date)

9. such option is not transferable by an employee other than by will or the laws of descent and distribution, and is exercisable, during his or her lifetime, only by him or her.

* A highly compensated employee under IRC § 414(q) is any employee who (1) was a 5-percent or more owner at any time during the year or the preceding year, or (2) for the preceding year had compensation from the employer in excess of $95,000 (in 2005, annually indexed for inflation) and, if the employer elects, was in the top 20 percent of employees by compensation.

OTHER REQUIREMENTS

In addition to the nine specific requirements listed previously, the employee who is granted an option must remain an employee of the employer corporation (or parent or subsidiary corporation) beginning with the grant date and ending on the day three months before the exercise date. What this means is that if the employee leaves the employ of the employer corporation, he or she has three months from the time he or she leaves to exercise the option.

Generally, if the employee disposes of the stock acquired through an ESPP after the two-year and one-year holding periods (discussed under ISOs), he or she may treat any resulting gain as long-term capital gain. However, a special rule applies where the option price is between 85 percent and 100 percent of the fair market value of the stock at the grant date. In this case, if the employee disposes of the stock after the two-year and one-year holding periods or dies while owning the stock, he or she must include as compensation income (not as a capital gain) an amount equal to the lesser of (1) the excess of the fair market value of the stock at the sale date or date of death over the amount paid for the stock under the option, or (2) the excess of the fair market value of the stock at the grant date over the option price. The remainder of any gain on sale during the employee's lifetime is treated as long-term capital gain. At the employee's death, his or her estate or heirs receive a stepped-up basis to the fair market value at the date of death; in other words, any remaining gain may never be subjected to income tax.

Example: John's employer, XYZ Corporation, granted John an option under its employee stock purchase plan to buy 100 shares of stock of XYZ for $20 per share at a time when the stock had a fair market value of $22 per share. Eighteen months later, when the value of the stock was $23 per share, John exercised the option, and 14 months after that he sold his stock for $30 per share. In the year of sale, John must report as wages the difference between the option price ($20) and the value at the time the option was granted ($22). The remainder of his gain ($8 per share) is capital gain, figured as follows:

Selling price ($30 x 100 shares)	$3,000
Purchase price (option price)	
($20 x 100 shares)	$2,000
Gain	$1,000
Amount reported as wages	
[($22 x 100 shares) - $2,000]	$ 200
Amount reported as capital gain	**$ 800**

If the employee does not meet the holding period requirement, he or she recognizes ordinary income to the extent that the stock's fair market value at the exercise date exceeded the option price. The amount of ordinary income reportable is not limited to the total gain realized from the sale of the stock. If the difference between the stock's fair market value at the exercise date and the exercise price exceeds the total gain realized from the sale (fair market value at date of sale versus exercise price), the entire amount of ordinary income must be reported.

Example: The facts are the same as in the previous example, except that John sold the stock only 6 months after he exercised the option. Since John did not hold the stock long enough, he must report $300 as wages and $700 as capital gain, figured as follows:

Selling price ($30 x 100 shares)	$3,000
Purchase price (option price)	
($20 x 100 shares)	$2,000 ✓
Gain	**$1,000** ·
Amount reported as wages	
[($23 x 100 shares) - $2,000]	$ 300
Amount reported as capital gain	
[$3,000 - ($2,000 + $300)]	**$ 700**

Tax Treatment to Employees

If the requirements of IRC § 423 are met, there is no gross income for participating employees on receipt of an option to purchase stock under an employee stock purchase plan, even though the exercise price of the stock may be less than the fair market value at the time. Nor will the employee recognize income on the exercise of the option and acquisition of the stock at a subsequent date. To receive this favorable tax treatment, however, the employee must meet certain requirements. As mentioned previously, the employee may not dispose of the stock within two years from grant of the option and within one year from its exercise or it is considered to be a **disqualifying disposition**. In this event, he or she will be taxed at ordinary income tax rates in the year of disposition on the difference between the fair market value of the stock at the exercise date, and the option strike price when the option was exercised. Further, the income will be considered compensation and will be subject to FICA withholding. Any remaining gain is treated as capital gain.

The following information is taken from the testimony of Frederic W. Cook, chairman of Frederic W. Cook & Company in New York City before the House Committee on Ways and Means' Subcommittee on Oversight in an October 12, 2000 hearing on employee stock options.

Table 18.1: Comparison of Stock Option Plans

| | Limits | Employee Taxation | | | Corporate Deduction | | |
		At Grant	At Exercise	At Sale	At Exercise	At Sale	Employment Taxes on Gain
Nonqualified Options IRC § 83	None	None	Ordinary income	Capital gain/loss on excess	Yes	No	Yes
Incentive Stock Options IRC § 422	$100,000 vesting limit/yr 100% FMV option price 10 yr max.	None	None, but gain is subject to AMT	Capital gains on full gain	No	No	No
Employee Stock Purchase Plans IRC § 423	$25,000/yr max. All employees eligible 85% option price	None	None	15% discount is ordinary income; remainder is capital gain	No	No	No

Tax Treatment to the Employer

The employer does not get a corporate income tax deduction at the date of grant or of exercise of options acquired under an employee stock purchase plan. However, as discussed earlier, if the employee disposes of the stock received in less than the two-year and one-year holding periods, a disqualifying disposition occurs and he or she must report any gain as ordinary income. As before, the employer is able to claim a deduction equal to the amount of ordinary income reported.

Nonqualified Employee Stock Purchase Plans

Not every employee stock purchase plan meets the requirements of IRC Section 423. When the requirements are not met, however, the stock purchase plan results in taxation similar to any non-statutory stock option plan. There is no taxation to the employees when they receive the options, but when the stock is purchased, they report the difference between the fair market value of the stock and any discount in price as ordinary income.

The Future of Equity Based Compensation

Ownership in one's own company has long been part of the American worker's dream. When an employee owns stock in his or her employer, there is, at some level, a realization that "them" has become "us." For generations employees have said that the company owners get rich from their efforts. Employee stock purchase plans permit employees to be owners. This does, however, also bring home the realization that there is risk in company ownership.

When large corporations vie for talented leaders, they have often used stock ownership as an incentive to lure those executives. Further, they generally believed that giving stock options to key leaders would entice them to perform well. However, in the shadow of the major corporate collapses of 2001 and 2002, where executives who had been granted stock options managed to sell millions of dollars worth of stock before the companies stock value collapsed, a number of large corporations (including Cendent, Allstate, General Motors, Microsoft and the Washington Post) reported publicly that they would no longer include stock options in executive compensation packages. Instead, in the future, these companies would use more traditional methods of adding to the executives' compensation, such as issuance of restricted stock (discussed in chapter 19).

As noted above, some argue that stock options provide an incentive to executives to work at peak performance levels. This may or may not have influenced how the executives operated in those companies that suffered. One issue that has been brought forward is that in some cases, executives focused their efforts on making the market value of the stock increase while neglecting sound corporate operations. Stock performance is not always driven by the same decisions as long-term operating performance. It has been argued that some top executives made decisions that had a very positive effect on the stock, selling their optioned shares when prices were high with knowledge that eventually the operations of the company would suffer and the stock would drop in value. It is hard to imagine that any of them did this with the intent of causing the company to collapse.

However, the perception held by many individuals is that stock options provide incentive to make the stock valuable at the cost of corporate stability. In this atmosphere, changes in how executives are given equity-based compensation are occurring. It will probably take a few years, and greater economic stability, before the long-term result of these changes will be known.

IMPORTANT CONCEPTS

Disqualifying disposition

Nonqualified stock options

Employee stock purchase plan (ESPP)

Nonstatutory stock options

Incentive stock options (ISO)

Substantially vested

QUESTIONS FOR REVIEW

1. What are the one-year limits for stock options under an ISO and ESPP?

2. What purposes are served by the use of incentive stock options?

3. What are the income tax ramifications of an employee stock purchase plan?

4. What differences exist between nonstatutory and statutory executive stock options?

5. What are the rules for qualifying an ISO plan?

6. Who may be excluded and who must be excluded from an ESPP?

7. For which types of companies are equity-based compensation plans appropriate and for which are they inappropriate?

8. What requirements exist for employee participants in an ESPP to receive the greatest income tax benefits?

SUGGESTIONS FOR ADDITIONAL READING

Consider Your Options: Get the Most Out of Your Equity Compensation, Kaye Thomas, Fairmark Press, Inc., 2005.

Current Practices in Stock Option Plan Design, 2nd ed., Corey Rosen, et. al, National Center for Employee Ownership, 2001.

Employee Benefits, 7th ed., Burton T. Beam, Jr. and John J. McFadden, Real Estate Education Company, 2005.

Stock Options: An Authoritative Guide to Incentive and Nonqualified Stock Options, 2nd ed., Robert Pastore, PCM Capital Publishing, 2000.

The Stock Options Book, 6th ed., Scott Rodrick, National Center for Employee Ownership, 2004.

The Tools & Techniques of Employee Benefit and Retirement Planning, 9th ed., Stephan R. Leimberg and John J. McFadden, National Underwriter Company, 2005.

CHAPTER NINETEEN

Equity-Based Compensation: Restricted Stock, Shadow Stock Arrangements, and Performance Unit or Share Plans

• • •

Rewarding executives with stock or hypothetical stock are additional methods of equity-based compensation. In some cases this gives the impression of ownership of the actual shares of stock. In other cases it provides the executive with the financial benefits of stock ownership without giving him or her actual shares of stock or stock options.

When you have completed this chapter you will be able to:

- Describe the provisions of restricted stock and shadow stock arrangements
- Describe performance unit and share plans
- Describe the tax treatment of various types of equity-based compensation, including restricted stock and shadow stock arrangements
- Describe the circumstances under which it would be appropriate to use each form of equity-based compensation

RESTRICTED STOCK PLANS

Under a restricted property or restricted stock plan, the employee receives property, but his or her rights to keep or dispose of the property are subject to a substantial risk of forfeiture. The property must have been transferred to the employee in recognition of the performance of, or refraining from performance of, services. This is true whether the related services were performed in a past year or the current year, or are to be performed in the future. Ordinarily, the property is stock of the employer, and the forfeiture provision typically requires the employee to perform substantial services for the employer for a specified minimum amount of time. If the employee does not meet this requirement, he or she will forfeit the stock or other property. Restricted stock can be considered another form of "golden handcuffs" in that it creates a substantial penalty for leaving the employing company prematurely, going to work for a competitor, being discharged either for cause or for a specific reason (e.g. embezzlement or disclosure of trade or marketing information), or starting a competing business. Usually, the employee is taxed in the year in which the receipt of the property is no longer subject to a substantial risk of forfeiture, or, if earlier, when the property can be transferred by the employee free of risk of forfeiture. But a special provision under IRC § 83 permits the employee to elect to be taxed on the property in the year in which the property is initially transferred or granted to the employee.

Issuing new shares of restricted stock tends to dilute ownership of the employer corporation. As a result, its use may be particularly undesirable for closely held corporations since shareholders of these corporations seldom want to share control or profits, or share company assets upon sale or liquidation of the business.

Restricted stock plans have increased in popularity beginning in 2003 relative to NQSOs (discussed in chapter 18) as a means of rewarding executives and other employees. This is due primarily to the relatively poor stock market performance of many stocks beginning in 2000 which has adversely affected the value of stock options and the increased interest of the Financial Accounting Standards Board (FASB) in the expensing of stock options on the financial statements of issuing companies.

IRC § 83 requires an individual who performed services for a corporation and who was compensated in restricted stock, to include in gross income the excess of:

1. the fair market value of the property (determined without regard to any lapse restriction, e.g., one that requires an employee to sell the stock back to the employer corporation) at the first time that the rights of the person having a beneficial interest in that property are (a) transferable or (b) not subject to a substantial risk of forfeiture, whichever occurs earlier, over

2. the amount (if any) paid for the property, by the person who performed the services.

If the property is sold after that time, the excess of the selling price over the fair market value of the property at the time the income is recognized is treated as a capital gain. Conversely, if less than the fair market value is obtained upon the sale of the property, the employee recognizes a capital loss. Also, if the employee (or other person holding a beneficial interest in the property) receives income from that property, such as dividends received on restricted stock shares, while it is nonvested (that is, while there is a substantial risk of forfeiture) the amount received is treated as additional compensation to the employee.

Example: In 2005, the Davis Company granted one of its employees, Bennett, the right to purchase 25 shares of the Davis Company stock for $2,000. Bennett's rights to the shares are subject to a substantial risk of forfeiture which will end in 2009. In 2005, the 25 shares were worth $3,000, and they are worth $8,000 in 2009 at the time the risk of forfeiture ends. Under IRC § 83(a), Bennett will include $6,000 ($8,000 - $2,000) as ordinary income in 2009. If Bennett sold the stock for $9,000 in 2011, he would recognize a long-term capital gain of $1,000 ($9,000 - $8,000).

However, if the restricted stock is sold before the property becomes transferable or before it is no longer subject to a substantial risk of forfeiture, the amount includible in the employee's gross income is the excess of the selling price over the amount paid for the property, if any. A potential problem for an employee is where he or she has to include an amount in gross income and pay the income tax before he or she has the funds from the restricted stock. Section 83 may force an employee to sell the property in the same year the income is recognized to raise the funds to pay the tax. Of course, the employee may be able to obtain a loan using the stock as collateral.

When employer stock is used in a restricted stock plan, the stock certificates usually bear a "legend" or statement imprinted on them indicating that transfer and ownership of the shares are subject to a restricted property plan. This puts any potential buyer or other recipient on notice that the employee is not entitled to sell, give away, or otherwise transfer the shares without restrictions.

The IRC § 83(b) Election

Instead of recognizing income under the general rules of IRC § 83(a), the employee can elect to be taxed under the provisions of Section 83(b). This election permits the employee to recognize as income in the year in which the restricted property is granted, the excess of the fair market value of the property at the time of the grant minus the amount, if any, that must be paid for the property. Since the employer receives a corresponding tax deduction, one disadvantage to the employer is that it loses control over the amount or timing of that deduction. If the employee makes such an election and the property is later transferred by the employee, any increase in value of the property, after the time the right to the property is granted to the employee, will be treated as a capital gain. This election can be particularly advantageous since the maximum rate on long-term capital gains is 15 percent (5 percent for taxpayers in the 10 or 15 percent regular marginal income tax rates). The only catch is that if the property is forfeited after making such an election, the employee is not permitted any deduction on account of the amount previously included in income. But the employee can claim a capital loss for the amount paid for the property, if any, minus the amount which the individual receives from the employer as a result of the forfeiture.

Example: Assume the same facts as in the previous example. If Bennett made the IRC § 83(b) election, he would have to recognize $1,000 of income ($3,000 - $2,000) in 2005. He would have a long-term capital gain of $6,000 ($9,000 - $3,000) when the stock is sold in 2011. However, if he forfeited the stock prior to 2009, no deduction would be permitted on account of the $1,000 previously included in gross income. He would only be permitted a $2,000 long-term capital loss on his initial stock purchase (i.e., if the employer provided no reimbursement). The holding period would begin with the grant date.

An employee who has made the Section 83(b) election and who receives dividends or other income from the property, will not have such income treated as compensation income. Beginning in 2003, dividends received from restricted stock are considered qualifying dividends taxed at a top rate of 15 percent (5 percent for taxpayers with a marginal tax rate of 10 or 15 percent). If the Section 83(b) election were not made, dividends received on the restricted stock would be treated as compensation received which would be fully taxable at regular rates and also would be subject to payroll taxes.

The primary downside of making the Section 83(b) election is the unfavorable tax treatment applicable to a forfeiture of the restricted property. If the rights to the restricted property are forfeited, no deduction is permitted to the employee for the amount that was previously included in gross income as a result of making the election. However, a capital loss will be permitted if the employee received less than the amount paid for the property. If more is received, the excess is treated as a capital gain.

Example: Bentley Corporation gives its employee, Jones, the right to buy 100 shares of its stock at $40 per share at a time when the stock is worth $140 per share. However, Jones must return the stock to the corporation for $40 per share if he should leave the employ of Bentley Corporation for any reason within three years after the transfer. If Jones makes the Section 83(b) election, he will include $10,000 [100 shares x ($140 - $40)] in the year of the transfer. His basis in the stock becomes $14,000. But if he forfeits the right to the stock, no deduction is permitted for the $10,000 previously included in income.

The Section 83(b) election must be made within 30 days after the transfer of the property. It can even be made before the date of the transfer. There are many technical requirements that must be met in order to effectively make the election.

Of course, the main advantages of making the election are that any increase in value of the property after the making of the election is taxed as a capital gain and that the employee will not have to pay tax on that further appreciation until he or she disposes of the property and can use the proceeds to pay the tax due. If the election is not made, tax will have to be paid in the year the property becomes vested whether or not it is sold.

The choice to make the Section 83(b) election then comes down to (1) no income recognition in the year in which the property is transferred and the recognition of ordinary compensation income in the year in which the property becomes substantially vested, minus the amount paid for the property, versus (2) recognition of ordinary income equal to the value of the property at the time of the transfer minus the amount paid for the property and the possibility of capital gain income in the future. In general, the decision depends on the following factors:

1. The market value of the property at the time of the transfer
2. The amount paid for the property, if any
3. The expected market value of the property when the property becomes substantially vested
4. The marginal income tax rate of the employee in the year of the transfer
5. The expected marginal income tax rate of the employee applicable to ordinary compensation income in the year the property becomes substantially vested
6. The expected marginal income tax rate of the employee applicable to capital gains in the year the property is sold
7. The expected after-tax rate of return of the employee on investments
8. The probability that the property will become substantially vested (that is, the probability that the employee will satisfy the restriction(s) constituting the substantial risk of forfeiture); and
9. The length of time the employee expects to retain the property

The executive making a Section 83(b) election is, in effect, gambling that the stock will increase substantially in value from the date of the election and that the stock will not be forfeited before the executive is able to sell or dispose of it without restriction.

SHADOW STOCK ARRANGEMENTS

There are two general types of shadow stock arrangements under which executives are compensated, typically in cash, in a manner that tracks the value of the employer's stock. These are phantom stock plans and stock appreciation rights (SARs). Such plans create a non-existent security that mimics the corporate stock, or create a non-existent security that eliminates the market variability, thereby eliminating the chance that an executive receiving these benefits will lose value merely because the stock market as a whole drops. In reality, no firm distinction is drawn between phantom stock plans and SARs by employee benefits practitioners. But in general, a phantom stock benefit usually refers to a plan formula based upon an amount of shares of employer stock, established for an employee when the plan is adopted, with a provision that the employee receives either the actual shares or equivalent cash at the date of payment. A SAR formula provides that the employee's future benefits are to be determined by a formula based on the appreciation value of the company's stock over the period between adoption of the plan and the date of payment. Generally, no actual shares are set aside, nor are shares of stock necessarily actually distributed. The value of employer stock simply is the measure by which the benefits are valued. Shadow stock arrangements tend to match the size of benefits with company success.

Phantom Stock Plans

A phantom stock plan is a method of providing deferred compensation (discussed in greater depth in chapter 17) by means of an unfunded and unsecured employer promise to pay cash, stock, or other property to the employee. These plans create "phantom stock" on the employer's books, which track the employer's actual stock performance as an incentive to spur the performance of the executive or other key employee. Phantom stock does not actually provide a share in the ownership of the business, so it can be useful when the employer wants to give a key executive the financial benefits of the growing value of the business as an incentive to perform, without future ownership rights. By using this approach, ownership of the business is not diluted, there is no battle for future control of the company, and there are no troublesome minority shareholder problems. Phantom stock is generally turned into cash on a specified date.

Actual Stock Value

Phantom stocks are typically geared to the actual value of the stock when the plan is initiated. The employer makes a book entry reflecting the amount of phantom stock granted to the employee based on his or her compensation agreement. The employer is, therefore, investing in its own theoretical stock (rather than its actual shares) at a hypothetical value as of the date of grant of the stock. Subsequently, the investment tracks the performance of the actual closely held stock, increasing or decreasing in value as does the real stock.

When the employee retires, dies, becomes disabled, or otherwise terminates his or her employment, the theoretical investment, valued to reflect cumulative gains and losses, is paid to the employee or his or her designated beneficiaries. Usually, the employer decides whether to pay this amount in cash or actual stock and likewise controls the event or date that triggers payment to the employee.

Other plans are designed to remove market volatility from the benefit. As long as the company grows and remains profitable, the value of the hypothetical stock reflects the actual value of the company rather than a depressed value that might occur whenever the entire stock market experiences a downturn. With a closely held corporation, there is no market to follow, as a few individuals hold all of the shares, so the business can use any reasonable approach to valuing the stock.

Benefits of Stock Without Drawbacks of Ownership

Under a phantom stock plan, an executive receives value for company growth without any effect on real stock ownership. Also, the executive bears no risk of loss, since he or she makes no financial investment in phantom shares and does not have to maintain the substantial risk of forfeiture required by certain other deferred-compensation arrangements (as described in chapter 17).

The major drawback to the plan involves having to determine a value for the closely held stock at various times. Since the business has a liability for the ultimate payment to the executive, for accounting purposes, this value is important. Not only can frequent appraisals of stock value be expensive and perhaps controversial, but closely held stock may also be subject to such vagaries as family problems or the death of a key management person. To avoid these pitfalls, some plans do not tie the value of the cash distributions payable to the employee to the value of the real stock.

While the employee bears the risk that this compensation may never materialize, the employee also realizes the tax advantage of recognizing no income unless and until a payment takes place. If the employee receives cash, stock, or a combination of both, the entire value of property received is reported as ordinary income and is subject to normal withholding tax rules. Any stock received has a basis equal to that of the full value reported.

Stock Appreciation Rights (SARs)

Stock appreciation rights (SARs) are, in effect, cash options that entitle the employee to whom they are granted an amount of cash determined by reference to the price of the employer's stock. (See the example below regarding how SARs and phantom stock are different.) Like phantom stock, a stock appreciation right (SAR) is a theoretical unit pegged to the value of the common stock of an employer, does not require cash to create, and does not dilute business ownership. SARs even have the same purpose as phantom stock: to give selected employees a vested interest in the success of the business without the attendant dilution risks to the current owners. What differentiates the two types of shadow stock arrangements is that, with phantom stock, the employee cannot choose the date on which to exercise the stock; in contrast, the employee can make this choice with a SAR.

If, for example, Pete Martin, the new CEO of Arc-Right Corporation (ARC), was granted a SAR with respect to 10,000 shares of stock, the SAR entitles him to be paid by ARC, the difference between the fair market value of ARC's stock at the time of exercise of the SAR and the fair market value of the stock at the time the SAR was granted. If the SAR is granted when the value of the stock is $1.00 per share and the SAR is exercised when the fair market value is $2.50 per share, Pete will be entitled to $1.50 per share, or $15,000. If instead, Pete had been granted phantom stock, he would be entitled to 10,000 shares of phantom stock with a value of $25,000. With phantom stock, the full value of the stock is awarded. With SARs, only the appreciation on the stock is awarded, based on the assumption that the value of the stock when the employee started was already there, and that the employee will benefit from the growth of the business that he or she theoretically helped create.

Other Important Points About SARs

In many cases, SARs are granted in connection with the grant of either a qualified or nonqualified stock option. The SAR is then exercisable at the same time as the stock option so that the employee has funds with which to purchase the stock or has cash compensation if he or she does not wish to purchase the stock. Normally, the number of shares subject to the stock option is reduced by the number of shares that may be obtained by exercise of the SAR. This means that if the employee exercises 2,000 SARs, he or she may use the cash to exercise the stock options, but even if he or she does not, the number of remaining stock options is reduced by the number of SARs exercised. The actual result depends on the wording of the grant of the stock options or SAR.

SARs are similar to NQSOs (discussed in chapter 18) in that the employee enjoys the economic benefits of stock ownership from the potential appreciation in the value of the stock without risk of loss. SARs differ from NQSOs in that NQSOs require a cash payment from the employee in acquiring the stock, whereas SARs provide a cash payment to the employee, with no transfer of stock to the employee. SAR plans, like NQSOs, are very flexible. Because they are nonstatutory plans, SARs have no restrictions on transferability, prices, or holding periods. This permits the employer to design SAR plans to suit its desires, as well as those of the employee.

Income Taxation of SARs

Like NQSOs, income from SARs has historically not been recognized at the time of grant but only when the SAR is exercised with such income equal to the amount resulting from the exercise of the SAR (see the 10,000-share example above), and as long as the grant is made at the fair market value of the stock. Contemporaneously, the employer is allowed a deduction for the payment, subject to normal withholding tax rules.

With the enactment of the American Jobs Creation Act of 2004 (signed by President Bush on October 22, 2004), the future income taxation of SARs may be affected to some extent. The American Jobs Creation Act added Section 409A to the Internal Revenue Code and directed the Internal Revenue Service to issue guidance within 60 days of enactment on the application of this new IRC section to, among other things, stock appreciation rights. Guidance was issued by the IRS in December 20, 2004 in IRS Notice 2005-1. Additional guidance will be issued during 2005 and eventually Treasury Regulations will be issued. As a result, it is difficult to draw firm conclusions about the position of the IRS on the income taxation of SARs at this time.

The guidance provided in IRS Notice 2005-1 is somewhat confusing and unclear. It seems to say that in order to receive the same income tax treatment that was applicable prior to the American Jobs Creation Act, SARs must meet the following four requirements:

1. The SAR grant price that is used to calculate gain at exercise must not be discounted from the fair market value of the underlying stock on the date the right is granted;

2. The stock that is subject to the right is traded on an established securities market;

3. Only traded stock of the company may be delivered in settlement of the right upon exercise (for stock-settled SARs); and

4. The SAR does not include any feature for the deferral of compensation other than the deferral of income recognition until the exercise of the right.

As additional guidance is issued and Treasury regulations are issued in this area, the income taxation of SARs should become more clear. However, it does appear that the most likely user of SARs, closely held businesses, will not be able to use them since their stock is seldom traded on an established securities market.

PERFORMANCE UNITS AND PERFORMANCE SHARES

Performance units or performance shares, as the name implies, are used to compensate key employees for achieving a contractually specified level of success, usually over a number of years. The most common goals are stated in terms of growth in earnings-per-share (EPS), although some goals are tied to divisional sales or similar measures, depending upon the particular employee's job responsibilities. **Performance unit** programs are valued at a designated amount or tied to some measure of performance while the value of **performance shares** is pegged to the value of the employer's stock. These programs usually provide for payment in either cash or shares of actual stock. Typically, the employer gives the employee the option to either receive a performance unit or to exercise a stock option when the earnings goal has been achieved or the stock has increased in value to the target amount.

Like phantom stock, performance unit or share plans are ordinarily unfunded and unsecured promises to pay. They are used more frequently in publicly held corporations, but can also be used in closely held corporations. In an effort to accurately measure actual performance against the target, the value of each unit must be established at the beginning of the program.

When the performance period ends, the employer makes an award in cash and/or stock if the performance target was achieved. Some plans permit deferral of the payment beyond the performance period if the plan document is carefully constructed to avoid constructive receipt.

There is another, similar, type of plan, known as a "performance cash plan." Under this type of plan, the amount earned by the executive *does not* depend on the value of the company's stock, but rather the maximum amount available as an award is pre-established. Performance cash plans are often used when the employer and employee want to recognize that stock values do not necessarily reflect the success of the business. The payment is subsequently made if the company reaches certain defined performance goals, typically after a stated period of time has elapsed. When the employee receives the cash award, it is taxable at that time with the employer entitled to a corresponding tax deduction.

Generally, these plans are used and operated with the long-term success of the business in mind. However, there have been instances in recent years where compensation plans tied to stock value have resulted in officers and senior management employees manipulating the business to maximize the value of the stock for their own personal benefit when they knew, or reasonably should have known that their actions would result in significantly poor long-term performance and even collapse of the business. It is this result that has led to changes in the law related to compensation through the use of stock related plans.

IMPORTANT CONCEPTS

IRC § 83(b) Election   Phantom shares

Performance share plans   Restricted stock purchase plans

Performance unit plans   Stock appreciation rights

QUESTIONS FOR REVIEW

1. What is restricted stock?

2. What is the purpose of a business using restricted stock as a form of compensation?

3. What concerns of business owners are addressed by the use of restricted stock plans, shadow stock plans, or SARs?

4. When will an employee who obtains restricted stock be taxed on it?

5. How do SAR plans generally operate?

6. What is the key feature of shadow stock?

7. What differences exist between phantom stock and SARs?

8. How do performance unit and performance share plans operate?

9. What is the difference between a performance unit plan and a performance share plan?

SUGGESTIONS FOR ADDITIONAL READING

Consider Your Options: Get the Most Out of Your Equity Compensation, Kaye Thomas, Fairmark Press, Inc., 2005.

Current Practices in Stock Option Plan Design, 2nd ed., Corey Rosen, et al, National Center for Employee Ownership, 2001.

Employee Benefits, 7th ed., Burton T. Beam and John J. McFadden, Real Estate Education Company, 2005.

Executive Stock Options and Stock Appreciation Rights, in the Employment Law Series, Herbert Kraus, Law Journal Seminars Press, 1994.

Restricted Stock for Employee Motivation, Reward, and Retention, Elizabeth Arreglado, Conference Board, 1992.

Stock Options: An Authoritative Guide to Incentive and Nonqualified Stock Options, 2nd ed., Robert Pastore, PCM Capital Publishing, 2000.

The Stock Options Book, 6th ed., Scott Rodrick, National Center for Employee Ownership, 2004.

The Tools & Techniques of Employee Benefit and Retirement Planning, 9th ed., Stephan R. Leimberg and John J. McFadden, National Underwriter Company, 2005.

CHAPTER TWENTY

Business Applications of Insurance

• • •

Life insurance and disability insurance have many applications in a business setting beyond their use as employee benefits. These products can permit the orderly change of ownership, prevent bankruptcy, and provide benefits to key employees. This chapter will introduce a number of uses for life and disability insurance when purchased by businesses and/or their owners.

When you have completed this chapter you will be able to:

- Describe how key person life insurance may be used to protect a closely-held business
- Explain transfer for value as it pertains to life insurance
- Explain business ownership transfer issues
- Describe the various types of buy/sell plans used to ensure the continuation of a closely-held business
- Compare and contrast cross-purchase buy-sell agreements with stock redemption (entity-purchase) buy-sell agreements
- Describe how split-dollar insurance may be used in a business context
- Describe the design and benefits of an executive bonus (or Section 162) plan using life insurance
- Describe the structure and operation of death-benefit-only (DBO) plans
- Describe how business overhead insurance and disability buy-sell insurance are used to ensure the continuation of closely-held businesses

KEY PERSON LIFE INSURANCE

Circuit Judge Staley of the U.S. Courts of Appeals, third circuit, once ruled "[W]hat corporate purpose could be considered more essential than key man insurance? The business that insures its buildings and machinery and automobiles from every possible hazard can hardly be expected to exercise less care in protecting itself against the loss of two of its most vital assets—managerial skill and experience."[1]

Who has not heard corporate leaders say that people are the company's most important assets—only to have said leaders turn around to remind their employees that no one is irreplaceable? In many businesses there are a few key people who account for a disproportionate amount of corporate profit. Recognizing this fact is important, and failure to prepare for the possible loss of those individuals can be damaging to large corporations and fatal to small businesses.

For example, Karen Brown is the sales manager for Stop Squeak, a wholesale business that sells various lubricants. Most buyers view lubricants as a commodity and typically look for the lowest price with no consideration for other factors. When Karen started at Stop Squeak, she quickly developed great relationships with the company's customers. As time went on, she made sure that all new sales staff kept the customers she had cultivated happy with Stop Squeak's products and service. Stop Squeak's owners have credited her skills with doubling the company's profits each year for the past five years. Because of relationships she has nurtured, Karen still works directly with the company's top 12 customers, who provide more than 25 percent of the company's total sales. If Karen were to die, it is likely that the company would suffer a substantial loss of business. Her leadership and instincts are essential for the continued growth and stability of Stop Squeak.

It is quite reasonable for the company to purchase a substantial amount of life insurance on Karen's life to cover the costs of maintaining corporate profitability while they find and develop her replacement.

Key person life insurance is life insurance applied for, owned by, and payable to the business on the life of key individuals. Premiums are not deductible, and death benefits are income-tax free, with the condition that the death benefit, minus the premiums paid, will create "adjusted current earnings and profits," and may result in alternative minimum tax (AMT). There is a small exemption for corporations with average annual gross receipts of less than $7.5 million. However, a large "C" corporation could be required to pay up to 20% of the net death benefits received in the form of alternative minimum tax. Additionally, the increase in the cash values beyond the total premiums paid potentially creates an annual AMT liability. The AMT is not often applicable, but is a possibility. The best way to avoid the impact of the AMT is to purchase additional life insurance to cover the anticipated AMT. The details of the alternative minimum tax are beyond the scope of this text.

---

[1] *Emeloid Co., Inc. v. Commissioner of Internal Revenue*, 189 F.2d 230, page 233.

Who might be considered a key person?

- A leading sales person
- An unusually imaginative product developer
- An owner/employee who has personally signed for corporate debt
- An individual working in a business that requires certain licensing if these businesses depend on licensed employees for the business to operate (i.e, physicians, professional engineers, insurance agents, accountants, or lawyers)
- Anyone whose death might result in a substantial drop in productivity as a result of the potentially negative psychological impact on the rest of the workforce
- A company "rainmaker" (a person who brings in business)

What are some reasons for wanting the death benefit available?

- To replace expected loss of profits
- To assure shareholders of the stability of the company stock and/or dividends
- To cover the cost of the search for a replacement
- To fund various obligations of the company, such as retirement benefits or health benefits
- To satisfy creditors who are concerned about the importance of certain individuals to the profitability of the business
- To help during a difficult period of adjustment after the death of certain employees
- To cover any debt for which the key person may have been required to sign
- To provide an orderly termination of the business when the key person is, in essence, the whole business

How Key Person Life Insurance Works

Prior to the purchase of the life insurance policy, a corporate resolution should be adopted emphasizing that the insurance is being purchased for the purpose of indemnifying the business for the loss of the key employee. It should also include language that states that the indemnification for that loss is the sole purpose of the insurance. The resolution may also address long-term disability and include the purchase of disability insurance to serve the same purpose. There does need to be a written record of the reason for buying the life insurance.

Typically, businesses purchase permanent insurance on key employees, treating the policies as an asset with an increasing value rather than merely an expense. If the employee lives to retirement age, the company can use the value in the policy to fund promised retirement benefits or for any other purpose. A business may also choose to keep the insurance in effect until the insured employee dies. This allows the business to recover the insurance premiums paid, as well as any payments made to his or her heirs.

It is important that the employer, rather than the key person, apply for the policy in order to avoid transfer-for-value problems (discussed later in this chapter) and inclusion of the life insurance in the estate of the insured. Generally, as long as the insured employee has no incident of ownership in the policy, the policy will not be included in his or her estate. It is possible that merely having the contractual right to purchase the policy upon terminating employment could cause inclusion of the death benefits in his or her estate, even though all of the proceeds are payable to the corporation. To prevent the employee from being taxed on the premiums paid by the employer, the employee must not be given any right to policy proceeds or values.

Other Income Tax Issues

The Internal Revenue Code imposes an accumulated earnings tax on businesses that accumulate earnings beyond their reasonable business needs. There is a safe harbor amount of $250,000 that is reduced to $150,000 for some personal service corporations. Life insurance cash values can be characterized as accumulated earnings, but many courts have found that insuring key individuals is a reasonable business purpose. Death benefits received by an employer on a key person life insurance policy generally will not give rise to the accumulated earnings tax as long as the proceeds are used for the purposes intended.

In many instances, corporations pay the premiums on key person policies by borrowing against the cash values of those policies. Generally, interest on life insurance policy loans is not deductible as a business expense. However, there is an exception under IRC Section 264(e) for key person policy loans that meet the following requirements:

- First, the aggregate amount of indebtedness with respect to each key person may not exceed $50,000 with a maximum of five key persons.
- Second, there is an interest rate cap tied to Moody's Corporate Monthly Average Bond Yield for corporate bonds.

As discussed earlier, the employer gets no deduction for the premium because it owns the policy and receives the proceeds—with the possible exception of corporate AMT—income-tax free. Because the policy is owned by the business and payable to the business, there are no tax ramifications for the employee.

Review the table at the end of the chapter to compare key attributes of various life insurance plans used as employee benefits.

TRANSFER FOR VALUE

As previously stated, IRC § 101(a) provides that the death benefits of life insurance are generally income-tax free to the beneficiary. The primary exception to this rule is when there is a transfer for value.

A transfer for value occurs when the owner of a life insurance policy transfers ownership of the policy to someone else for valuable consideration (any form of payment). The amount of the payment is often equal to the cash surrender value or the interpolated terminal reserve (a number available only from the insurance company actuaries). However, it can be a very different amount, as in the case of a viatical settlement. The subsequent owner may be an individual, a business, or a trust.

When a transfer for value occurs, the death benefit, minus the amount paid for the policy but including premiums paid subsequent to the transfer, is taxed as ordinary income. No matter how long the policy is owned, it will not result in a capital gain.

There are exceptions that permit a transfer that retains the income-tax-free nature of the death benefit. Once a policy has been transferred for value, that "taint" remains with the policy unless it is transferred according to one of the exceptions to the transfer for value rule shown below. Any of these exceptions operates to "wash away" the taint of a prior transfer for value.

- Transfer of the policy to the insured
- Transfer to a partner of the insured (business partnership)
- Transfer to a partnership in which the insured is a partner
- Transfer to a corporation of which the insured is a shareholder or officer
- Transfer in which the transferee's basis is determined in whole or in part by reference to the transferor's basis (i.e., a "substituted" or "carryover" basis), as with a gift or transfer from one business to a successor business

When there is a transfer to the insured, the amount paid for the policy makes no difference.

When transferring a policy to a partner or a partnership in which the insured is a partner, it does not matter if the policy has anything to do with the partnership. On the other hand, if two individuals are the owners of XYZ Corporation, and they want to obtain policies on each other for a buy-out plan (discussed later in this chapter), they may choose to transfer existing life insurance to one another to fund it. Normally, this would result in a transfer for value; transfer to a co-shareholder is not one of the exceptions. However, if they also have a bona fide partnership that they use for other purposes, the exchange of policies does meet the exception rules and will not be a transfer for value.

Financial planners need to recognize that while a transfer to a corporation of a life insurance policy on an individual who is an officer or shareholder is not a transfer for value, a transfer from one shareholder to another is a transfer for value.

In addition to the exceptions enumerated in IRC § 101(a), it is important to remember that every transfer of a life insurance policy is not necessarily a transfer for value. One clear example is when the policy is given as a gift. This generally happens when the insured makes an absolute assignment of the policy to a family member for "love and affection," with no consideration paid. In this case, the recipient of the policy has the same basis in the policy as the original owner. Additionally, a business might transfer a policy from one business entity to another, incident to a tax-free reorganization. When the new business takes ownership of the assets and assumes the liabilities of the other business, it acquires those assets with the same tax basis as the original owner, including life insurance policies the business may have owned. Therefore, this would not involve or constitute a transfer for value. The key for these two forms of transfer is that the basis is the same with the new owner as it was with the prior owner.

A financial planner must be vigilant in avoiding an unintentional transfer for value. For example, if a gift of a life insurance policy is made to a family member, but the policy has a policy loan outstanding, and the new owner assumes that loan, the new owner is deemed to have paid that amount for the policy. If the amount of the loan exceeds the original owner's basis, the recipient receives the policy subject to the transfer for value rules. It is not always clear whether a loan that is less than the basis in the policy for the owner will trigger a transfer for value if he or she transfers the policy as a gift to another and the new owner assumes the policy loan. During these transfers all of the rules should be carefully observed to ensure the transfer is an exception to the transfer for value rule. When there is any question about whether the transfer is an exception, the advice of an expert is necessary.

In-Depth: Partnership Issues

Businesses operated as partnerships have some unique issues. A partner may not transfer his or her shares to another person without the consent of the other partners. No one can be forced to be in a partnership with another person, and all partners must agree to be partners with one another. If one partner dies, the partnership no longer exists. The remaining partners may form a new partnership, but if there is no written agreement to continue the business, the deceased partner's heirs may force a liquidation to be assured of receiving their fair share.

Limited liability companies (LLCs) operate like partnerships and generally have the same issues as partnerships.

All partners in a partnership share the net income and losses equally unless there is a written agreement to the contrary. The partnership is not a tax paying entity; all income and losses flow through it to the partners. Again, without an agreement to the contrary, this equal sharing of the income is not affected by the amount of time spent working in the business or the percentage of partnership income earned by each partner. If one partner becomes disabled, he or she will not be able to contribute to the partnership's income, but would still be paid his or her share of that income.

If one of the partners becomes disabled in a three-person partnership, the other two might have to work 50 percent more to receive the same income. If the partnership income drops by one third, the remaining two partners will receive only two thirds of their prior income and the disabled partner will also receive two thirds of his or her prior income while not working.

Unless the partnership agreement provides otherwise, a permanently disabled partner will share in the income of the business until death or until the partnership terminates. If the partnership terminates, generally each partner is entitled to an equal share of any assets. From a pure business sense, the non-disabled partners may want to determine the value of the assets at the time that the disabled partner becomes disabled and pay the disabled partner for his or her share, then re-form the partnership with the remaining partners. However, an ongoing business, regardless of its form, is generally worth more than the assets, and the disabled partner may dispute the value of the business, creating a difficult situation for all. Additionally, the actions and ethics of the non-disabled partners may be a concern.

BUSINESS OWNERSHIP TRANSFER ISSUES

Business continuation for large corporations with hundreds or thousands of shareholders is generally not a problem. The board of directors changes over time; the board is responsible for hiring new executive talent. However, the picture is quite different for smaller businesses. When there are only a few shareholders or owners, transferring the ownership of that business to ensure operations beyond the lives of its founders, requires planning. Business continuation planning is a very important activity for any small business owner. Without it, the chances of the business continuing after the deaths of the present owners are slim.

This section will deal only with ownership transfer issues related to life and disability insurance. It is only an introduction to certain issues that must be considered when discussing buy-sell agreements.

Business interests change hands on a regular basis. In large corporations with publicly traded stock, ownership may change every day the stock exchanges are open. Because some shareholders hold so much of the stock, control does not change hands as easily. With small corporations, especially those that do not have stock traded on an exchange, ownership changes hands far less often, but it can still happen.

One business may buy another business in what is known as an acquisition. A business may also combine its assets and operations with another business in a merger. When the owner of an incorporated business dies, his or her shares of stock will change hands. The heirs may inherit those shares, or an agreement may be in place to transfer those shares to other owners. In some cases, business owners may merely sell their share of a business to another individual.

If a business owner dies and leaves his or her shares to family members, the remaining owners are forced into business with individuals who may not know anything about the business, or who have goals or desires that conflict with the needs of the business. This type of situation can potentially be very destructive.

Regardless of how a small business is owned, two of the greatest concerns for an owner and his or her family when an owner dies or becomes disabled are: (1) who is going to receive that owner's share of the business; and (2) how the disabled owner or decedent's heirs will get his or her fair share of the business value.

From the perspective of the other owners, the questions are much the same. They want to know with whom they will be in business, and, if they have the opportunity to buy the deceased owner's share, how much will they pay and how will they pay for it. Other employees will be concerned about whether or not the business will even survive.

As mentioned in the discussion of the accumulated earnings tax, most businesses do not maintain large surpluses. Usually the IRS will not designate excess accumulations as reasonable if their primary purpose is to buy out an owner who dies or becomes disabled. There are more reasonable approaches than the use of excess accumulations for securing funding for needs arising out of the loss of an owner, specifically life insurance.

Valuing an owner's interest in the business upon his or her death is another important issue. Small businesses do not generally have a ready market and are not easily valued. Quite often the IRS contests the valuation of a business interest, especially if the business did not make a provision for determining its value before the owner's death. The IRS may contest the valuation less often when such provisions have been made.

How ownership is to change hands can also affect the process of valuing a business. If a business is left to natural heirs, the owner(s) may want the value to be low to reduce potential estate taxes. Unless the scheduled temporary elimination of the estate tax becomes permanent (it is now scheduled to disappear for one year and then be reinstated), estate valuation will remain a very important issue.

On the other hand, if an owner's share is to be purchased by other owners, the selling owner will want a high value, and those who are buying will seek a low value. The lowest value for a business is most often the liquidation value. The valuation of businesses is well beyond the scope of this text, but a wide range of values for a small business could reasonably be supported. Different appraisers assign different values for different reasons.

The following section explains the primary methods of transferring ownership that deal with the issues mentioned above.

Buy/Sell Agreements

When one owner of a business dies, his or her share of the business will be left to heirs (according to a will), or sold to someone else. The most logical buyers for the deceased owner's share of the business are any other owners, or the business itself. There are two general approaches to buy/sell agreements: cross purchase and entity.

A **cross purchase agreement** is an agreement that states that if any owner of a business dies or becomes disabled, the other owners will purchase his or her share. (Note: Although they should, not all agreements cover the issue of disability.)

With an **entity agreement**, also known as a **stock redemption agreement** for corporations, the business itself will purchase the deceased or disabled owner's share.

In some situations a combination of the two, called a **hybrid agreement**, is used. This may involve the sale of stock to other owners and the business. It may also involve a more flexible approach that gives the other owners the option to purchase the shares before the business gets the right to buy them.

Both of these options include a written agreement that establishes a number of specific items:
- The date of the contract and who is involved with the agreement
- A description of the business purpose for the agreement
- When the agreement will be invoked or "triggered" (e.g., death, retirement, disability, bankruptcy, or divorce of an owner or a dispute among the owners)

- How the business interest is to be valued (e.g., fixed price, formula, appraisal)
- The manner in which the purchase price will be paid (e.g., cash, promissory notes, deferred payment terms)
- What happens in the case of bankruptcy, dissolution, or receivership of the business

The buy/sell agreement will also include:

- An acceptance by all who sign the agreement that they and/or their estates will sell their share of the business to the identified buyer(s) under the terms of the agreement upon the occurrence of any "triggering" event (alternately, an acceptance by all who sign to sell the ownership interest to the other owners or the business itself, at the price determined by the agreement prior to being able to sell the interest to a third party, regardless of the amount offered by a third party)
- A requirement for mediation or arbitration when there is a dispute regarding the terms of the agreement
- A statement specifying the jurisdiction under whose laws the agreement is to be interpreted

The problems that arise when the agreement is in place can be just as serious as when no plan is in place. If the agreement includes a fixed price and is out of date, the heirs of a deceased owner may be very unhappy with the outcome of the sale of the business interest. They could make life unpleasant for the remaining owners.

An agreement requires all parties to comply with its terms, but if the buyers have no money to make the purchase, the estate/heirs may realize substantially less money than anticipated and it may take much longer to receive it. If the ultimate payment for the business interest is realized more than nine months after death, the estate value may well be substantially greater than the actual amount received. The potential exists for the estate taxes on the business interest to be greater than the net amount realized on the sale or liquidation of the business. Further, if there is inadequate money available to pay for the interest, the business may be liquidated with the heirs of the deceased owner being the only ones to get anything.

If all of the valuation requirements are met, and all of the owners are unrelated, except for their common business, the valuation of the business interest will generally stand up to IRS scrutiny and be considered adequate for estate valuation. If owners are related, the IRS may contest the value provided by the agreement as being unreasonably low as an effort to avoid or reduce estate taxes.

There are virtually no disadvantages to a funded buy-sell agreement. Their primary advantages are:

- Assurance of a definite price and buyer under mutually agreeable conditions
- Creation of an automatic market for the business interest
- Assured continuity for the customers, creditors, and employees of the business
- Assurance that active owners retain business control
- Provision of estate value for planning purposes under most circumstances

Whenever there are certificates (stock or otherwise) that are evidence of ownership, in conjunction with a valid buy/sell agreement, the certificates should generally include a legend (printed statement) stating that transfer of ownership of those interests is subject to a binding buy/sell agreement and the agreement itself should require that each stock certificate be marked with this legend. For added protection, this limitation should also be included in the charter of the business.

Valuation

Competent business valuation is a profession unto itself. There are many ways to value a business, and a detailed discussion is beyond the scope of this text, but some understanding of its concepts is useful in recognizing valuation issues.

One of the greatest problems with closely held businesses is that members of the same family often own them and the buy-sell agreement may be used as a means to transfer the business interest to a family member for an amount less than the fair market value of that interest. By doing so, the deceased owner's estate saves estate taxes and the interest is transferred to the person(s) that he or she selects. When a buy-sell agreement involves family members, the IRS may look at it very closely. The IRS will attempt to answer the following questions:

- Is the agreement for a bona fide business purpose?
- Is the agreement a device to transfer the business to other family members, specifically the "natural objects of the transferor's bounty," (direct descendants) for less than full and adequate consideration?
- Are the terms of the agreement comparable to an arm's-length agreement that would be used with non-relatives?

For any valuation to be accepted by the IRS, it must be an arms-length agreement. This means that it must be a value that would be acceptable between unrelated parties.

Besides agreement by the owners to a specific value, there are three general methods of determining the value of a business: book value, fixed price, and by formula. If the transfer price resulting from the use of one of these three methods is significantly below the fair market value of the interest, then the buy-sell agreement might not be determinative in establishing the estate value for the closely held stock. Fair market value (FMV) is what a willing and informed seller and buyer would agree is a fair price when neither is under any pressure to complete the transfer of ownership. If a business' stock is sold on a stock exchange, the value of the stock on that exchange is the FMV. Assets such as buildings, equipment, and inventory would have their value adjusted to recognize their current value in the market. This is the value of a business as an ongoing enterprise.

One problem with the use of FMV is determining the current value of buildings and equipment. This usually requires an appraisal, which can be expensive. It is often necessary to have more than one appraisal completed to ensure that the value so determined is reasonable. As many homeowners have learned, an appraised value and the amount a building will sell for may be quite different.

To reduce the cost of determining the FMV and to speed up the process, it is permissible for the agreement to state that the owners will determine the FMV informally, by agreement, at the time of the triggering event. This may sound like a good idea, and it may be easy for all owners to agree on a value when no transfer is imminent. However, if one owner becomes ill and is to be bought out, he or she may believe a higher value is appropriate than may the other owners. If one owner dies, the heirs may believe the remaining owners are not being fair.

Book Value

Book value is generally based on accounting records, and it is the value of assets according to the books of the business minus any recorded liabilities. In many cases, this value is not representative of the actual value of a business. Equipment and buildings are depreciated over time and their true value may be substantially different from the accounting value assigned to them. Likewise, inventory would typically be carried at cost, but the accounting records may not make any adjustment for obsolete or damaged inventory. However, if the equipment owned by a business and all of its inventory are obsolete due to changing technology, the book value of the business may exceed FMV.

Fixed Price

The buy-sell agreement can state that the sales price is a specific amount at the date the agreement is signed and then require that the board of directors meet annually thereafter to review and adjust this price, if necessary. Typically, the board of directors neglects to conduct this annual review. Failure to do so, when required by the agreement, would very likely cause that part of the agreement to be unenforceable and, thus, not valid for estate or gift tax purposes.

Formula

If the industry has a known and widely used formula for valuing similar businesses, then the buy-sell agreement could use that formula as the basis for determining the buy-back price. The formula may be a multiple of the company's gross sales or a multiple of its net income. For example, a rule of thumb value for a hotel might be 2.5 times its annual sales. A hotel with annual sales of $500,000 would then be said to be worth $1,250,000.

Even if there is an industry wide formula that is widely known, the agreement must relate that industry norm to the company being valued. It is not adequate to put the industry standard in the agreement without explaining why it is the appropriate measure for the particular company. In the example above, if the particular hotel performed consistently above or below the industry average, use of the formula without adjustment would be inappropriate.

NEED TO KNOW: WHAT'S A BUSINESS WORTH?

Bill West started Bill's Builder's, Inc. (BBI) when he was 28 years old, out of the back of his pickup truck. Now that he is in his 60s, his business grosses millions of dollars a year and he has been approached by a potential buyer who is willing to pay him $3 million for his business. Fifteen years earlier, in a divorce proceeding, Bill had to obtain a business valuation of BBI. He spent $10,000 on getting the valuation. Enough has changed that he knows his old valuation is no longer valid. The $3 million sounded good to him, and instead of spending thousands of dollars on a valuation which may decrease what he gets, increase what he might get, or "blow the deal out of the water," he accepted the offer. In the real world, professional business valuations are often required for legal proceedings, and are often not considered at the time of sale. The value of any asset is based on what a willing buyer and a willing seller agree to, neither one being under any duress to complete the transaction.

As an alternative to actually placing the valuation formula in the buy-sell agreement, the agreement can simply state that the valuation at the trigger date will be the FMV of the interest to be transferred and will be determined by an independent business appraiser. If the appraisal determines FMV, then this may be the best and most cost-efficient approach of all, despite the extra up-front cost of the approach. The resulting value might be used for both an outside sale as well as the buy-sell agreement. Also, it can avoid disputes with the IRS and disgruntled owners or heirs. However, as pointed out above, different appraisals may give widely different results, so even this approach is not perfect.

Valuation Discounts

There are a number of discount opportunities when valuing a small business. Each discount is considered on its own merits and in total could result in a value reduction from full value of 25 percent or more.

Minority Discount

The IRS and the courts have agreed that sometimes the value of a transferred ownership interest is less than what the full value of that interest would be by simply multiplying the FMV of the business as a whole by the percent transferred. This is known as a minority interest discount. The reasoning behind it is that a buyer of 10 percent of a business would not pay 10 percent of the full FMV of the business since he or she may have little or no say in the operation of the company nor in its distributions to owners. This lack of control results in less value to the buyer and results in a discount. This is true regardless of the family relationship of the shareholder transferring his or her interest to other shareholders.

Lack of Marketability Discount

Another common valuation discount is that resulting from the fact that there may be no ready market for the company's stock or that the shareholder agreements place restrictions on the transferability of shares. The courts have established a list of factors to be considered in arriving at a lack of marketability discount, including:

1. The value of a similar corporation's public and private stock
2. An analysis of the company's financial statements
3. The company's dividend-paying capacity and payment history
4. The nature of the corporation, history, industry position, and economic outlook
5. Management
6. Degree of control transferred
7. Restriction on transferability
8. Investor's holding period
9. The company's redemption policy
10. Costs associated with a public offering of the stock

Discounts of from 25 to 40 percent are routinely accepted by the IRS and the courts.

Key Person Discount

If the person departing (i.e., due to retirement, death, or disability) is a key person in the company, the loss may impact the value of the business. Several factors may support this type of valuation discount, including:

1. A lack of trained personnel to take the place of the key person

2. The amount of life insurance that would be received by the company for the death of the individual

3. The company's ability to hire a competent replacement

4. The amount of compensation that the key person received

5. The degree of involvement of the key person in the day-to-day operations of the business

Triggering Events

Typical triggering events include death, retirement, disability, inability of an owner to continue, divorce, disagreements among the owners, and an owner's insolvency or bankruptcy. For obvious reasons, determining death as a triggering event is rarely a problem. An owner's death will cause a business interest to change hands. Normally a deceased executive could bequeath the business interest to a family member or it could go into the general estate for distribution to residuary beneficiaries. The buy-sell agreement can facilitate this transfer by permitting the inheritance of the business interest or it can block the inheritance by forcing the interest of the deceased owner to be sold to specified parties (usually either the business itself or the remaining business owners) and thus keep the actual ownership of the business inside the circle of present owners.

Retirement, or any other action of an owner to leave the company, is often a second trigger. For the purposes of our discussion, retirement may include any occurrence of one owner leaving the business. For some businesses, retirement may not trigger a buy/sell agreement. Owners may retire, in that they do not work in the business daily, but may remain owners in an advisory capacity, retaining a salary and other benefits. It is important that the buy/sell agreement price is one that is applicable in life as well as at death. The same pricing method used for a transfer at death is used when an owner leaves the business for any reason. The wants and needs of the owners will dictate how this trigger is activated.

When an owner becomes disabled, it is more difficult to determine if there has been a triggering event. Will he or she recover? How long is the disability expected to last? Can the owner still provide services to the business? In spite of a positive prognosis, at what point does an extended disability trigger the buy/sell agreement? Disability is not always clear-cut. How long should a disability last before it triggers the buy/sell agreement? Would the disability have to be total and permanent? Would it have to be measured by activities of daily living? Would partial disabilities trigger the agreement? What happens if the agreement is triggered, and shortly thereafter the individual recovers? Adopting a statement that defines a triggering disability generally protects owners from these problems. All owners must recognize that such a statement will apply to each of them if disabled.

Disability as a triggering event may be of more importance in a partnership or another pass-through entity that requires the owners to share the profits of the business. A disabled owner may not be able to contribute to the success of the business. Yet if he or she remains an owner, he or she will share in the business' success. From the standpoint of the disabled owner, he or she may now have higher living expenses and could need the funds he or she would receive from selling his or her business interest. The buy-sell agreement would provide the disabled owner with a market and fair price for his or her interest as soon as the trigger is activated.

In-Depth: Disability

Let us look at an example, based on a true case. Mac and Jake started a small manufacturing company together. Mac could bid jobs and schedule the work with the best of them; Jake made practically all of the sales calls in the early years, and he was the one that the employees admired, liked, and respected. Jake and Mac had a buy/sell agreement, but it did not cover disability.

At age 48, Jake had a stroke that left him unable to write or speak, but he continued to come into the plant and greet the employees. They were happy to see him and appreciated what little he could do. Obviously, sales calls were out of the question for him, and responding to questions from customers was impossible. Because Mac generally irritated most employees, Jake's position changed from manager to good will ambassador. Jake continued to receive his salary and kept the employees happy with his presence, allowing the company to grow until the two owners could sell it and retire wealthy. Without Jake the company may have failed because of poor employee relations, so in this circumstance, it may seem the buy-sell agreement was not needed.

But what would have happened if the roles had been reversed. If Mac had the stroke and was unable to write or talk, he would be unable to contribute much to the company. If Mac were to earn his salary while disabled, the company would have received no benefit for the salary paid to him, and he would instead drain company profits. As the company is a partnership and Mac and Jake are equal partners (without a disability clause in their buy-sell agreement), they would receive the same income each year.

In a professional practice, normally each of the owners is required to possess a valid license to practice. If, for some reason (such as conviction for a felony), an owner is required to surrender his or her professional license to the appropriate licensing entity, he or she will be unable to continue as a principal of the firm. This eventuality may be provided for in a buy-sell agreement. In fact, the agreement may cover nearly any situation in which an owner does not continue in the business, including if an owner is fired.

In community property states, a husband and wife may have an equal ownership interest in a business. If the couple were to obtain a divorce, the ownership interests are divided equally. If one of the spouses was not active in the business, it may not be in the best interest of either the business or the uninvolved spouse to have a portion of the business owned by such a party. The buy-sell agreement can stipulate a mandatory buy-back of any interest transferred in a divorce.

An additional trigger may be that of disagreement among the owners. Typically, such a trigger is activated by one owner writing a letter expressing his or her desire to purchase the other ownership interests in the entity for a specific price. Usually, the other owners have a period of time to respond to the letter by either agreeing to sell their ownership interests under the terms offered in the letter or by writing a letter in which they offer to buy the ownership interest of the author of the first letter under the same terms that were just offered to them. Therefore, the recipient of the letter can decide whether to sell or buy. This type of triggering event can be problematical if there is a disparity between the personal wealth of the owners. This could force the less wealthy owners to sell their interests to the wealthy owner. Moreover, in the situation where there are several younger owners and one older owner, the younger owners could conspire to drive the older owner out before the retirement provisions of the agreement are triggered.

If it becomes necessary for an owner to declare personal bankruptcy, all of his or her assets become available to the owner's personal creditors. Normally, a business will find it objectionable to have an ownership interest subjected to an owner's personal creditors. Accordingly, buy-sell agreements often contain a bankruptcy or insolvency trigger requiring the business or the remaining owners to purchase the ownership interest of such an owner. Of course, the bankruptcy court will review the transaction to ensure that the agreement is binding and legal and that the price paid is fair.

Funding

It has been said that an unfunded agreement is worse than no agreement at all because in such a case there are legal obligations to sell and to buy, but no money to complete the transaction.

Funding can be accomplished in a number of ways. A seller of a business interest, whether it is the departing owner or heirs, typically wants a lump sum payment, and agreements often call for it. This requires that a large amount of cash must be available at the time of the triggering event. A sinking fund may be established to create the fund, but unfortunately, that approach may take longer than the time the owners have and may trigger the accumulated earnings tax.

Another option is for the buyer of the business interest to borrow the money. This will mean that the buyer(s) will pay the price of the business interest plus interest. This can be done in two ways. The agreement may state that a lump sum is to be paid; this requires borrowing from an outside source. This brings up a question of availability. If a closely held business is losing one of its owners, the loss may affect the willingness of a lender to provide funds that are to be repaid from business earnings. The other way is to permit payment for the business interest over time—this is essentially borrowing from the seller of the business interest. In this case, the buy-sell agreement should specify all of the terms of the note that will be used to pay for the retiring owner's interest in the business, including the term, frequency of payments, and the rate of interest. If an inadequate interest rate is charged, the IRS will impute additional interest to bring the rate to a reasonable market rate. Each payment received by the seller consists of an interest portion and a principal portion. The interest received in each payment is ordinary income to the seller, while the principal portion consists of a return of capital and gain. The nature of the gain is determined by the kind of asset that was sold and the holding period for the asset sold at the time of the sale. The seller is not taxed on the return of capital and the gain portion of the payment is taxed at long- or short-term capital gain rates or other tax rates depending on the nature of the gain. Where a deferred sale is between related parties (as defined in IRS § 453), and the gain is from the sale of depreciable property, then all of the gain is treated as ordinary income and all of the gain must be recognized in the year of the sale (unless it can be shown to the IRS that the transaction did not have the avoidance of taxes as one of its principal purposes). Moreover, if there is an installment sale between related parties and the buyer disposes of the property within two years of the original sale, then the installment gain that has not yet been recognized under the contract must be reported in the year in which the property is sold.

The final and most commonly used method is life insurance. If the type of agreement used is a cross purchase agreement (discussed later in this chapter), the owners purchase insurance on one another. If it is an entity agreement (discussed later in this chapter), the business purchases insurance on each of the owners. If a hybrid agreement is used (discussed later in this chapter), the owners and the business may purchase life insurance on the parties to the agreement.

When life insurance is used, care must be taken to avoid a transfer for value (discussed earlier and later in this chapter) that could render the insurance proceeds taxable. It is possible that an entity purchase agreement will make the death proceeds, in excess of the premiums paid, partially subject to the alternative minimum tax. This is not a possibility when the insurance policy owners are individuals.

The greatest difficulty in using life insurance is to have an adequate amount of insurance. If the price of the business interest is stated in the agreement, determining the appropriate amount of life insurance is easy. If a formula is used, the formula is applied and the amount of insurance is purchased. If using a universal life insurance policy, an additional death benefit may be added to the policy as the value increases. However, the owners may not always be insurable, or at least insurable at standard rates. When this happens, alternatives must be considered.

It is common for an agreement to stipulate that when adequate insurance benefits are not available, the business interest will be purchased over a period of time at an agreed-upon interest rate. This interest rate may be fixed in the agreement or be based on a readily available index interest rate such as the prime rate or the Applicable Federal Rate as determined by the federal government. This takes care of the problem of not having adequate funds available if an owner becomes disabled or leaves the business for any other reason.

In addition to certain possible income tax consequences discussed later in this chapter, there are some drawbacks to using life insurance to fund a buy-sell agreement, including:

- The potential uninsurability of one of the business owners or the presence of a health condition that makes the acquisition of suitable insurance prohibitively expensive
- The existence of a wide disparity in the ages of the owners thereby increasing the cost of coverage on the older owners
- The nondeductibility of the premium payments for federal income tax purposes unless they are treated as compensation income to the individual insured owners
- The complexity and cost of maintaining life insurance on all of the owners in a cross-purchase agreement (discussed later in this chapter)

Disability Buy/Sell Insurance

When a business owner dies, his or her share of the business must be transferred to someone. Because this fact is so obvious, business owners rarely resist establishing and funding a buy-sell agreement for this possibility. Unfortunately, many business owners do not accept as readily the possibility of a long-term disability creating the same problems. For disability, there are specific disability buy-out policies available. These policies generally have a one- to two-year elimination period. They pay benefits only when there is a total disability as defined by contract. The benefits may be provided as a lump sum, as periodic payments over a number of years, or a combination of the two. There are also limitations on the maximum amount available, and insurers seldom will provide an amount in excess of 80 percent of the value of the business.

Some companies offering disability buy/sell insurance offer a waiver of premium benefit. Once the insured has been disabled by the terms of the contract for 90 days, the premium paid for those 90 days is generally returned and future premiums are waived until the insured has met the elimination period or until the insured physically improves and is thus no longer disabled as defined by the contract terms.

The greatest benefit of using a disability buy/sell policy is that the insurance company, which is a disinterested third party, determines when the individual is disabled. The use of a third party to make this determination eliminates the possibility that the disabled person feels that the other owners are trying to push him or her out. The decision is objective and based on contract terminology adopted before the disability begins.

Types of Buy-Sell Agreements

A buy-sell agreement is between one business owner who agrees to sell his or her interest in the business to the entity itself, the other business owners, a combination of the entity and the other business owners, an Employee Stock Ownership Plan (ESOP) or a non-owner under the terms described in the agreement. There are various advantages and disadvantages to any combination. We will discuss in this section the various types of agreements and their pros and cons.

Cross Purchase Agreement

If a cross purchase agreement is used, the owners agree to buy each other's interest after a triggering event. If there are two owners, each agrees to purchase the business interest of the other. If there are five owners, the agreement typically stipulates that each owner agrees to buy 25 percent of another owner's interest when he or she leaves the business, but the possibilities are numerous. For instance, if owner A dies or leaves the company, B and C will keep their present ownership interests and owners D and E will each buy one half of A's interest. It is possible—but not common—to have different agreements for each of the owners.

It is reasonable to use different valuation methods, or at least different values, when certain owners leave. If one owner is the heart and soul of the business, his or her absence will affect the business more than if another owner leaves. If different valuation methods are used for different owners, the business and the owners will need to be well prepared to explain the discrepancy to the IRS, which would certainly question the differing methods used to determine the value of the business.

The typical agreement keeps each owner in possession of a similar level of control held before the one owner left. If there are five owners, four of which own 15 percent of the business, and the remaining owner holds 40 percent of the business, then when one of the 15 percent owners dies, the 40 percent holder will typically purchase more of the deceased owners share than will the others. If the 40 percent owner dies, the others may well purchase equal percentages of his or her share of the business.

Advantages

Cross purchase agreements have a number of advantages. First, when owners purchase the interest of a departing or departed owner, the tax basis of their investment in the business increases by the purchase price. This reduces the income taxes payable when the surviving purchasers' business interests are eventually sold. The agreement can effect a change of control when specific individuals are no longer there. Assume each of five owners has 100 shares with a basis of $100 per share, or $10,000. After one owner's shares have been purchased, the remaining owners would have 125 shares each. However, if the departing shareholder received $1 million for his or her shares, each of the other owners has a basis that is increased by $250,000, which would be the amount paid by each surviving owner for those additional 25 shares. When all five owners were in place, two of them together held only 40% of the business. When one is gone, any two hold 50%. While the possibility of a decision making stalemate are all but impossible with five owners, it is quite possible with four equal owners.

Other advantages include: (1) life insurance death benefits are received income-tax-free unless there has been a transfer for value of the policies involved; (2) ownership is restricted to the present owners; (3) the money being used for the purchase is an asset of the purchasing owners, rather than that of the business; (4) the policies owned by the other owners on the life of the deceased owner are not included in the estate of the deceased owner; (5) if the seller is an owner, he or she may treat any gain on sale as capital gain (regardless of the character of the corporation's underlying assets); and (6) if the seller is the estate of a deceased owner and the stock is sold shortly after the owner's death, there is usually little or no gain realized by the estate under current estate and income tax laws.

Disadvantages

There are also disadvantages. The number of required life insurance policies to fund such an agreement can become overwhelming. When the funding of the agreement comes from life insurance, a formula is used: The number of policies is the number of owners times the number of owners minus one. If there are three owners, there are 3 x 2 = 6 policies. If there are five owners, there will be 5 x 4 = 20 policies. This is necessary so that each surviving owner can purchase the shares of any one of the other owners. An alternative is to have the owners set up a legitimate partnership that will purchase and hold the life insurance for the benefit of the partners. This would reduce the number of policies to the number of owners. When one owner dies, the death benefit is received income-tax free and is used to purchase the ownership interest of the deceased owner, whose heirs obtain a stepped-up basis of that interest resulting in no capital gains tax, if sold immediately. Of course, if a partnership is used, the life insurance benefits are assets of the partnership, and the decedent's heirs have a claim to a proportionate share of that as well.

Other disadvantages include: (1) that the money to fund the life insurance, or eventually the note to buy the retiring business interest, may have to come either from the resources of each shareholder outside of the business or somehow through the business. The funds from the business, depending on the type of business, may be taxable to the owner on the way out of the business; (2) the premiums used to fund a buy-sell agreement are not deductible by the business owners.; (3) the cash values (plus premiums paid but unearned on the date of death) of the policies the decedent owned on the surviving shareholders' lives will be included in his or her estate. Once an owner leaves, the policies he or she owns on the others need to be transferred in such a manner as to ensure adequate funds for future buyouts; and (4) if the corporation pays the life insurance premiums, it is likely to be considered a distribution of dividends to the owners. (If the proceeds are payable to the estate or personal beneficiary of the owner, the premiums are includable in the owner's income.)

Generally, under a cross purchase agreement, the business owners should be the applicants, owners, beneficiaries, and premium payors for policies on other owners and not on policies on their own lives.

Entity or Stock Redemption Agreement

This form is similar to a cross purchase, but in this case, the business entity itself buys the business interest. Entity purchase agreements are easy to establish. When funded with life insurance, only one policy is required per owner. When one owner dies or becomes disabled, the entity receives the insurance proceeds and purchases the interest of the departed owner. The tax basis of each of the remaining owners is unchanged (except in the case of a partnership or LLC). Their relative ownership interests change, but only to the extent that the business interest of the owner who is no longer there has been absorbed by the business.

For example, if five owners held 100 shares each of XYZ Corp. stock, and XYZ Corp. purchased the stock of one owner who left, there would then be 400 shares outstanding instead of 500. Each remaining owner would now have 25 percent of the outstanding stock instead of 20 percent, but their tax basis will not have changed. If their original basis in the stock was $100 per share, or $10,000, they would still have a $10,000 basis, even if the business paid the departed owner $1 million for his or her shares. The same voting power issues as mentioned previously would apply to this scenario.

Advantages

The advantages of an entity or stock redemption agreement include: (1) the relative simplicity of administration (fewer life insurance policies and only one buyer); (2) the death benefits are received regular income-tax-free (unless there has been a transfer for value of the life insurance policies) but if the business is a large C corporation, they may be subject to the alternative minimum tax (AMT) of up to 15 percent of the proceeds [this is not an issue when the business is an S corporation, partnership, or small C corporation ($5,000,000 or less in average gross receipts for the previous 3 years)]; (3) if the buy-sell agreement is triggered by the retirement of an owner, the entity can make the note payments and deduct the interest expense as a business deduction; (4) the ownership interest purchased is no longer outstanding and the remaining owners now own a larger percentage of the business; (5) premium payments not taxed to the insured shareholder as either a constructive dividend or salary; (6) proceeds are not included in the deceased owner's estate if the corporation is the owner and beneficiary of the policies; (7) cash values accumulated in life insurance policies used to fund such an agreement are not subject to the accumulated earnings tax (satisfy a reasonable business need).

Disadvantages

Some of the disadvantages include: (1) most states prohibit an entity from buying back its equity interests if it does not have earnings and profits sufficient to do so (only applies where retained earnings are low); (2) life insurance premiums are not deductible by the entity and not taxable to the insured owner; and (3) danger that the IRS will treat the redemption price amount as a dividend to the selling shareholder unless certain tests are met under IRS § 302 or 303.

Generally, under a stock redemption agreement, the corporation should be the applicant, owner, beneficiary, and premium payor.

Hybrid or Wait-and-See Agreement   *Corp. has 1st option to purchase stock*

The hybrid agreement is sometimes called the **wait-and-see** form of buy/sell and is generally the most beneficial because of its flexibility. This type of agreement may be appropriate when the corporation or surviving shareholders may not have sufficient funds to purchase the interest of a deceased owner; when the financial circumstances of the corporation and owners are uncertain; or when the parties want to allow for possible future changes in the tax laws. It permits a deferral of the decision as to the eventual purchaser of the business interests until the occurrence of a triggering event. Under this type of agreement, the corporation has the first option to purchase any or all of the exiting shareholder's stock within a specified time period. In the event that this first option is not exercised during the established timeframe, the remaining shareholders then acquire an option to purchase the stock. Any stock unacquired after the expiration of the remaining shareholder's option must be purchased by the corporation. It is important that these three option stages occur in this order. If the corporation had the second option (rather than the first and third options), it would be considered by the IRS to be relieving the shareholders of an obligation to purchase stock and would accordingly be treated as a constructive dividend.

Employee Stock Ownership Plan (ESOP) Agreement

In certain cases, an Employee Stock Ownership Plan (ESOP) can be established to purchase the retiring shareholder's ownership interest. An ESOP is a tax-qualified defined contribution plan that is designed to invest primarily in qualifying stock of the employer. Normally, the plan borrows money from a commercial lender to buy qualified employer stock with the loan secured by the stock and guaranteed by the employer-corporation. Subsequently, the corporation makes tax-deductible contributions to the ESOP and the plan uses these contributions to make the loan payments. As the loan is paid off and the shares collateralizing the loan are released, the plan assigns the stock to the employee participants. After a participant retires or dies, he or she is entitled to the full value of his or her account.

Advantages

The advantages of an ESOP include: (1) the employer is in a better cash position and not deprived of working capital by large plan contributions; (2) the plan provides an employee incentive to remain with the employer; (3) there is a ready market for minority interests in the employer securities; (4) the appreciation in value of the securities is not taxed while in the plan; and (5) there are some very favorable tax treatments available to both the stockholder who sells shares to an ESOP, as well as the corporation who sponsors the plan. For instance, the corporation's payments made to buy the company stock are deductible expenses similar to other defined contribution plans including principal payments on the loans to purchase the company stock. Additionally, dividends paid for stock held in an ESOP are deductible against the income of the paying corporation. The owner of the shares sold to the ESOP can make an election to defer the recognition of the long-term capital gain to the extent the proceeds are rolled over into a qualified investment within a specified amount of time.

Disadvantages

The disadvantages of an ESOP include: (1) dilution of ownership; (2) those who are charged with operating it have fiduciary responsibility and the liability that goes with it; (3) employees who have a beneficial interest in the ESOP, but no actual shares, are not privy to information disclosed only to shareholders even though it directly affects the value of their interest; (4) there may be a negative impact on the balance sheet of the company; (5) third party valuation of the stock value can be quite expensive; and (6) any offers made to purchase stock for the ESOP must be made pro-rata to all shareholders. If a retiring shareholder wants to sell all of his or her stock, the plan must be willing to purchase a proportionate share from all other shareholders. And, of course, the employee benefits of the plan are funded solely with employer stock

Third Party Agreement

A buy-sell agreement can include a non-owner as the purchaser of a withdrawing owner's interest. This would be the case when there are one or more owners and a key employee. Normally, the agreement will give the key person (or other third party) the right-of-first-refusal to purchase all or a portion of the retiring or deceased owner's interest. Of course, it is still necessary to obligate the entity itself and/or the remaining owners to buy the retiring or deceased owner's interest in case the third party fails to exercise his or her option to purchase the interest. There are a number of situations where the involvement of a non-owner in the agreement is a viable option, and sometimes the only viable option.

Which Type of Buy/Sell Agreement Is Best? *NEED To Compare tax brackets*

Consideration needs to be given to the comparative tax brackets of the entity and the owners in deciding on the type of buy-sell agreement. For instance, if the corporation is in a higher income tax bracket than the individual shareholders, it may be wise to make tax-deductible salary payments or bonuses to the shareholders and have them buy and own the insurance on a cross purchase basis. If the opposite situation applies, use of a stock redemption plan may be more appropriate. If the corporation pays the premiums directly, it may be treated as a dividend to the owner of the policy.

The increase in basis when a cross purchase plan is used is a very important consideration and will become far more important if the estate tax is completely eliminated. If the owners started out with a cross purchase and then decided to stop buying so many policies, and/or the value of the business grew faster than the rate at which they were able to provide adequate insurance, they might want the business to be involved in at least part of the transaction. Changes in circumstances and tax law may well call for changes in the plan used.

Buy/Sell Transfer for Value Issues

Once a deceased owner's shares have been purchased, his or her estate still owns insurance on the other owners, assuming a cross purchase agreement was used. It is considered a transfer for value if these policies are transferred to any stockholder other than the insured. This is another reason that leads some advisors to recommend that all owners of a closely held corporation also establish a partnership with the same owners. A transfer of a policy to a business partner in a partnership is an exception to the transfer for value rule. The partnership does need to be a legitimate organization. It may do little but purchase and lease equipment to the corporation. However, the partnership also needs to have a buy/sell agreement. The downside of using a partnership to own life insurance policies for a cross purchase agreement is that when one owner dies, the value of the partnership immediately increases by the amount of insurance proceeds received by it.

When changing from one form of buy/sell to another, there may or may not be transfer for value problems. If the change is from a cross purchase to a corporate stock redemption plan, there is no problem. Transfer of a policy to a corporation of which the insured is a shareholder or officer is one of the exceptions to the transfer for value rule. If the change is from a corporate stock redemption plan to a cross purchase agreement, all of the policy transfers will be transfers for value.

SPLIT DOLLAR LIFE INSURANCE

Split-dollar life insurance is not a specific type of policy but a method of paying for and owning permanent life insurance. The general purpose of split-dollar life insurance is to provide permanent life insurance on the life of key executives as a benefit, using corporate dollars rather than personal dollars. The plans generally provide that the business will have all of its payments eventually returned. Split-dollar insurance can also be used as a method of paying for life insurance to be used to fund a buy/sell agreement when the employee who owns the policy is not the insured.

While it is usually applied in a business setting, it can be used whenever one party who has money wants to help another individual purchase life insurance, but ultimately wants his or her money back.

The employer pays all or a portion of the premium for life insurance that has most of the death benefit going to the beneficiary designated by the insured. There are two general approaches: collateral assignment and endorsement.

The employee and the employer enter into an agreement that specifies the approach to be used. The following are the most common approaches, but the specifics of the plans can be just about anything the employer and employee find agreeable.

Under the **endorsement method**, both the employer and the insured apply for and own the policy. The insured owns the death benefit and the business owns the cash values. Generally, the business pays the premium, and the insured employee either reports as income an amount equal to the premium minus the increase in the cash value, or the term insurance rates from the government's Table 2001 premiums.

The endorsement method gives the employer greater control over the policy and is relatively simple to administer. Some states prohibit loans to officers and directors, who are often beneficiaries of split-dollar plans. This approach prevents any appearance of loans. If the company decides to implement a split-dollar plan and the insured's health deteriorates, using a key-person policy is possible.

In the **collateral assignment** method the insured, or policy owner, applies for the policy and assigns it to the employer. The employer generally makes loans to the individual to pay the premiums. Although it may seem the employer is merely making payments to the insurance company, the agreement specifies that the employer is to be reimbursed at the death of the insured for the amounts paid by it to that date, making the payments tantamount to loans in the eyes of the IRS.

The advantages to collateral assignment split-dollar are that it provides more protection for the employee, and if the employee's health deteriorates, existing policies owned by the employee can be used, reducing his or her out-of-pocket cost for the insurance.

Terms of the Plan

There is no single specific set of terms that defines how split-dollar plans may be established. In the **standard** or **classic plan** the employer pays an amount equal to the increase in the cash value. This means that in the early years of the policy the insured will be paying most of the premium, providing him or her with minimal, if any, benefit other than that obtained by buying life insurance.

The first alternative is a **level premium plan**. In such a plan the employee pays a level amount for the first five or 10 years. This makes it more of a benefit to the employee. Over the long run, the total paid by the employee and employer is essentially the same as with the standard plan approach. The downside of this plan is that if it terminates within the first 10 years or so, the cumulative cash value may not be adequate to reimburse the employer for all of the payments it made. As long as the employee's share of the premium is at least an amount equal to the IRS Table 2001 premiums, he or she will have no additional income to report.

The next alternative is the **employer-pay-all plan.** As the name indicates, the employer pays the entire premium. The employee reports as income the value of the death benefit as determined by the IRS Table 2001. If it is a collateral assignment plan, the loan amount will result in income on the imputed interest under IRC § 7872. The disadvantage of this approach is the same as for the level premium plan: If the plan terminates in the early years, the employer will not have all of its payments reimbursed.

The final alternative is the **2001 offset plan**. With this plan the employee pays the premium identified in the IRS Table 2001, which is the economic benefit cost of the death benefit, and the employer pays the balance. In some cases the employer will pay a "bonus" to the employee that covers the employee's cost for the economic benefit–perhaps enough to cover the income tax on it as well.

At the time of this publication, the taxation of split-dollar plans is in flux. The IRS has issued proposed regulations that have added some level of uncertainty.

Split-Dollar Plan Variations

Recent changes in the tax laws have resulted in the structuring of variations on split dollar plans for tax and financial reasons. We will discuss a few of these recent variations.

Equity Split-Dollar Plans

Equity split-dollar plans are not truly separate. These are split-dollar plans where the employer's economic interest in the policy is limited to its actual payments made. The result is that over time, the insured/owner may build substantial equity in the policy. Because of this, the IRS states that the portion of the equity build-up that inures to the insured/owner each year should be taxed as earned income (Technical Advice Memorandum 9604001). Furthermore, if the split-dollar plan had an irrevocable life insurance trust as the owner of the employee's interest, then the amount of the equity buildup subject to income taxes, as well as the economic value of the death benefit from Table 2001 rates or PS38 (joint term life insurance premiums) rates would be considered a gift from the employee to the trust.

If the insured is not a majority shareholder of the business and there is a substantial risk of forfeiture of the accumulations in the policy by the employee, then it may be possible to avoid having the accumulating equity taxed as current income to the employee.

IRS Notice 2001-10 restates and expands the provisions of TAM 9604001. It includes two major provisions. First, it requires the payments to a split-dollar plan made by an employer to be characterized in one of three ways: a loan, an investment in the contract for the benefit of the employer, or as compensation to the employee. Secondly, it states that Table 2001[2], a table of term insurance rates, replaces the earlier PS-58 rates that were much higher. This applies to all taxpayers rather than to a specific case as does a private letter ruling (PLR), including TAM 9604001. A notice is a statement by the IRS that provides interim guidance until a more formal IRS ruling is issued.

The notice creates clarity but also some confusion. If the parties consistently characterize and treat the transaction as a loan, it will generally be considered a loan. This prevents the employee from having to worry about whether the employer's payment is considered income. With a collateral assignment form of split-dollar (where the employer does not own any portion of the policy), the transaction is automatically a loan by the nature of the agreement. If the policy is collateral for repayment of the money paid by the employer, there is no other way the payment can be characterized. The IRS has not yet offered its opinion on this tax treatment.

If the employer does not consistently treat the payments as loans, IRC Sections 61 and 83 outline the results:

- The employer will be considered to have become a beneficial owner of the policy through its share of the premium payments
- The employee will have received income equal the value of the current life insurance protection minus any premium payments made by the employee

---

[2]In 2003, an insurer's published term rates may be used in place of Table 2001 rates if they are lower. After 2003 the insurer must show, through actual sales of these policies, that the rates are being used and not merely created for purposes of being less than Table 2001 rates.

- Any dividends payable as a benefit of the policy to the employee will be received by the employee as earned income
- The cash value that is vested in the employee, less any payments made by the employee that contributed to the increase in cash value, will be treated as earned income by the employee

There are some additional and confusing provisions in this IRS Notice. The nature of a notice is that it is interim guidance. Unfortunately, in some cases, final regulations and clarification of terms take years.

Split-Dollar Rollout

Before 1986, the interest on life insurance policy loans was deductible. Split-dollar plans were often sold to employees or third parties with this in mind. The employee's out-of-pocket cost for the policy could be recovered by taking out a policy loan. Premiums were then paid by the employee or third party sometimes using policy loans. Once the policy cash value was adequate to pay back the employer, the plan was terminated. The business could be paid back in one of three ways:

- The employee buys the policy from the employer for cash, which could come from a policy loan. The employer pays tax on any excess of sale proceeds over the employer's basis.
- The policy is transferred to the insured and the employer reports as taxable income to the insured an amount equal to its interest in the policy. The employee may use a policy loan to pay the resulting income tax.
- The policy is purchased from the employer over time by using the policy dividends to make payments. The dividends so used are taxable to the employee.

Interest rates were reasonably good, and with tax-deductible loan interest payments employees were able to obtain policies with increasing cash values at a substantially lower out-of-pocket cost than if they had originally purchased them individually. With the elimination of the deduction for the interest paid on policy loans, the use of rollouts diminished substantially.

Without the deductible interest there are still times when a rollout makes sense. Because the employee reports as taxable income the Table 2001 rates, it may be more beneficial to rollout the policy before the employee reaches an advanced age and for the employee to pay the premium thereafter. If an employee is leaving the company and needs the life insurance, he or she may want to keep that policy. This may well be the case if he or she has reduced insurability.

Reverse Split-Dollar Plan

In a reverse split-dollar plan, the employee generally has the primary claim on cash values up to the aggregate of his or her premium payments, and the business receives the balance of the death benefit. This can represent a significant employee benefit as policy cash values build up over the years tax free. In a closely held corporation, the death benefit might be used to fund a stock redemption buy/sell agreement. This was fairly beneficial when the PS-58 rates were used—the employer was essentially paying for part of the cash value build-up that was owned by the employee. The Table 2001 rates are lower, so the employee will be paying more. The purpose behind the plan was to provide some indemnification to the employer if the employee died, but mostly it was to have the employee own an asset with values that increased quite rapidly relative to the amount paid into it. One of the biggest concerns was the possibility that the death benefit would be included in the estate of the insured if he or she were a majority shareholder. A method of maximizing the benefit of a reverse split-dollar plan is to terminate the plan once the cash values are increasing at a much faster rate than the premiums paid. The insured employee ends up with a bargain priced life insurance policy and the employer has effectively transferred part of that value to the employee with no personal income taxes being paid.

Now, however, reverse split-dollar plans may be dead. In 2002 the IRS published Notice 2002-59 which prevents split-dollar plans from using the PS 58 rate table, table 2001 or an insurer's alternative term premium rates to determine the cost of the insurance. These have been the only options for valuing the death benefit cost under more straightforward split-dollar plans. The notice made no provision for dealing with existing plans which, upon publication of the notice, immediately became non-compliant with the notice. However, as this is merely a notice and not a revenue ruling, regulation, TAM or in any other form that constitutes enforceable tax law, any enforcement of this may lead to litigation. Since the IRS was silent on this issue for about 35 years, it is uncertain how the courts will deal with it. There is no proposed date for issuing regulations covering these changes, nor are there hearings scheduled for it.

Split-Dollar and ERISA

While split-dollar insurance plans are generally considered ERISA plans by being "an employee welfare benefit plan," they can avoid the problem of reporting. As long as a split-dollar plan is an "insured" plan maintained for a select group of management or highly compensated employees, it does not have to meet the reporting and notice requirements of other ERISA plans. However, ERISA does require a written document, a "named fiduciary", and a formal claims procedure for such plans.

Other Tax Issues Applicable to Split-Dollar Plans

The employer cannot deduct any portion of its premium contribution even for the part that results in taxable compensation income to the employee.

Review the table at the end of the chapter to compare key attributes of various life insurance plans used as employee benefits.

Changes in 2003

As you read above, under the classic type of split-dollar life insurance plan, the employer pays part of each premium equal to the increase in the cash surrender value (CSV) of the policy each year. The employee pays the balance of the annual premiums. Under the endorsement method in which the employer is the owner of the contract, the employer endorses the contract to specify the portion of the proceeds payable to the employee's beneficiary. Under the collateral assignment method, the employee is treated as the owner of the contract; the employer's premium payments are characterized as loans from the employer to the employee. The employer's interest in the proceeds of the contract is designated as collateral security for its loans.

Typically, when the employee dies, the employer is paid an amount equal to the CSV of the policy and the deceased employee's beneficiary receives the balance of the policy proceeds. The amount paid to the employer is taxable while the amount received by the beneficiary is generally excludable from taxation under Code Section 101(a).

For over 30 years, the income tax treatment of such arrangements had been controlled by IRS Revenue Ruling 64-328, which was issued in 1964. However, without a change in tax law, in January 1996, the IRS issued Technical Advice Memorandum (TAM) 9604001 in which it made a minor change to the taxation of cash values when they exceeded the employer's interest in the policy. Then in January 2001, the IRS issued Notice 2001-10 by which it eliminated the government-created P.S. 58 tables, replacing them with a new Table 2001. Notice 2001-10 included some interim guidance as to how to apply the Table 2001 rates and helped to reduce previous abuses in this area. In January 2002, Notice 2002-8 was issued with new interim guidance and revocation of Notice 2001-10. The Treasury Department then released Proposed Regulations regarding split-dollar plans in July 2002. Public hearings were held on these proposed regulations in October 2002; in May 2003 the IRS and Treasury Department released additional guidance for the proposed regulations. Finally, on September 17, 2003, final regulations, containing a few additional changes, became effective for split-dollar arrangements entered into or materially modified after that date.

The main purpose of the final regulations is to tax the portion of the equity in a split-dollar plan that belongs to the employee and which was created by payments made by the employer. Prior to this new guidance, under the classic type of split-dollar plan, the employee was taxed on the net premium cost of current insurance (i.e., the value of the insurance protection) minus the amount of the premium paid by the employee, if any. This net premium cost was determined by reference to the P.S. 58 tables and later by Table 2001.

Under the IRS final regulations, the tax treatment of split-dollar arrangements is based on the nature of the arrangement, rather than how the parties would or would not like to characterize the arrangement. In general, the final regulations provide two mechanisms (called regimes) for determining the tax consequences of such arrangements, including equity split-dollar arrangements:

- The first, the economic benefit regime, has brought about a change in the income tax treatment of the endorsement form of split-dollar plans and non-equity collateral assignment plans. The income tax treatment depends on the relationship between the parties. The owner of the policy, generally the employer, is treated as giving an economic benefit to the insured non-owner. If the arrangement is between an employer and an employee, the transfer is treated as compensation to the employee. If a corporation pays the premiums for life insurance on a stockholder, it is treated as a dividend. And if the relationship is non-compensatory, the benefit is treated as a gift. Taxation, if any, occurs in the year the economic benefit is received.

- The second regime, the loan regime, is applicable to equity collateral assignment plans where the employee is the owner of both the policy and the cash value and where the employer is the non-owner. In such cases, the non-owner (the employer) is treated as a lender and the employee (the owner) is treated as the borrower; the employer advances funds or (premiums) to finance the split-dollar plan owned by the employee, who is treated as the borrower. If the insured (the employee) is not charged a specified interest rate on the series of loans (premium payments), he or she is considered to have received taxable income in the amount of the imputed interest at the Applicable Federal Rate (APR). In general, the taxation of the benefits under such loan arrangements depends upon whether the loan is a demand loan or a term loan. If it is considered a demand loan, the determination of the amount of income recognized is made at the end of each year for which the loan is outstanding. The determination of income with respect to term loans is made in the year in which the loan originates.

A safe harbor provision was included in the final regulations to freeze the tax treatment of plans put in place prior to the effective date of the final regulations, provided such plans stay in place with no substantial changes. There was also a very short window of opportunity that provided that the employee would not be taxed on his or her equity if the plan was terminated prior to January 1, 2004, or if all employer's payments (prior to and after January 1, 2004) are treated as loans as of that date. If these rules are not followed, the equity will be taxable income to the employee when he or she receives it or the policy upon termination of the split-dollar arrangement.

One of the most important issues for existing plans is that the plan participants obtain competent legal and tax advice regarding the effects of the new regulations on their plan prior to making any changes or distributions. At the effective date of the regulation, a specialist in this area should have been used to prepare an analysis, and at various times in the future, of the effect of terminating the plan. As with any new regulations, it is likely to take months or years to clarify the many questions brought about by this change.

Even with no change in the tax laws related to split-dollar plans, these changes did not come as a complete surprise, although they took nearly 40 years to occur. For most of those years, split-dollar plans were put in place as a way to transfer business assets to chosen employees, usually owners, without having the transfer be taxable.

Finally, under the provisions of the Sarbanes Oxley Act of 2002, split-dollar collateral arrangements, a loan regime, involving executives and directors of publicly-held companies may now be illegal in that the law prohibits loans to executives and/or directors.

IRC § 162 PLANS

IRC §162 discusses reasonable compensation. The key provisions involve how much compensation is reasonable, and what qualifies as compensation. For example, the nephew of an executive who cannot seem to hold a job is hired as a mailroom assistant at an annual salary of $85,000. That is not reasonable compensation. An executive who is responsible for the operations of a $250 million subsidiary of a multi-national corporation is paid $500,000 plus maximum contributions to his retirement plan, provided a country club membership used for entertaining clients, a chauffeured limousine, a personal assistant, and a private chef for in-office meals. The latter may be considered reasonable compensation in a specific set of circumstances.

Some companies choose to use §162 plans as an alternative to split-dollar insurance, as we will discuss later in the chapter. These plans are far less complex and rarely attract IRS scrutiny. If a business pays the premium (for non-shareholder employees) on personally owned life insurance or bonuses an amount equal to the premium on the life insurance, that is deductible by the business and reportable as earned income by the employee (as long as the total compensation is reasonable). In some cases the business not only pays the premium, it may also pay an additional amount to cover the income taxes on the premium. For this reason, this approach to paying for life insurance is often called an **executive bonus plan**. All payments made to the employee, as long as the total compensation is reasonable, are deductible by the employer.

The board of the corporation should adopt a resolution that it will provide this form of compensation to the individual(s) it chooses to benefit. The resolution should state the benefit to the corporation for providing this bonus, which helps provide substantiation that it is being paid as part of a reasonable compensation plan under Section 162. There is usually an agreement with the employee as well that the employer is paying this as part of his or her compensation and that the plan may be terminated at any time.

Because the employee is the owner of the insurance, the proceeds of the policy are paid to his or her designated beneficiaries income-tax free. If the policy is owned by an irrevocable life insurance trust, and the employee has not had any incident of ownership for three years or more, the proceeds will also be out of the estate of the employee. Even though payments made for the insurance come from either the employee or the corporation, that in itself will not cause inclusion of the death benefit in the estate of the employee. Of course, since the employer is taking a deduction for the premium paid as part of the employee's compensation, the employee will have it included in his or her W-2 form as taxable income.

Review the table at the end of the chapter to compare key attributes of various life insurance plans used as employee benefits.

DEATH BENEFIT ONLY PLANS

Death Benefit Only (DBO) plans are a variation of deferred compensation plans. They typically operate to defer an employee's income, to be paid as a death benefit to his or her heirs. DBO plans provide no benefit to the employee during his or her lifetime.

These plans are used where the employee is likely to have a large estate tax or has a substantial insurance need because of having a young family. As long as it is properly established, the death benefits will not be included in the estate of the employee. It is critical that the employee have less than 50 percent ownership of the business.

The corporation is the owner and beneficiary of the policy, which is why the proceeds are outside the estate of the insured. Because the death benefits, with the possible exception of alternative minimum tax, are income-tax free to the employer, the premiums are not deductible. However, when the benefits are paid to the heirs of the employee, they are deductible by the corporation. The disadvantage of the death benefit only plan is that with the corporation taking a deduction for the payment, the payment is ordinary income to the heirs, even though the money was made available through life insurance.

To keep the proceeds outside of the employee's estate, there must be no benefits of any kind related to the policy available to the employee during his or her lifetime. Furthermore, once the plan is established, he or she may not have any right to change the beneficiary. If the employer also provides a non-qualified deferred compensation plan that will pay benefits to the employee during his or her life, the DBO plan will not be excluded from the employee's estate. Neither long-term disability plans nor qualified retirement plans affect the estate exclusion of a DBO plan.

To ensure the deductibility of the benefits when paid to the employee's heirs, the plan must be in writing and identified as a benefit for actual services rendered.

OVERHEAD EXPENSE INSURANCE

When a business is dependent on the specific skills of one, or only a few individuals, a disability of that individual will create substantial problems for the business. This issue arises in small businesses such as accounting, law, and medical practices, where the licensed professionals are responsible for the primary income of the business.

Disability income insurance replaces a portion of the lost income for an individual who becomes disabled. But how does a business pay its bills when a key income provider is not able to work? If the business has a single owner/income earner, his or her individual disability income insurance coverage amount is based on the net income from the business after payment of rent, utilities, salaries, leases, etc. Because it is the net income that is covered, the business expenses are obviously not covered.

To solve this problem, the insurance industry developed disability overhead expense insurance. This is a policy that makes payments to the business because of the disability of a prime income source. There is a wide range of disability overhead expense policies. For some companies, the elimination period may be as short as 30 days, and with others, the shortest is 90 days. Some companies require the elimination period to be met by consecutive days while others permit short breaks of a few days which gives the individual an incentive to see if working is possible.

The payment of benefits may require total or partial disability, so it is important to review the specific policy's definitions. Benefit periods generally run from one to two years. While the benefit may be listed as a monthly amount, it often is aggregated so that if higher expenses are experienced in the early months following the onset of a disability and are then reduced over time, the payments can match the need. Even if a policy is set up to pay $2,000 per month for 18 months ($36,000) total, it may pay benefits for a shorter or longer period of time, depending on the actual expenses of the business. The policies do not generally pay a flat amount regardless of the expenses incurred. They pay an amount to cover the actual expenses. The procedure for doing this varies by company.

As long as the business has expenses, and the insured meets the definition of disabled as specified in the policy, benefits will be paid to the limits of the contract. It does not make a difference whether the disability is expected to be temporary or permanent.

All insurance companies that offer disability overhead expense insurance cover certain expenses. Some companies are more generous than others. The following list shows expenses that may or may not be covered by a specific policy.

- Lease, rent, or mortgage payments
- Utilities
- Liability insurance
- Property taxes
- Salaries/wages of support staff
- Accounting and legal services
- Salary or contract payment for replacement professional services
- Professional trade dues and subscriptions
- Equipment leases
- Other fixed expenses normally incurred in running the business

Payment of the premium for overhead expense insurance is deductible. The benefits are taxable, but are immediately offset by the deduction for business expenses.

In-Depth: Comparison of Life Insurance Policies

A number of different life-insurance policies are used to provide key person life insurance and executive benefits. The ones discussed here are summarized below.

	Split Dollar Endorsement form	Split Dollar Collateral Assignment Form	Sec 162 Exec Bonus	Key Employee	Death Benefit Only
Beneficiary	Employer and employee's named beneficiary	Employer and employee's named beneficiary	Designated beneficiary	Employer	Employer
Employer Deduction	No	Yes–to extent of imputed interest	Yes	No	Only for payment to employee's heirs; not for premiums paid
Taxable to Employee	Table 2001 rates	Yes–to extent of imputed interest	Whole premium	No	No
Taxable to Heirs	No	No	Possible estate taxes	No	Yes

IMPORTANT CONCEPTS

Book Value

Hybrid agreement

Business valuation

Key Person Life Insurance

Buy/Sell agreement

Overhead expense insurance

Collateral assignment method

Reasonable compensation

Cross purchase agreement

Reverse Split Dollar

Death Benefit Only (DBO) plans

Section 162 plans

Disability Buy/Sell

Split-dollar life insurance

Endorsement method

Split-dollar rollout

Entity purchase agreement

Stock redemption agreement

Equity Split Dollar

Table 2001

Executive bonus plan

Transfer for value

Fair market value

Wait-and-see agreement

Loan regime

Economic benefit regime

$5000 = ?

$5000 = ?

$2000 = ?

$5000 = ?

next week

QUESTIONS FOR REVIEW

1. With what is IRC §162 concerned?

2. What are the benefits of using a hybrid buy/sell agreement?

3. Why would a business want to purchase key person insurance?

4. Compare a stock redemption buy/sell agreement with a cross purchase buy/sell agreement.

5. What would cause a DBO plan to result in taxable income to the insured?

6. What is the transfer for value rule?

7. What are the exceptions to the transfer for value rule?

8. How does disability overhead expense insurance work?

9. What are the issues of concern when transferring business ownership of a small business to the next generation?

10. What are the differences between a collateral assignment (loan regime) and endorsement method (economic benefit regime) of establishing a split-dollar plan?

SUGGESTIONS FOR ADDITIONAL READING

AALU Washington Report; AALU Bulletin no. 02-104; Aug. 20, 2002

Comprehensive Split Dollar, 4th ed., Louis R. Richey, Lawrence Brody, and Ronald Floridis, National Underwriter, 1983.

Employee Benefits, 7th ed., Burton T. Beam, Jr. and John J. McFadden, Real Estate Education Company, 2005.

Fundamentals of Risk and Insurance, 9th ed., Emmett J. Vaughan and Therese M. Vaughan, Wiley, 2003.

Introduction to Risk Management and Insurance, 8th ed., Mark Dorfman, Prentice Hall, 2004.

Life and Health Insurance, 13th ed., Skipper and Black, Prentice Hall, 2000.

Principles of Risk Management and Insurance, 9th ed., George E. Rejda, Addison Wesley, 2004.

Tax Facts 2005, National Underwriter 2005.

The Tools & Techniques of Life Insurance Planning, 3rd ed., Stephan R. Leimberg, National Underwriter, 2004.

Index

• • •

A

Abandonment of property provision, 217

Absolute liability, 17

Accelerated death benefits
    group life insurance, 332
    individual life insurance, 104 105, 125
    long-term care, 195 196
    taxation, 105

Accidental death
    accidental death provision, 47, 55
    accidental means provision, 55
    normal benefit (ADB), 47, 55

Accidental death and dismemberment (AD&D)
    group life insurance, 332-333
    health care plan, 158
    individual life insurance, 56

Accidents, automobile. *See Personal auto policy (PAP)*

Accumulation fund, 37-38, 92

Achievement awards, 397

Activities-of-daily living (ADL), 193 194, 196

Actual cash value (ACV), 24, 213

Additional insurance rider (AIR), 178, 180

Adjustable life insurance, 39

Adjustment fund, 69

Adoption assistance plans, 317, 387

Adult day care, 198

Adverse deviation, 2

Adverse selection
    defined, 13-14
    health insurance, 134, 141
    life insurance, 32

Aftermarket parts, 249-250

Age, misstatement
    disability income insurance, 180
    life insurance, 46, 331

Agency, legal doctrine, 126

AIDS, and life insurance policies, 103-105

Aleatory contracts, 22

All-terrain vehicles, 254

Alternative minimum tax (AMT)
    and incentive stock options (ISO), 424-428
    and key person life insurance benefits, 448

A.M. Best, insurance company rating, 118-119

American Association of Insurance Services (AAIS), 213

American Jobs Creation Act (2004), 417-418, 442

Americans with Disabilities Act (ADA), 382

Animals, personal liability coverage, 220, 244

Annually renewable term (ART) life insurance, 32

Annuitant, 108

Annuities, 106-111

    administrative charges, 108

    annuitization, 107, 110

    contracts, parties involved, 108

    death benefit, 109-111

    deferred, 106

    distribution options, 108-109

    equity indexed, 107

    fixed, 106

    fixed premium, 106

    flexible premium, 106

    immediate, 106

    compared to mutual funds, 109-110

    surrender charges, 107

    taxation of, 110-111

    variable, 106

Antiques

    cars, auto insurance, 253

    homeowners insurance exclusion, 228

Any occupation, 169-170, 352

    modified, 170

Any willing provider, 134

Appraisal

    homeowners insurance coverage, 217

    of personal property, 21

Archer accounts. *See Medical savings accounts (MSA)*

Art, insuring, 228

Asset risk, 120

Assets, 70-71, 77

Assigned risk plans, 258

Assignment

    group life insurance, 330

    homeowners insurance, 221

    individual life insurance, 21-22

Assisted living facilities, 198-199

Assumption of risk, 18, 269-270

Athletic facilities, 400

Attractive nuisances, 16, 266

Authorized control RBC level, 120

Automatic premium loans, 48

Automobile insurance

    assigned risk plans, 258

    automobile insurance plan, 258

    deductibles, 6, 254

    distress risk companies, 258

    forms of, 242

    joint underwriting associations, 258

    reinsurance pools, 258

    single limit coverage, 245

    split limit coverage, 245

    See also Commercial automobile insurance; Personal auto policy (PAP)

Automobiles, accidents and reduced value, 250

Average earnings clause, 181

Aviation-related deaths, 47

B

Bailee

    bailee liability, 299, 304

    defined, 304

Bailment, 304

Bailor, 304

Balanced Budget Act (1997), 150

Bankruptcy
  of business owner, 461
  and COBRA coverage, 347
  inadequate insurance issue, 255
  insurance companies, 122
  of liable party, 268, 273
Bed reservation, 203
Belth, Joseph M., 95
  method, 95-96
Beneficiary
  of annuity, 108, 110
  complications related to, 52-53
  group life insurance, 329
  individual life insurance, 46, 51-54
Benefit trigger, 194
Bereavement leave, 380
Bilateral contract, 22
Binding authority, 127
Blackout period, 72-73
Blanket bond, 300
Blanket coverage
  commercial property, 293
  homeowners insurance, 213, 227
Blue Cross/Blue Shield
  dental care plans, 368
  health insurance, 142-143
  long-term care plans, 197
Boats. *See Watercraft*
Boiler and machinery insurance, 296-297
Bond, 300-301
Bonuses, 316, 400, 406
Book value, 457
Breakpoint, 135
Broad form homeowners insurance, 213, 222-224
Builder's risk coverage, 293
Building codes, 217

Business interruption insurance, 294-296
Business ownership
  business property on premises, 229
  buy/sell agreements, 454-468
  death of owner, 453-454
  disability of owner, 459-460, 463
  valuation of business, 456-459
  See also Commercial insurance; Key person life insurance; Partnerships; Professional liability insurance; Self-employed
Buy/sell agreements, 454-468
  advantages of, 455
  choosing agreement, 467
  cross purchase agreements, 454, 463-465
  disability buy/sell insurance, 463
  employee stock ownership plans (ESOP) agreements, 466-467
  entity agreements, 454
  entity/stock redemption agreement, 465-466
  funding methods, 461-462
  hybrid agreements, 454, 466
  third party agreements, 467
  transfer-for-value, 462, 467-468
  triggering events, 459-461
  valuation of business, 456-459
  written features of, 454-455

C

Cafeteria plans, 358-361
  changes to, 360
  doctrine of constructive receipt, 359
  flexible spending accounts (FSA), 361-366
  safe harbor test, 359
  taxation, 359-361
  types of, 359-360

Cancellation clause
   group insurance policy, 331
   individual insurance policy, 221
Capital consumption, 83
Capital retention, 83
Capitation, 135, 148
Caps, 135
Captive agents, 126
Caregiver coverage, 204
Cargo insurance, 298
Cash accumulation method, 98-99
Cash dividends, 49
Cash value
   actual, 24, 213
   cash value accumulation test, 58
   whole life insurance, 35
Catastrophe, umbrella liability coverage, 282-283
Certified Automotive Parts Association (CAPA), 250
Chartered property casualty underwriter (CPCU), 212
Children
   dependent care assistance plans, 385-387
   family leave, 380-383
   health insurance for, 159, 163
   life insurance for, 43
   negligence, exclusion from, 267
   on property, owner obligations, 266
   Social Security benefits, 72
Chronic illness
   defined, 105
   and life insurance policies, 103-105
   preexisting condition, 139
Citibank method, 67
Claims made, 281
Classic cars, insuring, 253

Clothing allowance, 317
COBRA coverage, 343-347
   benefits, 344, 346-347
   election period, 346
   eligibility, 344-345
   employer bankruptcy, 347
   legal aspects, 159, 322, 343
   notice requirements, 346
   periods of coverage, 345
Coinsurance
   health insurance, 135
   homeowners insurance, 225
Collapse of dwelling, 215
Collateral assignment
   defined, 21
   life insurance, 48
   split-dollar insurance, 469
Collateral source rule, 268
Collision coverage, 245-251, 256
Commercial automobile insurance, 305-307
   business auto, 306
   garage coverage, 306
   motor carriers, 306
   truckers coverage, 306
Commercial general liability (CGL) coverage, 302
Commercial insurance
   automobile, 305-307
   boiler and machinery, 296-297
   business owners policy (BOP), 307
   commercial package policy (CPP), 307
   crime insurance, 300-301
   liability, 301-305
   portfolio programs, 291
   property, 290-296
   transportation, 297-300

Commercial liability insurance, 301-305
  bailee liability, 304
  directors/officers errors and omissions, 303
  employer's liability, 306-307
  excess liability, 304-305
  general liability, 302-303
  liquor liability, 303
  pension fiduciary liability, 303
  pollution liability, 304
  umbrella policies, 305
  underground storage tank, 304
Commercial package policy (CPP), 307
Commercial property insurance, 290-296
  blanket insurance, 293
  builder's risk, 293
  business interruption, 294-296
  condo association, 292
  extra expense, 294, 296
  full-value reporting clause, 293
  functional building valuation, 291
  functional personal property valuation, 291
  glass, 292
  leasehold interest, 294
  manufacturer's selling price, 292
  newly acquired buildings, 292
  non-owned detached trailers, 292
  rain/weather insurance, 296
  range of coverage, 290
  spoilage, 292
Common disaster clause, 48
Commutative contracts, 22
Company action RBC level, 120
Company cars, insuring, 249
Comparative negligence, 18, 271
Comprehensive homeowners insurance form, 224

Comprehensive personal liability coverage.
    See Personal liability insurance
Computers, insuring, 230
Concealment, 23
Conditional contracts, 26
Conditional renewability, 184
Condominiums
  association coverage, 292
  homeowners insurance, 224
Consent, implied, 266
Consolidated Omnibus Budget and
    Reconciliation Act (COBRA). *See COBRA
    coverage*
Constructive receipt
  defined, 383
  nonqualified deferred compensation plans, 412
Consumer-directed health insurance plans, 342
Contents/personal property insurance, 215,
    223-224, 227-228
Contingent liability, 302
Continuing care retirement communities
    (CCRCs), 197, 199
Contract owner, 108
Contracts, 19-26
  aleatory, 22
  annuity, 108
  assignment of, 21-22
  bilateral, 22
  commutative, 22
  components of, 19-20
  concealment, 23
  conditional, 26
  of indemnity, 21
  misrepresentation, 22-23
  parol evidence rule, 25
  personal, 21
  reformation of, 26

rescission of, 26

unilateral, 22

of utmost good faith, 22

void and voidable, 20

waiver and estoppel, 25-26

warranty, 23

Contractual liability, 302

Contributory negligence, 18, 271

Controlled forms, 298

Conversion privilege

group life insurance, 329-330

term life insurance, 35, 48, 89, 124-125

Co-payments

as cost-shifting, 338

group health insurance, 338, 343

individual health insurance, 135-136, 147-149

Corporations, and risk sharing, 7

Cost containment

group health insurance, 337-338

individual health insurance plans, 136

Cost-of-living rider

disability income insurance, 178

long-term care insurance, 203-204

Cost shifting

group health insurance, 338

Medicare, 338

Counterfeit money coverage, 216

Creditable coverage, 348

Credit card losses, 216

Credit risk, 120

Crime insurance, 300-301

employee theft coverage, 300-301

exclusions, 301

non-employee crime coverage, 301

special cause of loss, 299

Criminal wrongs, 265

Critical risks, 30

Cross purchase agreements, 454, 463-465

Current-assumption whole life insurance, 45

Current causation, 233

Custodial care, 198

D

Damages, 267-269

bankruptcy of liable party, 268

collateral source rule, 268

death of liable party, 268

general, 268

and joint liability, 268-269

punitive, 268

special, 267

Day care centers, 317

Death

bereavement leave, 380

of business owners, 453-454

of business partner, 452

premature, 4

Death Benefit Only (DBO) plans, 475-476

Death benefits

annuities, 109-111

life insurance. *See Life insurance death benefits*

Social Security, children of deceased parents, 72

Debit cards losses, 216

Debris removal, 215

Decreasing term life insurance, 33

Deductibles

auto insurance, 254

as cost-shifting, 338

defined, 6

group health insurance, 338, 343

individual health insurance, 136, 138, 144-145, 150

Medicare, 152-154

Deferred annuities, 106

Deferred compensation

    nonqualified deferred compensation plans, 407-418

    phantom stock plans, 440-441

    qualified deferred compensation plans, 408-410

Delta Dental care plans, 368

De minimis fringe benefits, 390-391, 400

Demutualization, 121

Dental insurance. *See Group dental insurance*

Dependent care assistance plans, 385-387

Dependent life insurance, 332

Depositors' forgery coverage, 216

Deregulation, and insurance industry, 121

Direct losses, 5

Disability

    of business owners, 459-460, 463

    of business partner, 452

    Medicare coverage, 139

    presumptive, 55, 125, 177

    as risk, 4

Disability income insurance, 167-188

    accidental death and dismemberment (AD&D) benefit, 56

    any occupation, 169

    average earnings clause, 181

    basic facts, 168-169

    canceling, 184

    change of occupation, 177

    cost-of-living rider, 178

    disability buy/sell insurance, 463

    earned income, 172-173

    elimination period, 173

    employer offered plans, 314

    exclusions, 179

    facility of payment clause, 179

    front-end-cost-of-living rider, 178

    group plans. *See Group disability income insurance*

    guaranteed insurability, 179-180

    long-term care, 180, 196-197

    loss of income, 171-172

    maximum benefit period, 173

    maximum monthly benefit payment, 174-175

    misstatement of age, 180

    modified any occupation, 170

    needs analysis, 185-186

    nonoccupational coverage, 180

    occupational class, 175-176, 187

    own occupation, 170, 186-187

    partial disability, 180-181

    preexisting conditions, 176, 188

    presumptive disability, 177

    probation period, 177

    rehabilitation, 181

    renewability, 184-185

    residual disability, 181-182

    social insurance rider, 182-183

    Social Security provided. *See Social Security disability income*

    specialty letter, 170

    split definition, 171

    taxation of benefits, 187

    underwriting, 169, 186-188

    waiver of premium, 35, 54-55, 184

Discounts

    auto insurance, 257

    qualified employees, 389

    valuation of business, 458-459

Disputes, contracts., 25-26

Disqualifying disposition, 431-432

Dissatisfiers, 313

Distress risk companies, 258

Dividends, life insurance. *See Life insurance dividends*

Doctrine of constructive receipt, 359

Doctrine of insurable interest, 24

Dogs, free bite laws, 244

Double indemnity, 55

Dread disease policy, 157

Dual capacity situation, 307

Dwelling insurance coverage, 213-214, 223, 235-236

Dynamic risk, 4

E

Earned income, 172-173

Earthquakes, 224, 230-231

Economic benefit doctrine, 413

Economic Growth and Tax Relief Reconciliation Act (EGTRRA), 408

Education funding

    education assistance programs, 385

    education reimbursement programs, 316

    life insurance needs analysis, 72, 79

    qualified tuition reduction plans, 393

Elimination period

    disability income insurance, 173

    long-term care insurance, 202

Employee assistance programs (EAP), 317, 398

Employee benefits, 312-324

    cash payments, 316

    commonality among companies, 318

    employee benefit planning, 323-324

    health care plans, 314

    insurance. *See Group insurance*

    legal requirements, 312-313

    satisfiers/dissatisfiers, 313

    services provided, 316-317

    time not worked payments. *See Employee benefits (non-insurance)*

Employee benefits (non-insurance), 374-383

    adoption assistance plans, 317, 387

    athletic facilities, 400

    bereavement leave, 380

    de minimis benefits, 390-391, 400

    dependent care assistance plans, 385-387

    education assistance programs, 385

    employee achievement awards, 397

    employee assistance programs (EAP), 317, 398

    employee discounts, 389

    executive benefits, 406-407

    family leave, 380

    and financial planning, 402

    financial planning programs, 398

    golden parachutes, 396-397

    holiday bonuses, 400

    holidays, paid, 315, 376-377

    jury duty, 315, 380

    legal services plans, 398-399

    meals/lodging, 383-385, 391

    military reserve time, 315, 380

    moving expenses, 316, 392

    no-additional cost services, 388

    nondiscrimination rules, 401

    nonqualified deferred compensation plans, 407- 418

    personal time off (PTO) plans, 379-380

    qualified plans, 323

    retirement planning services, 317, 392-393

sabbaticals, 315, 381

severance pay, 393-394

sick-pay/sick-leave, 315, 353, 374-375, 377

taxation, 388, 401

transportation benefits, 389-390, 391

tuition reduction plans, 393

vacation days, 315, 377-378

voluntary employee benefit association (VEBA), 394-396

wellness programs, 317, 400

working conditions, 389-390

Employee Retirement Income Security Act (ERISA)

on employee benefit programs, 322-323, 393

on split-value insurance plans, 472

on top hat plans, 411

Employee stock ownership plans (ESOP) agreements, 466-467

Employee stock purchase plan, 428-433

disqualifying disposition, 431-432

features of, 428-429

nonqualified, 433

requirements of, 429-431

taxation, 431-433

Employee theft coverage, 300-301

Employer's liability insurance

third-party suits, 307

workers compensation, 306-307

Endorsement method, 468

Endorsements

homeowners insurance, 213, 228-230

personal liability insurance, 279

Entity agreements, 454

Equity-based compensation

employee stock purchase plan, 428-433

future view, 433

performance cash plan, 443

performance shares, 443

performance unit programs, 443

restricted stock plans, 436-439

shadow stock arrangements, 439-441

stock appreciation rights (SARs), 441-442

stock options, 422-428

Equity indexed annuities, 107

Equity split-dollar plans, 470-471

Errors and omissions insurance, 281, 303

Estate taxes

financing with life insurance, 89

life insurance proceeds, 61

Estoppel, 26

Ethical code, insurance companies, 124

Excess benefits plans, 411

Excess liability insurance, 304-305

Exchanges, life insurance policies, 60-61

Exclusions

auto insurance, 246-247

disability income insurance, 179

group dental insurance, 369

health insurance, 137

homeowners insurance, 227-229

personal liability insurance, 274-279

Exclusive provider organizations (EPO), 149

Executive bonus plans, 475

Executive compensation

benefits package, 406-407

fringe benefits. *See Employee benefits (non-insurance)*

nonqualified deferred compensation plans, 407-418

reasonable compensation, 474-475

See also Equity-based compensation

Executive life insurance. *See Key person life insurance*

Exempt employees, 381

Exercise facilities, 317

Experience rating, 320, 338-339

Extended term life insurance, 50

Extra expense coverage, 294, 296

F

Facility of payment clause, 179

Fair market value (FMV), 456-457

Family leave, 380

Family and Medical Leave Act (FMLA), 381-383

Federal Emergency Management Agency (FEMA), 235

Federal regulation, group insurance, 321-323

Fifth dividend option, 49-50

Fifty percent rule (Wisconsin Rule), 18, 271

Financial loss, homeowners insurance coverage, 216

Financial Planning Practice Standards, 66

Financial planning programs, 398

Financial risk, 4

Financial surety bonds, 416

Firearms, homeowners insurance limit, 229

Fire department service charge, 216

First to die life insurance, 89

Fitch Ratings, 118-119

Fixed annuities, 106

Fixed interest, 36, 38

Fixed premium annuities, 106

Flexible premium adjustable life insurance. *See Universal life insurance*

Flexible premium annuities, 106

Flexible spending accounts (FSA), 361-366

employee access to funds, 364

enrollment form, 363

forfeited deferrals, 364

mid-year changes, 365

rules, 362-363

Floaters, 213, 229, 299

Flood insurance

commercial, 296

flood hazard areas, 235

homeowners insurance, 235

Following-form liability policy, 304

Formulary, 137

Founder's policies, 102

401(k) qualified retirement plan, deferral amounts, 408

49 percent rule, 18

Fraternal societies, life insurance provider, 127-128

Fraud

age misstatement, 46, 180, 331

automobile claims, 252

homeowners insurance claims, 221, 232

Free bite laws, 244

Freight insurance, 298

Fringe benefits. *See Employee benefits (non-insurance)*

Front-end-cost-of-living rider, 178

Fuel oil leakage, 279

Full-value reporting clause, 293

Functionally equivalent, 224

Fundamental risk, 5

Funded, secured plans, 417

Funded, unsecured plans, 416

Furs, homeowners insurance limit, 229

G

Garage coverage insurance, 306

Gatekeepers, primary care physicians (PCP) as, 135, 137, 140, 148

General average, 298

General damages, 268

Gift taxes, life insurance proceeds, 61-62

Glass coverage
    commercial property insurance, 292
    homeowners insurance coverage, 216, 218

Golden parachutes, 396-397, 407

Good neighbor provision, 272

Government action, homeowners insurance, 232, 234

Government bodies, negligence, exclusion from, 267

Grace period, 47, 331

Graded premium life insurance, 35-36

Gratuitous bailment, 304

Group dental insurance, 367-369
    benefits, 368-369
    exclusions, 369
    incentive-based plans, 367
    indemnity plans, 367
    integrated plans, 368
    managed care plans, 367

Group disability income insurance, 185, 350-354
    disability, definitions of, 351-352
    to executives, 406
    limitations of, 351
    long-term policies, 350
    non-occupational, 351
    offsets, 352
    planning for, 353-354
    return-to-work provisions, 352-353
    short-term policies, 350, 376

sick-leave plans, 353, 374-375

taxation, 354

underwriting, 351

Group health care plans, 340-349
    consumer-directed plans, 342
    deductibles/co-payments, 343
    eligibility, 340-341
    for executives, 406
    groups/associations offering, 341
    health reimbursement arrangements (HRAs), 366
    health savings accounts (HSA), 366
    high-deductible plans, 366
    Medicare coordination, 340
    multi-employer plans (MEPs), 341-342
    participation requirements, 341
    taxation, 349
    third-party administrator, 341-342

Group health insurance, 336-340
    COBRA extension, 159, 322, 343-347
    coordination of benefits, 337
    cost containment/cost shifting, 337-338
    as employee benefit, 314
    experience rating, 338-339
    and HIPAA, 347-349
    compared to individual, 141-142
    open-enrollment periods, 339
    plans. *See Group health care plans*
    underwriting, 339

Group insurance, 319-323
    cafeteria plans, 358-361
    contracts, 319
    contributory/noncontributory funding, 365
    disability income, 185, 350-354
    experience rating, 320
    flexible spending accounts (FSA), 361-366

group dental insurance, 367-369

health, 336-349

life, 89, 314, 328-336

long-term care insurance, 195, 369

premiums, 320

regulation of, 321-323

underwriting, 320-321

See also specific types of insurance

Group life insurance, 89, 314, 328-336

accelerated death benefits, 332

accidental death & dismemberment (AD&D), 332-333

assignment, 330

beneficiary designation, 329

benefit levels, 328

claims, 331

continuation of coverage, 331-332

conversion, 329-330

dependent life, 332

to executives, 407

insurability, 329

in nonqualified deferred compensation plans, 415

ordinary life, 335

ownership, 330

paid-up life, 335

permanent life, 335

portability of, 332

provisions, 331

retired lives reserves, 336

settlement options, 331

supplemental, 333

taxation of, 333-334

term life, 328-334

termination, 331

underwriting, 329

universal life, 336

Group/practice model HMO, 147

Guaranteed insurability

disability income insurance, 179-180

life insurance, 56-57, 125

Guaranteed renewability, 184

Guaranteed replacement cost coverage, 227

Guideline premium and corridor test, 58

H

Hail damage, 216

Hazards

homeowners policy, 213

and risk, 3

Health care coordinator, 204

Health care plans, 142-160

accidental death and dismemberment (AD&D) plan, 158

accreditation of, 139

choosing plan/coverage, 158-160

COBRA coverage, 159

dread disease policy, 157

employer offered plans, 314

group versus individual plans, 141-142

group plans. *See Group health care plans*

Health Insurance Portability and Accountabiliy Act (HIPAA), 159, 322, 347-348

health savings accounts (HSA), 137, 145-146

high-deductible health care plan (HDHC), 138, 144

hospital expense coverage, 142

hospital indemnity plans, 157

indemnity plans, 141, 157

major medical coverage, 143

managed-care plans, 138, 147-150

marketplace, changes in, 150-151

Medicaid, 138

medical savings accounts (MSA), 139, 144

Medicare, 139, 152-156, 158

needs analysis, 161-163

physician's expense coverage, 143

self-funded plans, 140-141

surgical expense coverage, 143

taxation of, 161

temporary/interim insurance, 151

underwriting, 142

Health insurance, 134-140

   adverse selection, 134, 141

   any willing provider, 134

   breakpoint/stop-loss limit/cap, 135

   capitation, 135, 148

   for children, 159, 163

   coinsurance, 135

   co-payments, 135-136

   cost containment, 136

   coverage, extent of, 141

   covered person, 136

   deductibles, 136, 138

   exclusions, 137

   formulary, 137

   gatekeeper, 137

   group insurance. *See Group health care plans; Group health insurance*

   insured, 138

   limitations, 138

   performance measures for, 137

   plans. *See Group health care plans; Health care plans*

   pre-certification, 139

   preexisting condition, 139, 142, 151

   primary care physician (PCP), 135, 137, 140, 148

   provider, 140

   third-party administrator (TPA), 140

   uninsurable persons, options for, 159

   uninsured, problem of, 151

   usual customary and reasonable (UCR) rates, 140, 143

Health Insurance Portability and Accountability Act (HIPAA) (1996)

   and COBRA coverage, 159, 322, 347-348

   on creditable coverage, 348

   on long-term care insurance, 194-196

   on preexisting conditions clause, 348

   purposes of, 347-348

   on terminally/chronically ill, 105

Health maintenance organizations (HMOs), 147-148

   long-term care plans, 197

   Medicare HMOs, 153

   primary care physician (PCP), 135, 137, 140

   types of, 147

Health reimbursement arrangements (HRAs), 366

Health savings accounts (HSA)

   group plans, 366

   individual plans, 137, 145-146

   tax benefits, 145-146

Hedging, as risk transfer, 7

High-deductible health care plans (HDHC), 137-139

   group plans, 342, 366

   health savings account (HSA), 137, 145-146

   medical savings accounts (MSA), 139, 144-146

Hold-harmless agreements, as risk transfer, 7

Holidays

   bonuses, 400

   paid, 315, 376-377

Home health care benefits, 198, 204

Homeowners insurance, 211-237

abandonment of property provision, 217

appraisal, 217

basic facts, 212

basic/standard coverage, 222

broad form/named peril coverage, 213, 222-224

building code update, 217

chartered property casualty underwriter (CPCU), 212

collapse of dwelling, 215

comprehensive form, 224

contents/personal property (Coverage C), 215, 223-224, 227-228

debris removal, 215

dwelling (Coverage A), 214, 223, 235-236

earthquakes, 224, 230-231

exclusions, general, 231-234

exclusions, personal property, 228-229, 234-235

exclusions, theft losses, 234-235

financial loss, 216

fire department service charge, 216

flood insurance, 235

forms, 222-224

glass, replacement, 216, 218

guaranteed replacement cost coverage, 227

hail damage, 216

home-work situation, 237

inflation guard endorsement, 227-228

inland marine policy, 229-230, 236

insurable interest/limit of liability, 218

insured's duties, 218

landlord's furnishings, 216

landscape damage, 217

loss assessment, 217

loss to pair clause, 218

loss settlement provision, 218

loss of use (Coverage D), 215, 223

mobile homes, 236

mortgage clause, 218

needs analysis, 237

no benefit to bailee clause, 218-219

nuclear hazard, 219, 232

older homes, 224

open perils coverage, 222, 224, 228

other structures (Coverage B), 215, 223, 230, 237

our option clause, 219, 226

personal liability (Coverage E). See Personal liability coverage

property removal, 217

recovered property, 219

renter's policy, 224

repairs, 217

replacement cost calculations, 225-227

suit against us clause, 219

terms related to, 213-214, 221

theft losses, 216, 219, 234-235

title insurance, 236

unit-owners/condo form, 224

volcanic eruption, 219

wedding presents, 236

Homeowners insurance concepts

actual cash value, 213

assignment, 221

blanket coverage, 213, 227

cancellation clause, 221

coinsurance requirement, 225

concealment of fraud, 221

death, 221

dwelling, 213

endorsement, 213

floaters, 213

forms, 213

functionally equivalent, 224

hazards, 213

homeowner's policy, 213

insurable interest, 214

liberalization clause, 221

loss assessment, 214

loss settlement, 214

nonrenewal, 221

open peril, 214

peril, 214

personal property, 214

policy period, 221

replacement cost, 214

scheduled property, 214

subrogation, 221

Homestead exemption, Medicaid, 207

Hospital expense coverage, 142

Hospital indemnity plans, 142, 157

Hull insurance, 298

Human life value, 67

Hybrid agreements, 454, 466

I

Illness, as risk, 4

Illustrations, life insurance policies, 92, 94-95

Immediate annuities, 106

Implied consent, 266

Incentive-based dental plans, 367

Incentive stock options (ISO), and alternative minimum tax (AMT), 424-428

Incontestability clause, 46, 331

Indemnity

assurance of, 23-25

contracts of, 21

defined, 23

Indemnity plans

coverage limits, 140-141

group dental insurance, 367

hospital-only coverage, 142, 157

Independent practice association (IPA) model HMO, 147

Indeterminate premium life insurance, 44

Indirect losses, 5

Individual health plans. *See Health care plans*

Inflation

homeowners insurance rider, 227-228

long-term care insurance rider, 200

present value of annuity due (PVAD), 67, 71-75

Inland marine insurance

commercial policy, 298-300

controlled/uncontrolled forms, 298

homeowners policy, 229-230, 236

Insect damage, 215

Insurable interest

defined, 24, 218

homeowners insurance, 218

Insurance, 11-17

actual cash value (ACV), 24

adverse selection, 13-14

contracts, 19-26

function of, 14

insurable interest doctrine, 24

insurable risk, identifying, 14-15

language of policies, 283

legal terms related to, 16-17

other insurable provisions, 25

premiums, 11-12

probability theory, 12-13

as risk management, 6-7

See also specific type of insurance

Insurance industry

company bankruptcies, 122

competitiveness, factors in, 117

and deregulation, 121

regulation of, 115-116

See also Life insurance companies

Insurance Marketplace Standards Association (IMSA), 122-123

code of ethics, 124

Insurance Services Office (ISO), 213, 242

Insured's duties, 218

Integrated dental plans, 368

Intentional loss, 232

Intentional tort, 16

Interest-adjusted cost indices

interest-adjusted net payment index, 93

interest-adjusted surrender cost index, 93

Interest-only settlement, 51

Interest sensitive whole life insurance, 44

Interim insurance, 151

Intermediate care, 198

International Risk Management Institute (IRMI), 300

Interpolated terminal reserve, 61-62

Invitees, 16, 266

IRC § 79, 332-333

IRC § 83(b) election, restricted stock plans, 436-439

IRC § 101(a), 57, 334

IRC § 125, 359

IRC § 132, 383, 388, 390-391

IRC § 162, 385, 389, 401

IRC § 414(q), 396, 401

IRC § 422, 424, 428, 432

IRC § 423, 428, 431-433

IRC § 1035 exchange, 44, 57, 60

IRC § 7872, 406

Irrevocable life insurance trust (ILIT), 61

J

Jewelry, insuring, 229

Joint and full survivor benefits, 53-54

Joint mortgage term life insurance, 40

Joint underwriting associations, 258

Jury duty, 315, 380

Juvenile insurance, 43, 58

K

Key person discount, 459

Key person life insurance, 448-478

and alternative minimum tax (AMT), 448

comparison of policies, 478

key persons, positions of, 449

overhead expense insurance, 476-477

taxation, 450-452

transfer-for-value, 450-452

L

Lack of marketability discounts, 458

Landlord's furnishings, 216

Landscape damage, 217

Lapse ratio, 124

Last clear chance, 18, 270

Law of Large Numbers, 12

Leasehold interest coverage, 294

Legal fees coverage

homeowners insurance, 216

legal services plans, 398-399

personal liability insurance, 220, 272

tort system, 280

Level premium term life insurance, 32

Liability

    absolute/strict, 17, 264

    commercial, areas of, 302

    contingent, 302

    contractual, 302

    general, for business, 302

    joint/several, 268-269

    legal tests for, 264-269

    liability risk, 5

    negligence, 18, 264-267

    product, 302

    proximate cause, 269

    vicarious, 17, 266-267

    See also Negligence

Liability coverage

    auto insurance, 243-245, 253, 255

    cost increase of, 305

    necessity of, 283

    See also Commercial liability insurance; Personal liability coverage; Professional liability coverage

Liberalization clause, 221

Licensee, 16, 266

Life events, 365

Life insurance

    adjustable, 39

    assignment of, 21-22

    for buy/sell agreement funding, 462

    choosing, tips for, 44

    contracts. *See Life insurance contracts*

    death benefit, *See Life insurance death benefits*

    dividends, *See Life insurance dividends*

    family policies, 41-42

    first to die/second to die policies, 89

    founder's policies, 102

    graded premium, 35-36

    group plans. *See Group life insurance*

    hybrid policies, 36

    indeterminate premium, 44

    interest-sensitive, 44

    juvenile, 43, 58

    key person, 448-478

    low-load/no-load, 45

    mortgage term, 40

    participating/nonparticipating policies, 33

    permanent, 34-39

    policy riders. *See Life insurance contracts*

    as risk management, 30-31

    selection of policy. *See Life insurance needs analysis; Life insurance policy analysis*

    split-dollar, 468-474

    survivorship life, 40-41

    term, 32-34

    transfer for value, 450-452

    universal life, 34, 36-39

    valued policies, 21

    variable, 42

    whole life, 35, 42-45

Life insurance companies, 115-129

    agents, captive/non-captive, 126

    agents vs. producers, 126-127

    bankruptcies, 122

    binding authority, 127

    demutualization, 121

    ethical code, 124

    fraternal societies as, 127-128

    general information, 123-124

    Insurance Marketplace Standards Association (IMSA), 122-123

    and life insurance needs, 124-125

limited options, 129

mutual holding company, 121-122

policyholder support services, 125

ratings system, 118-119

riders, importance of, 125

risk-based capital (RBC) ratio, 120-121

underwriting, 128-129

Life insurance contracts, 46-48

accidental death & dismemberment (AD&D), 56

accidental death benefit (ADB), 47, 55

accidental means, 55

aviation and war-related deaths, 47

beneficiary, 46

collateral assignment, 48

common disaster, 48

conversion privilege, 35, 48, 89, 124-125

death benefit changes, 47

disability waiver of premium, 54-55

extended term, 50

grace period, 47

guaranteed insurability, 56-57, 125

incontestability clause, 46

loan-related provisions, 48

long-term care rider, 195-196, 200

misstatement of age, 46

nonforfeiture options, 39, 50

ownership, 46

payor death, 54

presumptive disability, 55, 125

reduced paid-up insurance, 50

reinstatement, 47

riders, 43, 125

settlement options, 51-54

spendthrift provision, 57

suicide, 47

surrender value, 50

Life insurance death benefits

accelerated, 104-105

changes, to life insurance policy, 47

contract riders. See Life insurance contracts

defined, 31

first to die/second to die, 89

settlement options, 51-54

taxation of proceeds. See Life insurance taxation

universal life insurance, 37, 47

viatical agreements, 103-104

Life insurance dividends, 49-50

accumulate at interest, 49

cash option, 49

fifth dividend option, 49-50

illustrations, problems in, 94-95

and net cost method, 92-93

paid-up dividend additions, 49

participating policies, 33

premium reduction, 49

taxation of, 60

Life insurance needs

Life insurance needs analysis, 65-83

adjustment fund in, 69

Begin mode for calculator, 71

blackout period, 72-73

and capital retention, 83

Citibank method, 67

dependents income, planning for, 71-72

duration of need, 89-91

for education funding, 72, 79

example of, 76-82

general guidelines, 88-89

human life value, 67

insurance company, choosing, 124-125

multiples of income, 67-68

present value of annuity due (PVAD), 67, 71-75

process in, 70-75

retirement funding, 73-75, 81

straight income method, 68

term versus permanent, 90-91

Life insurance policy analysis, 91-105

accelerated death benefits, 104-105, 125

Belth Method, 95-97

cash accumulation method, 98-99

illustrations, problems related to, 92, 94-95

interest-adjusted cost indices, 93

Linton yield method, 99-101

net cost method, 91-93

net payment index, 93-94

for replacement of policy, 101-103

surrender cost index, 93

viatical agreements, 103-104

yearly price of protection method, 95-97

Life insurance taxation, 57-62

and accelerated payments, 105

cash value accumulation test, 58

dividend, taxation of, 60

estate taxes, 61

gift taxes, 61-62

group life insurance, 333-334

guideline premium and corridor test, 58

interpolated terminal reserve, 61-62

IRC § 101(a), 57, 334

IRC Section 1035 Exchange, 60-61

irrevocable life insurance trust (ILIT), 61

modified endowment contracts (MECs), 58-59

policy loans, 57, 60

7-pay test, 58-59

transfer for value rule, 59

viatical agreements, 105

Life support, 55

Limited-pay life insurance, 35

Limited payment plan, 200-201

Limit of liability, 218

Linton yield method, 99-101

Liquor liability coverage, 303

Living benefits rider, 195-196

Loans

to executives, 406

life insurance policies, 48

life insurance taxation, 57, 60

Lodging, meals/lodging benefit, 383-385

Long-tail coverage, 281

Long-term care facilities

adult day care, 198

assisted living facilities, 198-199

continuing care retirement communities (CCRCs), 197, 199

custodial care, 198

home health care benefits, 198, 204

homeowners insurance coverage, 230

intermediate care, 198

nursing homes, 199

skilled nursing care, 198

Long-term care insurance, 191-208

activities-of-daily living (ADL) concept, 193-194, 196

bed reservation, 203

benefit trigger, 194

caregivers, benefits to, 204

choosing policy, 200-202

cognitive impairment, 193

from continuing care retirement communities (CCRCs), 197

cost-of-living increase, 203-204

costs versus benefits, 200, 202

deductibility of premiums, 194-195

from disability income insurance, 180, 196-197

elimination period, 202

equipment supplied by, 204

evolution of, 192-193

group plans, 195, 369

health care coordinator, 204

of HMOs, 197

inflation rider, 200

length of coverage, 202-203

life insurance riders for, 195-196, 200

limited payment plan, 200-201

Medicaid, 207-208

medical necessity trigger, 194

Medicare benefits, 156, 192, 206

needs analysis, 201-202

nonforfeiture benefits, 194

personal care advocate, 204

qualified policies, 194-195

respite care, 204

restoration of benefits, 204-205

return of premium, 205

shared benefits, 205

single premium life conversion to, 43, 196

sources of coverage, 195

spousal discount, 203

substantial assistance, 193

underwriting, 205-206

waiver of premium, 203

Long-term disability income policies, 350

Loss assessment

homeowners insurance coverage, 217

personal liability coverage, 273

Loss discovery coverage, 299

Losses

direct/indirect, 5

insurance as protection, 14-15

management of, 6-10

pre/post-loss objectives, 30

Loss of income, disability insurance, 171-172

Loss to pair clause, 218

Loss prevention, as risk reduction, 7

Loss settlement, 214

Loss sustained coverage, 299

Loss of use, 215, 223

Low-load life insurance, 45

Lump sum payment, 50

M

Major medical coverage, 143

Malpractice insurance, 281-282

Managed-care plans, 147-150

costs, factors in, 134

defined, 138

dental plans, 367

exclusive provider organizations (EPO), 149

health maintenance organizations (HMOs), 147-148

point-of-service (POS) plans, 149

preferred provider organizations (PPO), 148-149

provider-sponsored organizations, 150

Mandatory control RBC level, 120

Manufacturers output coverage, 300

Manufacturer's selling price, 292

Maternity benefits, 141

Maternity leave, 315-316

Maximum benefit period, 173

Maximum monthly benefit payment, 174-175

McCarran-Ferguson Act (1945), 115

Meals/lodging benefit, 383-385, 391

Medicaid, 207-208

defined, 138

homestead exemption, 207

long-term care, 207-208

transfer of assets rules, 208

Medical necessity trigger, 194

Medical payments coverage

personal auto policy (PAP), 243, 255

personal liability coverage, 221, 223, 272

Medical savings accounts (MSA), 139, 144

tax benefits, 144

See also Health savings accounts (HSA)

Medicare, 152-156

cost shifting, 338

defined, 139

group plan coordination with, 340

long-term care, 156, 192, 206

Medicare Advantage, 152-153, 158

Medicare HMOs, 139, 153, 158

Medigap, 153-156, 206

Parts A and B, 143, 152-153, 155

Parts C and D, 152, 154

prescription drug benefit, 152-154, 156

provider-sponsored organizations, 150

with Social Security disability income, 152

usual customary and reasonable (UCR) rates, 143

Medicare Prescription Drug Improvement and Modernization Act (2003), 145

Medigap, 153-156

elements of plans, 155-156

and long-term care, 206

Memorabilia, insuring, 228-229

Mental impairment

long-term care benefits, 193

negligence, exclusion from, 267

Military reserve time, 315, 380

Minority discounts, 458

Minors, contracts with, 20

Misrepresentation, 22-23

Mobile homes, 236

Modified any occupation, 170

Modified endowment contracts (MECs), 43, 58-59, 196

Modified whole life insurance, 42-43

Mold, toxic, 233-234

Moody's insurance company rating, 118-119

Morale hazard, 3

Moral hazard, 3

Mortgage clause, 218

Mortgage term life insurance, 40

Motor carriers coverage, 306

Motorcycles, 254

Motor homes, 254

Moving expenses fringe benefit, 316, 392

Multi-employer plans (MEPs), 341-342

Multi-employer trusts (METs), 341-342

Multiples of income, 67-68

Mutual benefit bailment, 304

Mutual funds

compared to annuities, 109-110

taxation, 109

Mutual holding company, 121-122

N

Named peril coverage (broad form), 213, 222-224

National Association of Insurance Commissioners (NAIC), 32, 93, 103, 116, 120, 150, 154, 194, 232

National Committee for Quality Assurance (NCQA), 137, 139

National Flood Insurance Program (NFIP), 235

National Guard, 315, 380

Natural disasters, 4, 15

Neglect exclusion, 232

Negligence

comparative, 18, 271

contributory, 18, 271

damages, 267-269

defenses for, 18, 269-271

exclusions from, 267

injured party participation, 270-271

as matter of law, 17

negligent entrustment, 266-267

per se, 17, 265

proximate cause, 269

prudent man rule, 264

pure comparative, 18

res ipsa loquitur, 17, 265

unintentional tort, 17

Net cost method, 91-93

Net-level premiums, 59

Net payment index, 93-94

No-additional cost services, 388

No benefit to bailee clause, 218-219

No-fault auto insurance, 259-260

No-load life insurance, 45

Nonbuilding replacement cost, 230

Non-captive agents, 126

Nondiscrimination rules, 401

Nonexempt employees, 381

Nonforfeiture options

life insurance, 39, 50

long-term care insurance, 194

Nonoccupational coverage

group disability income insurance, 351

individual disability income insurance, 180

Nonparticipating life insurance policies, 33

Nonqualified deferred compensation plans, 407-418

and American Jobs Creation Act (2004), 417-418

design of, 410-411

excess benefits plans, 411

funded, secured plans, 417

funded, unsecured plans, 416

compared to qualified plans, 408-410

salary continuation plans, 411

supplemental executive retirement plans (SERPs), 411

taxation, 412-414

top hat plans, 411

unfunded, secured plans, 414-416

unfunded, unsecured plans, 414

Nonqualified employee stock purchase plan, 433

Nonqualified stock options (NQSO), 422-424

fair market value, 423

taxation, 422-424

Nuclear hazard, 219, 232

Nursing homes, 199

O

Occupational change, disability insurance, 177

Occupational class, disability insurance, 175-176, 187

Occurrence form, 280-281

Ocean marine insurance, 297-298

Off-balance sheet risk, 120

Offsets, 352

Old age, dependency as risk, 4

Older homes, 224

Omnibus Budget and Reconciliation Act (OBRA), 154

Open-enrollment periods, 339

Open perils coverage
    auto insurance, 246
    homeowners insurance, 222, 224, 228
Optional renewability, 185
Ordinary life insurance, 335
Other insurable provisions, 25
Other structures, 215, 223, 230, 237
Our option, 219, 226
Overhead expense insurance, 476-477
Ownership
    group life insurance, 330
    individual life insurance, 46
Own occupation, 170, 186-187, 351

P

Paid-up dividend additions, 49
Paid-up life, 335
Parol evidence rule, 25
Partial disability, 180-181
Participating life insurance policies, 33
Particular average, 298
Particular risk, 5
Partnerships
    death of partner, 452
    disabled partner, 452
    key person life insurance, 448-478
Payor death provision, 54
Pension fiduciary liability, 303
Performance cash plan, 443
Performance unit programs, 443
Perils
    open perils coverage, 222, 224, 228
    personal, types of, 4
    and risk, 3

Period certain guarantee, 108
Permanent insurance
    group life, 335
    individual life insurance, 34-39, 90-91
    versus term, 90-91
Personal auto policy (PAP), 242-260
    accident, meaning of, 260
    antique/classic cars, 253
    claims, traditional, 259
    company cars/rentals, 249
    cost of, 256-258
    covered auto criteria, 247-248, 253-254
    discounts, 257
    duties after loss, 251
    extended liability, 253
    general provisions, 251-253
    high-risk drivers, plans for, 258
    liability coverage, 243-245, 253, 255
    medical payments coverage, 243, 255
    motor home, 254
    named non-owner, 254
    no-fault system, 259-260
    non-owned auto coverage, 248-251, 254
    other than collision perils, 246-247
    physical damage coverage, 245-251, 256
    physical damage exclusions, 246-247
    snowmobile, 254
    split-limit/single-limit liability, 245
    termination/renewal/transfer, 252-253
    uninsured/underinsured motorists, 243, 248-249
Personal care advocate, 204
Personal contracts, 21
Personal injuries, 279

Personal liability insurance, 271-279
  automobile policy, 220-221, 223
  coverage options, 220
  duties after loss, 273
  employer offered plans, 314
  endorsements, 279
  exclusions, 274-279
  first aid costs, 273
  good neighbor provision, 272
  individuals covered, 272
  insureds, definition of, 220
  legal fees, 220, 272
  limit of liability, 273
  loss assessment coverage, 273
  medical payments to others, 221, 223, 272
  needs analysis, 284-285
  personal injuries, 279
  severability of insureds, 221, 274
  suit against us, 274
  umbrella coverage, 282-283
Personal property
  appraisal of, 21
  contents/personal property insurance, 215, 223-224, 227-228
  defined, 5
  exclusions, 228-229, 234-235
  open perils coverage, 228
  scheduled, 214, 229-230
  secondary residence, 227
  unscheduled, 227
Personal risk, 4-5
Personal time off (PTO) plans, 379-380
Phantom stock plans, 440-441
  actual stock value, 440
  negative aspects, 440-441
  taxation, 441

Physical hazards, 3
Physician's expense coverage, 143
Point-of-service (POS) plans, 149
Policy period, 221
Policy persistency, 124
Pollution liability insurance, 279, 304
Poor, Medicaid, 138
Portfolio programs, 291
Post-claim underwriting, 128-129, 178
Post-loss objectives, 30
Power failure, 231
Preadmission testing, 338
Pre-certification, 139
Predetermination of benefits, 368-369
Preexisting conditions
  disability income insurance, 176, 188
  HIPAA on, 348
  individual health insurance, 139, 142, 151
Preferred provider organizations (PPO), 148-149
  limitations of, 148-149
  swing plans, 148
Pre-loss objectives, 30
Premiums
  disability waiver of, 35, 54-55
  group health insurance, 339
  group insurance, 320
  individual health insurance, 134, 161
  life insurance, 11-13
Prescription drugs
  formulary, 137
  Medicare benefit, 152-154, 156
Present value of annuity due (PVAD), 67, 71-75
Presumptive disability, 55, 125, 177
Primary care physician (PCP), 135, 137, 140, 148
Probability distribution, 12-13
Probability theory, related to insurance, 12-13

Probation period, 177

Product liability, 302

Product recall, 303

Professional liability insurance, 280-285

    claims made, 281

    errors and omissions, 281

    long-tail coverage, 281

    malpractice insurance, 281-282

    occurrence form, 280-281

Profit-sharing plans, 316

Property

    owner obligations/duties, 266, 270

    See also Personal property

Property insurance. *See Commercial property insurance; Homeowners insurance*

Property removal coverage, 217

Property risk, 5

Providers, 140

Provider-sponsored organizations, 150

Proximate cause, 269

Prudent man rule, 264, 271

Punitive damages, 268

Purchase option, 56-57, 125

Pure comparative negligence, 18

Pure risk, 5

Pure rule, 271

Q

Qualification trigger, 194

Qualified deferred compensation plans

    compared to nonqualified plans, 408-410

    taxation, 408-409

Qualified plans, 323

R

Rabbi trust, 416

Rain insurance, 296

Ratings, life insurance companies, 118-119

Real property, 5

Reasonable compensation, 474-475

Reasonable repairs, 217

Recovered property, 219

Reduced paid-up insurance, 50

Re-entry term life insurance, 32

Reformation, contracts, 26

Regulation XXX, 32-33, 123

Regulatory action RBC level, 120

Rehabilitation coverage, 181, 352

Reinstatement of life insurance, 47

Reinsurance companies, 34-35

Reinsurance pools, 258

Relative frequency interpretation, 12

Rental car coverage, 249-251

Rental property

    contents/personal property (Coverage C), 215, 223-224, 227-228

    personal liability insurance, 279

Repairs, homeowners insurance, 217

Replacement cost

    defined, 214, 225

    homeowners insurance, 225-227

Rescission, 26

Reserve funds, 415

Residual disability benefits, 181-182

Res ipsa loquitur, 17, 265

Respite care, 204

Restricted stock plans, 407, 436-439

    features of, 436

        IRC 83(b) election, 436-439

Retired lives reserves, 336

Retirement
    age and Social Security, 73
    Medicare, 152-156
Retirement communities, continuing care
    retirement communities (CCRCs), 197
Retirement income
    annuities, 106-111
    life insurance needs analysis, 73-75, 81
    plans. *See Retirement plans*
Retirement planning services benefit, 317, 392-393
Retirement plans
    employer offered plans, 314, 323
    401(k) qualified retirement plan, 408
    nonqualified deferred compensation plans,
        407-418
Return-to-work provisions, 352-353
Reverse split-dollar plan, 471-472
Revocable trusts, 415
Riders
    defined, 43
    life insurance. *See Life insurance contracts*
Risk
    assumption of, 18
    defined, 2
    insurable, identifying, 14-15
    perils/hazards, 3
    risk exposures, types of, 5-6
    types of, 3-6, 30
    Risk associated with failure of others, 6
Risk-based capital (RBC) ratio, 120-121
Risk management, 6-10
    life insurance as, 30-31
    method, choosing, 10
    pre/post-loss objectives, 30-31
    risk avoidance, 6
    risk reduction, 7

risk retention, 6
risk sharing, 7
risk transfer, 7
rules of, 8-10
Running-down clause, 298

S

Sabbaticals, 315, 381
Safe harbor test, 359
Salary continuation plans, 353, 411
Satisfiers, 313
Savings plans, 316
Schedule bond, 300
Scheduled personal property, 214, 229-230
Second to die life insurance, 89
Secular trusts, 417
Security reduction, as loss control, 7
Self-employed
    disability income insurance, 176
    group health care plans, 341
    homeowners insurance option, 237
    individual health insurance. *See Health care
        plans*
Self-funded health insurance plans, 140-141, 149
Service area, 147
Settlement options
    group life insurance, 331
    individual life insurance, 51-54
7-pay test, 58-59
Severability of insured's, 221, 274
Severance pay
    golden parachutes, 396-397, 407
    plan requirements, 393-394
Shadow stock arrangements, 439-441
    phantom stock plans, 440-441

stock appreciation rights (SARs), 441-442

Shared benefits, 205

Short-term disability income policies, 350, 376

Sick-pay/sick-leave, 315, 353, 374-375, 377

Simplified underwriting, 329

Single-limit liability, 245

Single premium life insurance, conversion to long-term care insurance, 43, 196

Skilled nursing care, 198

Small Business Administration (SBA), 48

Snowmobiles, 254, 279

Social insurance rider, 182-183

Social Security benefits

blackout period, 72-73

calculating future benefits, 74

children of deceased parents, 72

normal retirement age, 73

parent of surviving child, 72

Social Security disability income

disability, definition of, 169

Medicare with, 152

and social insurance rider, 182-183

Sole proprietors. *See Self-employed*

Special cause of loss, 299

Special damages, 267

Special homeowners coverage, 222, 224, 228

Specialty letter, 170

Specified income option, 108

Specified payment period, 108

Speculative risk, 5

Spendthrift provision, 57

Split definition, 171

Split-dollar insurance, 468-474

collateral assignment, 469

endorsement method, 468

equity split-dollar plans, 470-471

and ERISA, 472

reverse split-dollar plan, 471-472

split-dollar rollout, 471

taxation, 472-474

terms of plans, 469

Split-limit liability, 245

Spoilage coverage, 292

Spousal long-term care insurance discount, 203

Staff model HMO, 147

Standard & Poors rating, 118-119

Static risk, 4

Stock appreciation rights (SARs), 441-442

features of, 441-442

taxation, 442

Stock companies, demutualization formation, 121

Stock options, 407, 422-428

comparison of plans, 432

incentive, 424-428

nonqualified, 422-424

Stock redemption agreement, 465-466

Stolen property. *See Theft losses*

Stop-loss limit, 135

Straight income method, 68

Strict liability, 17, 264

Subrogation, 221

Substantial assistance, 193

Substantial risk of forfeiture, 413

Suggestion awards, 316

Suicide, life insurance, 47

Sunk costs, 97

Supplemental executive retirement plans (SERPs), 411

Surgical expense coverage, 143

Surgical opinions, second, 338

Surrender charges, 107

Surrender cost index, 93

Surrender value, 50

Survivorship life insurance, 40-41

Swing plans, 148

T

Taxation

    adoption assistance plans, 387

    alternative minimum tax (AMT), 424-427

    of annuities, 110-111

    cafeteria plans, 359-361

    dependent care assistance plans, 386-387

    employee stock purchase plan, 431-433

    fringe benefits, 388, 401

    golden parachutes, 396

    group disability income insurance, 354

    group health care plans, 349

    incentive stock options (ISO), 424-427

    individual disability income benefits, 187

    individual health care plans, 161

    key person life insurance, 450-452

    life insurance proceeds. *See Life insurance taxation*

    loans to executives, 406

    long-term care insurance premium deduction, 194-195

    medical/health savings accounts, 137, 139, 144-146

    mutual funds, 109

    nonqualified deferred compensation plans, 412-414

    nonqualified stock options (NQSO), 422-424

    phantom stock plans, 441

    qualified deferred compensation plans, 408-409

    restricted stock plans, 436-439

    sick-leave plans, 374-375

    split-dollar insurance, 472-474

    stock appreciation rights (SARs), 442

    voluntary employee benefit association (VEBA), 395

Tax Reform Act (1986), 43

Temporary insurance, 151

Terminally ill person, defined, 105

Term life insurance, 32-34

    buy term, invest difference concept, 90, 98

    choosing policy, 34-35, 89

    conversion privileges, 35, 48, 89, 124-125

    decreasing term, 33

    yearly renewable/annually renewable (YRT/ART), 32

Theft losses coverage, 216, 219, 234-235

Third-party administrator (TPA), 140

Third party agreements, 467

Third-party guarantee, in nonqualified deferred compensation plans, 416

Third-party over suits, 307

Thrift plans, 316

Time not worked payments. *See Employee benefits (non-insurance)*

Title insurance, 236

Top hat plans, 411

Torrens System, 236

Tort feasor, 268

Torts

    defined, 265

    intentional, 16

    survival of tort actions, 17

    unintentional, 17

Towing coverage, 250

Trailers

    commercial property insurance, 292

        homeowners insurance limit, 229, 235

Transfer-for-value
   buy/sell agreements, 462, 467-468
   key person life insurance, 450-452
   rule, 59, 105
   taxation, 451-452
Transportation expenses
   auto insurance coverage, 250-251
   fringe benefit, 389-390, 391
Transportation insurance, 297-300
   inland marine insurance, 298-300
   ocean marine insurance, 297-298
Trespassers, 16, 266
Truckers coverage insurance, 306
Trusts
   irrevocable life insurance trust (ILIT), 61
   in nonqualified deferred compensation plans, 415-417
Tuition reimbursement. *See Education funding*
20-pay life insurance policy, 35

U

Umbrella policies
   commercial liability, 305
   personal liability, 282-283
Uncertainty, defined, 2
Uncontrolled forms, 298
Underground storage tank liability, 304
Underwriting
   defined, 32
   disability income insurance, 169, 186-188
   group disability income insurance, 351
   group health insurance, 339
   group insurance, 320-321
   group life insurance, 329
   health insurance plans, 142

life insurance, 128-129
long-term care insurance, 205-206
post-claim, 128-129, 178
simplified, 329
Unfunded, secured plans, 414-416
Unfunded, unsecured plans, 414
Unilateral contracts, 22
Uninsured/underinsured motorists coverage, 243, 248-249
Unintentional tort, 17
Unit-owners, 224
Universal life insurance, 36-39
   accumulation fund, 37-38, 92
   death benefits, 37
   defined, 34, 36
   disability waiver of premium, 54
   fixed interest form, 36, 38
   group plans, 336
   pros/cons of, 38-39, 47, 92
   separate accounts, 36
   variable forms, 36-37
   withdrawals/loans, 60
Usual customary and reasonable (UCR) rates, 140, 143
Utmost good faith contracts, 22

V

Vacation days, 315, 377-378
Valuable papers insurance, 300
Valuation of business, 456-459
   book value, 457
   fair market value (FMV), 456-457
   key person discount, 459
   lack of marketability discounts, 458
   minority discounts, 458

valuation formula, 457-458

Valuation methods, homeowners insurance, 225-226

Valued policies, 21

Variable annuities, 107

Variable life insurance, 42

Variable payout annuity, 109

Variable universal life insurance, 36-37

Vesting trusts, 415

Viatical agreements, 103-105

    taxation, 105

Vicarious liability, 17, 266-267

Voidable contract, 20

Void contract, 20

Volcanic eruption, 219

Voluntary employee benefit association (VEBA), 394-396

Welfare benefit plans, voluntary employee benefit association (VEBA), 394-396

Wellness programs, 317, 400

Whole life insurance, 42-45

    current-assumption, 45

    decreasing term as rider, 33

    defined, 35

    group plan, 335

    hybrid policies, 36

    interest sensitive, 44

    juvenile insurance, 43

    limited-pay life insurance, 35

    modified type, 42

    single premium, 43

Wisconsin rule, 271

Workers compensation, 303, 306-307, 351

Working condition fringe benefits, 389-390

W

Wait-and-see buy/sell agreements, 466

Waiver of premium

    disability income insurance, 184

    long-term care insurance, 203

Waivers, contracts, 25-26

War

    death in, life insurance, 47

    homeowners exclusion, 232

Warranty, 23

Watercraft

    homeowners insurance limit, 229, 235

    personal liability coverage, 220, 279

Water damage coverage, 231

Weather insurance, 296

Wedding presents, 236

Weiss Research rating, 118-119

Y

Yearly price of protection method, 95-97

Yearly renewable term (YRT) life insurance, 32